D1739951

A Comparative Grammar, Volume I

Franz Bopp, Edward Backhouse Eastwick

BIBLIOBAZAAR

Copyright © BiblioBazaar, LLC

BiblioBazaar Reproduction Series: Our goal at BiblioBazaar is to help readers, educators and researchers by bringing back in print hard-to-find original publications at a reasonable price and, at the same time, preserve the legacy of literary history. The following book represents an authentic reproduction of the text as printed by the original publisher and may contain prior copyright references. While we have attempted to accurately maintain the integrity of the original work(s), from time to time there are problems with the original book scan that may result in minor errors in the reproduction, including imperfections such as missing and blurred pages, poor pictures, markings and other reproduction issues beyond our control. Because this work is culturally important, we have made it available as a part of our commitment to protecting, preserving and promoting the world's literature.

All of our books are in the "public domain" and many are derived from Open Source projects dedicated to digitizing historic literature. We believe that when we undertake the difficult task of re-creating them as attractive, readable and affordable books, we further the mutual goal of sharing these works with a larger audience. A portion of Bibliobazaar profits go back to Open Source projects in the form of a donation to the groups that do this important work around the world. If you would like to make a donation to these worthy Open Source projects, or would just like to get more information about these important initiatives, please visit www.bibliobazaar.com/opensource.

A

COMPARATIVE GRAMMAR

OF THE

SANSKṚIT, ZEND,

GREEK, LATIN, LITHUANIAN, GOTHIC, GERMAN,

AND SCLAVONIC LANGUAGES.

BY

PROFESSOR F. BOPP.

TRANSLATED FROM THE GERMAN

BY

EDWARD B. EASTWICK, F.R.S., F.S.A., M.R.A.S.

OF MERTON COLLEGE, OXFORD, MEMBER OF THE ASIATIC SOCIETIES OF PARIS AND
BOMBAY, OF THE GERMAN ORIENTAL SOCIETY, AND OF THE PHILOLOGICAL
SOCIETY OF LONDON, HONORARY MEMBER OF THE MADRAS LITERARY
SOCIETY, PROFESSOR OF ORIENTAL LANGUAGES AND LIBRARIAN IN
THE EAST-INDIA COLLEGE, HAILEYBURY, AND TRANSLATOR OF
THE SARTASHT NÁMAH, THE KISSAH-I-SANJÁN, THE PREM
SÁGAR, THE BÁGH-O-BAHÁR, THE GULISTÁN, THE
ANVÁR-I-SUHAILÍ, ETC. ETC. ETC.

VOL. I.

SECOND EDITION.

WILLIAMS AND NORGATE,

LONDON, 14, HENRIETTA STREET, COVENT GARDEN; AND
EDINBURGH, 20, SOUTH FREDERICK STREET.

1856.

TO

THE CHAIRMAN, THE DEPUTY CHAIRMAN,

AND

THE DIRECTORS

OF THE

HONORABLE EAST-INDIA COMPANY,

THE MUNIFICENT PATRONS OF INDIAN LITERATURE,

THIS TRANSLATION OF A WORK,

WHICH IRREFRAGABLY DEMONSTRATES THE COMMON ORIGIN

OF THE

LANGUAGES OF INDIA AND OF EUROPE,

IS, WITH THEIR PERMISSION, RESPECTFULLY INSCRIBED

BY THEIR

MOST FAITHFUL AND OBEDIENT SERVANT,

THE TRANSLATOR.

PREFACE

SECOND EDITION.

In giving to the Public this Second Edition of the English Translation of Bopp's great work on Comparative Grammar, it is right to state that the version has been approved by Professor Bopp himself, and that it has been again very carefully compared with the original; so that numerous errors, which, from the great length of the work were perhaps hardly to be avoided in a first edition, have now been corrected. The appearance of the original, too, in parts, and at considerable intervals of time, led to some inconsistencies in the translation in the mode of expressing the value of certain letters; but care has been taken to rectify this defect, also, in the present edition. The Table of Contents is altogether new, and will be found to be very much more copious than the German.

Those who wish for an Introductory Notice before commencing the study of the Grammar, or who mean to content themselves with a general notion of what has been achieved by the Author, may refer to the "Edinburgh Review," No. CXCII. p. 298, and the "Calcutta Review," No. XXIV. p. 468. It will be there seen that this Work has created a new epoch in the science of Comparative Philology, and that it may be justly assigned a place in that department of study corresponding to that of "Newton's Principia in Mathematics, Bacon's Novum Organum in Mental Science, or Blumenbach in Physiology." The encomiums of the Reviewer have in fact been justified by the adoption of the Work as a Lecture Book at Oxford, and by the extensive use which Rawlinson and other eminent scholars have made of it in their researches.

It remains to be added, that while the Notes and Preface made by Professor Wilson, the former Editor, have been retained, I must be myself held responsible for the errors and defects, whatever they may be, of the present edition.

EDWARD B. EASTWICK.

HAILEYBURY COLLEGE,
February, 1854.

PREFACE

FIRST EDITION.

—•—

The study of Comparative Philology has of late years been cultivated in Germany, especially, with remarkable ability and proportionate success. The labours of Grimm, Pott, Bopp, and other distinguished Scholars, have given a new character to this department of literature; and have substituted for the vague conjectures suggested by external and often accidental coincidences, elementary principles, based upon the prevailing analogies of articulate sounds and the grammatical structure of language.

But although the fact that a material advance has been made in the study of Comparative Philology is generally known, and some of the particulars have been communicated to the English public through a few works on Classical Literature, or in the pages of periodical criticism; yet the full extent of the progress which has been effected, and the steps by which it has been attained, are imperfectly appreciated in this country. The study of the German language is yet far from being extensively pursued; and the results which the German Philologers have developed, and the reasonings which have led to them, being accessible to those only who can consult the original writers, are withheld from many individuals of education and learning to whom the affinities of cultivated speech are objects of interest and inquiry. Translations of the works, in which the information they would gladly seek

for, is conveyed, are necessary to bring within their reach
the materials that have been accumulated by German in-
dustry and erudition, for the illustration of the history of
human speech.

Influenced by these considerations, Lord FRANCIS EGERTON
was some time since induced to propose the translation
of a work which occupies a prominent place in the literature of Comparative Philology on the Continent—the
Vergleichende Grammatik of Professor BOPP of Berlin. In
this work a new and remarkable class of affinities has
been systematically and elaborately investigated. Taking
as his standard the Sanskrit language, Professor BOPP has
traced the analogies which associate with it and with each
other—the Zend, Greek, Latin, Gothic, German, and Sclavonic tongues: and whatever may be thought of some
of his arguments, he may be considered to have established
beyond reasonable question a near relationship between
the languages of nations separated by the intervention of
centuries, and the distance of half the globe, by differences
of physical formation and social institutions,—between the
forms of speech current among the dark-complexioned
natives of India and the fair-skinned races of ancient and
modern Europe;—a relationship of which no suspicion
existed fifty years ago, and which has been satisfactorily
established only within a recent period, during which the
Sanskrit language has been carefully studied, and the principles of alphabetical and syllabic modulation upon which its
grammatical changes are founded, have been applied to its
kindred forms of speech by the Philologers of Germany.

As the Vergleichende Grammatik of Professor BOPP is
especially dedicated to a comprehensive comparison of languages, and exhibits, in some detail, the principles of the
Sanskrit as the ground-work and connecting bond of the
comparison, it was regarded as likely to offer most interest to the Philologers of this country, and to be one of

the most acceptable of its class to English students: it was therefore selected as the subject of translation. The execution of the work was, however, opposed by two considerations—the extent of the original, and the copiousness of the illustrations derived from the languages of the East, the Sanskrit and the Zend. A complete translation demanded more time than was compatible with Lord F. EGERTON's other occupations; and as he professed not a familiarity with Oriental Literature, he was reluctant to render himself responsible for the correctness with which the orientalisms of the text required to be represented. This difficulty was, perhaps, rather over-rated, as the Grammar itself supplies all the knowledge that is needed, and the examples drawn from the Sanskrit and Zend speak for themselves as intelligibly as those derived from Gothic and Sclavonic. In order, however, that the publication might not be prevented by any embarrassment on this account, I offered my services in revising this portion of the work; and have hence the satisfaction of contributing, however humbly, to the execution of a task which I consider likely to give a beneficial impulse to the study of Comparative Philology in Great Britain.

The difficulty arising from the extent of the original work, and the consequent labour and time requisite for its translation, was of a more serious description. This, however, has been overcome by the ready co-operation of a gentleman, who adds a competent knowledge of German to eminent acquirements as an Oriental Scholar. Having mastered several of the spoken dialects of Western India, and made himself acquainted with the sacred language of the Parsees during the period of his service under the Presidency of Bombay, Lieutenant EASTWICK devoted part of a furlough, rendered necessary by failing health, to a residence in Germany, where he acquired the additional qualifications enabling him to take a share in the translation of the Vergleichende Grammatik. He has accordingly translated all those portions of the Comparative Grammar, the rendering of which was incompatible with the leisure of the Noble Lord with whom the design originated, who has borne a share in its execution, and who has taken a warm and liberal interest in its completion.

The Vergleichende Grammatik, originally published in separate Parts, has not yet reached its termination. In his first plan the author comprised the affinities of Sanskrit, Zend, Greek, Latin, Gothic, and its Teutonic descendants. To these, after the conclusion of the First Part, he added the Sclavonic. He has since extended his researches to the analogies of the Celtic and the Malay-Polynesian dialects, but has not yet incorporated the results with his general Grammar. The subjects already treated of are quite sufficient for the establishment of the principles of the comparison, and it is not proposed to follow him in his subsequent investigations. The first portions of the present Grammar comprise the doctrine of euphonic alphabetical changes, the comparative inflexions of Substantives and Adjectives, and the affinities of the Cardinal and Ordinal Numerals. The succeeding Parts contain the comparative formation and origin of the Pronouns and the Verbs: the latter subject is yet unfinished. The part of the translation now offered to the public stops with the chapter on the Numerals, but the remainder is completed, and will be published without delay.

With respect to the translation, I may venture to affirm, although pretending to a very slender acquaintance with German, that it has been made with great scrupulousness and care, and that it has required no ordinary pains to render in English, with fidelity and perspicuity, the not unfrequently difficult and obscure style of the original.

H. H. WILSON.

October, 1845.

PREFACE.

—o—

I CONTEMPLATE in this work a description of the comparative organization of the languages enumerated in the title page, comprehending all the features of their relationship, and an inquiry into their physical and mechanical laws, and the origin of the forms which distinguish their grammatical relations. One point alone I shall leave untouched, the secret of the roots, or the foundation of the nomenclature of the primary ideas. I shall not investigate, for example, why the root *i* signifies "go" and not "stand"; why the combination of sounds *stha* or *sta* signifies "stand" and not "go." I shall attempt, apart from this, to follow out as it were the language in its stages of being and march of development; yet in such a manner that those who are predetermined not to recognise, as explained, that which they maintain to be inexplicable, may perhaps find less to offend them in this work than the avowal of such a general plan might lead them to expect. In the majority of cases the primary signification, and, with it, the primary source of the grammatical forms, spontaneously present themselves to observation in consequence of the extension of our horizon of language, and of the confronting of sisters of the same lingual stock separated for ages, but bearing indubitable features of their family connection. In the treatment, indeed, of our European tongues a new epoch could not fail to open upon us in the discovery of another region in the world of language, namely, the Sanskrit,* of which it has been demonstrated, that, in its

---

* *Sanskrita* signifies "adorned, completed, perfect"; in respect to language, "*classic*"; and is thus adapted to denote the entire family or race." It is compounded of the elements *sam*, "with," and *krita* (nom. *kritas, kritâ, kritam*), "made," with the insertion of a euphonic *s* (§§. 18. 96.).

grammatical constitution, it stands in the most intimate relation
to the Greek, the Latin, the Germanic, &c.; so that it has
afforded, for the first time, a firm foundation for the comprehension of the grammatical connection between the two
languages called the Classical, as well as of the relation of
these two to the German, the Lithuanian, and Sclavonic.
Who could have dreamed a century ago that a language
would be brought to us from the far East, which should
accompany, *pari passû*, nay, sometimes surpass, the Greek
in all those perfections of form which have been hitherto
considered the exclusive property of the latter, and be
adapted throughout to adjust the perennial strife between
the Greek dialects, by enabling us to determine where each
of them has preserved the purest and the oldest forms?

The relations of the ancient Indian languages to their
European kindred are, in part, so palpable as to be obvious
to every one who casts a glance at them, even from a distance: in part, however, so concealed, so deeply implicated in
the most secret passages of the organization of the language,
that we are compelled to consider every language subjected
to a comparison with it, as also the language itself, from new
stations of observation, and to employ the highest powers of
grammatical science and method in order to recognise and
illustrate the original unity of the different grammars. The
Semitic languages are of a more compact nature, and,
putting out of sight lexicographical and syntactical features,
extremely meagre in contrivance; they had little to part
with, and of necessity have handed down to succeeding ages
what they were endowed with at starting. The tricon-
sonantal fabric of their roots (§. 107.), which distinguishes this
race from others, was already of itself sufficient to designate the
parentage of every individual of the family. The family bond,
on the other hand, which embraces the Indo-European race
of languages, is not indeed less universal, but, in most of its
bearings, of a quality infinitely more refined. The members
of this race inherited, from the period of their earliest youth,

endowments of exceeding richness, and, with the capability
(§. 108.), the methods, also, of a system of unlimited composition and agglutination. Possessing much, they were able
to bear the loss of much, and yet to retain their local life ; and
by multiplied losses, alterations, suppressions of sounds, con-
versions and displacements, the members of the common
family are become scarcely recognisable to each other
It is at least a fact, that the relation of the Greek to the
Latin, the most obvious and palpable, though never quite
overlooked, has been, down to our time, grossly misunderstood ; and that the Roman tongue, which, in a grammatical
point of view, is associated with nothing but itself, or with
what is of its own family, is even now usually regarded as
a mixed language, because, in fact, it contains much which
sounds heterogeneous to the Greek, although the elements
from which these forms arose are not foreign to the Greek
and other sister languages, as I have endeavoured partly
to demonstrate in my " System of Conjugation." *

The close relationship between the Classical and Germanic
languages has, with the exception of mere comparative lists
of words, copious indeed, but destitute of principle and
critical judgment, remained, down to the period of the appearance of the Asiatic intermediary, almost entirely unobserved,
although the acquaintance of philologists with the Gothic dates
now from a century and a half; and that language is so perfect
in its Grammar and so clear in its affinities, that had it been
earlier submitted to a rigorous and systematic process of comparison and anatomical investigation, the pervading relation

---

* Frankfort. a. M. 1816. A translation of my English revision of
this treatise (" Analytical Comparison of the Sanskrit, Greek, Latin and
Teutonic Languages," in the "Annals of Oriental Literature," London
1820.) by Dr. Pacht is to be found in the second and third number of the
second annual issue of Seebode's new Record of Philology and Pæda-
gogical science. Grimm's masterly German Grammar was unfortunately
unknown to me when I wrote the English revision, and I could then
make use only of Hickes and Fulda for the old German dialects.

of itself, and, with it, of the entire Germanic stock, to the
Greek and Roman, would necessarily have long since been
unveiled, tracked through all its variations, and by this time
been understood and recognised by every philologer.[*] For
what is more important, or can be more earnestly desired by
the cultivator of the classical languages, than their comparison
with our mother tongue in her oldest and most perfect form?
Since the Sanskrit has appeared above our horizon, that element
can no longer be excluded from a really profound investigation
of any province of language related to it; a fact, however,
which sometimes escapes the notice of the most approved
and circumspect labourers in this department.[†] We need

---

[*] Rask has been the first to supply a comprehensive view of the close
relationship between the Germanic and the Classical Languages, in his
meritorious prize treatise "On the Thracian Tribe of Languages," completed in 1814 and published in 1818, from which Vater gives an extract
in his Comparative Tables. It cannot be alleged as a reproach against
him that he did not profit by the Asiatic intermediary not then extensively known; but his deficiency in this respect shews itself the more
sensibly, as we see throughout that he was in a condition to use it with
intelligence. Under that deficiency, however, he almost everywhere
halts halfway towards the truth. We have to thank him for the
suggestion of the law of displacement of consonants, more acutely
considered and fundamentally developed by Grimm (§. 87., and see
Vater, §. 12.).

[†] We refer the reader to the very weighty judgment of W. von. Humboldt on the indispensable necessity of the Sanskrit for the history and
philosophy of language (Indische Bibl. I. 133). We may here borrow,
also, from Grimm's preface to the second edition of his admirable
Grammar, some words which are worthy of consideration (I. vi.): "As
the too exalted position of the Latin and Greek serves not for all
questions in German Grammar, where some words are of simpler and
deeper sound, so however, according to A. W. Schlegel's excellent remark, the far more perfect Indian Grammar may, in these cases, supply
the requisite corrections. The dialect which history demonstrates to be
the oldest and least corrupted must, in the end, present the most profound rules for the general exposition of the race, and thus lead us on to
the reformation, without the entire subversion of the rules hitherto
discovered, of the more recent modes of speech."

not fear that that practical and profound research in *utráque linguâ*, which is of most importance to the philologer can suffer prejudice by extension over too many languages; for the variety vanishes when the real identity is recognised and explained, and the false light of discrepancy is excluded. It is one thing, also, to learn a language, another to teach one, *i.e.* to describe its mechanism and organization. The learner may confine himself within the narrowest limits, and forbear to look beyond the language to be studied: the teacher's glance, on the contrary, must pass beyond the confined limits of one or two members of a family, and he must summon around him the representatives of the entire race, in order to infuse life, order, and organic mutual dependency into the mass of the languages spread before him. To attempt this appears to me the main requirement of the present period, and past centuries have been accumulating materials for the task.

The Zend Grammar could only be recovered by the process of a severe regular etymology, calculated to bring back the unknown to the known, the much to the little; for this remarkable language, which in many respects reaches beyond, and is an improvement on, the Sanskrit, and makes its theory more attainable, would appear to be no longer intelligible to the disciples of Zoroaster. Rask, who had the opportunity to satisfy himself on this head, says expressly (V. d. Hagen, p. 33) that its forgotten lore has yet to be rediscovered. I am also able, I believe, to demonstrate that the Pehlvi translator (tom. II. pp. 476, et seq.) of the Zend Vocabulary, edited by Anquetil, has frequently and entirely failed in conveying the grammatical sense of the Zend words which he translates. The work abounds with singular mistakes; and the distorted relation of Anquetil's French translation to the Zend expressions is usually to be ascribed to the mistakes in the Pehlvi interpretations of the Zend original. Almost all the oblique cases, by degrees, come to take rank as nominatives; the numbers, too, are sometimes mistaken. Further, we find forms

of cases produced by the Pehlvi translator as verbal persons,
and next these also confounded with each other, or translated
by abstract nouns.* Anquetil makes, as far as I know, no

---

* I give the Zend expressions according to the system of representation
explained in §. 30., annexing the original characters, which are exhibited
in type for the first time in this book, and which were lately cut at the
order of the Royal Society of Literature by R. Gotzig, according to the
exemplar of the lithographed M.S. of M. Burnouf. I give the Pehlvi
words exactly according to Anquetil (II. 435.): ‌ﺍﻫﻣﺎﻛﻢ *ahmákĕm,*
"ἡμῶν," P. *rouman* (cf. p.502, roman, "nos"), A. "*je*," "*moi*;" ‌ ‌
ahubya, "*bonis*" (with dual termination, §. 215.), P. *avaéh*, A. "*bon*,"
"*excellent*;" ‌ ‌ *aêtê*, "*hi*," "*ii*," P. *varman*, "*is*," A. "*lui*;"
‌ ‌ *anh m*, "I was," or also "I am," P. *djanounad*, "he is," A. "*il
est*;" ‌ ‌ *anheus*, "*mundi*," P. *akhé*, A. "*le monde*;" ‌ ‌
avaêshaüm, "*horum*," P. *varmouschan*, "*ii*," A. "*eux*;" ‌ ‌ *baraiti*,
"*fert*," P. *dadrouneschné*, "the carrying" (*eschné*, in Pehlvi, forms abstract
substantives), A. "*il porte*," "*il execute*," "*porter*;" ‌ ‌ *bis*, "twice,"
P. *dou*, "two," A. "*deux*;" *bérétebïö* (‌ ‌) *baratibyô*, "*ferenti-
bus?*" unquestionably a plural dative and ablative, P. *dadrouneschné*, "the
carrying," A. "*porter*;" ‌ ‌ *tê*, "*tui*," P. *tou*, "*tu*," A. "*tui*;" ‌ ‌
tácha, "*eaque*" (neut. §. 231.), P. *zakedj*, A. "*ce*;" ‌ ‌ *jatô*, "the
smitten" (cf. Sansk. *hatas* from *han*), P. *maitouned*, "he smites," A. "*il
frappe*;" ‌ ‌ *janat*, "he smote," P. *maitouneschné*, "the smiting,"
A. "*frapper*;" ‌ ‌ *zañthra*, "*per genitorem*," P. *zarhounad*, "*gi-
gnit*," A. "*il engendre*;" ‌ ‌ *stri*, "*femina*," P. *vakad*, A. "*femelle*;"
‌ ‌ *strīm*, "*feminam*," P. *vakad*, A. "*femelle*;" ‌ ‌ *stárañm*,
"*stellarum*," P. *setaran*, A. "*les étoiles*;" ‌ ‌ *fra-dátái*, "to
the given," or "especially given," P. *feraz dcheschné* (*nomen actionis*),
A. "*donner abondamment*;" ‌ ‌ *gaêthanañm*, "*mundorum*,"
P. *guehan* (cf. ‌ ‌), A. "*le monde*;" ‌ ‌ *gâtúmcha*, "*locum-
que*," P. *gáh*, A. "*lieu*;" ‌ ‌ *nars*, "of the man," P. *guebna hamat
adrak*, A. "*un homme*;" ‌ ‌ *nara*, "two men," P. *guebna hamat dou*,
A. "*deux hommes*;" ‌ ‌ *náirikunañm*, "*feminarum*," P. *nai-
rik hamat sé*, A. "*trois (ou plusieurs) femmes*;" ‌ ‌ *thryañm*,
"*trium*," P. *sevin*, A. "*troisième*;" ‌ ‌ *vahm mcha*, "*præcla-
rumque*," P. *néaeschné*, "*adoratio*," A. "*je fais néaesch*;" ‌ ‌ *rah-
mái*, "*præcluro*," P. *néaesch, konam*, "*adorationem facio*," A. "*je bénis

et

remark on the age of the Vocabulary to which I advert; while he ascribes to another, in which the Pehlvi is interpreted through the Persian, an antiquity of four centuries. The

---

et fais néuesch." I do not insist on translating the adjective ٮڡٮ٭٭ *vahma* by "*præclarus,*" but I am certain of this, that *vahmĕm* and *vahmái* are nothing else than the accusative and dative of the base *vahma;* and that ٮٮ٭ٮڡٮ٭٭ *vahmái* could be the first person of a verb is not to be thought possible for a moment. Anquetil, however, in the interlinear version of the beginning of the V. S. attempted by him, gives two other evident datives compounded with the particle ٭٭ *cha*, "and," as the first person singular of the present, viz. ٮٮ٭٭٭٭ ٭٭٭٭٭ *csnaothrái-cha*, ٮٮ٭٭٭٭٭٭٭٭٭ *frasastayaĕ-cha* (see §. 164.), by "*placere cupio,*" "*vota facio.*" One then sees, from the examples here adduced, the number of which I could with ease greatly increase, that the Pehlvi Translator of the said Vocabulary has, no more than Anquetil, any grammatical acquaintance with the Zend language, and that both regarded it rather in the light of an idiom, poor in inflexions; so that, as in Pehlvi and Modern Persian, the grammatical power of the members of a sentence would be to be gathered rather from their position than from their terminations. And Anquetil expressly says (II. 415.): "*La construction dans la langue Zende, semblable en cela aux autres idiômes de l'Orient, est astreinte à peu de regles* (!). *La formation des tems des Verbes y est à peu près la même que dans le Persan, plus trainante cependant, parce qu'elle est accompagnée de toutes les voyelles* (!). How stands it, then, with the Sanskrit translation of the Jzeschne made from the Pehlvi more than three centuries before that of Anquetil. This question will, without doubt, be very soon answered by M. E. Burnouf, who has already supplied, and admirably illustrated (Nouv. Journ. Asiat., T. III. p. 321), two passages from the work in a very interesting extract from its Commentary on the V. S. These passages are, however, too short to permit of our grounding on them overbold inferences as to the whole; moreover, their contents are of such a nature that the inflexionless Pehlvi language could follow the Zend original almost verbatim. The one passage signifies, "I call upon, I magnify the excellent pure spell, and the excellent man, the pure and the strict, strong like Dámi (? cf. Sansk. *upamána*, "similarity;" and V. S., p. 423, *dámóis drujó*) Izet." It is, however, very surprising, and of evil omen, that Neriosengh, or his Pehlvi predecessor, takes the feminine genitive *dahmayás* as a plural genitive, since this expression is evidently, as Burnouf rightly remarks, only an epithet of *áfritóis.* I abstain from speaking of the dubious expressions *dámóis upamanuhĕ*, and content myself

one in question cannot therefore be ascribed to any very late
period. The necessity, indeed, of interpretation for the Zend
must have been felt much sooner than for the Pehlvi, which
remained much longer current among the Parsee tribes. It
was therefore an admirable problem which had for its solution
the bringing to light, in India, and, so to say, under the very
eye of the Sanskrit, a sister language, no longer understood,
and obscured by the rubbish of ages ;—a problem of which the
solution indeed has not hitherto been fully obtained, but beyond
doubt will be. The first contribution to the knowledge of
this language which can be relied on—that of Rask—namely,
his treatise " On the age and authenticity of the Zend Language
and the Zend-Avesta," published in 1826, and made generally
accessible by V. d. Hagen's translation, deserves high honour
as a first attempt. The Zend has to thank this able man
(whose premature death we deeply deplore) for the more
natural appearance which it has derived from his rectification
of the value of its written characters. Of three words of
different declensions he gives us the singular inflections, though
with some sensible deficiencies, and those, too, just in the places
where the Zend forms are of most interest, and where are some
which display that independence of the Sanskrit which Rask
claims, perhaps in too high a degree, for the Zend ; a language
we are, however, unwilling to receive as a mere dialect of
the Sanskrit, and to which we are compelled to ascribe an
independent existence, resembling that of the Latin as compared with the Greek, or the Old Northern with the Gothic.
For the rest, I refer the reader to my review of Rask's and
Bohlen's treatises on the Zend in the Annual of Scientific
Criticism for December 1831, as also to an earlier work
(March 1831) on the able labours of E. Burnouf in this newly-

self with having pointed out the possibility of another view of the construction, different from that which has been very profoundly discussed
by Burnouf, and which is based on Neriosengh. The second passage
signifies, " I call upon and magnify the stars, the moon, the sun, the
eternal, self-created lights !"

opened field. My observations, derived from the original texts edited by Burnouf in Paris, and by Olshausen in Hamburgh, already extend themselves, in these publications, over all parts of the Zend Grammar; and nothing therefore has remained for me here, but further to establish, to complete, and to adjust the particulars in such a manner that the reader may be conducted on a course parallel with that of the known languages, with the greatest facility towards an acquaintance with the newly-discovered sister tongue. In order to obviate the difficulty and the labour which attend the introduction of the learner to the Zend and Sanskrit—difficulty sufficient to deter many, and to harass any one—I have appended to the original characters the pronunciation, laid down on a consistent method, or in places where, for reasons of space, one character alone is given, it is the Roman. This method is also perhaps the best for the gradual introduction of the reader to the knowledge of the original characters.

As in this work the languages it embraces are treated for their own sakes, *i. e.* as objects and not means of knowledge, and as I aim rather at giving a physiology of them than an introduction to their practical use, it has been in my power to omit many particulars which contribute nothing to the character of the whole; and I have gained thereby more space for the discussion of matters more important, and more intimately incorporated with the vital spirit of the language. By this process, and by the strict observance of a method which brings under one view all points mutually dependent and mutually explanatory, I have, as I flatter myself, succeeded in assembling under one group, and in a reasonable space, the leading incidents of many richly-endowed languages or grand dialects of an extinct original stock. Special care has been bestowed throughout on the German. This care was indispensable to one who, following Grimm's admirable work, aimed at applying to it the correction and adjustment that had become necessary in his theory of relations, the discovery of new affinities, or the more precise definition of those discovered, and to catch, with greater truth, at every step of grammatical progress, the

monitory voices of the Asiatic as well as the European sisterhood.
It was necessary, also, to set aside many false appearances of affinity; as, for example, to deprive the *i* in the Lithuanian *geri* of
its supposed connection with the *i* of Gothic, Greek, and Latin
forms, such as *gôdai, ἀγαθοι, boni* (see p. 251, Note †, and compare Grimm I. 827. 11); and to disconnect the Latin *is* of *lupis*
(*lupibus*) from the Greek *ις* of λύκοις (λύκοι-σι). As concerns
the method followed in treating the subject of Germanic
grammar, it is that of deducing all from the Gothic as the
guiding star of the German, and explaining the latter simultaneously with the older languages and the Lithuanian. At the close
of each lecture on the cases, a tabular view is given of the results
obtained, in which every thing naturally depends on the most
accurate distinction of the terminations from the base, which
ought not, as usually happens, to be put forward capriciously,
so that a portion of the base is drawn into the inflection, by
which the division becomes not merely useless, but injurious,
as productive of positive error. Where there is no real
termination none should be appended for appearance sake : thus,
for example, we give, §. 148, p. 164, the nominatives χώρα,
terra, giba, &c., as without inflection cf. §. 137. The division
gib-a would lead us to adopt the erroneous notion that *a* is the
termination, whereas it is only the abbreviation of the *ô* (from the
old *â*, §. 69.) of the theme.* In certain instances it is extraordi-

---

* The simple maxim laid down elsewhere by me, and deducible only
from the Sanskrit, that the Gothic *ô* is the long of *a*, and thereby when
shortened nothing but *a*, as the latter lengthened can only become *ô*, extends its influence over the whole grammar and construction of words, and
explains, for example, how from *dags*, "day " (theme *DAGA*), may be derived, without change of vowel, *dôgs* (*DÔGA*), " daily "; for this derivation is absolutely the same as when in Sanskrit *rájata*, "argenteus," comes
from *rájata*, "argentum," on which more hereafter. Generally speaking,
and with few exceptions, the Indian system of vowels, pure from consonantal
and other altering influences, is of extraordinary importance for the elucidation of the German grammar : on it principally rests my own theory of
vowel change, which differs materially from that of Grimm, and which I
explain by mechanical laws, with some modifications of my earlier defini-
tions,

narily difficult in languages not now thoroughly understood to hit on the right divisions, and to distinguish apparent terminations from true. I have never attempted to conceal these difficulties from the reader, but always to remove them from his path.

The High German, especially in its oldest period (from the eighth to the eleventh century), I have only mentioned in the general description of forms when it contributes something of importance. The juxta-position of it in its three main periods with the Gothic, grammatically explained at the close of each chapter, is sufficient, with a reference also to the treatise on sounds intended to prepare and facilitate my whole Grammar, after the ·model of my Sanskrit Grammar. Wherever, in addition, explanatory remarks are necessary, they are given. The second part will thus begin with the comparative view of the Germanic declensions, and 1 shall then proceed to the adjectives, in order to describe their formations of gender and degrees of comparison ; from these to the pronouns.

As the peculiarities of inflection of the latter must have, for the most part, already been discussed in the doctrine of the universal formation of the cases, inasmuch as they are intimately connected and mutually illustrative, what will remain to be said on their behalf will claim the less space, and the main compass of the second division will remain for the verb. To the formation and comparison of words it is my intention to devote a separate work, which may be considered as a completion of its antecedent. In this latter the particles, conjunctions, and original prepositions, will find their place, being, I consider, partly offshoots of pronominal roots, and partly naked roots of

---

tions, while with Grimm it has a dynamic signification. A comparison with the Greek and Latin vocalism, without a steady reference to the Sanskrit, is, in my opinion, for the German more confusing than enlightening, as the Gothic is generally more original in its vocal system, and at least more consistent than the Greek and Latin, which latter spends its whole wealth of vowels, although not without pervading rules, in merely responding to a solitary Indian *a* (*septimus* for *septamas*, *quatuor* for *chatvár-as* τίσσαρ-ις, *momordi* f r *mamardu*).

this class of words,* and which will, therefore, be treated in
this point of view among the pronominal adjectives.† It is
likely that a chasm in our literature, very prejudicial to inquiries
of this kind, may be shortly filled up by a work ready for the
press, and earnestly looked for by all friends of German and
general philology, the Old High German Treasury of Graff.
What we may expect from a work founded on a comprehensive
examination of the MS. treasures of libraries national and
foreign, as well as on a correction of printed materials, may be
gathered from a survey of the amount contributed to knowledge
in a specimen of the work, small, but happily selected, " The
Old High German Prepositions."

---

* I refer the reader preliminarily to my two last treatises (Berlin, Ferd.
Dümmler) " On Certain Demonstrative Bases, and their connection with
various Prepositions and Conjunctions," and " On the Influence of Pronouns on the Formation of Words." Compare, also, C. Gottl. Schmidt's
excellent tract " Quæst. Gramm. de Præpositionibus Græcis," and the
review of the same, distinguished by acute observations, by A. Benary,
in the Berlin Annual (May 1830). If we take the adverbs of place in
their relation to the prepositions—and a near relation does exist—we shall
find in close connection with the subject a remarkable treatise of the
minister W. von Humboldt, "On the Affinity of the Adverbs of Place to
the Prepositions in certain Languages." The Zend has many grammatical
rules which were established without these discoveries, and have since
been demonstrated by evidence of facts. Among them it was a satisfaction
to me to find a word, used in Sanskrit only as a preposition (*ava*, "from,")
in the Zend a perfect and declinable pronoun (§. 172.). Next we find
sa-cha, "*isque*," which in Sanskrit is only a pronoun, in its Zend shape
ᴧᴨᴧᴊᴇᴠ *ha-cha* (§. 53.), often used as a preposition to signify "out of";
the particle ᴧᴊᴩ *cha*, "and," loses itself, like the cognate *que* in *absque*, in
the general signification.

" Remark.—What in §. 68. is said of the rise of the *u* or *o* out of the
older *a* is so far to be corrected according to my later conviction, that
nothing but a retroactive influence is to be ascribed to the liquids; and
the *u* and the *o*, in forms like *plintemu* (*mo*), *plintyu*, are to be exempted
from the influence of the antecedent consonants."

† The arrangement thus announced, as intended, has undergone, as will
be seen, considerable modification.—*Editor.*

P. BOPP.

BERLIN, 1833.

COMPARATIVE GRAMMAR.

CHARACTERS AND SOUNDS.

Sanskrit writing distinguishes the long from their corresponding short vowels by particular characters, slightly
differing from these latter in form. We distinguish the long
vowels, and the diphthongs **ए** *e* and **ओ** *o*, which spring from
i and *u* united with an antecedent *a*, by a circumflex. The
simple vowels are, first, the three, original and common to all
languages, *a, i, u,* short and long; secondly, a vowel *r*, peculiar to the Sanskrit, which I distinguish by *r*, and its long
sound by *r̄*. The short *r* (**ऋ**) is pronounced like the consonant *r* with a scarcely-distinguishable *i*, and in European
texts is usually written *ri̇*; the long *r̄* (**ॠ**) is scarcely to
be distinguished from the union of an *r* with a long *i*. Both
vowels appear to me to be of later origin; and *r* presents
itself generally as a shortening of the syllable *ar* by suppression of the *a*. The long *r̄* (**ॠ**) is of much rarer occurrence. In declension it stands only for a lengthening of the *r*,
where, according to the laws of the formation of cases, a short
vowel at the end of the inflective base must be lengthened;
and in the conjugation and formation of words, those roots to
which grammarians assign a terminating **ऋ** *r̄* almost always
substitute for this unoriginal vowel **अर्** *ar*, **इर्** *ir*, **ईर्** *ir̄*, or,
after labials, **अर्** *ūr*. The last simple vowel of the Sanskrit
writing belongs more to the grammarians   [G. Ed. p. 2.]
than to the language: it is in character, as well as in pronunciation, an union of an **ल्** *l* with **र्** *r* (**ऌ**), or, when
lengthened, with **र्** *r̄* (**ॡ**). We require no representative
for this vowel, and shall not further advert to it.

2. Sanskrit possesses two kinds of diphthongs. In the one,

B

a short *a* united with a following *i* becomes ए *é* (equivalent
to the French *ai*), and with *u* becomes ओ *ó* (equivalent to
the French *au*); so that neither of the united elements is
heard, but both melt into a third sound.   In the second kind,
a long *á* with a following *i* becomes ऐ *ai*, and with *u*,
औ *au*, as in the German words *waise*, *baum*; so that the
two elements form indeed one syllable, but are both audible.
In order, however, to fix the observation on the greater
weight of the *a* in this diphthong, we write *ái* for ऐ, and *áu*
for औ.   That in ए *é* and ओ *ó* a short, in ऐ *ái* and औ *áu*,
a long *a* is bound up, I infer from this, that where, in order
to avoid a hiatus, the last element of a diphthong merges
into its corresponding semi-vowel, out of ए *é* and ओ *ó* proceed the sounds अय् *ay* and अव् *av* (with short *a*), but out
of ऐ *ái* and औ *áu* proceed *áy* and *áv*.   If, according to
the rules of combination, a concluding आ *á*, with an इ *i*,
ई *í*, or उ *u*, ऊ *ú* of a following word, be contracted, like the
short *a*, into ए *é* and ओ *ó*, but not into ऐ *ái* and औ *áu*,
this, in my view, is to be understood as if the long *a*, before
its combination with the initial vowel of the following word,
had shortened itself.   This should the less surprise us, as the
long *a* before a dissimilar vowel of an appended inflexion or
a suffix entirely disappears; and, for example, ददा *dadá*
with उस् *us* makes neither ददौस् *daddus*, nor ददोस् *dadós*,
but ददुस् *dadus*.   The opinion I have already expressed on
[G. Ed. p. 3.]   this point I have since found confirmed
by the Zend; in which ﺳﻮ *ái* always stands in the place
of the Sanskrit ऐ *ái*, and ﻋﻮ *áo* or ﻳﺳﻮ *áu* for औ *áu*.   In
support, also, of my theory, appears the fact, that a concluding *a* (short or long) with a following ए *é* or ओ *ó*, becomes ऐ *ái* and औ *áu*; of which it is to be understood, that
the short *a* contained in *é* and *ó* merges with the antecedent
a into a long *a*, which then, with the *i* of the diphthong *é*,
becomes *ái*, and with the *u* of *ó*, becomes *áu*.   For example,
ममैतत् *mamáitat*, from मम एतत् *mama état*, is to be understood

as if the diphthong ए *ê* united its first element *a* with the preceding *a* into *â*, and with this, further united its last element (*i*) into ऐ *âi*.

3. Among the simple vowels the old Indian alphabet is deficient in the designation of the Greek epsilon and omicron (ε and ο), whose sounds, if they existed when the Sanskrit was a living language, yet could only have evolved themselves, subsequently to the fixing of its written character, out of the short *a*; for an alphabet which lends itself to the subtlest gradations of sound would assuredly not have neglected the difference between *ă, ĕ,* and *ŏ,* if the sounds had been forthcoming.* It is important here to observe, that in the oldest Germanic dialect, namely, the Gothic, the sounds and characters of the short *e* and *o* are also wanting, and that either *a, i,* or *u* corresponds, in that dialect, to our German short *e.* For example, *faltha,* " ich falte," " I fold ;" *giba,* " ich gebe," " I give." In the Zend the Sanskrit व *a* remains usually ᴧ *a,* or has changed itself, according to certain   [G. Ed. p. 4.]
rules, into ᶓ *ĕ.*   Thus, for example, before a concluding *m* we always find ᶓ *ĕ*; compare the accusative ᶓᶓᾖ᷍ᴏᴣ *puthrĕ-m* " filium" with पुत्रम् *putra-m*; and its genitive ᴩᴏᴡᴧᾖᴏᴣ *puthra-hĕ* with पुत्रस्य *putra-sya.*   In Greek the Sanskrit व *a* becomes *ă, ε,* or *o,* without presenting any certain rules for the choice on each occasion between these three vowels; but the prevailing practice is, that in the terminations of nominal bases the Greek *o* answers to the Indian व *a,* except in the vocatives, where an ε is substituted.   In the Latin, besides *ă, ĕ,* and *ŏ, u* also is employed, in the terminations of nouns of the second declension and of the first person plural, as also in some adverbial suffixes, to replace the Sanskrit व *a.*

4. As in the Greek the short Sanskrit *a* is oftener replaced by ε or *o* than by a short *a,* so the long वा *â* is oftener re-

---

* Grimm, Vol. i. p. 594; with whom I entirely concur in this matter; having long abandoned a contrary opinion, which I maintained in 1819 in the Annals of Oriental Literature.

presented by η or ω than by a long alpha: and though in the Doric the long α has maintained itself in places where the ordinary dialect employs an η, no similar trace of the long *ā* for ω is to be found. दधामि *dadhâmi* "I place," becomes τίθημι; ददामि *dadâmi*, "I give," δίδωμι; the dual termination ताम् *tâm* answers to την, and only in the imperative to των: on the other hand, the आम् *âm* of the genitive plural is always represented by ων. Never, if we except peculiarities of dialect, does either η or ω stand for the Indian diphthongs ए *ê* or ओ *ô*, formed by इ *i* or an उ *u* following a long *â*: for the first, the Greek substitutes ει or οι (because for अ *a*, and also for α, ε and ο are the substitutes), and for the last, ευ or ου. Thus, एमि *êmi*, "I go," becomes είμι; पतेस् *patês*, "thou mayest fall," πίπτοις; वेद *vêda*, "I know," οἶδα; गो *go*, mas. fem. "a bullock or heifer," βοῦς. From this dropping of the *i* or *u* in the Indian diphthongs *ê* and *ô* it [G. Ed. p. 5.] may happen that α, ε, or ο, answer to these diphthongs; thus, एकतरस् *êkataras*, "one of two," becomes ἑκάτερος; देवृ *dêvri*,* "brother-in-law," Latin, *levir* (nom. देवा *dêvâ*, accus. देवरम् *devar-am*), becomes δαήρ (from δαϝήρ, δαιϝήρ); देवस् *dêva-s*, "God," Θεός; and the ο in βοός, βοΐ, stands for βου-ός, βου-ί, the *u* of which must have passed into ϝ, and certainly did so at first, as is proved by the transition into the Latin *bovis, bovi*, and the Indian गवि *gavi* (locative) from *gô-i*.

5. In Latin we sometimes find the long *e*, which, however, may be shortened by the influence of the following consonant, arising from the mixture of *a* and *i*, as in the abovementioned word *lêvir*, and in the subjunctive *amêmus* cf. कामयेम *kâmayêma* from *kâmaya-ima*.

6. If we inquire after the greater or less relative weight of the vowels of different quality, I have discovered, by

---

* The original has *devr*, but, as observed in p. 1, in European texts it is usual to write *ṛi* for ऋ; and the absence of any sign for the vowel sound is calculated to cause embarrassment: it seems advisable, therefore, to express ऋ by *ṛi*.—*Editor.*

various but sure appearances, which I shall further illustrate
in my treatise on Forms, that in Sanskrit व *a* and वा *d* are
graver than the corresponding quantity of the vowel *i*; and
this discovery is of the utmost importance for every Treatise
on special as well as comparative Grammar. It leads us, in
particular, to important discoveries with respect to the Germanic modification of vowels. In Latin, also, the *i* may be
considered as lighter than *a*, and generally takes the place of
the latter when a root with an original *a* would otherwise be
burthened with a reduplication of sound. Hence, for example,
abjicio for *abjacio*, *tetigi* for *tetagi*. I am compelled by this
view to retract an earlier conjecture, that the *i* in *tetigi* was
produced by a virtue of assimilation in the termination *i*. I
have also to relieve myself from my former theory, that the *e*
in words like *inermis*, *imberbis*, instead of [G. Ed. p. 6.]
inarmis, *imbarbis*, springs from a retrospective power of
assimilation in the following *i*, after the fashion of the modification of the vowel in German (Grimm, p. 80), and must
place it in the same class with the *e* in such forms as *abjectus*
and *tubicen*. The Latin radical *a*, for instance, is subject to
a double alteration, when the root is burthened with antecedent syllables or words: it becomes *i* in open syllables, but
e if the vowel is pressed upon by a following consonant un-
attended by a vowel. Hence we have *tubicen*, *abjectus*, in
contrast to *tubicinis*, *abjicio*; and *inermis*, *imberbis*, not *inirmis*,
imbirbis: on the contrary, *inimicus*, *insipidus*, not *inemicus*,
insepidus. In connection with this stands the transition of the
first or second declension into the third. As *us* is the masculine
form for *a*, we ought to say *inermus*, *imberbus*; but *inermis*,
imberbis, and other such forms, owe their origin to the lesser
weight of the *i*. With the displacement of the accent, where
it occurs, this change of the vowel has nothing to do; but the
removal of the accent and the weakening of the vowel are
nearly related, and are both occasioned by the composition.
In the Lithuanian we find similar appearances; as, for ex-

ample, *pónas* " lord," at the end of compounds, is weakened into *punis*, as *rótponis*, " councillor," Germ. *rathsherr*."

7. Sanskrit Grammar gives no certain indication of the relative weight of the *u* with regard to the other original vowels. The *u* is a vowel too decided and full of character to allow of its being exchanged in this language, in relief of its weight, for any other letter. It is the most obstinate of all, and admits of no exclusion from a terminating syllable, in cases where *a* and *i* admit suppression. Nor will it retire [G. Ed. p. 7.]   from a reduplicated syllable in cases where *a* allows itself to be weakened down to *i*. Thus in Latin we have *pupugi, tutudi*; while *a*, in cases of repetition, is reduced to *i* or *ĕ* (*tetigi, fefelli*, &c.)   In the Gothic, also, the *u* may boast of its pertinacity: it remains firm as the terminating vowel of nominal bases where *a* and *i* have undergone suppression, and in no single case has it been extinguished or transmuted. No power, however, exists which will not yield at last to time; and thus in the High German, whose oldest records are nearly four centuries younger than Ulphilas, the *u* has, in many cases, given way, or become in declension similar to *i*.

8. If, in the matter of the relative dignity of the vowels, we cast a glance at another race of languages, we find in Arabic the *u* taking precedence in nobility, as having its place in the nominative, while the declension is governed by the change of the terminating vowel; *i*, on the contrary, shews itself to be the weakest vowel, by having its place in the genitive, the most dependent case of the Arabic, and one which cannot be separated from the governing word. *I*, also, is continually used in cases where the grammatical relation is expressed by a preposition. Compare, also, in the plural, the *úna* of the nominative with the termination *ína* of the oblique cases. *A* stands between the strong *u* and the weaker *i*; and under the threefold change of vowels has its place in the accusative, which admits of more freedom than the genitive. In the

oblique cases, however, of nouns, and in the two-fold change of vowels, it stands opposed to the *u* of the nominative, and in the dependent subjunctive of the verb to the *u* of the independent indicative.

9. Between the vowels and the consonants, or at the close of the list of vowels, are commonly placed two signs, the sounds of which are rather to be considered as ap- [G. Ed. p. 8.] pendages to, or modifications of, the preceding vowels, than as independent sounds, and take, also, no place in the alphabet of the Native Grammarians, inasmuch as they are considered neither as consonants nor vowels, but rather as complements to the latter. The first, which we distinguish by *ṅ*, is called *Anuswâra*, " echo ;" and is, in fact, a thick nasal echo, which I think is best represented by the nasal *n* at the end of a French syllable. The weakness of its expression is discernible in the fact that it does not, like a consonant, impede the euphonic influence of an *i* or *u* on a following *s*, (see Sanskrit Grammar, R. 101ᵃ). It has its place before semi-vowels (य *y*, र *r*, ळ *l*, व *v*), sibilants, and *h ;* and we might thence term it the nasal of the two last lists of consonants, and assign its alphabetical place between them. A concluding म *m*, followed by a consonant of the said two lists, passes into Anuswâra ; for example, तस्याम् *tasyâm*, " in this," becomes तस्यां *tasyâṅ*, with the French nasal pronunciation of the *n*, if such a word as रात्रौ *râtrâu*, " in the night," come after. In connection with the स *s* of a verbal termination, a radical न् *n* also passes into Anuswâra ; as, हंसि *haṅsi*, " thou killest," from हन् *han*. Great confusion, however, has arisen from the circumstance that the Indian copyists allow themselves to express the unaltered concluding म *m*, as well as all the nasal alterations, and, in the middle of words, each of the six nasal sounds (the proper Anuswâra included), by Anuswâra.* I have

---

* The practice is not unauthorized by rule. A final म is convertible to Anuswâra before *any* consonant (Pán. 8. 3. 23.); and a medial न or म is

convertible

endeavoured, in my Grammar, to remedy this confusion in the simple theory of Anuswâra. My predecessors in the treatment of Sanskrit Grammar make no distinction between the real and the supposititious Anuswâra. Colebrooke gives it, in [G. Ed. p. 9.]   general, the pronunciation of *n*, and calls it " a shortening of the nasal consonants at the end of a syllable," which leads to the error, that each of the nasal characters, even the concluding न *n*, may be abbreviated into Anuswâra. Forster expresses it by the *n* in the English word *plinth;* Carey and Yates by the English combination *ng;* Wilkins by *m*. All substitute it for the concluding म of grammatical terminations : and as they give rules for the transition of the Anuswâra into म or न, the necessary consequence occurs, that we must write *abhavan* or *abhavang,* " I was ;" *dantan* or *dantang,* "a tooth;" not *abhavam, dantam*. Colebrooke, on the other hand, expressing a Sanskrit inscription in Roman letters (Asiatic Transactions, Vol. VII.) gives the proper termination *m*, and before *t*, by a euphonic rule, *n* ; but he maintains the original *m* before sibilants and half vowels where Anuswâra is due; as *vidwishâm śrîmad,* for विद्वषां *vidwishân*. On the other hand, F. von Schlegel and Frank write *n*, for the value of Anuswâra, in the place of *m* in several grammatical terminations. The first, for example, gives *danan,* "a gift," for *dânam ;* the second, *ahan* for *aham,* " I." A. W. von Schlegel gives rightly *m* instead of a spurious or representative Anuswâra at the end of words; and makes, for example, the infinitive termination in *tum*, not in *tun* or *tung*. He nevertheless, on this important point of grammar, retains the erroneous opinion, that the Anuswâra is a variable nasal, which, before vowels, must of necessity pass into *m* (Preface to the Bhag. Gita, p. xv.); while the direct converse is the fact, that the concluding *m* is

convertible to Anuswâra before any consonant except a semi-vowel or a nasal. (Ib. 8. 3. 24.) Such are the rules   In practice, the mutation of the final म is constant : that of the medial nasal is more variable, and in general the change occurs before the semi-vowels and sibilants.—*Editor.*

the variable nasal, which, under certain conditions, passes into the proper Anuswâra; but before vowels is necessarily retained, both in writing and pronunciation. [G. Ed. p. 10.] That Von Schlegel also still continues the original म् *m* at the end of words as an euphonic alteration of the dead sound of Anuswâra appears from his mode of printing Sanskrit text, in which he makes no division between a concluding म् *m* and the commencing vowel of the following word ; while he does make a division after न् *n*, and thereby shews that he admits a division after terminating letters which remain unaffected by the influence of the letters which follow. If, however, we write तान् अब्रवीत् *tân abravit*, " he said to them," we must also write ताम् अब्रवीत् *tâm abravit*, " he said to her ;" not तामब्रवीत् *tâmabravit*, for the म of ताम् *tâm* is original, and not, as Von Schlegel thinks, begotten out of Anuswâra. The conjecture of C. Lassen (Ind. Bibl. Book III. p. 39), that the Anuswâra is to be understood, not as an after sound (*Nachlaut*), nor as an echo (*Nachhall*), but as a sound which regulates itself by that which follows—as it were the term *Nachlaut*, with the accent on *laut**—appears to me highly improbable. Schlegel's *nasalis mutabilis* would indeed be justified by this view, and the imputation of error removed from the Iudian Grammarians, to whom we willingly concede a knowledge of the value of the Sanskrit signs of sound, and whom we are unwilling to censure for designating a half sound as mutable, in a language whose termi-

---

* This seems intended for an explanation, for Lassen has nothing like it. I have not found an etymological explanation of the term in any grammatical commentary ; but it may be doubted if the explanation of the text, or that given by Lassen, be correct. Anuswâra may indeed be termed *sequens sonus* ; but by that is to be understood the final or closing sound of a syllable. Any other nasal may be used as the initial letter of a syllable ; but the nasal Anuswâra is exclusively an "after" sound, or final. It is not even capable of blending, as it were, with a following vowel, like a final *n* or *m*, as in *tân-* or *tâmabravit*. It is the legitimate representative of either of the other nasals when those are absolutely terminal,

nating sounds are almost always governed by the following
words.   It is true the half sound owes its being to the muta-
bility of a concluding *m*, but is not mutable itself, since it never
has an independent existence of its own at the end of any word :
in the middle, however, of a radical syllable, as दंश् *danś*,
हिंस् *hins*, it is susceptible of expulsion, but not of alteration.

[G. Ed. p. 11.]   That the Indian Grammarians, however,
consider the *m* and not the *ṅ* as the original but mutable
letter in grammatical terminations, like अम् *am*, भ्याम् *bhyâm*,
&c., appears from the fact that they always write these
terminations, where they give them separate, with the labial
nasal, and not with Anuswâra.   If it be objected that this is
of no importance, as dependent on the caprice of the editor
or copyist, we can adduce as a decisive proof of the just
views of the Indian Grammarians in this respect, that when
they range the declensions of words in the order of their
terminating letters, the Pronouns इदम् *idam*, and किम् *kim*,
in which they consider the *m* as primitive, are treated when
the turn comes of the labial nasal *m*, and together with
प्रशाम् *praśâm*, "quiet," from the root शम् *śam*.   (Laghu-
Kaumudî, p. 46.)

10. The deadened nasal, which is expressed in the Lithuanian
by particular signs over the vowel which it follows, appears
to be identical with the Sanskrit Anuswâra; and we write it
in the same manner with *ṅ*.   At the end of words it stands
for the remainder of an ancient *m*, in the accusative singular
for example; and the deadening of *n* before *s* into *ṅ* presents

---

terminal, and in pronunciation retains their respective sounds, according
to the initial consonant of the following word.   Again, with regard to its
relation to the semi-vowels and sibilants, it may be regarded as appropriate
to them merely in as far as neither of the other nasals is so considered.
In this sense Anuswâra may be termed a subsidiary or supplemental sound,
being prefixed with most propriety to those letters which, not being classed
under either of the five series of sounds, have no rightful claim to the
nasals severally comprehended within each respective series.—*Editor.*

a remarkable accordance with the Sanskrit rule of euphony before mentioned. From *laupsin-u*, "I praise," therefore comes *laupsinsu*, "I shall praise;" as in Sanskrit हंस्यामि *hansyámi*, "I shall kill," from the root हन् *han*. In the Prâkrit, not only the म् *m*, but the न् *n*, at the end of words, has always fallen into Anuswâra; without regard to the following letters. Thus we read in Chezy's edition of the Sakuntalâ, p. 70, भवं, which is certainly to be pronounced, not *bhaavam*, but *bhaavan*, for भगवन् *bhagavan*; [G. Ed. p. 12.] कुधं *kudhan*, for कुधम् *kudham*.[*]

11. The second of the signs before mentioned is named Visarga, which signifies abandonment. It expresses a breathing, which is never primitive, but only appears at the end of words in the character of an euphonic alteration of स् *s* and र् *r*. These two letters (*s, r*) are very mutable at the end of words, and are changed into Visarga before a pause or the deadened letters of the guttural and labial classes (§. 12.). We write this sign *h́* to distinguish it from the true ह *h*.

12. The proper consonants are classed in the Sanskrit alphabet according to the organs used in their pronunciation; and form, in this division, five classes. A sixth is formed by the semi-vowels, and a seventh by the sibilants and the ह *h*. In the first five ranks of these consonants the single letters are so arranged, that the first are the surd or hard consonants, the thin (*tenues*), and their aspirates; next, the sonant or soft, the medials, and their aspirates, each class being completed by its nasal. The nasals belong, like the vowels and semi-vowels, to the sonants; the sibilants to the surd or hard. Every thin and every medial letter has its corresponding aspirate. The aspirates are pronounced, like their

---

[*] No native scholar would read these as *bhaavan* or *kudhan*, as the text affirms, but *bha-avam, kudham*, agreeably to the final म represented by Anuswâra.—*Editor.*

respective non-aspirates, with a clearly audible *h*; thus, for example, त *th*, not like the English *th*; फ *ph*, not *f* or *φ*; and ख *kh*, not like the Greek *χ*.* In an etymological point of view it is important to observe that the aspirates of different organs are easily exchanged with each other; thus, भर *bhar*, धर *dhar*, (भृ *bhri*, धृ *dhri*, §. 1.) "to bear," "to hold," are perhaps originally identical. धूमस् *dhuma-s*, [G. Ed. p. 13.] "smoke," is, in Latin, *fumu-s*. In Greek, *θάνω*, as well as *φένω*, is related to हन् *han*, from धन् *dhan*, "to kill." The Gothic *thliuhan* is the German *fliehen*, Old High German *vliuhan*.

13. The first class is that of the gutturals, and includes the letters क *k*, ख *kh*, ग *g*, घ *gh*, ङ *n*. The nasal of this class is pronounced like the German *n* before gutturals, as in the words *sinken*, *enge*, so as to prepare for the following guttural. In the middle of words it is only found before gutturals; and, at the end, supplies the place of म *m* when the following word begins with a guttural.† We write it without the distinctive sign, as its guttural nature is easily recognised by the following consonant. The aspirates of this class are not of frequent use, either at the beginning or end of words. In some Greek words we find *χ* in the place of ख *kh*: compare *ὄνυξ*, *ὄνυχ-ος*, with *nakha*, "a nail;" *κόγχη*, *κόγχος*, with *sankha*, "shell;" *χαίνω*, *χανῶ*, with *khan*, "to

---

* The original here adds—"We designate the aspirate by a comma, as *t'*, *d'*, *b'*." The use of such a mark is, however, unsightly, and appears likely to cause occasional perplexity and doubt. It seems therefore preferable to adhere to the usual mode of expressing the aspirated letters, as *dh*, *bh*, and the like. It is only necessary to remember that *th* and *ph* are the letters *t* and *p* with an aspiration, and not the *th* and *f* of the English alphabet—*Editor.*

† A careful examination will perhaps shew that the several nasals of the Sanskrit alphabet are mere modifications of one sound, according to the manner in which that is affected by a succeeding letter; and that the modifications prevail equally in most languages, although it has not been thought necessary to provide them with distinct symbols.—*Editor.*

dig." As regards the sonant aspirates, the ग gh of gharma, "heat" (in Greek θέρμη), has passed into the aspiration of another organ; लघु laghu, "light," has laid aside the guttural in the Latin levis, and, in virtue of the i, changed the u into v. The guttural has kept its place in the German leicht, the English light, and the Old High German lihti.

14. The second class is that of the palatals; and includes the sounds ch and j, with their aspirates and nasal. We write च ch, छ chh, ज j,* झ jh,* न n. This class is an offshoot from the preceding, and to be considered as a softening of it. It is only found before vowels and weak consonants (semi-vowels and nasals); and before strong consonants, and at the end of a word, generally retires into the class from which it springs. Thus, for example, the base   [G. Ed. p. 14.] वाच् vâch, "speech," "voice" (cf. vox), makes, in the uninflected nominative, वाक् vâk; in the instrumental and locative plurals, वाग्भिस् vâg-bhis, वाक्षु vâkshu. In the cognate languages we have to look for, in the place of the letters of this class, first, gutturals; next labials, on account of their mutual affinity; thirdly, the sounds of t, as, according to pronunciation, the first element of the palatals is a t or d; fourthly, sibilants, as being the last element in the letters of this class. Compare पचामि pachâmi, "I cook" (inf. paktum, part. pass. pakta), with coquo, πέπω (πέπτω, πέττω, πέσσω); चतुर् chatur, "four," nom. चत्वारस् chatwâras, with qualuor, τέτταρες, τέσσαρες, Gothic fidvôr, Lithuanian ketturi; पञ्चन् panchan, "five" (nom. accus. pancha), with quinque, πέντε, πέμπε, Gothic fimf, Lithuanian penki; राजन् râjan, "king," with rex, regis; राजत râjata, nom. râjatam, "silver" (from râj, "to shine"), with argentum, ἄργυρος; जानु jânu, "knee," with genu, γόνυ. With regard to the aspirates of this class, the chh, as an initial letter in some words, answers to sc, σκ; छिन्ध chhind-

---

* The original has ǵ and ǧ; but the appropriate symbols in English are j and its aspirate.

mas, " we cleave," चिन्दि *chhinadmi,* " " I cleave," answers
to the Latin *scindo;* छाया *chhâyâ,* " shadow," to the Greek
σκιά. As the terminating letter of a root *chh* answers, in
प्रछ् *prachh,* " to ask," to the Gothic *h* in *frah,* "I or he asked,"
and to the German and Latin *g* in *frage, rogo,* in case that
the latter, as I suspect, is a modification of *progo.* The nasal
of this class, for which we require no distinctive sign, as it
only precedes palatals, deviates but slightly from the sound
of the guttural *n,* and is pronounced nearly like *nj.*

15. The third class is called that of the linguals or cerebrals,
and embraces a peculiar kind of sounds of *t,* together with its
[G. Ed. p. 15.]   nasal; a kind not original, but which has
developed itself from the ordinary class of *t* sounds. We distinguish them by a point under the letter, thus, ट *t,* ठ *th,*
ड *d,* ढ *dh,* ण *n.* In the Prâkṛit this class has obtained great
supremacy, and has frequently supplanted the ordinary *t.*
We there find, for example, भोडु *bhôḍu,* for भवतु *bhavatu,* " let
it be ;" and पढम *paḍhama,* for प्रथम *prathama,* " the first."
With regard to the nasal, the substitution of ण for न is
nearly universal. The Indian Grammarians approach the
Prâkṛit nearer than the Sanskrit, when at the beginning of
roots they use the same substitution. The practice, also,
which we have condemned (§. 9.), of using Anuswâra for
म *m,* at the end of words, is more Prâkṛit than Sanskrit.
At the beginning of words these letters are seldom found in
Sanskrit, but they are found as terminations to a certain
number of roots ; for example, अट् *aṭ,* " to go." They are
pronounced by bending back the tongue against the roof of
the mouth, by which a hollow sound is expressed, as if from
the head.* The nasal of this class has sometimes overstepped
the limits of its usual laws : it is found before vowels, which

---

* Here, also, it may be doubted if similar modifications of the dental
sounds are not discoverable in languages which do not express them by
separate symbols. The *t* of the Italian *tutto* is the Sanskrit ट.—*Editor.*

is not the case with the nasals of the preceding classes ; yet never at the beginning of words.

16. The fourth class embraces the dentals, or the sounds which properly answer to the common *d* and *t*, together with the common *n*, which belongs to them, त *t*, थ *th*, द *d*, ध *dh*, न *n*. Of the aspirates of this organ, we have to remark, that थ *th*, in an etymological respect, never—at least in no instance of which we are aware—is represented in Greek by θ, but always like the natural *t*, by τ. On the other hand, ध *dh* does correspond to θ, which also sometimes represents द *d*. Thus the imperative ending धि *dhi*, in Greek becomes θι ; मधु *madhu*, "honey," "wine," is μέθυ ; दधामि *dadhâmi*, "I place," τίθημι ; दुहितर् *duhitar* [G. Ed. p. 16.] (दुहितृ *duhitri*, §. 1.), "daughter," θυγάτηρ ; द्वार् *dwâr*, f. and *dwâra*, neut. (nom. *dwâram*), "door," θύρα ; देव *dêva*, Lithuan. *diewas*, "God," Θεός. With regard to the hard aspirate, compare the terminations τε and τον with थ *tha* and थस् *thas*, the former in the plural, the second in the dual of the present and future ; στήσω with स्थास्यामि *sthâsyâmi*, "I shall stand"; ὀστέον with अस्थि *asthi*, "bone"; in the Latin, *rota* with रथ *ratha*, "carriage"; and in the Gothic, the ending *t*, in the second person singular of the preterite, with *tha* ; for example, *vais-t*, "thou knewest," with वेत्थ *vêt-tha*. From the beginning of words in the Sanskrit this aspirate is nearly excluded.

17. The interchange of *d* and *l* is well known. Upon it, among other instances, is founded the relation of *lacryma* to δάκρυ, δάκρυμα. In Sanskrit, also, an apparently original द *d* often corresponds to the *l* of cognate European languages ; for example, दीप् *dîp*, "to light," दीप *dîpa*, "lamp," becomes λάμπω, λαμπάς ; देह *dêha*, "body," Gothic *leik*. On this relation also rests, as I have shewn elsewhere, the relation of our *lf*, Gothic *lif*, in *elf*, *zwölf*, Gothic *tvalif*, to दशन् *daśan*, δέκα. As also the second consonant has undergone alteration, and has migrated from the gutturals into the

labials; and as, moreover, the number "ten," taken alone, is, in Gothic, *taihun*, in German *zehn*, its origin from *lif* was deeply concealed; and even the Lithuanian *lika*, which accompanies the simple numbers in their compounded forms from eleven to twenty, remained long under my notice without result. The fact, however, that one and the same word may, in the course of time, assume various forms for various objects, proved, as it is, by numberless examples, requires no further [G. Ed. p. 17.]   support. With respect to the affinity of λίκος in ἠλίκος, &c., and of the Gothic *leiks* in *hvêleiks*, "like to whom?" to इष *dṛiśa*, Prâkṛit दिस *disa*, "like," I refer the reader to my Treatise on the Pronoun and its influence (Berlin, published by Dümmler); and only remark, in addition, that by this analogy of λίκος, *leiks*, I was first led to that of *lif* to δέκα; while the Lithuanian *lika* had not yet attracted my observation.

18. The labial class comes next, namely, प *p*, फ *ph*, ब *b*, भ *bh*, म *m*. The hard aspirate *ph* is among the rarer letters; the most usual words in which it occurs are, फल *phala*, "fruit," फेन *phêna*, "foam," and the forms which come from the root फुल्ल *phull*, "to burst, blow, bloom." The sonant aspirate भ *bh* belongs, together with ध *dh*, to the most frequent of the aspirates. In the Greek and Latin, φ and *f* are the letters which most frequently correspond to this भ *bh*, especially at the beginning of words; for example, भृ *bhṛi*, "to bear," *fero*, φέρω; भू *bhû*, "to be," *fu-i*, φύ-ω. भ *bh* is also often represented by *b* in Latin, especially in the middle of words. The *f* of *fero* becomes *b* in certain compounds which rank as simple words with a derivable suffix, as *ber*, *brum*, *brium*, in words like *saluber*, *candelabrum*, *manubrium*. Thus the *f* of *fu* appears as *b* in the forms *amabam*, *amabo*, which I have recognised as compounds, and which will be hereafter explained. The dative and ablative termination plural भ्यस् *bhyas*, becomes *bus* in Latin. The nasal of this class, म *m*, is subject, at the end of a word, to several alterations, and only remains fast before a pause, a

vowel, or letters of its own class: it otherwise governs itself according to the nature of the following letters, and may pass, in this manner, into any of the four preceding nasals, and weakens itself into the softened nasal sound   [G. Ed. p. 18.] of the proper Anuswâra, if followed by a semi-vowel, a sibilant, or ह़ *h.* *M* has also a full right to the name of a mutable nasal. It is, however, not beseeming, when, in editions of a text otherwise conspicuous for accuracy, we find म, though protected in its original condition by a pause, or by the following letters, written as Anuswâra.

19. The semi-vowels follow next: य़ *y,* ऱ *r,* ल़ *l,* व़ *v.* We distinguish *y* by the sound of our German *j,* or the English *y* in the word *year.* As the Latin *j* in English has the sound of a softened *g,* so in Prâkṛit य़ *y* often passes into ज़ *j;* and in Greek, upon this exchange of sound rests the relation of ζεύγνυμι, ζυγός, &c. to the root युज yuj, "to bind," and that of the verbs in ἄζω to the Indian verbs in अयामि *ayâmi;* for ζ is *ds,* but the sound *dsch* is not to be looked for in the Greek. The relation of the Persian جوان *javân,* "young," to the Sanskrit Theme युवन *yuvan,* Lat. *juvenis,* belongs to this place. By *v* we here designate the sound of the German *w* and English *v.* After consonants, as त्वाम् *twâm,* "thee," this letter takes the pronunciation of the English *w.* The occasional hardening of the *v* into a guttural deserves mention here; thus, in Latin, *vic-si* (*vixi*), *victum,* spring from *viv;* and in *facio* I recognise the Sanskrit causal भावयामि *bhâv-ayâ-mi,* "I make to be," from the root भू *bhû.* The connection between *fac-tus* and *fio* is practically demonstrated. Refer back, in the Old and Modern Greek, to the occasional hardening of the Digamma into γ (cf. C. G. Schmidt in the Berlin Jahrbuch, 1831, p. 613.). The voice cannot dwell on व़ *v* or य़ *y;* and these two letters are therefore, as in the Semitic languages, excluded from the end of words: [G. Ed. p. 19.] therefore the word दिव् *div,* "Heaven," forms its nominative, which ought to be *div* (*divs* being forbidden, see §. 94.),

c

from बी *dyô.* Nominal bases in *y* do not exist. र *r* at the end
of a word is subject to many alterations, and is interchange-
able with स *s.* In places where the concluding *s,* by favour
of the following letter, is retained, र *r* becomes स *s* ; and, on
the other hand, remains unaltered in places where स *s* becomes र *r,* namely, before vowels and sonant consonants.

20. The semi-vowels, by reason of their tractable and fluent
nature, are easily interchanged. For instance, in the more
recent Sanskrit works ल *l* often stands for र *r.** We often,
also, find in the cognate European languages *l* for व *v.* On
this interchange is founded the relation of the Latin suffix *lent*
(*e. g. opulens*), and of the Gothic *laud*(a)-*s*† (see §. 116.), in
hvêlauds, "quantus," *svalauds,* "tantus," *samalauds,* "just so
much," to the Sanskrit वम *vant* (in the strong case, §. 119.),
in words like धनवम *dhanavant,* "endowed with wealth,"
तावम *tâvant,* "so much," यावम *yâvant,* "how much." On
the change between *v* and *r* is founded, as I believe, the relation of the Old High German *pir-u-mês,* "we are" (sing. *pim,*
भवामि *bhav-â-mi*), to भवामस *bhav-â-mas ;* as also that of *scrir-*
-u-mês, "we shriek," to श्रावयामस *srâv-ayâ-mas,* "we make
to hear" (§. 109.); as also that of *triusu,* "I fall," from the
[G. Ed. p. 20.]   root *trus,* to the Sanskrit ध्वंस *dhwans,* "to
fall ;"‡ and of the Cretan τρέ "thee" from τϝέ, to the Sanskrit
twâ. The semi-vowel *l* is also exchanged with the nasals;
thus, अन्यस *anya-s,* "the other," becomes *alius* in Latin, and

---

* It is scarcely correct to say "often," as the instances are rare: nor
are they restricted to recent works. Menu has *asîlka* for *asrîka.—Ed.*

† Grimm (iii. p. 46) assumes an adjective *lauds,* "great;" which, as
far as the Gothic at least is concerned, might be dispensed with, as it is
of the greatest antiquity as a suffix, and does not appear alone as an
adjective, even in the oldest periods.

‡ *Dh,* according to §. 16., = the Greek 9; and to the 9, according
to §. 87., corresponds the old High German *t.* The *u* of *trus,* from the
old *a,* may be produced by the influence of the *r,* or of the dropped
nasal.

वमारस antara-s, "the other," alter; वद् vad, "to speak," answers to the Gothic lath-ôn, "called," "invited," ga-lathôn, "called together": ध्मा dhma, "to blow," answers to flare. (§. 109.) Compare, also, balbus with βαμβαίνω.

21. The last class embraces the sibilants and h: श् ś, ष् sh, स s, and ह h. The first sibilant is spoken with a slight aspiration, and usually written by the English sh.* It belongs to the palatal class, and thence supplies the place of the third or proper स s when a hard palatal च ch or छ chh follows; for instance, रामश् चरति râmaś charati, instead of रामस् चरति râmas charati, "Râmas goes." In its origin, श् ś appears to have sprung from k; and in Greek and Latin we find κ and c regularly corresponding to the Sanskrit श् ś. The Gothic substitutes h in pursuance of the law of change of sound; but the Lithuanian stands the nearest to the Sanskrit with reference to this letter, and has in its stead a sibilant compound sz, pronounced like sh. Compare decem, δέκα, Gothic taihun, Lithuan. dészimtis, with दशन् daśan (nom. दश daśa); canis, κύων, Gothic hunds, Lithuan. szuo (gen. szuns), with श्वन् śwan (nom. श्वा śwâ, gen. शुनस् śunas, κυνός), "dog;" δάκρυ, lacrima, aszara, f. with अश्रु aśru n. "tear;" equus (= ecvus), Lith. aszwa f. "mare," with अश्व aśwa (nom. अश्वस् aśwas), "horse;" szaka f. with शाखा śâkhâ "bough." The Lith. szwenta-s, "holy," answers to the Zend spênta (§. 50.). At the end of a word, and in the middle before strong consonants, श् ś is not allowed, although admitted as an euphonic substitute for a concluding स s before an initial hard palatal. Otherwise श् ś usually falls back into the sound from which [G. Ed. p. 21.] it appears to have originated, namely, k. In some roots, however, श् ś passes into ट् ṭ; for instance, दृश् dṛiś, "seeing," and विश् viś, "a man of the third caste," form, in the uninflected nominative, दृक् dṛik, विट् viṭ. The second sibilant, ष् sh, is pronounced like our sch, or sh in English, and

---

* More usually s; the sh is reserved for the cerebral sibilant.—Editor.

belongs to the lingual class.   It often steps, according to
certain rules into the place of स s ; thus, for instance, after
क् k, स s never follows, but only ष sh ; and the ξ, x, in Greek
and Latin, are regularly represented by क्ष ksh.   Compare
दक्षिण dakshina, with dex-ter, δεξίος, Lithuanian dészinè, " the
right hand."   Of the vowels, i, u, and ri, short or long, are
averse from स s, to which a and á alone are inclined.   After the
first-named vowels, स s passes into ष sh ;   for instance, तनोषि
tanôshi, instead of तनोसि tanôsi (extendis).   As an initial, ष sh
is extremely rare : the Indian grammarians, however, write
the roots which, under certain circumstances, change स s into
ष sh, from the first with a ष sh.   A word which really begins with ष sh is षष् shash, " six;" to which the Lith. szeszi, a
plural nominative, answers most nearly, while other cognate
languages indicate an original ordinary s.   At the end of a
word, and in the middle before other strong consonants, such
as ट t, ठ th, ष sh is not permitted, but in most roots passes
into क् k, but with some into ट t: the number six, mentioned
above, becomes, in the uninflected nominative, षट् shat.

22. The third sibilant is the ordinary s of all languages, but
which, at the end of Sanskrit words, holds a very insecure position, and by certain rules is subjected to transmutation into
श ś, ष sh, र r, : ah or h Visarga (§. 11.), and u; and only remains unaltered before t and th.   We write, for example, सूनुस्
तरति súnus tarati, " the son passes over," but तरति सूनु: tarati
[G. Ed. p. 22.]   súnuh, सूनुश् चरति súnuś charati (it), सूनुर्
भवति súnur bhavati (est).   This sensitiveness against a concluding स s can only have arisen in the later period of the
language, after its division ; as in the cognate languages the
concluding s remains unaltered, or where it has been changed
for r does not return into its original form.   Thus, in the
decree against Timotheus (Maittaire, §. 383-4.) ρ everywhere
stands for ς: Τιμόσεορ ὁ Μιλήσιορ—παραγινόμενορ—λυμαίνε-
ται τὰρ ἀκοὰρ τῶν νέων, &c.*   The Sanskrit could not endure

----
* Cf. Hartung, p. 106.

r before *t*. The Latin protects the *s* usually at the end of words; but in the classical period generally sacrifices it, when between two vowels, to the *r*; for instance, *genus, generis,* for *genesis;* a contrast to forms found in Varro and Festus, such as *plusima, fœdesum, meliosem, majosibus,* in which the *s* evinces its original existence in the history of the language (see §. 127.). The accusative form *arbosem,* recorded by Festus, is more startling, for here *r* is the original form, if, as I can hardly doubt, *arbor, arbos,* is related to the word of such frequent occurrence in the Zend-Avesta, ᴡᴊᴜᴊᴊᴊᴊ *urvara,* "tree." This expression is not wanting in the Sanskrit, (उर्वरा *urvará;*) but it signifies, according to Wilson, "fruitful land," and "land" in general.

23. ह *h* belongs to the letters which, in Sanskrit, are never admitted at the end of words, nor in the middle before strong consonants. In these places it passes, by certain rules, into त् *t,* द् *d,* क् *k,* or ग् *g.* In Greek we often find χ in the place of the Sanskrit ह *h:* compare χειμών, *hiems,* with हिम *hima,* "snow," "rime;" χαίρω with हृषामि *hrish-*   [G. Ed. p. 23.] *yámi, gaudeo;* χήν with हंस *hansa,* "goose;" χθές, *heri,* with ह्यस् *hyas,* "yesterday;" ὄχος with वह *vah,* "to transport." We also find κ, c, for *h:* compare καρδία, *cor,* Gothic *hairtó,* with हृद् *hrid* (n. हृदय *hridaya*), "heart." We sometimes, but rarely, find the spiritus asper substituted for *h;* for instance, αἱρέω, हरामि *hardmi,* "I take away." The Lithuanian exhibits sometimes *sz* for *h;* for instance, *asz,* "I," for अहम् *aham, szirdis* f. "heart," for हृद् *hrid.* This letter stands sometimes in Sanskrit for a mutilation of other aspirated consonants, of which the aspiration alone has been suppressed; thus, instead of the imperative ending धि *dhi,* we generally find *hi;* on which account the grammarians accept हि *hi,* and not धि *dhi,* as the original ending, and assume that *hi* passes into *dhi,* for euphonic reasons, after consonants. The root ग्रह् *grah,* "to take," is written in the Vedas ग्रभ् *grabh,* and answers thus more nearly to the German *greifen,* and the Persian *giriftan.*

We give here a general view of the Sanscrit characters, with their respective values.

VOWELS.

ग a, आ á, इ i, ई í, उ u, ऊ ú, ऋ ṛi, ॠ ṛí.

ANUSWÂRA AND VISARGA.

· ṅ,　　: aḣ.

CONSONANTS.

Gutturals	क k,	ख kh,	ग g,	घ gh,	ङ n.
Palatals	च ch,	छ chh,	ज j,	झ jh,	ञ n.
Linguals	ट ṭ,	ठ ṭh,	ड ḍ,	ढ ḍh,	ण ṇ.
Dentals	त t,	थ th,	द d,	ध dh,	न n.
Labials	प p,	फ ph,	ब b,	भ bh,	म m.
Semi-Vowels	य y,	र r,	ल l,	व v.	
Sibilants and Aspirates,	श ś,	ष ṣh,	स s,	ह h.	

[G. Ed. p. 24.]　　The vowel characters given above are found only at the beginning of words; and in the middle or end of a word are supplied in the following manner : ग a is left unexpressed, but is contained in every consonant which is not distinguished by a sign of rest (ˌ) or connected with another vowel. क k is thus read ka; and k by itself, or the absence of the a, is expressed by क्. इ i, ई í, are expressed by ि, ी, and the first of these two is placed before, the second after, the consonant to which it relates; for instance, कि ki, की kí. For उ u, ऊ ú, ऋ ṛi, ॠ ṛí, the signs ु, ू, ृ, ॄ, are placed under their consonants; as, कु ku, कू kú, कृ kṛi, कॄ kṛí. For ए é and ऐ ái, े and ै are placed over their consonants; as, के ké, कै kái : को ó and कौ áu are written by omission of the ग, which is here only a fulcrum; as, को kó, कौ káu. The consonants without vowels, instead of appearing in their entire shapes, and with the sign of rest, are usually written so that their distinctive sign is connected with the following consonant; for instance, for त, ष, य, we have त्, ष्, य्; and thus matsya is written मत्स्य, not मत्ष्य; for त् + स we have त्स; and for क् + ष we have क्ष.

25. The Sanskrit letters are divided into hard or surd, and soft or sonant. Surd are, all the tenues, with their corresponding aspirates; and in fact, according to the order given above, the first two letters in each of the first five rows, also the three sibilants. Soft are, the medials, with their aspirates, the **ह**, the nasals, semi-vowels, and all vowels. Another division also appears to us convenient—that of the consonants into strong and weak; in which the nasals and semi-vowels come under the denomination of weak; the remaining consonants under that of the strong. The weak consonants and vowels exercise no influence, as initial letters of inflections and suffixes, in the formation of words, on the terminating   [G. Ed. p. 25.] letters of a root; while they themselves are compelled to accommodate themselves to a following strong consonant.

26. With regard to the vowels, it is of consequence to direct the observation to two affections of them, of frequent occurrence in the development of forms of Sanskrit; of which the one is called Guna, or virtue; the other Vriddhi, increase or augmentation. My predecessors in grammatical inquiry have given no information as to the essence, but have only expounded the effects of these vowel alterations; and it was only in my critical labours upon Grimm's German Grammar* that I came upon the trace of the true nature and distinctive qualities of these affections, as also of the law by which Guna is usually produced and governed, and at the same time of its hitherto undetected existence in the Greek and Germanic, and, most conspicuously, in the Gothic. My views in this particular have since derived remarkable confirmation from the Zend, with relation to which I refer to §. 2., in which, as I flatter myself, I have dealt successfully with an apparent contradiction to my explanation. Guna consists in prefixing short *a*, and Vriddhi in prefixing a long one: in both, however, the *a* melts into a diphthong with the primitive vowel,

---

* Berlin Journal, Feb. 1827, p. 254.

according to certain euphonic laws. इ *i*, namely, and ई, melt
with the अ *a* of Guna into ए *ê;* उ *u,* अ *û,* into ओ *ô.*   These
diphthongs, however, dissolve again before vowels into अय् *ay*
and अव् *av;* ऋ *ṛi* and ॠ *ṝi* become, in virtue of the action of
Guna, अर् *ar;* by that of Vṛiddhi, आर् *âr.*   As in Greek the
[G. Ed. p. 26.]   short Sanskrit *a* is frequently replaced by
ε; so we find the Guna here, when a radical *i* or *u* is prolonged
by prefixing an ε.   As in the Sanskrit the root इ *i,* " to go,"
forms, by the Guna modification, एमि *êmi* (from *a-imi*), " I
go," in contrast to *imas,* " we go ;" thus in Greek also we
have εἶμι in contrast to ἴμεν.   As the root बुध् *budh,* in several
tenses in the three numbers, rises, in virtue of Guna, into
बोध् *bôdh* (from *baudh*), for instance, बोधामि *bôdhâmi,* " I know ;"
so in the Greek * the root φυγ (ἔφυγον), in the present becomes φεύγω.   In the Gothic, in the strong form of Grimm's
8th and 9th conjugations, the radical vowel, strengthened by
a in the singular of the preterite, stands in the same contrast to the *i* and *u* of the plural, as is the case in the corresponding tense of the Sanskrit.   Compare *baug,* " I bent," in
contrast to *bugum,* " we bent," with the Sanskrit form of the
same signification, singular बुबोज *bubhôja,* plural बुबुजिम
bubhujima, of the root भुज् *bhuj;* compare *vait,* " I know," in
contrast with *vitum,* " we know," with the Sanskrit forms of
the same signification, वेद *vêda* (from *vaïda*), विदिम *vidima,*
from the root विद् *vid,* " know," which, like the corresponding Gothic and Greek root, employs the terminations of the
preterite with a present signification.

27. We have, however, the Sanskrit Guna in yet another
form in the Gothic—a form which I have but lately discovered, but of which the historical connection with the
Sanskrit modification appears to me not the less certain.   I
once thought that I had accounted in a different manner for
the relation existing between *biuga,* " I bend," and its root

---

* Regarding Greek οι as Guna of ι, see §. 491.; and as to Guna in Old
Sclavonic and Lithuanian, see §§. 255.b) *f),* 741., 746.

bug, and I conceived myself bound to ascribe generally, in the present tense, to the prevalent *i* of terminations a retro-active influence. It now, however, seems to me indisputable that Grimm's 8th and 9th conjugations of the   [G. Ed. p. 27.] first class correspond to my first Sanskrit conjugation (r. 326.); so that the Guna *a* of the special tenses has been weakened to *i,* while the monosyllabic preterite maintains the Guna vowel in the more important shape of *a*; just as in the 10th, 11th, and 12th conjugations, according to Grimm's division, the radical *a,* which has remained in the preterite singular, is, in the present and other tenses, weakened to *i*; so that, for instance, *at,* "I" and "he eat," corresponds to the root अद् *ad,* "to eat;" but in the present, *ita* stands in place of the form अद्मि *admi,* "I eat." *

28. The Zend possesses, besides the Sanskrit Guna, which has remained everywhere where it stands in Sanskrit, a vowel application peculiar to itself, which likewise consists in ల *a,* and which was first observed by M. E. Burnouf.† The vowels which admit this addition in the interior, but not at the end of words, are, first, the short *i,* *u,* *o;* 2dly, the Guna diphthongs *ê* and *ô.* The two latter are the most usually befriended by this addition, and *ê* takes it in all cases where the opportunity occurs, both as an initial letter, and even at the end of words wherever the dependent particle ల *cha,* "and," is appended to it; hence, for example, *nairê,* "homini," *âthre,* "igni"; but *naraêcha,* "hominique," *âthraêcha,* "ignique." Also where an *ê* stands in two consecutive syllables, an *a* is placed before each. Hence, for instance, *aêtaêibyô,* from एतेभ्य *êtêbhyas.* The only case in which, ex-

---

* It would be difficult to adduce a better instance of the phonetic deficiencies of our English alphabet than this sentence, in which I am forced to translate the present and past tenses of *essen* by the same characters. What foreign student could guess or remember that the one is pronounced *eet,* the other *ett* ? The preterite "ate" is obsolete.—*Translator.*

† N. Journ. Asiat., T. III. p. 327.

cepting at the actual end of the word, ‌‌ *é* remains without
the preceding ‌‌ *a*, is when it is produced by the influence of
a ‌‌ *y*, out of ‌‌ *a* or ‌‌ *â*.   We say, indeed, ‌‌

[G. Ed. p. 28.]   *yaëibyô*, "*quibus*," from ‌‌ *yébhyas;* but
not ‌‌ *âyaëié*, but ‌‌ *âyéié,* " I glorify," from
the Sanskrit root, which has been lost, for the verb ‌‌ *yaé,*
from which comes ‌‌ *yaśas*, "glory."   Yet we find, for
‌‌ *yéri*, "if" (cf. ‌‌ *yadi*), sometimes, though perhaps
erroneously, also ‌‌ *yaëzi*.   The addition of the ‌‌ *a*
before ‌‌ *ô* is just as unlimited, but the occasion is far less
frequent.   Examples of it are, ‌‌ *aôzô*, "strength," from
‌‌ *ôjas;* ‌‌ *kërënaôt*, "he made," from ‌‌ *kri*, according to the fifth class, for ‌‌ *akrinôt;* ‌‌ *mraôt*,
"he spoke," from ‌‌ *abrôt*, which would be the regular
form, instead of ‌‌ *abravít* (Gramm. Crit. r. 352.).   We
also find ‌‌ *mraôm*, "I spoke," for ‌‌ *abrôm*, which
would be the form used were, in the Sanskrit adjunct
tenses, as in the Greek, a mere nasal, and not ‌‌ *am*, the
suffix of the first person.   The vowels ‌‌ *i* and ‌‌ *u* are
much more sparing in their attraction of the ‌‌ *a* now in
question : they refuse it always at the beginning of words,
and in the middle before two consonants ; and if transferred
from the end of a word to its middle, by an adventitious termination or word, they do not acquire the capacity of being
wedded to an ‌‌ *a*.   We say, for example, ‌‌ *imĕm*,
" this" (accus.), not ‌‌ *aimĕm;* ‌‌ *mithwana*,
"a pair," not ‌‌ *maithwana;* ‌‌ *gairibyô*,
" *montibus*," not ‌‌ *gairaibyô*.   The ‌‌ *u* also, according to set rules, very frequently abstains from the ‌‌ *a;*
for instance, ‌‌ *urunô,* (*animæ*,) not ‌‌ *uraunô*, from
‌‌ *urvan;* on the contrary, ‌‌ *tauruna*, "young,"
from ‌‌ *taruna*.   Where, however, the Sanskrit ‌‌ *u* is
replaced by ‌‌ *o* (§. 32.), an ‌‌ *a* is placed before it, as well
at the beginning as before two consonants ; and in this case
‌‌ *o* stands in this respect in the same category as ‌‌ *é* and
[G. Ed. p. 29.]   ‌‌ *ó*.   Compare ‌‌ *raoch,* "light," with

ह्रच् *ruch;* ᏩᏫᏫᏫᏫᏫ *śaochantaṁm* (*lucentium*) with शुच्यताम् *śuchyatám;* ᏫᏫᏫᏫ *aocta,* "he spoke," with उक्त *ukta,* which I form, by theory, after the analogy of अक्षिप्त *akshipta* (Gram. Crit. r. 389.), leaving out the augment.

29. In the Vriddhi modification, the vowels इ *i,* ई *í,* melt with the preceding आ *á* into ऐ *ái;* उ *u,* ऊ *ú,* into औ *áu;* ऋ *ṛi,* ॠ *ṛí,* into आर् *ár.* The simple vowel अ *a,* as also the diphthongs ए *e* and ओ *o,* which would produce the same effect by Guna as by Vriddhi—for *a + a,* like *á + a.* makes *á; a + é,* like *á + é,* makes *ái; a + ó,* like *á + ó,* makes *áu*—are capable of only one higher modification, and reserve this one for cases where grammatical laws demand the highest step, namely, Vriddhi, and remain in the cases of Guna unaltered, unless extraordinary grounds of exception occur. It may be convenient here to give a connected summary of the results produced by Guna and Vriddhi.

Primitive Vowels, अ *a,* आ *á,* इ *i,* ई *í,* उ *u,* ऊ *ú,* ऋ *ṛi,*
Guna . . . . ए *é,* ए *é,* ओ *ó,* ओ *ó,* अर् *ar,*
Vriddhi . . . . आ *á,* ... ऐ *ái,* ऐ *ái,* औ *áu,* औ *áu,* आर् *ár,*[*]

Primitive Vowels, ऋ *ṛí,* ए *é,* ऐ *ái,* ओ *ó,* औ *áu.*
Guna . . . . . . अर् *ar,* ... ...
Vriddhi . . . . आर् *ár,* ऐ *ai,* ... औ *áu,* ...

30. We now proceed to the exposition of the Zend writing, which, like the Semitic, proceeds from right to left, and towards the comprehension of which Rask has contributed valuable corrections, which give the language an appearance more natural and more in consonance with the Sanskrit than it assumed in the hands of former commentators, Anquetil's pronunciation having admitted much that was heterogeneous, especially in the vowels. We follow the order of the Sanskrit

---

* According to original Grammars the Guna letters are *a, e, o;* the Vriddhi, *á, ai, au;* the two first, *a* and *á,* being severally substituted for the vowel sounds of *ri, lri,* in combination with the semi-vowels *r* and *l,* as *ar, al, ár, ál.—Editor.*

alphabet in giving the corresponding value of each letter in
[G. Ed. p. 30.]   the Zend. The Sanskṛit short व *a* has two,
or rather three, representatives; the first is ◡, which Anquetil pronounces as *a* or *e*, but Rask, certainly with truth,
limits to *a*.   The second is ६, which Rask pronounces like
the short *æ* of the Danish, or like the short German *ä*, as in
Hände, or as *a* in *cane* in English, and *e* in the French *après*.
I consider this ६ as the shortest vowel, and write it *ĕ*.   We
often find it inserted between two consonants which form a
double consonant in the Sanskṛit; for instance, ◡◡६◡◡◡◡
dadarĕśa (pret. redupl.), for the Sanskṛit ददर्श *dadarśa*, "he"
or "I saw;" ◡◡◡६◡◡◡ *dadĕmahí* (V. S. p. 102), "we give,"
for the Vêda form ददर्मसि *dadmasi*.   This shortest *ĕ* is also
always appended to an originally terminating *r*. Thus, for instance, ६◡◡◡◡◡◡ *antarĕ*, "between," ६◡◡◡◡◡ *dâtarĕ*, "giver,"
"creator," ६◡◡◡◡ *hvarĕ*, "sun," stand for the corresponding
Sanskṛit forms अन्तर् *antar*, दातर् *dâtar*, स्वर् *swar*, "heaven."
It is worthy also of remark, that always before a final
६ *m*, and generally before a final ◡ *n*, and frequently before
an intermediate vowelless ◡ *n*, the older व *a* becomes ६ *ĕ*.
Compare, for instance, ६६◡◡◡◡ *puthrĕ-m*, "*filium*" with पुत्रम्
putra-m; ◡६◡◡◡ *anh-ĕn*, "they were," with आसन् *âsan*, ἦσαν;
६६◡◡६◡ *hĕnt-ĕm*, "the existing one," with सन्तम् *sant-am*,
præ-sentem, ab-sentem.   This retro-active influence of the
nasal reminds us of the shortening power of the Latin termination *m*; as, for instance, *stĕm, stĕmus* (Sanskṛit तिष्ठेयम्
tishthéy-am, तिष्ठेम *tishthéma*).

31. Anquetil entirely refuses to admit into his alphabet a
letter differing but little from the ६ *ĕ* above discussed, but
yet distinct from it by rule in practice, namely, ६, which
Rask teaches us to pronounce like a long Danish *æ*. We find
this letter usually in connection with a following ◡ *u*, and
this vowel appears to admit, with the excep-   [G. Ed. p. 31.]
tion of the long ◡ *â*, no vowel but this ६ before it. We write
this ६ *e* without the diacritic sign, inasmuch as we represent
the ◡, like the Sanskṛit ए, by *ê*. *Eu* ◡६ corresponds etymo-

logically to the Sanskrit वो *ô*, or diphthong formed by व *a*
and उ *u;* thus, for example, the nominal bases in *u*, which
in the Sanskrit genitive, by the influence of Guna, *i.e.* by the
prefixing of a short *a*, make *ô-s*, form, in Zend, ꜟꜟ *eus*.
Compare, for instance, ꜟꜟ *paśeus* with पशोस् *paśôs*,
from *paśu*, "*pecus*." And yet the Sanskrit *ô* does not universally become *eu* in Zend, but often remains as it is, and
specially in cases where it arises out of the termination *as*,
by the solution of the *s* into *u*. According to its pronunciation, ꜟꜟ *eu* would appear to be a diphthong, and to form
but one syllable, as in our German words *heule*, *Leute*, &c.
The long *a* (*â*) is written ꜟꜟ.

32. Short and long *i* are represented, as are long and
short *u*, by special characters, ꜟ *i*, ꜟ *î*, ꜟ *u*, ꜟ *û*: Anquetil,
however, gives to the short *i* the pronunciation *e*, and to the
short *u* (ꜟ) that of *o;* while, according to Rask, only ꜟ is
pronounced as short *o*.[*] This short *o* frequently holds the
etymological place of the Sanskrit उ *u*, and never corresponds
to any other Sanskrit vowel. For the diphthong वो *âu*, in
particular, we have generally the Zend ꜟꜟ *âo:* we yet find,
sometimes, also ꜟꜟ *âu;* for instance, ꜟꜟ *gâus*, "*bos*," is
more frequent than ꜟꜟ *gâos*, for the Sanscrit गौस् *gâus*.

33. The Sanskrit diphthong *ê*, formed out of *a + i*, is represented by ꜟ, which, especially as a terminating letter, is
also written ꜟ, and which we, as in Sanskrit, represent by *ê*.
We must here, however, observe, that the Sanskrit ए *ê* is not
always preserved as ꜟ *ê* in the Zend, but is sometimes replaced by ꜟ *ôi*, which appears to prevail particularly after
a preceding ꜟ *y*, especially at the end of   [G. Ed. p. 32.]
words. The Vriddhi diphthong ऐ *âi* (out of *â + i*) is always
represented by ꜟ *âi; ô*, either by the equivalent ꜟ—for
which we often find ꜟ *o* substituted by the neglect of copyists—or by the above-mentioned ꜟ *eu*, which, according to
rule, before a terminating ꜟ *s* replaces the Indian वो *ô;*

---

* But see §. 447. Note.

so that a termination in ᠊ᠣᠰ *ôs* is unheard of in the Zend.
For the Vṛiddhi diphthong औ *âu* (out of *â + u*) we generally find *âo*, for which there is a special character ᠊ᠣᠣ;
more rarely ᠊ᠣᠣ *âu*. It would appear that ᠊ᠣᠣ *âi*, ᠊ᠣᠣ *aô*,
᠊ᠣᠣ *âu*, and the ᠊ᠣᠣ *ôi* which replaces ᠊ᠣ *ê*, should be pronounced as diphthongs, *i.e.* as monosyllables.

34. Anuswâra and Visarga do not exist in Zend, unless we
admit the nasal specified in §. 61. as answering to the sound
of the Sanskṛit Anuswâra. We proceed meanwhile, for the
present, to the proper consonants. The first letter of the
Sanskṛit guttural class has divided itself into two characters
bearing reference to different functions, ᠊ᠣ and ᠊ᠣ; of which
the first, which we represent by *k*, only appears before vowels
and » *v*; the other, which we write *c*, precedes especially
consonants, excepting » *v*. Compare, for instance, ᠊ᠣᠣ *kô*,
᠊ᠣᠣ *kâ*, ᠊ᠣᠣ *kaṭ*, (*quis, quæ, quid*), ᠊ᠣᠣ *hakĕrèṭ*, " once,"
᠊ᠣᠣ *karôiti*, " he made," ᠊ᠣᠣ *kva*, " where," with को *kô*,
का *kâ*, किम् *kim*, सकृत् *sakṛit*, करोति *karôti*, and क्व *kwa*: on the
other hand, ᠊ᠣᠣ *csathra*, " king," with क्ष *kshatra*;
᠊ᠣᠣ *hicti*, " pouring out" (V. S. p. 198), with सिक्ति *sikti*
(from सिच् *sich*). In what manner the pronunciation of this
᠊ᠣ *c* differs from that of the ᠊ᠣ *k* can indeed hardly be defined with certainty: it is probably softer, weaker than that
of the ᠊ᠣ *k*, which latter is fenced in by no strong consonants.
Rask selects for it the character *q*, without observing that this
letter prefers only to precede consonants, and in this position
[G. Ed. p. 33.]   always corresponds to the Sanskṛit क *k*.
Burnouf considers ᠊ᠣ as an aspirate, and writes ᠊ᠣᠣ
takhmahê. He writes, on the other hand, the letter ᠊ᠣ, which
Rask treats as an aspirate, with *q*. Burnouf has not yet given
his reason, which I think, however, I can guess, namely, that
᠊ᠣ *c* is found before *r*, which, according to Burnouf's just

---

* ᠊ᠣᠣ *ôs*, according to Burnouf, occurs occasionally as the termination
of the genitive singular of the *u*-bases for the more common ᠊ᠣᠣ *eus*;
e.g. ᠊ᠣᠣ *bâzaôs*, " *brachii.*"

remark, generally confers an aspirate upon a preceding consonant. I consider this reason, however, as insufficient; and think that ଓ *c* stands before *r*, because, as we have before remarked, all consonants, *v* excepted, only admit before them that modification of the *k* sound which is expressed by ଓ. It would be impossible for ⟩ *r*, and the other letters of similar agency, to convey aspiration to the preceding hard guttural if ख *kh* be not extant in Zend; so that, for instance, the root खन् *khan*, "to dig," sounds *kan* in Zend. There are, however, some words in which ख *kh* is represented by ଓ. From खर *khara*, "ass," we find the accusative *carĕm*; and we find, also, the ख *kh* of सखि *sakhi*, "friend," replaced by *c*; the accusative, for instance, सखायम् *sakháyam* transformed into *hacđim*. It may therefore remain a question whether ⟩ *k* or ଓ *c*, in respect of their sounds, have the better right to be referred to ख *kh*; but this much is certain, that ख *k* before vowels and before व *v* is only represented by ⟩ in Zend; before other consonants only by ଓ; which latter we shall, till better advised, continue to render by *c*.

35. Anquetil ascribes to ଓ the value of *kh*, and to both the pronunciation *kh*; while Rask considers the latter alone, by reason of the aspiration stroke which he recognises, as aspirated, and compares it to the Spanish *x* and the Arabic خ, and our German *ch*. Burnouf renders [G. Ed. p. 34.] *kh* by *q*; and observes (l. c. p. 345) that the Sanskrit syllable स्व *swa* becomes *qa* in Zend, namely, in स्वप्न *swapna*, "sleep," written, according to Burnouf, *qafna*, and in स्व *swa* (*suus*), "his." We are inclined to add to these examples, *khanha*, (nom.) accus. *khanhrĕm*, from स्वसा *swasá*, "sister" (*soror*); स्वसारम् *swasáram* (*sororem*); and *kharĕno*, "splendour," as related to स्वर् *swar*, "heaven," and सुर् *sur*, "to shine." We must, however, at the same time, remark, that स्व *sw* does not universally become *kh*, and that स्व *swa* in particular, in an isolated position and with a possessive signification, much oftener appears in the shape of *hva*,

or that of ‏ﺳﻮﺳﻢ‎ *hava.* We render ‏ﺧﻮ‎ by *kh,* and support our
view of its aspiration more on the fact, that in modern Persian
it corresponds frequently to ‏چ‎, our *ch,* than on the circumstance that Rask has marked it as aspirated. This modern
Persian ‏چ‎ is pronounced, indeed, at present, without aspiration, like an Italian *c* before *a, o, u;* but its value in Arabic,
and the choice of this letter, so powerfully aspirated in the
Arabic to designate a special guttural sound, in true Persian
words, seems to indicate an intrinsic stronger or milder aspiration. As ‏ﺧﻮ‎ *kh* is derived from the Sanskrit स्व *swa,* it was
not applied to replace the क *k* before letters, which would
without it produce an aspiration. It may also be here convenient to remember that either *u* or *v* (‏ﻭ‎) accompanies the
Persian ‏چ‎ when the latter replaces at the beginning of a
[G. Ed. p. 35.]   word the Sanskrit स्व *sw.* It is true that ‏ﻭ‎ *v*
is no longer sounded before long vowels, but it must originally
have had its influence on the pronunciation, and cannot have
been introduced into writing entirely without object, and for
the mere employment of the copyist. Compare ‏ﺧﺪﺍ‎ *khudá,*
"God," with स्वदत्त *swadatta,* "self-given;" for which, in Zend,
we have, under a more regular participial form (see Gramm.
Crit. r. 608), ‏ﺧﺪﺍﺗﻪ‎ *khadáta**; which Anquetil, or his
Pârsî teacher, always understands in the sense of, "given
through God," deceived, probably, by the resemblance of
sound to ‏ﺧﺪﺍ‎ *khudá;* while Neriosengh properly translates it
by स्वयन्दत्त *swayandatta.* The Persian ‏ﺧﺪﺍ‎ *khudá* is, however,
as Burnouf correctly assumes, actually related to the Zend
‏ﺧﺪﺍﺗﻪ‎ *khadáta,* so as to have its name based in the idea,
"created by itself," while in its form it has been mutilated of
one syllable. In Sanskrit we find both स्वभू *swabhú,* "self-
existent," and also the more common स्वयम्भू *swayambhú,* as
appellations of Brahma and Vishṇu. That, however, as has
often been maintained, our word "God" is really related to

---

* This word comes from the root *dhá,* "to place," not from *dá,* "to
give," see §. 637.

خدا khudá, and that its primal signification has thus been discovered through the Zend, we are forced still to doubt. We
will here only call to mind that the Germanic forms, especially
in the older dialects, in general approximate much more to
the Sanskrit than to the modern Persian. स्व *sw*, in particular, in the Gothic, either remains unaltered, or becomes
sl (§. 20.). The pronominal syllable स्व *swa* exhibits itself in
the Gothic as a pronominal adverb, *sva* (*so*) "thus;" and with
an instrumental form, *svē* (*wie*) "how." The neuter substantive *svēs* (Theme *svēsa*) means *Eigenthum*, "property," as
in Sanskrit the neuter स्व *swa*. I know of no certain form in
which a Germanic *g* or *k* corresponds to a Sanskrit स्व *sw* or a
Persian خ *kh*. To return, however, to the   [G. Ed. p. 36.]
Persian خُ *khu* = स्व *sw* : compare خفتن *khuftan*, "to sleep,"
with स्वप् *swap* ; خواب *kh*(*w*)*áb*, "sleep," with स्वाप *swápa* ;
خواندن *kh*(*w*)*ándan*, "to sing," with स्वन् *swan*, "to sound ;"
خواهر *kh*(*w*)*áhar*, "sister," with स्वसृ *swasri*, Gothic *svistar* ;
خرشید *khur-shíd*, "sun," Zend هوَرَ *hvarĕ*, with स्वर् *swar*,
"heaven." In some words خ *kh* corresponds to a Sanskrit *k*
before *r*, in which position the Zend loves an aspiration ; in
the modern Persian, however, a vowel intrudes between the
guttural and the *r*; thus, خرامیدن *khirám-ídan*, "to proceed
with pomp," corresponds to the Sanskrit क्रम् *kram*, "to go,"
"to step ;" and خریدن *khirídan*, "to buy," to the Sanskrit
equivalent root क्री *krí*. The Persian خ *kh* answers to the
Sanskrit aspirated ख *kh*, in the word خر *khar*, "ass"
(Sanskrit खर *khara*).

36. The guttural ग, and its aspirate घ, are represented by
ع *g* and ع *gh*. The Sanskrit घ *gh* has, however, sometimes
dismissed the aspiration in Zend; at least گرما *garĕma*,
"heat" (θέρμη and *Wärme*), answers to the Sanskrit घर्म
gharma : on the other hand, the ghna in ورثرغن *verĕthraghna*, "victorious," corresponds to the Sanskrit घ्न *ghna* at
the end of compounds; for instance, in शत्रुघ्न *satru-ghna*, "enemy
slayer." The Zend ورثرغن *verĕthraghna* properly signi-

fies, like the word so often used in the same sense *ѵѵҳ҃ҽ҄҅ҽҍҩ*
vĕrĕthra-zan, "killer of Vṛitra," and proves a connection between the Zendish and Indian mythologies, which, however,
in consequence of the obscuration of meanings in Zend, and
the oblivion of the old Myths, now only exists in affinities of
speech. "Killer of Vṛitra" is one of the most usual titles of
honour of the prince of the lesser gods, or Indra, who, from
his slaughter of the dæmon Vṛitra, of the race of the Dâ-
[G. Ed. p. 37.]   nawas, bears this name.

We shall discuss the nasals apart in §. 60.

37. Of the Sanskṛit palatals the Zend has only the *tenuis*;
namely ѵ *ch* (= च), and the *media*, namely ѵ *j* (= ज): the
aspirates are wanting, which is not surprising, as they are of
rare occurrence in the Sanskṛit. The following are examples : *ѕҩѕѵ҄ҩѵ charaiti*, "he goes," Sanskṛit चरति *charati*;
ҩҍѵҩҩҩ҃ѵ chathwârô, "four" (nom. plur. masc.) Sansk. चत्वार्ऎ
chatwdras, चत्वारॊ *chatwârô*; *ҩѵҩҩҍ adjô*, "strength," Sansk.
ओजस् *ôjas*, ओजॊ *ôjô*. It is, however, to be observed, that,
while the Sanskṛit *ch* remains, by rule, unaltered in Zend, the
sonant *j* is often replaced by other letters; and first, by ҫ *z*;
for instance, *ѵҩҩҍҫ zâta*, "born," Sansk. जात *jâta*; secondly,
by ҩ *sh*; for instance, *ѵҽҩ shĕnu*, "knee," Sansk. जानु *jânu*.

38. The modification of the sounds of *t*, peculiar to the
Sanskṛit, contained in the third row of consonants, is wanting
in the Zend. We pass, therefore, to the ordinary sounds of
that letter, the dentals. These are, ѵ *t* (त), ҩ *th* (थ), ѵ *d*
(द) ѵ *dh* (ध), together with a *t* (ѵ), peculiar to the Zend,
of which more hereafter. The ѵ *t* is like the guttural which
we represent by *k* (ѵ), in this respect, that its position is
almost limited to one preceding vowels. Before ҍ *r* and
ҩ *w*, and sometimes before ѵ *y*, in order to gratify the
affection of the latter for an aspirate, the aspirated ҩ *th*
steps in. Thus, for instance, ҫѵҩҩҩ *thwanm* signifies "thee,"
while the nominative is written ҫѵѵ *tûm*, and the genitive
ѵ҃ѵѵ *tava*; and the word ҍҩҩѵ *âtar*, "fire," nom. ѵѵҍҩҩѵ

âtars, makes, after rejection of the *a* which preceded *r*, ᴊᴏ⁶ˢᴊ *âthrê*, "*igni*," ᴩᴊᴏ⁶ˢᴊ *âthrat̤*, "*ab igne*," &c. If, however, the *t* be protected by a preceding consonant, excepting *n̆*, the succeeding semi-vowel is thereby de- [G. Ed. p. 38.] prived of its retro-active power. We find, for instance, ᴊᴩᴏˢˢᴧ *vaśtra*, not ᴊ⁶ˢˢᴧ *vaśthra*, "garment," "vest;" but we have ᴊ⁶ᴖᴄ *manthra*, "speech," not ᴊᴩᴖᴄ *mantra*, from the root ᴩᴊᴄ *man*. At the end of a word, and, which rarely occurs, before strong consonants, (§. 25.) at the beginning also, and middle of a word, the Sanskṛit *t* (त) is represented by a special letter, namely, by ᴩᴏ, which we, with Burnouf, write *t̤*, but formerly wrote with a simple *t* undotted below, because no change is possible with ᴩᴏ or ⑥. Rask represents it by *th*, because he recognises the sign of aspiration. I am unable, however, to assent to the universal validity of this sign of Rask's, and I incline to rejecting the aspirate, as in Sanskṛit, from the end of words. We should also remember that the diphthong *ê* is written ᴩᴏ as well as ᴩᴏ; the last, which prevails at the end of words, with a stroke similar to that which distinguishes our ᴩᴏ from ᴩᴏ. Before consonants, for instance, in the word ᴑᴩᴩᴏˢᴐᴩᴏ *tkaêshô*, the sounding of *th* would be more precarious than that of *t̤*, in case this *th* did not somewhat partake of a sibilant sound. I think, however, that ᴩᴏ *t̤* has merely a feebler pronunciation than ᴩᴏ *t*, and is, so to say, the last breathing of *t*; as, in Sanskṛit, *s* and *r*, at the end of words, are diluted to Visarga (§. 11.); and as त *t*, in Prâkṛit, and also in Greek, is, at the end of words, altogether suppressed.

39. ᴄ is the ordinary *d* द, and ᴄᴄ according to Rask's just remark, its aspirate *dh*. This represents the Sanskṛit ध *dh*, for instance, in the imperative ending धि. The Zend, moreover, favours ᴄᴄ *dh* for ᴄ *d* in the middle of words between two vowels. We find, for instance, ᴊᴩᴏˢᴄ *dâta*, "given," but ᴊᴄˢᴄᴄ *dadhâmi*, Sanskṛit ददामि *dadâmi*, "I give"; and ᴊᴩᴏˢᴄᴄᴄᴄ *mazda-dhâta*, [G. Ed. p. 39.|
D 2

"given by Ormusd," "created "; ـﻮﺮﻳ *yêdhi*, " if," Sanskrit यदि *yadi ;* ـﺪﺎﭘ *pâdha*, "foot," Sansk. पाद *pâda*.

40. The labial class embraces the letters و *p,* ﻮ *f,* ﻮ *b,* and the nasal of this organ ﻮ *m,* of which more hereafter. و *p* answers to the Sanskrit प *p,* and is transformed into ﻮ *f* by the retro-active aspirative power of a following ﻮ *r,* ﻮ *s,* and ﻮ *n ;* whence, for instance, the preposition प्र *pra* (pro, πρό) becomes, in Zend, ﻮﻮ *fra ;* and the primitive words ﻮﻮ *ap,* " water " (*aqua,* and perhaps ἀφρός), ﻮﻮﻮ *kĕrĕp,* "body," form in the nominative, ﻮﻮﻮ *âfs,* ﻮﻮﻮ *kĕrĕfs ;* on the other hand, in the accusative, ﻮﻮﻮ *âpĕm,* ﻮﻮﻮ *kĕrĕpĕm,* or ﻮﻮﻮ *kĕhrpĕm.* In regard to the power which resides in *n* of aspirating a *p,* compare ﻮﻮﻮ *tafnu,* "burning," from the root ﻮﻮ *tap,* with the derivative from the same root ﻮﻮﻮ *âtâpayêiti,* " he shines" (See Vendidâd Sâde, p. 333), and the plural ﻮﻮﻮ *csafna,* "nights," with the ablative singular ﻮﻮﻮ *csaparât* (Vendidâd Sâde, p. 330), in which, even in the root, the interchange between *n* and *r* is observable, as the same takes place in the Sanskrit between अहन् *ahan* and अहर् *ahar,* "day." (Gramm. Crit. r. 228. annot.) Originally— *i.e.* standing for itself, and not proceeding from the و *p* by the influence described—ﻮ *f* is of very rare occurrence. In some instances known to me it corresponds to the Sanskrit भ *bh,* which, however, for the most part, in the Zend has rejected the aspiration. In Anquetil's Vocabulary we find *nâfo,* " navel," which in Sanskrit is written नाभि *nâbhi ;* and in the fem. accus. plural, of frequent occurrence in the Zend-Avesta, ﻮﻮﻮ *hufĕdhrîs,* we recognise the Sanskrit सुभद्र *subhadra* "very fortunate," "very excellent," also a title of Vishnu.

41. We come now to the semi-vowels, and must, in order to follow the order of the Sanskrit alphabet, discuss *y* in the [G. Ed. p. 40.]　next place, by which we express the sound of the German and Italian *j,* the English consonantal *y.* This

semi-vowel is written at the beginning of words by ‮س‬ or
‮ح‬, and in the middle by the duplication of the *u* ‮ננ‬, as in
the Old High German we find *w* expressed. This semi-vowel,
and the vowels which correspond to it, ‮נ‬ *i* and ‮נ‬ *í*, introduce
into the preceding syllable an ‮נ‬ *i*; an interesting phenomenon, first observed by Burnouf (l. c. pp. 340, 341), and which
in its principle is connected with the German vowel modification (§. 73.). We are obliged to ascribe a similar influence
also to the diphthong ‮ס‬ *é* where it stands at the end of a
word. Frequent occasion for this presents itself in the dat.
sing. and the third pers. pres. of the middle verb. For instance, ‮سננס‬ *nairé*, "*homini*," for ‮سננ‬ *naré*, is frequent;
but ‮سנננסנ‬ *naraécha*, "*hominique*," is an exception. The
vowels after which, by the attractive power of the letters
mentioned, an ‮נ‬ *i* is placed, are ‮ננ‬ *a*, ‮ננ‬ *á*, ‮נ‬ *u*, ‮נ‬ *û*, ‮ס‬ *é*, ‮נ‬ *ô*,
as to which we must also observe, that *u*, in the case of a
succeeding *i*, is lengthened. Examples are: ‮سננסננن‬ *mai-*
dhya (मध्य *madhya*) "middle"; ‮سננננن‬ *nairya*, "man";
‮سננننن‬ *bavaiti*, "he is"; ‮سננننن‬ *dadhâiti*, "he gives";
‮سننننننن‬ *âtâpayéiti*, "he shines"; ‮سننננن‬ *kĕrĕnôiti*,
"he makes"; ‮سننננن‬ *stâidhi*, "praise," instead of ‮ססننن‬
studhi, from the root ‮ננن‬ *stu* (ष्टु); ‮ننננננ‬ *tûirya*, "the
fourth," from चतुर् *chatur*, with the त *cha* suppressed [*];
‮ننननننن‬ *dhuirya*, an adjective, derived from ‮ننننن‬ *ahura*.
With regard to the influence of ‮ננ‬ *y* we must observe, that
it does not mix up an ‮נ‬ *i* with a vowel immediately preceding, but only with one separated from it by one consonant; for if there be two, unless the first be ‮نن‬ *n*, the retro-
active power of *y*, *i*, or *î*, is neutralized; thus ‮سננننن‬ *asti*,
not ‮سננننن‬ *aisti*, stands for "he is"; on the other hand we
have ‮سننننننن‬ *bavainti*, Sansk. भवन्ति *bhavanti*, "they are."
Several other consonants also resist simply   [G. Ed. p. 41.]
this power of attraction; thus we have ‮נננننن‬ *dakhyu*, not

---

[*] Or more immediately from the Sanskrit ordinal तुर्य्य *turyya* or तुरीय
turiya, "fourth."—*Editor.*

ﺩﺍﯾﺨﯿﻮ *daikhyu*, "land," "province"; and the *i* of the
personal terminations ﻣﯽ *mi* and ﻫﯽ *hi*, or ﺷﯽ *shi*, obtain
no influence over the preceding syllable. In the same manner, in the first person plural, ﻣﻬﯽ *mahi*, not ﻣﺌﻬﯽ *maihi*,
corresponds to the Veda termination मसि *masi*; and in the
genitive of the stems, or inflective bases, in ﺍ *a*, ﺍﻫﯽ
a-hê, not ﺍﺋﻬﯽ *aihê*, stands for अस्य *a-sya*.

42. ﯼ *y* sometimes also exerts that disturbing influence
on a following ﺍ *a* or ﺁ *â*, which is equivalent to the insertion of a vowel, or of *i*, and consequently effects their
transmutation into ﻩ *ê**; thus the bases of nouns in

---

* The expression of the text is "äufsert umlautenden Einfluss." It is
hardly possible to render into English without circumlocution certain
terms which the philologers of Germany have invented and adopted to
express the various modifications of the Indo-Germanic vowel; such as,
Ablaut, Auflaut, Inlaut, Umlaut. Whether these terms have in themselves the virtue of suggesting to a Teutonic ear the particular modification
of the vowel to which they are respectively applied may be doubted; but
if to the student and the teacher they answer the purpose of a *memoria
technica*, their use is fully justified by the necessity of the case, and the
practice of a language which possesses a singular and inexhaustible power
of progress and adaptation to exigencies. In our language, it seems to us
that the uncouthness of such compounds as Upsound, Offsound, and In-
sound, could hardly be compensated by any advantage to be derived from
their use; and we therefore purpose, in the course of this work, where any
of these terms occur in the original, to retain them in their German shape.
Of these terms, *Ablaut* and *Umlaut* are those which chiefly, if not alone,
are used by our author. *Inlaut* is, we believe, merely the Sanskrit *Guna.*
The meaning of the two former, and their distinction from each other,
may best be explained by the following extract from our author's excellent work the Vocalismus, p. 10.

"I designate," he says, "by the term *Ablaut*, a change of the root
vowel, which is distinguished from the *Umlaut* by the fact that it is not
produced by the influence of the vowel of the termination; for *Umlaut* is
a mere affection, disturbance (*Trübung*) of the primary sound, through
which that sound becomes more homogeneous with the vowel of the termination; while in the *Ablaut*, without any *recognised* external cause, it
makes room for another, and, in general, totally different sound; as in
Gothic, *nima*, 'I take'; *nam*, 'I took.' I say, without any *recognised* external

ᴊᴜᴙ *ya* form, in the genitive, ᴘᴊᴙᴙᴙᴊᴜᴙ *yĕ-hĕ*, instead of
ᴘᴊᴜᴙᴊᴙᴙᴊᴙ *ya-hĕ*; and, with the verb, the old Sanskrit य *ya*
or या *yá* of the fourth and tenth classes, in the present
singular becomes ᴙᴘᴊᴙ *yĕ*.   Compare ᴊᴄ᷂ᴙᴊᴊᴊᴜᴙᴊᴜ᷂ᴘᴜᴙ *dĭá-*
payĕmi, ᴊᴜᴙᴙᴙᴊᴊᴊᴜᴙᴊᴜᴙᴘᴜᴙ *dĭápayĕhi*, ᴊᴘᴊᴊᴙᴙᴊᴊᴊᴜᴙᴊᴜᴙᴘᴜᴙ *dĭápayĕiti*,
with the Sanskrit वातापयामि *dĭápayámi*, वातापयसि *dĭápayasi*,
वातापयति *dĭápayati*.   In the last syllable, ᴊᴜᴊᴊ *ya* before ᴄ *m*,
according to rule, becomes ᴣ *í*; and after the same
analogy, ᴄᴊᴜᴙᴙ *vam* becomes ᴄᴣ *úm*.   We find, therefore,
for instance, ᴄᴣᴣᴊᴣᴙᴘ *túirím*, "quartum," from ᴊᴜᴊᴊᴣᴊᴣᴙᴘ *tái-*
rya; and ᴄᴣᴙᴘᴘᴊᴣᴄ *thrishúm*, "tertiam partem," ᴄᴣᴘᴘᴙᴙᴣᴄᴊᴜᴘ
chathrushúm, "quartam partem," from ᴊᴜᴙᴙᴘᴘᴊᴣᴄ *thrishva*,
ᴊᴜᴙᴙᴘᴘᴊᴣᴄᴊᴜᴘ *chathrushva*.   This appearance is to be thus
understood, that the antecedent semi-vowel, after the suppression of the *a*, passes into its corresponding vowel, which,
however, according to the rule of §. 64., must be a long one.
The ᴊᴊ *y*[*], after its influence has transformed ᴊᴜ *a* into
ᴙᴘ *e*, is often itself suppressed; thus we find ᴄᴊᴙᴊᴜᴊᴊᴙᴙᴊᴜᴙᴙᴙᴜᴘᴊᴊᴅ
frádnĕšaĕm, "I shewed," from प्रादेशयम् *prádĕšayam*, which

---

ternal cause; because I think I can shew that the *Ablaut* also is produced
by the particular quality and condition of the termination. Whether,
however, we seek for the radical vowel in the present or the preterite, the
change is equally one quite different from that of the Indian *Guna* or
Vriddhi, and in this respect, that it is a positive change; while in Sanskrit
the root vowel is not in fact changed, but only receives an increment, and
that increment always one and the same, with which it diphthongizes itself, as in Greek, ι and υ with ε, λειπω, φευγω. In respect of signification,
likewise, there is a difference between the Indian *Guna* and *Vriddhi* and
Germanic *Ablaut*; for the *Ablaut* has acquired for itself a significatory
power for grammatical purposes, even if, as I conjecture, it did not originally possess such: the contrast between the present and the past seems
to rest upon it, and there are indications that the latter is expressed by this
change. In Sanskrit, *Guna* and *Vriddhi* present no indication of this significatory power, but, merely in the character of diphthongizing modifications, accompany those inflections which do signify grammatical relations."
 Further illustrations of these latter remarks are to be found in the
Note 4, which Professor Bopp has appended to the above passage of the
Vocalismus. — *Trans.*
 [*] Cf. p. 963, Note.

according to the rule of the tenth class, would be formed from विश् *diś*. The genitive termination स्य *sya* appears everywhere reduced into ങ്ക് *hê*. The semi-vowels ᘔᘔ *y* and » *v* are generally suppressed after preceding conso-

[G. Ed. p. 42.]   nants*; and thus, also, the imperative ending स्व *swa* gives up its *w*.

43. In Sanskrit, य *y* is sometimes, for euphony, inter-posed between two vowels (Gram. Crit. rr. 271. 310. 311.); but this does not uniformly occur.   In Zend, the interposi-tion of *y* between ᕯ *u*, ᕧ *û*, and a following ᖵ *ê*, seems to amount to a law.   Thus the Sanskrit ब्रुवे *bruvê*, "I say" (from ब् and ए, Gram. Crit. r. 55.), becomes, in Zend, ങ്ക്ᘔᘔᖵᖵ *mrûyê* (§. 63.); and the neuter form द्वे *dvê*, "two," after the vocalization of the *w* into *u*, takes the form ങ്ക്ᘔᘔᖵᖵ *duyê*.

44. We have already remarked (§. 30.) with respect to ᖵ *r*, that at the end of a word an ᖶ *ê* is always appended to it; for instance, ᖶᘔᖵᖵᖵ *dâtarê*, "Creator," "Giver"; ᖶᘔᘔᖵ *hvarê*, "Sun," instead of ᘔᖵᖵᖵ *dâtar*; ᘔᘔᖵ *hvar*. In the middle of a word, where an ᖵ *h* is not introduced according to §. 48., the union of ᖵ *r* with a following con-sonant is mostly avoided; so, indeed, that to the originally vowelless *r* an ᖶ *ê* is appended: thence, for instance, ᘔᘔᖶᖵᘔᘔᖵᖵ *dadarêsa*, from दद्र् *dadarśa*, "*vidi*," "*vidit*"; or the *r* is transposed, in the same manner as is usual in the Sanskrit for the avoidance of the union of र *r* with two following con-sonants. (Gram. Crit. r. 34ᵇ.)   Hence, for instance, ᘔᘔᘔᖵ᙭ᘔᘔ *âthrava*, "priests" (nominative), accus. ᖶᖶᘔᘔᘔᘔᖵ᙭ᘔᘔ *âthra-vanêm*, from the theme ᖵᘔᘔᖵᘔᖵᘔᘔ *âtarvan*, which in the weak cases (§. 129.) contracts itself into ᖵᖵ᙭ᘔᘔ *âthurun* or ᖵᖵ᙭ᘔ᙭ᘔᘔ *âthaurun*. (§. 28.)   To this, also, pertains the fact that poly-syllabic stems (or uninflected bases) in ᘔᘔ *ar*, at the be-ginning of compounded forms, transpose this syllable into ᘔᖵ *ra*; and thus ᘔᖵ᙭ᘔᘔ *âthra*, "fire," stands instead of

------

* But see § 721.

ꭵꭴꙅꭴ *áthar.** The combinations ꭻꭻ⁷ *ry*, [G. Ed. p. 43.]
»⁷ꭷ *urv*, are only permitted where a vowel follows, and the
combination ꭴⁱꭴ *ars* only as a termination, and in the middle
of a word before ꝓ *t*; for instance, ꭴꭻꭻⁱꭻꝓ *táirya*, "the
fourth"; ꭴꭻꭻⁱꭴꭴꮭ *vairya*, "strong"; ꭵꭴ»⁷ *urvan*, "soul"
ꭴꭵ»⁷ꭴꭴꮃ *haurva*, "whole" (?); ꭴⁱꭴꝓꭴꭴ *átars*, "fire" (nominative); ꭴⁱꭴꭻ *nars*, "of a man"; ꭴꝓꭴꭴⁱꭴꭻ *harstn*, "ploughed";
but ꭴꭴꭻⁱꮲꭴꝓ *chathrus*, "four times," for ꭴꭴⁱꮲꭴꝓ *chathurs*,
since here no *a* precedes the *rs*.

45. It is worthy of remark, that in the Zend the *l* is wanting, as in Chinese the *r*, while, nevertheless, it exists in the
modern Persian, and shews itself in words which are not of
Semitic origin. The Sanskrit व *v* has three representatives
in the Zend, ꮭ, », and ꝏ. The two first are so far distinguished from each other in their use, that ꮭ corresponds to the
Sanskrit *v* only at the beginning, and » only in the middle
of words; for instance, Ꝗꭷꭴꮭ *vaêm*, " we," = वयम् *vayam*,
ꭴ»ꭴꝓ *tava* (*tui*) = तव *tava*. This distinction, as Rask justly
assumes, is only graphic. ꝏ, which I, with Burnouf, render by *w*, most frequently occurs after ꮲ *th*, so that » never
accompanies an antecedent ꮲ *th*. On the other hand we find »
much oftener than ꝏ after the aspirated medials of this class.
Perhaps the law here obtains that the ꝏ *dh*, which, according to §. 39., stands for ꭻ *d* (द),is only followed by », while
an original ꝏ *dh*, corresponding to a Sanskrit ध *dh*, only
appears in conjunction with ꝏ. Thus Ꝗꭴ»ꝏꭻꭻ *dadhvâo*,
" having created," "given," from the root ꭴꭻ *dâ*†, answers
to the Sanskrit nom. दधात् *dadwân*; while the accusative,
of frequent occurrence in the Vendidâd, Ꝗꝝꭻꭴꭴꝏꝏꭻ *adhwânĕm*,
seems to be identical with the Sanskrit अध्वानम् *adhwânam*,
" viam." (Vend. Olsh. p. 18.) After other consonants than

---

* By *Stämme*, the author here evidently means the crude derivative
words which serve as Stems or Bases to inflected words, or those in combination with inflectional terminations; thus *áthru* for *áthar*, forms
áthrava, áthravanĕm, not *átharva, átharvanam*, &c.—*Editor.*

† The root corresponds to the Sanskrit *dhâ*, see §. 637.

ᘓ *th* and ℺ *dh*, ᴕ *w* appears not to be admitted, but only
» *v*; on the other hand, ᴕ *w* much prevails between two *i*'s
or ى *i* and ﺝﺝ *y*, in which position » *v* is not allowed.
[G. Ed. p. 44.]   Thus we read in the Vendidâd (Olsh. p. 23),
the nominatives ᙏᙏᴕﺝﺝﻭ *driwis*, " beggar," (?) and ᙏᙏﻮﺝﺝ
daiwis, "a worshipper of Daêva." ᙏᙏﺝᴕﺝﺝﻭ *daiwis* however,
as derived from *daêva* through the suffix ى *i*, seems to me
dubious, and I prefer the variation ᙏᙏﺝ»ﻡᙏﻭ *daêvis*. Or is it
between *ê* and *i* also that ᴕ *w* only can be allowed? Another
instance is, ﺝﺝᴕﺝﺍ *aiwyô*, " *aquis*," as dative and ablative
plural; an interesting form which long remained a mystery
to me, but which I am now in condition to explain. It springs
from the root ﻉᙏ *ap*, "water" in such a manner, that after
suppression of the *p*,[*] the Sanskrit termination भ्यस् *bhyas*,
which elsewhere, in the Zend, appears only as ﺝﺝﺝ *byô*,
has weakened itself to ﺝﺝﺝᴕ *wyô*, and, according to §. 41., has
introduced an ى *i* into the base.   Another instance in which
भ *bh* has weakened itself in the Zend into a semi-vowel,
and obtained the form ᴕ *w* in virtue of its position between
two ى *i*'s, is the very common preposition ᙏﻉᴕﺝﺍ *aiwi*, for
which, however, ﺝﺍﺝᙏ *aibi* is sometimes substituted. It may
be appropriate here to remark that भ *bh* appears in the
Zend, in other company, in the enfeebled shape of » *v*.
We find, namely, the base उभ *ubha*, " both," not only in the
shape ᙏﺝﻭ *uba*, but also in that of ᙏ»ᴕᙏ *aova* (§. 28.), the
neuter dual form of which I think I recognise in the Vend. S.
p. 88., where ᴕﻡﺝﻉᙏ ᴕﺝﺝﻉﻉﺍ ﺝﺝﺝﺝﺍﻍ ᴕᙏ»ﺍﺍ *aorê ya*ᘔ*nô*
amêshê spêntê, can hardly signify any thing else than " *ambos*
† *venerans Amschaspantos*" (*non conniventes Sanctos*, see Nalus,
vv. 25, 26.) Anquetil interprets (T. 3, p. 472.) *orê*, by " *tous
deux.*" We have still another position to mention, in which
[G. Ed. p. 45.]   the semi-vowel ᴕ *w* appears, namely,
before ﺍ *r*, in which connection the softer *w* is more appro-

---

[*] Compare, in this respect, अभ्र *abhra*, "cloud," for अब्भ्र *ab-bhra*,
"water-bearing,"and theZend ᙏﻭﻉﺍᙏ *â-bêrêta*, nom. "water-bearer."
† Burnouf reads *abi* (*i.e.* "over")and makes *yaine*, signify "reverence."

priate than the harder » *v.* The only example of this case is the feminine ᴊᴜⱢᴏᴏⱤ ᴊᴜ *śuwrâ,* "sword," "dagger," in which we believe we recognise the Sanskrit शुभ्र *śubhra,* "shining,"•
As to the pronunciation of the ᴏᴏ *w,* I think, with Burnouf, that it accords with the English *w,* which also is akin to the Sanskrit व *v* after consonants. Rask reverses the powers, pronouncing the Zend ᴏᴏ as the English *v,* and the letters ᴌ and » as the English *w.*

46. I have not detected in the *v* and *w* a power of attraction similar to that which belongs to the ᴊᴊ *y,* as described in §. 41., unless the term ᴊᴜ»ᴌᴊᴜᴡ *haurva,* "all," which often occurs, as well as ᴊᴏᴊᴊᴌᴌ *víśpa,* is derived from the Sanskrit सर्व *sarwa,* "all." I have, however, already elsewhere ascribed to the corresponding vowel › *u* a power of attraction, howbeit sparingly exerted; in virtue of which, for instance, the base ᴊᴜ»ᴌᴊᴘᴊᴜ *âtarvan,* "priests," in the weak cases (see §. 129.), after that ᴊᴜᴌ *van* has contracted itself into ᴊ› *un,* by the influence of this *u,* also converts the *a* of the preceding syllable into *u;* hence, for instance, in the dative, ᴘᴊᴊᴌᴊᴘᴊᴜ *âtaurunê* for ᴘᴊᴊᴌᴊᴘᴊᴜ *âtarunê.* The Sanskrit तरुण *taruṇa,* "young," is, in Zend, ᴊᴊᴌᴘ *turuna* or ᴊᴊᴌᴊᴜᴘ *tauruna* (§. 28.); and वसु *vasu,* "thing," "riches,"

[G. Ed. p. 46.] has, by the influence of the concluding *u,* converted itself into ›ᴜᴌᴌ *vôhu.*

47. Burnouf was the first to remark on the fact, peculiar to the Zend, that the semi-vowels are fond of communicating an aspiration to a preceding consonant; and we (§. 40.) have ascribed a similar influence to ᴊᴜ *s* and ᴊ *n,* and find ourselves compelled to assign the same also to the

---

• The accusative ᴄᴊᴌᴏᴏᴊᴊ *śuwraṁm,* appears in Olshausen, p. 13, with the variation ᴄᴊᴌᴌᴊᴊ *śufraṁm.* (§. 40.) Then we often find the instrumental ᴊᴊᴊᴌᴏᴏᴊᴊ *śuwrya,* for which, however, we must read ᴊᴊᴊᴊᴌᴏᴏᴊᴊ *uwraya,* if *śuwrya* be not derivable from a Theme ᴌᴏᴏᴊᴊ *śuwri,* after the analogy of सुन्दरी *sundari,* from सुन्दर *sundara.* (Gramm. Crit. r. 270.)

labial nasal, by which, for instance, the feminine participle
जग्मुषी *jagmushí* has changed itself to ﺩﺩﻮﻳﭼﺭﺣﺳﻳ *jaghmúshí*.
The dental medial is free from this influence, for we find
ﺩﻣﻳﻖ *dva,* "two," ﺩﻣﻳﻖﻳﻖ *drucs,* "a demon," (accus. ﻖﻳﻖﺩﻳﻖ
drujĕm,) not ﺩﻣﻳﻖﻳﻖ *dhrucs,* ﻖﻳﻖﺩﻳﻖ *dhrujĕm.* The guttural
medial is, however, exposed to this influence, as in the
abovementioned instance of *jaghmúshí.* We have, on the
other hand, adduced, in §. 38., a limitation of this appearance.
The aspirating virtue of the ﺩﺩ *y* is less potent than that of
the *ʔ r* and ﻮﻓ *w,* and we find *y* often preceded by the un-
aspirated *t*; for instance, in ﺩﺩﻳﻖﻳﻖ *bitya,* "the second,"
ﺩﺩﻳﻖﻳﻖﻳﻖ *thritya,* "the third": on the other hand, we have
ﺩﺩﻳﻖﻳﻖﻳﻖ *mĕrĕthyu,* "death," Sansk. मृत्यु *mrityu.*

48. In connection with the above rule stands the phenomenon, that before *r,* when followed by any consonant not
a sibilant, an *h* is usually placed; for instance ﺩﻳﻖﻳﻖﻳﻖﻳﻖ
mahrka, "death," from the root ﻳﻖﻳﻖ *mar* (मृ *mri,*) "to die";
ﻖﻳﻖﻳﻖﻳﻖ *kehrpĕm,* or ﻖﻳﻖﻳﻖ *kĕrĕpĕm,* "the body" (nom.
ﺩﺩﻳﻖﻳﻖ *kĕrĕfs*); ﺩﻳﻖﻳﻖ *vĕhrka,* or ﺩﻳﻖﻳﻖﻳﻖ *vĕrĕka,* "wolf,"
(वृक *vrika.*) The semi-vowel *y* also, which only appears before vowels, sometimes attracts an ﻮ *h* ; thus, ﺩﺩﻳﻖﻳﻖﻳﻖ
thwahya, "through thee," corresponds to the Sanskrit त्वया
twayá; and the word ﺩﺩﻳﻖﻳﻖﻳﻖﻳﻖ *csahya* (nom. त्स्वया

[G. Ed. p. 47.] *csahyô* adduced by Rask, stands for ﺩﺩﻳﻖﻳﻖﻳﻖ
csaya and comes from the root ﺩﻳﻖﻳﻖ *csi,* "to rule," (क्षि *kshi.*)

49. We come now to the sibilants. The first, a palatal,
pronounced in Sanskrit with a gentle aspiration, श्, which
we express by *ś* in Sanskrit, and *s* in Zend, is written ﺩ in
the latter. Its exact pronunciation is scarcely ascertain-
able. Anquetil assigns it that of the ordinary *s.* It in
general occurs in those positions in which the Sanskrit in
corresponding words has its श् *ś*; thus, for instance, *daśa,*
"ten," *śata,* "hundred," *paśu,* "beast," are common to both
languages. In this respect ﺩ *s* has spread itself wider in
Zend than in Sanskrit; that before several consonants,

namely, ℘ *t*, ⸱ *k*, and ∫ *n*, as well at the beginning as in
the middle of words—in the latter place, however, only
after ↄↄ *a*, ↄↄↄ *d*, and ↄↄ *aṅ*—it corresponds to the Sanskrit
dental or ordinary *s* स्. Compare ⸱⸱ↄↄↄ *stârô*, "the stars,"
with स्तारस् *stâras*; ⸱⸱ↄↄↄↄ *stâômi*, "I praise," with स्तौमि
stâumi; ⸱ↄↄↄ *asti*, "he is," with अस्ति *asti*; ⸱ↄↄↄↄ
aitaṅm, "ossium," with अस्थि *asthi*; ⸱ↄↄↄↄↄↄ *shanda*,
"shoulder," (?) with स्कन्ध *skandha*; ↄↄↄ *snâ*, "to purify,"
with स्ना *snâ*, "to bathe." We might infer from this circumstance that *s* ↄↄ was pronounced as a simple *s*, yet it
may have to do with a dialectical preference for the sound
sh, as happens with the German *s* in the Suabian dialect,
and pretty universally at the beginning of words before *t*
and *p*. It is further to be remarked, that *s* ↄↄ occurs also
at the end of words after ↄↄ *aṅ*. The occasion for this presents itself in the nom. sing. masc. of bases in ℘ↄↄↄ *nt*.

50. The semi-vowel » *v* is regularly hardened into ↄ *p*
after ↄↄ *s*; hence, for instance, ↄↄↄↄↄↄ *spâ*, "canis." ↄↄↄↄↄↄ
spânĕm "canem," ↄↄↄↄↄↄ *vîspa*, "all," [G. Ed. p. 48.]
ↄↄↄↄↄↄ *aspa*, "horse," corresponding to the Sanskrit श्वा *svâ*,
श्वानम् *svânam*, विश्व *viswa*, अश्व *aswa*. ↄↄↄↄↄↄↄↄ *spenta*, "holy,"
is not corresponded to by a Sanskrit श्वन्त *swanta*, which must
have originally been in use, and which the Lithuanian
szanta-s indicates. From the Zend ↄↄↄↄↄↄ *aspa*, the transition is easy to the Greek ἵππος, which is less obvious in the
case of the Indian *aswa*.

51. For the Sanskrit lingual sibilant ष् *sh*, the Zend
supplies two letters, ↄↄ and ↄↄↄ. The first, according to
Rask, is pronounced like the ordinary *s*, and therefore like the
Sanskrit dental *s* स्; while ↄↄↄ has the sound of ष् = *sh*,
and marks this by a stroke of aspiration. We therefore write
it *sh*.* Rask observes that these two letters are often interchanged in MSS.; which he accounts for by the circumstance

* It is in this Translation given *sh* without any mark. *Sh* denotes the
Sansk. ष्.

that ᴡᴏ is used in the Pehlevi for *sh*, and that the Parsî
copyists have been long better acquainted with the Pehlevi
than the Zend. We find, also, in the Codex edited by Burnouf,
ᴡᴏ almost everywhere corresponding to ष *sh*. We recognise,
however, from the text edited by Olshausen of a part of the
Vendidâd, and the variations appended, that although in etymological respects ᴡᴏ as well as ᴄᴘ corresponds to the Sanskṛit ष *sh*, the principal position of ᴡᴏ is before strong consonants (§. 25.) and at the end of words; a position of much
importance in the Zend, and which requires attention in the
cases of other classes of letters. In this respect ᴡᴏ resembles, among the dentals, ᴘ *t*, among the gutturals ᴏᵟ *c*,
and among the nasals principally ᴊᴊ *n*. At the end of
words, indeed, ᴡᴏ *s* corresponds to the Sanskṛit स *s*, but yet
[G. Ed. p. 49.]   only after such letters as, in the middle of
a word, would, according to Rule 101(ᵃ) of my Sanskṛit Grammar, change an original स *s* into ष *sh*; namely, after vowels
other than *a* and *â*, and after the consonants ᴏᵟ *c* and � *r*.
Hence, for instance, the nominative ᴡᴊᴘᴊᴡᴏ *paitis*, "Lord,"
ᴡᴏᴊᴊᴊᴡᴏ *pasus*, "beast," ᴡᴏᴣᴘᴡ *âtars*, "fire," ᴡᴏᴏᵟᴣᴣ *drucs*,
"dæmon," from the theme ᴊᴊᴣᴣ *druj*. On the other hand,
ᴊᴊᴩᴣᴡ *baraṅs*, "bearing," from ᴘᴊᴊᴣᴡ *barant.*[*] In the
word ᴡᴊᴊᴊᴊᴡᴏᵟ *csvas*, "six," it is true a terminating ᴡᴏ *s*
stands after *a*; but it does not here replace a Sanskṛit स *s*,
but the original ष *sh* of षष् *shash*. As evidence of the use
of ᴡᴏ *s* for ष *sh* before strong consonants, we may adduce
the very usual superlative suffix ᴡᴘᴡᴊ *ista* (*i. e.* ιστος),
corresponding to the Sanskṛit ष्ठ *ishtha.* Other examples
are ᴡᴘᴡᴣᴊ *karsta*, "ploughed," for कृष्ट *krishṭa*. In the
word ᴡᴊᴊᴊᴊᴊᴡᴏ *sayana* "camp," ᴡᴏ stands irregularly for
ᴊᴣ *s*, which latter was to be anticipated from the Sanskṛit शयन *sayana* (cf. *saêtê*, §. 54.) In the fem. numeral

---

* I retain here the original *t*, since the theme of the word does not
appear in use. ᴘ *t* must otherwise have been changed for ᴘ *t*.

ৠ৶ᴠᴠᴖৢ *tisarô,* "three" (Olsh. p. 26), the ᴠᴠ might seem questionable, for the Sanskrit form is तिस्रस् *tisras,* and स् according to §. 53., becomes ᴡ *h.* The स्, however, is here in a position (after इ *i*) in which the Sanskrit favours the conversion of स् *s* into ष् *sh*; and on this rests the Zend form ৠ৶ᴠᴠᴖৢ *tisarô.* That it does not, however, stand as ৠ৶ᴗ৶ᴖৢ *tisharô,* as we might expect from §. 52., is certainly not to be ascribed to the original existence of ᴠᴠ *a*, for ৠ৶ᴠᴠᴖৢ *tisarô* stands for ৠ৶ᴠᴖৢ *tisrô,*

52. ৩ৢ stands for the Sanskrit ष् *sh* be-   [G. Ed. p. 50]
fore vowels and the semi-vowels ৶ৢ *y* and » *v*; compare ৻৩ৢৰৣᴠᴖᴠ *aêtaêshanm* and ᴠᴠᴠৢᴠᴖᴠ *aêtaêshva,* with इतेषाम् *êtéshâm,* "*horum,*" and इतेषु *êtéshu,* "*in his*"; ᴠৢৢ৻ৢ *mashya,* "man," with मनुष्य *manushya.* Yet ৩ৢ *sh* does not unite itself with an antecedent ৫ *c*; but for the Sanskrit क्ष् *ksh* we find almost everywhere in Olshausen's text, and without variation, ᴠᴠৢ *cs*; hence, for instance, ᴠৠৢᴠᴠৢৢ *csathra,* "king." Sanskrit क्षत्र *kshatra,* "a man of the war-like or royal caste."   The word of frequent occurrence, ᴠৢৠ৶ᴠ৶ৢৢ *cshnaôma,* and the third person connected with it, ৵ৢᴖৢৢᴖৢ৻৶ᴠ৶ৢৢ *cshnaômayêiti,* we must, on a double ground, reject, and prefer the variation given at p. 33, since ᴠᴠ *s* here is prolonged, as well by the preceding *c* as by the following *n.* It is, however, worthy of remark, that the Sanskrit क्ष् *ksh* in many Zend words abandons the guttural, and appears as ৩ৢ *sh.* For instance, दक्षिण *dakshina,* "*dexter,*" becomes ᴠৢৢৢৢৢ৶ *dashina* (Lithuan. *deszinè,* "the right hand"), and अक्षि *akshi,* "eye," becomes ৶৩ৢᴠ *ashi,* which, however, seems only to occur at the end of possessive compounds (Bahuvrîhi).

53. ᴡ *h* is never, in etymological respects, the repre-sentative of the Sanskrit ह् *h,* but of the pure and dental sibilant स् *s.* Before vowels, semi-vowels, and *m,* in Zend, this letter invariably becomes ᴡ, possibly because स्व *sw* (§. 35.) takes the shape ৸ *kh*; while before *n,* and such con-sonants as cannot unite with a preceding *h,* (§. 49.) it is to be looked for in the shape of ᴠᴠ *s.*   The   [G. Ed. p. 51.]

roots which begin with स्प *sp* and स्फ *sph* have not yet been detected by me in the Zend; but I am convinced that स्पृश *spriś*, for instance, "to touch," could not begin otherwise in Zend than with ᭁᳲᳲ *śp*.   Compare, for instance—

ZEND.		SANSKRIT.	
ᳲᳲᳲ	*hâ*, "they,"	सा	*sâ.*
ᳲᳲᳲᳲᳲ	*hapta*, "seven,"	सप्त	*sapta.*
ᳲᳲᳲᳲᳲ	*hakĕrĕṭ*, "once,"	सकृत्	*sakrit.*
ᳲᳲᳲᳲ	*ahi*, "thou art,"	असि	*asi.*
ᳲᳲᳲᳲᳲ	*ahmâi*, "to this,"	अस्मै	*asmâi.*
ᳲᳲᳲᳲ	*hvarĕ*, "sun,"	स्वर्	*swar*, "heaven."
ᳲᳲᳲ	*hva*, "his,"	स्व	*swa.*

The word ᳲᳲᳲᳲᳲ *hizva*, "tongue," from जिह्वा *jihwa*, deserves mention, because the sibilant quality of the ज *j* is treated as श *s*, and replaced by ᳲ *h* (§. 53.).

54. I do not remember to have met with an instance of the combination ᳲᳲ *hr*; the Sanskrit word सहस्र *sahasra*, "thousand," which might give occasion for it, has rejected the sibilant in the last syllable, and taken the shape ᳲᳲᳲᳲᳲᳲ *hazaṇra*. If, in the word ᳲᳲᳲᳲᳲ *huska*, "dry," Sansk. शुष्क *śushka*, ᳲ replaces the Sansk. श *ś*, we must remember that the Latin *siccus* indicates a Sansk. स *s*, because *c* regularly answers to श *ś*. In many instances of Sanskrit roots beginning with स *s*, the corresponding Zend form may be grounded on the change which is effected on an initial स *s* by the influence of certain prepositions. (Gram. Crit. r. 80.)

[G. Ed. p. 52.]   Thus I believe I have clearly ascertained the existence of the Sanskrit participle सिद्ध *siddha*, "perfected," in the term of frequent occurrence in the Vendidâd ᳲᳲᳲᳲᳲᳲ *shâistĕm*; after the analogy of ᳲᳲᳲᳲᳲ *irista*, "deceased," from ᳲᳲᳲ *irith* (see §. 99.) Olshausen notifies (p. 29) as variations of ᳲᳲᳲᳲᳲᳲ *shâistĕm* — ᳲᳲᳲᳲᳲᳲ *sâistĕm*, ᳲᳲᳲᳲᳲᳲ *shâistim*, ᳲᳲᳲᳲᳲᳲ *shdistim*, and ᳲᳲᳲᳲᳲᳲ *shâistĕm*. In all these forms, the long *a* presents a difficulty; for, according to §. 28., सिध् *shidh* would give the form ᳲᳲᳲᳲ *shaidh*; and this, with the suffix *ta*,

سرهسردبى *shaista*, in the nom. and accus. neut. ٤٤هسردبى *shâistĕm*. What Anquetil (vol. II. p. 279) translates, *Juste juge du monde qui existe par votre puissance, vous qui êtes la pureté même, quelle est la premiere chose qui plaise à cette terre (que nous habitons), et la rende favorable*, runs in the original (Olsh., p. 29, Burnouf, p. 137), وسرهسلك ع سرسهرکسرردبى ٤هکسردردبى ٤هسردردبى. سرىرىرى ٤هرى سرسردبى ٤سرەسى٤. سرو، سرهسلرىرى ٤سرەسى٤ سرورسى ٤٤٤كى، سردبى سرهسردردبى. *Dâtarĕ gaĕthananm astvaitinanm ashâum! kva paoirím anhâo zĕmô shâistĕm?* "*Creator mundorum existentium, pure! ubi (quid) primum hujus terræ perfectum (bonum?*")

55. The nominative pronominal base स्य *sya* (Gramm. Crit. r. 268), in the Veda dialect, is under the influence of the preceding word; and we see in Rosen's specimen, p. 6, this pronoun, when it follows the particle उ *u*, converted into श्य *shya*, after the analogy of rule 101ᵃ of my Grammar. I have detected a similar phenomenon in the Zend pronouns; for we find روبى *hê*, "*ejus*," "*ei*," which is founded on a lost Sanskrit से *sê* (cf. मे *mê*, "*mei*," "*mihi*," and ते *tê*, "*tui*," "*tibi*"), when it follows سرروبرى *yêzi*, "if," taking the form روسى *sê* (more correctly, perhaps, روبى *shê*); for instance, at p. 37 of Olshausen: while on the same page we find روبى سرسررروبرى *yêzicha hê*, (*und wenn ihm*,) [G. Ed. p. 53.] "and if to him." In the following page we find a similar phenomenon, if, as I can hardly doubt, ٤سربى *shâo* (thus I read it with the variation), corresponds to the Sanskrit असौ *asâu* ("*ille*," "*illa*"): سرهعسسرلىوبى سردجك ٤سرسربى ٤سربى ٤٤ ىر ٤هربىرى، سرهوبرلربسدبى، *Nôiṭ zi ím zâo shâo yâ* (text, ٤سرجك *yâo*) *dareghа akarsta* (text, سرهوبرلربوبرى *adarsta*), "For not this earth which lies long unploughed."

56ᵃ). An وبى *h* standing between *a* or *â* and a following vowel is usually preceded by a guttural nasal (ع *n*); and this appendage seems indispensable—I remember, at least, no exception—in cases where the following vowel is *a*, *â*, or *ĕ*. We find, for instance, سرروبرسربررسررسردبى *usazayaṇha*, "thou wast born"; while in the active the personal ending سربى *hi* of the present admits no nasal; and we find, for instance, ‌‌‌ـ‌‌ـ‌ـ *ahi*, "thou art," ‌‌‌ـ‌‌‌ـ‌‌ *bacsahi*, "thou givest," not ‌‌‌ـ‌‌ـ *aṇhi*, ‌‌‌ـ‌‌‌ـ‌‌ *bacsaṇhi*.

56*b*). The termination *as*, which in Sanskrit only before sonant consonants (§. 25.) and ‌‌‌ *a*, dissolves its ‌‌ into ‌‌ *u*, and contracts the latter together with the preceding *a* into ‌‌‌ *ô* (compare the French *au*, from *al*): this ancient termination *as* appears in Zend, as also in Prâkrit and Pali, always under the shape of *ô*. On the other hand, the termination *ás*, which in Sanskrit before all sonant letters entirely abandons the *s*, in Zend has never allowed the concluding sibilant entirely to expire, but everywhere preserves its fusion in the shape of ‌‌ *o* (for

[G. Ed. p. 54.]   *u*); and I consider myself thereby strongly supported in a conjecture I enounced before my acquaintance with Zend,[*] that in Sanskrit the suppression of a terminating *s* after *á* had preceded the vocalization of this *s* into *u*. It is remarkable that where, in Zend, as above observed, an ‌‌ *ṇ* precedes the ‌‌ *h* which springs out of the *s* of the syllable *ás*, or where, before the enclitic particle ‌‌‌ *cha*, the *s* above mentioned is changed into ‌‌ *ś*, together with these substantial representatives of the *s*, its evaporation into ‌‌ *o* is also retained, and the sibilant thus appears in a double form, albeit torpid and evanescent. To illustrate this by some examples, the Sanskrit मास् *mâs*, "*luna*"— an uninflected nominative, for the *s* belongs to the root— receives in Zend the form ‌‌‌ـ‌‌ *mâo*, in which *o* represents the Sanskrit *s*; माश् *mâś-cha*, "*lunaque*," gives us ‌‌‌ـ‌‌ـ *mâoścha*, and मासम् *mâsam*, "*lunam*," ‌‌‌ـ‌‌ـ *mâoṇhĕm*; so that in the two last examples the Sanskrit sibilant is represented by a vowel and a consonant. The analogy of *mâoṇhĕm*, "*lunam*," is followed in all similar instances; for example, for आस *ása* "*fuit*," we find ‌‌‌ـ‌‌ـ *áoṇha*, and for आसाम् *ásám*, "*earum*," ‌‌‌ـ‌‌ـ *áoṇhaṅm*[†].

---

[*] Observations, rule 78 of the Latin edition of Sanskrit Grammar.

[†] Burnouf is of a different opinion as to the matter in question, for in
the

57. Two sibilants remain to be mentioned, namely, ς and
ↄ, of which the former was probably pronounced like the
French *z*, and may therefore be replaced   [G. Ed. p. 55.]
by that letter.   Etymologically this letter answers to the
Sanskṛit ह *h* for the most part, which never corresponds
to the Zend ↄ *h*.   Compare, for example,

SANSKRIT.		ZEND.
अहम् *aham,* "I,"	६ॣॢ५५ *azĕm.*
हस्त *hasta,* "hand,"	५५०५५५ *zasta.*
सहस्र *sahasra,* "thousand,"	५५०५५५ *hazaṇra.*
हन्ति *hanti,* "he strikes,"	५०५५५५ *zainti.*
वहति *vahati,* "he carries,"	५०५५५५ *vazaiti.*
"bears,"		
हि *hi,* "for,"	५५ *zi.*
जिह्वा *jihwâ,* "tongue,"	५५५५५ *hizva,* (§. 53.)
महत् *mahat,* "great,"	५५५६ *mazô* (from *mazas,*
	acc. ६ॣॢ५५५५६ *mazaṇhĕm.*)

58. Sometimes ς *z* appears also in the place of the Sanskṛit ज *j;* so that the sibilant portion of this letter, pronounced *dsch,* is alone represented, and the *d* sound suppressed (see §. 53.).   Thus ५५५५ *yaz,* "to adore," answers
to the Sanskṛit यज् *yaj* ; ५५५५५ *zaôsha,* "to please," springs
from the Sanskṛit root जुष् *jush,* "to please *or* gratify."
Thirdly, the Zend *z* represents also the Sanskṛit ग *g,* which
is easily accounted for by the relationship between *g* and *j*.
The Indian *gô,* (accus. *gâm,*) *bos* and *terra,* has, in Zend,
as also in Greek, clothed itself in two forms ; the first

---

the Nouveau Journ. Asiatique, tom. iii. p. 342, speaking of the relation of
mâoṇho to *mananhô,* without noticing the analogies which occur in cases
of repetition, *mâosh-cha,* "*lunaque,*" *urvâraosh-cha,* "*arboresque,*" he says,
" In *mâonghô,* there is perhaps this difference, that the *ngh* does not replace the Sanskṛit *s,* for this letter has already become *o* in consequence
of a change of frequent occurrence which we have lately noticed.

signification has maintained itself in Zend, but in Greek
has given way to the labial; and βοῦς and ₄₀ₔₐₒₚ *gdos*, or
₄₀ᵢₐₐₒ *gdus*, correspond to the Sanskrit nom. गौष् *gáus*.

[G. Ed. p. 56.]   For the signification "earth" the Greek
has preserved the guttural, which in Zend is replaced by *z*.
The nom. ₆ₐₛ *zdo* supposes an Indian form गाष् *gás*, for
गौष् *gáus*; in the accusative, ₆ₐₛ *zanm* agrees, in respect
of inflection, as closely as possible with गाम् *yám* and γῆν.

59. ᚕ is of less frequent use, and was probably pronounced like the French *j*: we write it *zh*. It is observable,
that as the French *j* in many words corresponds to the Latin
semi-vowel *j*, and derives from it its own developement, so
also sometimes, in Zend, ᚕ *zh* has arisen out of the Sanskrit य *y*. Thus, for instance, यूयम् *yúyam*, "you," (*vos*),
becomes ₆ₐₛᚕᵧₐₛ *yúzhĕm*. Sometimes, also, ᚕ *zh* has
sprung from the sound of the English *j*, and corresponds to
the Sanskrit ज *j*, as in ᵢᚕᚕᚕ *zhĕnu*, Sanskrit जानु *jánu*, "knee."
Finally, it stands as a terminating letter in some prefixes, in
the place of the Sanskrit dental स *s* after *i* and *u*; thus,
ₛₚₐₐₐᚕᵤₓₐₛᵢ *nizhbaraiti*, "he carries out"; ₆ₐₚₐₛᚕᵧₓₛᵢ
duzh-úctĕm, "ill spoken": on the other hand, ₆ₐₚₐₛ₆ₐₛ
dus-matĕm, "ill thought."

60. We have still to elucidate the nasals, which we have
postponed till now, because for them a knowledge of the
system of the other sounds is indispensable. We must first
of all mention a difference from the Sanskrit, that in Zend
every organ has not its particular nasal; but that here, in
respect of *n*, two main distinctions are established, and that
these mainly depend on the circumstance whether *n* precedes
a vowel or a consonant. In this manner *ſ* and *ₐₛ* are so
contrasted, that the first finds its place chiefly before whole
and half vowels, and also at the end of words; the latter only
[G. Ed. p. 57.]   in the middle of strong consonants. We
find, for instance, ₛₚₐₐₐₛᵤₐₛₚₐₛₚₐₛₐ *hankárayémi*, "I glorify";
ₐₚₚₐₛₐ *pancha*, "five"; ₆ₐₚₐₛₐₛₐₓ₀ₚₐₛ *búshyantĕm*: on the

other hand, ⁀ nâ (nom.) "man"; ⁀ nôit̤, "not"; ⁀
barayĕn, "they might bear"; ⁀ anya, "the other."
Concerning the difference between ⁀ and ⁀—a difference
not recognised in European alphabets—it is probable that
⁀, being always fenced in by strong consonants, must have
had a duller and more suppressed sound than the freer ⁀;
and by reason of this weak and undecided character of its
pronunciation, would appear to have applied itself more
easily to every organ of the following letter.

61. Still feebler and more undecided than ⁀, perhaps
an equivalent to the Indian Anuswâra, we conjecture to
have been the nasal ⁀, which is always involved with ⁀ a,
and which seems from its form to have been a fusion of
⁀ and ⁀. We find this letter, which we write aṅ, first,
before sibilants, before ⁀ h, like the Anuswâra, and before
the aspirates ⁀ th and ⁀ f; for instance, ⁀ csayańs,
"regnans," accus. ⁀ csayantĕm; ⁀
zaṅhyamâna, a part of the middle future of the root ⁀ zan,
"to beget," but, as it seems to me, with a passive signification ("qui nascetur." Vend. S. pp. 28 and 103.); ⁀
maṅthra, "speech," from the root ⁀ man; ⁀ jaṅfnu,
"mouth," probably from the Sanskrit जप् jap, "to pray,"
§. 40., and with the nasal inserted. Secondly, before a
terminating ⁀ m and ⁀ n. We have here to observe that
the Sanskrit termination आम् âm is always changed to
⁀ aṅm in Zend; for intance, ⁀ dadhaṅm, "I gave,"
Sanskrit अददाम् adadâm; ⁀ pâdhanaṅm, "pedum,"
Sans. पादानाम् pâdânâm; and that the ter- [G. Ed. p. 58.]
mination of the third person plural, अन् an, provided the a do
not pass into ĕ, always appears as a double nasal ⁀ aṅn.*

62. For the nasal, which, according to §. 56., is placed as
an euphonic addition before the ⁀ h, which springs from
स s, the Zend has two characters, ⁀ and ⁀, to both which

---

* The termination aṅn from ân belongs to the potential, precative, and
subjunctive.

Anquetil assigns the sound *ng*.* We write them ṇ, in order
to avoid giving the appearance of a *g* preceded by a guttural *n* to this guttural, which is only a nasal precursor of
the following ᴡ *h*. As to the difference in the use of these
two letters, ʒ always follows *a* and *áo* ; ᴊ, on the contrary,
comes after *i* and *e*, for which the occasion is rare. For
instance, in the relative plural nom. ᴘᴜᴡᴊᴦᴏᴘᴜ *yênhê*, " *qui*,"
and in the fem. pron. genitives, as ᴇᴜᴡᴠᴊᴊᴜ *ainháo*, " *hujus*,"
which often occurs, but as often without ᴊ *i*, and with ʒ *ṇ*,
ᴇᴜᴡᴠʒᴜ *aṇháo*. What phonetic difference existed between ʒ
and ᴊ we cannot venture to pronounce. Anquetil as we
have seen, assigns the same pronunciation to each; while Rask
compares ᴊ with the Sanskrit palatal ञ *n*, and illustrates
its sound by that of the Spanish and Portuguese ñ.

63. The labial nasal ᴄ *m* does not differ from the Sanskṛit म: it must, however, be remarked, that it sometimes
takes the place of *b*. At least the root ब्रू *brú*, " speak," in
Zend becomes ᴘ⁷ᴄ *mrú* ; as ᴄᴣᴊ⁷ᴄ *mraôm*, " I spoke," ᴘᴣᴊᴊ⁷ᴄ
mraôt, " he spoke" : in a similar manner is the Indian
मुख *mukha*, " mouth," related to the Latin *bucca* ; and not
    [G. Ed. p. 59.]   much otherwise the Latin *mare* to the
Sanskṛit वारि *vári*, " water." I consider, also, *multus* related to बहुल *bahula*, the Greek πολύς, and the Gothic *filu*.

64. A concluding ᴄ *m* operates in a double manner on
a preceding vowel. It weakens (see §. 30.) the ᴊ *a* to ᴇ *ĕ* ;
and, on the other hand, lengthens the vowels *i* and *u* ;
thus, for instance, ᴄᴊᴘᴊᴊᴓ *paitim*, " the Lord," ᴄʒᴘᴊᴘ *tanúm*,
" the body," from the bases ᴊᴘᴊᴊᴓ *paiti*, ʒᴘᴊᴘ *tanu*. In
contradiction to this rule we find the vocative of frequent
occurrence, ᴄʒᴊᴡᴇᴘᴊ *ashâum*, " pure." Here, however,
ʒᴊ *âu*, as a diphthong, answers to the Sanskrit ओ *âu*, the
last element of which is not capable of further lengthening

---

* Burnouf also writes the first of these *ng*. I have done the same in
my reviews in the Journal of Lit. Crit.

The form in question is a contraction of the theme *ashavan;* with an irregular conversion of the concluding *ʃ n* into *ç m.*

65. We give here a complete summary of the Zend characters.

Simple Vowels: *ɴ a, ε ĕ, ç e; ɴ â; ɟ i, ɟ í; ɔ u,* *o, ʒ ú.*

Diphthongs: *ɴ, ɴ ĕ, ɟ ôi; ɟɴ âi; ô, ɢɴ âo, ɔɴ âu.*

Gutturals: *ʒ k* (before vowels and *» v*), *ɑ c* (principally before consonants), *ɢ kh* (from *sw*, before vowels and *ɟɟ y*); *ɑ g, ʒ gh.*

Palatals: *ɴ ch, ʒ j.*

Dentals: *ɟ t* (before vowels and *ɟɟ y*), *ɴ ṭ* (before consonants and at the end of words), *ɑ th* (before whole and semi-vowels), *ʒ d, ɑ dh.*

Labials: *ɟ p, ɟ f* (the latter before vowels, semi-vowels, nasals, and *ɴ s*), *ɟ b.*

Semi-vowels: *ɑ, ɴ, ɟɟ y* (the two   [G. Ed. p. 60.] first initial, the last medial), *ʔ, ɟ r* (the last only after *ɟ f*), *ɢ, » v* (the first initial, the last medial), *ɑ w.*

Sibilants and *h:* *ɴ s,* *ɢɴ sh, ɴ s, ɑ zh* (or like the French *j*), *ʒ z, ɴ h.*

Nasals: *ɟ n* (before vowels, semi-vowels, and at the end of words), *ɴ n* (before strong consonants), *ɴ aṇ* (before sibilants, *ɴ h, ɑ th, ɟ f, ç m,* and *ɟ n*), *ʒ ṇ* (between *ɴ a* or *ɢɴ âo,* and *ɴ h,* and between *a* and *r*[*]), *ɟ ṇ* (between *ɟ i* or *ɴ ĕ,* and *ɴ h*), *ç m.*

Remark also the Compounds *ɴ* for *ɴɴ ah,* and *ɴ* for *ɴɴ st.*

66. We refrain from treating specially of the Greek, Latin, and Lithuanian systems of sounds, but must here devote a closer consideration to the Germanic. The Gothic *a,* which, according to Grimm, is always short, answers

---

* E.g. *ɴʒɢɴ hazaṇra,* "a thousand."

completely to the Sanskrit *a*; and the sounds of the Greek
e and *o* are wanting, in their character of degeneration
from *a*, in Gothic as well as in Sanskrit.   The ancient
a has not, however, always been retained in Gothic; but
in radical syllables, as well as in terminations, has often
been weakened to *i*, or has undergone suppression; often,
also, by the influence of a following liquid, has been converted into *u*.   Compare, for instance, *sibun*, "seven," with
सप्तन् *saptan*; *taihun*, "ten," with दशन् *daśan*.

67. We believe ourselves authorized to lay down as a
law, that व *a* in polysyllabic words before a terminating *s*
is everywhere weakened into *i*, or suppressed; but before
a terminating *th* generally appears as *i.*   A concluding व *a*
in the Gothic either remains unaltered, or disappears: it
never becomes *i.*

68. In the Old High German the Gothic *a* either remains
[G. Ed. p. 61.]   unaltered, or is weakened to *e*, or is changed
by the influence of a liquid to *u* = perhaps *o*.   According to
this, the relation of the unorganic *e* to the Gothic *a* is the
same as that of the Gothic *i* (§. 66.) to व *a ;* compare, for
instance, in the genitive of the bases in *a* वृकस्य *vrika-sya*,
Gothic *vulfi-s*, Old High German *wolfe-s*.   In the dative plural
wolfu-m stands to *vulfa-m* in the same relation as above (§. 66.),
sibun to *saptan*.   The precedence of a liquid has also, in Old
High German, sometimes converted this *a* into *u* or *o*; compare *plinte-mu(mo)*, *cœco*, with the Gothic *blindamma*.   Also
after the German *j* or *y*, which in Sanskrit (य *y*) belongs as
a semi-vowel to the same class as *r*, the Old High German
seems to prefer *u* to *a*; thence *plintju*, without *j* also *plintu*,
"*cœca*," as a fem. nom. sing., and neuter nom. acc. voc.
plural; *plinta* "*cœcam*."   The *u* of the first person present, as
kipu, "I give," Gothic *giba*, I ascribe to the influence of
the dropped personal letter *m*.   Respecting the degeneration of the original *a* sound to *u* compare also §. 66.   In
the Old High German inseparable preposition *ki* (our
German *ge*) = Gothic *ga*, Sanskrit स *sa* or सम् *sam*, we

have an example in which the Gothic-Sanskrit *a* has become *i*.

69, For the Sanskrit **श** *á*, the Gothic, which has no long *a*, almost always substitutes *ô* (§. 4.), and this *ô*, in cases of abbreviation, falls back into the short *a*. Thus, for instance, in Grimm's first fem. declension of the strong form, the nom. and accus. sing. *ô* is softened to *a*, whence *giba*, *gibô-s* (§. 118.). Generally in the Gothic polysyllabic forms, the concluding **श** *á* is shortened to *a*; and where *ô* stands at the termination, an originally succeeding consonant has been dropped; for instance, in the gen. plur. fem. *ô* stands for **शाम्** *ám*. Sometimes, also, in the Gothic, *ê* corresponds to the Sanskrit *á*, as in the gen. plur. masc. and neuter. In the Old High German the Gothic *ô* either   [G. Ed. p. 62.] remains *ô*, as in the gen. plur., or divides itself into two short vowels; and, according to differences of origin, into *ou*, *ua*, or *uo*; of which, in the Middle High German, *uo* prevails; while in the Modern High German the two divided vowels are contracted into *ú*.   For the Gothic *ê* = **श** *á*, the Old, Middle, and Modern High German have preserved the old *á*, except in the gen. plural.

70. For **इ** *i* and **ई** *í* the Gothic has *i* and *ei*; which latter, as Grimm has sufficiently shewn, is everywhere to be considered as long *i*, and also in Old and Middle High German is so represented. We, together with Grimm, as in the case of the other vowels, designate its prolongation by a circumflex. In the Modern High German the long *i* appears mostly as *ei*; compare, for instance, *mein* with the Gothic genitive *meina*, and the Old and Middle High German *mîn*. Sometimes a short *i* is substituted, as in *lich*, answering to the Gothic *leiks*, "like," at the end of compounds. On the long *i*, in *vîr*, "*nos*," Gothic *veis*, we can lay no stress, as we match the dat. sing. *mîr* also with the Gothic *mis*. It is scarcely worth remarking that we usually, in writing, designate the elongation of the *i* and other vowels by the addition of an *h*.

71. While the original व *a* has undergone many alterations in the Germanic languages, and has produced both
i and *u*, I have been able to detect no other alterations in
i and *í* than that *i* is as often suppressed as *a*; but it never
happens, unless some rare exceptions have escaped me, that
i is replaced by a heavier vowel *a* or *u*.* We may lay
[G. Ed. p. 63.]   it down as a rule, that final *i* has given
way in German everywhere, as it has generally in Latin.
Compare.

SANSKRIT.	GREEK.	LATIN.	GOTHIC.
परि *pari*,	περί,	*per*,	*fair*. (§. 82.)
उपरि *upari*,	ὑπέρ,	*super*,	*ufar*.
अस्ति *asti*,	ἐστί,	*est*,	*ist*.
सन्ति *santi*,	ἐντί,	*sunt*,	*sind*.

72. Where a concluding *i* occurs in Gothic and Old High
German it is always a mutilation of the German *j* (or *y*) together with the following vowel; so that *j*, after the suppression of this vowel, has vocalized itself. Thus the uninflected
Gothic accus. *hari*, "*exercitum*," is a mutilation of *harya*.† The
Sanskrit would require *harya-m;* and the Zend, after §. 42.,
meeting the Germanic half way, *hari-m*. Before a concluding *s* also, in the Gothic, इ *i* is usually suppressed ; and
the Gothic terminating syllable *is*, is mostly a weakening
of *as*, §. 67.   In Old High German, and still more in Middle
and Modern High German, the Gothic *i* has often degenerated into *e*, which, where it occurs in the accented syllable,
is expressed in Grimm by *ë*. We retain this character. We
have also to observe of the Gothic, that, in the old text, *i*

---

* The Sanskrit पितृ *pitṛi*, "father," probably stands for पातृ *pátṛi*,
"ruler"; and the European languages have adhered to the true original.
(Gramm. Crit. r. 178, Annot.)

† In the text *harja;* but in order to shew more exactly the connection
with the Sanscrit य *y*, vide §. 68. 1. 12. ; and as the *j* is simply and universally pronounced *y*, the German *j* will be represented by *y* in this
translation.

at the beginning of a syllable is distinguished by two dots above, which Grimm retains.

73. As in Zend (§. 41.), by the attractive force of *i, î,* or *y,* an *i* is introduced into the antecedent syllable ; so also, in Old High German, the corresponding sounds have obtained an assimilating power; and frequently an   [G. Ed. p. 64.] *a* of the preceding syllable is converted into *e,* without any power of prevention on the part of either a single or double consonant. Thus, for instance, we find from *ast,* " branch," the plural *esti;* from *anst,* "grace," the plural *ensti;* and from *vallu,* "I fall," the second and third persons *vellis, vellit.* This law, however, has not prevaded the Old High German universally : we find, for instance, *arpi,* "*hereditas,*" not *erpi;* *zahari,* "*lacrymæ,*" not *zaheri.*

74. In the Middle High German, the *e,* which springs from the older *i,* has both retained and extended the power of modification and assimilation; inasmuch as, with few limitations, (Grimm, p. 332,) not only every *a* by its retrospective action becomes *e,* but generally, also, *â, u,* and *o* are modified into *æ, ü,* and *ö;* *ô* into *œ,* and *uo* into *ue.* Thus the plural *geste, dræte, brüche, küche, læne, gruese,* from *gast, drât, bruch, koch, lôn, gruoz.* On the other hand, in the Old High German, the *e* which has degenerated from *i* or *a* obtains no such power ; and we find in the genitive singular of the above words, *gaste-s, drate-s,* &c., because the Old High German has already, in the declension of the masculine *i* class, reduced to *e* the *i* belonging to the class, and which in Gothic remains unaltered.

75. The *e* produced in Old and Middle High German by the modification of *a,* is retained in the Modern High German, in cases where the trace of the original vowel is either extinguished or scarcely felt; as, *Ende, Engel, setzen, netzen, nennen, brennen;* Goth. *andi, aggilus, satyan, natyan, namnyan, brannyan.* Where, however, the original vowel is distinctly opposed to the change, we place *ä,* short or

[G. Ed. p. 65.]   long, from short or long *a*; and in the same relation, *ä* from *u*, *ö* from *o*, *äu* from *au*; for instance, *Brände, Pfäle, Dünste, Flüge, Köche, Töne, Bäume*, from *Brand, Pfál*, &c.

76. For उ *u*, ऊ *ú*, the Gothic has *u*, which is generally short. Among the few examples cited by Grimm, p. 41, of long *u*, we particularize the comparative *sútizô*, the essential part of which corresponds to the Sansk. स्वादु *swádu*, "sweet," (ἡδύ-ς), and in which the long *u* may stand as a compensation for the absence of the *w(v)*, which becomes vocalized. In Old High German it seems to me that *púam*, "to dwell," and *trúén*, "to trust," correspond to the Sanskrit roots भू *bhú*, "to be," ध्रु *dhrú* "to stand fast"—from which comes ध्रुव *dhruva*, "fast," "constant," "certain" (Gramm. Crit. r. 51.)—with the Guna form of which (§. 26.) the Goth. *bauan, trauan*, is connected; cf. भवितुम् *bhav-itum*, "to be," ध्रवितुम् *dhrav-itum*, "to stand fast." The Middle High German continues the Gothic Old High German *ú*, but the Modern High German substitutes *au*, whence *bauen, trauen, Taube* (Gothic *dúbô*).

77. As out of the Sanskrit उ *u*, in Zend, the sound of a short ل* has developed itself (§. 32.), thus, also, the Gothic *u* shews itself, in the more recent dialects, oftener in the form of *o* than in its own. Thus have the Verbs in the Old and Middle High German (Grimm's 9th conjug.) preserved a radical *u* in the plur. of the pret., but replaced it by *o* in the passive part. Compare, for instance, *bugum*, "we bend," *bugans*, "bent," with Old High German *pukumés, pokanér*, Middle High German *bugen, bogen*. The example adduced shews, also, the softening of the old *u* to *e*, in unaccented syllables, in Middle High German as in Modern High German; so that this unaccented *e* may represent all original vowels—*a*, *i*, *u*; and we may lay it down as a rule, that all long and short vowels in the last syllable of poly-

---

* Cf. §. 447. Note.

syllabic words, are either worn away or softened down to a
mute *e*.

78. For the diphthongs ए *ê* $(a + i)$ and   [G. Ed. p. 66.]
ओ *ô* $(a + u)$, the Gothic has *ai* and *au*, which are also
monosyllabic, and were perhaps pronounced like ए *ê* and *ô*.
Compare *bavaima*, "*ædificemus*" with भवेम *bhavêma*, "*simus*";
sunau-s, "of a son," with its equivalent सुनोस् *sunô-s*. Where
these Gothic diphthongs *ai* and *au* have maintained themselves
unaltered in value, they then appear, in writing, as *ê* and *ô*,*
which must be considered as contractions of $a + i$ and $a + u$;
as in the Latin *amêmus*, from *amaïmus* (§. 5.); and as in
the almost solitary case of *bôs*, the long *o* of which is the
result of a contraction of $a + u$, whose latter element appears
again before vowels in the independent shape of *v* (*bovis*,
bovem), while the first element *ă*, in its degeneration,
appears as *ŏ* (§. 3.). Compare,

SANSKRIT.	GOTHIC.	OLD HIGH GERMAN.
चरेम *charêma* (*eamus*),	*faraima*,	*varêmês*.
चरेत *charêta* (*eatis*),	*faraith*,	*varêt*.
तेभ्यस *têbhyas* (*his*),	*thaim*,	*dêm*.

79. In like manner, in all subjunctives, and in the pronominal declension in which the adjective bases in *a* take
part, an Old High German *ê* corresponds to the Sanskrit
ए *ê* and Gothic *ai*. The Middle High   [G. Ed. p. 67.]
German has shortened this *ê*, as standing in an unaccented
terminating syllable (*varen*, *varet*). Besides this, the Middle
High German has, in common with the Old High German,

If, however, the Gothic diphthongs in question were not pronounced
like their etymological equivalents ए *ê* and ओ *ô*, but, as Grimm con-
ceives, approximate to the Vriddhi-change (§. 26.) ऐ *ai* and औ *au*: in
such case the High German *ê*, *ô*, as opposed to the Gothic *ai*, *au*, are not
merely continuations of these Gothic diphthongs: but the pronunciation
assigned by the Sanskrit to the union of *a* with *i* or *u*, must have been
first introduced into the Germanic, under certain conditions, in the eighth
century.

preserved the diphthong *ê* where it stood in radical syllables under the protection of a following *u, r* (out of the older *s*), or *h (ch)*, even in cases where one of these letters had been dropped, or where *u* had vocalized itself into *v* or *o*. (Grimm. pp. 90. 343).   Compare,

GOTHIC.	OLD HIGH GERMAN.	MIDDLE HIGH GERMAN.
aiv, " *ævum,*"	*êwîn.*	
snaivs, " *nix,*"	*snêv,*	*snê.*
mais, " *magis,*"	*mêr,*	*mê.*
laisyan, " *docere,*"	*lêran,*	*lêren.*
laihv, " *commodavit,*"	*lêh*	*lêch.*

In the Modern High German this *ê* is partly preserved, partly replaced; for instance, *mêr (mehr), Schnê (Schnee), Sêle* (Gothic *saivala*); but *ich lieh, gedieh*. (Grimm. p. 983.).

80. As the *ê* for the Gothic *ai*, so the *ô* for *au*, in the Old and Middle High German, is favoured by certain consonants ; and those which favour the *ô* are the more numerous.   They consist of the dentals (according to the Sanskrit division, §. 16.) *t, d, z*, together with their nasal and sibilant (*n, s*) ; further, the semi-vowel *r*; and *h*, which, as a termination in Middle High German, becomes *ch* (See Grimm, pp. 94. 345).   The roots, which in the Gothic admit the Guna modification of the radical *u* by *a*, in the preterite singular, oppose to the Gothic *au*, in Middle and Old High German, a double form; namely, *ô* under the condition above mentioned, and next *ou*, §. 34., in the absence [G. Ed. p. 68.] of the letter which protects *ô*.   For instance, Old High German *zôh*, Middle High German *zôch (traxi, traxit)* Gothic *tauh*, Sanskrit दुदोह *dudôha (mulxi, mulsi,)* ; but *pouc, bouc, flexi, flexit*, Gothic *baug*, Sanskrit बुभोज *bu-bhôja.* The Modern High German exhibits the Gothic diphthong *au*, either, like the Middle and Old High German, as *ô*, and in a more extended degree, and subject to the modification of §. 75; or next, shortened to *o*,

the particulars of which will be explained under the verb; or, thirdly, as *au*; for instance, *daupya*, " I baptize," *hlaupa*, " I run"; or, fourthly, as *eu*, §. 83.

81. As Ulfilas, in proper names, represents both *ε* and *αι* by *ai*, and likewise *o* and *αυ* by *au* (*Paitrus*, *Galeilain*, *apaustaulus*, *Paulus*); and as, in the next place, not every Gothic *ai* and *au* in the cognate dialects is represented in like manner, but in some cases the Gothic *ai* is replaced in Old High German by a simple *i* or *ë*, and *au* by *u* or *o* (§. 77.); but in the others, *ai* is replaced by *ê*, or (§. 85.) by *ei*, and *au* by *ô* or (§. 84.) *ou*; therefore Grimm deduces from these facts a double value of the diphthongs *ai* and *au*; one with the accent on the last element (*aí*, *aú*), another with the accent on the *a* (*ái*, *áu*). We cannot, however, give implicit belief to this deduction of the acute author of the German system of sounds, and prefer assuming an equal value in all cases of the Gothic *ai* and *au*, although we might support Grimm's view by the fact, that, in Sanskrit, ए *ê*, ओ *ô*, never replace his *aí* and *aú*; but everywhere, where occasion occurs, do replace *ái* and *áu*. We think, however, that the difference is rather phonetic than etymological. As concerns the *ai* and *au* in proper names, it may be accounted for, inasmuch as the Gothic was   [G. Ed. p. 69.] deficient in equivalents for these non-primitive vowels, which have degenerated from the original आ *a*. Could Ulfilas have looked back into the early ages of his language, and have recognised the original idenity of *ε* and *o* with his *a*, he would perhaps have used the latter as their substitutes. From his point of sight, however, he embraced the *ai* and *au*, probably because these mixed diphthongs passed with him as weaker than the long *ê* and *ô*, *ejusdem generis,* = (आ *â*). It is important here to observe, that in Greek also *αι* is felt as weaker than *η* and *ω*, as is proved by the fact that *αι* does not attract the accent towards itself (*τύπτομαι* not *τυπτόμαι*. The expression of the Greek *αι* and *αυ* by

the Gothic *ai* and *au* requires the less justification, because even if *ai* was pronounced like ए *ĕ*, and *au* like ओ *ŏ*, yet the written character presents these diphthongs as a still perceptible fusion of *a* with a following *i* or *u*.

82. As to the other statement, namely, that not every Gothic *ai* and *au* produces the same effect in the younger dialects, nor has the same foundation in the older Sanskrit, it might be sufficient to observe upon one feature of dialect peculiar to the Gothic, that *h* and *r* do not content themselves with a pure preceding *i*, but require it to be affected by Guna (§. 26.); thus, *ai* for *i*, and *au* for *u*; while other dialects exhibit the *i* and *u* before *h* and *r* in the same form as before every other consonant. The relation of the Gothic to their Sanskrit equivalents,

GOTHIC	SANSKRIT.
saihs, "six,"	षष् *shash*,
taihun, " ten,"	दशन् *dasan*,
faihu, " cattle,"	पशु *pasu*,
svaihra " father-in-law,"	श्वशुर *swasura*,
taihsvô, "dextera,"	दक्षिणा *dakshinâ*,
hairtô, "heart,"	हृद् *hrid* (from *hard* §. 1.),
bairan, "to bear,"	भर्तुम् *bhartum*,
distairan, "to tear,"	दरितुम् *dar-i-tum*,
stairnô, "star,"	तारा *târâ*.

[G. Ed. P. 70.]

is not so to be understood as though an *i* had been placed after the old *a*, but that, by the softening down of the *a* to *i* (§. 66.), the forms *sihs*, *tihun*, had been produced; out of which, afterwards, the Guna power arising from *h* and *r* had produced *saihs*, *taihun*, *bairan*. The High German has, however, remained at the earlier stage; for Old High German *sëhs*, (Anglo-Saxon, "six,") and *tëhan* or *tëhun*, &c., rest upon an earlier Gothic *sihs*, *tihun*. Thus, *tohtar* rests on an earlier Gothic *duhtar*, for the Guna form *dauhtar*, Sanskrit दुहितर् *duhitar*, (दुहितृ *duhitri*, §. 1.) "daughter." Where the

Sanskrit व*a* has preserved itself in the Gothic unaltered, that is, not weakened to *i*, the occasion is absent for the development of the diphthong *ai*, since it is not the *a* before *h* and *r* which demands a subsequent addition, but the *i* which demands a precedent one; compare *ahtau*, " eight," with वरी *ashtáu*.*

83. The alterations to which the simple vowels have been subjected appear again in the simple elements of the diphthongs, as well in the relation of the Gothic to the Sanskrit, as in that of the younger Germanic dialects to the Gothic. Thus the *a* element of the diphthong वो *ó* shews itself often in the Gothic, and in certain places in a regular manner, as *i* (§. 27.); and in the same places the *a* contained in ए *é* (*a* + *i*) becomes *i*, which, with the second element of the diphthong, generates a long *i* (written as *ei*, §. 70.). The Gothic *iu* has either retained that form in Old High German, or has altered sometimes one, sometimes both of its constituents. Thus have arisen *io*, *ëo*. [G. Ed. p. 71.] There is a greater distance to be passed in Otfrid's theory of the substitution of *ia* for *iu*, which cannot fail to surprise, as we know that a simple *u* never becoms *a*.† In Middle High German *iu* has either remained unaltered, or has been changed to *ie*, which is as old as the latest Old High German, as it is found in Notker. In Modern High German the substitution of *ie* for the old *iu* is that which princi-

---

* *Ahtau=ashtáu* is perhaps the only case in which the Gothic *au* corresponds to the Sanskrit Vriddhi diphthong वौ *áu*; on the other hand, *au* often answers to वो *ó*=(*a*+*u*).

† There is yet another *ia* in Old High German, namely, that which Grimm (p. 103) very acutely represents as the result of a contraction, and formerly dissyllabic, to which, therefore, there is no counterpart diphthong in Gothic. The most important case will be discussed under the head of the verb, in preterites, such as *hialt*, " I held," Gothic *haihald*. After this analogy *fiar*, " four," (according to Otfrid), arose out of the Gothic *fidvor*, in this way, that, after the extrusion of the *dv*, the *ó* passed into its corresponding short vowel.— *Grimm*, p. 193.

F

pally prevails, in which, however, the *e* is only visibly retained, for phonetically it is absorbed by the *i.* Compare *ich biele* with the Gothic *biuda, giesse* with *giula.* Besides this form, we also find *eu* in place of the old *iu* or still older *au*, in cases, namely, where *e* can be accounted for as the result of a no longer perceptible modification (Grimm, p. 523, §. 75.); compare *Leute* with the Gothic *laudeis*, Old High German *liuti,* "people"; *Heu,* "hay," with Goth, *havi,* "grass." Usually, however, the Gothic has already acquired an *iu* in place of this *eu*, and the original *au* (which becomes *av* before vowels) is to be sought in the Sanskrit; for instance, *Neune,* "nine," Old High German *niuni,* Gothic *niuneis,* Sanskrit नवन् *navan* (as theme); *neu,* "new," Old High German *niwi* (indeclinable), Gothic *nivi-s,* Sanskrit नवस् *nava-s.* This *e*, however, is difficult to account for, in as far as it is connected with the *Umlaut,* because it corresponds to an *i* in Middle and Old High German ; and this vowel, of itself answering to an *i* or *y* in the following syllable, is capable of no alteration through their power of attraction.   Long *u* for *iu,* equivalent to a transposition of the diphthong, is found in *lügen,* " to lie," *trügen,* "to deceive," Middle High German *liugen, triugen.*

[G. Ed. p. 72.]   84. Where the *a* element of the Sanskrit ओ *ó* retains its existence in the Gothic, making *au* the equivalent of *ó,* the Middle High German, and a part of the Old High German authorities, have *ou* in the place of *au,* although, as has been remarked in §. 80, under the influence of certain consonants *ó* prevails. Compare Old High German *pouc,* Middle High German *bouc,* with the Gothic preterite *baug,* "*flexi.*"   The *o* of the High German *ou* has the same relation to the corresponding Gothic *a* in *au,* as the Greek *o* in βοῦς bears to the Sanskrit व *a,* which undergoes a fusion with उ *u* in the ओ *ó* of the cognate word गो *gó.* The oldest Old High German authorities (Gl. Hrab. Ker. Is.) have *au* for the *ou* of the later (Grimm. p. 99); and as, under the conditions specified in §. 80., they also exhibit *ó*, this tells in favour of Grimm's assumption, that *au* in the Gothic and oldest High German was pronounced like our German *au*, and thus not like the Sanskrit ओ *ó* (out of *a + u*). In 'this case, in the Gothic *ai*, also, both the letters must have been sounded, and this diphthong must be only an etymological, and not a phonetic equivalent of the Sanskrit ए *é*.

85. In the Gothic diphthong *ai* the *a* alone is susceptible of alteration, and appears in High German softened down to *e*, in the cases in which the *é*, contracted from *ai* (§. 78.), does not occur. In Modern High German, however, *ei*, in pronunciation, = *ai*. Compare

GOTHIC.	OLD HIGH GERMAN.	MIDDLE HIGH GERMAN.	MODERN HIGH GERMAN.
haita, " *voco*,"	*heizu,*	*heize,*	*heisse.*
skaida, " *separo*,"	*skeidu,*	*scheide,*	*scheide.*

86. (1.) Let us now consider the consonants, preserving the Indian arrangement, and thus examining   [G. Ed. p. 73.] the gutturals first. Of these, the Gothic has merely the *lenuis* and the medial (*k, g*); and Ulfilas, in imitation of the Greek, places the latter as a nasal before gutturals; for instance, *drigkan*, "to drink"; *briggan*, "to bring"; *tuggó*, "tongue"; *yuggs*, "young"; *gaggs*, "a going" (subst.). For the compound *kv* the old writing has a special character, which we, like Grimm, render by *qv*, although *q* does not appear elsewhere, and *v* also combines with *g*; so that *qv* (=*kv*) plainly bears the same relation to *gv* that *k* bears to *g*; compare *sigqvan*, "to sink," with *siggvan*, "to read," "to sing." *H* also, in Gothic, willingly combines with *v*; and for this combination, also, the original text has a special character; compare *saihvan*, *leihvan*, with our *sehen*, *leihen*. In respect to *h* by itself we have to observe that it often appears in relations in which the dentals place their *th* and the labials their *f*, so that in this case it takes the place of

kh, which is wanting in the Gothic. In this manner is *aih* related to *aigum*, "we have," as *bauth* to *budum*, and *gaf* to *gêbum*. Probably the pronunciation of the Gothic *h* was not in all positions the same, but in terminations, and before *t* and *s*, if not generally before consonants, corresponded to our *ch*. The High German has *ch* as an aspirate of the *k*: for this *tenuis*, however, either *k* or *c* stands in the older dialects, the use of which, in Middle High German, is so distinguished, that *c* stands as a terminating letter, and in the middle of words before *t*, and *ch* also stands for a double *k*. (Grimm, p. 422.) This distinction reminds us of the use of the Zend ꝏ *c* in contrast to ꝗ *k*, as also of the ꝗ *t* in contrast to ꝗ *t*. (§§. 34. 38.)

(2.) The palatals and linguals are wanting in Gothic, as in Greek and Latin; the dentals are, in Gothic, *t*, *th*, *d*, [G. Ed. p. 74.] together with their nasal *n*. For *th* the Gothic alphabet has a special character. In the High German *z* (=*ts*) fills the place of the aspiration of the *t*, so that the breathing is replaced by the sibilation. By the side of this *z* in the Old High German, the old Gothic *th* also maintains its existence.[*] There are two species of *z*, which, in Middle High German, do not agree with each other. In the one, *t* has the preponderance, in the other, *s*; and this latter is written by Isidor *zs*, and its reduplication *zss*, while the reduplication of the former he writes *tz*. In the Modern High German the second species has only retained the sibilant, but in writing is distinguished, though not universally, from *s* proper. Etymologically, both species of the Old and Middle High German *z* fall under the same head, and correspond to the Gothic *t*.

(3.) The labials are, in Gothic, *p*, *f*, *b*, with their nasal

---

[*] Our Modern High German *th* is, according to Grimm (p. 525), inorganic, and to be rejected. "It is, neither in pronunciation nor origin, properly aspirated, and nothing but a mere tenuis."

m. The High German supplies this organ, as the Sanskrit does all, with a double aspiration, a surd $(f = \text{ष } ph)$ (see §. 25.) and a sonant, which is written *v*, and comes nearer to the Sanskrit भ *bh.* In Modern High German we perceive no longer any phonetic difference between *f* and *v*; but in Middle High German *v* shews itself in this manner softer than *f*, in that, first, at the end of words it is transformed into *f*, on the same principle by which, in such a position, the medials are converted into tenues; for instance, *wolf* not *wolv*, but genitive *wolves;* second, that in the middle before surd consonants it becomes *f*, hence *zwelve* becomes *zwelfte, fünve* becomes *funfte, funfzic.* At the beginning of words *f* and *v*, in Middle High German, seem of equal signification, and their use in the MSS. is precarious, [G. Ed. p. 75.] but *v* preponderates (Grimm, pp. 339. 400). It is the same in Old High German; yet Notker uses *f* as the original primarily existing breathing-sound, and *v* as the softer or sonant aspiration, and therefore employs the latter in cases where the preceding word concludes with one of those letters, which otherwise (§. 93.) soften down a tenuis to its medial (Grimm, pp. 135, 136); for instance, *demo vater, den vater,* but not *des vater* but *des fater.* So far the rule is less stringent (observes Grimm), that in all cases *f* may stand for *v*, but the converse does not hold. Many Old High German authorities abandon altogether the initiatory *v*, and write *f* for it constantly, namely, Kero, Otfrid, Tatian. The aspiration of the *p* is sometimes, in Old High German, also rendered by *ph*, but, in general, only at the beginning of words of foreign origin, *phorta, phenning;* in the middle, and at the end occasionally, in true Germanic forms, such as *wërphan, warph, wurphumês,* in Tatian; *limphan* in Otfrid and Tatian. According to Grimm, *ph*, in many cases, has had the mere sound of *f*. "In monumental inscriptions, however, which usually employ *f*, the *ph* of many words had indisputably the sound of *pf;* for example, if Otfrid

writes *kuphar*, " *cuprum*," *scepheri*, " Creator," we are not to
assume that these words were pronounced *kufar, sceferi* "
(p. 132).   In Middle High German the initial *ph* of foreign
words of the Old High German has become *pf* (Grimm,
p. 326).   In the middle and at the end we find *pf*, first, always
after *m*, *kumpf*, " *pugna*," *tampf*, " *vapor*," *krempfen*, " *contra-
here*," in which case *p* is an euphonic appendage to *f*, in order
to facilitate a union with *m*.   Secondly, in compounds with the
inseparable prefix *ent*, which, before the labial aspirates, lays
aside its *t*, or, as seems to me the sounder supposition, converts
that letter, by assimilation, into the labial tenuis.   Hence, for
[G. Ed. p. 76.]   instance, *enp-finden*, later and more harmonious *emp-finden*, for *ent-finden*.   Standing alone, nevertheless, it appears, in Middle High German, *vinden*, but *v* does not
combine with *p*, for after the surd *p* (§. 25.) the surd aspirate
is necessary (see Grimm, p. 398).   Thirdly, after short vowels
the labial aspirates are apt to be preceded by their tenues, as
well in the middle as at the end of words : just as in Sanskrit
(Gramm. Crit. r. 88.) the palatal surd aspirate between a short
and another vowel or semi-vowel is preceded by its tenuis ;
and, for instance, पृच्छति *prichchhati* is said for पृच्छति *prichhati*.
" *interrogat*," from the root प्रच्छ *prachh*.   In this light I
view the Middle High German forms *kopf*, *kropf*, *tropfe*,
klopfen, *kripfen*, *kupfen* (Grimm, p, 398).   In the same words
we sometimes find *ff*, as *kaffen*, *schuffen*.   Here, also, *p* has
assimilated itself to the following *f*; for *f*, even though it be
the aspirate of *p*, is not pronounced like the Sanskrit फ *ph*,
that is, like *p* with a clearly perceptible *h*; but the sounds
p and *h* are compounded into a third simple sound lying
between the two, which is therefore capable of reduplication,
as in Greek φ unites itself with θ, while *ph* + *th* would be impossible.

(4.) The Sanskrit semi-vowels are represented in Gothic
by *j* (=*y*), *r, l, v*; the same in High German ; only in Old
High German Manuscripts the sound of the Indo-Gothic *r*

(our *w*) is most usually represented by *uu*, in Middle High German by *vv*: *j* (or *y*) in both is written *i*. We agree with Grimm in using *j* (or *y*) and *w* for all periods of the High German. After an initial consonant in Old High German, the semi-vowel *w* in most authorities is expressed by *u*; for instance, *zuelif*, " twelve," Gothic *tvalif*. As in the Sanskrit and Zend the semi-vowels *y* and *v* often arise out of the corresponding vowels *i* and *u*, so also in the   [G. Ed. p. 77.] Germanic; for instance, Gothic *suniv-ê*, "*filiorum*," from the base *sunu*, with *u* affected by Guna (*iu*, §. 27.). More usually, however, in the Germanic, the converse occurs, namely, that *y* and *v*, at terminations and before consonants, have become vocalised (see §. 73.), and have only retained their original form before terminations beginning with a vowel; for if, for instance, *thius*, " servant," forms *thivis* in the genitive, we know, from the history of the word, that this *v* has not sprung from the *u* of the nominative, but that *thius* is a mutilation of *thivas* (§. 116.); so that after the lapse of the *a* the preceding semi-vowel has become a whole one. In like manner is *thivi*, " maid-servant," a mutilation of the base *thivyô* (§. 120.), whose nominative, like the accusative, probably was *thivya*, for which, however, in the accusative, after the *v* had become vocalized, *thiuya* was substituted.

(5.) Of the Sanskrit sibilants, the Germanic has only the last, namely, the pure dental स *s*. Out of this, however, springs another, peculiar, at least in use, to the Gothic, which is written *z*, and had probably a softer pronunciation than *s*. This *z* is most usually found between two vowels, as an euphonic alteration of *s*, but sometimes also between a vowel and *v*, *l*, or *n*; and between liquids (*l*, *r*, *n*) and a vowel, *y* or *n*, in some words also before *d*; finally, before the guttural medial, in the single instance, *azgô*, " ashes"; everywhere thus before sonants, and it must therefore itself be considered as a sonant sibilant (§. 25.), while

s is the surd.   It is remarkable, in a grammatical point of
view, that a concluding *s* before the enclitic particles *ei* and
uh, and before the passive addition *a*, passes into *z*; hence, for
instance, *thizei* "*cujus*," from *this* "*hujus*," *thanzei* "*quos*,"
from *thans* "*hos*," *vileizuh* "*visne*" from *vileis* "*vis*," *haitaza*
"*vocaris*," from *haitis* "*vocas*," or rather from its earlier form
  [G. Ed. p. 78.]   *haitas*.   The root *slêp*, "to sleep," forms,
by a reduplication, in the preterite, *saizlêp*, "I *or* he slept."
Other examples are, *izvis*, "*vobis*," "*vos*," *razn* "house," *talzyan*,
"to teach," *marzyan*, "to provoke," *fairzna*, "heel."   The
High German loves the softening of *s* into *r*, especially
between two vowels (see §. 22.); but this change has not
established itself as a pervading law, and does not extend
over all parts of the Grammar.   For instance, in Old High
German, the final *s* of several roots has changed itself into
r before the preterite terminations which commence with a
vowel; on the other hand, it has remained unaltered in the
uninflected first and third pers. sing. indicative, and also
before the vowels of the present.   For example, from the
root *lus*, comes *liusu*, "I lose," *lôs*, "I *or* he lost," *lurumês*
"we lost."   While in these cases the termination takes *s*
under its protection, yet the *s* of the nominative singular,
where it has not been altogether dropped, is everywhere
softened down to *r*; and, on the other hand, the concluding
s of the genitive has, down to our time, remained unaltered,
and thus an organic difference has arisen between two cases
originally distinguished by a similar suffix.   For instance,

GOTHIC.	OLD HIGH GERMAN.	MODERN HIGH GERMAN.
Nominative . . *blind'-s*,	*plintê-r*,	*blinde-r*.
Genitive . . . *blindi-s*,	*plinte-s*,	*blinde-s*.

87. The Germanic tongues exhibit, in respect of consonants, a remarkable law of displacement, which has been
first recognised and developed with great ability by Grimm.
According to this law, the Gothic, and the other dialects,

with the exception of the High German, in relation to the Greek, Latin, and, with certain limits, also   [G. Ed. p. 79.] to the Sanskrit and Zend, substitute aspirates for the original tenues, *h* for *k*, *th* for *t*, and *f* for *p*; tenues for medials, *t* for *d*, *p* for *b*, and *k* for *g*; finally, medials for aspirates, *g* for *χ*, *d* for *θ*, and *b* for *f*. The High German bears the same regular relation to the Gothic as the latter to the Greek, and substitutes its aspirates for the Gothic tenues and Greek medials; its tenues for the Gothic medials and Greek aspirates; and its medials for the Gothic aspirates and Greek tenues. Yet the Gothic labial and guttural medial exhibits itself unaltered in most of the Old High German authorities, as in the Middle and Modern High German; for instance, Gothic *biuga*, "*flecto*," Old High German *biuga* and *piuka*, Middle High German *biuge*, Modern High German *biege*. For the Gothic *f*, the Old High German substitutes *v*, especially as a first letter (§. 86. ₃.). In the *t* sounds, *z* in High German (=*ts*) replaces an aspirate. The Gothic has no aspiration of the *k*, and either replaces the Greek *κ* by the simple aspiration *h*, in which case it sometimes coincides with the Sanskrit ॡ *h*, or it falls to the level of the High German, and, in the middle or end of words, usually gives *g* instead of *k*, the High German adhering, as regards the beginning of words, to the Gothic practice, and participating with that dialect in the use of the *h*. We give here Grimm's table, illustrating the law of these substitutions, p. 584.

Greek	. . . . . .	P		B	F	T	D	Th	K	G	Ch
Gothic	. . . . . .	F		P	B	Th	T	D		K	G
Old High German,		B (V)	F	P		D	Z	T		G	Ch	K

[G. Ed. p. 80.]

EXAMPLES.*

SANSKṚIT.	GREEK.	LATIN.	GOTHIC.	OLD HIGH GERM.
पादस् *pâda-s*,	*πούς, ποδ-ός*,	*pes, pedis*,	*fôtus*,	*vuoz*.
पञ्चन् *panchan*,	*πέμπε*,	*quinque*,	*fimf*,	*vinf*.
पूर्ण *pûrṇa*,	*πλέος*,	*plenus*,	*fulls*,	*vol*.
पितृ *pitṛi*,	*πατήρ*,	*pater*,	*fadrein*†,	*vatar*.
उपरि *upari*,	*ὑπέρ*,	*super*,	*ufar*,	*ubar*.
	κάνναβις,	*cannabis*,	. .	*hanaf*.
भञ्ज् *bhanj*,	. .	*frangere*,	*brikan*,	*prëchan*.
भुज् *bhuj*,	. .	*frui, fructus*,	*brûkôn*,	*prûchôn*.
भ्रातृ *bhrâtṛi*	. .	*frater*,	*brôthar*,	*pruoder*.
भृ *bhṛi*,	*φέρω*,	*fero*,	*baira*,	*piru*.
भ्रू *bhrû*,	*ὀφρύς*,	. .	. .	*prawa*.
कपाल *kapâla*, m. n.,	*κεφαλή*,	*caput*,	*haubith*,	*houpit*.
त्वम् *twam* (nom.),	*τύ*,	. .	*thu*,	*du*.
तम् *tam* (acc.),	*τόν*,	*is-tum*,	*thana*,	*dën*.
त्रयस् *trayas* (n. pl.),	*τρεῖς*,	*tres*,	*threis*,	*drî*.
अन्तर *antara*,	*ἕτερος*,	*alter*,	*anthar*,	*andar*.
दन्तम् *danta-m* (acc.),	*ὀδόντ-α*,	*dentem*,	*thuntu-s*,	*zand*.
द्वौ *dwau* (n. *du*),	*δύο*,	*duo*,	*twai*,	*zuênê*.
दक्षिणा *dakṣhiṇâ*,	*δεξία*,	*dextra*,	*taihswô*,	*zësawa*.
उद *uda*,	*ὕδωρ*,	*unda*,	*watô*,	*wazar*.
दुहितृ *duhitṛi*,	*θυγάτηρ*,	. .	*dauhtar*,	*tohtar*.
[G. Ed. p. 81.] द्वार् *dwâr*,	*θύρα*,	*fores*,	*daur*,	*tor*.
मधु *madhu*,	*μέθυ*,	. .	. .	*mëto*.
श्वन् *śwan*,	*κύων*,	*canis*,	*hunths*,	*hund*.
हृदय *hṛidaya*,	*καρδία*,	*cor*,	*hairtô*,	*hërza*.
अक्ष *akṣha*,	*ὄκος*,	*oculus*,	*augô*,	*ouga*.
अश्रु *aśru*,	*δάκρυ*,	*lacrima*,	*tagr* m.,	*zahar*.
पशु *paśu*,	. .	*pecus*,	*faihu*,	*vihu*.

* The Sanskṛit words here stand, where the termination is not separated from the base, or the case not indicated, in their crude or simple form (theme); of the verb, we give only the bare root.

† "Parents."

SANSKRIT.	GREEK.	LATIN.	GOTHIC.	OLD HIGH GERM.
श्वशुर *swaśura,*	ἐκυρός,	*socer,*	*svaihra,*	*suehur.*
दशन् *dasan,*	δέκα,	*decem,*	*taihun,*	*zëhan.*
ज्ञा *jnâ,*	γνῶμι,	*gnosco,*	*kan,*	*chan.*
जाति *jâti,**	γένος,	*genus,*	*kuni,*	*chuni.*
जानु *jânu,*	γόνυ,	*genu,*	*kniu,*	*chniu.*
महत् *mahat,*	μέγαλος,	*magnus,*	*mikils,*	*mihil.*
हंस *hansa,*	χήν,	*anser,*	*gans,*	*kans.*
ह्यस् *hyas,*	χθές,	*heri,*	*gistra,*	*këstar.*
लिह् *lih,*	λείχω,	*lingo,*	*laigô,*	*lëkôm.*

88. The Lithuanian has left the consonants without displacement in their old situations, only, from its deficiency in aspirates, substituting simple tenues for the Sanskrit aspirated tenues, and medials for the aspirated medials. Compare,

LITHUANIAN.	SANSKRIT.
rata-s, " wheel,"	रथस् *ratha-s,* "waggon."
búsu, " I would be,"	भविष्यामि *bhavishyâmi.*
ka-s, " who,"	कस् *ka-s.*
dümi, " I give,"	ददामि *dadâmi.* [G. Ed. p. 82.]
pats, "husband," "master,"	पतिस् *pati-s.*
penki, " five,"	पञ्चन् *panchan.*
trys, "three,"	त्रयस् *trayas* (n. pl. m.)
keturi, "four,"	चत्वारस् *chatwâras* (n. pl. m.)
ketwirtas, "the fourth,"	चतुर्थस् *chaturtha-s.*
szaká, f. "bough,"	शाखा *śâkhâ.*

Irregular deviations occur, as might be expected, in individual cases. Thus, for instance, *naga-s,* "nail" (of the foot or finger), not *naka-s,* answers to the Sanskrit नखस् *nakhas.* The Zend stands, as we have before remarked, in the same rank, in all essential respects, as the Sanskrit,

* From *jan,* "to be born."

Greek, and Latin. As, however, according to §. 47., certain consonants convey an aspiration to the letter which precedes them, this may occasion an accidental coincidence between the Zend and the Gothic; and both languages may, in like manner and in the same words, depart from the original tenuis. Compare,

GOTHIC.	ZEND.	SANSKRIT.
thir (theme), " three,"	ᒍᎧ thri,	त्रि tri.
thus, " to thee,"	thwûh,	ते twê.*
fra, (inseparable prep.)	fra,	प्र pra
friyô, " I love,"	âfrínámi,†	प्रीणामि prínámi.
ahva ‡, " a river,"	âfs	अप् ap (theme).

[G. Ed. p. 83.] I pronounce this coincidence between the Gothic and the Zend aspirates accidental, because the causes of it are distinct; as, on the one side, the Gothic accords no aspirating influence to the letters v and r (truda, trauan, trimpan, tvai), and, in the examples given above, th and f stand, only because, according to rule, Gothic aspirates are to be expected in the place of original tenues; on the other side, the Zend everywhere retains the original tenues, where the letters named in §. 47. do not exhibit an influence, which is unknown to the Gothic; so that, quite according to order, in by far the majority of forms which admit of comparison, either Gothic aspirates are met with in the place of Zend tenues, or, according to another appointment of the Germanic law of substitution, Gothic tenues in that of Zend medials. Compare,

---

* Twê occurs as an uninflected genitive in Rosen's Veda-Specimen, p. 26, and may, like the mutilated ते tê, be also used as a dative.

† "I bless," from the Sanskrit root prî, "to love," united with the prep. a.

‡ Ahva. The Sanskrit-Zend expression signifies " water " ; and the Gothic form developes itself through the transition, of frequent occurrence, of p to k, for which the law of substitution requires h (see also aqua).

GOTHIC.	ZEND.
thu, " thou,"	ᵹᵽ *tûm.*
fidvôr, (ind.) " four,"	ᵹᵌᵐᵌᵍᵌ *chathwârô* (n. pl. m.)
fimf,	ᵌᵐᵌ *pancha.*
fulls, " full,"	ᵌᵌᵌ *përënô* (n. m.)
fadrein, " parents,"	ᵌᵌᵌ *paitar-ëm* (*patrem*).
faths, " master,"	ᵌᵌᵌ *paiti-s.*
faihu, " beast,"	ᵌᵌᵌ *pasu-s.*
faryith, " he wanders,"	ᵌᵌᵌ *charaiti.*
fôtu-s, " foot,"	ᵌᵌᵌ *pâdha* (§. 39.)
fraihith, " he asks,"	ᵌᵌᵌ *përësaiti.*
ufar, " over,"	ᵌᵌᵌ *upairi,* (§. 41.)
af, " from,"	ᵌᵌᵌ *apa.*
thai, " these,"	ᵌᵌ *të.*
hvas, " who,"	ᵌᵌ *kô.* [G. Ed. p. 84.]
tvai, " two,"	ᵌᵌᵌ *dva.*
taihun, " ten,"	ᵌᵌᵌ *dasa.*
taihsvô, " right hand,"	ᵌᵌᵌ *dashina,* "*dexter.*"

In the Sanskrit and Zend the sonant aspirates, not the
surd, as in Greek, (ह *h* too is sonant, see §. 25.) correspond,
according to rule, to the Gothic medials : as, however, in the
Zend the *bh* is not found, ᴊ *b* answers to the Gothic *b.*
Compare,

GOTHIC.	ZEND.	SANSKRIT.
bairith, " he carries,"	ᵌᵌᵌ *baraiti,*	बिभर्ति *bibharti.*
brôthar, " brother,"	ᵌᵌᵌ *brâtarëm* (acc.)	भ्रातरम् *bhrâtaram* (acc.)
bai, " both,"	ᵌᵌ *uba,*	उभौ *ubhâu* (n. ac. v. du.)
brûkan, " to use,"		भुज् *bhuj,* " to eat."
bi (prep.)	ᵌᵌ *abi,* ᵌᵌᵌ *aiwi,*	अभि *abhi.*
midya, " middling,"	ᵌᵌᵌ *maidhya,*	मध्य *madhya.*
bindan, " bind,"	ᵌᵌᵌ *bandh,*	बन्ध् *bandh.*

89. Violations of the law of displacement of sounds, both by
persistence in the same original sound, or the substitution of
irregular sounds, are frequent in the middle and at the end of

words. Thus, in the Old High German *vatar*, the *t* of the
Greek πατήρ remains; in the Gothic *fadrein*, "*parentes*," *d* is
substituted irregularly for *th*. The same phenomenon occurs
in the cases of the Old High German *olpenta*, and the Gothic
ulbandus, contrasted with the τ of ἐλεφαντ- ; thus, also, the *t*
of चतुर् *chatur*, "*quatuor*," has become *d* in the Gothic
fidvôr instead of *th*; but in High German has entirely disappeared.   The *p* of the Sanskrit root स्वप् *swap*, (Latin
sopio,) "sleep," has been preserved in the Gothic *slêpa*, and
[G. Ed. p. 85.]   the Old High German *slâfu* stands in the
Gothic category, but the Sanskrit root is more faithfully
preserved in the Old High German in *in-suepyu* (*sopio*, see
§. 86. 4.)

90. Nor have the inflexions or grammatical appendages
everywhere submitted[*] to the law of displacement, but have,
in many instances, either remained faithful to the primary
sound, or have, at least, rejected the particular change prescribed by §. 87. Thus the Old High German has, in the
third person, as well singular as plural, retained the original
t; compare *hapêt*, " he has," *hapênt*, " they have," with *habet*,
habent: the Gothic, on the contrary, says *habaith*, *haband*;
the first in accordance with the law, the last in violation of
it, for *habanth*. Thus, also, in the part. pres., the *t* of the old
languages has become, under the influence of the preceding
n, not *th* but *d*; the *t* of the part. pass., however, is changed
before the *s* of the nom. into *th*, but before vowel termina-

---

* It would be better to regard the phenomenon here discussed by assuming *d* as the proper character of the third person in Gothic ; and
viewing the Old High German *t* as the regular substitute for it. The
d has been retained in the Gothic passive also (*bair-a-da*), and the active
form *bairith* is derivable from *bairid*, in that the Gothic prefers the aspirates to the medials at the end of a word. The same is the case with the
part. pass., the suffix of which is, in Gothic, *da*, whence, in Old High German, in consequence of the second law for the permutation of sounds,
comes *ta* ; so that the old form recurs again, re-introduced by a fresh corruption.

tions, by an anomalous process, into *d*; after the same principle by which the *th* of the third person before the vowel increment of the passive is softened to *d*; so that *da**, instead of *tha*, corresponds to the Greek το, of ἐτύπτετ-ο, and to the Sanskrit त *ta*, of अभवत *abhavata.* The Old High German, on the other hand, has preserved the original *t* in both participles: *hapêntêr, hapêtêr*, Gothic *habands*, genitive *habandins; habaiths*, gen. *habaidis.*

91. Special notice is due to the fact, that in the middle of words under the protection of a preceding consonant, the old consonant often remains without displacement, sometimes because it chimes in well with the preceding sound, sometimes because, through regard for the preceding letters, alterations have been admitted other than those which the usual practice as to displacement would lead us to expect. Mute consonants (§. 25.), among which, in   [G. Ed. p. 86.] the Germanic, the *h* must be reckoned, where it is to be pronounced like our *ch*, protect a succeeding original *t*. Thus, अष्टौ *ashtâu*, "eight," ὀκτώ, "*octo*," is in Goth. *ahtau*, in Old High German *ahtô*: नक्तम् *naktam* (adverbial accusative), "night," νύξ, νυκτός, "*nox*," "*noctis*," is in Gothic *nahts*, Old High German *naht.* The liquids, on the other hand, like the vowels, which they approach nearest of all consonants, affect a *d* or *th* after themselves. From these euphonic causes, for instance, the feminine suffix ति *ti* in Sanskrit, in Greek σις, as ποίησις, which designates abstract substantives, appears in Gothic in three forms, *ti, di,* and *thi.* The original form *ti* shews itself after *f*, into which *p* and *b* mostly resolve themselves, and also after *s* and *h*; for instance, *anst(i)s* (§. 117.), "grace," from the root *an*, Old High German *unnan*, "to be gracious," with the insertion of an euphonic *s*: *fralust(i)s*, "loss," (from *lus*, pres. *liusa*): *maht(i)s*, "strength," (from *magan*): *fra-gift(i)s*," betrothment," (from *gib, gaf*), also *fragibts*, perhaps erroneously, as *b* has little

---

  * *Da* is an abbreviation of *dai* = G. ται Sansk. *tê*, s: e §. 406.

affinity with *t*: *ga-skafl(i)s*, "creation," (from *skap-an*). The
form *di* finds its place after vowels, but is able, where the
vowel of the suffix falls away, *i. e.* in the nom. and accus.
sing., to convert *d* into *th*, because *th* can, more easily than *d*,
dispense with a following vowel, and is a favourite letter at
the end of words and before consonants, though *d* also is
tolerated in such a position. Hence the root *bud*, "to bid,"
(pres. *biudn*, §. 27.) forms, in the uninflected condition of the
pret., *bauth*, in the plur. *bud-um*; and the nominal base,
mana-sê-di, "world," (according to Grimm's well-founded
interpretation, "seed, not seat, of man,") forms in the nom.
and accus. *mana-sêths*, *mana-sêth*, or *mana-sêds*, *mana-sêd;*
but in the dat. *mann-sêdai* not -*sêthai*. On the other hand,
after liquids the suffix is usually *thi*, and after *n*, *di*: the
dental, however, once chosen, remains afterwards in every
position, either without a vowel or before vowels; for instance,
gabaurths, "birth," dat. *gabaurthai*; *gafaurds*, "gathering"
[G. Ed. p. 87.]   (from *far-yan*, "to go"), gen. *gafaurdais:*
gakunths, "esteem," gen. *gakunthais*; *gamunds*, "memory,"
gen. *gamundais*; *gaqvumths*, "meeting," dat. *gaqvumthai*, dat.
plur. *gaqvumthim*. From the union with *m*, *d* is excluded.
On the whole, however, the law here discussed accords remarkably with a similar phenomenon in modern Persian,
where the original *t* of grammatical terminations and suffixes
is maintained only after mute consonants, but after vowels
and liquids is changed into *d*: hence, for instance, *girif-tan*,
"to take," *bas-tan*, "to bind," *dâsh-tan*, "to have," *pukh-tan*,
"to cook": on the other hand, *dâ-dan*, "to give," *bur-dan*, "to
bear," *âm-dan*, "to come." I do not, therefore, hesitate to
release the Germanic suffix *ti*, and all other suffixes originally
commencing with *t*, from the general law of substitution of
sounds, and to assign the lot of this *t* entirely to the controul
of the preceding letter. The Old High German, in the case
of our suffix *ti*, as in that of other suffixes and terminations
originally commencing with *t*, accords to the original *t* a

far more extensive prevalence, than does the Gothic; inasmuch as it retains that letter, not only when protected by *s, h,* and *f,* but also after vowels and liquids—after *m* an euphonic *f* is inserted;—and the *t* is only after *l* changed into *d.* Hence, for instance, *ans-t,* "grace," *hlouft,* "course," *mah-t,* "might," *sâ-t,* "seed," *kipurt,* "birth," *var-t,* "journey," *mun-t,* "protection," *ki-wal-t,* "force," *scul-t, schuld,* "guilt," *chumft,* "arrival."

92. The law of substitution shews the greatest pertinacity at the beginning of words, and I have found it everywhere observed in the relation of the Gothic to the Greek and Latin. On the other hand, in some roots which are either deficient or disfigured in the Old European languages, but which are common to the Germanic and the Sanskrit, the Gothic stands on the same footing with   [G. Ed. p. 88.] the Sanskrit, especially in respect of initial medials. Thus, बन्ध् *bandh,* "to bind," is also *band* in Gothic, not *pand*; ग्रह् *grah,* in the Vedas ग्रभ् *grabh,* "to take," "seize," is *grip* (pres. *greipa* with Guna, §. 27.) not *krip*;[*] to गा *gâ* and गम् *gam,* "to go," correspond *gagga,* "I go," and *ga-tvâ,* "street;" दह् *dah,* "to burn," is, in Old High German, *dahan* (δαίω), "to burn," "to light." I can detect, however, no instance in which Gothic tenues correspond to Sanskrit as initial letters.

93(ᵃ). We return now to the Sanskrit, in order, with relation to the most essential laws of sound, to notice one adverted to in our theory of single letters; where it was said of several concurrent consonants that they were tolerated neither at the end of words, nor in the middle before strong consonants, and how their places were supplied in such situations. It is besides to be observed, that, properly, tenues alone can terminate a Sanskrit word; but medials, only before sonants, (§. 25,) may either be retained, if they originally terminate an inflective base, or take the place of a tenuis

---

[*] The Latin *prehendo* is probably related to the Sanskrit root ग्रह् *grah,* through the usual interchange between gutturals and labials.

or an aspirate, if these happen to precede sonants in a
sentence.   As examples, we select हरित् *harit*, (*viridis*),
" green," वेदविद् *véda-vid*, "skilled in the Véda," धनलभ् *dhana-
labh*, "acquiring wealth." These words are, according to
§. 94., without a nominative sign.   We find, also, अस्ति हरित्
asti harit, "he is green," अस्ति वेदवित् *asti vedá-vit*, अस्ति धनलप्
asti dhana-lap; on the other hand, हरिद् अस्ति *harid asti*, वेदविद्
अस्ति *vedavid asti*, धनलब् अस्ति *dhana-lab asti*; also, हरिद् भवति
harid bhavati, &c.   With this Sanskrit law the Middle High

[G. Ed. p. 89.]   German is very nearly in accordance, which
indeed tolerates aspirates at the end of words, contrary to the
custom of the Sanskrit, only with a conversion of the sonant
v into the surd *f*, see §. 86. 3.; but, like the Sanskrit, and
independent of the law of displacement explained in §. 87.,
supplies the place of medials at the end of words regularly
by tenues.   As, for example, in the genitives *tages, eides,
wibes*, of which the nom. and accus. sing., deprived of the
inflexion and the terminating vowel of the base, take the
forms *tac*, (§. 86. 1.) *eit, wip*.   So also as to the verb; for
instance, the roots *trag, lad, grab*, form, in the uninflected
1st and 3d pers. sing. pret., *truoc, luot, gruop*, plur. *truogen,
luoden, gruoben*.   Where, on the other hand, the tenuis or
aspirate (*v* excepted) is radical, there no alteration of sound
occurs in declension or in conjugation.   For instance, *wort,*
gen. *wortes*, not *wordes*, as in Sansk. ददत् *dadat*, "the giver,"
gen. ददतम् *dadatas*, not ददद्स *dadadas*, but विद् *vit*, "knowing,"
gen. विदस् *vidas*, from the base विद् *vid*.   In Old High
German different authorities of the language are at variance
with respect to the strict observance of this law.   Isidor is
in accordance with it, insomuch that he converts *d* at the
end into *t*, and *g* into *c*; for instance, *wort, wordes*; *dac,
dages*.   The Gothic excludes only the labial medials from
terminations, but replaces them, not by tenues, but by
aspirates.   Hence *gaf*, "I gave," in contrast to *gébum*, and
the accusatives *hlaif, lauf, thiuf*, opposed to the nominatives
hlaibs, laubs, thiubs, gen. *hlaibis*, &c.   The guttural and dental

medials (*g, d*) are tolerated by the Gothic in terminations; yet even in these, in individual cases, a preference appears for the terminating aspirates. Compare *bauth,* " I or he offered," with *budum,* " we offered," from the root *bud;* *haitad-a* "*nominatur*" with *hailith* (§. 67.) "*nominat;* *aih,* " I have," " he has," with *aigum,* " we have."

[G. Ed. p. 90.]   93(ᵇ). In a sense also opposed to that of the above-mentioned Sanskrit law, we find, in Old High German, yet only in Notker, an euphonic relation between terminating and initial letters of two words which come together. (Grimm, pp. 130, 138, 181). As in Sanskrit the tenuis appears as an essential consonant, fit for the conclusion of a sentence, but exchangeable, under the influence of a word following in a sentence, for the medials; so with Notker the tenuis ranks as a true initial; stands therefore at the beginning of a sentence, and after strong consonants; but after vowels and the weakest consonants the liquid is turned into a medial. Thus, for instance, *ih pin,* " I am," but *ih ne bin;* *ter dag,* " the day," but *tes tages;* *mit kote,* " with God," but *minan got,* " my God."

94. Two consonants are no longer, in the existing condition of the Sanskrit, tolerated at the end of a word, but the latter of the two is rejected. This emasculation, which must date from an epoch subsequent to the division of the language, as this law is not recognised either by the Zend or by any of the European branches of the family, has had, in many respects, a disadvantageous operation on the Grammar, and has mutilated many forms of antiquity required by theory. In the High German we may view, as in some degree connected with this phenomenon, the circumstance that roots with double liquids—*ll, mm, nn, rr*— in forms which are indeclinable (and before the consonants of inflexions) reject the latter of the pair. In the case, also, of terminations in double *h* or *t,* one is rejected. Hence, for instance, from *stihhu* (*pungo*) *ar-prittu* (*stringo*), the 1st and 3d pers. pret. *stah, ar-prat.* In Middle High German,

in declensions in *ck, ff*, the last is rejected; for instance, *boc,* gen. *bockes; grif, griffes: tz* loses the *t*; for instance, *schaz, schatzes.*

95. Between a final न *n* and a suc-   [G. Ed. p. 91.]
ceeding *t* sound — as which the palatals also must be reckoned, for च *ch* is equivalent to *tsh*—in the Sanskrit an euphonic sibilant is interposed, from the operation of the following *t*; and न, by this sibilant, is converted, §. 9., into Anuswâra; for instance, अभवंस् तत्र *abhavans tatra,* (*abhavan-s-tatra*), "they were there." With this coincides the circumstance, that, in High German, between a radical *n* and the *t* of an affix, an *s*, in certain cases, is inserted; for instance, from the root *ann,* "to favour," comes, in Old High German, *an-s-t,* "thou favourest," *on-s-ta* or *onda,* "I favoured," *an-s-t,* "favour"; from *prann* comes *prun-s-t,* "ardour"; from *chan* is derived *chun-s-t,* "knowledge," our German KUNST, in which, as in BRUNST and GUNST, (from *gönnen,* probably formed from the *ann* before noticed, and the preposite *g(e).*) the euphonic *s* has stood fast. The Gothic exhibits this phenomenon nowhere, perhaps, but in *an-s-ts* and *allbrun-s-ts* 'holocaustum.' In Old High German we find still an *s* inserted after *r,* in the root *tarr*; hence, *tar-s-t,* "thou darest," *tor-s-ta,* I dared." (Cf. §. 616. 2d Note.)

96. In Sanskrit the interposed euphonic *s* has extended itself further only among the prefixed prepositions, which generally enter into most intimate and facile connection with the following root. In this manner the euphonic *s* steps in between the prepositions सम् *sam,* अव *ava,* परि *pari,* प्रति *prati,* and certain words which begin with क *k.* With this the Latin *s* between *ab* or *ob* and *c, q,* and *p,* remarkably accords[*],

[G. Ed. p. 92.]   which *s, ab* retains even in an isolated position, when the above-mentioned letters follow. To this we also refer the *cosmittere* of Festus, instead of *committere*

---

[*] We scarcely think it necessary to defend ourselves for dividing, with Vossius, *ob-solesco,* rather than with Schneider (p. 571) *obs-olesco.*

(Schneider, p. 475), unless an original *smitto*, for *mitto*, is involved in this compound. In the Greek, ς shews an inclination for connection with τ, θ, and μ, and precedes these letters as an euphonic link, especially after short vowels, in cases which require no special mention. In compounds like σακες-πάλος I reckon the ς, in opposition to the common theory, as belonging to the base of the first member (§. 128.). We have yet to consider a case of the interpolation of an euphonic labial, which is common to the Old Latin and Germanic, and serves to facilitate the union of the labial nasal with a dental. The Latin places *p* between *m* and a following *t* or *s*; the Gothic and Old High German *f* between *m* and *t*. Thus, *sumpsi, prompsi, dempsi, sumptus, promptus, demptus ;* Gothic *andanum-f-ts*, "acceptance"; Old High German *chum-f-t*, "arrival." In Greek we find also the interpolation of an euphonic β after μ, of a δ after ν, of a θ after σ, in order to facilitate the union of μ, ν, and σ with ρ and λ (μεσημβρία, μέμβλεται, ἀνδρός, ἱμάσθλη—see Buttman, p. 80); while the Modern Persian places an euphonic *d* between the vowel of a prefixed preposition and that of the following word, as *be-d-ú*, "to him."

97. The Greek affords few specimens of variability at the end of words, excepting from peculiarities of dialect, as the substitution of ρ for ς. The alteration of the ν in the article in old inscriptions, and in the prefixes σύν, ἐν, and πάλιν, seems analogous to the changes which, according to §. 18., the terminating म *m*, in Sanskrit, undergoes in all cases, with reference to the letter which follows. [G. Ed. p. 93.] The concluding ν in Greek is also generally a derivative from μ, and corresponds to this letter, which the Greek never admits as a termination in analogous forms of the Sanskrit, Zend, and Latin. N frequently springs from a final ς; thus, for instance, μεν (Doric μες) and the dual τον answer to the Sanskrit personal terminations मस् *mas*, थस् *thas*, तस् *tas*. I have found this explanation, which I have given elsewhere, of the origin of the ν from ς

subsequently confirmed by the Prâkṛit, in which, in like manner, the concluding *s* of the instrumental termination plural भिस् *bhis* has passed into the dull *ṅ* (Anuswâra, §. 9.), and हिं *hiṅ* is said for .*bhis.*   An operation, which has a prejudicial effect on many Greek terminations, and disturbs the relation to cognate languages, is the suppression of the *t* sound at the end of words, where, in Sanskrit, Zend, and Latin it plays an essential part. In respect of the vowels, it is also worthy of notice, that in Sanskrit, but not in Zend, at the meeting of vowel terminations and commencements, a hiatus is guarded against, either by the fusion of the two vowels, or, in cases where the vowel has a cognate semi-vowel at its command, by its transition into this latter, provided the vowel following be unlike. We find, for instance, अस्तीदम् *astídam,* "*est hoc,*" and अस्त्य् अयम् *asty ayam,* "*est hic.*"   For the sake of clearness, and because the junction of two vowels might too often give the appearance of two or more words to one, I write in my most recent text अस्ती 'दम्, in órder, by an apostrophe which I employ as a sign of fusion, to indicate that the vowel which appears wanting in the दम् *dam* is contained in the final vowel of the preceding word. We might, perhaps, still better write अस्ती॒ 'दम्, in order directly [G. Ed. p. 94.]   at the close of the first word to shew that its final vowel has arisen out of a contraction, and that the following word participates in it.*

98. We have now to consider the alterations in the middle of words, *i.e.* those of the final letters of the roots and nominal bases before grammatical endings, and we find, with respect to these, most life, strength, and consciousness in the Sanskrit; and this language is

---

* We cannot guide ourselves here by the original MSS., as these exhibit no separation of words, and entire verses are written together without interruption, as though they were only a series of senseless syllables, and not words of independent place and meaning. As we must depart from Indian practice, the more complete the more rational the separation.

placed on the highest point of antiquity, insomuch as the signification of every radical portion is still so strongly felt, that while it admits of moderate changes, for the avoiding of harshness, it never, if we except some vowel elisions, permits the radical sense to be obliterated, or rendered irrecognisable by concessions too great, or transitions too daring. Yet does the Sanskrit, more than any of its kindred, afford a field for the conflict of unsociable consonants, a conflict, however, which is honourably and strenuously maintained. The Vowels and weak consonants, (§. 25.) of grammatical endings and suffixes exert no influence over preceding consonants; but strong consonants, if surd (§. 25.), require a tenuis, and if sonant a medial, before them. Thus, त t and थ th allow only of क k, not ख kh, ग g, घ gh preceding them; only त t, not थ th, द d, ध dh; while on the other hand, ध dh allows only ग g, not क k, ख kh, घ gh; only द d, not त t, थ th, ध dh; only ब b, not प p, फ ph, भ bh to precede it. The [G. Ed. p. 95.] roots and the nominal bases have to regulate their final letters by this law; and the occasion frequently presents itself, since, in comparison with the cognate languages, a far greater proportion of the roots connect the personal terminations immediately with the root; and also among the case terminations there are many which begin with consonants (भ्याम् bhyâm, भिस् bhis, भ्यस् bhyas, सु su). To cite instances, the root अद् ad, "to eat," forms अद्मि admi, "I eat"; but not अत्सि adsi (for s is surd), nor अद्ति ad-ti, अद्थ ad-tha, but अत्सि at-si, अत्ति at-ti, अत्थ at-tha: on the other hand, in the imperative, अद्धि ad-dhi, "eat." The base पद् pad, "foot," forms, in the locative plural, पत्सु pat-su, not पद्सु pad-su; on the other hand, महत् mahat, "great," forms, in the instrumental plural, महद्भिस् mahad-bhis not महत्भिस् mahat-bhis.

99. The Greek and Latin, as they have come down to us, have either altogether evaded this conflict of consonants, or exhibit, in most cases, with regard to the first of any two contiguous consonants, a disposition to surrender it, or

at least an indifference to its assistance towards the signification of the word, since they either abandon it altogether, or violently alter it, *i.e.* convey it beyond the limits of its proper organ. These two languages afford fewer occasions for harsh unions of consonants than the Sanskrit, principally because, with the exception of ʼΕΣ and ʼΙΔ in Greek, and *ES, FER, VEL, ED*, in Latin, as ἐσ-τί, ἐσ-μέν, ἐσ-τέ, ἴδ-μεν, ἴσ-τε, *est, estis, fer-t, fer-tis, vul-t, vul-tis*, no root, terminated by a consonant, joins on its personal terminations, or any of them, without the aid of a connecting vowel. The Greek perf. pass. makes an exception, and requires euphonic alterations, which, in part, come within the natural limits recognised by the Sanskrit, and, in part, overstep them.

[G. Ed. p. 96.] The gutturals and labials remain on the ancient footing, and before σ and τ observe the Sanskrit law of sound cited in §. 98.; according to which κ-σ(ξ), κ-τ, π-σ, π-τ, are applied to roots ending in κ, γ, χ, or π, β, φ, because the surd σ or τ suffers neither medials nor aspirates before it; hence τέτριπ-σαι, τέτριπ-ται, from ΤΡΙΒ, τέτυκ-σαι, τέτυκ-ται, from ΤΥΧ. The Greek, however, diverges from the Sanskrit in this, that μ does not leave the consonant which precedes it unaltered, but assimilates labials to itself, and converts the guttural, tenuis and aspirate into medials. For τέτυμ-μαι, τέτριμ-μαι, πέπλεγ-μαι, τέτυγ-μαι, we should, on Sanskrit principles, write (§. 98.) τέτυπ-μαι, τέτριβ-μαι, πεπλεκ-μαι, τετυχ-μαι. The *t* sounds carry concession too far, and abandon the Sanskrit, or original principle, as regards the gutturals; inasmuch as δ, θ, and ζ (δσ), instead of passing into τ before σ and τ, are extinguished before σ, and before τ and μ become σ (πέπεισ-ται, πέπει-σαι, πέπεισ-μαι, instead of πέπειτ-ται, πέπειτ-σαι, πεπειθ-μαι, or πεπειδ-μαι. The Greek declension affords occasion for the alteration of consonants only through the ς of the nominative and the dative plural termination in σι; and here the same principle holds good as in the case of the verb, and in the formation of words: *kh* and *g* become, as in Sanskrit, *k* (ξ=κ-ς), and *b* and *ph* become *p*.

The *t* sounds, on the other hand, contrary to the Sanskrit, and in accordance with the enfeebled condition, in this respect, of the Greek, vanish entirely. We find πού-ς for πότ-ς, που-σί for ποτ-σί, which latter naturally and originally must have stood for ποδ-σ, ποδ-σι.

100. In Latin the principal occasion for the alteration of consonants presents itself before the *s* of the perfect and the *t* of the supine, or other verbal substantive or adjective (participles) beginning with *t*; and it is in   [G. Ed. p. 97.] accordance with the Sanskrit law cited §. 98., and the original condition of the language, that the sonant guttural passes, before *s* and *t*, into *c*, the sonant labial into *p*, as in *rec-si* (*rexi*), *rectum* from *reg*, *scripsi*, *scriptum* from *scrib*. It is also in accordance with the Sanskrit that *h*, as a sonant (§. 25.) and incompatible with a tenuis, becomes *c* before *s* and *t*; compare *vec-sit* (*vexit*), with the word of like signification अवाक्षीत् *a-vák-shít*. If of the two final consonants of a root the last vanishes before the *s* of the perfect tense (*mulsi* from *mulc* and *mulg*, *sparsi* from *sparg*), this accords with the Sanskrit law of sounds, by which, of two terminating consonants of a ˚nominal base, the last vanishes before consonants of the case terminations. *D* ought to become *t* before *s*; and then the form, so theoretically created, *claut-sit* from *claud*, would accord with the Sanskrit forms, such as अतौत्सीत् *a-táut-sit*, "he tormented," from तुद् *tud*. Instead, however, of this, the *d* allows itself to be extinguished; so, however, that, in compensation, a short vowel of the root is made long, as *di-vi-si*; or, which is less frequent, the *d* assimilates itself to the following *s*, as *cessi* from *ced*. With roots in *t*, which are rarer, assimilation usually takes place, as *con-cus-si* from *cut*; on the other hand, *mi-si*, not *mis-si*, for *mit-si*, from *mit* or *mitt*. *B*, *m*, and *r* also afford instances of assimilation in *jus-si*, *pres-si*, *ges-si*, *us-si*.* A third resource, for the avoidance

---

* Compared with the Sanskrit, in which उष् *ush* signifies "burn"; the sibilant must here pass for the original form.

of an union, very natural, but not endurable in this weakened state of the language, *ts*, is the suppression of the
latter of these two letters, which is also compensated by
the lengthening of a short radical vowel; thus,[*] *sĕdi* from
[G. Ed. p. 98.]   *sĕd*, *vĭdi* from *vĭd*. I believe, at least, that
these forms are not derivable from *sedui, vidui*, and I class
them with forms like *fōdi* from *fōd, lēgi*, for *lec-si*, from *lĕg*,
fugi, for *fuc-si*, from *fŭg*. To these probably also belong *cāvi*,
fāvi, *fōvi*, for *pāvi, vōvi*, from *căv*, &c. A *cavui*, &c. is hardly
conceivable; *cavi* could never have had such an origin. I
conjecture forms such as *cau-si, fau-si*, after the analogy of
cautum, fautum; or *moc-si* (*moxi*), after the analogy of *vic-si*,
con-nic-si. (§. 19.) Possibly a *moc-si* form might derive probability from the adverb *mox*, since the latter is probably
derived from *mov*, as *cito* is from another root of motion.
The *c* of *fluc-si, struc-si*, (*fluxi*, &c.) *fluxum, structum*, must,
in the same manner, be considered as a hardening of *v*;
and a *flu-vo, stru-vo*, be presupposed, with regard to which
it is to be remembered, that, in Sanskṛit also, *uv* often developes itself out of उ *u* before vowels (Gram. Crit. r. 50.[']);
on which principle, out of *flu, stru*, before vowels, we might
obtain *fluv, struv*, and thence before consonants *fluc, struc*.
Thus, also, *fructus* out of *fruv-or* for *fru-or*. In cases of *t*
preceded by consonants, the suppression of *s* is the rule,
and *ar-si* for *ard-i* an exception. *Prandi, frendi, pandi,
verti*, &c., are in contrast to *ar-si* and other forms, like
mulsi above mentioned, in their preserving the radical letter
in preference to the auxiliary verb; and they accord in
this with the Sanskṛit rule of sound, by which the *s* of
अतौत्सम् *atâut-sam*, अक्षैप्सम् *akshaip-sam*, &c., for the avoidance
of hardness, is suppressed before strong consonants, and
we find, for instance, अतौत *atâut-ta*, instead of अतौत्स *atâut-
sta*. The perfects *scĭdi, fĭdi*, are rendered doubtful by
their short vowel, and in their origin probably belong
to the reduplicated preterites, their first syllable having

---

[*] Cf. §. 547., and for the whole §. cf. §§. 547. 576. 579.

perished in the lapse of time: in other   [G. Ed. p. 99.]
respects, *fīdī, scīdi*, correspond to *tutŭdi, pupŭgi*, not to speak
of *tetĭgi*, the *i* of which latter is not original.

101. The suffixes employed in the formation of words
and beginning with *t*, for the representation of which the
supine may stand, deserve special consideration, in regard
to the relations of sound generated by the conflict between
t and the preceding consonant. According to the original
law observed in the Sanskṛit, a radical *t* ought to remain
unaltered before *tum*, and *d* should pass into *t*; as, भेत्तुम्
bhēttum, "to cleave," from भिद् *bhid*. According to the degenerated practice of the Greek, a radical *d* or *t* before *t*
would become *s*. Of this second gradation we find a remnant in *comes-tus, comes-tura*, analogous to *es-t, es-tis*, &c.
from *edo*: we find, however, no *comes-tum, comes-tor*, but
in their place *comesum, comesor*. We might question whether, in *comēsum*, the *s* belonged to the root or to the suffix; whether the *d* of *ed*, or the *t* of *tum*, had been changed
into *s*. The form *com-es-tus* might argue the radicality of
the *s*; but it is hard to suppose that the language should
have jumped at once from *estus* to *ēsus*, between which two
an *essus* probably intervened, analogous to *cessum, fissum,
quassum*, &c., while the *t* of *tum, tus*, &c., assimilated itself
to the preceding *s*. Out of *essum* has arisen *ēsum*, by the
suppression of an *s*, probably the first; for where of a pair
of consonants the one is removed, it is generally the first,
(εἰμί from ἐσμί, πο-σί from ποδ-σί,) possibly because, as in
§. 100., an auxiliary verb is abandoned in preference to a
letter of the main verb. After that the language had, through
such forms as *ē-sum, cā-sum, divi-sum, fis-sum, quas-sum*,
habituated itself to an *s* in suffixes properly beginning with a
t, *s* might easily insinuate itself into forms where it did not
owe its origin to assimilation. *Cs* (*x*) is a   [G. Ed. p. 100.]
favourite combination; hence, *fic-sum, nec-sum*, &c. for *fic-
tum, nec-tum*. The liquids, *m* excepted, evince special incli-

nation for a succeeding *s*, most of all the *r* ; hence, *ter-sum*, *mer-sum*, *cur-sum*, *par-sum*, *ver-sum*, in contrast to *par-tum*, *tor-tum*: there are also cases in which *r*, by a conversion into *s*, accommodates itself to *t*, as in *ges-tum*, *us-tum*, *tos-tum*.* This answers to the Sanskrit obligatory conversion of a concluding *r* into *s* before an initial *t* ; as, भ्रातस् तारय माम् *bhrâtas târaya mâm*, " brother save me," instead of भ्रातर् *bhrâtar*: on the other hand, in the middle of words *r* remains unaltered before *t* ; hence, for instance, भर्तुम् *bhartum*, not भस्तुम् *bhastum*, "to bear." *L* exhibits in the Latin the forms *fal-sum*, *pul-sum*, *vul-sum*, in contrast to *cul-tum ;* *n* exhibits *ten-tum*, *can-tum*, opposed to *man-sum*. The other forms in *n-sum*, except *cen-sum*, have been mulcted of a radical *d*, as *ton-sum*, *pen-sum*.

102. In the Germanic languages, *t* alone gives occasion for an euphonic conversion of a preceding radical consonant; for instance, in the 2d pers. sing. of the strong preterite, where, however, the *t* in the Old High German is retained only in a few verbs, which associate a present signification with the form of the preterite. In the weak preterites, also, which spring from these verbs, the auxiliary *t*, where it remains unaltered, generates the same euphonic relations. We find in these forms the Germanic on the same footing as the Greek, in this respect, that it converts radical *t* sounds (*t*, *th*, *d*, and in Old and Middle High German *z* also) before a superadded *t* into *s*. Hence, for instance, in [G. Ed. p. 101.] Gothic *maimais-t* (*abscidisti*), for *maimait-t*, *fai-fals-t* (*plicavisti*), for *fai-falth-t*, *ana-baus-t* (*imperasti*), for *ana-baud-t*. In Old and Middle High German *weis-t*, " thou knowest," for *weiz-t*. The Gothic, in forming out of the root *vit*, in the weak preterite, *vis-sa* ("I knew "), instead of

---

* The obvious relationship of *torreo* with τέρσομαι, and तृष् *trish* from तर्ष् *tarsh*, argues the derivation of the latter *r* from *s*. Upon that of *uro* from उष् *ush*, see §. 97.

vista, from *villa,* resembles, in respect of assimilation, the
Latin forms mentioned in §. 101., such as *quas-sum* for *quas-*
tum, from *quat-tum.* The Old High German, however, which
also adopts *wis-sa,* but from *muoz* makes not *muos-sa,* but
muo-sa, corresponds, in the latter case, to such Latin forms,
as *ca-sum, clau-sum.* The case is different in Old High German with those verbs of the first weak conjugation, which,
having their syllables made long generally through two
terminating consonants in the preterite, apply the *t* of the
auxiliary verb directly to the root. Here the transition of *t*
into *s* does not occur, but *t, z,* and even *d,* remain unaltered;
and only when another consonant precedes them *t* and *d* are
extinguished, *z* on the contrary remains; for instance, *leit-ta,*
"DUXI," *ki-neiz-ta,* "AFFLIXI," *ar-ôd-ta,* "VASTAVI," *walz-ta,*
"VOLVI," *liuh-ta,* "LUXI," for *liuht-ta;* *hul-ta,* "PLACAVI," for
huld-ta. Of double consonants one only is retained, and of *ch*
or *cch* only *h*; other consonantal combinations remain, however, undisturbed, as *ran-ta,* "CUCURRI," for *rann-ta;* *wanh-ta,*
"VACILLAVI," for *wanch-ta;* *dah-ta,* "TEXI," for *dacch-ta.* The
Middle High German follows essentially the same principles,
only a simple radical *t* gives way before the auxiliary verb,
and thus *lei-te* is opposed to the Old High German *leit-ta;* on
the other hand, in roots in *ld* and *rd* the *d* may be maintained,
and the *t* of the auxiliary be surrendered—as *dulde,* "TOLERAVI"
—unless we admit a division of *dul-de,* and consider the *d* as
a softened *t.* The change of *g* into *c* (§. 98.) is natural, but
not universal; for instance, *anc-te,* "ARCTAVI," for *ang-te;* but
against this law *b* remains unaltered. [G. Ed. p. 102.]
Before the formative suffixes beginning with *t**, both in Gothic
and High German, guttural and labial tenues and medials are
changed into their aspirates, although the tenuis accord with
a following *t.* Thus, for instance, in Gothic, *vah-tvô,*

---

* With the exception of the High German passive part. of the weaker
form, which, in the adjunction of its *t* to the root, follows the analogy of
the pret. above described.

" watch," from *vak*; *sauh-t*(*i*)*s*, " sickness," from *suk*; *mah-t*(*i*)*s*, " might," from *mag*; *ga-skaf-t*(*i*)*s*, " creation," from *skap*; *fragif-t*(*i*)*s*, " betrothment," from *gib*, softened from *gab*; Old High German *suht, maht, ki-skaft*, " creature," *kift*, " gift." The dentals replace the aspirate *th* by the sibilant (*s*), as is the case in Gothic before the pers. character *t* of the preterite, as *th* cannot be combined with *t*. The formation of words, however, affords few examples of this kind: under this head comes our *mast*, related to the Gothic *mats*, " food," and *matyan*, " to eat." In Gothic, the *s* of *blôstreis*, " worshipper," springs from the *t* of *blôtan*, " to worship": *beist*, " leaven," comes probably from *beit* (*beitan*, " to bite," Grimm, ii. p. 208). The Zend accords, in this respect, with the Germanic*, but still more with the Greek, in that it converts its *t* sounds into ം *s*, not only before ൦ *t*, but also before Ჿ *m*; for instance, ൰ഷ *irista*, " dead," from the root ൳ *irith*; ൰ഷ *basta*, " bound," from ൌ *bandh*, with the nasal excluded; as in Modern Persian بستـه *bastah*, from بند *band*; ൬ഷ *aêsma*, " wood," from इध्म *idhma*.

103. It is a violation of one of the most natural laws of sound, that, in Gothic, the medial *g* does not universally pass into *k* or *h* (= *ch*), before the personal character *t* of [G. Ed. p. 103.]　the pret., but generally is retained; and we find, for instance, *ôg-t*, " thou fearest," *mag-t*, " thou canst†"; and yet, before other inflections formed with *t*, the *g* undergoes an euphonic transition into *h*, as for instance, *ôh-ta*, " I feared," *mah-ts*, " might."

104. When in Sanskrit, according to §. 98., the aspiration of a medial undergoes a necessary suppression, it falls back, under certain conditions and according to special laws, upon the initial consonant of the root, yet only upon a medial, or throws itself onward on the initial consonant of

---

* Cf. the Sclavonic and Lithuanian, §. 457.

† No other roots in *g* in this person are to be found in Ulfilas.

the following suffix. We find, for instance, भोत्स्यामि *bhot-syámi,* "I shall know," for बोध्स्यामि *bódh-syámi;* वेदभुत् *véda-bhut,* "knowing the vedas," for बुध *budh;* बुद्ध *bud-dha,* "knowing," for बुध्त *budhta;* धोक्ष्यामि *dhók-shyámi,* "I shall milk," for दोह्स्यामि *dóh-syámi;* दुग्ध *dug-dha,* "milked," for दुह्त *duh-ta.* In Greek we find a remarkable relic of the first part of the transposition of the aspirate,[*] in the necessary suppression of the aspirate in some roots which begin with *t* and end with an aspirate before σ, τ, and μ, letters which admit of no union with an aspirate, and in its being thrown back on the initial letter, by which process τ becomes θ. Hence, τρέφω, θρέπ-σω, (θρέψω), θρεπτήρ, θρέμ-μα; ταφή, θάπ-τω, ἐτάφην, τέθαμ-μαι; τρύφος, θρύπ-τω, ἐτρύφην, θρύμ-μα; τρέχω, θρέξομαι; θρίξ, τριχός, ταχύς, θάσσων. In the spirit of this transposition of the aspirate, ἐχ obtains the spiritus asper when χ is obliged to merge in the tenuis, (ἐκτός, ἔξω, ἕξις).[†]

---

[*] See J. L. Burnouf in the Asiatic Journal, III. 368; and Buttmann, pp. 77, 78.

[†] It is usual to explain this appearance by the supposition of two aspirations in the root of these forms, of which one only is supposed to appear in deference to the euphonic law which forbids the admission of two consecutive aspirated syllables. This one would be the last [G. Ed. p. 104.] of the two, and the other would only shew itself when the latter had been forced to merge in the tenuis. Opposed, however, to this explanation is the fact, that, on account of the inconvenience of accumulated aspirates, the language has guarded itself in the original formation of its roots against the evil, and has never admitted an aspirated consonant at once for the initial and final letter of a root. In Sanskrit, the collection of whose roots is complete, there is no such instance. The forms, however, ἐθάφθην, τεθάφθαι, τεθάφθω, τεθάφαται, τεθράφθαι, ἐθρέφθην,, present a difficulty. These, perhaps, are eccentricities of usage, which, once habituated to the initial aspiration by its frequent application to supply the place of the terminating one, began to assume its radicality, and extended it wider than was legitimate. We might also say, that since φθ (as χθ) is so favourite a combination in Greek that it is even substituted for πθ and βθ—while, according to §. 98., an original φθ ought to become πθ—on this ground the tendency to aspiration of the root remained unsatisfied by ἐτάφθην &c.; and as if the φ only existed out of reference to the θ, the original terminating aspirate necessarily fell back on the radical initial. This theory, which seems to me sound, would only leave τεθάφαται to be explained.

OF THE ROOTS.

[G. Ed. p. 105.] 105. There are in Sanskrit, and the languages which are akin to it, two classes of roots : from the one, which is by far the more numerous, spring verbs, and nouns (substantives and adjectives) which stand in fraternal connection with the verbs, not in the relation of descent from them, not begotten by them, but sprung from the same shoot with them. We term them, nevertheless, for the sake of distinction, and according to prevailing custom, Verbal Roots; and the verb, too, stands in close formal connection with them, because from many roots each person of the present is formed by simply adding the requisite personal termination. From the second class spring pronouns, all original prepositions, conjunctions, and particles : we name them Pronominal Roots, because they all express a pronominal idea, which, in the prepositions, conjunctions, and particles, lies more or less concealed. No simple pronouns can be carried back, either according to their meaning or their form, to any thing more general, but their declension-theme (or inflective base) is at the same time their root. The Indian Grammarians, however, derive all words, the pronouns included, from verbal roots, although the majority of pronominal bases, even in a formal respect, are opposed to such a derivation, because they, for the most part, end with *a*: one, indeed, consists simply of *a*. Among [G. Ed. p. 106.] the verbal roots, however, there is not a single one in *ă*, although long *a*, and all other vowels, ‌औ *áu* excepted, occur among the final letters of the verbal roots. Accidental external identity takes place between the verbal and pronominal roots; *e.g.* इ *i* signifies, as a verbal root, " to go," as a pronominal root, " he," "this."

106. The verbal roots, like those of the pronouns, are

monosyllabic; and the polysyllabic forms represented by the grammarians as roots contain either a reduplicate-syllable, as जागृ *jágri*, " to wake," or a preposition which has grown up with the root, as अवधीर् *ava-dhír*, " to despise "; or they have sprung from a noun, like कुमार् *kumár*, " to play," which I derive from कुमार *kumára*, " a boy." Except the law of their being monosyllabic, the Sanskrit roots are subjected to no further limitation, and their one-syllableness may present itself under all possible forms, in the shortest and most extended, as well as those of a middle degree. This free state of irrestriction was necessary, as the language was to contain within the limits of one-syllableness the whole body of fundamental ideas. The simple vowels and consonants were not sufficient: it was requisite to frame roots also where several consonants, combined in inseparable unity, became, as it were, simple sounds; *e.g.* स्था *sthá*, " to stand," a root in which the age of the co-existence of the *s* and *th* is supported by the unanimous testimony of all the members of our race of languages. So also, in स्कन्द् *skand*, " to go," (Lat. *scand-o*) the age of the combination of consonants, both in the beginning and ending of the root, is certified by the agreement of the Latin with the Sanskrit. The proposition, that in the earliest period of language a simple vowel is sufficient to express a verbal idea, is supported by the remarkable concurrence of   [G. Ed. p. 107.] nearly all the individuals of the Sanskrit family of languages in expressing the idea " to go " by the root *i.*

107. The nature and peculiarity of the Sanskrit verbal roots explains itself still more by comparison with those of the Semitic languages. These require, as far as we trace back their antiquity, three consonants, which, as I have already elsewhere shewn,* express the fundamental

---

* Trans. of the Hist. Phil. Class of the R. A. of Litt. of Berlin for the year 1824, p. 126, &c.

H

idea by themselves alone, without the aid of vowels; and
although they may be momentarily compressed into one
syllable, still, in this, the combination of the middle radical
with the first or last cannot be recognised as original and
belonging to the root, because it is only transitory, and
chiefly depends on the mechanism of the construction of
the word.   Thus, in Hebrew, *kâtûl*, "slain," in the fem.,
on account of the addition *âh* contracts itself to *ktûl* (*ktûl-
-âh*); while *kôtêl*, "slaying," before the same addition, com-
presses itself in an opposite manner, and forms *kôtlâh.*
Neither *ktûl*, therefore, nor *kôtl*, can be regarded as the root;
and just as little can it be looked for in *ktôl*, as the *status con-
structus* of the infinitive; for this is only a shortening of the
absolute form *kâtôl*, produced by a natural tendency to pass
hastily to the word governed by the infinitive, which, as it
were, has grown to it.   In the imperative *ktôl* the abbreviation is not external, subject to mechanical conditions, but
rather dynamic, and occasioned by the hurry with which a
command is usually enunciated.   In the Semitic languages,
in decided opposition to those of the Sanskṛit family, the
vowels belong, not to the root, but to the grammatical motion,
the secondary ideas, and the mechanism of the construction of
[G. Ed. p. 108.]   the word.   By them, for example, is distinguished, in Arabic, *katala*, "he slew," from *kutila*, "he was
slain"; and in Hebrew, *kôtêl*, "slaying," from *kâtûl*, "slain."
A Semitic root is unpronounceable, because, in giving it
vowels, an advance is made to a special grammatical form, and
it then no longer possesses the simple peculiarity of a root
raised above all grammar.   But in the Sanskṛit family of
languages, if its oldest state is consulted in the languages which
have continued most pure, the root appears as a circumscribed
nucleus, which is almost unalterable, and which surrounds
itself with foreign syllables, whose origin we must investigate, and whose destination is, to express the secondary
ideas of grammar which the root itself cannot express.

The vowel, with one or more consonants, and sometimes without any consonant whatever, belongs to the fundamental meaning: it can be lengthened to the highest degree, or raised by Guna or Vṛiddhi; and this lengthening or raising, and, more lately, the retention of an original *a*, opposed to its weakening to *i* or change to *u* (§§. 66., 67.), belongs not to the denoting of grammatical relations, which require to be more clearly pointed out, but, as I imagine I can prove, only to the mechanism, the symmetry of construction.

108. As the Semitic roots, on account of their construction, possess the most surprising capacity for indicating the secondary ideas of grammar by the mere internal moulding of the root, of which they also make extensive use, while the Sanskrit roots, at the first grammatical movement, are compelled to assume external additions ; so must it appear strange, that F. von Schlegel,* while he   [G. Ed. p. 109.] divides languages in general into two chief races, of which the one denotes the secondary intentions of meaning by an internal alteration of the sound of the root by inflexion, the other always by the addition of a word, which may by itself signify plurality, past time, what is to be in future, or other relative ideas of that kind, allots the Sanskrit and its sisters to the former race, and the Semitic languages to the second. "There may, indeed," he writes, p. 48, "arise an appearance of inflexion, when the annexed particles are melted down with the chief word so as to be no longer distinguishable ; but where in a language, as in the Arabic, and in all which are connected with it, the first and most important relations, as those of the person to verbs, are denoted by the addition of particles which have a meaning for themselves individually, and the tendency to which suffixes shews itself deeply seated in the language, it may there be safely assumed that the same may have

---

* In his work on the language and wisdom of the Indians.

occurred in other positions, where the annexation of particles of a foreign nature no longer admits of such clear
discrimination: one may at least safely assume that the
language, on the whole, belongs to this chief race, although
in this single point, by admixture or artificial adornment,
it has adopted another and a higher character." We must
here preliminarily observe, that, in Sanskrit and the languages connected with it, the personal terminations of the
verbs shew at least as great a similarity to isolated pronouns as in Arabic. How should any language, which
expresses the pronominal relations of the verbs by syllables
annexed either at the beginning or end of the word, in the
choice of these syllables avoid, and not rather select, those
which, in their isolated state, also express the corresponding
[G. Ed. p. 110.]   pronominal ideas? By inflexion, F. von
Schlegel understands the internal alteration of the sound of
the root, or (p. 35) the internal modification of the root, which
he (p. 48) opposes to addition from without. But when from
δo or δω, in Greek, comes δίδω-μι, δώ-σω, δo-θησόμεθα, what
are the forms μι, σω, θησόμεθα, but palpable external additions to the root, which is not at all internally altered, or
only in the quantity of the vowel? If, then, by inflexion,
an internal modification of the root is to be understood,
the Sanskrit and Greek &c. have in that case—except the
reduplication, which is supplied by the elements of the root
itself—scarce any inflexion at all to shew. If, however,
θησόμεθα is an external modification of the root δo, simply
because it is combined with it, touches it, with it expresses
a whole; then the idea of sea and continent may be represented as an internal modification of the sea, and vice versâ.
P. 50, F. von Schlegel remarks: "In the Indian or Grecian
language every root is truly that which the name says,
and like a living germ; for since the ideas of relation are
denoted by internal alteration, freer room is given for
development, the fulness of which can be indefinitely

extended, and is, in fact, often wondrously rich.   All, however, which in this manner proceeds from the simple root,
still retains the stamp of its relationship, adheres to it, and
thus reciprocally bears and supports itself."   I find, however, the inference not established ; for from the capability
of expressing ideas of relation by internal alteration of the
root, how can the capability be deduced of surrounding the
(internally unalterable) root indefinitely, with foreign syllables
externally added?   What kind of stamp of relationship is
there between μι, σω, θησόμεθα, and the   [G. Ed. p. 111.]
roots to which these significative additions are appended ?
We therefore recognise in the inflexions of the Sanskrit
family of languages no internal involutions of the root, but
elements of themselves significative, and the tracing of the
origin of which is the task of scientific grammar.   But even
if the origin of not a single one of these inflexions could be
traced with certainty, still the principle of the formation
of grammar, by external addition, would not, for that
reason, be the less certain, because, at the first glance, in
the majority of inflexions, one discovers at least so much,
that they do not belong to the root, but have been added
from without.   A. W. von Schlegel, also, who, in essential
points, assents to the above-mentioned division of languages,* gives us to understand, with regard to the so-called

---

* Nevertheless, in his work, "*Observations sur la langue et la littérature
provençales*," p. 14, &c., he gives three classes, viz. *Les langues sans aucune
structure grammaticale, les langues qui emploient des affixes, et les langues
à inflexions.* Of the latter, he says : "Je pense, cependant, qu'il faut
assigner le premier rang aux langues à inflexions.   On pourroit les appeler
les langues organiques, parce qu'elles renferment un principe vivant de
développement et d'accroissement, et qu'elles ont seules, si je puis m'exprimer ainsi, une végétation abondante et féconde.   Le merveilleux
artifice de ces langues est, de former une immense variété de mots, et de
marquer la liaison des idées que ces mots désignent, moyennant un assez
petit nombre de syllabes qui, considérées séparément, n'ont point de signification

inflexions, that they are not modifications of the root, but
foreign additions, whose characteristic lies in this, that
[G. Ed. p. 112.] regarded, *per se*, they have no meaning.
In the Semitic, the appended grammatical syllables or inflexions have no meaning, at least in so far that they do not,
any more than in Sanskrit, occur isolated in a completely
similar state. In Arabic, for instance, *antum*, and not *tum*,
is said for "ye"; and in Sanskrit *ma*, *ta*, and not *mi*, *ti*, are
the declinable bases of the first and third person; and *at-Ti*,
"he eats," has the same relation to *TA-m*, "him," that in
Gothic *IT-a*, "I eat," has to the monosyllabic *AT*, "I ate."
The reason for weakening the *a* of the base to *i* is probably,
in the different cases of the two sister languages, the same,
viz. the greater extent of the form of word with *i* (comp.
§. 6.) If, then, the division of languages made by F. von
Schlegel is untenable, on the reasons on which it is
founded, still there is much ingenuity in the thought of a
natural history or classification of languages. We prefer,
however, to present, with A. W. von Schlegel (l. c.), three
classes, and distinguish them as follows: first, languages
with monosyllabic roots, without the capability of composition,
and hence without organism, without grammar. This class
comprises Chinese, where all is hitherto bare root, and the
grammatical categories, and secondary relations after the

---

fication, mais qui déterminent avec précision le sens du mot auquel elles
sont jointes. En modifiant les lettres radicales, et en ajoutant aux racines
des syllabes dérivatives, on forme de mots dérivés de diverses espèces, et
des dérivés des dérivés. On compose des mots de plusieurs racines pour
exprimer les idées complexes. Ensuite on décline les substantifs, les
adjectifs, et les pronoms, par genres, par nombres, et par cas; on conjugue
les verbes par voix, par modes, par temps, par nombres, et par personnes,
en employant de même des désinences et quelquefois des augmens qui, séparément, ne signifient rien. Cette méthode procure l'avantage d'énoncer
en un seul mot l'idée principale, souvent déjà très-modifiée et très-com-
plexe, avec tout son cortége d'idées accessoires et de relations variables.

main point, can only be discovered from the position of the roots in the sentence.* Secondly, languages with monosyllabic roots, which are capable of combination, and obtain their organism and grammar nearly in this way alone. The chief principle of the formation of words, in this class, appears to me to lie in the combination of verbal and pronominal roots, which together represent, [G. Ed. p. 113.] as it were, body and soul (Comp. §. 100.). To this class belongs the Sanskrit family of languages, and moreover all other languages, so far as they are not comprehended under 1. and 3., and have maintained themselves in a condition which renders it possible to trace back their forms of words to the simplest elements. Thirdly, languages with dissyllabic verbal roots, and three necessary consonants as single vehicles of the fundamental meaning. This class comprehends merely the Semitic languages, and produces its grammatical forms, not simply by combination, like the second class, but by a mere internal modification of the roots. We here gladly award to the Sanskrit family of languages a great superiority over the Semitic, which we do not, however, find in the use of inflexions as syllables *per se* devoid of meaning, but in the copiousness of these grammatical additions, which are really significative, and connected with words used isolated ; in the judicious, ingenious selection and application of them, and the accurate and acute defining of various relations, which hereby becomes possible; finally, in the beautiful adjustment of these additions to a harmonious whole, which bears the appearance of an organized body.

109*. The Indian Grammarians divide the roots according to properties, (which extend only to the tenses which

---

* We find this view of the Chinese admirably elucidated in W. von Humboldt's talented pamphlet, "*Lettre à M. Abel Remusat, sur la nature des formes grammaticales en général, et sur le génie de la langue chinoise.*"

I call the special tenses,* and to the part. pres.,) into ten
classes, all of which we have re-discovered in the Zend also,
and examples of which are given in the following paragraph.

[G. Ed. p. 114.]   We shall here give the characteristics of
the Sanskrit classes, and compare with them those which
correspond in the European sister languages.

(1.) The first and sixth class add व a to the root; and
we reserve the discussion of the origin of this and other
conjugational affixes for the disquisition on the verb.   The
point of difference between the first class of nearly 1000
roots (almost the half of the entire number) and the sixth
class, which contains about 130 roots, lies in this, that the
former raise the vowel of the root by Guna (§. 26.), while
the latter retain it pure; e.g. बोधति bódhati, "he knows,"
from बुध budh (1.); तुदति tudati, "he vexes" (comp. tundit),
from तुद् tud (6.)   As व a has no Guna,† no discrimination can
take place through this vowel between the classes 1. and 6.:
but nearly all the roots which belong to either, having व a
as the radical vowel, are reckoned in the first class.   In Greek,
e (before nasals o, §. 3.) corresponds to the affix व a; and
λείπ-ο-μεν,‡ φεύγ-ο-μεν, from ΛΙΠ, ΦΥΓ (ἔλιπον, ἔφυγον),
belong to the first class, because they have Guna (§. 26.);
while, e.g. θίγ-ο-μεν, θλίβ-ο-μεν, &c., fall under the sixth
class.‖   In Latin we recognise, in the third conjugation,

---

* In Greek, the present (indic. imper. and optat., the form of the Greek
subjunct. is wanting in Sanskrit) and imperfect correspond to them; beyond which certain conjugation-signs do not extend.   In German, the
present of every mood corresponds.

† The accent here distinguishes the 1st cl. from the 6th. e.g. for pátati
did it belong to the 6th. cl., we should have patáti.

‡ We give the plural, because the singular, on account of abbreviation,
makes the thing less perspicuous.

‖ Sanskrit long vowels admit Guna only when they occur at the end of
the root, but in the beginning and middle remain without admixture of
the व a; so do short vowels before double consonants.

which I would raise to the first, the cognate of the Sanskrit first and sixth class, since we regard the addition *i* as a weakening of the old *a* (§. 8.); and *e. g. legimus* has the same relation to λέγ-ο-μεν, that the genitive *ped-is* has to ποδ-ός where the Sanskrit has likewise *a* (पद्‍ [G. Ed. p. 115.] *pad-as*). In *leg-u-nt*, from *leg-a-nti*, the old *a*, through the influence of the liquid, has become *u* (Comp. §. 66.). In German, all the primitive (strong) verbs, with the exception of some remains of the fourth class (No. 2.), stand in clear connection with the Sanskrit first class, which is here, for the first time, laid down in its full extent.* The व *a* which is added to the root has, in Gothic†, before some personal terminations, remained unchanged; before others, according to §. 67., and as in Latin, been weakened to *i*; so, *hait-a*, " I am called," *hait-i-s, hait-i-th*, 2d pers. du. *hait-a-ts;* pl. *hait-a-m, hait-i-th, hait-a-nd*. The radical vowels *i* and *u* keep the Guna addition, as in Sanskrit, only that the *a* which gives the Guna is here weakened to *i* (§. 27.), which, with a radical *i*, is aggregated into a long *i* (written *ei*, §. 70.): hence *keina* (= *kína*, from *kiina*), "I germinate," from *KIN*; *biuga*, "I bend," from *BUG*, Sanskrit भुज् *bhuj*, whence भुग्न *bhugna*, "bent." The diphthongs *ai, au*, as in Sanskrit ए and ओ (§. 2.), are incapable of any Guna; as are *é* (= वा, §. 69.) and *a*. The Sanskrit radical vowel व *a* has, however, in Gothic, experienced a threefold destiny. It has either remained unaltered in the special tenses, and is lengthened in the preterite, except in reduplicate roots (*i.e.* to *ô*, see §. 69.)—

---

* I have already, in my Review of Grimm's Grammar, expressed the conjecture that the *a* of forms like *haita, haitam, haitaima*, &c. does not belong to the personal termination, but is identical with the व *a* of the Sanskrit 1st and 6th classes; but I was not then clear regarding the Guna in the present in all roots with vowels capable of Guna. (See Ann. Reg. for Crit. of Litt., Book II. pp. 282 and 259.)

† We make frequent mention of the Gothic alone as the true starting-point and light of German Grammar. The application to the High German will hereafter present itself.

thus, *e.g. far-i-th*, " he wanders," answers to वरति *charati*
[G. Ed. p. 116.] (§. 14.), and *fôr*, " he wandered," to चचार
chachâra ; or, secondly, the old *a* shews itself in the special
tenses weakened to *i*, but retained in the monosyllabic singular of the preterite : so that here the stronger *a* (§. 8.) corresponds to the weaker *i* in the same way that, in the first case,
the *ô* (= वा *â*) does to the short *a*.   The root वद् *ad*, " to
eat," in Gothic, according to §..87., forms *AT*; hence, in the
present, *ita* ; in the sing. pret., *at, as-t, at*.   The third fate
which befalls the *a* of the root in Gothic is a complete
extirpation, and compensation by the weaker *i*, which is
treated like an original *i*, existing in the Sanskrit ; *i.e.* in the
special tenses it receives Guna by *i*, and in the pret. sing. by
a (§. 27.), but in the pret. pl. it is preserved pure.   To this
class belongs the *KIN*, " to germinate," mentioned above,
pres. *keina*, pret. sing. *kain*, pl. *kin-um*.   The corresponding
Sanskrit root is जन् *jan*, " to produce," " to be born " (see
§. 87.) : the same relation, too, has *greipa, graip, gripum*,
from *GRIP*, " to seize," to ग्रभ् *grabh* (Vêda form) : on the
other hand, *BIT*, " to bite," * (*beita, bait, bitum*), has an
original *i*, which exists in Sanskrit (comp. भिद् *bhid*, " to
cleave ") ; just so, *VIT*, " to know," Sanskrit विद् *vid*.

(2.) The fourth class of Sanskrit roots adds to them the
syllable य *ya*, and herein agrees with the special tenses of
the passive ; and from the roots which belong to it spring
chiefly neuter verbs, as *e.g.* नश्यति *naśyati*, " he perishes,"
Their number amounts altogether to about 130. The German
has preserved one unmistakeable remnant of this class, in
those strong verbs which again lay aside, in the preterite, the
syllable *ya* (weakened to *yi*), which is added to the root in the
[G. Ed. p. 117.]   special tenses ; *e.g. vahs-ya*(Zend ﺭﻭﺍﺱﺳﻮﺥﻭ﮺
ucs-yann, " *crescebant*," Vendidâd S. p. 257), " *cresco*," *vahs-
yi-th*, " *crescit*," pret. *vôhs*.

---

* Occurs only with the prep. *and*, and with the meaning " to scold,"
but corresponds to the Old High German root *BIZ*, " to bite."

(3.) The second, third, and seventh classes add the personal termination direct to the root; but in the cognate European languages, to facilitate the conjugation, these classes have mainly passed over to the first class; *e. g. ed-i-mus*, not *ed-mus* (as a remnant of the old construction *es-t*, *es-tis*), Gothic *it-a-m*, Old High German *iz-a-mês* not *iz-mês*, answering to the Sanskrit अद्मस् *ad-mas*. The second class, to which अद् *ad* belongs, leaves the root without any characteristic addition, with Guna of the vowels capable of Guna before light terminations, which must be hereafter explained; hence, *e.g.* एमि *êmi*, corresponding to इमस् *imas*, from इ *i* "to go," as in Greek εἶμι to ἴμεν. It contains not more than about seventy roots, partly terminating in consonants, partly in vowels. In this and the third-class, the Greek exhibits roots, almost entirely ending in vowels, as the above mentioned Ἱ, ΦΑ, ΓΝΩ (γνῶ-θι), ΔΩ, ΣΤΑ, ΘΗ, ΦΥ (ἔφυν), ΔΥ, &c. To the consonants the direct combination with the consonants of the termination has become too heavy, and Ἐ Σ alone (because of the facility of σμ, στ) has remained in the Sanskrit second class, as the corresponding root in Latin, Lithuanian, and German. Hence, अस्ति *asti*, ἐστί, Lithuan. *esti*, *est*, Gothic and High German *ist*. In the Latin there fall also to the second class, *I, DA, STA, FLA, FA*, and *NA*; and also *in-quam*, whence *QUA* weakened to *QUI*, is the root, which, in Gothic, appears as *QUAT*, weakened to *QUIT*, with the accretion of a *T*. *FER* and *VEL* (*VUL*) have preserved some persons of the ancient construction.* [G. Ed. p. 118.] The third class is distinguished from the second by a syllable of reduplication in the special tenses, and has maintained itself under this form in Greek also, and Lithuanian. In

---

* Five roots of the second class introduce in Sanskrit, between the consonants of the root and the personal termination, an इ *i*, as रोदिमि *rôd-i-mi*, "I weep," from रुद् *rud*. I can, however, no longer believe that the *i* of the Latin third conjug. is connected with this इ *i*, as there is scarce any doubt of its relationship with the अ *a* of the very copious first class.

Sanskrit it comprehends about twenty roots; *e. g.* ददामि *dadâmi,* δίδωμι, Lithuanian *dudu;* दधामि *dadhâmi,* τίθημι (§. 16.); जजन्मि *jajanmi,* " I beget," comp. γί-γν-ο-μαι. The seventh class, of about twenty-four roots, introduces, in the special tenses, a nasal into the root, which is extended before the light personal terminations to the syllable *na;* *e. g.* भिनद्मि *bhinadmi,* "I cleave," भिन्मस् *bhindmas,* " we cleave." The Latin has kept the weaker form of this nasalization, but has further added to the root the affix of the first class (p. 114 G. Ed.); hence *findo, find-i-mus.* From the Greek come to be here considered roots, like ΜΑΘ, ΛΑΒ, ΘΙΓ, in which the inserted nasal has been repeated further on in the word, with the prefixed *a,* and, like the Latin *find-i-mus,* is connected with the affix of the first class; thus, μανθ-άν-ο-μεν, λαμβ-άν-ο-μεν, θιγγ-άν-ο-μεν.

(4.) The fifth class, of about thirty roots, has *nu;* and the eighth, with ten roots, which, excepting कृ *kri,* " to make," all terminate in न् *n* or ण् *n,* has *u* for its characteristic addition: the *u,* however, of these two classes is lengthened before the light terminations by Guna, which in the corresponding Greek appended syllables, νυ and ν, is supplied by lengthening the υ; thus, *e. g.* δείκνῦμι, δείκνῠμεν, as in Sanskrit आप्नोमि *âp-nô-mi,* " ad-ip-is-cor," आप्नुमस् *âp-nu-mas,* "*adipiscimur.*" An example of the eighth class is तन् *tan,* "to extend," whence तनोमि *tan-ô-mi*=τάν-ῠ-μι, तनुमस् *tan-u-mas*=τάν-ῠ-μες. With the उ *u, v,* of the eighth class, is probably connected

[G. Ed. p. 119.]   the *v* in some Gothic strong verbs, where, however, it adheres so firmly to the root, that, in a German point of view, it must be regarded as a radical. Hence it is not dropped in the preterite, and receives, in the special tenses, like all strong verbs, the affix of the Sanskrit first class; *e, g. saihva,** "I see," *sahv,* " I saw."

(5.) The ninth class adds ना *nâ* to the root, which syllable, before heavy terminations, instead of being shortened

---

* I now consider the *v* of *saihva* and similar verbs as purely euphonic, cf. §. 86. and Latin forms like *cogno, linquo, stinguo.*

to न na, replaces the heavy आ *á* by the lighter इ *í* (§. 6.), and is thus weakened to नी *ní*. *E.g.* from मृद् *mrid*, " to crush," (comp. *mordeo*) comes मृद्नामि *mridnámi*, मृद्नीमस् *mrid-nímas*. In this is easily perceived the relationship with Greek formations in *νημι* (*νᾱμι*) *νᾰμεν*; *e.g.* δάμνημι, δάμνα-μεν. As ᾰ, *e*, and *o*, are originally one, formations like *τέμ-νο-μεν* belong to this class, only that they have wandered into the more modern ω-conjugation at a remote period of antiquity; for more lately *νεω* would not have become *νω* from *νημι*.

(6.) The tenth class adds अय *aya* to the root, but is distinguished from the other classes in this farther important point, that this affix is not limited to the special tenses: the final *a* of अय *aya* is peculiar to them, but अय् *ay* extends, with very few exceptions, to all the other formations of the root. All causals, and many denominatives, follow this class, and, indeed, from every root a causal can be formed by the addition अय् *ay*, which is always accompanied by Guna of the middle vowel of the root capable of Guna, or by Vriddhi of every radical final vowel and of a middle *a* belonging to the root; *e.g.* वेदयति *véd-aya-ti* " he makes to know," from विद् *vid*; श्रावयति *śráv-aya-ti*, "he makes to hear," from श्रु *śru*. We recognise, in German, the affix अय *aya* at least in two shapes : in the one   [G. Ed. p. 120.] the first *a*, in the other the last, is lost, and in the latter case *y* has become *i*; so that I have no longer any scruple in tracing back Grimm's first and third conjugation of the weak form to a common origin. According to all probability, however, the verbs with the affix *ô* also (as Old High German *manôn*, " to mention," " to make to think,") belong to this class, regarding which we will speak further under the verb. The Old High German gives *é* as the contraction of *a + i*, (see §. 78.), but retains its *é* more firmly than the Gothic its *ai*, which, in several persons, sinks into a simple *a*. Compare Gothic *haba, habam, haband*, with Old High German *hapém, hapémes, hapént*. Very remarkable, however, is the concurrence of the Prâkrit with the Old High German and the Latin of the 2d conj. in this point, that it in like manner has contracted the affix चय *aya* to ए *ê*. Compare Sanskrit मानयामि *mânayâmi*, " I honour," Prâkrit माणेमि *mânêmi*,[*] Old High German, *var-manêm*, " I despise," Latin *moneo*:

[G. Ed. p. 121.]

SANSKRIT.	PRÂKRIT.	OLD HIGH GERMAN.	LATIN.
मानयामि *mânayâmi*	माणेमि *mânêmi*	*var-manêm*	*moneo*
मानयसि *mânayasi*	माणेसि *mânêsi*	*manês*	*monês*
मानयति *mânayati*	माणेदि *mânêdi*	*manêt*	*monet*
मानयामस् *mânayâmas*	माणेम्ह *mânêmha*	*manêmes*	*monêmus*
मानयथ *mânayatha*	माणेध *mânêdha*	*manêt*	*monêtis*
मानयन्ति *mânayanti*	माणेन्ति *mânênti*	*manênt*	*monent*

In regard to those weak verbs, which have suppressed the first vowel of the Sanskrit चय *aya*, and give therefore *ya* as affix, we will here further recall attention to the forms *iga* (*ige*), which occasionally occur in Old High German and Anglo Saxon, whose connection with चय *aya* is to be traced thus, that the semi-vowel *y* has become hardened to *g*, (comp. §. 19.), and the preceding *a* weakened to *i*. In Greek, the cognate verbs to the Sanskrit of the tenth class are to

---

* I am not at present able to adduce this verb from the edited texts: it is, however, certain, that *mânayâmi* in this dialect can have no other sound but *mânêmi*. The conjugation is supported by other examples of this class, as *chintêmi*, "I think" (from *chintayâmi*), *nivêdêmi* (from *nivêdayâmi*). In the plural the termination *mha* is nothing else than the appended verb substantive (Sansk. *smas*, "we are"). In the third pers. pl., together with *mânenti* the forms *mânaanti* and *mânanti* are also admissible. The Indian Grammarians assume for the Sanscrit a root *mân*, " to honour": more probably, however, the verb, for which this root is supplied, is only a denominative from *mâna*, " honour"; and this substantive itself a derivation from *man*, " to think," whence *ava-man*, " to despise," as in Old High German *var-MAN* (by Otfrid, *fir-MON*). The root, therefore, which is contained in *varmanêm* is identical with the Gothic *MAN* (*man*, " I mean," " I think," pl. *munum* see §. 66.). To this class belongs, also, the Latin *monere*, as, " to make to think" (Old High German *manôn*), the radical *o* for *a* of which we explain by the principle of §. 66. (see, also, §. 3.); while the *i* of *memin-i* is a weakening of the original *a*, explained by §. 6.

be looked for in those in αω, εω, οω; in Latin, besides the
2d conjugation compared above, most verbs of the 1st and 4th
also belong to this affinity. We shall recur to them when
speaking of the verb.

109ᵇ. In order to adduce single examples of the mul-
tiform construction of the roots, let us examine the order
of the final letters; but we will select only such examples
as are common to the Sanskṛit and several sister languages. The greatest forbearance, however, is requisite,
as an authenticated comparison of all that admits of comparison would easily swell to a book, which shall hereafter
be devoted to this subject.*

(1.) Roots ending with a vowel:—   [G. Ed. p. 122.]

"There are, as has been already remarked (§. 105.), no
roots in व a; but roots in आ â are numerous. Thus गा˙ gâ,†
"to go," contained in the Latin navi-ga-re; also, perhaps,
in fati-gare, the first member of which belongs to fatiscor,
fessus; in Greek, βίβημι answers to जगामि jagâmi, and rests
on the frequent interchange of gutturals and labials; Gothic
ga-thvô, "a street," (see p. 102. G. Ed.); Zend ܝܘܘ gâ-tu,
"a place," (nom. ܡܘܘ gâtus; Old High German gâ-m,
"I go," = जगामि ja-gâ-mi; not therefore, as Grimm conjectures (p. 868), by syncope from gangu, but, with a more
ancient and regular foundation, only with a suppression of
the Sanskṛit syllable of reduplication, introduced, therefore,
from the third into the second class (see p. 117. G. Ed.), as in
Latin, da-mus answering to δίδο-μεν. Thus, also, stâ-m,
stâ-s, stâ-t, in like manner, with suppressed reduplication,
corresponds to ἵ-στη-μι (for σίστημι), and to the Sanskṛit
root स्था sthâ, which is irregularly inflected, तिष्ठामि tishṭhâmi,
तिष्ठसि tishṭhasi, तिष्ठति tishṭhati, for tasthâmi, tasthâsi, tasthâti,

---

* Somewhat that pertains to this subject I have already put together
very concisely at the end of my Sanscrit Glossary.

† The attached cyphers denote the classes described in §. 109ᵃ.

which will be more closely considered hereafter. The Latin, in root and inflexion, most resembles the Old High German: the Zend, however, in its ﺟﻌﻤﻌﺮﻮﺟﻮ *histámi** (for *sistámi*, see §. 53.), appears in a genuine Greek dress. Observe, also, the ﻢﻌﺮﻮﺟﻮﺮﺟﻮﻮ *rathaêstáo*, "warrior," which occurs so often in the Zend-Avesta, properly "chariot stander," with *o* for *s* as the sign of the nominative. How, then, in Old High German, comes from *STA* the extended form of the root *STANT*, whence the present *stantu*, "I stand," and preterite *stuont*, "I *or* he stood"; for which the Gothic has *standa*, *stóth*? We will here only preliminarily remark, that we have observed in Zend also, in some roots terminating in *á*, an inclination to connect themselves with a *t*-sound. Thus we find, from ﻮﺟﻮ *sná*, "to wash," "to purify," (Sansk. स्ना *sná*, "to bathe,") whence *snáta*, "purified," in Vend. S. p. 233, frequently ﻮﺟﻮﺮﺟﻮﻮﻮﻮﻮ *fra-snádhayĕn* "*lavent*"; from ﻮﺟﻮ *dá*, "to lay," (Sans. धा *dhá*, p. 118 G. Ed.), we find ﻮﺟﻮﻮﻮﻮﺮﻮﻮﻮ *nidaithyaĭn*, "*deponant*" (as Vendidâd S. pp. 205 and 206, ﻮﺟﻮﻮﻮﻮﻮ ﻢﻌﻌﺮ ﻮﺟﻮﻮﺮﻮ *huskĕ zĕmĕ nidaithyaĭn*, "*in siccâ terrâ deponant*"): from the same root we find the imperative [G. Ed. p. 123.] form, ﻮﺟﻮﻮﻮﻮﻮﻮ *ni-dá-thâma*, "*deponamus*" (Vend. S. p. 208, ﻮﺟﻮﻮﻮﻮﻮ ﻮﻮﻮﻮﻮﻮﻮﻮﻮﻮﻮﻮﻮ ﻮﻮﻮ *kva naraĭm isritanaĭm tanûm barâma Ahura mazda kva nidálhâma*, "*Quo hominum mortuorum corpus feramus, ubi deponamus*"?). Of the Germanic we will further remark, that the root मा *má*, "to measure" (cf. μέ-τρον), has connected itself with a *t*-sound, and forms, in Gothic, *MAT*, present *mita* (§. 109ª. 1.). ज्ञा *jná*, "to be acquainted with," "to know," ΓΝΩ, *GNA* (*gnarus*) Old High German *CHNÁ* (§.87.); whence *chná-ta*, "I knew," annexing the auxiliary verb direct, as in Latin (*g*)*no-vi*. To

---

* I believe I may deduce this form from the 3d pers. pl. ﻮﺟﻮﻮﻌﺮﻮﺮﻮﺟﻮﻮ *histĕnti* (cf. ἵσταντι) in the V. S. p. 183: more on this head under the verb.

the special form, जानामि *jânâmi*, for ज्ञानामि *jnâ-nâ-mi*, may belong the Gothic root *KANN*, Old High German *CHANN*
(*kann, chan*, "I know," see §. 94., *kunnum, chunnum*, "we
know," see §.66.). ध्मा[1] *dhmâ*, "to blow," alters itself in the
special forms to धम् *dham*, Latin *FLA*, according to the
second class (§. 109ᵃ ₃.), Old High German *PLÂ* (§§. 12. 20.),
whence *plâ-ta*, "*flavi*." As in Sanskrit, from the above-mentioned धम् *dham*, comes the nominal base धमनी *dhamanî*,
"a vein"; so may the Gothic base *BLOTHA* (nom. acc.
blôth, "blood") come here also under consideration. We
pass on to roots in *i*, and have to remark that the root
mentioned at p. 107. G. Ed., इ *i*, "to go," is not unknown
in German. We find it in the Gothic imperative *hir-i*, "come
here"; du. *hir-yats*; pl. *hir-yith*. I believe, too, that in the
irregular preterite *iddya*, "I went," the *i* alone can be assumed as the root. In Zend occurs صومشى *aêi-ti*, "he goes"
(from एति *êti*, according to §§. 29. 41.), Lithuan. *ei-ti*. ऋ[5]
sri, "to go," with the prep. उत् *ut*, "to raise itself"; hence,
उच्छ्रित *uchchhrita*, "raised," "high"; compare *cre-sco, cre-vi*
(see §. 21.), Old High German *SCRIT*, "to step," with the
addition of a *t*, as in the case of *mat*, from मा *mâ*: perhaps
the Latin *gradior*, as well as *cresco*, might be here included,
the Guna form of the vowel, as in श्रयति *sray-a-ti*, "he
goes," being observed. स्मि *smi*, "to smile," Old High
German *SMIL*; प्री[°] *prî*, "to love," Zend فري *frî* (§. 47.), Goth.
friyô, "I love" (§. 87.), compare प्रिय *priya*, "dear." भी[3] *bhî*,
"to fear," बिभेमि *bibhê-mi*, "I fear"; Lithuan. *biyau;* Gothic
fiya, "I hate" (*fiyais, fiyaith*), *fiyands*, "foe"; Old High German *vîêm* or *fîêm*, "I hate": the Greek φέβ-ο-μαι answers to
the Sanskrit reduplication of *bibhêmi;* so that, contrary to
the common rule, the aspirates have remained in the prefix,
but in the base itself have become medials, and this has left
only β as the whole root, as in Sanskrit *da-d-mas*, "we give,"
for *da-dâ-mas*, δί-δο-μες. Perhaps, also, [G. Ed. p. 124.]
ΦΙΔ, φείδομαι, is to be referred to the roots in *i*, so that an

I

unorganic dental affix would be to be assumed. श्री² *śi,*
"to lie," "to sleep," with irregular Guna in the middle;
hence *śé-té* = κεῖ-ται. ह्री³ *hrî,* "to be ashamed"; Old High
German *HRU,* "to repent" (*hriw-u, hrou, hru-umés,* see
p. 115. G. Ed.). Of roots in *u,* द्रु¹ *dru,* "to run," द्रवति *drav-
a-ti,* "he runs" may furnish, through the Guna form, the
Greek δρά-σκω, δι-δρά-σκω, which appears hence to derive
its α with suppression of the digamma: the μ of δρέμω, however, might pass as a hardening of the व *v* (§. 63.), and
δρέμ-ο-μεν, δρέμ-ε-τε, &c., therefore represent most truly the
forms *drav-á-mas, drav-a-tha.* प्लु¹ *plu,* "to go," "to swim,"
"to float" (प्लव *plava,* "a ship."), Latin *FLU.* The Greek
πλέω, πλόω is again not to be so regarded as if the old *u* had
been corrupted to *e* or *o,* but πλέ(*F*)ω, πλο(*F*)ω supply the place
of the Guna form in *plav-é* (of the middle voice), 3d pers.
plav-a-té: the future πλεύσω, the *v* having the Guna (§. 26.),
answers to प्लोष्ये *plô-shyé;* Lithuan. *plaukiu,* "I swim," with
a guttural added, as in Latin *fluc-si* from *fluv* (p. 98.
G. Ed.). Old High German *VLUZ,* "to flow," pre-sup-
poses the Gothic *FLUT* (§. 87.); with the favourite dental
addition, with which all final vowels are so commonly
invested. श्रु⁵ *śru,* "to hear," ΚΛΥ (§§. 20., 21.), Gothic
HLIU-MAN (nominative *hliuma*), "ear," as "hearer,"
with weakened Guna (§. 27.); with regard to the *kl* for
śr, compare, also, *clunis* with श्रोणी *śrônî, f.* "hip.")
Lithuan. *klausau,* "I hear." Perhaps *erudio,* as "to make
hear," is to be referred to this class: the derivation from *e*
and *rudis* is little satisfactory. Anquetil introduces a Zend
erodé, célebre, (κλυτός), which I have not yet found in the original text, but I meet with the causal form ᵴᵍᵃᵎᵎ
śrávayémi (Sansk. श्रावयामि *śrávayámi*), "I speak," "recite"
(V. S. p. 39). The Old High German, *scrirumés,* "we have
exclaimed," gives *SCRIR* as the root, and rests probably on
the form *śráv* (§. 20.), with a thinning of the *á* to *i* (§. 66.);
the present and sing. preterite, however, have lost the *r* (*scriu*

for *scriru, screi* for *screir*), like the Greek κλή-σω, κέκλη-κα, &c.
The Latin *clamo*, however, has the same relation to श्राव् *śrâv*
that *mare* has to वारि *vâri*, "water" (§. 63.), and δρεμ to
द्रव् *drav*, from द्रु *dru*, "to run." ᚹᚣ *hu*[5], "to extol," "to
glorify" (ᚫᚣᚱᚹ *hunûta*, "he celebrated," V. S. p. 39.), is
probably the root of the Greek ὕμνος (ὕμ(ε)νος), which I do
not like to regard as an irregular derivative from ὕδω.
पू *pû*[1. 9.] "to purify," *PUrus*. This root is the verbal
parent of the wind and fire, which are both represented
as pure. पवन *pavana* (with Guna and *ana* [G. Ed. p. 125.]
as suffix) is "the wind," and the corresponding Gothic *FÔNA*
(neut. nom. acc. *fôn*, see §. 116.) is "fire," which in Sanskrit
is called पावक *pâv-a-ka*, with Vriddhi and *aka* as suffix.
The relation of *FÔNA* to पवन *pavana* resembles that of the
Latin *mâlo* from *mavolo*; the loss of the syllable व *va*
is replaced by the lengthening of the *a* (§. 69.). The Greek
πῦρ and Old High German *VIURA* (nom. acc. *viur*), the
latter with weakened Guna (§. 27.), and *ra* as suffix, both
fall to the root, पू *pû*. ब्रू *brû*[2], "to speak," Zend ᚫᚣᚷ *mrû*
(*e.g.* ᚷᚱᚫᚣᚷ *mrad-m*, "I spoke," V. S. p. 123.); the Greek
ῥέ(F)ω rests on the Guna form ब्रवीमि *brav-i-mi*, and has,
as often happens, lost the former of two initial consonants
(cf. also ῥέω, ῥεύω, and *ruo*, with स्रु *sru*, "to flow"). The
Old High German *SPRAH*, or *SPRAHH* (*sprihhu*, "I
speak," *sprah*, "I spoke") appears to have proceeded from
ब्रव् *brav*, by hardening the व *v* (see §. 19.), and prefixing an
s akin to the *p*. भू *bhû*, "to be," Zend ᚫᚣ *bû*, Lithuan. *BU*
(future *bûsu*, "I will be"), Latin *FU*, Greek ΦΥ. Probably, also, BY, in πρέσ-βυ-ς, πρεσβύτης, &c., is only
another form of this root (cf. §. 18.); so that πρές would
have to be regarded as a preposition from πρό (प्र *pra,*)
essentially distinguished only by a euphonic Σ (cf. §. 96.).
Moreover, the base πρέσβυ has a striking resemblance to
प्रभु *prabhu* (*excelsus, augustus*), literally, "being before."
In Old High German *pim* or *bim* corresponds to the

Sanskṛit भवामि *bhavâmi*: more exact, however, is the corre-
spondence in the plural of *pir-u-mês*, *pir-u-t*, to *bhav-â-mas*,
"*sumus*," *bhav-a-tha*, "*estis*" (see §. 19.). To this class belongs,
also, *PŪ*, "to dwell" (*pû-ta*, "I dwelt"), as the Sanskṛit वस्
vas "to dwell," in German *VAS*, *WAS*, has become *seyn*. In
Sanskṛit, too, from भू *bhû*, "to be," comes the substantive
bhav-ana "house," as place of being. The Gothic *baua*,
"I build," may be regarded as the causal of the idea "to
be," like the Latin *facio* (§. 19.): its conjugation answers
also to भावयामि *bhâvayâmi*, "I make to be," which, in Prâkṛit, may sound *bhâvêmi*, *bhâvêsi*, *bhâvêti* (Gothic *baua*,
bauais, *bauait*). See p. 121 G. Ed. Sanskṛit roots ending in
diphthongs (ए *ê*, ओ *ô*, ऐ *âi*; there are no roots in औ *âu*)
follow in their formations, in many respects, the analogy of
roots in आ *â*. We abstain from adducing examples of
them, as they also offer little occasion for comparison.

(2.) Roots terminating with a consonant. We shall give
[G. Ed. p. 126.] only a few examples, in which we compare
roots with the same vowel, and proceed in the order, *a, i, u*.
According to §. 1. we do not allow the vowel ऋ *ri* and ॠ *rî*
to belong to the root. Long radical vowels before a final
consonant are rare; and the majority of them are probably
not original.

The most numerous class of roots ending with a consonant has a medial व *a*. So वच्[1.2] *vach*, Zend ᭄ᮙᮩ *vach*
(ᮀᮥᮞ᭄᮪ᮨ *aôita*, "*dixit*," Vend. S. p. 124), Greek ΕΠ for ϜΕΠ
(§. 14.), Latin *VOC*, Old High German, *WAH*, *WAG* (*ki-
wahu*, "*mentionem facio*," pret. *ki-wuoh* pl. *ki wuogumês*).
प्रछ्[6] *prachh*, Zend ᮠᮨ᮲ᮩ᮪ *përës*, Gothic *FRAH*; pres पृच्छामि
pṛichchhâmi, ᮡᮙ᭄ᮩ᮪᮲ᮩ᮪᮪ *përësâmi*, *fraiha* for *friha* (see §. 82.
and §. 109ᵃ. 1.); the Latin *ROG* (*rogo*, *interrogo*) appears to
be abbreviated from *FROG*. पत्[1] *pat*, "to fall," "to fly,"
Zend ᮞᮩ᮪ *pat*, "to fly" (Vend. S. p. 257. ᮲ᮩ᮪᮲᮪ᮩ᮪ ᮣᮩ᮪ᮣᮩ ᮡᮩᮢᮩ
᮲᮪ᮙᮩ᮪ᮩ ᮠᮩ᮪ᮞ᮪ ᮲᮪ᮩᮩᮙᮩ *yat frâ vayô patañn urvara ucsyañn,*
"where birds fly, trees grow"). One sees clearly from this

that, in Greek, πίπτω, πετάω, πετάομαι, πέτομαι, πτῆμι, &c.
belong to a common root ΠΕΤ; Latin *PET*, *peto*, *im-peto*,
præpetes, *penna* by assimilation for *pet-na*. In Gothic
FATH, or, with the vowel weakened, *FITH*, might be
looked for. To the latter corresponds, according to §. 87.,
Old High German *VED*, in *ved-ara*, "feather," वद् [l. 10.]
vad, "to speak," Latin *VAD*, contained in *vas*, *vad-is*. From
वद् *vad* proceeds the abbreviated form उद् *ud*, to which pertains 'ΥΔ (ὕδω, ὑδέω, ὕδης). The Old High German gives
WAZ (*var-wizu* "*maledico*"), with *z* for *d*, according to §. 87.,
and the vowel of the base lengthened, as in वादयामि *vâdayâmi*,
according to the tenth class. सद्[0] *sad*, "to sink, with the
prep. नि *ni*, "to set oneself down"; Latin *SED*, *SID*, *sido*,
sedeo; Greek 'ΕΔ, 'ΙΖ, ἕδος, ἕδρα, ἵζομαι; Gothic *SAT*
(§. 87.), *sita*, "I sit" (p. 116 G. Ed.). अन्[2] *an*, "to blow,"
"to breathe," अनिल *anila*, "wind," Gothic *AN*, *usana*,
"I expire," cf. ἄνεμος, "*animus*." जन्[3] *jan*, "to beget,"
Zend ᭪ᨈ᨟ *zan* (§. 58.), ᨁᨳ᨟᭪᨟ *zazâmi*, "I beget," Sanskrit
जजन्मि *jajanmi*, Greek ΓΕΝ, Latin *GEN* (γίγνομαι, γένος,
gigno, *genus*), Gothic *KIN*, "to germinate," (p. 116 G. Ed.);
kuni, "gender" (§. 66.). कर्[8] *kar* (कृ *kri*), e.g. करोति *karôti*,
"*facit*": this root, in Zend, follows the fifth class; *e.g.*
᭪ᨁᨳ᨟᭪᨟᭪ *kĕrĕnaôiti* (§. 41.), "*facit*," ᭪ᨳ᨟᭪᨟᭪᨟ *kĕrĕnaôt*, "*fecit*," ᭪ᨳ᨟᭪᨟᭪ *kĕrĕnûidhi*, "*fac*"; Old High German *kara-
wan* or *garawan*, "to prepare"; Latin *creo*, *cura* (cf. कुरु
kuru, "*fac*"), *ceremonia*, and with *p* for *c* (§. 14.), *paro*; Greek
κραίνω, κρά-τος; with π, πράσσω, πρακ-σω,   [G. Ed. p. 127.]
πρᾶγ-μα, where the guttural appears to be a hardening of the
व् *v* (§. 19.), *e.g.* of कुर्वन्ति *kurvanti*, "*faciunt*" (from *kur-u-
-anti*). वह्[1] *vah*, "to drive," "to carry," Zend ᨟᭪᭪ *vaz* (§. 57.),
Latin *VEH*, Greek ὄχος, "wagon," as bearer, carrier, for
Ϝόχος. श्वस्[2] *śvas*, "to breathe," cf. *spiro*, according to
§§. 50. and 22. ग्रह्[9.10.] *grah*, "to take": the original
form, occurring in the Vedas, is ग्रभ् *grabh*. To this the
Zend form belongs, according to the tenth class, and,

indeed, so that the ᴎ *bh* appears before vowels as » *v*, but before ℘ *l* as ᴣ *p*.   Thus we read in the Vend. S. p. 155:

[Zend script] ashâum; yêzi nôiṭ uzvarêzyâṭ yô narêm âgĕrĕptĕm âgeurvayêitĕ, kâ hĕ aṡti chitha? "Pure! si non dimittit, qui hominem captum capit (i. e. tenet), quænam ei est pœna"?*   In the European sister languages I believe I recognise this root in three forms: the Gothic *GRIP* has been already mentioned (p. 116 G. Ed.), likewise *prehendo* (§. 92. note): by changing the medials into their tenues, ΚΛΕΠ also seems to belong to this class, Gothic *HLIF*, "to steal," *hliftus*, "thief." Finally, also, in Greek, γρῖπος, γρῖφος, "the net," stands quite isolated, and appears to me to be related to the Indian ग्रभ् *grabh*, by changing the *a* into *i*. आस्² *âs*, "to sit," Greek 'ΗΣ a remnant of the second class, terminating in a consonant to be supplied at §. 109ᵃ. s.; ἦσ-ται answers exactly to आस्ते *âs-tĕ* (middle voice), and hence ἧμαι stands for ἦσμαι, as εἰμί for ἐσμί (Sanskrit *asmi*). भ्राज्¹ *bhrâj*, "to shine," Zend *[Zend]* bĕrĕz (§. 58). or† *[Zend]* barĕz, whence the part. pres. *[Zend]* bĕrĕzant, nom. m. *[Zend]* bĕrĕzaṅs, "splendens," "altus," very frequently occurs. This Zend form prepares the way for the Old High German root *PERAH*, whence *PERAH-TA*‡, nom. *perah-t*, "fulgidus." To this root belongs, also, our *Pracht*. The Greek language gives ΦΛΕΓ (§. 20.) a cognate root, and thus [G. Ed. p. 128.] points to a Sanskrit short *a* for the long one. The cognate root in Latin is *FLAG*, *flagro*. छिद्⁷ *chhid*, "to cleave," *SCID*, *scind-i-mus* = *chhindmas* (§. 14.): ΣΧΙΖ, perhaps also ΣΚΙΔ, σκίδνημι, &c. belong to this place; the form is more genuine, and the ideas, too, of

---

* Anquetil translates, "*Si celui qui a commis l'Aguereṡté ne reconnoit pas sa faute quelle sera sa punition.*"

† Cf. p. 1281. Note *

‡ The *h* (in the sense of *ch*) corresponding to the *j*, γ, accords with §. 87., but is moreover favoured by the following *l*.

clearing, dispersing, separating, are kindred ones. The Gothic *SKAID*, "to separate," if the relationship is certain, has a stiffened Guna, so that *ai* appears to belong to the root. According to §. 87., however, the Gothic form should be *SKAIT* and the Old High German *SKEIZ* for *SKEID*. फ़िद़[2] *vid*, "to know," Zend وِيد *víd*, 'ΙΔ; Gothic *VID*, Old High German, *VIZ*; in the Latin *VID*, and in εἴδω, "I see," the seeing is regarded as something, which "makes to know," and the conjugation of *video* is causal, according to p. 121 G. Ed. Thus, also, another root, signifying "to know," namely बुध़ *budh*, has, in Zend, gained the meaning "to see."[*] According to the tenth class, and with the prep. *ni*, *VID*, in Zend, signifies "to summon" (نِيْوَاذْهَيَمِي *nivaêdhayêmi*, "invoco," see §. 28.) In Gothic, *VIT* receives through the prep. *in* the meaning "to adore" (*inveita, invait, invitum*). दिश़[6] *diś*, "to shew," Zend دِيش़ *diś*[10]; hence فْرَدَئِشَيُو *fradaêśayô*, "thou shewest" (Vend. S. p. 123), Greek ΔΙΚ, with Guna δείκνυμι, according to the fifth class; Latin *DIC*, in *dico*, as it were, "to point out," and *dicis* (*dicis causa*). In Gothic, the rule laid down in §. 87. requires the form *TIH*, and this root, combined with *ga*, signifies "to announce" (*ga-teiha, ga-taih, ga-taihum*, for *ga-tihum*, according to §. 82.). On the other hand, in *taikus*, "sign," the law for the transposition of letters is violated. जीव़[1] *jîv*, "life;" Lithuanian *gywa-s*, "alive," *gywenú* "I live," *gywata* "life;" Gothic *QUIVA*, nom. *quivs*, "alive"; Latin *VIV*, as it appears from *QUIV*, as *bis* from *duis* (Sansk. द्विस़ *dwis*), *viginti* from *tviginti*. The Zend has dropped either the vowel or the *v* of this root. Hence, *e.g.* جْوَ *jva*, nom. جْوُو *jvô*, "living," (V. S. p. 189); and هُوجِيتَيُو *hu-jîtayô*, "bonam vitam habentes" (l. c. p. 222), from هُوجِيتِي *hu-jîti*. From *jî*, the root, would become, with Guna, *jayámi*, on which rests the Greek ζάω, the *j* having

---

[*] Vide Gram. Crit. p. 328.

fallen out (§. 14.); but βίος also belongs to this root, and finds a medium of comparison with जीव् *jîv*, in the Latin *vivo*. Of roots with *u*, रुच्[1] *ruch*, "to shine," and रुद्[2] *rud*, "to weep," may serve as examples; the former, in Zend, is ‏روچ‎ *raôch*, (§§. 28. 32.), and follows the tenth class, *e. g.* ‏راوچاييتى‎

[G. Ed. p. 129.]   *raochayêiti, "splendet."* In Latin correspond *LUC, luc-s, luceo* (§. 20.) and *RUD*: the Greek has, in both roots, replaced the *r* by *l*, and presents, for comparison, ΛΥΚ (ἀμφιλύκη, λυκόφως) and ΛΥΖ; to the former, λύχνος, λυχνεύω, &c., has the same relation that, in Zend, ‏تفنوس‎ *tafnu-s*, "burning," has to the root ‏تپ‎ *tap* (§. 40.) We must assign λευκός also, with Guna, to the root ΛΥΚ. The Gothic gives *LUH* for *LUK*, according to §. 87.; whence, with the original, or with weakened Guna (§§. 26., 27.), spring forms like *lauhmôni*, "lightning," *lauhatyan*, "to lighten," *liuhath*, "light." Without Guna, and preserving the old smooth letter, stands *lukarn* (theme, *lukarna*, neut.), "lamp," rather isolated. A root corresponding to रुद् *rud* is wanting in Gothic, but the Old High German has for it, quite regularly according to §. 87., *RUZ*, "to weep" (*riuzu, rôz* for *rauz*, according to §. 80., *ruzumês*). भूष्[1] *bhûsh*, "to adorn," is perhaps contained in the Latin *or-no*, with loss of the initial letter, as *amo* in relation to कामयामि *kâmayâmi*, "I love." With regard to the *r* for ष् *sh*, advert to the relation of *uro* to उष् *ush*, "to burn," सेव्[1] *sev*, "to honour," मेध् *mêdh*, "to think"(?). The latter cannot hitherto be quoted as a verb: it springs, however, from मेधस् *mêdhas* and मेधा *mêdhâ*, "understanding." unless it should be preferred to assume for these words a root *midh*, which, however, the Grammarians do not exhibit. The Gothic has, for comparison, *MIT*, whence *mitô*. "I think": the Greek furnishes an analogous word to *sev*, viz. ΣΕΒ, σέβω. (§. 4.)

110. From the monosyllabic roots proceed nouns, substantive and adjective, by the annexation of syllables,

which we should not, without examination, regard as not,
per se, significative and, as it were, supernatural mystic
beings; to a passive belief in whose undiscoverable nature
we are not willing to surrender ourselves. It is more
natural to suppose that they have or had meaning, and
that the organism of language connects that which has a
meaning with what is likewise significative. Why should
not language denote accessory ideas, by accessory words
appended to the root? Language, which possesses both
sense and body, infuses sense and imparts form to every
word. The object of nouns is to represent   [G. Ed. p. 130.]
persons or things, to which that which the abstract root expresses adheres; and hence it is most natural to look for
pronouns in the elements used in the formation of words, as
the bearers of qualities, actions, and conditions, which the
root expresses *in abstracto.* There appears, too, in reality,
as we shall develope in the chapter on the pronouns, a com-
plete* identity between the most important elements in
the formation of words and some pronominal bases which
are declined even in an isolated state. But it is not surprising that several of the elements of verbal formation, in
the class of independent words, should not admit of more
certain explanation; for these affixes have their origin in
the most obscure and early epoch of language, and subsequently they have themselves lost all consciousness as to
whence they have been taken, on which account the appended suffix does not always keep equal pace with the
alterations which, in the course of time, occur in the corresponding isolated word; or it has been altered while the
other remains unchanged. Still, in individual cases, we
may remark the admirable exactitude with which the
appended grammatical syllables have maintained them-

---

* I direct attention preliminarily to my treatise " On the Influence of
Pronouns in the Formation of Words " (Berlin, by F. Dümmler).

selves through thousands of years in an unaltered form; I say, we may remark this from the perfect accordance which exists between various individuals of the Sanskrit family of languages, although these languages have been removed, as it were, from each other's eyes since time immemorial, and every sister dialect has, since that removal, been left to its own fate and experience.

111. There are also pure radical words, *i.e.* those of which the theme, without suffix of derivation or personality, repre-

G. Ed. p. 131.]   sents the naked root, which are then united in declension with the syllables which denote the relations of case.   Except at the end of compounds, such radical words are, in Sanskrit, few in number, and are all feminine ab-stracts;   as, भी *bhí,* "fear," युध् *yudh,* "contest," मुद् *mud,* "joy."   In Greek and Latin the pure root is the most rare form of the word; but it does not always appear as an abstract substantive.   As, for instance, *e.g.* φλογ (φλόκ-ς), ὀπ (ὄπ-ς). νιφ (νίπ-ς), *leg (lec-s), pac (pac-s), duc (duc-s), pel-lic (pel-lec-s).* In German, commencing even with the Gothic, no pure radical words exist, although, by reason of the abbrevia-tion of the base of the word in the singular, many words have assumed that appearance; for from the abbreviation of these verbal bases, which has been constantly extending during the lapse of time, it is precisely the most modern dialects which appear to exhibit the greatest number of naked roots as nouns. (cf. §. 116.)   Naked roots seem most generally used at the end of compounds, on account of the clogging of the preceding part of the word.   According to this principle, in Sanskrit, every root can, in this position, designate the agent by itself;   as, *e.g.* धर्मविद् *dharma-vid,* "duty-knowing."   In Latin, the use of these compounds is as frequent as in Sanskrit, only that, according to §. 6., a radical *a* is weakened to *i* or *e*; thus, *carni-fic (fec-s), tubi-cin (cen).*   An example in Greek is χερνιβ (for -νιπ from νιπ-τω).   Sanskrit roots which end with short vowels, as फिज *ji*, " to conquer," are, in compounds of this kind, supported by the addition of a *t*, which so much the more appears to be a simple phonetic affix without signification, that these weakly-constructed roots appear to support themselves on an auxiliary *t* before the gerundial suffix *ya* also. Thus, *e. g.* खगेजित *svarga-jit*, " conquering the heaven," विजिज्य *vi-jit-ya*, " by conquering." In Latin I find [G. Ed. p. 132.] interesting analogies to these formations in *IT* and *STIT*, from the roots *I* and *STA*, the latter weakened to *STI* according to §. 6. Thus, *com-it* (*com-es*), "goer with"; *equ-it* (*equ-es*), "goer on horseback"; *al-it* (*al-es*), "goer with wings"; *super-stit* (*-stes*), "standing by." The German has in this way supported throughout with a *t* several roots terminating with a vowel, and hence given to this letter the character of radicalism, as above mentioned (p. 123 G. Ed.) in *MAT*, from मा *má;* " to measure."

FORMATION OF CASES.

112. The Indian Grammarians take up the declinable word in its primary form, *i.e.* in its state when destitute of all case-termination ; and this bare form of the word is given also in dictionaries. In this we follow their example; and where we give Sanscrit and Zend nouns, they stand, unless it is otherwise specified, or the sign of case is separated from the base, in their primary form. The Indian Grammarians, however, did not arrive at their primary forms by the method of independent analysis, as it were by an anatomical dissection or chemical decomposition of the body of language ; but were guided by the practical use of the language itself, which, at the beginning of compounds—and the art of composition is, in Sanscrit, just as necessary as that of conjugation or declension— requires the pure primary form ; naturally with reservation of the slight changes of the adjoining limits of sound, rendered necessary at times by the laws of euphony. As the primary form at the beginning of compounds can represent every relation of case, it is, as it were, the case general, or the most general of cases, which, in the unlimited use of compounds, occurs more frequently than any other. Nevertheless, the Sanskrit language does not everywhere remain true to the strict and logical principle usually [G. Ed. p. 134.] followed in composition ; and as if to vex the Grammarians, and put their logic to the test, it places as the first member of the compounds in the pronouns of the first and second person the ablative plural, and in those of the third person the nom. and acc. sing. of the neuter, instead of the true primary form. The Indian Grammarians, then, in

this point, have applied to the cases furnished to them by
the language, and take the augmented अस्मत् *asmat* or
अस्मद् *asmad*, "from us," युष्मत् *yushmat* or युष्मद् *yushmad*,
"from you," as the starting-point in the declension, or as
the primary form, although in both pronominal forms only
व *a* and यु *yu* belong to the base, which, however, does not
extend to the singular. That, however, in spite of this
error, the Indian Grammarians understand how to decline
the pronouns, and that they are not deficient in external
rules for this purpose, is a matter of course. That the
interrogative, in its declension, resembles bases in *a*, cannot escape any one who holds the neuter किम् *kim* for the
original indeclinable form of the word. Pânini settles the
matter here with a very laconic rule, when he says (edit.
Calc, p. 969) किम: क: *kimah kah*, i. e, *ka** is substituted for
kim. If this strange method were to be followed in Latin,
and the neuter *quid* in like manner regarded as the
theme, then, in order to get at the dative *cu-i* (after
the analogy of *fructui*), one would have to say "*quidis cus*,"
or "*quidi cus*." In another place (p. 825), Pânini forms
from *idam*, "this" (which in like manner has the honour
of passing for a base) and *kim*, "what?" a copulative
compound; and by इदंकिमोर् ईइकी *idankimôr iski*, the Gram-
marian teaches that the putative bases in   [G. Ed. p. 135.]
the formations under discussion substitute for themselves
the forms *î* and *kî*.

113. The Sanskrit, and the languages akin to it, which
in this respect have still kept upon the old footing, distinguish, besides the two natural genders, another—the
neuter, which the Indian Grammarians call Klîva, *i. e.* eu-
nuch; which appears to be a peculiarity of the San-

---

* He forms, namely, from *kim*, regarded as a base, *kim-as*, which
in reality does not occur, and which has, for the sake of euphony, here
become *kimah*.

skrit, or most perfect family of languages. According to
its original intention this gender had to represent inanimate nature, but it has not everywhere confined itself to
these old limits: the language imparts life to what is
inanimate, and, on the other hand, (according to the view
then taken,) impairs the personality of what is by nature
animate. The feminine in Sanskrit, both in the base and
in the case-terminations, loves a luxurious fullness of
form; and where it is distinguished from the other
genders in the base or in the termination, it marks this
distinction by broader, and more sonant vowels. The
neuter, on the other hand, prefers the greatest conciseness,
but distinguishes itself from the masculine, not in the base,
but only, in the most conspicuous cases, in the nominative
and its perfect counterpart the accusative; in the vocative
also, when this is the same as the nominative.

114. Number, in Sanskrit and its sister languages, is
distinguished, not by a particular affix denoting the number,
but by the selection or modification of the case-syllable,
so that, with the case-suffix, the number is at once known;
e. g. bhyam, bhyâm, and bhyas are cognate syllables, and,
among other relations, express that of the dative; the first
in the singular (only in the pronoun of the 2d person, तुभ्य
tubhyam, " to thee "), the second in the dual, the third in the
plural. The dual, like the neuter, in course of time is the first
to be lost with the weakening of the vitality   [G. Ed. p. 136.]
of the view taken by the senses, or is more and more straitened
in its use, and then replaced by the abstract plural expressive
of infinite number. The Sanskrit possesses the dual most
fully, both in the noun and in the verb, and employs it everywhere where its use could be expected. In the Zend, which
otherwise approximates so closely to the Sanskrit, it is
found very rarely in the verb, more frequently in the
noun. The Pali has only as much left of it as the Latin,
viz. a remnant of it in two words, which signify "two"

and "both"; in the Prâkṛit it is entirely wanting. Of
the German languages, only the eldest dialect, the Gothic,
possesses it, but merely in the verb; while, on the contrary, in the Hebrew (speaking here of the Semitic
languages) it is retained only in the noun, in disadvantageous contrast with the Arabic, which, in many other
respects also, is a more perfect language, and which maintains the dual in equal fulness in the verb also; while in
the Syriac it has been almost entirely lost in the noun as
well as in the verb.*

115. The case-terminations express the reciprocal relations of nouns, *i.e.* the relations of the persons spoken of, to
one another, which principally and originally referred only
to space, but from space were extended also to time and
cause. According to their origin, they are, at least for the
most part, pronouns, as will be more clearly developed
hereafter. Whence could the exponents of the relations
of space, which have grown up with the primary words
into a whole, have better been taken, than from those
words which express personality, with their inherent secondary idea of room, of that which is nearer or more distant,
of that which is on this or that side? [G. Ed. p. 137.]
As also in verbs the personal terminations, *i.e.* the pronominal
suffixes—although, in the course of time, they are no longer
recognised and felt to be that which, by their demonstrable
origin, they imply and are—are replaced, or, if we may
use the expression, commented on by the isolated pronouns
prefixed to the verb; so, in the more sunken, insensible
state of the language, the spiritually dead case-terminations
are, in their signification of space, replaced, supported, or ex-

---

* Regarding the character, the natural foundation, and the finer gradations in the use of the dual, and its diffusion into the different provinces
of language, we possess a talented inquiry, by W. von Humboldt, in the
Transactions of the Academy for the year 1827; and some which have been
published by Dümmler.

plained by prepositions, and in their personal signification by the article.

116. Before we describe the formation of cases in the order in which the Sanskrit Grammarians dispose them, it appears desirable to give the different final sounds of the nominal bases with which the case-suffixes unite themselves, as well as to point out the mode in which the cognate languages are in this respect related to one another. The three primary vowels (a, i, u) occur in Sanskrit, both short and long, at the end of nominal bases; thus, **च** a, **ई** i, **उ** u; **आ** $á$, **ई** $í$, **ऊ** $ú$. To the short a, always masculine or neuter, never feminine, a, corresponds in Zend and Lithuanian, and also in German, where, however, even in the Gothic (in Grimm's first strong declension), especially in substantives, it is only sparingly retained: in more modern dialects it is commonly supplanted by a more recent u or e. In Greek, the corresponding termination is the o of the second declension (*e.g.* in λόγο-ς): and o was also the termination of the Latin noun in ancient times; but in the classic period, although sometimes retained, it was commonly changed to u in the nom. and accus. sing. (of the second declension). An old a, however, is still left in *cola, gena, cida*, at the end of compounds, where, however, from the want of other analogies, it is used in declension similarly to the feminine [G. Ed. p. 138.] originally long a, on which account the nominative is written, not *colas, genas, cidas*, but *cola*, &c. The Grecian masculines of the first declension in $á$-ς,[*] with the η-ς which has proceeded therefrom, must likewise, according to their origin, be compared with the Sanskrit masculine short a, to which, in regard of quality and preservation of the nominative sign, they have remained faithful, while the o of the second declension has preserved its old original brevity. Their identity with bases in o is excellently shewn by the genitive in ov, which does not at all

* Cf. p. 1294. l. 20. G. Ed.

suit a theme in α or η; and further, from such compounds
as μυροπώλη-ς, παιδοτρίβη-ς, in which the vowel that has
been added to the roots ΠΩΛ and ΤΡΙΒ supplies the place
of the Sanskrit a in similar compounds for which, in Greek, o
usually stands.

117. To the short i, which occurs in the three genders,
the same vowel corresponds in the cognate languages. In
German it is to be looked for in Grimm's fourth strong
declension, which I shall make the second; where, however, from the destructive alterations of time, it becomes
nearly as hard as the a of the first declension. In Latin,
i is interchanged with e; hence *facile* for *facili*, *mare*
for *mari*, Sanskrit वारि *vâri*, " water." In Greek, before
vowels the ι is generally weakened to the unorganic ε. The
short u also shews itself in Sanskrit in the three genders,
as in Greek υ, and u in Gothic, where it distinguishes itself
from the a and i in that it is retained as well before
the s of the nominative as in the uninflected accusative.
In Latin the corresponding letter is the u of the fourth
declension.

118. The long vowels (â, î, û) belong, in Sanskrit, principally to the feminine (see §. 113.), are never found in the
neuter, and occur in the masculine very rarely. In Zend
the long final a has generally been shortened in polysyllabic
words; as it has in Gothic, in which bases [G. Ed. p. 139.]
in ô correspond (§. 69.) to the Sanskrit feminine bases in â,
and the ô in the uninflected nom. and accus. sing. is shortened
to a, with the exception of the monosyllabic forms *sô*, "she,"
"this," Sanskrit सा *sâ*, Zend *hâ*; *hvô*, " which?" Sanskrit
and Zend *kâ.* The Latin, also, in the uninflected nom. and
voc., has shortened the old feminine long a; but the Lithuanian has, in the nom., maintained the original length. In
Greek, the Doric ᾱ approaches most nearly to the Sanskrit
feminine आ *â*, which the common dialect has sometimes
preserved, sometimes shortened, sometimes transformed
into η.

K

119. The long *í* appears, in Sanskrit, most frequently as a characteristic addition in the formation of feminine bases, thus, the feminine base महती *mahatí* (*magna*) springs from महत् *mahat*. The same holds good in Zend. Moreover, the feminine character *í* has been preserved most strictly in Lithuanian, where, for example, in the part. pres. and fut. an *i* is added to the old participial suffix *ant*, and *ésant-i*, "the existing," *bú-sent-i*, "that that shall be," correspond to the Sanskrit सती *sat-í* (for *asati* or *asanti*), भविष्यन्ती *bhav-i-shyanti*. In Greek and Latin this feminine long *i* has become incapable of declension; and where it has still left traces, there a later unorganic affix has become the bearer of the case-terminations. This affix is, in Greek, either α or δ; in Latin, *c*. Thus, ἡδεῖα corresponds to the Sanskrit स्वाद्वी *swádw-í*, from स्वादु *swádu*, "sweet"; -τρια, -τριδ, e.g. ὀρχήστρια, ληστρίς, ληστρίδ-ος, to the Sanskrit त्री *trí*, e.g. जनित्री *janitrí*, "genitress," to which the Latin *genitri-c-s*, *genitri-c-is*, corresponds; while in the Greek γενέτειρα, and similar formations, the old feminine *i* is forced back a syllable. This [G. Ed. p. 140.] analogy is followed by μέλαινα, τάλαινα, τέρεινα, and substantive derivations, as τέκταινα, Λάκαινα. In θεράπαινα, λέαινα, the base of the primitive is, as in the nom. masc., shortened by a τ. In θέαινα, λύκαινα, it is to be assumed that the proper primitive in ν or ντ has been lost, or that these are formations of a different kind, and correspond to the rather isolated word in Sanskrit इन्द्राणी *Indrání*, as the wife of Indra, as derived from इन्द्र *Indra*, is termed. The cases where the feminine *i* is solely represented by α are essentially limited to feminine derivatives from forms in ντ, where τ passes into σ: the preceding ν, however, is replaced by υ or *ι*, or the mere lengthening of the preceding vowel, or it is assimilated to the σ:

hence, ουσ-α,   εισ-α,   εσσ-α,   ᾱσ-α*,   ῡσ-α

for   οντ-α,   εντ-α,   εντ-α,   αντ-α,   υντ-α.

---

* In Doric subsequent and original αισ-α.

To this analogy belong, moreover, the feminine substantives, like θάλασσα, βασίλισσα, μέλισσα, which J. Grimm (II. 328.) very correctly, in my opinion, compares with forms like χαρί-εσσα, μελιτό-εσσα, and explains the double σ by gemination or assimilation. The feminine formations by a simple α instead of the original ι are most corrupt, and, relatively, the most recent; and herein the Greek is not supported by any of the cognate languages. The Latin, its twin-sister, which otherwise runs parallel to it, leaves, in the part. pres. and other adjective bases terminating with a consonant, the feminine undistinguished from the masculine through all the cases, since it has no longer the power of declining the old *i.*

120. The German, too, can no longer fully decline the old feminine *i;* and the Gothic, by a foreign affix, introduces it into the *ô* declension, but in the singular of substantives shortens the syllable *yô* in the   [G. Ed. p. 141.] uninflected nominative and vocative to *i,* in the adjective to *ya.* More commonly, however, the old bases in *i* are introduced, by the frequently employed affix of an *n,* into the so-called weak declension; and as *i* in Gothic is denoted by *ei,* so to the Sanskrit feminine participial bases in वती *antí,* and to the fem. comparative bases in ईयसी *íyasí,* correspond the forms *ndein, izein,* regarding the nominative of which refer to §. 142.

121. The long *u* (*û*) appears, in Sanskrit, rather seldom at the end of primary forms, and is for the most part feminine. The words most in use are वधू *vadhû,* "a wife," भू *bhû,* "earth," श्वश्रू *śvaśrû,* "mother-in-law" (*socrus*), भ्रू *bhrû,* "eyebrow." To the latter corresponds ὀφρύς, likewise with the long *v,* the declension of which, however, is not different from that of the short *v;* while in Sanskrit the long *u* is distinguished from the short feminine *u* in the same way as ई *í* from इ *i.* But few monosyllabic primary forms end, in Sanskrit, with diphthongs, not any at all with ए *é;* with ऐ *ái* (from *á + i,* see §. 2.) only रै *rai,* masc. "thing," "riches"; in

K 2

the nom. irregularly रास् *rá-s* for रस् *rái-s*. In this is recognised the Latin *re-s*. Still I do not believe that Latin bases
in *ē* should therefore be looked upon as corresponding to
the Sanskrit रे *ái*; for, in the first place, the Latin *ē* corresponds elsewhere to the Sanskrit ए *ê* (from *ă + i*), never to
ái; secondly, the connection of the *ē* of the fifth declension
with the originally long *a* of the first is not to be mistaken (to which it bears the same relation that the Ionic
η does to the Doric *ā*), for many words with the same meaning belong to the A and E declension; and, for example,
a suffix which is employed for the formation of abstracts
from adjectives is sounded as well *tiē* as *tia* (*planitie-s*,
[G. Ed. p. 142.] *planitia, canitie-s, canitia*); and *iē-s*, and *ia*,
in the formation of primitive and derivative words—like
effigie-s, effigia, pauperie-s, pauperia—are clearly one and the
same suffix, identical with the Sanskrit या *yá*, which is used
for the same purpose, and the Greek *ία*, Ionic *ίη*. Let us now
consider the objections which are opposed to the original
identity of the feminine *ē* and *a*. The most weighty is
the *s* in the nom. sing. and pl.: *ē-s, ē-s* for *ē, ei*, as *musa*,
musæ (*musai*), κεφαλή, κεφαλαί. As regards the *s* in the
singular, it is, if the identity with the first declension be
authentic, very remarkable; and forms like *species, canities*,
seem to be true lingual patriarchs: for the Sanskrit, like the
Zend, Greek, Gothic, Lithuanian, exhibits the absence of the
nominative sign in the corresponding feminine bases in *a*.
I have, however, never considered as original the abandonment of the nominative sign, and the complete equal-
ization with the primary form in सुता *sutá*, "daughter," and
similar words, although it has appeared to me as losing
itself very deeply in far-distant ages. The Latin, however, in some other points of Grammar, shews greater
antiquity than the Sanskrit and Greek, as, for example
(to confine the present instance to the nominative case),
participial nominatives, like *amans, legens*, are better and

older forms than the Sanskrit and Greek, like गुदन् *tudan*,
λέγων, τιθείς, because they have preserved the nominative *s* together with the nasal, and therein stand on
the same footing with Zend forms, like ᛘᛕᛘ *bavaṅś*,
"being." I cannot, therefore, find, in the retention of
the nominative sign in the fifth declension, any decisive
argument against its original identity with the first. We
will treat hereafter of the *s* of the nominative plural. In
the genitive singular the common form *ei* answers to *deae*
(*deai*), the more rare, however, and better, in *ēs* to *familias*.
Schneider searches, but fortunately without [G. Ed. p. 143.]
success, for genitives like *die-is*: we require them as little,
perhaps, as a *familia-is*, Let *dies* be written with Greek
letters διη-ς, and then, perhaps, a *die-is* will be as little required as a δικη-ος. Although a few bases of the third declension, by rejecting a consonant or an entire syllable, have
passed into the fifth declension, we will not therefore infer
that all bases in *e* have arisen from such an abbreviation. If
QUIET, after rejecting the *t*, could be declined according to
the fifth declension, then must there necessarily have formerly been a fifth, *i.e.* there must have been bases in *ē*,
otherwise from *QUIET* could only have come *QUII* (*quies*,
quiis, like *cædes*); *i.e.* in spite of the rejection of the *t*
it must have continued in the third declension. The connection between *rē-s* and the abovementioned Sanskrit रै *rāi* is,
in my opinion, to be arrived at through the irregular
nominative राः *rā-s*; and according to this *re-s* would be
supported on an old *ā*: it answers to राः *rā-s* as *rē-bus* to
राभ्यस् *rā-bhyas*, and as in Greek γῆ-ν to the Sanskrit गाम्
gām, "*terram*," which, in the remaining cases, has गो *gô* for
its base. In Lithuanian there are feminine primary forms
in *e* (Ruhig's third declension) which resemble the Greek η
in the suppression of the singular nominative sign, but in the
nominative plural in *e-s* approach more closely the Latin
in *ē*.

122. Primary forms in द्यौ *dyô* are rare in Sanskrit: the only ones known to me are द्यौ *dyô*, "heaven," and गौ *gô* : the former is feminine, and properly proceeds from दिव् *div* (a radical word from दिव् *div*, "to shine") by the vocalization of the व् *v*, after which the vowel इ *i* becomes its semi-vowel य् *y*. In the accusative the *ô* bases change this diphthong into *â*. To the *â* thus obtained in द्याम् *dyâ-m*,

[G. Ed. p. 144.]   गाम् *gâ-m*, corresponds the Latin *e* of *die-m*, the Greek η, Doric α, of γῆ-ν, γᾶ-ν: the Latin *e*, however, is rendered short by the influence of the final *m*: the original language requires *diē-m*. In Sanskrit, also, from दिव् *div*, "to shine," are derived appellations of day; as on the other side, in Latin, those for the heaven—*divum, sub divo, sub dio* —viz. दिवा *divâ*, as an adverb, "by day," and used as a primary form at the beginning of compounds; and also दिवस *divasa*, masc., and द्यु *dyu*, neuter (a contraction from *div*), which latter signifies both "day" and "heaven." To द्यु *dyu* answers, after rejecting the *d* (as *viginti* for *dviginti*), the Latin *Ju* of *Ju-piter*, "heavens-lord or father": the oblique cases *Jov-is, Jov-i, Jov-em* answer better to the broader theme द्यौ *dyô*, whence the dative द्यवे *dyav-ê*, and the locat. द्यवि *dyav-i*. The *Djovis*, moreover, furnished by Varro, deserves mention, as that which keeps most faithfully to the ancient form. The Grecian Ζεύς signifies, therefore, in accordance with its origin primarily, "heaven": I form its relation to द्यौ *dyô* thus, that after dropping the द् *d* the following semi-vowel य् *y* became ζ (§. 19.). The oblique cases, on the contrary (Διός, Διΐ, &c.), belong to the Sanskrit द्यु *dyu*, and must originally have had a digamma, proceeding by the natural law of sound from *u*, after which change the semi-vowel *j* must have become a vowel. Διός has the same relation to ΔιϜός, that, in Latin, *sub dio* has to *sub divo*.

123. Let us now consider the second of the abovementioned primary forms in *ô*, viz. गौ *gô*. It has several

meanings; but the most common are "bull," as masculine,
and "cow" and "earth" as feminine. Both significations
have in Zend, as in Greek, divided themselves into two
forms. The Greek has preserved for the meaning "earth"
the old guttural. With regard to the vowel, γῆ, γᾶ follows the
example of the Indian accusative, where, as has been already
remarked, गाम् *gâm* (γῆν) stands for *gô-m*   [G. Ed. p. 145.]
or *gav-am*. For the meaning "ox" the Greek has preserved
the old diphthong—(for, for गौ *ô* = *a* × *u* may very well be
expected, according to §. 4., *ov*)—but has exchanged the guttural medials for labials, as, p. 122 G. Ed., βίβημι for जगामि
jagâmi. The base BOY before vowels must originally have
become BOF; thus, in the dative, βοϜ-ί would answer to the
Sanskrit locat. गवि *gav-i*, and the Latin dative *bov-i*; but in
the present state of the language the middle digamma
between two vowels has always been dropped; and there
is not, as with the initial digamma, the medium of metre
for replacing it in the oldest writings. Only theory and
comparative grammar can decide here. The Latin has,
in the word *bō-s*, changed the vowels (*a* + *u*)—(which were
originally of different kinds, but have been united into a
diphthong)—into a homogeneous mass (cf. §. 4.), the nature
of whose contraction, however, discloses itself before vowel
inflexions, since the *u*-half of *BŌ* becomes *v*, and the short *a*
is resolved into the form of a short *o*; thus, *bov-i* answers
to the Sanskrit locat. गवि *gav-i*. The Zend for the meaning
"earth" has changed the guttural of the word under discussion into *z*, and gives in the nominative ꞡꭒꭤ *zâo* for
ꭤꭒꭤ *zâs* (§. 56ᵇ.), in the accusative ꭞꭤꭤ *zañm* (§. 61.): I am
not able to adduce other cases. For the meaning "ox"
the guttural has remained in Zend, and the nominative
is then ꭤꭒꭤꭤꭤ *gâu-s* or ꭤꭒꭤꭤꭤ *gâo-s*.

124. I know only two words in Sanskrit which terminate
in नौ *ûu*—नौ *nûu*, "ship," and ग्लौ *glûu*, "moon": the former
has navigated very far on the ocean of our wide province of

language, without, however, in Sanskrit, having arrived at a
secure etymological haven. I believe नौ *nâu* to be an abbreviation of *snau* (cf. ῥέω, ῥεύω, *ruo*, with स्रु *sru*, p. 125 G. ed.),
[G. Ed. p. 146.]   and that it therefore proceeds from the root
स्ना *snâ*, "to bathe," which originally, perhaps, may also have
meant "to swim," and with which νάω, νέω, *na-to*, appear to
be connected. नौ *nâu* would consequently be a radical word;
and in regard to the vowel would stand for *nâ*, according to
the analogy of ददौ *dadâu* (*dedi*, *dedit*) for *dadâ*, from *dadâ-a*.
As *a*, according to §. 6., is a grave vowel, the Greek cannot
represent the Sanskrit Vriddhi-diphthong औ *âu* better than
by *αυ*, while ओ *ô* (from short *a + u*) is commonly represented by *ευ* or *ου*. Hence नौस् *nâu-s* and ναῦ-ς correspond
as exactly as possible; the *υ* of NAY, however, like that
of BOY, has maintained itself only before consonants; and
the digamma, which replaces it, is lost before vowel inflexions; νῆ-ες, νᾶ-ες, are from ναϜ-ες (Sansk. नावस् *nâv-as*),
as βό-ες from βόϜ-ες. The Latin has given this word a
foreign addition, and uses *navi-s*, *navi-bus*, for *nau-s*, *nau-bus*.*
As the semi-vowel *v* is easily hardened to a guttural
(§. 19.), we have here also, for *nau*, *nâv-am*, a sister form
in our *Nachen*, Old High German *naccho*, "ship," gen. dat.
nacchin.

125. We pass over to the consonants: of these, *n*, *t*, *s*,
and *r* appear in Sanskrit most frequently at the end of
primary forms; all other consonants occur only in radical
words, which are rare, and in some nominal bases of uncertain origin. We consider next the more rare or radical
consonants. Of gutturals (*k*, *kh*, *g*, *gh*) we find none at

---

* Thus in German an *i* has been added to the above-mentioned गो
gô, which, however, according to §. 117., is suppressed, together with the
case sign in Old High German; hence *chuo*, "cow," gen. *chuvi*, where
the *i* does not belong to the case designation, but to the here uninflected
base.

the end of the nominal bases most in use; in Greek and
Latin, on the contrary, they are of frequent occurrence;
c is in Latin both radical and derivative, [G. Ed. p. 147.]
g only radical—*DUC, VORAC, EDAC, LEG.*   In Greek,
κ, χ, and γ are only radical, or occur in words of unknown
origin, as ΦΡΙΚ, ΚΟΠΑΚ, 'ΟΝΥΧ (Sanskrit *nakha*), ΦΛΟΓ.
Of the palatals, *ch* and *j* in Sanskrit occur most frequently in
वाच् *vâch*, "speech, voice" (*VOC*, 'ΟΠ); राज् *râj*, "king," the
latter only at the end of compounds; असृज् *asrij*, "blood"
(*sanguis*): in Zend we have درُج *druj*, f., as name of an
evil demon, probably from the Sanskrit root द्रुह् *druh*, "to
hate."   Of the two classes of the *T*-sound, the first, or
lingual (ड् *t*, &c.), is not used at the end of nominal bases;
and therefore the second, dental, or proper *T*-class, is so
much the more frequently employed.   Still द् *d*, ध् *dh*, occur
only in radical words, and therefore seldom; थ् *th* perhaps
only in पथ् *path*, as the secondary theme of पथिन् *pathin*,
"way"; nom. पन्थास् *panthâs*, from पन्थस् *panthas*, which I
think I again recognise in the Latin *PONT, pons*.   Other
examples are, अद् *ad*, "eating," at the end of compounds,
and युध् *yudh*, f., "strife."   The letter त् *t* is so much the
more common, that several of the most frequently employed
suffixes end with it, as that of the part. pres. in अत् *at* or
अन्त् *ant*, Greek and Latin *nt*.   The Greek, besides τ, exhibits also δ and θ at the end of primary forms which are not
radical; still ΚΟΡΥΘ and 'ΟΡΝΙΘ appear to me to be properly compounds, and to contain the roots ΘΗ, ΘΕ (the vowel
being dropped) as their last member; and according to this,
ΚΟΡΥΘ would properly mean "what is placed on the head";
so in Sanskrit, शरद् *śarad*, "autumn," "rainy season,"
which Grammarians explain by a suffix *ad*, in my opinion
means nothing but "water giving," and contains the root
दा *dâ*, "to give," with â suppressed.   'ΟΡΝΙΘ finds in
Greek itself no etymology: the Sanskrit offers for its explanation अरणि *arani* (according to the pronunciation of Ben-
gal, *oroni*), "wood"; and if ὄρνι is con-   [G. Ed. p. 148.]

nected therewith, we may refer to θέω, " to run," in respect
to the θ: " bird" therefore would derive its name from its
going in the wood; while in Sanskṛit, from its passage
through the air, it is called, among other names, विहग
viha-ga. Regarding the later origin of the δ in feminine
bases in ιδ, an account is given in §. 119.; that is to say,
patronymics in ιδ may be compared with Sanskṛit ones in ἰ,
e.g. भैमी bhaimî, " the daughter of Bhîma. Probably, too,
the δ in feminine patronymics in αδ is a later addition; they
spring, like those in ιδ, not from their masculines, but directly
from the primary word of the masculine, and, in my opinion,
stand in sisterly, not in filial connection with them. In
Latin, d appears as a more modern affix in the base PECUD,
which the Sanskṛit, Zend, and Gothic terminate with u
(Sans.-Zend, paśu, Goth. faihu). In Gothic, primary forms
with a final T-sound are chiefly limited to the part. pres.,
where the old t appears changed into d, which remains
without extraneous addition: there only, however, where
the form stands substantively; otherwise, with the exception of the nominative, it is conducted by the affix an
into a more current province of declension. The more
modern German dialects under no circumstances leave the
old T-sound without a foreign addition commixed with
the base. In Lithuanian the participial suffix ant, in regard of the nom. sing. ańs for ants, rests exactly upon
the Latin and Zend step, which extends beyond the Sanskṛit; but in most of the remaining cases the Lithuanian
cannot decline any more consonants, i.e. cannot unite
them with pure case terminations, but transports them
always, by a more modern affix, into a vowel-declension;
and, indeed, to the participial suffix ant is added the
[G. Ed. p. 149.]   syllable ia, by the influence of which
the t experiences the euphonic transformation into ch
(= tsch*). The nasal of this dental T-class, viz. the

---

* This sound is expressed by cs, as in Mielcke's edition of Ruhig's
Grammar.

proper *n*, belongs to those consonants which occur most frequently at the end of nominal bases. In the German all the words of Grimm's weak declension like the Sanskrit, and the masculine and feminine in Latin, reject in the nominative the *n* of the base, and thereby have a vowel termination. The Lithuanian presents the same appearance in the nominative, but in most of the oblique cases adds to a base in *en* sometimes *ia*, sometimes a simple *i*.

126. Primary forms with a final labial, including the nasal (*m*) of this organ, appear in Sanskrit only in naked roots, as the last member of compounds, and here, too, but seldom. In isolated use, however, we have अप् *ap* (probably from the root आप् *áp*, "to take in," "to comprehend"), "water," which is used only in the plural; in Zend, however, in the singular also.* In Greek and Latin, also, bases in *p*, *b*, *φ*, are either evidently radical, or of unknown origin, with probably radical letters at the end; or in Latin they have suppressed, in the nominative, a vowel belonging to the base; and so, as in [G. Ed. p. 150.] German, the first and fourth strong declensions, according to Grimm, have only the appearance of a base terminating with a consonant. Of this kind is *plebs*, from *plebis;* to explain which it is not requisite to turn, with Voss, to the Greek πλῆθος: one must keep to the Latin root *PLE*. The derivative *bis*, *bes*, I explain like *bus, bundus, bilis, bam,*

---

* The Latin adds an *a* to this old consonantal base, and thus arises, according to the frequent interchange of *p* with *qu* (cf. *quinque* with पञ्चन् *panchan*), *aqua*; on the other hand, *am-nis* rests on the form *ap*, as *somnus* for *sopnus*, and σεμνός, for σεβνός, in analogy with a Sanskrit euphonic law (Gramm. Crit. r. 58.). The Sanskrit has from the same root another neuter, आपस् *ápas*, in which we recognise the Latin *æquor*, which therefore would not proceed from *æquus*, but is transferred from the waves, or the mirror of the sea, to other things of a similar nature. In Greek, ἀφρός appears to belong to the same origin.

bo (*amabam*, *-bo*), as from the root *FU*, "to be," which, like *FER*, often changes the *B* in its middle into *F* (§. 18.). Without appealing to the cognate languages, it is difficult, in Latin, to distinguish those bases which truly and originally terminate in a consonant from those which only appear to do so; for the declension in *i* has clearly operated on the consonantal declension, and introduced an *i* into different places in which it is impossible it could have stood originally. In the dative and ablative plural, the *i* of forms like *amantibus*, *vocibus*, admits of being explained as a conjunctive vowel, for facilitating the affix; it is, however, in my opinion, more correct to say that the bases *VOC*, *AMANT*, &c., because they could not unite with *bus*, have, in the present state of the Latin language, been lengthened to *VOCI*, *AMANTI*; so that we ought to divide *voci-bus*, *amanti-bus*, just as at §. 125. it was said of the Lithuanian, that in most cases it extends its participial bases in *ant* to *anchia* (euphonic for *antia*). This view of forms like *amanti--bus* is proved to be the more probable, in that in the genitive plural also before *um*, as before the *a* of neuters, an *i* frequently finds its place, without its being possible to say that in *amanti-um*, *amanti-a*, the *i* would be necessary to facilitate the annexation of the ending. On the other hand, *juveni-s*, *cani-s*, forming the genitives *canu-m*, *juven--um*, remind us of older bases in *n*; as in Sanskrit श्वन् *śwan*, "a dog" (abbreviated शुन् *śun*), and युवन् *yuvan*, "young" (abbreviated यून् *yún*), in Greek κύων, abbreviated [G. Ed. p. 161.] KYN, really close their theme with *n*. The German resembles the Latin in this point, that for the convenience of declension it has added an *i* to several numerals, whose theme originally terminated with a consonant; thus, in Gothic, from *FIDVŌRI* (Sanskrit चतुर् *chatur*, in the strong cases §. 129. चत्वार् *chatwár*) comes the dative *fidvôri-m*. The themes सप्तन् *saptan*, "seven," नवन् *navan*, "nine," दशन् *daśan*, "ten," by the addition of an *i*,

in Old High German mould themselves to *SIBUNI,
NIUNI, ZEHANI*; which forms, at the same time, pass as
masculine nominatives, as these cases, in Old High German,
have lost the case-suffix *s*. The corresponding Gothic
nominatives, if they occurred, would be *sibunei-s, niunei-s,
taihunei-s*. More on this point hereafter.

127. Of the semi-vowels (*y, r, l, v*), I have never
found in Sanskrit य *y* and ऌ *l* at the end of bases, and
व *v* only in the word दिव् *div*, before mentioned, which
contracts itself in several cases to द्यौ *dyô* and द्यु *dyu*. On
the other hand, र occurs very frequently, especially in
words which are formed by the suffix तर् *tar*,[*] to which, in
the cognate languages, likewise correspond bases in *r*.
Moreover, *r* in Latin appears frequently as an alteration
of an original *s*, as, in the comparative suffix *ior* (Sanskrit ईयस् *íyas*); and, further, as an abbreviation of *ri-s,
re*, as *l* for *li-s, le*; or, in the second declension, as abbreviated from *ru-s*; as in Gothic, *vair*, "man," for *vair(a)s*,
belongs to bases in *a* (§. 116.). In Greek 'ΑΛ appears as a
consonantal base; but in contrast with the   [G. Ed. p. 152.]
Sanskrit सलिल *salila*, "water," ἅλ-ς appears abbreviated
exactly in the same manner as μέγα-ς from μεγαλος.

128. Of the Sanskrit sibilants, the two first (श *ś*, ष *sh*),
as also the ह *h*, are found only in radical words, and therefore seldom; स *s*, on the contrary, concludes some very
common suffixes used in the formation of words, as अस् *as*,
which forms principally neuters, *e.g.* तेजस् *têjas*, "splendour,"
"strength," from तिज् *tij*, "to sharpen." The Greek appears to be without bases in Σ; this, however, proceeds
from the following reason, that this sibilant between two

---

[*] Bases in अर् *ar* in several cases, and in the primary form also at the
beginning of compounds, contract the syllable अर् *ar* to ऋ *ri*; and this
ऋ *ri* is regarded by the Grammarians as their proper final sound. (ʃ. 1.)

vowels, especially in the last syllable, is usually rejected;
hence, neuters like μένος, γένος (from ΜΕΝΕΣ, ΓΕΝΕΣ,
with change of the ε into ο), form in the genitive μένεος,
γένεος, for μένεσος, γένεσος.   The ς of the nominative,
however, belongs, as I have already elsewhere remarked,
to the base, and not to the case designation, as neuters
have no ς in the nominative.   In the dative plural, however, in the old epic language, the Σ, as it did not stand
between two vowels, maintained itself; hence τεύχεσ-σι,
ὄρεσ-σι; so likewise in compounds, like σακές-παλος, τελες-
φόρος, in which it would be wrong to assume the annexation
of a Σ to the vowel of the base.   In γῆρας, γήρα-ος, for
γήρασ-ος, after restoring the Σ of the base, the form of word
answers exactly to the Sanskrit जरस् *jaras*, "age," although
the Indian form is not neuter, but feminine.   In Lithuanian, another remarkable remnant of the Sanskrit suffixes
terminating with s has been preserved, viz. in the partic.
perf., in the oblique cases of which *us* corresponds to the
Sanskrit उष् *ush* (euphonic for उस् *us*) of the weakest cases
(§. 130.); still, in Lithuanian, on account of the above-
noticed incapacity for the declension of the consonants, the
old *us* is conducted, as in other similar cases, by the subsequent addition of *ia*, *a* or *i*, partly into the *a*, partly into the
[G. Ed. p. 163.] *i* declension; and only the nominative and
the vocative, which is the same with it, belong, in the singular,
to the consonantal declension.

129. The Sanskrit and Zend have eight cases, viz. besides those which exist in Latin, an instrumental and a
locative.   These two cases exist also in Lithuanian;
Ruhig calls the former the instrumental ablative, the latter
the local ablative; in Lithuanian, however, the proper ablative—which in Sanskrit expresses the relation " whence?"—
is wanting.   With reference to the primary form, which
in Sanskrit does not remain the same in all words, or

suffixes used in the formation of words through all the cases, a division of the cases into strong and weak is desirable for this language. The strong cases are the nominative, accusative, and vocative of the three numbers, with exception of the accusative plural, which, together with all the other cases, is weak. Where a double or triple formation of the primary form exists, there, with surprising regularity, the cases which have been designated as strong always exhibit the fullest form of the theme, which, from a comparison of languages, is proved to be the original one; while the other cases exhibit a weakened form of it, which appears also in the beginning of compounds, and hence is represented by the native Grammarians, according to §. 122., as the proper primary form. The pres. part. may serve as an example: it forms the strong cases with the suffix *ant*, but in the weak cases and in the beginning of compounds rejects *n*, which is retained by the cognate European languages, as also, for the most part, by Zend; so that बत् *at* is given as the suffix of this participle in preference to बत् *ant*. The root तुद् *tud*, "to vex," *e.g.* exhibits in the participle mentioned the form तुदन् *tu-dant* as the strong and original theme (cf. *tundent-em*), and तुदत् *tudat* as the weak theme; hence the masculine is declined,   [G. Ed. p. 154.]

		STRONG CASES.	WEAK CASES.
Singular :	Nom. Voc.	तुदन् *tudan*	. . . . . .
	Acc.	तुदन्तम् *tudantam*	. . . . . .
	Instr.	. . . . . .	तुदता *tudatá.*
	Dat.	. . . . . .	तुदते *tudaté.*
	Abl.	. . . . . .	तुदतस् *tudatas.*
	Gen.	. . . . . .	तुदतस् *tudatas.*
	Loc.	. . . . . .	तुदति *tudati.*
Dual :	Nom. Acc. Voc.	तुदन्तौ *tudantáu*	. . . . . .
	Instr. Dat. Abl.	. . . . . .	तुदद्भ्याम् *tudadbhyám.*
	Gen. Loc.	. . . . . .	तुदतोस् *tudatós.*

	STRONG CASES.	WEAK CASES.
Plural: Nom. Voc. . . .	तुदन्तस् *tudantas*	
Acc.	. . . . . .	तुदतस् *tudatas.*
Instr.	. . . . . .	तुदद्भिस् *tudadbhis.*
Dat. Abl.	. . . . . .	तुदद्भ्यस् *tudadbhyas.*
Gen.	. . . . .	तुदताम् *tudatâm.*
Loc.	. . . . . .	तुदत्सु *tudatsu.*

130. Where three formations of the primary form per-
vade the declension of a word or a suffix, the weakest form
of the theme there occurs in those weak cases whose terminations begin with a vowel, the middle form before those case-
suffixes which commence with a consonant. This rule makes
a division of the cases into strong, weaker or middle, and
weakest, desirable. (See Gramm. Crit. r. 185.)

131. In suffixes used in the formation of words, which in
Sanskrit separate into different forms, the Zend usually carries
the strong form through all the cases; for instance, the part.
pres. retains the nasal in most of the cases, which in Sanskrit
[G. Ed. p. 155.] proceed from the weakened theme. Words,
however, are not wanting which follow the theory of the
Sanskrit gradations of form. Thus, the Sanskrit base
श्वन् *śwan*, "hound," which in the weakest cases is contracted to शुन् *śun*, appears in Zend likewise in a double
form, and presents the weak genitive *śûn-ô* over against
the strong nominative and accusative *śpâ*, *śpân-ĕm*, Sanskrit श्वा *śwâ*, श्वानम् *śwânam* (§. 50.). The base *ap*, "water,"
which, in Sanskrit, in the strong cases has a long *â*, but
is not used in the singular, forms in the Zend the strong
sing. nom. ᵃⁿⁱ *âfs* (§. 40.), accus. ᵃⁿⁱ *âpĕm;* on the
other hand, *ap-ô*, "of the water," *ap-at*, "from the water," &c.*

---

* This word occurs in the Codex of the V. S., edited by Burnouf, very
frequently, and mostly with that quantity of the initial *a* which is
required by the theory; so that where that is not the case it can only
be imputed to an error in writing.

In the plural, where the Zend very frequently makes the nominative and accusative the same, confusion has, for this reason, crept in; and the weak ڛۏۑ *sûnô*, "*canes,*" is found for ڛۏۑ *spâno* in the nominative; and, on the other hand, the strong ڛۏ *ápô*, in the nominative as well as in the accusative.*

132. The Greek, in the declension of κύων, has limited the strong form to the nom. and voc. sing.: in   [G. Ed. p. 156.] some cognate words in ρ, however, in accordance with the Sanskrit, it has given the accusative also the strong form, in which the Gothic agrees with it. Compare πατήρ, πατέρα, πάτερ, πατρί, with पिता *pitá*, पितरम् *pitaram*, पितर् *pitar*, पितरि *pitri* (locat.); and the Gothic *brôthar*, as nom., accus., and vocat., opposed to *brôthrs*, "of the brother," *brôthr*, "to the brother," with the Sanskrit भ्राता *bhrátá*, भ्रातरम् *bhrátaram*, भ्रातर् *bhrátar*, dative भ्रात्रे *bhrátré*, locat. भ्रातरि *bhrátri*. According to the same principle in bases in *an*, in Gothic, the *a* in the genitive and dative sing. is weakened to *i* (§. 140.); while the nominative, accus., and vocat. retain the original *a*; *e. g.* *ahma, ahmin-s, ahmin, ahman, ahma,* from *AHMAN,* "spirit" (§. 140.).

133. As regards the mode of combining the final vowels of the primary forms with case-suffixes beginning with a vowel, we must first draw attention to a phenomenon, which is almost limited to the Sanskrit, and the dialects which

---

* I have, however, found also ڛۏ *apô* in the accusative; and am therefore in doubt, whether in this word, owing to the facile exchange of ۑ *a* and ۏ *á*, the confusion has not originated in mere graphical oversights. Thus, V. S. p. 21, we find: ڛۏۑ *ápô vanhuis vahistáo mazda-dhátáo ashaonis áyésé*, "*aquas puras, optimas, ab Ormuzdo creatas, mundas celebro*"; and ڛۏ *vîspáo ápô*, "*omnes aquas.*" On the other hand, in the page following: *imáo apas-cha zémas-cha urardós-cha áyésé,* "*has aquasque terrasque arboresque celebro.*"

L

approximate most nearly to it, as Pâli and Prâkṛit, through which, to avoid a hiatus, and to maintain pure the vowels of the base and of the termination, a euphonic *n* is introduced. This euphonic expedient cannot, in the extent in which it exists in Sanskṛit, belong to the original state of the language; otherwise it would not be almost entirely lost in the cognate European dialects, and even in the Zend. We therefore regard it as a peculiarity of the dialect, which, after the period of the division of languages, became the prevailing one in India, and has raised itself to be the universal written language in that country. It is necessary here to remark, that the Vêda language did not use the euphonic *n* so universally as the common Sanskṛit; and together with एना *énâ*, इना *inâ*, उना *unâ*, occur also अया *ayâ*, इया *iyâ*, उया *uyâ*. The euphonic *n* is most frequently employed by the neuter

[G. Ed. p. 157.] gender, less so by the masculine, and most rarely by the feminine: the latter limits its use to the plural genitive termination आम् *âm*, in which place it is introduced by the Zend also, although not as indispensably requisite. And it is remarkable, that precisely in this place in Old High German, and other Old German dialects, an *n* has been retained before the case-suffix; thus in Old High German, *ahô-n-ô,* " *aquarum*," from the feminine theme *AHŌ* (nom. *aha*). Besides the use of the euphonic *n*, there is further to be remarked, in Sanskṛit and Zend, the attachment of Guna to the vowels of the base (§. 26.) in certain cases, to which also the Gothic presents analogies.

SINGULAR.

NOMINATIVE.

134. Bases, of the masculine and feminine genders, ending with a vowel have, in the Sanskṛit family of languages, (under the limitation of §. 137.) *s* as nominative-suffix, which in Zend, after an *a* preceding it, always melts into *u*, and is then contracted with the *a* to *ô* (§. 2.), while this in Sanskṛit

takes place only before sonant letters (§. 25.)* Examples
are given at §. 148. I find the origin of this case-designation
in the pronominal base स sa, " he," "this," fem. सा sá; and
a convincing proof of this assertion is the fact, that the said
pronoun does not extend beyond the limits of the nom. masc.
and fem., but is replaced in the nom. neuter, and in the
oblique cases of the masculine, by त ta, and feminine ता
tá regarding which more hereafter.

135. The Gothic suppresses a and i be- [G. Ed. p. 158.]
fore the case-suffix s, except in monosyllabic bases, where
this suppression is impossible. Hva-s, " who ?" i-s, " he," are
used, but vulf-s, " wolf," gast-s, "stranger," for vulfa-s, gasti-s
(cf hosti-s, according to §. 87.). In masculine substantive
bases in ja (ya), however, the final vowel is retained, only
weakened to i (§. 66.); e. g. haryi-s, "army." If, however,
as is generally the case, the final syllable is preceded by a
long syllable, or by more than one, the ji (yi) is contracted
to ei (=î, §. 70.); e.g. ondei-s, " end," raginei-s, " counsel,"
for andyi-s, raginyi-s. This contraction extends also to the
genitive, which is in like manner denoted by s. To the
Gothic nominatives in yi-s correspond the Lithuanian, like
Atpirktoyi-s, "Saviour," the i of which has likewise arisen
from an elder a.† I deduce this from the majority of the
oblique cases, which agree with those of the a bases.
Where, however, in Lithuanian, a consonant precedes
the final syllable ya, which is the more common case,
there the y is changed into the vowel i, and the following i, which had arisen from a, is suppressed: hence,
yaunikki-s, "young man," for yaunikkyi-s from yaunikkya-s.
Hereto correspond in Gothic all adjective bases in ya,‡

* E g. सुतो मम sutó mama, "filius meus," सुतस् तव sutas tava, "filius tuus" (j. 22.).

† Through the influence of the y, in accordance with a Zend law of
euphony (§. 42.).

‡ Respecting the nom. e. g. of Gothic bases in ya, see p. 1309 G. Ed.,
Remark.

L 2

as *midi-s* "the middle" (man), for *midyi-s* from *midya-s*,
Sanskrit मध्यस् *madhya-s*, The Zend also, in the *vocalization** of the syllable *ya*, presents a remarkable analogy
to the Lithuanian and Gothic in contracting the syllable
ауٮ *ya* before a final ᶜ *m* regularly to ؟ *i*, as also ᴗᶜ *va*
to ؟ *û* (§. 42.).

136. The High German has, up to our time, preserved
the old nominative sign in the changed form of *r*; nevertheless, as early as in the Old High German, in pronouns
and adjectives only, with a vowel termination of the base.
[G. Ed. p. 159.]   The High German is, however, in this
point, superior to the Gothic in fulness, that in its *a* bases—
to which belong all strong adjectives—it has not suppressed
the vowel before the case-sign, but preserved it in the form
of *e*, which, in Old High German—as it appears through
the influence of the *r*—is long, but only in polysyllabic,
not in monosyllabic forms.   Thus, *e. g. plint-êr*, "*cæcus*,"
completes the Gothic *blind-s* for *blinda-s*; as to the Gothic
i-s, "he," corresponds *i-r*; Middle and New High German
e-r.   The Old Northern has likewise *r* as the nominative sign, and, in fact, everywhere where, in Gothic, *s*
stands.   In the other dialects the nominative character is
entirely lost.

137. Feminine Sanskrit bases in आ *â*, and, with very
few exceptions, polysyllables in इ *î*, together with स्त्री *strî*,
"wife," like the corresponding forms of the cognate languages, have lost the old nominative sign (with the exception
of the Latin *ê* bases, see §. 121.), and give the pure base : the
cognate languages do the same, the base having been weakened by the abbreviation of the final vowel.   In Gothic, *ô* becomes *a* (§. 69.); only *sô*, "this," and *hwô* "which?" remain
unshortened, on account of their being monosyllabic, as in
Zend ᴗᴗᴗ *hâ* and ᴗᴗ₎ *kâ* ; while in polysyllabic forms the

---

* I have used *vocalization* and *vocalize* to express the change of a semi-
vowel to its corresponding vowel.—*Trans.*

ᴍ *á* is shortened.   In Zend, ⸗ *í* also is shortened, even in
the monosyllabic ᴣᴍ *itrí*, "wife," see V. S. par. 136, (by
Olshausen), p. 28, where we read ᴍᴣᴍ *itri-cha*, "*femi-
naque*"; whilst elsewhere the appended ᴍᴇ *cha* preserves
the original length of the vowel.   Here, too, the Zend nominatives in ᴊᴇ *é* deserve to be mentioned, which seem very
similar to the Greek in *η*; as ᴊᴇᴣᴇ *pĕrĕné*, "*plena*," which
in the Vendidâd occurs very often in relation to ᴇᴍᴄ *záo*,
"earth," without my being able to remember that I have
found another case from ᴊᴇᴣᴇ *pĕrĕné*.   But from the
nom. ᴊᴊᴍᴄ *kainé*, "maid" (Sanskrit क्न्या [G. Ed. p. 160.]
kanyá), which is of frequent occurrence, I find the accus.
ᴇᴣᴊᴊᴍᴄ *kanyaṅm* (V. S. p. 420); this furnishes the proof
that the ᴊᴇ *é* in the nominative is generated by the euphonic influence of the suppressed ᴊᴊ *y* (§. 42.).   In ᴊᴊᴣᴍᴣ
bráturyé, "cousin," and ᴊᴊᴣᴣᴇ *túiryé*, "a relation in the
fourth degree" (V. S. p. 380), the ᴊᴊ *y* has remained; on
the other hand, in ᴊᴇᴍᴊᴊ *nyáké*, "grandmother," the
dropping of a ᴊᴊ *y* must be again assumed.   We cannot
here refrain from conjecturing that the *ē* also of the Latin
fifth declension, as with very few exceptions it is everywhere
preceded by an *i*, is likewise produced from *ā* by the influence of this *i*; so that the Latin here stands in reversed
relation to the Greek, where *ι* rejects the combination with
η, and preserves the original *α* (σοφία).

138. Bases of the masculine and feminine genders which
terminate with a consonant, lose, in Sanskrit, according to
§. 94., the nominative sign *s*; and if two consonants terminate the base, then, according to the same law, the latter of
these also is lost.   Hence, विभ्रत् *bibhrat*, for विभ्रत्स् *bibhrat-s*,
"the bearer"; तुदन् *tudan*, for तुदन्स् *tudant-s* "the vexer";
वाक् *vák* (from वाच् *vách*, f.), for वाक्ष् *vák-sh*, "speech."
The Zend, Greek, and Latin, in preserving the nominative
sign after consonants, stand in an older position than the
Sanskrit; Zend ᴍᴊᴍ *áf-s* (for *áp-s*, §. 40.), "water"

ᴍᴏᴅᴄ̓ᴇᴐ *k͏̈refs,* " body "; ᴍᴏᴏ̃ᴐᴌᴐ *druc-s* (from the base *druj*),
" a demon." The Latin and Greek, where the final consonant of the base will not combine with the *s* of the nominative, prefer abandoning a portion of the base, as χάρις for
χάριτ-ς, *comes* for *comit-s* (cf. § 6.). The Latin, Æolic, and
Lithuanian agree remarkably with the Zend in this point,
[G. Ed. p. 161.] that *nt,* in combination with *s,* gives the
form *ns;* thus *amans,* τιθένς, Lith. *sukans* (§. 10.), correspond to the Zend ᴊᴐᴧᴊᴊᴊᴧ»ᴍᴌᴧ *śrâvayans,* " the speaking "
(man).

139. A final *n* after a short vowel is, in Sanskṛit, no
favourite combination of sound, although one not prohibited.
It is expelled from the theme in the first member of a
compound, *e.g.* राजपुत्र *râja-putra,* " king's son," for राजन्पुत्र
rajan-putra ; and it is rejected in the nominative also, and
a preceding short vowel is lengthened in masculines ;
e.g. राजा *râjâ,* " king," from राजन् *râjan,* m. ; नाम *nâma,*
" name," from नामन् *nâman,* n. ; धनी *dhani,* m., धनि *dhani,* n.,
from धनिन् *dhanin,* "rich." The Zend in this agrees exactly
with the Sanskṛit ; but from the dislike to a long *a* at the
end, which has been before mentioned, omits the lengthening of the vowel ; *e.g.* ᴧᴊ»ᴧᴠᴋᴜᴊᴧ *ashava,* " the pure " (man),
from ⌐ᴧᴊ»ᴧᴠᴋᴜᴊᴧ *ashavan,* m. ; ᴧᴄ̧ᴋᴜᴊᴧᴪ *chashma,* " eye," from
⌐ᴧᴄ̧ᴋᴜᴊᴧᴪ *chashman,* n. The Latin follows the Sanskṛit in
the suppression of the *n* in the nominative, in the masculine, and feminine, but not in the neuter: *sermo,*
sermon-is, actio, action-is; but *nomen,* not *nome* or *nomo.*
The root *can* at the end of compounds, refrains from
rejecting the *n,* probably in order not to weaken still more
this weak radical syllable; thus *tubi-cen, fidi-cen, os-cen* (see
§. 6.). *Lien* is an abbreviation of *lieni-s ;* hence the retention of the *n* is not surprising. *Pecten* stands rather
isolated. In Sanskṛit the naked roots also follow the principle of the rejection of *n;* हन् "slaying," "smiting,"
nom. हा *hâ,* is, however, the only root in *n* which I have

met with so used. चन् *śwan* "hound," nom. चा *śwá*, which, in the weakest cases, contracts its theme to मुन् *śun*, is of obscure origin. The Latin has extended the base चन् *śwan*, in the nominative, by an unorganic addition, to *cani*; so युवन् *yuvan*, "young," has become *juveni* (cf. §. 126.). As regards the opposition [G. Ed. p. 162.] between *o* and *i*, by which, in several words—as *homo, homin- -is, arundo, arundin-is*—the nominative is distinguished from the oblique cases, this *o* appears to me a stronger vowel,* which compensates for the loss of the *n*, and therefore is substituted for the weaker *i*; according to the same principle by which, in Sanskṛit, the nom. चनी *dhaní,*† comes from धनिन् *dhanin*; and, in Lithuanian, bases in *en* and *un* give, in the nominative, *ŭ* (= *uo*) for *e* or *u*. Thus, from the bases *AKMEN*, "stone," *SZUN*, "hound," come the nominatives *akmŭ, szŭ*; as in Sanskṛit, from the primary forms of the same signification, चश्मन् *aśman*, चन् *śwan*, have arisen चश्मा *aśmá* and च *śwá*. It does not follow that *homin-is* has come from *homon-is*,‡ because the old language had *hemo, hemonis*, for *homo, hominis*; but *mon* and *min* are cognate suffixes, signifying the same, and were originally one, and therefore may be simultaneously affixed to one and the same word.

140. The German language also rejects a final *n* of the base in the nominative and in the neuter, in the accu-

---

* Although its quantity in the actual condition of the language is arbitrary, still it appears to have been originally long, and to imply a similar contrast to the Greek ην, εν-ος; ων, ον-ος. For the rest it has been already remarked, that between short vowels also exists a difference of gravity (§. 6.).

† In bases in चन् *an* the lengthening extends to all the strong cases, with the exception of the vocat. sing.; thus, not merely राजा *rájá*, "*rex*," but also राजानम् *ráján-am*, "*regem*," राजानस् *rájánas*, "*reges*."

‡ I now prefer taking the *i* of *homin-is*, &c., as the weakening of the *o* of *homo*. The relation resembles that of Gothic forms like *ahmin-is, ahmin*, to the nom and acc. *ahma, ahman*, which preserve the original vowel.

sative also, like Sanskrit.   In Gothic, in the masculine
and neuter—where alone, in my opinion, the *n* has an
old and original position—an *a* always precedes the *n*.
There are, that is to say, only bases in *an*, none in *in* and
un; the latter termination is foreign to the Sanskrit also.
[G. Ed. p. 163.]   The *a*, however, is weakened to *i* in the
genitive and dative (see §. 132.); while in Sanskrit, in these
cases, as especially in the weakest cases (§. 130.), it is entirely
dropped.*   Among masculine bases in *an*, in Gothic, exist
several words, in which *an* is the whole derivative-suffix,
and which therefore correspond to the Sansk. राजन् *ráj-an*,
"king," as "ruler."   Thus *AH-AN*, "spirit," as "thinker"
(*ah-ya*, "I think"), *STAU-AN*, "Judge" (*stau-ya*, "I judge"),
whence the nominatives *aha*, *staua*.   There are also, as in
Sanskrit, some masculine formations in *man*; as, *AHMAN*,
"spirit," nom. *ahma*, with which perhaps the Sansk. आत्मन्
átman, "soul," nom. आत्मा *átmá*, is connected; in case this
stands for *áh-man*, and comes from a lost root आह् *áh*,
"to think,"† where it is to be remembered that also the
root नह् *nah*, "to bind," has, in several places, changed its
h into *t*.   The Gothic *MILH-MAN*, nom. *milh-ma*, "cloud,"
appears to have sprung from the Sanskrit root *mih*, by the
addition of an *l*, whence, remarkably enough, by the suffix
a, and by exchanging the ह *h* for घ *gh*, arises the nominal base मेघ *mégha*, "cloud."   In Latin *ming-o* answers to
मिह् *mih*, and in Greek ὀ-μιχ-έω; the meaning is in the
three languages the same.

141. Neuter bases in *an*, after rejecting the *n*, lengthen,
in Gothic, the preceding *a* to *ó*, in the nominative, accusa-

---

* In case two consonants do not precede the termination अन् *an*;
e. g. आत्मन-अस् *átman-as*, not *átmn-as*, but नाम्नस् *námn-as*, not *náman-as*,
"*nominis*."

† Perhaps identical with the actually-occurring आह् *áh*, "to speak," as
मन् *man*, "to think," in Zend means also "to speak"; whence ᠊ᠣᠺᠣᡉᡑᡉ
manthra, "speech," and in Gothic *MUN-THA*, nom. *munths*, "mouth"
ᵍ. 66.).

tive, and vocative, which sound the same; [G. Ed. p. 164.]
so that in these cases the Gothic neuter follows the theory of
the strong cases (§. 129.), which the Sanskrit neuter obeys
only in the nom., accus., and vocat. plural, where, for example, चत्वारि *chatwár-i*, "four," with a strong theme, is
opposed to the weak cases like चतुर्भिस् *chaturbhis* (instr.),
चतुर्भ्यस् *chaturbhyas*. The *a*, also, of neuter bases in *an* is
lengthened in the nominative, accusative, and vocative plural
in Sanskrit, and in Gothic; and hence नामानि *námán-i*,
Gothic *namón-a*, run parallel to one another. However, in
Gothic *namn-a* also exists, according to the theory of the
Sanskrit weakest cases (§. 130.), whence proceeds the plural
genitive नाम्नाम् *námn-ám*, "*nominum*"; while the Gothic
namón-ê has permitted itself to be led astray by the example
of the strong cases, and would be better written *namn-ê* or
namin-ê.

142. In the feminine declension in German I can find
no original bases in *n*, as also in Sanskrit there exist no
feminines in *an* or *in*; but feminine bases are first formed
by the addition of the usual feminine character ई *í*; as,
राज्ञी *rájní*, "queen," from राजन् *rájan*; धनिनी *dhaniní*, "the
rich" (fem.), from धनिन् *dhanin*, m. n. "rich." Gothic feminine substantive bases in *n* exhibit, before this consonant,
either an *ó* (= वा, §. 69.) or *ei*: these are genuine feminine
final vowels, to which the addition of an *n* can have been
only subsequently made. And already, at §. 120., a close
connection of bases in *ein* (= *ín*) with the Sanskrit in ई *í*,
and Lithuanian in *i*, has been pointed out. Most substantive bases in *ein* are feminine derivatives from masculine-
neuter adjective bases in *a*, under the same relation, excluding the modern *n*, as in Sanskrit that of सुन्दरी *sundarí*,
"the fair" (woman), from सुन्दर *sundara* m. n. "beautiful."
Gothic substantive bases in *ein* for the most part raise
the adjective, whence they are derived, to an abstract;

---

* Vide p. 1083, Note.

[G. Ed. p. 165.]　*e.g. MANAGEIN,* "crowd, nom. *managei,* from the adjective base *MANAGA* (nominative masc. *manag-s,* neut. *managa-ta*); *MIKILEIN,* nom. *mikilei,* "greatness," from *MIKILA* (*mikil-s, mikila-ta*), "great." As to feminine bases in *ôn,* they have arisen from feminine bases in *ô*; and I have already observed that feminine adjective bases in *ôn*—as *BLINDŌN,* nom. *blindô,* gen. *blindôn-s*—must be derived, not from their masculine bases in *an,* but from the primitive feminine bases in *ô* (nom. *u,* Grimm's strong adjectives). Substantive bases with the genitive feminine in *ôn* presuppose older ones in *ô*; and correspond, where comparison is made with old languages connected in their bases, to Sanskrit feminines in *â,* Greek in *α, η,* Latin in *a*; and in these old languages never lead to bases with a final *n.* Thus, *TUGGŌN* (pronounced *tungôn*), nom. *tuggô,* answers to the Latin *lingua,* and to the Sanskrit जिह्वा *jihwâ,* (= *dschihwâ,* see §. 17.); and *DAURŌN,* nom. *daurô,* to the Greek *θύρα*; *VIDŌVŌN,* nom. *vidôvô,* "widow," to the Sanskrit विधवा *vidhawâ,* "the without man" (from the prep. वि *vi* and धव *dhava,* "man"), and the Latin *vidua.* It is true that, in *MITATHYŌN,* "measure," nom. *mitathyô,* the suffix *thyôn* completely answers to the Latin *tion, e.g.* in *ACTION;* but here in Latin, too, the *on* is a later addition, as is evinced from the connection of *ti-on* with the Sanskrit suffix ति *ti,* of the same import, and Greek *σι-ς* (old *τις*), Gothic *ti, thi, di* (see §. 91.). And in Gothic, together with the base *MITATHYŌN* exists one signifying the same, *MI-TATHI,* nom. *mitaths.* In *RATHYŌN,* nom. *rathyô,* "account," a relationship with *RATION,* at least in respect of the suffix, is only a seeming one; for in Gothic the word is [G. Ed. p. 166.] to be divided thus, *rath-yôn*: the *th* belongs, in the Gothic soil, to the root, whence the strong part. *rath-an(a)-s* has been preserved. The suffix *yôn,* of *RATHYŌN* therefore corresponds to the Sanskrit *yâ; e.g.* in विद्या *vid-yâ,* "knowledge." Of the same origin is *GA-RUN-YŌN,* nom. *garunyô,* "inundation."

143. If a few members of a great family of languages have suffered a loss in one and the same place, this may be accident, and may be explained on the general ground, that all sounds, in all languages, especially when final, are subject to abrasion; but the concurrence of so many languages in a loss in one and the same place points to relationship, or to the high antiquity of such a loss; and in the case before us, refers the rejection of an *n* of the base in the nominative to a period before the migration of languages, and to the position of the original site of the human races, which were afterwards separated. It is surprising, therefore, that the Greek, in this respect, shews no agreement with its sisters; and in its *v* bases, according to the measure of the preceding vowel, abandons either merely the nominative sign, or the *v* alone, never both together. It is a question whether this is a remnant of the oldest period of language, or whether the *v* bases, carried away by the stream of analogies in the other consonantal declensions, and by the example of their own oblique cases, which do not permit the remembrance of the *v* to be lost, again returned, at a comparatively later period, into the common and oldest path, after they had experienced a similar loss to the Sanskrit, Zend, &c., by which we should be conducted to nominative forms like εὐδαίμω, εὐδαιμο, τέρη, τέρε, τάλᾱ, τάλᾰ? I do not venture to decide with positiveness on this point, but the latter view appears to be the more probable. It here deserves to be   [G. Ed. p. 167.] remarked, that, in German, the *n*, which in Gothic, in the nominative, is always suppressed, has in more modern dialects made its way in many words from the oblique cases again into the nominative. So early as the Old High German this was the case; and, in fact, in feminine bases in *ín* (Gothic *ein*, §. 70.), which, in the nominative, oppose to the Gothic *ei* the full base *ín*: as *guotlihhín*, "glory" (see Grimm, p. 628). In our New High

German the phenomenon is worthy of notice, that many
original *n* bases of the masculine gender, through a confusion in the use of language, are, in the singular, treated
as if they originally terminated in *na;* *i.e.* as if they belonged to Grimm's first strong declension. Hence the *n*
makes its appearance in the nominative, and the genitive
regains the sign *s,* which, indeed, in Gothic, is not wanting in the *n* bases, but in High German was withdrawn
from them more than a thousand years since. Thus,
Brunnen, Brunnens, is used instead of the Old High German *prunno, prunnin,* and the Gothic *hrunna, brunnin-s.*
In some words, together with the restored *n* there occurs in
the nominative, also, the ancient form with *n* suppressed, as
Backe or *Backen, Same* or *Samen;* but the genitive has in
these words also introduced the *s* of the strong declension.
Among neuters the word *Herz* deserves consideration.
The base is, in Old High German, *HERZAN,* in Middle
High German *HERZEN;* the nominatives are, *herza,*
herze; the New German suppresses, together with the
n of *Herzen,* the vowel also, as is done by many masculine *n* bases; as, *e.g.* *Bär* for *Bäre.* As this is not a
transition into the strong declension, but rather a greater
weakening of the weak nominative, the form *Herzens,*
therefore, in the genitive, for an uninflected *Herzen,* is sur-

[G. Ed. p. 168.] prising. With this assumed or newly-re-
stored inflection *s* would be to be compared, in Greek, the
nominative ς, as of δελφί-ς, μέλα-ς; and with the *n* of *Brun-*
nen for *Brunne,* the ν of δαίμων, τέρην; in case, as is rendered probable by the cognate languages, these old forms
have been obtained from still older, as δελφί, μέλα, δαίμω, τέρη.
by an unorganic retrograde step into the stronger declension.*

---

* That, in Greek, the renunciation of a ν of the base is not entirely
unknown may be here shewn by an interesting example. Several
cardinal numbers in Sanskrit conclude their base with न *n;* viz.
panchan,

144. Bases in चर् *ar* (च *ri*, §. 1.) in Sanskrit reject the *r* in the nominative, and, like those in न *n*, lengthen the preceding vowel ; *e. g.* from पितर् *pitar*, " father," भ्रातर् *bhrâtar*, " brother," मातर् *mâtar*, "mother," दुहितर् *duhitar*, "daughter," come पिता *pitâ*, भ्राता *bhrâtâ*, माता *mâtâ*, दुहिता *duhitâ.* The lengthening of the *a* serves, I believe, as a compensation for the rejected *r*. As to the retention, however, through all the strong cases, excepting the vocative, of the long *a* of the agent, which corresponds to Greek formations in τηρ, τωρ, and to Latin in *tōr*, this takes place because, in all probability, in these words तार् *târ*, and not तर् *tar*, is the original form of the suffix; and this is also supported by the length of the suffix being retained in Greek and Latin through all the cases—τηρ, τωρ, *tōr*; only [G. Ed. p. 169.] that in Latin a final *r*, in polysyllabic words, shortens an originally long vowel. Compare

	SANSKRIT.	GREEK.	LATIN.
Nom. sing.	दाता *dâtâ*,	δοτήρ,	*datōr*,
Acc. sing.	दातारम् *dâtâr-am*,	δοτῆρ-α,	*datōr-em*,
N. A. V. dual,	दातारौ *dâtâr-au*,	δοτῆρ-ε,	. . . . . .
Nom. Voc. pl.	दातारस् *dâtâr-as*,	δοτῆρ-ες,	*datōr-es*.

The Zend follows the analogy of the Sanskrit, both in the rejection of the *r* in the nominative, and in the length

---

panchan, " five," *saptan*, " seven," *ashtan* with *ashtau*, " eight," *navan*, " nine," *dasan*, " ten." These numerals are, indeed, used adjectively, when they are not governed by the gender of their substantive, but display always a neuter form, and indeed, which is surprising, in the nominative, accusative, and vocative sing. terminations, but in the other cases the suitable plural endings ; *e. g.* पञ्च राजानस् *pancha* (not *panchânas*) *râjânas* " *quinque reges* "; on the other hand, पञ्चसु राजसु *panchasu râjasu* " *in quinque regibus*." To the neuter nominatives and accusative of the singular पञ्च *pancha*, सप्त *sapta*, नव *nava*, and दश *dasa*—which rest on the regular suppression of the *n*—answer the Greek πέντε, ἑπτά, ἐννέα, δέκα, with the distinction that they have become quite indeclinable, and retain the old uninflected nominative through all the cases.

of the preceding *a* of the noun agent, in the same places
as in the Sanrkrit, with the exception of the nominative singular, where the long *a*, as always when final, is shortened;
e. g. སྤ⁣⁣ *paita,* "father," སྤ⁣⁣ *dâta,* "giver," "Creator;"
acc. ⁣⁣ *paitar-ĕm,* ⁣⁣ *dâtâr-ĕm.*   In Lithua-
nian there are some interesting remains, but only of feminine bases in *er,* which drop this letter in the nominative, but in most of the oblique cases extend the old
er base by the later addition of an *i.*   Thus *motė,* "wife,"
duktė "daughter," answer to the abovementioned माता
mâtâ, दुहिता *duhitâ;* and, in the plural, *moter-ės, dukter-ės,* to
मातरस् *mâtar-as,* दुहितरस् *duhitar-as.*   In the genitive singular I regard the form *moter-s, dukter-s,* as the elder and
more genuine, and *moteriės, dukteriės,* as corruptions belonging to the *i* bases.   In the genitive plural the base
has kept clear of this unorganic *i;* hence, *moter-û, dukter-û,*
not *moteri-û, dukteri-û.*   Besides the words just mentioned,
the base *SESSER,* "sister," belongs to this place: it
answers to the Sanskrit स्वसर् *swasar,* nom. स्वसा *swasâ;* but
distinguishes itself in the nominative from *mote* and *duktr,*
in that the *e,* after the analogy of bases in *en,* passes into *û,*
thus *sessû.*

[G. Ed. p. 170.]   145. The German languages agree in their
r bases (to which but a few words belong denoting affinity)
with the Greek and Latin in this point, that, contrary to the
analogy just described, they retain the *r* in the nominative.
As πατήρ, μητήρ, θυγάτηρ, δαήρ (Sanskrit, देवर् *dêvar,* देवृ *dêvri,*
nom. देवा *dêvâ*), *frater, soror;* so in Gothic, *brôthar, svistar,*
dauhtar; in Old High German, *vatar, pruodar, suёstar, tohtar.*
It is a question whether this *r* in the nominative is a remnant of the original language, or, after being anciently
suppressed, whether it has not again made its way in the
actual condition of the language from the oblique cases
into the nominative.   I think the latter more probable;
for the Sanskrit, Zend, and Lithuanian are three witnesses

for the antiquity of the suppression of the r; and the Greek words like πατήρ, μήτηρ, σωτήρ, ῥήτωρ, exhibit something peculiar and surprising in the consonantal declension, in that ρ and ς not combining, they have not rather preferred giving up the base-consonant than the case-sign (as παῖς, ποῦς, &c.). It would appear that the form της is of later origin, for this reason, that the ρ having given place to the nominative ς, the form τη-ς, whence τηρ-ος should come, was, by an error of language, made to correspond to the η-ς of the first declension. The want of a cognate form in Latin, as in Zend and Sanskrit, as also the, in other respects, cognate form and similarity of meaning with तार tár, tō-r, τηρ and τωρ, speak at least plainly enough for the spuriousness and comparative youth of the nouns of agency in της.

146. Masculine and feminine primary forms in अस् as in Sanskrit lengthen the a in the nominative singular. They are, for the most part, compounded, and contain, as the last member, a neuter substantive in अस् as, as दुर्मनस् durmanas, " evil-minded," from दुस् dus   [G. Ed. p. 171.] (before sonant letters—§. 25.—दुर् dur) and मनस् manas, " mind," whence the nom. masc. and fem. दुर्मनास् durmanás, neut. दुर्मनस् durmanas. A remarkable agreement is here shewn by the Greek, in δυσμενής, ὁ, ἡ opposed to τὸ δυσμενές. The स् s of दुर्मनास् durmanás, however, belongs, though unrecognised, to the base; and the nominative character is wanting, according to §. 94. In Greek, on the other hand, the ς of δυσμενής has the appearance of an inflexion, because the genitive, &c., is not δυσμενεσ-ος, like the Sanskrit दुर्मनस् durmanas-as, but δυσμενέος. If, however, what was said at §. 128 is admitted, that the ς of μένος belongs to the base, and μένεος is abbreviated from μένεσ-ος, then in the compound δυσμενής also, and all similar adjectives, a Σ belonging to the base must be recognised, and the form δυσμενέσος must lie at the bottom of the genitive δυσμενέος. In the

nominative, therefore, either the ç belongs to the base, and then the agreement with दुर्मनास् *durmanás* would be complete; or the ç of the base has been dropped before the case-sign ç. The latter is, in my opinion, least probable; for the former is supported by the Latin also, where the forms which answer to the Sanskrit *as* bases are in the nom. masc. and fem. in like manner without the case-sign. Thus the Sanskrit comparative suffix is ईयस् *íyas*—the last *a* but one of which is lengthened in the strong cases, and invested with a dull nasal (Anuswâra, §. 9.)—in Latin, *iōr*, with the *s* changed into *r*, which so frequently happens; and the nominative in both genders is without the case-sign: the originally long *o*, however, is shortened by the influence of the final *r*. In the neuter *ŭs* corresponds to the Sanskrit अस् *as*, because *u* is favourable to a final *s*, and prevents its transition into *r*; hence *gravius* has the same relation to the Sanskrit गरीयस् *garíyas* (irregular from गुरु *guru*, "heavy,") as *lupus* to

[G. Ed. p. 172.]   वृकस् *vrikas*, only that the *s* of the nominative character in the latter belongs in the former to the base. The final syllable *ŭr*, though short, must nevertheless be held, in Latin, as graver than *ŭs*, and hence *gravior* forms a similar antithesis to *gravius* that in Greek δυσμενής does to δυσμενές, and in Sanskrit दुर्मनास् *durmanás* to दुर्मनस् *durmanas*.

147. In Lithuanian a nominative, which stands quite isolated, *mēnû* (= *mēnuo*), "moon" and "month," deserves here to be mentioned: it proceeds from the primary form *MENES**, and, in regard to the suppression of the final consonant and the transformation of the preceding vowel, has the same relation to it that, as above (§. 139.), *akmû* has

---

* The relation of this to मास् *mâs*, which signifies the same—from मास् *mâs*, "to measure," without a derivative suffix—is remarkable; for the interposed nasal syllable *ne* answers to the Sanskrit न *na* in roots of the seventh class (see p. 118); and in this respect *MENES* bears the same relation to the Latin *MENSI* that l. c. भिनद्मि *bhinadmi* does to *findo*.

to *AKMEN*, *sessŭ* to *SESSER :* in the oblique cases, also, the *s* of the base again re-appears, but receives, as in the *er* and *en* bases, an unorganic increase: thus the genitive is *menesio*, whence *MENESIA* is the theme ; as *wilko*, "*lupi*," from *WILKA*, nom. *wilka-s.*

148. In neuters, throughout the whole Sanskrit family of languages the nominative is identical with the accusative, which subject is treated of at §. 152. &c. We here give a general view of the nominative formation, and select for the several terminations and gender of the primary forms, both for these cases and for all others which suit our purpose, the following examples : Sanskrit वृक *vrika*, m. " wolf ;" क *ka*, " who ?" दान *dâna*, n. " gift ;" त *ta*, n. " this ;" जिह्वा *jihwâ*, f. " tongue ;" का *kâ*, " which ?" पति *pati*, m. " lord," " husband ;" प्रीति *priti*, f. " love ;" वारि *vâri*, n. " water ;" भविष्यन्ती *bhavishyanti*, " who is about to be ;" सूनु *sûnu*, m. " son ;" [G. Ed. p. 173.] तनु *tanu*, f. " body ;" मधु *madhu*, n. " honey," " wine ;" वधू *vadhû*, f. " wife ;" गो *gô*, m. f. " bullock," " cow ;" नौ *nâu*, f. " ship." Of the consonantal declension we select only such final consonants as occur most frequently, whether in single words or in entire classes of words: वाच् *vâch*, f. " speech "*; भरन्त् *bharant*, in the weakened form, भरत् *bharat* (§. 129.) m. n. " bearing," " receiving," from भर *bhar* (भृ *bhri*) cl. 1. ; आत्मन् *âtman*, m. " soul ;" नामन् *nâman*, n. " name ;" भ्रातर् *bhrâtar*, m. " brother ;" दुहितर् *duhitar*, f. " daughter ;" दातर् *dâtar*, m. " giver ;" वचस् *vachas*, n. " speech," Greek, ΕΠΕΣ. ἔπος (§§. 14. 128.), for FEΠEΣ, Fεπος. Zend, வேர்ka *vĕrhka*, m. " wolf ;" ka *ka*, m. " who ?" *dâta*, n. *datum ;* *ta*, n. " this ;" *hizvâ*, f. " tongue ;" *kâ*, " which ?"

---

* Masculines and feminines in the consonantal declension agree in all cases: hence an example of one of the two genders is sufficient. The only exception is the accusative plural of words denoting relationship in ऋर् *ar* (ऋृ, §. 114.), which form this case from the abbreviated theme in ऋ *ri*.

M

ﺳﻮﺳﻮ *paiti*, m. (§. 41.) "Lord;" ﺳﻮﺟﺎﻟﺴﻮ *áfriti*, f. "bless-
ing;" ﻟﺴﻮﻟﺞ *vairi*, n. "water;" ﭘﻮﺳﻮﺳﺪﺩﺩﺳﻮﺝﺩ *búshyainti*,
"who will be;" ﺳﻮﺳﻮ *pasu*, m. "tame animal;" ﺳﺠﻮﺳﻮ *tanu*,
f. "body;" ﺳﻮﻉﺝ *madhu*, n. "wine;" ﻟﺲ *gó*, m. f. "bullock,"
[G. Ed. p. 174.]   "cow"*; ﻣﺴﻮﻟﺞ *vách*, f. "speech," "voice"†;
ﻣﺴﻮﺳﻮﻟﺴﻮ *barant*, or ﻣﺴﻮﺝﻋﻠﺴﻮ *barént*, weakened form ﻣﺴﻮﻟﺴﻮ
barat, m. n. "bearing;" ﺳﻮﻉﺳﺪﺳﻮ *asman*, m. "heaven;" ﺳﻮﻉﺳﻮﺩ
náman (also ﺳﻮﻉﻧﻮﺩ *nańman*), n. "name;" ﻟﺴﻮﻣﺴﻮﻟﺴﻮ *brátar*,‡

---

* It has been remarked at §. 123 of the cognate nom. ﮔﺴﻮﺝ *záo*,
"earth," accus. ﻉﻧﻮﺝ *zańm*, that I have only met with these two cases.
The very common form ﻉﻉﺝ *zĕm*, which is found only in the other
oblique cases, is nevertheless represented by Burnouf, in a very interesting
article in the *Journal des Savans* (Aug. 1832), which I only met with
after that page had been printed, as belonging to the same theme.
I agree with him on this point at present, so much the rather as I believe
I can account for the relationship of ﺭﻭﻉﻉﺝ *zĕmé*, "*terræ*," (dat.) ﺳﻮﻉﻉﺝ
zĕmi, "*in terra*," &c. to the Sanskrit गवे *gavé*, गवि *gavi*. I do not doubt,
that is to say, that, in accordance with what has been remarked at §. 63.
and p. 114, the Zend ﻉ *m* is to be regarded as nothing else than the
hardening of the original *v*. The Indian गो *gó*, before vowel terminations
gav, would consequently have made itself almost unintelligible in the
meaning "earth," in Zend, by a double alteration; first by the transition
of *g* to *z*, in which *j* must be assumed as the middle step—in which
e.g. ﻉﺳﻮﺝ *jam*, "to go," from गम् *gam*, has remained; secondly, by the
hardening of the *v* to *m*. Advert, also, to the Greek δη, for γη, in δημήτηρ;
since δ and ﺝ *z*, from ज *j* (=*dsch*), have so divided themselves in the
sound whence they have sprung, that the Greek has retained the *T*-sound,
the Zend the sibilant.

† I cannot quote the nominative of this word; but it can only be
ﺳﻮﺟﺎﺳﻮﻟﺞ *vác-s*, as palatals before ﺳﻮ *s* change into ﺟﺎ *c*; and thus, from
ﺝﻟﺞ *druj*, "an evil demon," occurs very frequently the nom. ﺳﻮﺟﺎﺝﻟﺞ
druc-s. I have scarcely any doubt, too, that what Anquetil, in his
Vocabulary, writes *váhksch*, and renders by "*parler, cri*," is the nominative of the said base; as Anquetil everywhere denotes ﺟﺎ by *kh*, and
ﺳﻮ by *sch*.

‡ In the theme we drop, intentionally, the ﻉ *ĕ* required by §. 44, as it
is clear that ﻟﺴﻮﻣﺴﻮﻟﺴﻮ *brátar*, not ﻋﻟﺴﻮﻣﺴﻮﻟﺴﻮ *brátarĕ*, must be the base
word; ﻟﺴﻮﻣﺴﻮﻟﺴﻮ *baratar* also occurs, with ﺳﻮ *a* interposed.

m. "brother;" لو ـ ــو dughdhar, f. "daughter;" دلار ddlar, m. "giver," "creator;" وقود vachô, n. (§. 56ᵇ.) "word." It is not requisite to give here examples in Greek and Latin: from Lithuanian and Gothic we select the bases, Lith. *WILKA*, Goth. *VULFA*, m. "wolf;" Lith. *KA*, Goth. *HVA*, m. "who?" Lith. *GERA*, n. "good;" *TA*, n. "the;" Goth. *DAURA*, n. "gate," (Sanskrit, द्वार dwâra, n.); *THA*, n. "this;" Lith. *RANKA*, f. "hand;" Goth, *GIBŌ*, f. "gift" (§. 69.); *HVŌ*, f. "which?"; Lith. *PATI*, m. "Lord"*; Goth. *GASTI*, m. "stranger;" *I*, m. "he," n. [G. Ed. p. 175.] "it;" Lith. *AWI*, f. "sheep," (Sansk. अवि avi, m. cf. ovis, ὄϊς); Goth. *ANSTI*, f."mercy;" Lith. Goth. *SUNU*, m. "son;" Goth. *HANDU*, f. "hand;" Lith. *DARKU*, n. "ugly;" Goth. *FAIHU*, n. "beast;" Lith. *SUKANT*, m.† "turning ; Goth. *FIYAND*, m. "foe;" Lith. *AKMEN*, m. "stone;" Goth. *AHMAN*, m. "spirit;" *NAMAN*, n. "name;" *BRŌTHAR*, m. "brother;" *DAUHTAR*, Lith. *DUKTER*, f. "daughter."

SANSKRIT.	ZEND.	GREEK.	LATIN.	LITHUAN.	GOTHIC.
m. *vrika-s*,	*věhrkô*,‡	λύκο-ς,	*lupu-s*,	*wilka-s*,	*vulf s.*
m. *ka-s*,	*kô*,‡	....	....	*ka-s*,	*hva-s.*

* In the comp. *wiess-pati-s*, "landlord"; isolated *pat-s*, "husband," with *i* in the nominative suppressed, as is the case in Gothic in all bases in *i*. Compare the Zend ويس پيتي *vís-paiti*, "lord of the region."

† These and other bases ending with a consonant are given only in those cases which have remained free from a subsequent vowel addition.

‡ Before the enclitic particle *cha*, as well here as in all other forms, the termination *as*, which otherwise becomes *ô* (§. 56ᵇ.), retains the same form which, in Sanskrit also, अस् *as* assumes before च *cha*: hence is said věhrkaïcha, "lupusque," as in Sanskrit वृकश्च *vrikaïcha*. And the appended *cha* preserves the otherwise shortened final vowel in its original length: hence jihvâcha, "linguaque," bushyaintícha, "futuraque," brátâcha, "fraterque." Even without the at times the original length of the final vowel is found undiminished: the principle of abbreviation, however, remains adequately proved, and I therefore observe it everywhere in the terminations.

SANSKRIT.	ZEND.	GREEK.	LATIN.	LITHUAN.	GOTHIC.
n. dâna-m,	dâtĕ-m,	δῶρο-ν,	donum,	géra,	daur'.
n. ta-t,	ta-t,	τό,	is-tu-d,	ta-i,	tha-ta.
f. jihwâ,	hizva,*	χώρα,	terra,	rankà,	gibu.
f. kâ,	kâ,	....	....	....	hvô.
m. pati-s,	paiti-s,	πόσι-ς,	hosti-s,	pati-s,	gast'-s.
m.	....	....	i-s,	....	i-s.
f. prîti-s,	âfrîti-s	πόρτι-ς,	siti-s,	avi-s,	anst'-s.
n. vâri,	vairi,	ἴδρι,	mare,	....	....
n.	....	....	i-d,	....	i-ta.
f. bhavishyanti, bûshyainti*		....	....	bûsenti,	....
m. sûnu-s,	pusu-s,	ἰχθύ-ς,	pecu-s,	sunù-s,	sunu-s.
f. tanu-s,	tanu-s,	πίτυ-ς,	socru-s,	....	handu-s.
n. madhu,	madhu,	μέθυ,	pecu,	darkù,	faihu.
f. vadhû-s,	....	....	....	....	....
m. f. gâu-s,†	gâu-s,‡	βοῦ-ς,	bô-s,	....	....
f. ndu-s,	....	ναῦ-ς,	....	....	....
f. vâk,	vâc-s,	ὄπ-ς,	voc-s,	....	....
m. bharan,	baran-s,	φέρων,	feren-s,	sukan-s,	fiyand-s·
m. âtmâ,	asma,*	δαίμων,	sermo',	akmâ',	ahma'.
n. nâma',	nâma',	τάλαν,	nomen,	....	namô'.
m. bhrâtâ',	brâta',*	πατήρ,	frater,	....	brôthar.
f. duhitâ',	dughdha,*,	θυγάτηρ,	mater,	duktė,'	dauhtar.
m. dâtâ,	dâta',*	δοτήρ,	dator,	....	....
n. vachas,	vachô,*	ἔπος,	opus,	....	....

[G. Ed. P. 176.]

ACCUSATIVE.

SINGULAR.

149. The character of the accusative is *m* in Sanskṛit, Zend, and Latin; in Greek *ν*, for the sake of euphony. In Lithuanian the old *m* has become still more weakened to

---

* See the marginal note marked (‡) on the foregoing page.

† Irregularly for गोस् *gô-s*.

‡ Or ᵹᴀᴜ *gâos*, §. 33.

the dull re-echoing nasal, which in Sanskrit is called Anu-
[G. Ed. p. 177.] swâra, and which we, in both languages,
express by *n* (§. 10.). The German languages have, so early
as the Gothic even, lost the accusative mark in substantives
entirely, but in pronouns of the 3d person, as also in adjective bases ending with a vowel which follow their declension, they have hitherto retained it; still only in the
masculine: the feminine nowhere exhibits an accusative
character, and is, like its nominative, devoid of inflexion.
The Gothic gives *na* instead of the old *m*; the High
German, with more correctness, a simple *n*: hence, Gothic
blind-na, " *cæcum,*" Old High German *plinta-n,* Middle and
Modern High German *blinde-n.*

150. Primary forms terminating with a consonant prefix
to the case-sign *m* a short vowel, as otherwise the combination would be, in most cases, impossible: thus, in Sanskrit *am,* in Zend and Latin *ĕm,* appears as the accusative
termination*: of the Greek- *αν,* which must originally have
existed, the *ν* is, in the present condition of the language,
lost: examples are given in §. 157.

151. Monosyllabic words in *i, û,* and *du,* in Sanskrit,
like consonantal bases, give *am* in place of the mere *m,* as
the accusative termination, probably in order in this way
to become polysyllabic. Thus, भी *bhí,* " fear," and नौ *ndu,*
" ship," form, not *bhî-m* and *ndu-m,* as the Greek *ναῦ-ν* would

---

* From the bases ꝺ꜀꜀ *druj* and ꝺ꜀꜀ *vâch,* I find besides ꝺ꜀꜀ꝺ꜀
drujĕm, ꝺ꜀꜀ *vâchĕm,* in the V. S.; also frequently ꝺ꜀꜀ꝺ꜀ *drujim,*
ꝺ꜀꜀ *vâchim:* and if these forms are genuine, which I scarcely doubt,
they are to be thus explained—that the vowel which stands before *m* is
only a means of conjunction for appending the *m*; for this purpose, however, the Zend uses, besides the ꜀ *ĕ* mentioned at §. 30, not unfrequently
ꝺ *i*; *e g* for ꝺ꜀꜀ *dadĕmahi,* occurs also ꝺ꜀꜀ *dadimahi,*
and many similar forms; as ꝺ꜀꜀ *ui-i-mahi,* answering to the Sanskrit उश्मस् *uśmas* (in the Vêdas उश्मसि *uśmasi*), "we will."

[G. Ed. p. 178.]   lead us to expect, but मियम् *bhiy-am,* नावम् *nâv-am.* With this agree the Greek themes in ευ, since these give ε-α, from εF-α, for ευ-ν; *e.g.* βασιλέ(F)α, for βασιλευ-ν. It is, however, wrong to regard the Latin *em* as the true, originally sole accusative termination, and for *lupu-m, hora-m, fruc-tum, diem,* to seek out an older form *lupo-em, hora-em, fructu-em, die-em.* That the simple nasal suffices to characterize the accusative, and that a precursory vowel was only added out of other necessary reasons, is proved by the history of our entire family of languages, and would be adequately established, without Sanskrit and Zend, by the Greek, Lithuanian, and Gothic. The Latin *em* in the accusative third declension is of a double kind: in one case the *e* belongs to the base, and stands, as in innumerable cases, for *i*; so that *e-m,* of *igne-m* (Sanskrit अग्निम् *ayni-m*), corresponds to the Indian *i-m,* Zend *i-m,* Greek *ι-ν,* Lithuanian *i-ù,* Gothic *i-na* (from *ina,* "him"); but in the *em* of consonantal bases the *e* answers to the Indian *a,* to which it corresponds in many other cases also.

152. The Sanskrit and Zend neuter bases in *a,* and those akin to them in Greek and Latin, as well as the two natural genders, give a nasal as the sign of the accusative, and introduce into the nominative also this character, which is less personal, less animated, and is hence appropriated to the accusative as well as to the nominative in the neuter : hence, Sansk. शयनम् *śayana-m,* Zend ﻉ *śayanĕ-m,* "a bed"; so in Latin and Greek, *donu-m, δῶρο-ν.* All other bases, with but few exceptions, in Latin, remain in the nominative and accusative without any case character, and give the naked base, which in Latin, however, replaces a final *i* by the cognate *e*; thus, *mare* for *mari* corre-

[G Ed. p. 179.]   sponds to the Sanskrit वारि *vâri,* "water"; the Greek, like the Sanskrit and Zend, leaves the *ι* unchanged —ἴδρι-ς, ἴδρι, as in Sanskrit शुचिस् *śuchis,* शुचि *śuchi.* The following are examples of neuter *u* bases, which supply the place both of nominative and accusative: in Sanskrit मधु madhu, "honey," "wine," अश्रु aśru, "tear," स्वादु swddu, "sweet"; in Zend ﹖﹖﹖ vóhu, "wealth" (Sanskrit वसु vasu); in Greek μέθυ, δάκρυ, ἡδύ; in Latin pecu, genu. The length of this u is unorganic, and has probably passed into the nominative, accusative, and vocative from the oblique cases, where the length is to be explained from the suppressed case terminations. With regard to the fact that final u is always long in Latin, there is perhaps a reason always at hand for this length: in the ablative, for example, the length of the originally short u is explicable as a compensation for the case sign which has been dropped, by which, too, the ŏ of the second declension becomes long. The original shortness of the u of the fourth declension is perceivable from the dat. pl. ŭ-bus. The Σ, in Greek words like γένος, μένος, εὐγενές, has been already explained at §. 128. as belonging to the base: the same is the case with the Latin e in neuters like genus, corpus, gravius: it is the other form of the r of the oblique cases, like gener-is, corpor-is, gravior-is (see §. 127.); and corpus appears akin to the Sanskrit neuter of the same meaning, वपुस् vapus, gen. वपुषस् vapu-sh-as (see §. 19.), and would consequently have an r too much, or the Sanskrit has lost one.* The Σ also of neuter bases in T, in τετυφός, τέρας, does not seem to me to be the case sign, but an exchange with T, which is not admissible at the end, but is either rejected (μέλι, πρᾶγμα) or exchanged [G. Ed. p. 180.] for a cognate Σ, as πρός from προτί, Sanskrit प्रति prati.†

---

* Compare, in this respect, brachium, βραχίων, with बाहुस् báhu-s, "arm"; frango, ῥήγνυμι, with भनज्मि bhanajmi, "I break," भन्ज्मस् bhanjmas, "we break."

† With this view, which I have already developed in my treatise "On some Demonstrative Bases, and their connection with various Prepositions and Conjunctions" (Berlin, by Dümmler), pp. 4—6, corresponds, as to the essential points, what Hartung has since said on this subject

In Latin it is to be regarded as inconsistent with the spirit of the language, that most adjective bases ending with a consonant retain the nominative sign *s* of the two natural genders in the neuter, and in this gender extend it also to the accusative, as if it belonged to the base, as *capac-s felic-s, soler(t)s, aman(t)s*. In general, in Latin, in consonantal bases, the perception of the distinction of gender is very much blunted, as, contrary to the principle followed by the Sanskrit, Zend, Greek, and Gothic, the feminine is no longer distinguished from the masculine.

153. In Gothic substantives, as well neuter as masculine, the case sign *m* is wanting, and hence neuter bases in *a* stand on the same footing with the *i, u,* and consonantal bases of the cognate languages in that, in the nominative and accusative, they are devoid of all inflexion. Compare, with regard to the form of this case, *daur(a)* with द्वारम् *dwâram*, which has the same meaning. In Gothic there are no neuter substantives in *i*; on the other hand, the

[G. Ed. p. 181.] substantive bases in *ya*, by suppression of the *a* in the nominative and accusative singular (cf. §. 135.), gain in these cases the semblance of *i* bases; *e.g.* from the base *REIKYA*, "rich" (Sanskrit राज्य *râjya*, likewise neuter), comes, in the case mentioned, *reiki*, answering to the Sanskrit राज्यम् *râjya-m*. The want of neuter *i* bases

---

subject in his valuable work on "On the Cases," p. 152, &c.; where also the ρ of ἧπαρ and ὕδωρ is explained as coming from T, through the intervention of Σ. The Sanskrit, however, appears to attribute a different origin to the ρ of these forms. To यकृत् *yakrit* "liver" (likewise neuter), corresponds both *jecur* and ἧπαρ, through the common interchange between *k* and *p* : both owe to it their ρ, as ἧπαr-os does its r. ῞Ηπαr-os should be ἧπαρτ-os, Sanskrit यकृतस् *yakrit-as*. But the Sanskrit also in this word, in the weak cases, can give up the *r*, but then irregularly substitutes न *n* for त *t*, *e.g.* gen. यक्नस् *yakn-as* for यकनस् *yakanas*. With regard to the ρ of ὕδωρ, compare उद्र *udra*, "water," in समुद्र *sam-udra*, "sea."

in German is the less surprising, that in the cognate Sanskrit, Zend, and Greek, the corresponding termination in the neuter is not very common. Of neuter *u* roots the substantive declension has preserved only the single *FAIHU*, "beast." In Lithuanian the neuter in substantives is entirely lost, and has left traces only in pronouns and adjectives, where the latter relate to pronouns. Adjective bases in *u*, in this case, have their nominative and accusative singular in accordance with the cognate languages, without case sign; *e.g. darkù*, "ugly," corresponds as nominative and accusative neuter to the masculine nominative *darkù-s*, accusative *darku-n*. This analogy, however, is followed in Lithuanian, by •the adjective bases in *a* also; and thus *géra*, "good," corresponds as nominative and accusative to the masculine forms *géra-s*, *géra-n*,* which are provided with the sign of the case.

[G. Ed. p. 182.] 154. It is a question whether the *m*, as the sign of the nominative and accusative neuter (it is excluded from the vocative in Sanskrit and Zend), was originally limited simply to the *a* bases, and was not joined to the

---

* The *e* of neuter forms like *dide*, "great," from the base *DIDYA*— nom. masc. *didi-s* for *didya-s*, as §. 135.* *yaunikkis*, "youngling"—I explain through the euphonic influence of the suppressed *y*. As also the feminine originally long *a* is changed into *e* by the same influence, so is the nominative and accusative neuter in such words identical with the nominative feminine, which is likewise, according to §. 137, devoid of inflexion; and *dide* therefore signifies also "*magna*," and answers, as feminine, very remarkably to the Zend nominatives explained at §. 137., as ܠܘ ܓ̈ܘ *pérĕné*, ܠܘ ܓ̈ܘ *bráturyé*. In this sense are to be regarded, also, the feminine substantives in Ruhig's third declension, as far as they terminate in the nominative in *e*, as *giesme*, "song." As no masculine forms in *is* correspond to them, the discovery of the true nature of these words becomes more difficult; for the lost *y* or *i* has been preserved only in the genitive plural, where *giesmy-ú* is to be taken like *rank-ú* from *rankà, i.e.* the final vowel of the bases is suppressed before the termination, or has been melted down with it.

i and *u* bases also; so that, in Sanskrit, for *wtri* we had originally *vári-m*, for *madhu*, *madhu-m?* I should not wish to
deny the original existence of such forms; for why should
the *a* bases alone have felt the necessity of not leaving
the nominative and accusative neuter without a sign of
relation or of personality? It is more probable that the
a bases adhered only the more firmly to the termination
once assumed, because they are by far the most numerous,
and could thus present a stronger opposition to the destructive influence of time by means of the greater force
of their analogies; in the same way as the verb substantive, in like manner, on account of its frequent use, has
allowed the old inflexion to pass less into oblivion, and in
German has continued to our time several of the progeny of
the oldest period; as, for instance, the nasal, as characteristic
of the 1st person in *bi-n*, Old High German *pi-m* Sans. भवामि
bhavá-mi. In Sanskrit, one example of an *m* as the nominative and accusative sign of an *i* base is not wanting, although
it stands quite isolated; and indeed this form occurs in the
pronominal declension, which everywhere remains longest
true to the traditions of bygone ages. I mean the interrogative form किम् *ki-m*, "what"? from the base कि *ki*,
which may perhaps, in Sanskrit, have produced a *ki-t*,
which is contained in the Latin *qui-d*, and which I recognise again, also, in the enclitic चित् *chit*, weakened from कित्
ki-t. Otherwise *i* or *u*-bases of pronouns in the nominative accusative neuter do not occur; for अमु *amu*, "that"
(man), substitutes अदस् *adas*; and इ *i*, "this," combines with
[G. Ed. p. 183.] दम् *dam* (इदम् *idam*, "this"). Concerning
the original procedure of consonantal bases in the nominative
and accusative neuters no explanation is afforded by the pronominal declension, as all primary forms of pronouns terminate in vowels, and, indeed, for the most part, in *a*.

155. Pronominal bases in *a* in Sanskrit give *t*, in Zend *t*, as
the inflexion of the nominative and accusative neuter. The

Gothic gives, as in the accusative masculine, *na* for *m* or *n*, so here *ta* for simple *t*; and transfers these, like other peculiarities of the pronominal declension, as in the other German dialects, also to the adjective *a* bases; *e.g. blinda-ta,* "*cæcum,*" *midya-ta,* "*medium.*" The High German gives, in the older period, *z* instead of the Gothic *t* (§. 87.), in the most modern period, *s*. The pronominal base *I* (later *E*) follows in German, as in Latin, the analogy of the old *a* bases, and the Latin gives, as in the old ablative, *d* instead of *t*. The Greek must abandon all *T* sounds at the end of words: the difference of the pronominal from the common *o* declension consists, therefore, in this respect, merely in the absence of all inflexion. From this difference, however, and the testimony of the cognate languages, it is perceived that τό was originally sounded τοτ or τοδ, for a τον would have remained unaltered, as in the masculine accusative. Perhaps we have a remnant of a neuter-inflexion τ in ὅττι, so that we ought to divide ὅτ-τι; and therefore the double τ, in this form, would no more have a mere metrical foundation, than the double σ (§. 128.) in ὄρεσ-σι. (Buttmann, p. 85.)

156. We find the origin of the neuter case-sign *t* in the pronominal base त *ta*, "he," "this," (Greek TO, Goth, *THA,* &c.); and a convincing proof of the correctness of this explanation is this, that तत् *ta-t* "it" "this," stands, in regard to the base, in the same contrast with स *sa*, "he," सा *sá*, "she," as *t*, as the neuter case-sign, does to [G. Ed. p. 184.] the nominative *s* of masculine and feminine nouns (§. 134.). The *m* of the accusative also is, I doubt not, of pronominal origin; and it is remarkable that the compound pronouns *i-ma*, "this," and *a-mu*, "that," occur just as little as *ta* in the nominative masculine and feminine; but the Sanskrit substitutes for the base *amu*, in the nominative masculine and feminine singular the form *asáu*, the *s* of which, therefore, stands in the same relation to the *m* of अमुम् *amu-m*, "*illum,*" अमुष्य *amu-shya*, "*illius,*" and other oblique cases, as, among

the case-terminations, the sign of the masculine feminine
nominative to the *m* of the accusative and neuter nominative.   Moreover, in Zend is used ριδεις *imat*, "this," (n.)
(nom. accus.), but not *imó*, "this" (m.), but ερωσ *aëm* (from
श्रयम् *ayam*), and ε *im* (from इयम् *iyam*), "this" (f.). Observe
in Greek the pronominal base MI, which occurs only in the
accusative, and, in regard to its vowel, has the same relation to म *ma* (in the compounded base इम *i-ma*) that किम्
ki-m " what?" has to कस *ka-s* " who "?   The Gothic neut.
termination *ta* anwers, in respect to the transposition of
sound (§. 87.), to the Latin *d* (*id*, *istud*): this Latin *d*, however, seems to me a descent from the older *t*; as, *e.g.*, the
b of *ab* has proceeded from the *p* of the cognate श्रप *apa*,
ἀπό; and in Zend the *d* of εξως* *à-dëm*, "him," is clearly
only a weakening of the *t* of त *ta*, ιδε *ta*.†

[G. Ed. p. 185.]   157. To the Sanskrit *ta-t*, mentioned above,
Zend *ta-t*, Greek τό, &c., corresponds a Lithuanian *tai*, " the,"
as the nominative and accusative singular.   I do not believe,
however, that the *i* which is here incorporated in the base *T.*

---

* The *à* of *à-dëm* is the preposition corresponding to the Sansk. *à*.

† See my treatise " On the Origin of the Cases " in the Trans. of the
Berlin Academy for the year 1826.   As T in Greek easily becomes Σ (but a
final Σ has in many parts of Grammar become ν), Hartung founds on this,
in the pamphlet before mentioned, p. 154, the acute conjecture of an
original identity of neuters in ν (*m*) with those in *t*. We cannot, however, agree with him in this, because the *m*, on account of the origin
which we ascribe to this case-sign, is as little surprising in the nominative
of the neuter as in the accusative of the more animated genders; and
besides, a greater antiquity is proved to belong to the neuter *m*, through
the Sanskrit and Zend, than probably the ν sounds can boast, which, in
Greek, stand for an older Σ, as μεν for μες (मस *mas*), and in the dual των,
τον for यास *thas*, तास *tas*. What is wanting in the Greek, viz. a neuter
inflexion *s*, appears, however, to be possessed by the Sanskrit; and I am
inclined to divide the form अदस् *adas*, " that " (nom. accus.) into *a-da-s*,
and to explain it as a corruption of *a-da-t* (cf. Gramm. Crit. Addend. to
r. 299.); but to regard the syllable *da* as weakened from *ta*, as in the Zend
εξως *à-dë-m*, "him." We shall recur to this when treating of the
pronouns.

is any way connected with the neuter *t, d,* of the cognate languages: I should rather turn to a relationship with the *i* demonstrative in the Greek (ούτοσί, έκεινοσί), and to the इत् *it,* which is, in like manner, used enclitically in the Vêdas—a petrified neuter, which is no longer conscious of any gender or case; and hence, in several cases, combining with masculine pronouns of the third person.* This इत् *it,* is consequently the sister form of the Latin *id* and Gothic *i-ta,* which, in the Greek έκεινοσί, has, perhaps only from necessity, dropped the τ or δ, and which already, ere I was acquainted with the Vêda-dialect, I represented as a consistent part of the conjunctions चेत् *chêt* (from *cha + it*), "if," and नेत् *nêt* (*na + it*). [G. Ed. p. 186.]

The words mentioned at §. 148. form in the accusative:

SANSKRIT.	ZEND.	GREEK.	LATIN.	LITHUAN.	GOTHIC.
m. *vrika-m,*	*vĕhrkĕ-m,*	λύκο-ν,	*lupu-m,*	*wilka-ṅ,*	*vulf'.*
m. *ka-m,*	*kĕ-m,*	. . . .	. . . .	*ka-ṅ,*	*hwa-na.*
n. *dâna-m,*	*dâtĕ-m,*	δῶρο-ν,	*donu-m,*	*gêra,*	*daur'.*
n. *ta-t,*	*ta-t,*	τό,	*is-tu-d,*	*ta-i,*	*tha-ta.*
f. *jihwâ-m,*	*hizva-ṅm,*	χώρα-ν,	*terram,*	*ranka-ṅ,*	*giba.*
f. *kâ-m,*	*ka-ṅm,*	. . . .	. . . .	. . . , .	*hvô.†*

* Examples are given by Rosen in his Vêda Specimen, pp. 24, 25, which, though short, are in the highest degree interesting for Sanskrit and comparative Grammar; as, सइत् *saït,* "he," तमित् *tamit,* "him"; तयोरित् *tayôrit,* "of these two"; तस्माइत् *tasmâit,* "to him"; अस्माइत् *asmâit,* "to this" (m.). The Zend combines in the same way *jo e* or *i* with the interrogative: *kaiê* and *kaii,* "who"? occur frequently. Perhaps only one of the two modes of writing is correct. Cf. Gramm. Crit. Addend. to r. 270.

† One would expect *hvô-na,* or, with abbreviation of the base, *hva-na,* which would be the same as the masculine. With regard to the lost case-termination, it may be observed, that, in general, the feminines are less constant in handing down the old inflexions. A charge which is incurred by the Sanskrit in the nominative, since it gives *kâ* for *kâ-s** (§. 137.), is incurred by the Gothic (for in this manner the corruption spreads) in the accusative also.

* Cf. §. 386. p. 514.

	SANSKRIT.	ZEND.	GREEK.	LATIN.	LITHUAN.	GOTHIC.
m.	*pati-m,*	*paiti-m,*	πόσι-ν,	*hostem,*	*púti-ṅ,*	*gasl'.*
m.	....	....	....	....	....	*i-na.*
f.	*priti-m,*	*áfriti-m,*	πόρτι-ν,	*siti-m,*	*áwi-ṅ,*	*ansl'.*
n.	*vári,*	*vairi,*	ἴδρι,	*mare,*	....	...
n.	....	....	....	*i-d,*	....	*i-ta.*
f.	*bhavishyantím,*	*búshyainti-m,*	....	....	....*	...
m.*sûnu-m,*	*pasù-m,*	ἰχθύ-ν,	*pecu-m,*	*sunu-ṅ,*	*sunu.*
f. *tanu-m,*	*tanù-m,*	πίτυ-ν,	*socru-m,*	....	*handu.*
n. *madhu,*	*madhu,*	μέθυ,	*pecu,*	*darkù,*	*faihu.*
f. *vadhù-m,*	....	....	....	....	....
m.f.*gá-m,†*	*ga-ṅm,†*	βοῦ-ν,	*bov-em,*	....	....
f. *náv-am,*	....	ναῦ-ν,	....	....	....
f. *vách-am,*	*vách-ěm,*	ὄπ-α,	*voc-em,*	....	....

(left margin: [G. Ed. p. 187])

* The feminine participial bases in *i,* mentioned at §. 119., remain free from foreign commixture only in the nominative and vocative singular: in all other cases, to the old *i* is further added a more modern *a*; and the declension then follows *RANKA* exactly; only that in some cases, through the euphonic influence of the *i,* and in analogy with the Zend and the Latin fifth declension (§. 137.), the added *a* becomes, or may become, *e*: in the latter case the *i* is suppressed, as l. c. ro *ʃʒʒʃɡ kainé* for *kainyé* (§. 42.). Thus, from *sukanti,* "the turning" (f.), *sukusi,* "the having turned" (f.), and *suksenti,* "the about to turn," Mielcke gives the accusatives *sukan-czeṅ* (see. p. 138, Note) or *sukanczian, sukuseṅ,* and *suksenczeṅ* or *suk-senczian.* And even if, according to Ruhig (by Mielcke, pp. 3, 4), the *i* before *a, e, o, u* is scarcely heard, it must not therefore, in this case, as well as in those there enumerated, be the less regarded as etymologically present, and it was originally pronounced so as to be fully audible. From the feminine, where the *i,* as Sanskrit grammar shews, has an original position, this vowel appears to have made its way, in Lithuanian participial bases, into the oblique cases of the masculine, and to be here invested with a short masculine *a.* The accusative *sukanti-ṅ,* "the turning" (masc.), is therefore to be regarded in the same light as *yaunikki-ṅ,* from the theme *YAUNIKYA,* i.e. it stands for *sukantyi-ṅ* from *sukantya-ṅ,* and hence answers to the Zend accusatives, like ç,ʃ‍ʒ‍ʒ‍ϙ *túiri-m* for *táiryěm* (§. 42.), and to the Gothic, like *hari* from the base *HARYA* (§. 135.).

† See §. 122.

INSTRUMENTAL, DATIVE SINGULAR.

SANSKRIT.	ZEND.	GREEK.	LATIN.	LITHUAN.	GOTHIC.
m. bharant-am,	barĕnt-em,	φέροντ-α,	ferent-em,	. . . .	fiyand.
m. átmán-am,	asman-ĕm,	δαίμον-α,	sermon-em,	. . . .	ahman.
n. náma',	náma',	τάλαν,	nomen,	. . . .	namô.
m. bhrátar-am,	brátar-ĕm,	πατέρ-α,	fratr-em,	. . . .	bróthar.
f. duhitar-am,	dughdhar-ĕm,	θυγατέρ-α,	matr-em,	. . . .	dauhtar.
m. dátár-am,	dátár-ĕm,	δοτῆρ-α,	datōr-em,	. . . .	. . . .
n. vachas,	vachô,*	ἔπος,	opus,.	. . . .	. . . .

INSTRUMENTAL, DATIVE.

158. The instrumental is denoted in Sanskrit by आ á ; and this inflexion is, in my opinion, a   [G. Ed. p. 188.] lengthening of the pronominal base अ a, and identical with the preposition आ á, "to," "towards," "up to," which springs from this pronoun, and appears only as a prefix. The Zend á appears still more decidedly in its pronominal nature in the compound mentioned at §. 156. Note *, ؟ؘۦۑ á-dĕm, "him," "this," (m.) fem. ؟ؘۦؗۑ á-daṅm. As a case-sign, ۑ á generally appears abbreviated (see p. 163. Note ‡), even where this termination has been melted into one with a preceding ۑ a of the base ; so that in this case the primary form and the instrumental are completely similar ; e.g. ۑ؟۟ؤ۟ؗۑ zaôsha, "voluntarily," ۑ؟۟ؤ۟ؗۑ azaôsha, "involuntarily," (V. S. p. 12.) ۑ؟ؚ۟؟۟ؗۑ skyaôthna, "actione," often occur ; ۑ؟ۑ ana, "through this" (m.), ۑ؟؟ؚۦ۟ؗۑ paiti-bĕrĕta, "allevato."†   The long á appears in the instrumental only in monosyllabic bases in ۑ a ; thus ۑ؟۟ khá, "proprio" V. S. p. 46.), from the base ۑ؟۟ kha (Sanskrit ख swa, §. 35.). In Sanskrit a euphonic न n is added to bases ending with short vowels in the masc.

---

* See §. 56ᵇ.

† Cf. Gramm. Crit. r. 638. Rem. This interesting instrumental form was not known by Rask when he published his work on the Zend, and it was not easy to discover it, on account of its discrepancy from the San-skrit and the many other forms with final ۑ a.

and neut. genders;* a final स *a*, however, is, as in several other cases, changed into ए *ê*; and the आ *â* of the case-suffix is shortened, as it appears to me, by the influence of this clog of the base; as वृकेण *vrikê-n-a*, but अग्निना *agni-n-â*, वारिणा *vâri-n-â*, सूनुना *sûnu-n-â*, मधुना *madhu-n-â*, from वृक *vrika*, &c. The Vêdas, however, exhibit further remains of formations without the euphonic *n*, as स्वप्नया *swapnay-â* for स्वप्नेन *swapnê-n-a* from स्वप्न *swapna*, m. "sleep" (see §. 133.); उरुया *uru-y-â* for उरुणा *uru-n-a*, from उरु *uru*, "great," with a euphonic य् *y* (§. 43.); प्रबाहवा *prabâhav-â*, from प्रबाहु *prabâhu*, from बाहु *bâhu*, "arm," with the preposition [G. Ed. p. 189.] प्र *pra*. The Vêda-form स्वप्नया *swapnayâ*, finds analogies in the common dialect in मया *mayâ*, "through me," and त्वया *twayâ*, "through thee," from the bases *ma* and *twa*, the *a* of which in this case, as in the loc., passes into *ê*. And from पति *pati*, m. "Lord," and सखि *sakhi*, m. "friend," the common dialect forms instrumentals without the interposition of न् *n*, viz. पत्या *paty-â*, सख्या *sakhy-â*. Feminines never admit a euphonic *n*; but *â*, as before some other vowel terminations, passes into ए *ê*, that is to say, *i* is blended with it, and it is shortened to स *a*; hence, जिह्वया *jihway-â* (from *jihwê + â*). The Zend follows in this the analogy of the Sanskrit.

159. As *ê* in Gothic, according to §. 69., just like *ô*, represents आ *â*, so the forms *thê*, *hvê*, which Grimm (pp. 790. and 798.) regards as instrumentals, from the demonstrative base *THA* and the interrogative *HVA*, correspond very remarkably to the Zend instrumentals, as ‌‌‌ *khâ* from the base ‌‌‌ *kha*. We must, however, place also *srê* in the class of genuine Zend instrumental forms, which have been correctly preserved: besides *svê* from *SVA* is also.

---

* The original has "Stämmen gen. masc. und fem.;" but genitives of nouns in *a* do not take a euphonic *n*, nor do feminine nouns ending in short vowels use such an augment in the instrumental: here is no doubt some typographic error.—*Editor*.

in respect of its base, akin to ᴊᴡᴘ *khá* from *kha* (§. 35.).*
The meaning of *své* is "as" (ὡς), and the *só*, which has arisen
in High German from *sva* or *své*, means both "as" and
"so," &c. The case relations, however, which are expressed by
"as" and "so" are genuine instrumentals.† [G. Ed. p. 190.]
The Anglo-Saxon form for *své* is *svá*, in which the colouring
of the Zend ᴊᴡᴘ *khá* is most truly preserved.   The Gothic
sva, "so," is, according to its form, only the abbreviation of
své, as *a* is the short equivalent both of *é* and of *ó*: through
this abbreviation, however, *sva* has become identical with
its theme, just as ᴊᴧ *ana* in Zend is, according to §. 158.,
not distinguished from its theme.

160. ‡As the dative in Gothic and in Old High German
very frequently expresses the instrumental relation, and
the termination also of the dative is identical with the
Sanskrit-Zend instrumental character, shortened only, as
in polysyllabic words in Zend, it may be proper here to
describe at the same time the formation of the German
dative.   In *a* bases it is in Gothic, as in Zend, identical
with the theme, and from *VULFA* comes *vulfa*, as ᴊᴧᴘᴇᴘ
vĕhrka from *VEHRKA*.   Moreover, there are some other
remarkable datives, which have preserved their due length,
and answer to the monosyllabic instrumentals *thé*, *vé*, *své*,
which have been already explained, viz. *hvammé-h*, *hvar-
yammé-h*, "*cuique*," and *ainummé-hun*, "*ulli*," for *ainammé-*

---

* Grimm's conjectures regarding the forms *sva* and *své* (III. 43.) appear to me untenable; and an explanation of these forms, without the
intervention of the Sanskrit and Zend, is impossible.   More regarding this
at the pronouns.

† If "as" is regarded as "through which means, in which manner or
way," and "so" as "through this means, in this way," it is certain that
among the eight cases of the Sanskrit language there is none which would
be adapted in the relative and demonstrative to express "as" and "so."

‡ The German dat. sing. is according to §. 356. Rem. 3., to be everywhere identified with the Sanskrit dative; and so, too, the dat. pl. the *m*
of which approaches as closely to the Sansk. *bhyas*, Latin *bus*, Lith. *mus*,
as the instrumental termination *bhis*, Lith. *mis*.

N

hun (§. 66.).* Bases in *i* reject this vowel before the case-
sign; hence *gast'-a* for *gasti-a:* on the other hand, in the
u bases the termination is suppressed, and the base-vowel
receives the Guna: hence *sunau,* which will have been pronounced originally *su-nav-a* ; so that, after suppressing the
termination, the *v* has again returned to its original vowel
nature. The form *sunav-u* would answer to the Vêda form
प्रवाहवा *pra-bâhav-â.* In Zend, the bases which terminate
with ᜒ *i* and ᜒ *u,* both in the instrumental and before most
[G. Ed. p. 191.] of the other vowel terminations, assume
Guna or not at pleasure. Thus we find in the Vend. S. p. 469.
ᜒᜒᜒᜒᜒ *bâzav-a,* "*brachio,*" as analogous to प्रवाहवा *pra-*
-bâhav-â (§. 57.); on the other hand, p. 408, ᜒᜒᜒᜒᜒ *zanthwa*
from *zantu,* "the slaying," "killing." From ᜒᜒᜒᜒᜒ *pansnu,*
"dust," we find, l. c. p. 229, the form ᜒᜒᜒᜒᜒ *pansnâ,* which
Anquetil translates by "*par cette poussiere*"; and if the reading is correct, then *pansnâ,* in regard of the suppressed termination (compensation for which is made by lengthening
the base vowel), would answer to the Gothic *sunau.*

161. Bases ending with a consonant have lost, in German, the dative character: hence, in Gothic, *fiyand, ahmin,*
brôthr (§. 132.), for *fiyand-a, ahmin-a, brôthr-a.*† All feminines, too, must be pronounced to have lost the dative
sign, paradoxical as it may appear to assert that the Gothic
gibai, "*dono,*" and *thizai,* "*huic,*" *izai,* "*ei,*" do not contain
any dative inflexion, while we formerly believed the *ai* of
gibai to be connected with the Sanskrit feminine dative

---

* Here the appended particle has preserved the original length of the
termination, as is the case in Zend in all instrumentals, if they are combined with ᜒᜒᜒ *cha,* "and."

† The Old High German form *fatere* (for *fatera*), "*patri,*" proceeds,
as do the genitive *fatere-s,* and the accusative *fatera-n,* from a theme
FATERA, extended by *a.* The accusative *fatera-n,* however, is remarkable, because substantives, so early as in the Gothic, have lost the accusative sign, together with the final vowel of the base. In Old High German a
few other substantives and proper names follow the analogy of *FATERA.*

character र् *âi.* But as we have recognised in the masculine and neuter dative the Indo-Zend instrumental, we could not, except from the most urgent necessity, betake ourselves to the Sanskrit dative for explanation of the Gothic feminine dative. This necessity, however, does not exist, for, *e. g., hveilai, "albae,"* from *HVEITŌ* from *HVEITÂ,* may be deduced from the instrumental श्वेतया *śwêlay-â, "albâ,"* from श्वेता *swêlâ,* by suppressing the termination, and changing the semi-vowel to a vowel in the same manner as, above, *sunau* from *sunav-a,* [G. Ed. p. 192.] or as the fem. *handau, "manui,"* from *handav-a.* Analogous with *sunau, handau,* are also the dative feminine *i* bases; and, *e. g., anstai, "gratiæ,"* has the same relation to its theme *ANSTI* that *handau* has to *HANDU.*

162. In Old High German the forms *diu, hviu,* correspond to the Gothic instrumentals *thê, hvê;* but authorities differ as to the mode of writing them,[*] regarding which we shall say more under the pronouns. The form *hiu,* also, from a demonstrative base *HI,* has been preserved in the compound *hiulu* for *hiu-tagu,* "on this day," "to-day" (see Grimm, p. 794), although the meaning is here properly locative. The Gothic has for it the dative *himma-daga.* This termination *u* has maintained itself also in substantive and adjective bases masc. neut. in *a* and *i,* although it is only sparingly used, and principally after the preposition *mit* (see Graff, l. c. pp. 110, 111); *mit wortu,* "with a word," from *WORTA; mit cuatu,* "with good," from *CUATA; mit kastu,* "with a guest," from *KASTI.* It is here important to remark, that the instrumental in Sanskrit *very frequently expresses, *per se,* the sociative relation. We cannot, however, for this reason look upon this *u* case as generically different from the common dative, which, we have already remarked, is likewise of instrumental origin

---

[*] With reference to their use with various prepositions we refer our readers to Graff's excellent treatise, "The Old High German Prepositions," p. 181, &c.

and meaning : we rather regard the u^* as a corruption [G. Ed. p. 193.] (although one of very ancient date) of u, just as in the neuter plural of pronouns and adjectives a u corresponds to the short a of the Gothic and the older cognate languages. In Lithuanian the a bases form their instrumental in $\grave{u}$, which is long, and in which the final vowel of the base has been melted down. That this $\grave{u}$, also, has arisen from a long a, and thus, *e. g. diewù* is akin to the Zend ⲙⲱⲣⲱⲩⲅ *daêva*, "deo," for ⲙⲱⲣⲱⲩⲅ *daêvâ*, appears to me the less doubtful, as also in the plural *diewais* answers very surprisingly to ⲙⲱⲙⲱⲣⲱⲩⲅ *daêvâis*, देवैस् *dévâis*. Moreover, in many other parts of grammar, also, the Lithuanian $\grave{u}$ corresponds to the Sanskrit आ $\hat{a}$; *e. g.* in the plural genitive. In feminine a bases, also, in Lithuanian, the vowel of the base is melted down with that of the termination, but its quality is not changed ; as, *e.g. rankù* "*manu*," from *RANKÁ*. In all other bases *mi* stands as the termination, to which the plural instrumental termination *mis* has the same relation as, in Latin, *bis* to *bi* (*voBIS*, *tiBI*) ; and, according to §. 63., I do not doubt that in both numbers the m has arisen from b.

163. The bases given in §. 148. form, in the instrumental and in the Gothic, in the dative,

	SANSKRIT.	ZEND.	LITHUANIAN.	GOTHIC.
m.	*vrikê-n-a,*	*vĕhrka,*	*wilkù,*	*vulfa.*
f.	*jihway-â.*	*hizvay-a,*	*rankà,*	*gibai.*
m.	*paty-â,*	*paithy-a,*	*pati-mi,*	*gast'-a.*

* Contrary to Grimm's opinion, I cannot let the instrumental u pass as long, even not to notice its derivation from a short a ; for, first, it appears, according to Notker, in the pronominal forms *diu*, &c. without a circumflex (other instrumentals of the kind do not occur in his works) ; secondly, like the short a, it is exchanged for o (§. 77.) ; hence, *wio, wĕo,* with *wiu, wio-lih, huĕo-lih*, "*qualis*" (properly, "similar to whom") ; thirdly, the length of this u cannot be deduced from the Gothic forms *thé, hvé, své,* because these, in all probability, owe the retention of their long vowel to their being monosyllabic (cf. §. 137.).

	SANSKRIT.	ZEND.	LITHUANIAN.	GOTHIC.	
f.	prîty-â,	âfrithy-a,	awi-mi,	anslai.	[G. Ed. p. 194.]
f.	bhavishyanty-â,	bûshyainty-a,	. . . .	. . . .	
m.	sûnu-n-â,	pasv-a,	sunu-mi,	sunau.	
f.	tanw-â,	tanv-a,	. . . .	handau.	
f.	vadhw-â,	. . . .	. . . .	. . . .	
m.f.	gav-â.	gav-a,	. . . .	. . . .	
f.	nâv-â,	. . . .	. . . .	. . . .	
f.	vâch-â,	vâch-a,	. . . .	. . . .	
m.	bharat-â,	barěnt-a,	. . . .	fiyand.	
m.	âtman-â,	asman-a,	. . . .	ahmin.	
n.	nâmn-â,	nâman-a,	. . . .	namin.	
m.	bhrâtr-â,	brâthr-a,	. . . .	brôthr.	
f.	duhitr-â,	dughdher-a,	. . . .	dauhtr.	
m.	dâtr-â,	dâthr-a,	. . . .	. . . .	
n.	vachas-â,	vacanh-a,	. . . .	. . . .	

164. In Sanskṛit and Zend, *ê* is the sign of the dative, which, I have scarce any doubt, originally belongs to the demonstrative base *ê*, whence the nom. अयम् *ayam* (from *ê + am*), "this"; which, however, as it appears, is itself only an extension of the base व *a*, from which arise most of the cases of this pronoun (*a-smâi, a-smât, a-smin*, &c.); and regarding which it is to be observed, that the common *a* bases, also, in Sanskṛit in many cases extend this vowel to *ê* by the admixture of an *i* (§. 2.). The dative sign consequently would, in its origin, be most intimately connected with the case, which, as (§. 160.) was explained, denotes, in German, both the dative and instrumental relation, and occurs in Zend also with a dative signification.*

---

* *E. g.* Vend. 8. p. 45: ⟨Zend script⟩ *Haômô astzânâitibis dadhâiti csaitô-puthrìm*, "Hóm gives a splendid daughter to those who have not had offspring." The lithographed Codex, however, gives the form *astzânâitibis* as three words,

[G. Ed. p. 195.]   We have here further to remark, that in the pronoun of the 2d person the affix भ्यम् *bhyam* (from *bhi + am*) in तुभ्यम् *tu-bhyam*, " to thee," stands in evident relationship to the instrumental भिस् *bhis* in the plural. The feminine bases in *â, î, û,* and, at will also, those in *i* and *u,* prolong in Sanskrit the dative termination ए *ê* to ऐ *âi* ; with the final *â* of the base an *i* is blended ; hence जिह्वायै *jihwây-âi* from *jivâi-âi.* On the other hand, इ *i* and उ *u* receive the Guna augment before ए *ê*, but not before the broader ऐ *âi*; as सूनवे *sûnav-ê* from *sûnu.* In Zend, feminine *â* and *î*-bases, like the Sanskrit, have *âi* for their termination :   however, *hizvây-âi* is not used, but ‫جسوزوسرکیو‬ *hizvay-âi*, from the base *hizvâ,* as long vowels in the penultimate, in polysyllabic bases, are so frequently shortened. Bases in ‫ی‬ *i* have, in combination with the particle ‫چه‬ *cha,* preserved the Sanskrit form most truly, and exhibit, without exception in this case, the form ‫سایوسزوسی‬ *ay-aê-cha* (see § 28), *e. g.* ‫سایوسزوسپیولسی‬ *karstayaêcha,* " and on account of the ploughing," " in order to plough" (Vend. S. p. 198), [G. Ed. p. 196.]   from *karsle.* Without *cha,* however, the form ‫یوه‬ *eê* is almost the sole one that occurs, *e. y.* ‫یوهپولسی‬ *kharêleê,* " in order to eat," from ‫سپولیو‬ *kharêti.* This form, I doubt not, has arisen from ‫یوزوسی‬ *ay-ê,* by rejecting the semi-vowel, after which the preceding ‫س‬ *a* has become ‫ه‬ *e* (§. 31.).   Forms like ‫سوللرپو‬ *âfrîlê*[*] or ‫سوللرپوه‬ *âfrîte,* which sometimes occur, and are most corrupted, may

---

‫بیی‬ ‫یوزسوسیوپوسزو‬ ‫سزوزو‬ *azî zânâiti bis.* Such separations in the middle of a word are, however, in this Codex, quite common. I entertain no doubt of the correctness of the length of the *a,* both of *zâ* and *nâi*; and I anticipate a variety *azîzanaitibis* or—*bis.* Probably also *csaêtô* is to be read for *csîitô.* Anquetil translates: "O Hom, donnez à la femme, qui n'a pas encore engendré, beaucoup d'enfans brillans." We will return to this passage hereafter ; and we will here further remark that, at the same page of the Vend. S., the instr. ‫سیوزوزوس‬ *aêbis* also occurs in the sense of " to them."

   * Cf. p. 286 Note †.

rest on errors in writing.* Bases in *u* may take Guna ;
e.g. ⁓ *vaṇ-hav-ĕ* from ⁓ *vaṇhu,* "pure"; or not,
as ⁓ *rathv-ĕ* from ⁓ *ratu,* "great," "lord." The
form without Guna is the more common. A euphonic ⁓ *y*
also is found interposed between the base and the termination (§. 43.) *e.g.* ⁓ *tanu-y-ĕ,* "*corpori*."

165. Bases in ग *a* add to the case-sign *ĕ* also an ग *a* ;
but from ए *ĕ* (= *a* + *i*) and *a* is formed य *aya* ; and this,
with the *a* of the base, gives * áya,* thus वृकाय *vrikáya.*
Hence may have arisen, by suppressing the final *a,* the
Zendian ⁓ *vĕhrkái,* after which the preceding semi-
vowel must return to its vowel nature. It might, however, be assumed, that the Zend has never added an *a* to
the dative *ĕ,* and that this is a later appearance in Sanskrit,
which arose after the division of languages ; for from *a* + *ĕ*
is formed, quite regularly, *ái* (§. 2.). The Sanskrit forms
also, from the particle स्म *sma,* which is added to pronouns of the 3d person, the dative स्मै *smái* ; and thus, *e.g.*
कस्मै *kasmái,* " to whom"? answers to the Zend ⁓
kahmái. The Sanskrit, in this case, abstains from adding
the ग *a,* which is elsewhere appended to the dative ए *ĕ* ;
since स्म *sma,* already encumbered with the preceding principal pronoun, cannot admit any superfluity in its termination, and for this reason gives up its radi- [G. Ed. p. 197.]
cal ग *a* before the termination इन् *in* in the locative case
also, and forms *sm'-in* for *smĕn.*

166. The particle स्म *sma,* mentioned in the preceding section, which introduces itself between the base and the termination, not only in the singular, but (and this, in fact,
occurs in pronouns of the two first persons) in the plural also,
if not separated from both—as I have first attempted to shew

---

* ⁓ *áfríte* is undoubtedly incorrect: however, ع *e* is often
found erroneously for ⁓ *e* in other forms also.

in my Sanskrit Grammar—gives to the pronominal declension the appearance of greater peculiarity than it in fact possesses.   As this particle recurs also in the cognate European languages, and there, as I have already elsewhere partly shewn, solves several enigmas of declension, we will therefore here, at its first appearance, pursue all its modifications and corruptions, as far as it is possible.   In Zend, *sma,* according to §. 53., has been changed to *hma;* and also in Prâkrit and Pâli, in the plural of the two first persons, the *s* has become *h,* and besides, by transposition of the two consonants, the syllable *hma* has been altered to *mha; e.g.* Prâkrit अम्हे *amhê,* " we" (ἄμμες), Pâli अम्हाकम् *amhâkam,* Zend ᴄᴇᴣᴡᴄᴀ *ahmâkĕm,* ἡμῶν.   From the Prâkrit-Pâli *mha* we arrive at the Gothic *nsa* in *u-nsa-ra,* ἡμῶν, *u-nsi-s,** " *nobis,*" " *nos.*"   In that the Gothic has left the sibilant unaltered, it stands on an older footing than the Pâli and Prâkrit; and on the other hand, by the change of *m* into *n,* for more facile combination with the following *s,* it rests on a more modern stage.   We cannot, therefore, any longer assume the *ns* of *uns,* " *nos,*" to be

[G. Ed. p. 198.] the common accusative termination, as we have formerly done in unison with Grimm†—cf. *vulfa-ns, gasti-ns, sunu-ns*—and thence allow it, as though it had become a property of the base, to enter into some other cases, and connect it with new case-terminations.   To this is opposed, also, the 2d person, where *izvis* (*i-zvi-s*) stands in the accusative, and yet in essentials the two persons are identical in their declension; *uns,* " *nobis,*" " *nos,*" stands, therefore, for *unsi-s* (from *unsa-s*), and this has *s* as the case-suffix, and *u-nsa* (weakened from *u-nsi*) as the compound base.   And we

---

* The *a* being changed into *i,* according to r. 67.

† I. 813. "*unsara* appears to be derived from the accusative *uns,* as also the dative *unsis,* which, with *izvis,* preserves a parallel sound to the dative singular." Cf. I. 813. 34.

cannot, also, any longer regard the *u* of *unsa-ra,* "*nostri,*" &c. as the vocalized *v* of *veis,* "we," although the *i* of *izvara,* "*vestri,*" &c. can be nothing else than the vocalized *y* of *yus,* "your"; for in Sanskrit, also, the syllable य *yu* of *yûyam,* "ye," (§. 43.) goes through all the oblique cases, while in the 1st person the व *v* of वयम् *vayam,* "we," is limited to the nominative, but the oblique cases combine a base व *a* with the particle स्म *sma.* This *a,* then, in Gothic, through the influence of the following liquid, has become *u*; hence, *unsa-ra,* &c. for *ans-ara* (§. 66.).

167. As in Zend, the Sanskrit possessive स्व *swa* shews itself* in very different forms in juxta-position with different letters, so I believe I can point out the particle स्म *sma* in Gothic at least under four forms; namely, as *nsa, zva, gka,* and *mma.* The first has been already discussed; the second—*zva,* and in a weakened form *zvi*— occurs in the pronoun of the 2d person, in the place where the 1st has *nsa* (*nsi*); and while in the cognate Asiatic languages (Sanskrit, Zend, Pâli, Prâkrit), as also in Greek and Lithuanian, the two pronouns run quite   [G. Ed. p. 199.] parallel in the plural, since they both exhibit the interposed particle under discussion, either in its original form, or similarly modified, in Gothic a discrepancy has arisen between the two persons, in that the syllable *sma* has in them been doubly transformed. The form *zva* from *sma* rests, first, on the not surprising change of the *s* into *z* (§. 86. 5.); secondly, on the very common change of *m* and *v* (§. 63.).

168. From the Gothic downwards, the particle *sma* has been still further corrupted in the German dialects, in the pronoun of the 2d person, by the expulsion of the sibilant. The Old High German *i-wa-r* has nearly the same relation to the Gothic *i-zva-ra* that the Homeric genitive τοῖο has

---

* See Ann. of Lit. Crit. March 1831, p. 376, &c.

to the Sanskrit तस्य *tasya*, which is older than the Homeric form. Compare, without intervention of the Gothic, the Old High German *i-wa-r, i-u, i-wi-h,* with the Sanskrit *yu-shmá-kam, yu-shma-bhyam, yu-shmá-n,* and with the Lithuanian *yù-sú, yù-mus, yù-s:* thus it would be regarded as settled, that the *w* or *u* belongs to the base, but is not the corrupted remainder of a far-extended intermediate pronoun; and it would be incorrect to divide *iw-ar, iu-ih, iu,* for *i-wa-r,* &c. I, too, formerly entertained that erroneous opinion. A repeated examination, and the enlarged views since then obtained through the Zend, Prâkrit, and Pâli, leave me thoroughly convinced, that the Gothic intermediate syllable *zva* has not been lost in High German, but that one portion of it has been preserved even to our time (*e-ue-r* from *i-zva-ra, e-u-ch* from *i-zvi-s,* Old High German *i-wi-h*): on the other hand, the *u* of the base *yu* (युyu), as in Gothic so also in the oldest form of the High [G. Ed. p. 200.] German, is rejected in the oblique cases, both in the plural and in the dual[*]; and the Gothic *i-zva-ra,* Old High German *i-wa-r,* &c., stand for *yu-zva-ra, yu-wa-r.* The Old Saxon, however, and Anglo-Saxon, like the Lithuanian, shew themselves, in respect to the preservation of the base, more complete than the Gothic, and carry the *u,* which in Anglo-Saxon has become *o,* through all the oblique cases: *iu-we-r, ëo-ve-r, "vestri,"* &c. If merely the two historical extremes of the forms here under discussion—the Sanskrit and New German forms—be contrasted with one another, the assertion must appear very paradoxical, that *euer* and युष्माकम् *yushmákam* are connected, and, indeed, in such wise, that the *u* of *euer* has nothing

---

[*] So much the more remarkable is the *u,* which is still retained in the North Friesian dialect (Grimm, p. 814), where, *e. g. yu-nke-r, yu-nk,* in regard to the base, distinguishes itself advantageously from the Gothic *i-gqva-ra, i-nqvi-s.*

in common with the *u* of ई *yu*, but finds its origin in the *m* of the syllable स्म *sma*.

169. The distinction of the dual and plural in the oblique cases of the two first persons is not organic in German; for the two plural numbers are distinguished originally only by the case-terminations. These, however, in our pronouns are, in Gothic, the same; and the difference between the two plural numbers appears to lie in the base—*ugka-ra*,* νῶϊν, *unsa-ra*, ἡμῶν, ἱγϛνα-ρα, σφῶϊν, ἰϛνα-ρα, ὑμῶν. But from a more close analysis of the forms in the two plural numbers, and from the light afforded us by the cognate Asiatic languages, it appears that the proper base is also identical in the two plural numbers; and it is only the particle *sma* combined with it which has become doubly corrupted, and then the one form has become fixed in the dual, the other in the plural. The former comes nearest to   [G. Ed. p. 201.] the Prâkṛit-Pâli form म्ह *mha*, and between *u-nsa-ra* and *u-gka-ra* (=*u-nka-ra*) an intervening *u-nha-ra* or *u-mha-ra* must be assumed. At least I do not think that the old *s* became *k* at one spring, but that the latter is a hardened form of an earlier *h*, which has remained in the Prâkṛit and Pâli, as in the singular nominative the *k* of *ik* has been developed from the *h* of अहम् *aham*. The second person gives, in Gothic, *qv* (=*kv* §. 86. 1.) for *k*, while the other dialects leave the guttural the same form in both persons: Old High German, *u-ncha-r*, *i-ncha-r*; Old Slavonic, *u-nke-r*, *i-nke-r*; Anglo-Saxon, *u-nce-r*, *i-nce-r*. It would consequently appear proved that the dual and plural of the two first persons are not organically or originally different, but belong, as distortions and mutilations of different kinds, to one and the same original form; and that therefore these two pronouns have preserved the old dual just as little as

---

* It must not be overlooked, that here *g* before *k* only represents the nasal answering to *k* (86. 1.).

the other pronouns and all substantive and adjective declensions.

170. The fourth form in which स्म *sma* appears in Gothic is that which I first remarked, and which I have brought forward already in the "Annals of Oriental Literature" (p. 16). What I have there said, that the datives singular, like *thamma, imma*, have arisen, by assimilation, from *thasma, i-sma*, I have since found remarkably confirmed by the Grammar of the Old Prussian published by Vater, a language which is nearly connected with the Lithuanian and Gothic, since here all pronouns of the third person have *smu* in the dative. Compare, *e. g. antar-smu* with the Gothic *anthara-mma*, "to the other": *ka-smu* with the Gothic *hva-mma*, "to whom?" We have also shewn in Greek, since then, a remnant of the appended pronoun स्म *sma* similar to the Gothic, and which rests on assimilation,

[G. Ed. p. 202.] since we deduced the Æolic forms ἄ-μμ-ες, ὔ-μμ-ες, &c., from ἄ-σμε-ες, ὔ-σμε-ες, to which the common forms ἡμεῖς, ὑμεῖς, have the same relation that the Old High German *de-mu* has to the Gothic *tha-mma*, only that ἡμεῖς, ὑμεῖς, in respect to the termination εῖς, are more perfect than the Æolic forms, since they have not lost the vowel of the particle σμε, but have contracted με-ες to μεῖς.

171. The Gothic datives in *mma* are, as follows from §. 160., by origin, instrumentals,[*] although the particle *sma* in Sanskrit has not made its way into these cases, and *e. g.* तेन *téna*, "through him," not *tasména*, or, according to the Zend principle (§. 158.), *tasma* (for *tasmd*), is used ;—I say, according to the Zend principle; for though in this

---

[*] The difference between the forms *thé, hvé*, explained at §. 159., and the datives *tha-mma, hva-mma*, consists first in this, that the latter express the case relation by the affixed particle, the former in the main base; secondly, in this, that *thamma, hvamma*, for *thammé, hvammé*, on account of their being polysyllabic, have not preserved the original length of the termination (cf. §. 137.)

language *hma* has entered into the instrumental masculine
and neuter, this case in the base *ta* could only be ﻮﻼﻴﻮ *tahma*
or ﻮﻼﻴﻮ *tahmâ* (from *ta-hma-â*). In the feminine, as we
can sufficiently prove, the appended pronoun really occurs in
the instrumental; and while *e.g.* from the masculine and neuter
base ﻼﻴﻼ *ana*, "this" (m.), "this" (n.), we have found the
instrumental of the same sound ﻼﻴﻼ *ana* not *anahma*, from
the demonstrative base ﻼ *a* occurs rather often the feminine
instrumental ﻼﻴﻮ *ahmy-a*, from the fem. base ﻴﻮ *ahmî*,
increased by the appended pronoun.

172. The Sanskrit appended pronoun [G. Ed. p. 208.]
स्म *sma* should, in the feminine, form either स्मा *smâ* or स्मी
smí: on the latter is based the Zend form ﻴﻮ *hmí*, mentioned
at §. 171. But in Sanskrit the feminine form स्मी *smí* has
been preserved only in such a mutilated condition,* that before my acquaintance with the Zend I could not recognise it.
From *ta-smí* must come the dative *ta-smy-âi*, the gen. and
ablative *ta-smy-âs*, and the locative *ta-smy-âm*. These forms,
by rejecting the *m*, have become abbreviated to तस्यै *ta-sy-âi*,
तस्यास् *ta-sy-âs*, तस्याम् *ta-sy-âm;* and the same is the case
with the feminine pronoun *smí* in all similar compounds; so
that the forms mentioned appear to have proceeded from the
masculine and neuter genitive *tasya*, by the annexation of new
case-terminations. This opinion was the more to be relied
on, that in Gothic, also, the feminine forms *thi-zôs*, "*hujus*,"

---

* The Zend, too, has not everywhere so fully preserved the feminine
hmí, as in the instr. *a-hmy-a;* but in the genitive, dative, and ablative
has gone even farther than the Sanskrit in the demolition of this word,
and has therein rejected not only the *m* but also the *í*. The feminine
ﻮﻼﻴﻮ *a-ṇh-âo* (§. 56ᵃ.), "*hujus*," for *a-hmy-âo*, often occurs; and for it
also ﻮﻼﻴﻮ *aiṇh-âo*, in which the *i* is, to use the expression, a reflection of the lost य *y* (§. 41.). From another demonstrative base we find
the dative ﻮﻼﻴﻮ *ava-ṇh-âi*, and more than once the ablative
ﻮﻼﻴﻮ *ava-ṇh-ât* for *ava-hmy-âi*, *ava-hmy-ât*.

thi-zai, "*huic,*" might be deduced from the masculine genitive *this,* by the addition of the terminations *ôs* and *ai* ; and as, too, in Lithuanian, the whole of the oblique cases singular of the 1st and 2d person stand in close connection with the Sanskrit-Zend genitives मम *mama,* ᴊᴊᴊᴕ *mana,* तव *tava,* ᴊᴊᴊᴊᴕ *tava,* and have the same as base.   After discovering the Zend fe-

[G. Ed. p. 204.]   minine pronominal forms in *hmy-a* in the instrumental and locative—in the latter for *hmy-anm*—the above-mentioned forms in Sanskrit cannot be regarded otherwise than as abbreviations of *ta-smy-ai,* &c., as this is far more suited to the nature of the thing.   The Gothic forms then, *thizôs, thizai,* will be regarded as abbreviated, and must be divided into *thi-zô-s, thi-zai.* The masculine and neuter appended pronoun *sma* must, for instance, in Gothic give the feminine base *SMŌ* = स्मा *smâ,* as *BLINDŌ,* nom. *blinda,* "*circa,*" from *BLINDA,* m. n. (nom. *blind'-s, blinda-ta*).   *SMŌ,* however, by the loss of the *m,* as experienced by the Sanskrit in the feminine, has become *SŌ*; but the *s,* on account of its position between two vowels (according to §. 86. 5.), has become *z.* Therefore, *thi-zô-s* * has only *s* as case-sign, and the dative *thi-zai,* like *gibai* in §. 161., is without case character.   With the masculine and neuter genitive *thi-s,* therefore, *thi-zô-s, thi-zai,* have nothing in common but the demonstrative theme *THA,* and the weakening of its *â* to *i* (§. 66.).

173. Gothic adjective bases in *a* (Grimm's strong adjectives) which follow the pronominal declension, differ from it, however, in this point, that they do not weaken the final *a* of the base before the appended pronoun to *i,* but extend it to *ai,* and form the feminine dative from the simple theme, according to the analogy of the substantives : †   hence *blindai-zô-s, blindai,* not *blindi-zô-s, blindi-zai.*

---

* Cf. §. 356. Rem. 3. p. 501. last line but seven.

† With respect to the extension of the *a* to *ai,* compare the gen. pl. and Sanskrit forms, as *tê-bhyas,* " *iis,*" *têshâm,* "*eorum,*" for *ta-bhyas, ta-sâm.*

174. The Zend introduces our pronominal syllable *sma* in the form of *hma* also into the second, and probably into the first person too: we find repeatedly, in the locative, ᵧᵤᵤⳉⳃ *thwa-hm'-i*, instead of the Sanskrit   [G. Ed. p. 205.] तव *tway-i*, and hence deduce, in the 1st person, *ma-him'-i*, which we cannot quote as occurring. The Prâkṛit, in this respect, follows the analogy of the Zend; and in the 2d person gives the form तुमस्मि *tuma-sm'-i*, "in thee," or, with assimilation, तुमम्मि *tumammi*, with तुमे *tumê* (from *tuma-i*) and तइ *tai*; and ममस्मि *mama-sm'-i* or ममम्मि *mama-mmi*, "in me," together with the simple मइ *maé* and मइ *maï*.* Ought not, therefore, in German also, in the singular of the two first persons, a remnant of the pronominal syllable *sma* to be looked for? The *s* in the Gothic *mi-s*, "to me," *thu-s*, "to thee," and *si-s*, "to himself," appears to me in no other way intelligible; for in our Indo-European family of languages there exists no *s* as the suffix of the instrumental or dative. Of similar origin is the *s* in the plural *u-nsi-s*, "*nobis*," "*nos*," *i-zvi-s*, "*vobis*," "*vos*"; and its appearance in two otherwise differently denoted cases cannot therefore be surprising, because this *s* is neither the dative nor accusative character, but belongs to a syllable, which could be declined through all cases, but is here deprived of all case-sign. In *u-nsi-s*, *i-zvi-s*, therefore, the Sanskrit स्म *sma* is doubly contained, once as the base, and next as the apparent case-suffix. I am inclined, also, to affirm of the above-mentioned Prâkrit forms, *tu-ma-sm'i*, "in thee," and *ma-ma-sm'i*, "in me," that they doubly contain the pronominal syllable *sma*, and that the middle syllable has dropped a preceding *s*. For there is no more favourite and facile combination in our class of languages than of a pronoun with a pronoun; and what is omitted by one dialect in this respect is often afterwards supplied by another more modern dialect.

* See *Essai sur le Pali*, by E. Burnouf and Lassen, pp. 173. 175.

[G. Ed. p. 206.]   175. The *k* in the Gothic accusatives *mi-k*, *thu-k*, *si-k* (*me*, *te*, *se*), may be deduced, as above, in *u-gka-ra*, *νῶΐν*, &c., from *s*, by the hardening of an intervening *h*; so that *mi-s* is altered to *mi-h*, and thence to *mi-k*; and therefore, in the singular, as also in the plural, the dative and accusative of the two first persons are, in their origin, identical. In Old High German and Anglo-Saxon our particle appears in the accusative singular and plural in the same form: Old High German *mi-h* "me," *di-h*, "thee," *u-nsi-h*, "us," *i-wi-h*, "you"; Anglo-Saxon *me-c*, "me," *u-si-c*, "us," *thê-c*, "thee," *eo-vi-c*, "you": on the other hand, in the dative singular the old *s* of the syllable *sma* has become *r* in the High German, but has disappeared in the Old Saxon and Anglo-Saxon: Old High German *mi-r*, *di-r*; Old Saxon *mi*, *thi*; Anglo-Saxon *me*, *the*.

176. In Lithuanian स्म *sma* appears in the same form as in the middle of the above-mentioned (§. 174.) Prâkṛit forms; namely, with *s* dropped, as *ma*; and indeed, first, in the dative and locative sing. of the pronouns of the 3d person and adjectives; and, secondly, in the genitive dual of the two first persons: we cannot, however, refer to this the *m*, which the latter in some cases have in common with the substantive declension. The pronominal base *TA*, and the adjective base *GERA*, form, in the dative, *tá-mui*, "to thee," *gerá-mui*, "to the good" (shortened *tám*, *gerám*), and in the locative *ta-mè*, *gera-mè*; and if *-mui* and *-mè* are compared with the corresponding cases of the substantive *a* bases, it is easily seen that *mui* and *mè* have sprung from *ma*. The pronouns of the two first persons form, in the genitive dual, *mu-mû*, *yu-mû*, according to the analogy of *ponû*, "of the two lords."

---

* We have a remnant of a more perfect form of the particle स्म *sma* in the locative interrogative form *ka-mmè*, "where"? Sansk. कस्मिन् *ka-smin*, "in

177. Lithuanian substantives have *i* for　　[G. Ed. p. 207.]
the dative character, but *i* bases have *ei**; a final *a* before
this *i* passes into *u*; hence *wilku-i*. Although we must refuse
a place in the locative to the dative *i* of the Greek and Latin,
still this Lithuanian dative character appears connected with
the Indo-Zend *é*, so that only the last element of this diphthong, which has grown out of *a* + *i*, has been left. For
the Lithuanian has, besides the dative, also a real locative,
which, indeed, in the *a* bases corresponds exactly with the
Sanskṛit and Zend.

178. The nominal bases, Sanskṛit, Zend, and Lithuanian,
explained at §. 148., excepting the neuters ending with a
vowel and pronouns, to the full declension of which we
shall return hereafter, form in the dative:

	SANSKRIT.	ZEND.	LITHUANIAN.
m.	*vṛikâya,*	*vĕhrkâi,*	*wilku-i.*
f.	*jihwây-âi,*	*hizvay-âi,*	*ranka-i.*
m.	*paty-ê,†*	*paite-ê ?‡*	*pách-ei.*
f.	*prîtay-ê,*	*âfríte-ê,*	*áwi-ei.*
f.	*bhavishyanty-âi,*	*bûshyainty-âi,*	. . . .
m.	*sûnav-ê,*	*pasv-ê,*	*sunu-i.*

"in whom," which, according to the common declension, would be
क स्मे *kasmé* (from *kasma-i*). Compare the Gothic *hvamma*, "to whom?"
for *hvasma*.

* The form *áwiui*, with *áwiei* appears to admit of being explained as
arising from the commixture of the final vowel of the *a* bases.

† The form पत्ये *patyé* is, with respect to its want of Guna, irregular,
and should be पतये *patayé*.

‡ In combination with ‌cha we find in V. S., p. 473. ‌
paithyé-cha, and hence deduce for the instrumental (p. 193 G. Ed.) the form
paithya, while, according to ‌. 47., also *paitya* might be expected. From
‌*haci*, "friend," I find in V. S., p. 162, the instrumental ‌
hacaya with Guna, after the analogy of the ‌ *bázava*, mentioned
at ‌. 160.

o

	SANSKRIT.	ZEND.	LITHUANIAN.
f.	*tanuv-ė,*	*tanu-y-ė,**	. . . .
f.	*vadhw-ái,*	. . . .	. . . .
m. f.	*gav-ė,*	*gav-ė,*	. . . .
f.	*náv-ė,*	. . . .	. . . .
f.	*vách-ė,*	*vách-ė.*	. . . .
m.	*bharat-ė,*	*barėnt-ė,*	. . . .
m.	*átman-ė,*	*aśmain-ė,*	. . . .
n.	*námn-ė.‡*	*námain-ė,*	. . . .
m.	*bhrátr-ė,*	*bráthr-ė,*	. . . .
f.	*duhitr-ė,*	*dughdhĕr-ė,†*	. . . .
m.	*dátr-e,*	*dáthr-ė.*	. . . .
n.	*vachas-ė,‡*	*vachanh-ė,*	. . . .

---

* I give ro jjj jso *tanuyė* with euphonic *y*, because I have found this form frequently, which, however, cannot, for this reason, be considered as peculiar to the feminine ; and, instead of it, also *tanvė* and *tanavė* may be regarded as equally correct. Cf. §. 43., where, however, it is necessary to observe, that the insertion of a euphonic jj *y* between *u* and *ė* is not everywhere necessary ; and, for instance, in the dative is the more rare form.

† The ς *ė* in ro jς o o j g *dughdhėrė,* and in the instr. jo jς o o j g *dughdhėra,* is placed there merely to avoid the harsh combination of three consonants. I deduce these forms from the plural genitive ς ro jo o j g *dughdhĕr-ańm,* for ς ro jo o j g *dughdhr-ańm.*

‡ Respecting नाम्ने *námnė,* for नामने *námanė,* and so in the instrumental नाम्ना *námná,* for नामना *námaná,* see §. 140. In Zend, in this and similar words, I have not met with the rejection of the *a* in the weakest cases (§. 130.), but examples of its retention, *e. g.* in the compound *aoctó-náman,* whence the genitive *aoctó-námanó* (Vend. S. p. 4, and frequently). I consider the initial *a* in this compound as the negation, without euphonic *n* ; for in all probability it means "having untold (countless) names." Similar compounds precede, viz. $\varsigma$$\lambda$$j$$j$$ro$$j$$j$ $ro$$j$$j$$\varsigma$$j$$j$$j$$g$ $\psi$$j$$j$$\varsigma$$\lambda$$j$$j$ $\psi$$j$$j$$\varsigma$$\lambda$$j$$j$$\varsigma$ *hazanró-ghaóshahė baėvarĕ-chashmanó,* "of the thousand eared, ten thousand eyed." Cf. Anquetil II. 82. In words in *van*, on the other hand, $j$$j$ *a* is rejected in the weakest cases, and then the » *v* becomes ∍ *u* or $\downarrow$ *o*. Regarding the addition of the j *i* in ro j$j$$j$$j$$\varsigma$$j$$j$ *námainė,* see §. 41.

ABLATIVE.

179. The Ablative in Sanskrit has ऋ *t* [G. Ed. p. 209.]
for its character, regarding the origin of which there can no
longer be any uncertainty, as soon as the influence of
pronouns on the formation of cases has been recognised, as
we are conducted at once to the demonstrative base *ta*,
which already, in the neuter nominative, and accusative,
has assumed the nature of a case-sign, and which we shall
subsequently, under the verb, see receiving the function of
a personal termination. This ablative character, however,
has remained only in bases in व *a*, which is lengthened
before it; a circumstance that induced the Indian Grammarians, who have been followed by the English, to represent
वात् *dt* as the ablative termination. It would therefore be
to be assumed, that in वृकात् *vrikdt* the *a* of the base has
been melted down with the *d* of the termination.*

180. M. E. Burnouf† has been the first [G. Ed. p. 210.]
to bring home the ablative character to a class of words in
Zend which had lost it in Sanskrit, and whence it can be
satisfactorily inferred that a simple *t*, and not *dt*, is the true
ablative character. We mean the declension in *u*, of which
hereafter. As regards bases in *a*, which in Sanskrit alone
have preserved the ablative, we have to observe, that in

---

* I have drawn attention already, in the first (German) edition of my
Sanskrit Grammar, to the arbitrary and unfounded nature of this assumption (§§. 156. and 264.); and I have deduced from the ablatives of the
pronouns of the two first persons (*mat, twat*) that either *at* with short *a*, or,
more correctly, a simple *t*, must be regarded as the ablative termination.
This view I supported in the Latin edition of my Grammar, on the ground
that in old Latin also a simple *d* appears as the suffix of the ablative. But
since then the justness of my opinion regarding the Sanskrit ablative has
been still more emphatically confirmed by the Zend language, because the
Zend stands in a closer and more evident connection with the Sanskrit
than does the Latin.

† Nouveau Journal Asiatique 1829, tom. III. 311.

Zend also the short vowel is lengthened, and thus ونهرکاو
vĕhrkā-ṭ answers to वृकात् *vrikā-t.*   Bases in ى *i* have *ōi-t*
in the ablative; whence may be inferred in Sanskrit ablatives
like पतेत् *patē-t,* प्रीतेत् *prītē-t* (§. 33.), which, by adding Guna
to the final vowel, would agree with genitives in *ē-s.*   The
Zend-Avesta, as far as it is hitherto edited, nevertheless
offers but few examples of such ablative forms in ى *ōi-ṭ*:
I owe the first perception of them to the word آفریتوئو
āfrītōiṭ, "*benedictione,*" in a passage of the Vendidâd,[*] explained elsewhere, which recurs frequently.   Examples of
masculine bases are perhaps آزراتوشتروئو آزرایى *rajvit*
zaratustrōiṭ, "*institutione zarutustricā*" (V. S. p. 86), although
otherwise آزرایى *raji,* which I have not elsewhere met with,
is a masculine: the adjective base *zaratustri,* however, belongs to the three genders.   From گائیرى *gairi,* "moun-

[G. Ed. p. 211.] tain," occurs the ablative گاروئو *garōiṭ*
in the Yescht-Sâde.[†]   Bases in *u* have ائو *ao-ṭ*[‡] in the
ablative‖; and in no class of words, with the exception of

---

[*] See Gramm. Crit. add. ad r. 156.

[†] What Anquetil III. 170. Rem. 4, writes *guerōed* can be nothing else
than the ablative گاروئو *garōiṭ,* for Anquetil generally expresses
گ by *gu,* ى by *e,* ئو by *ōe,* and ق by *d.* The nominal base گائیرى *gairi,*
however, is treated in Zend as if *gari* was the original form, and the *i*
which precedes the *r* was produced by the final *i,* as remarked by
M. Burnouf in the article quoted at p. 173, and confirmed by the genitive
گاروئیس *garōis.* That, however, which is remarked by M. Burnouf,
l. c. with respect to the genitive, and of which the Vend. S. p. 64. affords
frequent proof in the genitive پاتوئیس *patōis,* must also be extended to
the ablative in *ōit;* and the *i,* which, according to §. 41., is adduced through
the final ى *i* of the base, is dropped again before this termination.

[‡] For this we also find ائو *eut;* e.g. مائینیئوت *mainyeuṭ* from
mainyu.

[‖] Interchanges of ب *o* and ب *ō* are particularly common, owing to the
slight difference of these letters. Thus, e.g. for مرائوت *mraōṭ,* "he
spoke," occurs very frequently مرائوت *mraoṭ;* the former, however, is,
as we can satisfactorily prove, the right reading; for, first, it is supported
                                                                                    by

that in *a*, does the ablative more frequently occur, although these words are in number but five or six, the ablative use of which is very frequent; e.g. *dâonhaôt*, "creatione," from *dâonhu*, in a passage explained elsewhere[*] *anhaô-t*, "mundo," from *anhu*; *tanaôt* "corpore," from *tanu*. Bases ending with consonants are just as little able to annex the [G. Ed. p. 212.] ablative *t* without the intervention of another letter, as the accusative is to annex *m* without an intermediate letter; and they have *at* as their termination, numerous examples of which occur; e.g. *ap-at*, "aquâ"; *âthr-at*, "igne"; *chashman-at*, "oculo"; *ndonhan-at* "naso"; *druj-at*, "dæmone"; *vîs-at*, "loco" (cf. *vicus*, according to §. 21.). Owing to the facile interchange of the *a* with *â*, *ât* is sometimes erroneously written for *at*; thus, Vendidâd S. p. 338, *saôchant-ât* for *saôchant-at* "lucente." Bases in *u* sometimes follow the

---

by the Sanskrit form अब्रोत् *abrôt*, for which the irregular form अब्रवीत् *abrav-ît* is used; and secondly, it answers to the 1st pers. *mraôm* (V. S. p. 123); thirdly, the Sanskrit ओ *ô* is, in Zend, never represented by *ao*, but by *ô*, before which, according to §. 28., another *a* is placed, hence *aô*: on the other hand, *ao* represents *u*, in accordance with §. 32 and §. 28. If, then, *paśu* formed in the ablative *paśaot*, this would conduct us to a Sanskrit पशोत् *paśu t*; while from the ablatives *âfrîtôi-t*, *zaratustrôi-t*, *garôi-t*, and from the analogy, in other respects, with the genitive, the Guna form, पशोत् *paśô-t* must be deduced. Moreover, in the Vend. S. the ablative form *aô-t* actually occurs; for at p. 102. (*hacha vanheaô-t mananh-at*, "from pure spirit") occurs *vanheaôt*, the ablative of *vanhu*; and the *e* preceding the *a* is an error in orthography, and *vanhaôt* is the form intended: p. 245 occurs *anhaôt*, "mundo," from *anhu*.

[*] Gramm. Crit. §. 640. ann. 2.

consonantal declension in having ‌‍‌ *aṭ* as the ablative termination instead of a mere *ṭ*; just as in the genitive, besides
a simple *s*, they exhibit also an *ó* (from *as*, §. 56[b].), although
more rarely.   Thus, for the above-mentioned ‌‍‌‍
tanaoṭ, "*corpore*," occurs also *tanv-aṭ* (Vend. S. p. 482).*
Feminine bases in ‌‍ *á* and *ɟ i* have ‌‍‌ *áṭ* in the ablative,
as an analogous form to the feminine genitive termination
वास् *ás*, whence, in the Zend ‌‍ *áo*; *e.g.* ‌‍‌‍‌
dahmay-áṭ, "*præclara*," from ‌‍‌‍ *ɟ dahmá*; ‌‍‌‍‌
urvaray-áṭ) "*arbore*," from ‌‍‌‍ *urvará*; ‌‍‌‍‌
[G. Ed. p. 213.]   *barĕthry-áṭ*, "*genitrice*," from ‌‍‌ *barĕ-*
thrî.† The feminine bases also in *u*, and perhaps also those
in *i*, may share this feminine termination ‌‍‌ *áṭ*; thus,
from *zantu*, "begetting," comes the ablative *zanthw-áṭ* (cf.
Gramm. Crit. §. 640. Rem. 2.).   Although, then, the ablative
has been sufficiently shewn to belong to all declensions in
Zend, and the ablative relation is also, for the most part,
denoted by the actual ablative, still the genitive not unfrequently occurs in the place of the ablative, and even
adjectives in the genitive in construction with substantives in the ablative.   Thus we read, Vend S. p. 479,
‌‍‌‍‌‍‌‍‌‍‌ *hacha*
avaṇháṭ‡ *riśaṭ yaṭ mázdayaśnôis*, "*ex hac terrd quidem maz-*
dayasnicá."

---

* Burnouf writes *tanavaṭ*, probably according to another Codex.
I hold both forms to be correct, the rather as in the genitive, also, both
tanv-ô and *tanav-ô* occur; and in general, before all terminations beginning
with a vowel, both the simple form and that with Guna are possible.

† Vendidâd Sâde, p. 436: ‌‍‌‍‌‍‌‍‌
‌‍‌‍‌‍‌‍ *Yatha vehrkó*
chathwarĕ-jangrô nishdarĕdairyáṭ barĕthryaṭ hacha puthrĕm, "As a wolf,
a four-footed animal, tears a child from its mother." This sentence is
also important as an example of the intensive form (cf. Gramm. Crit.
§. 303.)   The Codex, however, divides incorrectly *nishdarĕ dairyáṭ*.

‡ Regarding this form, see p. 172. Rem.

181. The Old Roman corresponds with the Zend in regard to the designation of the ablative; and in those two memorials of the language, that on the *Columna rostrata*, and the *S. C. de Bacchanalibus*, which are the most important inscriptions that remain, all ablatives end with *d*; so that it is surprising that the ablative force of this letter could be overlooked, and that the empty name of a paragogic *d* could be held satisfactory. Bases ending with a consonant use *ed* as ablative suffix, as in the accusative they have *em* instead of a simple *m*: hence, forms like *præsent-ed dictator-ed*, answer to the Zend *saôchant-at âthr-at* (*lucente igne*); while *navale-d* prædu-d, inallo-d mari-d, senatu-d*, like the above-mentioned Zend forms ᵱᵾᵷᵻᵾᵽ *garôi-t*, "*monte*," ᵱᵾᵷᵻᵾᵽ *tanaô-t*, "*corpore*," &c.; and in Sanskrit वृकात् *vṛikâ-t*, "*lupo*," have a simple *T* sound to denote the ablative. The Oscan also takes the ablative sign *d* through all declensions, as appears from the remarkable inscription of Bantia, *e.g. dolu-d* [G. Ed p. 214.] *mallu-d, cum preivatu-d, touta-d præsenti-d.†* It may be preliminarily observed, that, in the 3d person of the imperative, old Latin and Oscan forms like *es-tod, es-tud*—for *es-to*, and therefore with a double designation of person—correspond remarkably to similar Vêda forms with which we are hitherto acquainted only from Pânini ; *e.g.* जीवतात् *jîva-tât,* which signifies both "*vivat*" and "*vive*," but in the latter sense is probably only an error in the use of the language (cf. *vivito* as 3d and 2d person).

182. In classical Latinity a kind of petrified ablative form appears to be contained in the appended pronoun *met*, which may be transferred from the 1st person to the others also, and answers to the Sanskrit ablative *mat*, "from me." But it is possible, also, that *met* may have

---

* The *e* here belongs to the base, which alternates between *e* and *i*.
† See O. Müller's Etruscans, p. 36.

dropped an initial *s*, and may stand for *smet*, and so belong to the appended pronoun स्म *sma*, explained in §. 165.
&c., corresponding with its ablative *smât*, to which it
stands in the same relation that *memor* (for *mesmor*) does
to स्मृ *smṛi*—from *smar*, §. 1.—"to remember." The combination of this syllable, then, with pronouns of the three
persons, would require no excuse, for स्म *sma*, as has
been shewn, unites itself to all persons, though it must
itself be regarded as a pronoun of the 3d person.* The
conjunction *sed*, too, is certainly nothing but the ablative
of the reflexive; and *sed* occurs twice in the *S. C. de Bacch.*
as an evident pronoun, and, in fact, governed by *inter ;*
[G. Ed. p. 215.]   whence it may be assumed that *inter* can
be used in construction with the ablative, or also that, in the
old languages, the accusative is the same with the ablative:
the latter view is confirmed by the accusative use of *ted* and
med in Plautus.

† 183. In Sanskṛit the ablative expresses distance from a
place, the relation " whence ;" and this is the true, original
destination of this case, to which the Latin remained
constant in the names of towns.   From the relation
" whence," however, the ablative is, in Sanskṛit, transferred to the causal relation also; since that on account
of which any thing is done is regarded as the place whence
an action proceeds.   In this manner the confines of the ablative and instrumental touch one another, and तेन *téna* (§. 158.)
and तस्मात् *tasmât*, may both express "on account of which."
In adverbial use the ablative spreads still further, and in
some words denotes relations, which are otherwise foreign
to the ablative.   In Greek, adverbs in ως may be looked upon
as sister forms of the Sanskṛit ablative; so that ω-ς, from
bases in *o*, would have the same relation to the Sanskṛit

---

* The reduplication in *me-mor*, from *me-smor*, would be of the kind
used in Sanskṛit, *e.g. pasparśa*, "he touched," of which hereafter.

† Cf. the Gothic ablatives in *ó*, adduced in §. 294. Rem. 1. p. 384.

आत् *á-t*, from bases in *a*, that, *e.g.* δίδωσι has to द्दाति *dadá-ti.*
Thus, ὁμῶ-ς may be akin to the Sanskrit समात् *samá-t,*
"from the similar," both in termination and in base. In
Greek, the transition of the *T* sounds into ς was requisite, if
indeed they were not to be entirely suppressed*; and in
§. 152. we have seen neuter bases in τ, in the uninflected
cases, preserve their final letter from being entirely lost by
changing it into ς. We deduce, therefore,   [G. Ed. p. 216.]
adverbs like ὁμῶ-ς, οὕτω-ς, ὦ-ς, from ὁμῶ-τ, οὕτω-τ, ὦ-τ or
ὁμῶ-δ, &c., and this is the only way of bringing these formations into comparison with the cognate languages; and it is
not to be believed that the Greek has created for this adverbial relation an entirely peculiar form, any more than
other case-terminations can be shewn to be peculiar to the
Greek alone. The relation in adverbs in ω-ς is the same as
that of Latin ablative forms like *hoc modo, quo modo, raro,
perpetuo.* In bases ending with a consonant, ος for οτ might
be expected as the termination, in accordance with Zend
ablatives like ↄᙄᙄ↉ᙄᙄ *chashman-at,* "*oculo*"; but then
the ablative adverbial termination would be identical with
that of the genitive: this, and the preponderating analogy
of adverbs from *o* bases, may have introduced forms like
σωφρόν-ως, which, with respect to their termination, may be
compared with Zend feminine ablatives like ↄᙄↄↄ↉ᙄↄↄ
burēthry-át. We must also, with reference to the irregular length of this adverbial termination, advert to the
Attic genitives in ως for ος.†

---

* As, in οὕτω, together with οὕτω-ς, ὧδε, ἄφνω, and adverbs from
prepositions—ἔξω, ἄνω, κάτω, &c. It is here desirable to remark, that in
Sanskrit, also, the ablative termination occurs in adverbs from prepositions,
as अधस्तात् *adhastát,* "(from) beneath," पुरस्तात् *purastát,* "(from) before,"
&c. (Gram. Crit. §. 652. p. 273.).

† In compounds, remains of ablative forms may exist with the original
T sound retained. We will therefore observe, that in Ἀφροδίτη the first
member

THE GENITIVE.

[G. Ed. p. 217.]   184. In no case do the different members
of the Sanskrit family of languages agree so fully as in the
genitive singular; only that in Latin the two first declensions, together with the fifth, as well as the two first persons
of the pronouns, have lost their old termination, and have replaced it by that of the old locative. The Sanskrit terminations of the genitive are स् *s,* स्य *sya,* अस् *as,* and आस् *ás:*
the three first are common to the three genders: *as* is

---

member has a genuine ablative meaning; and as the division ἀφρο-δίτη
admits of no satisfactory explanation, one may rest satisfied with ἀφροδ-ίτη.
In Sanscrit, अभ्रादिता *abhráditá* would mean "the female who proceeded
from a cloud," for *abhrá-t* must become *abhrád* before *itá* (§. 93'.); and in
neuter verbs the otherwise passive participial suffix *ta* has usually a past
active meaning. Of this usage ιτη, in ἀφροδ-ίτη, might be a remnant, and
this compound might mean, therefore, "She who arose, who sprang, from
foam." The only difficulty here is the short vowel of οδ for ωδ. As regards the Sanskrit, here also the *s* of the ablative may in most declensions
rest on an exchange with an older *t* (cf. p. 184 G. ed. Note); and, as the
Zend gives us every reason to expect Sanskrit ablatives like *jihwáy-át,*
prité-t, súnó-t, bhavishyanty-át, átman-at; so it will be most natural to
refer the existing forms *jihwáy-ás, prité-s,* &c., where they have an ablative meaning, to the exchange of *t* with *s,* which is more or less in vogue
according to the variety of dialects; particularly as it is known, also, that,
vice versâ, according to certain laws, स् *s* passes into त् *t* (Gramm. Crit.
§. 100.). Consequently the identity between the genitive and ablative, in
most declensions, would be only external, and the two cases would vary
in their history; so that, *e.g. jihwáy-ás* would be, in one sense, viz. in that
of *linguæ,* independent and original; and in another, that of *linguá,* a
corruption of *jihwáy-át.* At the time when Sanskrit and Zend were separated from one another, the retention of the original *t* must have been
the prevailing inclination, and, together with it, may also its change into
s have arisen, as the Zend also uses, at times, the genitive form with an
ablative meaning (*e.g.* Vend. S. p. 177.).

principally confined to the consonantal bases,* and hence has the same relation to *s* that, in the accusative, *am* has to *m*, and, in the Zend ablative, *at* has to *t*.

185. Before the genitive sign स *s* the [G. Ed. p. 218.] vowels इ *i* and उ *u* take Guna; and the Zend, and in a more limited degree, also the Lithuanian and Gothic, share this augment. All *u* bases, for example, in Lithuanian and Gothic, prefix an *a* to their final vowel: hence the Lithuanian *sunaù-s* and Gothic *sunau-s* correspond to the Sanskrit सूनोस् *sûnôs* (*filii*) from *sunaus* (§. 2.). In the *i* bases in Gothic, Guna is restricted to the feminines; thus *anstai-s*, "*gratiæ*," answers to प्रीतेस् *prîtê-s*. Respecting Lithuanian genitives of *i* bases see §. 193. The High German has, from the earliest period, dropped the genitive sign in all feminines: in consonantal bases (§§. 125. 127.) the sign of the genitive is wanting in the other genders also.

186. The form which the Sanskrit genitive termination after consonants assumes, as it were of necessity (§. 94.), viz. *as* for *s*, has in Greek, in the form ος, passed over also to the vowels ι and υ and diphthongs terminating in υ; and genitives like πορτει-ς, ἰχθευ-ς, which would be in accordance with §. 185. are unheard of; but πόρτι-ος, ἰχθύ-ος answer, like ποδ-ός, to Sanskrit genitives of consonantal bases, as पदस् *pad-as*, "*pedis*," वाचस् *vâch-as*, "*vocis*." The Latin, on the other hand, answers more to the other sister languages, but is without Guna: so *hosti-s* is like the Gothic genitive *gasti-s*. In the *u* bases (fourth declension) the lengthening of the *u* may replace the Guna, or, more correctly, this class of words followed the Greek or consonantal principle, and the vowel dropped before *s* was compensated for by

---

* Besides this, it occurs only in monosyllabic bases in इ *i*, उ *û*, ए *ài*, and ौ *àu*; e.g. राय-अस् *rây-as*, "*rei*," नाव-अस् *nâv-as*, "*navis*:" and in neuters in इ *i* and उ *u*, which, by the assumption of an euphonic न् *n*, assimilate to the consonantal declension in most cases.

lengthening the *u*. The *S. C. de Bacch.* gives the genitive *senatu-os* in Grecian garb. Otherwise the termination *is* of consonantal bases is better derived from the Sanskrit अस्

[G. Ed. p. 219.] *as* than from the Greek *ος*, because the old Sanskrit *a* in other places in Latin has been weakened to *i*, as frequently happens in Gothic (§§. 66. 67.).

187. With regard to the *senatu-os* just mentioned, it is important to remark, that, in Zend also, the *u* bases, instead of annexing a simple *s* in the genitive, as ‏مَينيُوس‎ *mainyĕu-s,* "of the spirit," from *mainyu*, may, after the manner of consonantal bases, add ◌ *ò* (from *as*, cf. p. 212, G. Ed.), as ‏دَنهُو‎ *danhv-ò,* or ‏دَنهَوُ‎ *danhav-ò,* for *danheu-s* "*loci,*" from ‏دَنهُ‎ *danhu.* This kind of genitive occurs very frequently as a substitute for the locative, as also for the ablative (Vend. S. p. 177), more rarely with a genuine genitive meaning.*

188. Bases in अ *a,* and pronouns of the third person, of which only *amu* ends with a vowel other than *a*, have, in Sanskrit, the more full genitive sign स्य *sya*; hence, *e. g.* वृकस्य *vrika-sya,* "*lupi,*" तस्य *ta-sya,* "*hujus,*" &c., अमुष्य *amu-shya,*

---

* It might be assumed that as βασιλέος clearly stands for βασιλέϜος, βοός for βοϜός, ναός for ναϜός, (§. 124.), so also ἄστεος would stand for ἄστεϜος, and that ἄστεος, therefore, should be compared with the Zend genitives with Guna, as ‏دَنهَوُ‎ *danhav-ò.* The ε, therefore, in ἄστεος would not be a corrupted *υ* of the base, but the Guna vowel foreign to the base; but the *υ* of the base, which, according to the original law of sound, must become Ϝ before vowels, is, like all other digammas in the actual condition of the language, suppressed. The ε is certainly a very heterogeneous vowel to the *υ*, and the corruption of the latter to ε, in the middle of a word, would be a greater violation of the old relations of sound than the rejection of a *υ* sound between two vowels. The corruption of ĭ to ĕ is less surprising, and occurs also in Old High German (j. 72.). In Greek, also, a consonant *y* is wanting, but cannot have been originally deficient; and therefore the question might be mooted whether also πόλεως, σινάπεος may not stand for *pole-yòs, sinape-yos.*

"*illius,*" (§. 21.) In Zend this termination   [G. Ed. p. 220.]
appears in the form of *hê*, (§. 42.): hence, *e. g.* ᵰᵕᵂᵕ᷈ᵍᵎᵛᵧᵱ
vêhrkahê, "*lupi,*" ᵰᵕᵂᵚᵵᵶᵍᵱ *tûiryê-hê,* "*quarti,*" for *tûirya-hê.*

189. In Greek and Latin we have already, in another
place, pointed out a remnant of the genitive termination
रय *sya,* and, in fact, precisely in places where it might be
most expected.   As bases in व *a* correspond to the Greek
bases in *o,* and as σ in Greek at the furthest extremity of words
between two vowels is generally dislodged, I do not entertain the smallest doubt that the old epic genitive termination
in *ιo* is an abbreviation of σιo; and that *e. g.* in τοῖο = तस्य
ta-sya, the first *o* belongs to the base, and only *ιo* to the
case-sign.   As regards, however, the loss of the σ in τοῖο, the
Greek Grammar supplies us with another οῖο, where a Σ is
lost, the necessary and original existence of which no one
can doubt: ἐδίδοσο, and the ancient position of the Σ in the
second person, testify for διδοισο instead of διδοῖο, as for ἐλε-
γεσο instead of ἐλέγου, just as the Indian तस्य *ta-sya* for
το-σιο instead of τοῖο.   In the common language the *ι,* also,
has been dropped after the σ, and the *o* of the termination,
which has remained, has been contracted with that of the base
to *ου*; hence τοῦ from το-ο.   The Homeric form *ao* (Βορέαο,
Αἰνείαο) belongs likewise to this place, and stands for α-ιο,
and this for α-σιο (§. 116.).   The Latin has transposed our
रय *sya* to *jus,* with the change, which is so frequent, of the
old *a* before the final *s* to *u* (cf. वृकस् *vrika-s,* "*lupu-s,*" युनज्मस्
yunjmns, jungimus); hence, *hu jus, cu-jus, e-jus, illius* for *illi-
-jus,* &c.   I cannot, however, believe that the *i* of the second
declension is an abbreviation of οιο, of which the *ι* alone has
been retained;[*] for it is clear that *lupi* and   [G. Ed. p. 221.]
lupæ from *lupai* rest on the same principle; and if *lupi* proceeds from λύκοιο, whence can *lupai* be derived, as the corresponding Greek feminines nowhere exhibit an αιο or ηιο?

---

[*] Hartung's Cases, p. 211.

190. In Lithuanian the genitives of the *a* bases differ remarkably from those of the other declensions, and denote the case by *o*, in which vowel, at the same time, the final vowel of the base is contained; thus, *wilko*, " *lupi*," for *wilka-s*. It is probable that this *o* (*ō*) has arisen from *a-s*, according to a contraction similar to that in the Zend (§. 56ᵇ.). In old Sclavonic, also, *o* occurs, answering to the Sanskrit *as*; and *nebo*, gen. *nebese*, corresponds to the Sanskrit नभस् *nabhas*. That, however, the Lithuanian has left the syllable *as* in the nominative unaltered, but in the genitive has contracted it to *o*, may induce the remark, that like corruptions do not always find entrance in like places, if they have not raised themselves to a pervading law. In this manner, in Gothic, the old *a* has remained in the interrogative base *HVA* in the nominative (*hvas*), but in the genitive *hvi-s* the weakening to *i* has taken place; so that here, as in Lithuanian, only the more worthy powerful nominative has preserved the older more powerful form, and an unorganic difference has found its way into the two cases, which ought to be similar.

191. The Gothic has no more than the Lithuanian preserved a remnant of the more full genitive termination *sya*, and the Gothic *a* bases, in this case, resemble the *i* bases, because *a* before final *s* has, according to §. 67., become weakened to *i*; thus *vulfi-s* for *vulfa-s*; as also in Old Saxon the corresponding declension exhibits *a-s* together with *e-s*, although more rarely; thus, *daga-s*, " of the day,"

[G. Ed. p. 222.] answering to the Gothic *dagi-s*. The consonantal bases have, in Gothic, likewise a simple *s* for case-sign; hence, *ahmin-s*, *fiyand-s*, *brôthr-s* (§. 132.). The older sister dialects lead us to conjecture that originally an *a*, more lately an *i*, preceded this *s*—*ahmin-as*, *fiyand-as*, *brôthr-as*,—which, as in the nominative of the *a* bases (*vulf-s* for *vulfa-s*), has been suppressed. The Zend exhibits in the *r* roots an agreement with the Gothic, and forms, *e. g.* ⲱⲗⲟⲩ *nar-s*, " of the man," not *nar-ó*, probably on account of the nature of the *r* bordering on that of a vowel, and of its facile combination with *s*.[*]

192. Feminines in Sanskrit have a fuller genitive termination in bases ending with a vowel, viz. *ás* for simple *s* (see §. 113.); and, in fact, so that the [G. Ed. p. 223.] short-ending bases in इ *i* and उ *u* may use at will either simple म् *s* or आम् *ás*; and instead of प्रीतेस् *prité-s*, तनोस् *tanó-s*, also प्रीत्यास् *príty-ás*, तन्वास् *tanw-ás*, occur. The long vowels आ *á*, ई *í*, ऊ *ú*,[†] have always आस् *ás*; hence, जिह्वायास् *jihwáy-ás*, भविष्यन्त्यास् *bhavishyanty-ás*, वध्वास् *vadhw-ás*. This termination आस् *ás*, is, in Zend, according to §. 56[b]., sounded *áo*; hence, ϩϩϩϩϩϩϩϩϩϩ *hizvay-áo*, ϩϩϩϩϩϩϩϩϩϩ *bushyainty-áo*. In bases in ᳵ *i* and ᳵ *u* I have not met

---

[*] Hence I deduce the genitives ϩϩϩϩϩϩ *brátar-s*, ϩϩϩϩϩϩ *dughdhar-s*—which cannot be quoted—and the probability that the corresponding Sanskrit forms are properly *bhrátur*, *duhitur*, which cannot be gleaned from the Sanskrit alone, on account of §. 11., and by reason of the elsewhere occurring euphonic interchange of *s* and *r*. भ्रातुर् *bhrátur*, and similar forms, would therefore stand for -*urs*, and this apparently for *ars*, through the influence of the liquids; and, according to §. 94., they would have lost the genitive sign. The same is the case with the numeral adverb चतुर् *chatur*, "four times," for चतुर्स् *chaturs*; for which the Zend, by transposing the *r*, gives ϩϩϩϩϩ *chathrus* (§. 44.). The Indian Grammarians also, in the genitives under discussion, assume the absence of the genitive sign (Laghu-Kaumudí, p. 35). As, however, the Visarga, in क्रोष्टु *króshtu* (from the theme क्रोष्टर् *króshtar* or क्रोष्टृ *króshtri*, see §. 1.), may evidently stand as well for *s* as for *r*; so in such doubtful cases it is of no consequence to which side the Indian Grammarians incline, where arguments are not found in the Sanskrit itself, or in the cognate languages, which either confirm or refute their statements. And it is impossible, if the Visarga, in भ्रातुः *bhrátuh*, stands for *r*, that the preceding *u* can be a transposition of the final letter of the base (भ्रत् उर्), for this cannot be both retained in the form of *r*, and yet changed into *u* (cf. Colebrook, p. 55, Rem.)

[†] Only the few monosyllabic words make an exception. (Gramm. Crit. §. 130.)

with this termination; together with *âfrîtôi-s*, *taneu-s*, or *tanv-ô*, *tanav-ô*, I find no *âfrîthy-âo*, *tanv-âo*. The cognate European languages exhibit no stronger termination in the feminine than in the masculine and neuter; the Gothic, however, shews a disposition to greater fulness in the feminine genitive, inasmuch as the *ô* bases preserve this vowel in contradistinction to the nominative and accusative; but the *i* bases, as has been shewn above, attach Guna to this vowel, while the masculines do not strengthen it at all. Compare *gibô-s* with the uninflected and base-abbreviated nominative and accusative *giba*, and *anstai-s* with *gasti-s*. Respecting the pronominal and adjective genitives, as *thi-zô-s*, *blindai-zô-s*, see §. 172. The Greek, also, in its feminine first declension preserves the original vowel length in words which have weakened the nominative and accusative—σφύρᾱς, Μούσης, [G. Ed. p. 224.] opposed to σφῦρᾰ, σφύρᾰ-ν, μοῦσᾰν.* In Latin, also, *ā-s*, with the original length of the base *escās*, *terrās*, &c. stands opposed to *escă*, *escă-m*. It cannot be supposed that these genitives are borrowed from the Greek; they are exactly what might be expected to belong to a language that has *s* for the genitive character. That, however, this form, which no doubt extended originally to all *a* bases, gradually disappeared, leaving nothing but a few remains, and that the language availed itself of other helps, is in accordance with the usual fate of languages which continually lose more and more of their old hereditary possessions.

193. The Lithuanian, in its genitive *rank-ôs* for *rankâ-s*,

---

* The Attic termination ως is, perhaps, a perfect transmission of the Sanskrit आस् *âs*; so that forms like πόλε-ως answer to प्रीत्यास् *prity-âs*. Although the Greek ως is not limited to the feminine, it is nevertheless excluded from the neuter (ἄστεος), and the preponderating number of ι bases are feminine.

resembles the Gothic; and in some other cases, also, replaces the feminine _ā_ by a long or short _o_. It is doubtful
how the genitives of _i_ bases, like _awiės_, are to be regarded.
As they are, for the most part, feminine, and the few masculines may have followed the analogy of the prevailing
gender, the division _awi-ės_ might be made; and this might
be derived, through the assimilative force of the _i_, from
awi-ās (cf. p. 174, note*), which would answer to the Sanskrit genitives like प्रीत्याम् _prīty-ás_. If, however, it be compared with प्रीतेस् _prités_, and the _ė_ of _awiės_ be looked upon
as Guna of the _i_ (§. 26.), then the reading _awiės_ for _awėv_ is
objectionable. Ruhig, indeed, in his Glossary, frequently
leaves out the _i_, and gives _ugnės_, "of the fire," for _ugniės_;
but in other cases, also, an _i_ is suppressed before the _e_
generated by its influence (p. 174, note*); and, _e.g._, all
feminine bases in _yā_ have, in the genitive, _ės_ for _i-ės_ or _y-ės_,
as _giesmė-s_, for _giesmyės_, from _GIESMYÁ_ (see p. 169, note).
Therefore the division _awiė-s_ might also be made, and it
might be assumed that the _i_ bases have, in some cases, experienced an extension of the base, similar to those which
were explained in the note, p. 174 (cf. §. 120.). This
view appears to me the most correct, espe-   [G. Ed. p. 225.]
cially as in the vocative, also, _awiė_ answers to _giesme_ for
giesmye, or _giesmie_.

194. As regards the origin of the form through which,
in the genitive, the thing designated is personified, with
the secondary notion of the relation of space, the language
in this case returns back to the same pronoun, whence, in
§. 134., the nominative was derived. And there is a pronoun for the fuller termination also, viz. स्य _sya_, which occurs
only in the Vêdas (cf. §. 55.), and the _s_ of which is replaced
in the oblique cases likewise, as in the neuter, by _t_ (Gramm.
Crit. §. 268.); so that स्य _sya_ stands in the same relation to
त्यम् _tya-m_ and त्यत् _tya-t_ that स _sa_ does to तम् _ta-m_, तत् _ta-t_.
It is evident, therefore, that in स्य _sya_, त्य _tya_, the bases स _sa_,
त _ta_, are contained, with the vowel suppressed and united

P

with the relative base य *ya*. Here follows a general view
of the genitive formation :*

	SANSKRIT.	ZEND.	GREEK.	LATIN.	LITHUAN.	GOTHIC.
m.	*vṛika-sya,*	*vĕhrku-hĕ,*	λύκο-ιο,	. . . .	*wilkō,*	*vulfi-s.*
m.	*ka-sya,*	*ka-hĕ,*	. . . .	*cu-jus,*	*kō,*	*hvi-s.*
f.	*jihwáy-ás,*	*hizvay-áo,*	χώρᾱ-ς,	*terrā-s,*	*rankó-s,*	*gibó-s.*
m.	*patĕ-s,*	*patói-s,*	. . . .	*hosti-s,*	. . . . † *gasti-s.*	
	paty-us,	. . . .	πόσι-ος,	. . . .	. . . .	. . . .
f.	*prĭtĕ-s,*	*áfrĭtŏi-s,*	. . . .	*siti-s,*	. . . . † *anstai-s*	
	prĭty-ás,	. . . .	φύσε-ως,	. . . .	. . . .	. . . .
f.	*bhaviṣhyanty-ás,*	*báshyainty-áo,*	. . . .	. . . .	. . . .	. . . .
m.	*sûnô-s,*	*paśeu-s,*	. . . .	. . . .	*sunaù-s,*	*sunau-s.*
	. . . .	*paśv-ó,*	ἰχθύ-ος,	. . . .	. . . .	. . . .
f.	*tanô-s,*	*taneu-s,*	. . . .	*socrū-s,*	. . . .	*handau-*
	tanw-ás,	*tanv-ó,*	πίτυ-ος,	. . . .	. . . .	. . . .
f.	*vadhw-ás,*	. . . .	. . . .	. . . .	. . . .	. . . .
m.f.	*gô-s,*	*geu-s,*	βο(F)-ός,	*bov-is,*	. . . .	. . . .
f.	*náv-as,*	. . . .	νᾱ(F)-ός,	. . . .	. . . .	. . . .
f.	*vách-as,*	*vách-ó,‡*	ὀπ-ός,	*voc-is,*	. . . .	. . . .
m.	*bharat-as,*	*barĕnt-ó,§*	φέροντ-ος,	*ferent-is,*	. . . . ‖ *fiyand-i*	
m.	*átman-as,*	*aśman-ó,‡*	δαίμον-ος,	*sermon-is,*	*ákmen-s,*	*ahmin-s*
n.	*námn-as,*	*náman-ó,‡*	τάλαν-ος,	*nomin-is,*	. . . .	*namin-s*

[left margin: [Ø. Ed. p. 233.]]

---

* The meanings will be found in §. 148.

† See §. 193.

‡ See p. 168. Note †.

§ And ψρѕѕ *baratô* also may occur, according to the analogy of
ψρѕхсᶟᴇѕ *bĕrĕzató*, "*splendentis*," V. S. p. 87, and *passim*. The retention of the nasal in the genitive, however, as in all other cases, is the more
common form, and can be abundantly quoted. For ψρᵤᴡᴇᶟѕѕ *barĕntô*,
also ψρᵤᴡᴠѕѕ *barantô*, is possible, and likewise, in the other cases, the
older ѕ *a* for ᴇ *ĕ*. In some participles, as in ѕᴡᴊᴊᴊᴜᴠᶠ *fnuyańs* (nom.),
which is of constant recurrence as the usual epithet of agriculture
(ᴊᴊᴊᶌᴡᴊᴜᴠᴊ *vaiśtrya*) ᴇ *ĕ* never occurs.

‖ Vide §. 254. p. 302, Note ‡.

SANSKRIT.	ZEND.	GREEK.	LATIN.	LITHUAN.	GOTHIC.
m. *bhrâtur,*	*brâtar-s,*	πατρ-ος,	*fratr-is,*	....	*brôthr-s.*
f. *duhitur,*	*dughdhar-s,*†	θυγατρ-ός,	*matr-is,*	*dugter-s,*	*dauhtr-s.*
m. *dâtur,*	*dâtar-s,*	δοτῆρ-ος,	*dator-is,*	....	....
n. *vachas-as,*	*vachanh-ñ,*‡	ἔπε(σ)-ος,	*oper-is,*	....	....

THE LOCATIVE.

195. This case has, in Sanskṛit and Zend,§ *i* for its character, and in Greek and Latin‖ has received the function of the dative, yet has not suffered its locative [G. Ed. p. 227.] signification to be lost; hence, Δωδῶνι, Μαραθῶνι, Σαλαμῖνι, ἀγρῷ, οἴκοι, χαμαί; and, transferred to time, τῇ αυτῇ ἡμέρᾳ, τῇ αὐτῇ νυκτί. So in Sanskṛit, दिवसे *divasé,* "in the day;" निशि *niśi,* "in the night."

196. With अ *a* of the base preceding it, the locative इ *i* passes into ए *ê* (§. 2.), exactly as in Zend; but here, also, ओ *ôi* stands for ए *ê* (§. 33.); so that in this the Zend approaches very closely to the Greek datives like οἴκοι, μοί, and σοί, in which *i* has not yet become subscribed, or been replaced by the extinction of the base vowel. To the forms mentioned answers *maidhyôi,* "in the middle.' One must be careful not to regard this and similar phenomena as shewing a more intimate connexion between Greek and Zend.

197. In Lithuanian, which language possesses a proper locative, bases in *a* correspond in this case in a remarkable manner with the Sanskṛit and Zend, since they con-

---

* It would be better to read *bráthr-ô,* after the analogy of *dâthr-ô,* "*creatoris.*" (Burnouf, "Yaçna," p. 363, Note).

† The gen. of *dúghdar* is probably *dughdër-ô* (see p. 194, Note †).

‡ See p. 163, Note ‡.

§ Few cases admit of being more abundantly quoted in Zend than the locative, with which, nevertheless, Rask appears to have been unacquainted at the time of publishing his treatise, as he does not give it in any of his three paradigms.

‖ I now refer the Latin dative to the Sanskṛit dative, rather than to the locative; see p. 1227 G. Ed., Note †.

tract this *a* with the old locative *i*, which appears pure nowhere any more, to *è*; hence, *dievè*, "in God," from *DIEWA*, answers to देवे *dêvê*, ϵϵϵ *daêvê*. The bases which terminate with other vowels employ, however, in Lithuanian, without exception, *ye* as the locative termination, without any accent upon the *e*, a circumstance which must not be overlooked. This *e* is, perhaps, only an unorganic echo, which has occasioned the change of the old locative *i* into *y*, as, in Zend, the plural locative termination *su*, by adding an *a*, appears, for the most part, in the form of ϵϵϵ

[G. Ed. p. 228.] *shva*, or ϵϵϵ *hva*. To the Lithuanian *ye* answers also, in old Sclavonic, a locative termination *ye*, for which several declensions have the original pure *i*; so that *nebes-i*, "in Heaven," and *imen-i*, "in the name," agree most strictly with the Sanskrit नभसि *nabhas-i* and नामनि *nâman-i*, from नभस् *nabhas*, नामन् *nâman*.

198. Masculine bases in *i* and *u*, and, optionally, feminine bases also, have a different locative termination in Sanskrit, viz. औ *âu*, before which इ *i* and उ *u* are dropped; but in पति *pati*, "lord," and सखि *sakhi*, "friend," the *i* has remained in its euphonic change to य् *y*: hence, पत्यौ *paty-âu*, सख्यौ *sakhy-âu*. If we consider the vocalization of the *s* to *u*, shewn in §. 56[b]., and that, in all probability, in the dual, also, औ *âu* has proceeded from आस् *âs* (§. 206.); moreover, the circumstance that in the Vêdas the genitive occurs with a locative meaning (दक्षिणायास् *dakshiṇâyâs*, "*in dexterâ*," for दक्षिणायाम् *dakshiṇâyâm*, Pânini VII. 1. 39.); and, finally, the fact that, in Zend, masculines in *i* and *u* likewise employ genitive terminations with a locative signification; we shall be much disposed to recognise in this औ *âu*, from आस् *âs*, a sort of Attic or produced genitive termination.

199. In *u* bases, instead of the locative the Zend usually employs the genitive termination ϵ *ô* (from अस् *as*), while, in a genitive meaning, the form ϵϵϵ *eu-s* is more common; thus we read, in the Vend. S. p. 337., ϵϵϵ ϵϵϵ ϵϵϵ ϵϵϵ *aêtahmi aṅhvô yaṭ astvainti*, "in

hoc mundo quidem existente." This Zend termination *ô* (from
a + u) has the same relation to the Sanskrit *du* that a
short *a* has to a long *a*, and the two locative terminations
are distinguished only by the quantity of the first member
of the diphthong. On the other hand, we find in the
feminine base ‎ *tanu*, " body," very often the genuine
locative form ‎ *tanv-i*; and we do not doubt that, in
Sanskrit also, originally the *u* bases of the   [G. Ed. p. 229.]
three genders admitted in the locative the termination *i*
(सुन्वि *sunw-i*, तन्वि *tanw-i*, मध्वि *madhw-i*, or मधुनि *madhu-n-i*).
Bases in ‎ *i* employ, in the locative, the usual genitive
termination *ôi-s;* thus, in the Vend. S. p. 234, ‎
‎ *ahmi namânê yaṭ mâzdayaînôis*, " *in
hac terra quidem mazdayasnica*," which Anquetil renders by
" *dans le pays des mazdeïesnans*." In pronouns, also, though
they have a locative, the genitive sometimes occurs with
a locative meaning; *e. g.* Vend. S. p. 46, ‎
ainhê visê, " in this way," or " place," (cf. the feminine form
‎ *ainháo*, §. 172. Note.).

200. From the Zend and Sanskrit we have already been
compelled to acknowledge a connexion between the genitive
and locative; and as we have seen the locative replaced
by the genitive, so must we, in Latin, recognise a replacing
of the genitive by the locative. Through the formal
agreement of the corresponding Latin and Sanskrit termi
nation, and from the circumstance that the genitive occurs
with a locative meaning only in the two first declensions
(*Romæ, Corinthi, humi*), not in the third or in the plural (*ruri*
not *ruris*), M. Prof. Rosen was first induced to characterize
the Latin genitive of the two first declensions as borrowed
from the old locative; a view, the correctness of which I
do not doubt, and which I have already corroborated elsewhere by the genitives of the two first persons, in which *mei
tui*, agree most surprisingly with मयि *mayi* (from *mê-i*, §. 2.),
" in me," त्वयि *twayi* (from *twê-i*). Or ought, perhaps, a double
inflexion *i* to be assumed as the sign of both a genitive and

a locative dative?   Should *Romæ* (from *Romai*), *Corinthi*,
be on one occasion genitives and on another locatives, and
[G. Ed. p. 230.]   in their different meaning be also of
different origin?   And where, then, would the origin of the
genitive *Romæ* be found, as that of the locative has been
found already?   Should *mei, tui,* be compared, not with मयि
mayi, त्वयि *twayi,* μοί, τοί, but with मम *mama,* तव *tava,* μοῦ, τοῦ,
Goth. *meina, theina?*   As the cases, like their substitutes the
prepositions, pass easily from one relation of space to
another, and, to use the expression, the highest become the
lowest, nothing appears to me more probable, than that,
after the first declension had lost its *ā-s,* then the dative,
according to its origin a locative, necessarily became substituted for the genitive also.*   In the second declension the
form *o-i,* which belongs to the dative locative, corresponding
to the Greek ω, οι—and of which examples still remain
handed down to us (as *populoi Romanoi*)—has become doubly
altered: either the vowel of the base alone, or only that
[G. Ed. p. 231.]   of the termination, has been left, and the
first form has fixed itself in the dative, and the latter in the

---

* The assumption that a rejected *s* lies at the base of the genitives in *i,*
ae (*a-ī*) appears to me inadmissible, because in all other parts of Grammar
—numerous as the forms with a final *s* otherwise are—this letter has in
Roman defied all the assaults of time, and appears everywhere where the
cognate languages lead us to expect it : no *terræ* for *terras* (acc. pl.), no
lupi for *lupos,* no *amæ* for *amas,* &c.   The question is not here that of an
occasional suppression of the *s* in old poets, before a consonant in the word
following.   The genitives in *e-s* and *æ-s* occurring in inscriptions (*pro-
vincie-s, suæ-s,* see Struve, p. 7.) appear to be different modes of writing
one and the same form, which corresponds to the Greek η-ς for *ā-s* ; and
I would not therefore derive the common genitive *suæ*—older form *suai*—
from *suæs* with the *s* dropped.   The genitives in *us,* given by Hartung
(p. 161.) from inscriptions in Orelli (*nomin-us, exercitu-us, Castor-us,* &c.),
I am not surprised at, for this reason, that generally *us* is, in Latin, a
favourite termination for अस् *as ;* hence *nomin-us* has the same relation
to नाम्नस् *námn-as,* that *nomin-i-bus* has to नामभ्यस् *náma'-bhyas,* and
lupus to वृकस् *vrika-s.*

genitive, which is therefore similar to the nom. plural, where, in like manner, *Romani* stands for *Romanoi*. But the dative is not universally represented in Latin by a locative termination; for in the pronouns of the two first persons *mihi* answers to मह्यम् *ma-hyam*, from *ma-bhyam*, and *tibi* to तुभ्यम् *tu-bhyam;* as, however, the league between the dative and locative had been once concluded, this truly dative termination occurs with a locative meaning (*ibi, ubi*), while *vice versâ*, in Sanskrit, the locative very frequently supplies the place of the dative, which latter, however, is most usually expressed by the genitive, so that the proper dative is, for the most part, applied to denote the causal relation.

201. Pronouns of the 3d person have, in Sanskrit, इन् *in* instead of *i* in the locative, and the अ *a* of the appended pronoun स्म *sma* is elided (see §. 165.); hence, तस्मिन् *tasm'in*, "in him"; कस्मिन् *kasm'in*, "in whom ?" This *n*, which seems to me to be of later origin, as it were an *n* ἐφελκυστικόν, does not extend to the two first persons, and is wanting in Zend also in those of the third; hence, ahmi, "in this." As to the origin of the *i* signifying the place or time of continuance, it is easily discovered as soon as *i* is found as the root of a demonstrative; which, however, like the true form of all other pronominal roots, has escaped the Indian Grammarians.

202. Feminine bases ending with long simple vowels have, in Sanskrit, a peculiar locative termination; viz. आम् *âm*, in which, also, the feminines in short *i* and *u* may at will participate (cf. §. 192.); while the monosyllabic feminine bases in long ई *î* and ऊ *û*, for आम् *âm*, admit also the common इ *i*; hence, भियाम् *bhiy-âm* or भियि *bhiy-i*, "in fear," from भी *bhî*.[*] In Zend this termi- [G. Ed. p. 232.]

---

[*] Perhaps the termination *âm* is a corruption of the feminine genitive termination *âs* (cf. §. 198. दक्षिणायास् *dakshinâyâs* for *dakshinâyâm*), where it should be observed that in Prâkrit, as in Greek, a final *s* has frequently become a nasal.

nation *âm* has become abbreviated to *a* (cf. §. 214.); hence, ملكيهم *yahmy-a*, "in which," from ملكيم *yahmí* (cf. §. 172.). This termination appears, however, in Zend, to be less diffused than in Sanskrit, and not to be applicable to feminines in و *i* and و *u*. The form *tanwi* is clearly more genuine than the Sanskrit *tandu*, although from the earliest period, also, *tanwâm* may have existed.

203. We here give a general view of the locative, and of the cases akin to it in Greek and Latin (see §. 148.):

	SANSKRIT.	ZEND.	GREEK.	LATIN.	LITHUAN.
m.	vrikê,*	vĕhrkê,*	λύκῳ,	lup'-î,	wilkè.
f.	jihwây-âm,	hizvay-a,	χώρᾳ,	terra-i,	ranko-ye.
m.	paty-âu,†	. . . .	πόσι-ï,	host'-î,	páli-ye.
f.	prĭt'-âu,‡	. . . .	πόρτι-ï,	sit'-î,	awi-ye.
f.	bhavishyanty-âm,	bûshyainty-a,	. . . .	. . . .	
m.	sûn'-âu,	. . . .	ἰχθύ-ι,	pecu-î,	sunu-ye.
f.	tan'-âu,§	tanw-i,	πίτυ-ι,	socru-î,	. . . .
n.	madhu-n-i,	. . . .	μέθυ-ι,	. . . .	
f.	vadhw-âm,	. . . .	. . . .	. . . .	
m.f.	gav-i,	gav-i,	βο(F)-í,	bov-î,	. . . .
f.	ndv-i,	. . . .	νᾱ(F)-í,	. . . .	
m.	bharat-i,	barĕnt-i,	φέροντ-ι,	ferent-î,	. . . .
m.	âtman-i,	asmain-i,	δαίμον-ι,	sermon-i,	. . . .
n.	nâmn-i,	nâmain-i,	τάλαν-ι,	nomin-î,	. . . .
m.	bhrâtar-i,	brâthr-i?‖	πατρ-í,	fratr-î,	. . . .
f.	duhitar-i,	dughdhĕr-i?	θυγατρ-í,	matr-î,	. . . .
m.	dâtar-i,	dâthr-i?‖	δοτῆρ-ι,	dator-î,	. . . .
n.	vachas-i,	vacanh-i,	ἔπε(σ)-ι,	oper-î,	. . . .

Marginal note, left side: [G. Ed. p. 233.]

---

* See §. 196.   † See §. 198.   ‡ Or *prĭty-âm.*   § Or *tanw-âm.*

‖ The rejection of the *a* preceding the *r* in the theme seems to me more probable than its retention. The *i* of the termination is guaranteed by the other consonantal declension, which in this case we can abundantly enough exemplify. (Regarding *dughdhĕr-i,* see p. 194, Note †). That in Sanskrit *bhrâtar-i, duhitar-i, dâtar-i,* are used instead of *bhrâtri,* &c. is contrary

to

VOCATIVE.

204. The vocative in the Sanskrit family of languages has either no case-sign at all, or is identical with the nominative: the former is the principle, the latter the practical corruption, and is limited in Sanskrit to monosyllabic bases terminating in a vowel: hence, भीस् *bhí-s* "fear!" as κί-ς. A final *a* of the nominal [G. Ed. p. 234.] bases remains, in Sanskrit and Zend, unchanged; in Lithuanian it is weakened to *e*; and the Greek and Latin also, in the uninflected vocative of the corresponding declension, prefer a short *e* to *o* or *u*, which, under the protection of the terminations, appears as the final letter of the base. We must avoid seeing in λύκε, *lupĕ*, case terminations: these forms have the same relation to वृक *vṛika* that πέντε, *quinque*, have to पञ्च *pancha*; and the old *a*, which appears in λύκος as *o*, in *lupus* as *ŭ*, has assumed the form of *ĕ* without any letter following it. In Zend, the consonantal bases, when they have *s* in the nominative, retain it in the vocative also; thus, in the present participle we have frequently found the form of the nominative in the sense of the vocative.

205. Bases in *i* and *u* have, in Sanskrit, Guna; neuters, however, have also the pure vowel: on the other hand,

---

to the theory of the weakest cases (§. 130.), to which in other respects the locative belongs. As, however, bases in वर् *ar* (ऋ *ṛi*), with respect to the rejection and lengthening of the *a*, have a very great agreement with bases in *an*, it must here be further remarked, that these too, in the locative, do not strictly follow the suppression of the *a* in the weakest cases, which is conditionally prescribed in §. 140., but optionally retain the *a*, or reject it; so that with *námn-i* also *náman-i* is used. With *brátar-i*, however, exists no *bhrátr-i*, and the form *pitr-i*, given at §. 132. is an oversight: the Greek πατρ-ί may therefore, with respect to the shortening of the base, be better compared with the dative *pitr-ĕ*.

polysyllabic feminines in *i* and *ŭ* shorten this final vowel; while a final **या** *ă*, by the commixture of an *i*, becomes *ê* (§. 2.). The language, however, both by producing and shortening the final vowel, clearly aims at one and the same end, only by opposite ways; and this end, in fact, is a certain emphasis in the address. To the Guna form **वो** *ô*, from *a + u*, correspond remarkably the Gothic and Lithuanian; as *sunau, sunaù,* resembling the Sanskrit **सूनो** *sûnô,*[*] Gothic feminine bases in *i* do not occur in [G. Ed. p. 235.] Ulfilas in the vocative: as, however, they, in other respects, run parallel to the *u* bases, the vocative *anstai,* from *ANSTI,* might be expected as an analogous form to *handau.* The Lithuanian *i* bases in the vocative extend their theme in the same manner as in the genitive (§. 193.); so that, properly, there is no vocative of this class of words, and *awie* answers to *zwáke, giesme* (Ruhig's third declension), for *zwákie, giesmye.*[†] Masculine bases, in Gothic, in *i*, like the masculine and neuter *a* bases, have lost their final vowel in the vocative, just as in the accusative and nominative; hence *vulf', daur', gast'.* In bases in *n* the Gothic shares with the Latin the suppression of the final consonant, which has passed over from the nominative to the vocative; while only the Sanskrit and Zend again introduce

---

[*] The Zend can at will attach Guna to a final ꭥ *u*, or not; and we find both ꭥⲗⲗ mainyô and ꭥⲗⲗ mainyu as the vocative of ꭥⲗⲗ mainyu, "spirit." On the other hand, we have found a final ꭕ *i* only, without Guna; and indeed frequently ꭕⲗⲗ paiti, "lord." So Vend S. p. 456, ꭕⲗⲗ ꭥⲗⲗ ꭥⲗⲗ usihista namánô-paiti,"Arise, lord of the place!" The ꭕ *i* between the preposition and the verb serves as a conjunctive vowel, to assist the juncture of the words (cf. §. 150. Note).

[†] It follows from this, and from §. 193., that (§. 177.) I have incorrectly assumed *ei* as the termination in the dative. For *áwi-ei,* the division should be made thus, *áwie-i;* and this is analogous with *zwáke-i, giesme-i,* for *zwákie-i, giesmye-i.*

into the vocative the nasal which had been dropped in the nominative. Adjectives in German, with respect to the vocative, have departed from the old path, and retain the case-sign of the nominative; hence Gothic *blind's*, "blind!" In Old Northern, substantives also follow this irregular use of the nominative sign. The Greek has preserved a tolerable number of its vocatives pure from the nominative sign, and in some classes of words uses the bare base, or that abbreviation of it which the laws of euphony or effeminacy rendered requisite; hence, τάλαν opposed to τάλας, χαρίεν for χαρίεντ' opposed to χαρίεις, παῖ for παιδ opposed to παῖς. In guttural and labial bases the language has not got free of the nominative sign in the vocative, because κς and πς (ξ, ψ) are very favourite combinations, to which the alphabet also has paid homage by particular letters to represent them. Still the   [G. Ed. p. 236.] vocative ἄνα, together with ἄναξ, is remarkable, and has that sound which might be expected from a theme ἄνακτ', to which, in its uninflected state, neither κτ, nor, conveniently, even the κ, could be left. "For the rest it is easy to imagine (says Buttmann, p. 180), that particularly such things as are not usually addressed, prefer, when they happen to be addressed, to retain the form of the nominative, as ὦ πούς!" [*] The Latin has followed still farther the road of corruption in the vocative which was prepared by the Greek, and employs in its place the nominative universally, except in the masculine second declension. The substantive bases mentioned in §. 148. form, in the vocative,

---

[*] To this circumstance may also the re-introduction of the case-sign in the neuter be owing, while the Sanskrit employs the bare base. Moreover, this fact also may have co-operated towards the Greek more easily freeing itself in the vocative from the bare primary form, because it appears at the beginning of compounds much more rarely than in Sanskrit. (See §. 112.)

	SANSKRIT.	ZEND.	GREEK.	LATIN.	LITHUAN.	GOTHIC.
m.	vrika,	vĕhrka,	λύκε,	lupe,	wilke,	vulf'.
n.	dána,	dála,	δῶρο-ν,	donu-m,	. . . .	daur'.
f.	jihwĕ,	hizvĕ?	χώρα,	terra,	ranka,	giba?
m.	patĕ,	paiti,	πόσι,	hosti-s,	. . . .	gast'.
f.	prĭtĕ,	áfríti,	πόρτι,	siti-s,	. . . .	. . . .
n.	vári,	vairi,	ἴδρι,	mare,	. . . .	. . . .
f.	bhavishyanti,	bũshyainti,	. . . .	. . . .	. . . .	. . . .
m.	sunŏ,	paśu,	ἰχθύ,	pecu-s,	sunaù,	sunau.
f.	tanŏ,	tanu,	πίτυ,	socru-s,	. . . .	handau.
n.	madhu,	madhu,	μέθυ,	pecu,	. . . .	. . . .
f.	vadhu,	. . . .	. . . .	. . . .	. . . .	. . . .
m.f.	gáu-s,	gáu-s,	βοῦ,	bo-s,	. . . .	. . . .
f.	náu-s,	. . . .	ναῦ,	. . . .	. . . .	. . . .
f.	vák,	vác-s?	ὄπ-ς,	voc-s,	. . . .	. . . .
m.	bharan,	baran-s,	φέρων,	feren-s,	sukaṅ-s,	fiyand.
m.	átman,	aśman,	δαῖμον,	sermo',	ákmĕ',	ahma'.
n.	náman,	náman,	τάλαν,	nomen,	. . . .	namŏ'.
m.	bhrátar,	bráturĕ,*	πάτερ,	frater,	. . . .	bróthar.
f.	duhitar,	dughdharĕ,*	θύγατερ,	mater,	motĕ,	dauhtar.
m.	dátar,	dátare,*	δοτήρ,	dator,	. . . .	. . . .
n.	vachas,	vachŏ,	ἔπος,†	opus,	. . . .	. . . .

[G. Ed. p. 237.]

DUAL.

NOMINATIVE, ACCUSATIVE, VOCATIVE.

206. These three cases have, in Sanskrit, in the masculine and feminine, the termination औ áu, which probably
arose from आस् ás by vocalization of the s (cf. §§. 56ᵇ. and
198.), and is therefore only a stronger form of the plural
termination as. The dual, both in the cases mentioned and
in the others, prefers the broadest terminations, because
it is based on a more precise intention than the indefinite

---

* See §. 44.   † See §. 128.

plural, and needs, therefore, stronger emphasis, and more
lively personification. Compare, also, in the neuter, the
long *í* of the dual with the short *i* of the plural; as
चषुषी *aśruní* with चषूषि *aśrûṇi*.

207. While the Prâkṛit and Pâli have lost   [G. Ed. p. 238.]
the dual, the Zend has retained it; still, however, so that
instead of it the plural often occurs, and in the Vend. S.,
p. 203, [Zend] *â schĕnubyaschit*, "and as far as
the knees," is used with a plural termination. In the verb
the dual is still more rare; but here, however, it is not entirely lost, and many examples of it can be quoted in the
V. S.[*] The Sanskṛit termination औ *âu* occurs in the corresponding places in Zend in the form of [Zend] *âo*, which,
according to §. 56ᵇ., stands at the same time for the Sanskṛit
termination आस् *âs*, and gives an emphatic proof that the
Sanskṛit dual termination औ *âu* is nothing else than a corruption of आस् *âs*, and, in fact, an occasional one which
appears in grammar only once or twice (see §. 198.), while
the example herein given by the Sanskṛit has been raised
to a general principle by the Zend. This principle becomes almost irrefragable matter of fact from the consideration that the Zend has even actually retained, in the
dual, the sibilant before the particle [Zend] *cha*, and uses
âoś-cha, not *âo-cha*, as might have been expected if the
dual termination औ *âu*, in Sanskṛit, were the original form,
and not a corruption of आस् *âs*. Thus we read in the
Vend. S. p. 225, [Zend]
tâi ubaê hurvŏoś-cha amĕrĕtat-âoś-cha, "the two Haurvats and
Amertats."[†] What Anquetil, in his Voca-   [G. Ed. p. 239.]

---

[*] Cf. Gramm. Crit. Add. to r. 137.

[†] Cf. Anquetil II. 175. The two Genii, which Anquetil writes *Khordad* and *Amerdad*, appear very frequently in the dual, also with the termination *bya* (§. 212.); and where they occur with plural terminations,
this may be ascribed to the disuse of the dual, and the possibility of
replacing

bulary (p. 456), writes *naerekeïdo*, and renders by "*deux femmes*," can be nothing else than ـﺳﺪﺩﺯﺩﻭﺟﺪﺳﺠ *ndirikay-do*, from the base ﺳﺠﺪﺯﺟﻭﺳﺠ *ndirikd*. The form ـﺳﺪﺩﺯﺩﻭﺟﺪﺳﺠ *ndirikaydo* is, however, evidently more genuine than. ـﺳﺠﺪﺯﺟﻭﭘﺠ *ndirikê*; as, according to the Sanskrit principle (§. 213.), from a feminine base must have been formed *ndirikd*. From ﺳﺠﺠﺮ *bdzu*, Rask cites the form ـﺳﺠﺠﺮﺯﺟﺳﺠ *bdzvdo*, "arms," without remarking that it is a dual: it clearly belongs, however, to this number, which was to be expected referring to the arms; and ﺳﺠﺠﺮ *bdzu* forms, in the nominative plural, ﺳﺠﺠﺮﺯﺟﻳ *bdzvd* or ﺳﺠﺠﺮﺟﺳﺟﻳ *bdzavd*. Still, in the edited parts of the Zend-Avesta, examples are wanting of *bdzvdo*, regarding the genuineness of which, however, I have no doubt.

208. In the Vêda dialect, the termination शौ *du* occurs frequently abbreviated to *d*, so that the last element of the diphthong is suppressed. Several examples of this abbreviated form occur in Rosen's "Specimen"; as, अश्विना *asvin-d*, "the two Aswins," from *asvin*, and नरा *nard*, "two [G. Ed. p. 240.] men," which can be derived both from *nar*

---

replacing the dual in all cases by the plural. Thus we read, l. c. p. 211, *haurvatât-ô* and *amĕrĕt-aś-cha* as accusative, and with the fullest and perhaps sole correct reading of the theme. We will, however, not dwell on this point any longer here, but only remark, that *haurvatât* is very frequently abbreviated to *haurvat*, and the *d* of *amĕrĕtât* is often found shortened; whence, p. 104, ﺳﺠﺪﺯﺟﻭﺟﺳﺠ *haurvathya*, ﺳﺠﺪﺯﺟﻭﺟﻩﻉﻍﻍﺪﺳﺠ *amĕrĕtatbya*, (see §. 38.); ﺳﺠﺪﺯﺟﺳﺠﻭﺟﻩﻉﻍﻍﺪﺳﺠ *amĕrĕtata bya* is a palpable error. Undoubtedly, in the passage before us, for *hurvdoścha*, must be read either *haurvatâoścha*, or *haurvatâtâoścha*, or *haurvatatâoścha*. Compare l. c. p. 91, ﺳﺠﺪﺯﺟﻭﺟﺳﺠﺩﺳﺠﭘﺪﺳﺠ *haôrvatatâuś-cha* with the termination ﺳﺠﺩﺳﺠ *âuś* for ﺳﺠﭙﺠ *âoś* (cf. §. 33.), but incorrectly ﭘ *ô* for ﭘ *ô*. The two twin genii are feminine, and mean apparently, "Entireness" and "Immortality." The forms preceding them, therefore, *tôi* and *uhaê*, are likewise feminine; the former for ते *tê* (§. 33.), the latter for उभे *ubhê* (cf. §. 28.). We must also regard the dual form mentioned at §. 45. of the so-called *Amschaspants* not as neuter, but as feminine.

(न *nṛi*) and from *nara*, but which more probably comes from *nur*. In Zend the abbreviated termination from *du* is likewise employed, and, in fact, more copiously than the fuller termination; and we rejoice to see, in the Heaven of Ormuzd also, the twin pair called Indian, and celebrated for their youthful beauty. We read, namely, in Vend. S. p. 313, ꭳꭳꭲ꭮ꭲꭲ꭮ ꭳꭲꭲ꭮ꭲ꭮ ꭲꭲꭲ꭮ꭲꭲ꭮ *aśpinâ-cha yavanô yaz* (*maidhê*), "*Aśvinosque juvenes veneramur,*" which Anquetil renders by "*je fais Jzeschné à l'excellens toujours (subsistant*"). The Sanskrit अश्विना *aśvinâ* however, can, in Zend, give nothing but *aśpinâ* or *aśpina* (§. 50.): the former we owe here to the protecting particle ꭲꭲ *cha* (see p. 175, Note ‡ G. Ed.). The plural *yavan-ô* (from *yavanas*), referring to the dual *aśpinâ*, is worthy of remark, however (if the reading be correct), as it furnishes a new proof that, in the received condition of the Zend, the dual was near being lost: the verb being, for the most part, found in the plural when referring to nouns in the dual form.

209. From the Vêda termination *â*, and the short *a*,[*] which frequently stands for it in Zend, the transition is easy to the Greek ε, as this vowel, at the end of words, is a favourite representative of the old *ă*; and, as above, in the vocative (§. 204.), λύκε stood for वृक *vṛika*, ꭲꭲꭲꭲꭲ *vĕhrka*, so here, also, ἄνδρα (with euphonic δ) corresponds to the above-mentioned Vêda नरा *narâ*, and Zend ꭲꭲꭲ *nar-a*. Although, according to §. 4., ω also very frequently stands for आ *â*, still we must avoid regarding λύκω as the analogous form to वृका *vṛikâ*, or ꭲꭲꭲꭲꭲ *vĕhrkâ* (see §. 211.). That however, the Lithuanian dual *ù* of masculine   [G. Ed. p. 241.] bases in *a* (in the nominative) is connected with the Vêda and Zend dual termination spoken of, *i. e.* has proceeded from *ā*, I

---

[*] Thus, Vendidâd Sâde, p. 23, ꭲꭲꭲꭲꭲꭲ ꭲꭲꭲꭲꭲ *haurvata amĕrĕtâta*, "the two Haurvats and Amertats"; p. 136, and frequently, ꭲꭲꭲ ꭲꭲꭲ *dva nara*, "two men." Cf. Gramm. Crit. Add. to r. 137.

have the less doubt, because in the other declensions the Lithuanian dual also agrees in this case most strictly with the
Sanskrit, and the Lithuanian u or $\mathring{u}$ (uo) is, in some other
places, equally the representative of an old $\mathring{a}$ (see §. 162.);
compare, $d\breve{u}mi$, or $d\breve{u}du$, "I give," with दुदानि $dad\mathring{a}mi$;
$d\mathring{u}su$, "I will give," with दास्यानि $d\mathring{a}sy\mathring{a}mi$. And the monosyllabic pronominal bases also in a sound in the dual $\mathring{u}$;
thus $t\mathring{u}=$ ता $t\mathring{a}$, $k\mathring{u}=k\mathring{a}$. We hold, therefore, the Vêda
form वृका $vrik\mathring{a}$, the Zend ᵹᵉᶜʳᵏᵃ $v\breve{e}hrk\mathring{a}$, and the Lithuanian $wilk\mathring{u}$, as identical in principle: we are, at
least, much more inclined to this view of the matter
than to the assumption that the u of $wilk\mathring{u}$ is the last
portion of the Sanskrit diphthong औ $\mathring{a}u$, and that $wilk\mathring{u}$
belongs to the form वृकौ $vrik\mathring{a}u$. In the vocative the Lithuanian employs a shorter u, and the accent falls on the
preceding syllable: thus $wilku$, opposed to $wilk\mathring{u}$, in which
respect may be compared πάτερ opposed to πατήρ, and §. 205.

210. Masculine and feminine bases in i and u suppress,
in Sanskrit, the dual case termination औ $\mathring{a}u$, and, in compensation, lengthen the final vowel of the base in its unin-
flected form; thus, पती $pat\acute{\imath}$, from पति $pati$; सूनू $s\mathring{u}n\mathring{u}$, from
सूनु $s\mathring{u}nu$. The ᵍᵘᵃᵘᵈᵃ $b\mathring{a}zu$-do, "arms," (from $b\mathring{a}zu$) mentioned in §. 207., is advantageously distinguished from these
abbreviated forms. The curtailed form is not, however,
wanting in Zend also, and is even the one most in use.
From ᵐᵃⁱⁿʸᵘ $mainyu$, "spirit," we frequently find the dual
ᵐᵃⁱⁿʸᵘ $mainy\mathring{u}$: on the other hand, for ᵉʳᵉᶻᵘ $\breve{e}r\breve{e}z\mathring{u}$, "two
[G. Ed. p. 242.] fingers," we meet with the shortened form
ᵉʳᵉᶻᵘ $\breve{e}r\breve{e}zu$, which is identical with the theme (Vend. S.
p. 318, ᵉʳᵉᶻᵘ ᵈᵛᵃ dva $\breve{e}r\breve{e}zu$.

211. The Lithuanian, in its i and u bases, rests on the
above-mentioned Sanskrit principle of the suppression of
the termination and lengthening of the final vowel: hence,
$aw\grave{\imath}$, "two sheep" (fem.), answers to अवी $av\acute{\imath}$, from अवि avi;
and $sun\grave{u}$, "two sons," to सूनू $s\mathring{u}n\mathring{u}$. On this principle rests

also the Greek dual of the two first declensions.   If it be
not desired entirely to remove the ω of λύκω from a Grecian
soil, and banish it completely to India, it may be allowed
to seek its origin, not in the long a of वृका *vrikâ*, but in
the short o of the base, as the first declension has a long
a in the dual, because its bases terminate with a, although
in the common dialect this letter is very frequently represented by $η$.   Or may it, perhaps, have happened, that, in
the dual a of the first declension an $ι$ subscribed has been
lost, and thus τά for τᾷ would correspond to the Sanskrit
ते *tê* (from *tâ* + i or i)?   Be that as it may, still the dual
has always the quality a, because it is comprehended in the
base, and the ω of λύκω may be regarded as merely the
lengthening of the o of λύκο; for it must be assumed, that if
the Sanskrit a bases had preserved the short a in Greek, and
वृकस् *vrika-s* had become λύκα-ς, then the dual too would
be λύκᾱ, and not λύκω.

212. Neuters have, in the Sanskrit dual, for the termination of the cases under discussion, not ौ *âu*, but i, as in
the plural they have not *as* but short i (इ).   A final व a
of the base with this ई i passes into ए $ê$ (§. 2.); hence,
शते *satê*, "two hundred," from शतइ *sata-i*:   [G. Ed. p. 243.]
other vowels interpose a euphonic n; hence, तालुनी *tâlu-n-î*,
"two palates."   In Zend I can quote the neuter dual only in
the a bases; as, for example, we frequently find ιυρωυ
saitê (§. 41.), answering to the Sanskrit शते *satê*; and ιυϳϳυϳ
ιυϳϳυςϳυ *duyê hazanrê*, "two thousand," (§. 43.) for दे सहस्रे
duê sahasrê.

213. The Greek has renounced a termination distinguishing the neuter from the two natural genders; but
the Sanskrit appears to have extended the neuter i mentioned above also to the feminine $â$ bases.   But the coincidence of the feminine form जिह्वे *jihwê*, "two tongues,"
from जिह्वा *jihwâ*, with the neuter दाने *dânê*, "two gifts," is,
as the Zend instructs us, only external, and the two forms

Q

meet in quite different ways, and have such a relation to one another, that in *ddné*, from *ddna + é*, a dual termination, and, in fact, the usual one of neuters, is actually contained; but in फिन्रे *jihwé* the masculine-feminine termination *du* (from *ds*, §. 206.) is lost, but can, however, be again restored from the Zend form ⲅⲱⲁⲁⲁⲅ⳿ⲟⲁ⳿ⲁⲁⲟⲭ *ndirikay-do*, "two women." I believe, that is to say, that फिन्रे *jihwé* has arisen or been corrupted from फिन्रयौ *jihway-du** in such a manner, that after the termination has been dropped, the preceding semi-vowel has returned to its vowel nature, and has become a diphthong with the *d* of the base (see §. 2. and cf. p. 121 G. ed.). The dual *jihwé*, therefore, like the Gothic singular dative *gibai* (§. 161.) would have only an apparent termination, *i.e.* an extension of the base which originally accompanied the real case termination. In Zend, however, the abbreviated feminine dual form in ⲟⲟ *é* likewise occurs (§. 207. Note†), and is, indeed, the prevalent one; but it is

[G. Ed. p. 244.] remarkable, and a fair and powerful confirmation of my assertion, that even this abbreviated form in ⲟⲟ *é*, where the appended particle ⲁⲟⲁ *cha* stands beside it, has preserved the case sign *s*; and, as above, ⲁⲟⲁⲁⲅⲱⲁⲟⲟⲟⳍⲅⲅⲁ *ameretal-dos-cha*, "the two Amertats," so we find, Vend. S. p. 58, ⲟⲟⲟⳍⲩⲩⲅⲟⲁⲁ ⲁⲟⲁⲁⲟⲟⲟⲟⲟⳍⲅⲅⲁ *ameshes-cha spenté*, "and two Amshaspants" ("non-conniventesque sanctos," cf. सनिष *amisha* and Nalus V. 25, 26. and see §. 50.).†
The form ⲁⲟⲟⲟ *és* is to be deduced from the full form ⲁⲟⲅⲱⲁⲁⲁⲟ *ay-dos*; so that, after dropping the ⲅⲱⲁ *do*, the preceding *ay* must have been contracted to *é*, just as (p. 121

---

* Cf. the dual genitive and locative फिन्रयोस *jihway-ós*.

† The MS. has here ⲁⲟⲁⲁⲅⲟⲁⲅⲅⲁ *amesescha*, but ⲅ frequently occurs in the place of ⲟⲟ, although, as it appears, through an error. Cf. l. c. p. 88, ⲅⲟ,ⲟⲩⲅⲟⲁⲁ ⲟⲟⲁⲟⲟⲅⳍⲅⲁ ⲟⲟ/ⲁⲁⲁⲁⳍⳍ ⲟⲟ»ⲁⲁⲁⲁ *aoré yainó amesé spénte*; and see §. 51.

G. Ed.) in Prâkṛit, रमि *êmi* has arisen from the Sanskṛit अयामि *ayâmi*, by rejecting the *â*. We may support the derivation of जिह्वे *jihwê* from जिह्वयौ *jihway-âu*, by this circumstance, also, that in the Vêda dialect the feminine *i* bases may lose the dual termination *âu*, and then display the naked base; thus, in the scholia to Pâṇini, वाराही उपानही *vârâhî upânahâu*, "boar-leather shoes," for वाराह्यौ *vârâhyâu*. It is very remarkable, that even this Vêda form, only one example of which can be quoted, can be referred to the Zend language. We find, frequently, ﻦﺱﻭﺭﮔﻭ *tevishi* applied to feminine dual substantives (*e. g.* Vend. S. p. 225.); and I infer that its theme ends with a long, not a short *i*, from the frequently-occurring plural accusative ﻮﻥﺱﻭﺭﮔﻭ *tevishís* (Vend. S. pp. 99, 102).[*]

214. To the Sanskṛit-Zend feminine dual [G. Ed. p. 245.] forms in *ê* answer the Lithuanian in *i*, as *rankì*, from *RANKÂ;* so that of the diphthong ए *ê* only the last element is left. The Lithuanian forms the accusative dual, in contradistinction to the cognate languages, according to the analogy of the singular, by a ringing nasal, *e. g. witkun.* The Latin has preserved only in *duo* and *ambo* a remnant of the dual corresponding to the Greek, which, however, in the oblique cases, is replaced by plural terminations. Here follows a general view of the nominative, accusative, and vocative dual (see §. 148.).

---

[*] It is perhaps a participle of the reduplicated pret., according to the analogy of the Sanskṛit तेनिवस् *tênivas*, fem. तेनुषी *tênuṣhí* (Gramm. Crit. §. 603.); and indeed, from the root ﺗﻮ *tav*, "to be able," it may signify "powerful, strong." The ﮔ *e* for ﯗ *ê* is explained by the influence of the ﺭ *r.* And ﻮﺗﺍﯾﯙﺗﻰ *utayüitî* also is an adjective feminine dual; but I am unable to quote examples of the other cases of this word, from which to learn whether ﯼ *i* or ﺝ *i* is its final vowel.

	SANSKRIT.	ZEND.	GREEK.	LITHUANIAN.
m.	vrikáu,	vĕhrkáo,	....	
	vriká,	vĕhrká,*	λύκω,	N. wilkù, V. wílku.
n.	dáné,	dáté,	δώρω.	....
f.	....	hízvay-áo,	....	....
	jihwé,	hizvé,	χώρā,	N. rankì, V. ránki.
m.	pati,	paiti?	πόσι-ε,	N. patì, V. páti.
f.	pritì,	áfriti ?	πόρτι-ε,	N. awì, N. áwi.
n.	vári-ṇ-í,	....	ἴδρι-ε,	...

[G. Ed. p. 246.] [G. Ed. p. 247.]

---

* While consonantal bases occur in the dual both with a long and a short *a*, the *a* bases, contrary to the practice otherwise adopted of shortening a final *á*, exhibit in the nom. acc. dual, for the most part, the original long vowel. I deduce this, among other words, from the so-called *Amshaspants*, which, together with the feminine form noticed at §. 207. Note †., are found also as masculine ; e g. Vend. S. pp. 14. 30, 31, &c.: ꜱꜱꜱꜱ ꜱꜱꜱꜱꜱ ꜱꜱꜱꜱ *amĕshá spĕntá hucsathrá hudáonhó áyésé,* "I glorify the two Amshaspants (*non conniventesque sanctos*) the good rulers, who created good." If *amĕsha spĕntá* and *hucsathrá* were plural forms, the final *a* would be short, or at least appear much more frequently short than long ; while, on the contrary, these repeatedly recurring expressions, if I mistake not, have everywhere a long *a*, and only in the vocative a short *a* (Vend. S. p. 67. Cf. §. 209.). That the epithet *hudáonhó* is in the plural cannot incur doubt, from the dual nature of the *Amshasp* (cf. §. 208.): this resembles, to a certain degree, the use of adjective genitives referring to a substantive in the ablative, which was mentioned in §. 180. We find, also, the forms *amesháo spĕntáo* (Vend. S. p. 313.), which indeed might also be feminine plural forms, but shew themselves only as masculine duals, in the same meaning as the so frequent *ameshá spĕntá*. We find also, frequently, ꜱꜱꜱꜱꜱ ꜱꜱꜱꜱ *spĕnistá mainyú,* "the two most holy spirits" (p. 80), through which the dual form in *á* of bases in *a* is likewise confirmed in the most unequivocal manner. The answer to the query, Whether generally only two *Amshaspants* are to be assumed ? whether the genitive plural (*ameshananm spĕntananm*), and sometimes also the accusative plural, is only the representative of the dual, which is very uncertain and shaken in its use ? whether under the name *Amshaspants*, perhaps, we should always understand the Genii *Haurvat* (*Khordad*) and

Amertat

	SANSKRIT.	ZEND.	GREEK.	LITHUANIAN.
f.	bhavishyanty-áu,	búshyainti,	. . . .	. . . .
m.	súnú,	pasú,	ἰχθύ-ε,	N. sunù, V. súnu.
f.	tanú,	tanú,	πίτυ·ε,	. . . .
m.	madhú-n-í,	. . . .	μέθυ-ε,	. . . .
f.	vadhw-áu,	. . . .	. . . .	. . . .
m. f.	gav-áu,*	. . . .	βό(F)-ε,	. . . .
f.	náv-áu,	. . . .	νᾶ(F)-ε,	. . . .
f.	vách-áu,	vách-áo,	. . . .	. . . .

Amertat, and whether these two Genii, according to the principle of the Sanskrit copulative compounds, have the dual termination for this reason alone, that they are usually found together, and are, together, two? whether, in fine, these two twin-genii are identical with the Indian Aswinen, which were referred in §. 208. to the Zend-Avesta? The reply to all these queries lies beyond the aim of this book. We will here only notice that, Vend. S. pp. 80 and 422, the Genii *Haurvat* and *Amertat*, although each is in the dual, still are, together, named ‌‌‌‌‌‌ *spènistá mainyú mazdá tevíshí*, &c., "the two most holy spirits, the great, strong." As Genii, and natural objects of great indefinite number, where they are praised, often have the word *viṡpa*, "all," before them, it would be important to shew whether "all Amshaspants" are never mentioned; and the utter incompatibility of the *Amsh*. with the word *viṡpa* would then testify the impassable duality of these Genii. If they are identical with the celestial physicians, the Indian Aswinen, then "Entireness" and "Immortality" would be no unsuitable names for them. In Pánini we find (p. 803) the expressions मातरपितरौ *mátara-pitaráu* and पितरमातरा *pitara-mátará* marked as peculiar to the Vèdas. They signify "the parents," but, literally, they probably mean "two mothers two fathers," and "two fathers two mothers." For the first member of the compound can here scarcely be aught but the abbreviated dual *pitará*, *mátará*; and if this is the case, we should here have an analogy to the conjectured signification of *haurvát-a* and *amèrètát-a*.

* Bases in ओ *ó* form the strong cases (§. 120.) from ओ *áu*; those in अन् *an*, and nouns of the agent in तर *tar*, lengthen in those cases, with the exception of the vocative singular, the last vowel but one (see §. 144.).

	SANSKRIT.	ZEND.	GREEK.	LITHUANIAN.
	vâch-â,*	vâch-a,	ŏπ-ε,	. . . .
m.	bharant-âu,	barant-âo,	. . . .	. . . .
	bharant-â,	barant-a,	φέροντ-ε,	. . . .
m.	âtmán-âu,†	aśman-âo,	. . . .	. . . .
	âtmán-â,	aśman-a,	δαίμον-ε,	N. V. ákmen-u.
n.	nâmn-î,	. . . .	τάλαν-ε,	. . . .
m.	bhrâtar-âu,	brâtar-âo,	. . . .	. . . .
	bhrâtar-â	brâtar-a,	πατέρ-ε,	. . . .
f.	duhitar-âu,	dughdhar-âo, ...		. . . .
	duhitar-â,	dughdhar-a,	θυγατέρ-ε,	. . . .
m.	dâtâr-âu,†	dâtâr-ao,	. . . .	. . . .
	dâtâr-â,	dâtâr-a,	δοτῆρ-ε,	. . . .
n.	vachas-î,	. . . .	ἔπε(σ)-ε,	. . . .

[G. Ed. p. 248.]

INSTRUMENTAL, DATIVE, ABLATIVE.

215. These three cases have in the Sanskrit and Zend dual
a common termination; while in Greek the genitive has
joined itself to the dative, and borrowed its termination from
it. It is in Sanskrit भ्याम् bhyâm, which in Zend has been
abbreviated to بيا bya. Connected with the same is, first,
the termination भ्यम् bhyam, which, in the pronoun of the two
first persons, denotes the dative singular and plural, but
in the singular of the first person has become abbreviated
to ह्यम् hyam (§. 23). This abbreviation appears, however,
[G. Ed. p. 249.] to be very ancient, as the Latin agrees

---

* The Vêda duals in â are as yet only cited in bases in a, n, and ar
(ऋ, §. 1.); however, the Zend leads us to expect their extension to the
other consonantal declensions, as also the circumstance that, in other parts of
grammar, in the Vêdas â is occasionally found for âu, and other diphthongs; e.g. नाभा nâbhâ, as locative for नाभौ nâbhâu, from नाभि nâbhi,
"navel."

† See the marginal note marked (*), p. 229.

remarkably with it; and *mi-hi* corresponds to मह्यम् *ma-hyam*, as *ti-bi* does to तुभ्यम् *tu-bhyam*.   In the second place, भ्यस् *bhyas*, which expresses the dative and ablative plural, is pronounced in Zend *byô* (§. 56ᵇ.), in Latin *bus*, suppressing the *y*, and with the usual change of *as* into *us*.   The Lithuanian has *mus* for *bus* in the dative plural (§. 63.): this more complete form has, however, remained only in the pronoun of the two first persons, where *mu-mus*, "*nobis*," *yu-mus*, "*vobis*," are used as well as *mu-m's*, *yu-m's*; while in all other words we find simply *ms* as the sign of the dative—*wilka-ms*, &c.   In the dual dative the Lithuanian has only the *m* of the Sanskrit termination भ्याम् *bhyâm*, as *wilka-m*.   This *m* is, however, not the final letter of *bhyâm*, but the initial labial, *b*, in a nasal form (§. 63.)* : to me, at least, it appears improper to regard this dual termination otherwise than that of the cognate plural case ; and I have no doubt of the identity of the *m* of *wilka-m*, λύκοιν, with that of *wilka-ms* (for *wilka-mus*), λύκοις.   According to this explanation, therefore, the German plural dative corresponds to the Lithuanian dual dative, *vulfa-m*, *gasti-m*, *sunu-m*.†

216. A third form related to the dual ter-   [G. Ed. p. 250.] mination भ्याम् *bhyâm* is भिस् *bhis*, as sign of the instrumental plural.   This termination which is in Zend ᵂⱼᵤ *bis*,

---

* On the facile transition of *v* into *m* (cf. p. 114) rests also, I doubt not, the connexion of the termination युवाम् *yuvâm*, "ye two," आवाम् *âvâm*, "we two," with the common termination *âu*, before vowels *âv*, which in the pronouns spoken of has stiffened into *âm*, and in this form has remained even before consonants.   Whether the case is the same with the verbal third dual person ताम् *tâm* shall be discussed hereafter.

† Cf. Grimm, I. 828. 17, where the identity of the Lithuanian-German inflection *m* with the *b* (*bh* of the older languages) was first shewn.   When, however, Grimm, l.c., says of the Lithuanian that only the pronouns and adjectives have *ms* in the dative plural, the substantives simply *m*, this is perhaps a mistake, or the plural is named instead of the dual ; for Ruhig gives *ponams*, "*dominis*," *akims*, "*oculis*," &c.

(also ﺑﺲ *bis*), has in Latin fixed itself in the dative and
ablative,* which must together supply the place of the instrumental; while in Lithuanian, with the exchange of the
labial medial for the nasal of this organ (§. 63.), *mis* is the
property of the instrumental alone, so that *puti-mis* answers
to पतिभिस् *pati-bhis*, ﻣﺲﺳﻮﻣﺲ *paiti-bis*.

217. I have already elsewhere affirmed, that the Greek
termination φι, φιν, is to be referred to this place,† and what
is there said may be introduced here also. If φιν, and not
φι, be assumed to be the elder of the two forms, we may offer
the conjecture that it has arisen from φις, following the analogy
of the change of μες into μεν in the 1st person plural, which
corresponds to the Sanskrit *mas* and Latin *mus‡; φις* would
correspond to the Sanskrit *bhis* and Latin *bis*, in *nobis, vobis.*
Perhaps, also, there originally existed a difference between
φι and φιν (which we find used indifferently for the singular
and plural), in that the former may have belonged to the
singular, the latter to the plural; and they may have had
the same relation to one another that, in Latin, *bi* has to
bis in *tibi* and *vobis*; and that, in Lithuanian, *mi* has to *mis*
in *akimi*, "through the eye," and *akimis*, "through the
eyes." It has escaped notice that the terminations φι and

[G. Ed. p. 251.]   φιν belong principally to the dative: their
locative and instrumental use—αὐτόφι, θύρηφι, βίηφιν—is explained by the fact, that the common dative also has assumed
the sign of these relations.   The strict genitive use of the termination φι, φιν, may perhaps be altogether denied; for if prepositions, which are elsewhere used in construction with the

---

* In the 1st and 2d pronoun (*no-bis, vo-bis*), where *bis* supplies the
place of the *bus* which proceeds from भ्यस् *bhyas*.

† Trans. Berlin Academy, 1826.   Comparison of Sanskrit with its cognate languages, by Prof. Bopp.   Essay III. p. 81.

‡ Observe, also, that the Sanskrit instrumental termination *bhis* has
been, in Prákrit, corrupted to हिं *hiṅ*.

genitive, occur also with the case in φι, φιν, we are not compelled, on this account, to regard the latter as the genitive
or representative of the genitive. In general, all prepositions,
which are used in construction with the genitive, would,
according to the sense, be better used with an ablative or a
locative, if these cases were particularly represented in
Greek. The suffix θεν also, of genuine ablative signification,
expressing separation from a place, is incorrectly considered to represent the genitive termination, where the
latter, in the common dialect, has received the sign of the
lost ablative. In ὄσσε δακρυόφιν πίμπλαντο, δακρυόφιν would,
in Sanskṛit, be rendered by अश्रुभिस् aśrubhis : the relation
is entirely instrumental, and is not changed because the
verb mentioned is more usually, though less suitably, used
with the genitive. The same is the case with ὄσσε δακρυόφιν τέρσαντο. In Ἰλιόφι κλυτὰ τείχεα it is not requisite
to make Ἰλιόφι governed by τείχεα, but it may be regarded
as locative "to Ilium." And in Od. XII. 45. (πολὺς δ᾽ ἀμφ᾽
ὀστεόφιν θὶς ἀνδρῶν πυθομένων) there is no necessity to look
upon ὀστεόφιν as the genitive, for it can be aptly rendered
by ossibus. I know no passages besides where a genitive
meaning could be given to forms in φι and φιν. To the
accusative, likewise, the form φι, φιν, is foreign, and according to its origin does not suit it; nor does it appear in
the train of prepositions, which elsewhere occur with the
accusative, with the single exception of ἐς ἐννηφιν in Hesiod
(cf. Buttmann, p. 205). As to the opinion   [G. Ed. p. 252.]
of the old Grammarians, that φι, φιν, may stand also in the
nominative and vocative, and as to the impropriety of the ι
subscribed before this termination in the dative singular of
the first declension, we refer the reader to what Buttmann
(p. 205) has rightly objected on this head.

218. The neuters in Σ, mentioned in §. 128., are nearly
the only ones from bases ending with a consonant, which
occur in combination with φι, φιν, in forms like ὄχεσ-φι,

ὄρεσ-φι, στήθεσ-φιν, which have been misunderstood, because the Σ dropped before vowel terminations was not recognised as the property of the base. Of the other consonants, ν is the only one, and ΚΟΤΥΛΗΔΟΝ the only ν base, which occurs in combination with φιν; and since Ν does not combine with Φ so readily as Σ, it assumes an auxiliary vowel ο—κοτυληδόν-ο-φιν—after the analogy of compound words like κυν-ο-θαρσής. This example is followed, without the necessity for it however, by δάκρυ—δακρυόφιν; while ναῦ-φιν, in an older point of view, resembles exactly the Sanskrit नौभिस् náubhis; for in compounds, also, the base ΝΑΥ keeps free from the conjunctive vowel ο, on which account ναύσταθμον may be compared with Sanskrit compounds like नौस्थ náu-stha, " standing (being) in the ship."

219. But to return to the Sanskrit dual termination भ्याम् bhyám, it is further to be remarked, that before it a final आ a is lengthened; hence, वृकाभ्याम् vrikábhyám for वृकभ्याम् vrikabhyám. It hardly admits of any doubt, that this lengthening extended to the cognate plural termination भिस् bhis; and that hence, from वृक vrika also vriká-bhis would be found. The common dialect has, however, abbreviated this form to वृकैस् vrikáis, which is easily derived from vrikábhis by rejecting the bh; for ऐ ái is, according [G. Ed. p. 253.] to §. 2., = á + i. This opinion, which I have before expressed,* I can now support by new arguments. In the first place, which did not then occur to me in discussing this question, the pronouns of the two first persons really form from their appended pronoun स्म sma, smá-bhis; hence अस्माभिस् asmábhis, युष्माभिस् yushmábhis; which forms stand in the same relation to the वृकाभिस् vriká-bhis, assumed by me, that the accusatives अस्मान् asmán, युष्मान् yushmán, do to वृकान् vrikán, " lupos." Secondly, the opinion

* Trans. Berlin Academy, 1826. Comparison of Sanskrit with its cognate languages, by Prof. Bopp. Essay III. p. 70.

which I arrived at theoretically has, since then, been so far
practically established by the Vêda dialect, that, in it, from a
final व *a* not *á-bhis* but *é-bhis*, has been formed, according to
the analogy of the dative and ablative, as वृकेभ्यस् *vrikébhyas;*
hence, अश्वेभिस् *asvébhis*, "*per equos*," from अश्व *asva*. In the
common dialect the pronominal form एभिस् *é-bhis* "*per hos*,"
answers to this Vêda form, which must properly be derived from the pronominal base व *a*, which generally plays
the chief part in the declension of इदम् *idam*. Though, then, on
one side, from the pronoun व *a* springs the form एभिस् *é-bhis;*
on the other side, from अस्म *asma* and युष्म *yushma* proceed
the forms अस्माभिस् *asmábhis*, युष्माभिस् *yushmábhis;* and though
the Vêda dialect, in its substantive and adjective bases in *a*,
attaches itself to the former form, still no necessity hence
arises for supposing the abbreviated *áis* to be based on an
é-bhis,* as that could never lead to *áis*. Perhaps, however,
ábhis might become *ébhis*, either through the assimilative
force of the *i* of *bhis*, or through analogy to   [G. Ed. p. 254.]
the dative *é-bhyas*, the *é* of which may, in like manner, owe
its origin to the re-active influence of the य *y*.†

220. The Prâkrit has fully followed out the path commenced by the Vêda dialect, and changed into ए *é* the *á* of

---

* From *ébhis* would come, after rejecting the *bh*, not *áis*, but *ayis*, for
é, =*a+i*, cannot be combined with a following *i* into a diphthong, or, as
it is itself already a diphthong, into a triphthong.

† I do not regard the Vêda नद्यैस् *nadyáis*, for नदीभिस् *nadí-bhis*, as
an abbreviation of *nadi-bhis* (for after rejecting the *bh*, from *nadí+is*
would be formed *nadis*), but as a very common instrumental, for which
an extension of the base *nadí* to *nadya* is to be assumed. On the other
hand, the Zend pronominal instrumental *dís* mentioned by Burnouf
(Nouv. Journ. Asiat. III. 310.) may here be considered, which occurs frequently in the Jzeshne, and is probably an abbreviation of دیبیش *dibis* or
دیبیش *dibís*, from a base *di*, the accusative of which دیم *dim*, "him,"
is often found with *i* unlengthened, contrary to §. 64. The connection of
the base دی *di* with تـ *ta* cannot, on this account, be disputed.

asmá-bhis, yushmá-bhis, as also, in the locative plural, that of
asmásu, yushmásu; hence अम्हेहिं *amhé-hin,* तुम्हेहिं *tumhé-hin,*
अम्हेसु *amhésu,* तुम्हेसु *tumhésu.*   Moreover, in Prâkṛit, all other
a bases, as well pronouns as substantives and adjectives,
terminate the instrumental plural with एहिं *e-hin;* and thus
कुसुमेहिं *kusumé-hin,* "*floribus,*" (from *kusuma,*) answers to the
Vêda कुसुमेभिस् *kusumé-bhis.*   Before, however, the forms in
एभिस् *é-bhis,* एहिं *é-hin,* had arisen, from आभिस् *ábhis,* by the
change of *á* into *é,* *áis* must have proceeded by means of
rejection and contraction from that most early form.   This
form exists also in the oldest hymns of the Vêdas, together
with that in एभिस् *ébhis:* thus, in Rosen, p. 14, यज्ञैस् *yajnáis;*
pp. 15 and 21 अर्कैस् *arkáis.*   In Zend the abbreviated form
áis is the only one that occurs, which it does, indeed, extremely often.

221. Before the dual termination ༷༷༷ *bya* the Zend, in
[G. Ed. p. 255.]   its *a* bases, differs from the Sanskṛit in the
same way as the Zend and Prâkṛit do before the termination भिस् *bhis,* हिं *hin;* it employs, namely, *é* for *á:* but
from *vĕhrké-bya,* according to §§. 28. 41. comes *vĕhrkaéibya.*
Thus, in the Vendidâd, ༷༷༷ *hvaéibya*
pádhaéibya, "*suis pedibus,*" = स्वाभ्याम् पादाभ्याम् *swábhyám pádá-*
bhyám; ༷༷༷ *zastaéibya* (हस्ताभ्याम्) "*manibus.*"   But
in this case, also, the diphthong ए *é* is supplied by *ái* (§. 33.);
e.g. ༷༷༷ *ubóibya,* "*ambobus*" (Vend. S. p. 305.).   If in
this form the lost nasal be restored, and it be assumed (of
which I have no doubt) that the Greek dual termination *ιν* is an
abbreviation of the Sanskṛit *bhyám;*[*] then the Homeric forms
like ὤμοι-ιν are to be compared with the ༷༷༷ *ubói-bya*

_____

[*] By rejecting the labial, as in वृकैस् *vṛikáis* from वृकाभिस् *vṛikábhis,*
and by contracting the याम् *yám* to *ιν,* as when, in Sanskṛit, for *yashta,*
ishta is said, from *yaj,* "to sacrifice," and in Zend छ्ज् *im,* "*hæc,*" for
इयम् *iyam* (see, also, §. 42.).

above mentioned; where, therefore, the first ι would fall to
the base, which it lengthens, the other to the termination.
The third declension, by its forms like δαιμόν-οιν, might give
rise to the conjecture, that οιν and not ιν is the true termination: the latter, however, is shewn to be so from the two
first declensions, where ιν and not οιν is attached to the final
vowel of the base (Μούσα-ιν, λόγο-ιν).   In the third, therefore, we explain the o before ιν in the same manner as, §. 218.
before φιν (κοτυληδον-ό-φιν); viz. as a conjunctive vowel,
which has made its way from the bases which necessarily
have it, i. e. from those terminating in a consonant into
those which might dispense with it (into the bases in
ι and υ); as, in general, in the third declension the consonantal bases have given the tone, and have shewn the way
to the vowels ι and υ. It might, however, not   [G. Ed. p. 256.]
have been necessary for the conjunctive vowel o to make its
appearance between consonants and the termination, as
δαιμον-ιν could very easily be uttered; but the o of δαιμόνοιν
comes evidently from a time when the ιν was still preceded
by the consonant, which the corresponding Sanskrit termination bhyām leads us to expect; in all probability a φ; thus,
δαιμόν-ο-ιν, from δαιμον-ο-φιν.*   We should have, therefore,
here a different φιν from that which, in §. 217., we endeavoured to explain from φις, भिस् bhis: the nasal in the dual
(φ)ιν stands quite regularly for its predecessor m, as, in general, at the end of words.   In order to present to our

---

* The conjunctive vowel o, therefore, before the dual termination ιν,
has an origin exactly similar to that of the possessive suffix εντ, which has
been already elsewhere compared with the Sanskrit वन्त् vant. Εντ must
therefore have been originally pronounced Fεντ; and the conjunctive
vowel, which the digamma made requisite or desirable before consonantal
bases, and which, from thence, has extended itself to the whole third
declension, has remained also after the digamma has been dropped, and
thus πυρ-ό-εις answers to πυροῖν, from πυρ-ο-ῖν: on the other hand, τυρό-εις
to τύροιν (τυρο-ῖν).

view still more clearly how forms quite similar take root in the language as corruptions of preceding dissimilar forms, let the form ἔτυπτον be considered as the first person singular and third person plural; in one case from ἔτυπτομ, in the other from ἔτυπτοντ.

222. If the dual termination *ιν* be explained as a contraction of *bhyâm*, we shall have found, also, the origin of the dative plural termination *ιν*, which appears to have been changed in this number in the pronouns of one gender as it were by accident (ἡμ'-ῖν, ὑμ'-ῖν, σφ'-ίν, together with σφί-σι). The Greek, however, in this respect, is guided or misled by the Sanskrit; or, more correctly, the distinction of the plural dative of the pronouns of one gender is very ancient, and the Sanskrit has in them भ्यम् *bhyam* as termination (अस्मभ्यम् *asma-bhyam*, "nobis," युष्मभ्यम् *yushma-bhyam*, (G. Ed. p. 257.) "*vobis*"), opposed to the भ्यस् *bhyas* of all other words. From this *bhyam*, then, we arrive at *ιν* quite as easily, or more so, than from the dual termination *bhyâm* (cf. §. 42.). As, however, भ्यम् *bhyam*, and its abbreviated form ह्यम् *hyam*, according to §. 215., has also its place in the singular dative of the pronouns of one gender, but occurs nowhere else; as, moreover, the Latin also, in the pronouns referred to, has maintained a genuine dative termination, and to the common *i*, which is borrowed from the locative, presents in contrast the termination *bi* or *hi* (for *bhi*) (§. 200.); we can, therefore, in the singular *ιν* also of ἐμ'-ίν, τε-ίν, τ'-ίν, ίν, σφ'-ίν, see nothing else than an abbreviation of भ्यम् *bhyam*, a form which the Latin and Greek have shared in such a manner, that the former has retained the beginning and the latter the end. In the *i* both coincide.* The occasional accu-

---

* A short time since, Max. Schmidt, in his excellent treatise "Commentatio de Pronomine Græco et Latino" (p. 77), endeavoured to connect the termination *ιν* here treated of with the Sanskrit in a different way, by designating it as the sister form of the pronominal locative termination

sative use of this termination, in Theocritus, is to be explained from its original signification being no longer felt,
and the exchange of its v with that of the accusative thereby
caused.   On the other hand, we have in $\mu\acute{\iota}\nu$ and $\nu\acute{\iota}\nu$ real accusatives, and should therefore divide them $\mu\acute{\iota}$-ν, $\nu\acute{\iota}$-ν; and
not assume, with Buttmann (p. 296), a connection between
this form and the dative -$\bar{\iota}\nu$.

223. As to the origin of the case-suffixes   [G. Ed. p. 268.]
भिस् bhi-s, भ्याम् bhy-am, भ्याम् bhy-$\hat{a}m$, and भ्यस् bhy-as, which
begin with भ्य bhy (from भि bhi), we must notice, first,
their connection with the preposition अभि $abhi$, " to," " towards," "against,"(whence अभितस् $abhi$-tas, "at," cf. "$apud$").
However, in $abhi$ itself bhi is clearly, in like manner, the termination, and the demonstrative अ a the theme ; so that this
preposition, in respect to its termination, is to be regarded
as a sister form to the Latin ti-bi, si-bi, i-bi, u-bi;* just as
another preposition, which springs from the pronominal
base a, viz. अधि $adhi$, " over," finds analogous forms in the
Greek locatives, like $\ddot{o}$-$\theta\iota$, $\ddot{a}\lambda\lambda o$-$\theta\iota$, $o\dot{v}\rho\alpha\nu\acute{o}$-$\theta\iota$ (§. 16.).   Related
to the suffix धि dhi is ध dha, which has been retained in
the common dialect only in the abbreviation ha, in i-ha,
" here," and in the preposition sa-ha, " with"; but in the
Vêda dialect exhibits the original form and more extended
diffusion, and in the Zend, also, is found in several pro-

---

mination इन in (§. 201.).   In this view similar forms would be contrasted, exclusive of the length of the Greek $\iota\nu$, which, according to my
explanation, may pass as compensation for the a, which has been dropped.
Still I lay less stress on the difference of quantity than on this, that it is
precisely the pronouns of one gender in the Sanskrit, which exhibit in the
locative not in but the common i (§. 201.), but I attach still more weight
to what has been said above in support of my opinion.

* In Prâkṛit the termination हिं hin, which is connected with भि bhi
(cf. §. 217.), unites also with other pronominal bases, for the formation of
locative adverbs, as तहिं ta-hin, " there," कहिं ka-hin, " where ?"

nominal bases with a locative signification; *e. g.* ᴀᴏꞯᴊᴠ»ᴀᴊ
ava-dha, "here." In the Greek, compare θα of ἔνθα, opposed to θεν, from ἔνθεν, ἐμέθεν, &c., from धस् *dhas*, for
तस् *tas*, in अधस् *a-dhas*, "beneath": in which formations
ध् *dh* stands as a permutation of *t*, and occurs in this way,
also, in some other formations.* Therefore *dha, dhi,* are
to be derived from the demonstrative base त *ta*; but it is
more difficult to trace the origin of the भि *bhi* of अभि *abhi*
(Greek ἀμφί). I suspect that an initial consonant has been
[G. Ed. p. 259.] dropped. As in Greek, also, φίν is used for
σφίν, and as in Sanskrit विंशति *vinśati* "twenty," is clearly
an abbreviation of द्विंशति *dwinśati*, and in Zend ᴀᴜᴢ_ᴊ *bis*,
"twice," ᴀᴊᴊꝺᴊᴜ *bitya*, "the second," is used for ᴀᴜᴢ»ᵍ *dvis*,
(Sanskrit द्विस् *dwis*), ᴀᴊᴊꝺᴊ»ᵍ *dvitya* (Sanskrit द्वितीय *dwitiya*),
so भि *bhi* may be identical with the pronominal base स्व *swa*
or स्वि *swi*—whence the Greek σφεῖς, σφίν, φίν, &c.; and so
indeed, that after the *s* has been dropped, the following
semi-vowel has been strengthened or hardened, just as in
the Zend ᴀᴜᴢ_ᴊ *bis*, ᴀᴊᴊꝺᴊᴊ *bitya*, and the Latin *bis, bi.* The
changed sibilant might also be recognised in the aspiration of the भ *bh*, as, in Prâkṛit (§. 166.), स्म *sma* has become
म्ह *mha*; and, (which comes still closer to the case before us), in
Greek for σφίν is found also ψίν. And, in Sanskrit, that भ *bh*
should spring from *b + h* is not entirely unknown; and in
this way is to be explained the relation of भूयस् *bhúyas*,
"more," to बहु *bahu*, "much," the *a* being rejected (Gramm.
Crit. r. 251. Rem.).

224. The following will serve as a general view of the
dual termination under discussion, in Sanskrit, Zend, Greek,
and Lithuanian: —

---

* Among others, in the 2d person plural of the middle ध्वे *dhwé* and
ध्वम् *dhwam* for त्वे *twé*, त्वम् *twam*.

SANSKRIT.	ZEND.	GREEK.	LITHUANIAN.
m. *vṛikâ-bhyâm,*	*vĕhrkaêi-bya,* or *vĕhrkôi-bya,*	*λύκο-ιν,*	*wilka-m.*
f. *jihvâ-bhyâm,*	*hizvâ-bya,*	*χώρα-ιν,*	*ranko-m.*
m. *pati-bhyâm,*	*paiti-bya,*	*ποσί-ο-ιν,*	*pati-m.*
f. *tanu-bhyâm,*	*tanu-bya,*	*πιτύ-ο-ιν,*	....
f. *vâg-bhyâm,*	*vâch-e-bya,**	*ὀπ-ο-ῖν,*	....
m. *bharad-bhyâm,*	*baran'-bya,*	*φερόντ-ο-ιν,*	....
m. *âtma'-bhyâm.*†	*aśma'-bya,*	*δαιμόν-ο-ιν,*	....

[G. Ed. p. 260.]

---

* I deduce this form principally from the base *raoch*, "light," which often occurs in the terminations beginning with *b*, and always interposes *e* as conjunctive vowel—*raoch-e-bis*, *raoch-e-byô*. We find, also, *vi-vach-e-bis* (Vend. S. p. 63.). Bases in *r* interpose *ĕ*; those in *t*, when a vowel precedes that letter, conjoin the termination direct (*amĕrĕtâtaṭ-bya*, according to §. 38.): on the other hand, the *t* of *nt* is rejected; thus, V. S. p. 9. *bĕrĕzĕn'-bya*, "*splendentibus*," with *ṇ*, contrary to §. 60. The form *bruaṭ-byaṅm*, "*superciliis*," also deserves notice, because in this solitary word the case termination appears unreduced (§. 61.). The MS., however, as often as this word occurs, always divides the termination from the base (Vend. S. p. 269, twice, *brvaṭ byaṅm*; pp. 321 and 322, *barvaṭ byaṅm*, probably for *bravaṭ byaṅm*; so that it would seem that *brvaṭ* is the ablative singular of a theme *brû* (Sansk. *bhrû*). I have not found this word in any other case: it is not likely, however, that any thing but *brvat* or *brvant* is its theme: in the latter case it would be a participial form, and would demonstrate, that instead of the last consonant of *nt*, the last but one also may be rejected. Or are we to regard *brvaṭ byaṅm* as a form of that singular kind that unites with the termination of the ablative singular that of the dual, and thus *brû* would still be the theme?

† *N*, in Sanskrit and Zend, is rejected before case terminations beginning with a consonant; thus, in Greek, *δαίμο-σι*, and in Gothic *ahma'-m*.

SANSKRIT.	ZEND.	GREEK.	LITHUANIAN.
m. *bhrátri-bhyám,**	*bhrátar-ĕ-bya,*	πατέρ-ο-ιν,	. . . .
n. *vachô-bhyám,†*	*vachô-bya,*	ἐπέ(σ)-ο-ιν,	. . . .

GENITIVE, LOCATIVE.

[G. Ed. p. 261.] 225. These two cases, in Sanskrit, have the common termination बोस् *ôs*, which may be connected with the singular genitive termination. The following are examples: वृकयोस् *vrikay-ôs*, जिह्वयोस् *jihway-ôs* (cf. §. 158.), पत्योस् *paty-ôs*, तन्वोस् *tanw-ôs*, वाचोस् *vách-ôs*, भ्रात्रोस् *bhrátr-ôs*, वचसोस् *vachas-ôs*. In Zend this termination seems to have disappeared, and to be replaced by the plural; likewise in Lithuanian, where, *awy-û* is both dual and plural genitive.

PLURAL.

NOMINATIVE, VOCATIVE.

226. Masculines and feminines have, in Sanskrit, अस् *as* for the termination of the nominative plural, with which, as in the cognate languages, the vocative is identical in all declensions. I consider this *as* to be an extended form of the singular nominative sign *s*; so that in this extension of the case-suffix lies a symbolical allusion to plurality: and the *s*, which is too personal for the neuter, is wanting in that gender, in the singular and dual, as well as in the plural. The three numbers, therefore, with regard to their masculine-feminine termination or personal designation, are related to one another, as it were, like positive, comparative, and superlative, and the highest degree belongs to the dual. In Zend अस् *as* has, according to §. 56[b].

---

* अर् *ar* before case terminations beginning with consonants is shortened to ऋ *ri* (§. 127.).

† See §. 56[b].

become *ó* or ᴊᴊᴊ *aś* before the appended particles *cha* and *chit*; the Greek exhibits εϛ, under the restriction of §. 228.; the Latin *ēs*,* with unorganic length of quantity through the influence of the *s*; the Lithuanian has *ės* in bases in *r* but elsewhere simple *s*. Thus the words दुहितरस् *duhitar-as*, ᴊᴘᴊᴊᴊᴊ̂ᴊᴐ_ᴐ_ᴊᴓ *dughdhar-aś-cha*, θυγατέρ-εϛ, *dukter-ės*, *matr--es*, correspond with one another.

227. The *a* of the termination is melted   [G. Ed. p. 202.] down with a preceding ग *a* of the base to *á*; thus, वृकास् *vṛikás*, from *vṛika + as*, corresponds to the Gothic *vulfôs*, from *VULFAas* (§. 69.). In this concretion only, however, with the vowel of the base, the Gothic has preserved the full termination; but elsewhere, both with vowel and consonantal bases, the *s* alone of the old *as* is left, as in general the termination *as* in Gothic polysyllabic forms has everywhere been weakened to *is* or *s* (cf. §§. 135. 191.): hence, *sunyu-s*, *ahman-s*, for *suniv-as*, *ahman-as*. And आ *á*, too, is contracted with the termination *as* to *ás*; hence, जिह्वास् *jihwás*, for *jihwá-as*. It cannot, however, be shewn with certainty, from what has been just said, that the Gothic *gibôs*, from *GIBŌ*, has simple *s* or *as* (contracted with the base vowel to *ô = á*) for its case designation.

228. The masculine pronominal bases in *a* refuse, in Sanskrit, Zend, and Gothic, the full nominative designation, and in place of it extend the base by the addition of an *i*, which, according to §. 2., with the *a* of the base forms इ *é*,† for which, in Zend, is used ᴊᴑ *é* or ᴊᴘ *ói*;

---

* Vide §. 797. p. 1078.

† As ग *a* is lengthened in many other cases to इ *é*, and with this the case terminations are then first conjoined, there is good ground to assume that in ते *té*, and similar forms, no case designation at all is contained, and that the pronouns, as purely words of personality, find themselves sufficiently personified in this case through themselves alone; as in the singular *sa* is said for *sas*, in Sanskrit as in Gothic, and in Greek *ó* for *ós*; while in Latin, with *is-te* also *ipse* and *ille* are robbed of the nominative sign. This opinion is remarkably confirmed by the fact that अमी *amí* (Grimm.

hence, Sanskṛit तै *tê,* Zend ‌‌ *tê,* Gothic *thai,* "this,"
[G. Ed. p. 263.]   answering to the feminine form ताः *tâs,*
‌‌ *tâo* (§. 56".), *thâs.* To this corresponds, in Greek, τοί
(Doric for *oi*). In Greek and Latin, however, this *i*, which
practically replaces the termination *as* (ες, ēs), has not remained in the masculine pronominal bases in *o* (= व *a,*
§. 116.); but all other bases of the second, as of the first declension, have, in Greek and Latin, taken example from it; hence,
λύκοι, χῶραι, for λυκο-ες, χωρα-ες, *lupi* (from *lupoi*), *terræ*
(from *terrai*), for *lupo-es, terra-es.* The Latin fifth declension,
although in its origin identical with the first (§. 121.), has
preserved the old termination; hence, *rēs* from *rē-ēs,* as,
in Sanskṛit *jihwâs* from *jihwâ-as.* The Lithuanian has
fixed narrower restrictions than the Greek and Latin on
the misuse of the pronominal inflexion under discussion, or,
to speak more correctly, want of inflexion: it gives, indeed,
wilkai=λύκοι, *lupi,* but not *rankai,* but *rankos.* Honour,
therefore, to the Gothic! that in this respect it has not
overstepped by one hair the old Sanskṛit-Zend limits; for
that the adjective *a* bases, as they in general follow the
pronominal declension, give also *ai* for *ôs* (*blindai* "*cæci*") is,
therefore, no violation of the old law.

229. In Zend, in consonantal bases the dual termination
‌‌ *do* also (from ताः *âs,* §. 207.) occurs with a plural signification; thus, frequently, ‌‌ *vâch-do,* "*voces,*" ‌‌

Crit. §. 271.) shews itself clearly through most of the oblique cases, as
amí-byas, "*illis,*" *ami-shâm,* "*illorum,*" to be the naked theme. The form
which occurs in the Zend-Avesta ‌‌ *vîspeś-cha,* "*omnesque*"
(V. S. p. 49), considered as a contraction of *vîspay-aś-cha* (cf. §. 244.),
leads to the conjecture, that to तै *tê,* and similar uninflected forms, the
termination *as* also might attach itself; thus, तयस *tay-as.* In Zend, the
pronominal form in *ê* occurs, for the most part, in the accusative plural;
and thus the abovementioned *vîspeś-cha* l. c. stands probably as accusative, although, according to Anquetil's inaccurate translation, it might
be regarded as the nominative.

raoch-ōo, "*luces*," which forms cannot be regarded, perhaps, as regular plurals of bases in *d*; for I believe   [G. Ed. p. 264.]
I can guarantee that there exists no such base as ᭭᭭ *vāchā* and ᭭᭭ *raochā*.   The form ᭭᭭ *āonhā* in *a* bases, as ᭭᭭ *vēhrkāonhā*, "*lupi*," and "*lupos*," rests on that in the Vêdas, but which only occurs in the nominative, चासस् *āsas* (§. 56".); *e.g.* स्तोमासस् *stōmāsas*, "songs of praise," for स्तोमास् *stōmās*, from स्तोम *stōma*.*

230. Bases in *i* and *u* have, in Sanskrit, Guna; hence पतयस् *patay-as*, सूनवस् *sūnaw-as*, for *paty-as*, *sūnw-as*. The Gothic also has preserved this Guna, but in its weakened form *i* (§. 27.), which, before *u*, becomes *y; hence, *sunyu-s*, "sons," (for *suniu-s*, from *sunau-s*,) a form which would be unintelligible without the Guna theory, which has been shewn to belong to the German. In *i* bases the Guna *i* is melted down with that of the base to long *i* (written *ei*, §. 70.); hence, *gastei-s*, *anstei-s*, from *GASTI, ANSTI* (cf. p. 105.). The Zend employs Guna or not at pleasure; hence ᭭᭭ *paity-ō*, or *paitay-ō*,† ᭭᭭ *pasv-ō*, or *pasav-ō*.

231. Neuters have, in Zend, as in the cognate European languages, a short *a* for their termi-   [G. Ed. p. 265.]
nation‡; perhaps the remains of the full *as*, which belongs to the natural genders, after the *s*, which is too per-

---

* This form is, in my opinion, to be so regarded, as that, for greater emphasis, the termination *as* has been a second time appended to the termination, which had become concrete with the base.

† The *i*, which, according to §. 41., is blended with the base, remains in spite of the *a* preceding the *y*.

‡ Simple as this point is, I have nevertheless found it very difficult to come to a firm conclusion regarding it, although, from the first, I have directed my attention towards it. Burnouf has already (Nouv. Journ. Asiat. III. 309, 310) given the plural neuter form, and instituted comparisons with the Gothic and Greek, &c. But from forms like *hu-mata*, "*bene-cogitata*," "*hūcta*," "*bene-dicta*," it cannot be perceived what the neuter plural termination properly is; because, setting out with the Sanskrit, we are tempted to assume that the true termination in these forms has

sonal for the dead speechless gender, has been dropped.
[G. Ed. p. 266.] This *a* remains, then, in the accusative.
The masculine and feminine have, in the same case,
generally likewise *as* (Zend ꭶ *ô*, ᴧᴩᴊᴊᴧ *aścha*). The
following are examples: ᴧᴊᴧᴧᴧᴧᴩᴊᴧ *ashavan-a*, "*pura*;"
ᴧᴩᴊᴩᴊᴧᴄᴄᴇᴈᴊ *bĕrĕzant-a*, "*splendentia*;" ᴧᴩᴊᴊᴧᴒ *vâch-a*, "*verba*;"
ᴧᴑᴩᴊ *nar-a*, "*homines*;" ᴧᴩᴇᴒᴒᴊ *ast-a*, "*ossa*." In nominal bases in *a* the termination is melted down with
the vowel of the base: the *â* so produced has, however, in
the received condition of the language, according to a

---

has been dropped, and its loss either compensated by lengthening the final
vowel, or not. We must therefore direct our attention to bases with a
different termination than *a*, especially to such as terminate with a consonant. The examination of this subject is, however, much embarrassed,
in that the Zend, without regard to the gender of the singular, is prone,
contrary to natural expectation, to make every noun neuter in the
plural; an inclination which goes so far, that the numerous class of *a* bases
have hereby entirely lost the masculine nominative, and but sparingly
exhibit the masculine accusative. When, *e.g. mashya*, "human being,"
is, in the plural nominative, likewise, *mashya* (with *cha, mashyâ-cha*), here
I am nevertheless convinced that this plural *mashya*, or *mashyâ*, is not an
abbreviation of *mashyân* from *mashyâs* (§. 56ᵇ.), as in no other part of
Zend Grammar ᴧ *a* or ᴧᴑ *â* stands for आस् *âs*: I am persuaded that this
form belongs to the neuter. The replacing, however, of the plural masculine by neuters rests upon a deep internal feeling of the language;
for in the plural number it is clear that gender and personality are far in
the back ground. The personality of the individual is lost in the abstract
infinite and inanimate plurality; and so far we can but praise the Zend
for its evitation of gender in the plural. We must blame it, however, in
this point, that it does not, in all places, bring the adjectives or pronouns
into concord with the substantives to which they refer, and that in this
respect it exhibits a downright confusion of gender, and a disorder which
has very much impeded the inquiry into this subject. Thus, *e.g. vîspa
unaghra-raochâo* (not *raoch-â*), "all lights which have had no beginning";
tisarô (fem.) *śata* or *thrayô* (masc.) *śata*, "three hundred"; *chathwârô*
(masc.) *śata* "four hundred." In general the numbers "three" and
"four" appear to have lost the neuter; hence, also, *thrayô csafn-a*, "three
nights," *chathwârô csafn-a*, "four nights": in Vend. S. p. 237, on the other
hand, stands *tâ nara yâ*, "those persons who . . . ." I divide thus *nar-a*
although

principle often quoted, been again shortened, and remains
only in monosyllabic bases and before annexed particles.
The Gothic and Zend, in this respect, stand   [G. Ed. p. 267.]
very remarkably upon one and the same footing; for *thô*,
"*hæc*," is used (for *thd*, §. 69.), from *THAa*; *hvô*, "*quæ*," for
HVAa ; but *daura*, from *DAURA*, as, in Zend, ᚷᚦ *tâ*,
"*hæc*," ᚷᚲ *yâ*, "*quæ*," opposed to ᚷᚲᚾ *agha*, "*peccata*,"
from *agha*. It cannot, therefore, be said of the Gothic that
the *a* of the base has been dropped before that of the termi-

---

although the form might also belong to a theme *nara*, which also occurs,
but much less frequently than *nar*; whence also, elsewhere, the masculine
nar-ô taĕ-cha, "and those persons." From the theme *vâch*, "word,"
"speech," we find frequently *vâch-a* (also, erroneously as it appears,
vach-a); *e.g.* Vend. S. p. 34, ᚷᚲᚾᚲᛋᚷᛟᚷᛋᚲᚷᚾᛋᚲ ᚷᚲᚾᛋᚷᛟ ᚷᚲᚾᛋᚷᚾ ᚷᚲᚾᛋᚷ
vâcha humata hûcta hvarĕsta, "*verba bene-cogitata, bene-dicta, bene-peracta.*"
From ᚷᚲᛋᚲᚷᚾ *ashavan*, "pure," occurs very often the neuter plural
ashvana-a: as, however, the theme *ashavan* sometimes, too, although
very rarely, extends itself unorganically to *ashavana*, this form proves less
(though it be incorrect) that the neuter *ashavan-a* should be derived from
the unorganic extremely rare *ashavana*, than from the genuine and most
common *ashavan*, in the weak cases *ashaun* or *ashaon*. Participial forms,
too, in *nt* are very common in the neuter plural; and I have never found
any ground for assuming that the Zend, like the Pâli and Old High German, has extended the old participial theme by a vowel addition. In
the Vend. S., p. 119, we find an accusative *agha aiwishitâr-a*, "*peccata
corrumpentia* (?)." Anquetil renders both expressions together by "*la
corruption du cœur*" (II. 227.); but probably *aiwi-sitâra* stands for
-csitâra, and means literally "the destroying" (cf. क्षि *kshi*, intrans. "to
be ruined"). So much is certain, that *aiwi* is a preposition (p. 42), and
tar is the suffix used in the formation of the word (§. 144.), which is in
the strong cases *târ;* and from this example it follows, as also from *ashavan-a*, that where there are more forms of the theme than one, the Zend,
like the Sanskrit (see Gramm. Crit. r. 185. c.), forms the nominative, accusative, and vocative plural from the stronger theme. I refrain from adducing other examples for the remarkable and not to have been expected
proposition, that the Zend, in variance from the Sanskrit, forms its plural
neuters according to the principle of the Latin *nomin-a*, Greek τάλαν-*a*,
Gothic *namón-a* or *namn-a*.

nation, for it could not be dropped, because the base-vowel
and termination have been, from the first, concrete. The old
length of quantity might, however, be weakened: this is
the fate of long vowels especially at the end of words. It
cannot, therefore, be said of the Greek τὰ δῶρα and the
Latin *dona*, that the *a* entirely belongs to the termination,
This *a* is an old inheritance of the oldest date, from the
time when the second declension, to use the expression,
terminated its bases with *ă*. This *ă* has since then become, in Greek, *o* or ε (§. 204.), in Latin, *u, o,* or *e,* and has
maintained its ancient quality only in the plural neuter,
and the *ā,* which has grown out of *ă + ă,* has become
shortened. This *ă,* however, in contrast with its offspring
ŏ, ĕ, ŭ, may even pass for a more weighty ending, which
unites base and termination, than if δωρο or δωρε, *donŭ,*
donĕ, stood as the plural neuter.

232. Bases in *i* and *u* may, in Zend, suppress their final
vowel before the termination, and *u* may be suppressed and
replaced by lengthening the base-vowel: thus we read in
the Vend. S. pp. 46 and 48, ‍‍‍ᴧᴧᴧ *gara,* "hills," from ᴧᴧᴧ
gairi (see p. 196, Note†): on the other hand, p. 313, *gairis*
(fem.). That which Anquetil (II. 268.) renders by "*une
action qui empêche de passer le pont, le péché contre nature*,"
runs in the original (p. 119), ᴧᴧᴧᴧᴧᴧᴧᴧᴧᴧᴧᴧᴧᴧ
ᴧᴧᴧᴧᴧᴧᴧ *agha andpĕrĕtha skyaothna yă narô-vaipaya,*
[G. Ed. p. 208.] *i. e.* "the sins which stop the bridge, the
actions which . . . ."; and here it is evident that *andpĕrĕtha*
stands for *andpĕrĕthw-a,* for *pĕrĕtu* means actually "bridge."[*]

---

[*] Burnouf's MS. divides thus, *and pĕrĕtha,* which is following Olshausen (p. 6), but with the various reading *andpĕrĕtha.* I have no ground
for assuming that in Zend there exists a preposition *and,* "without," so
that *and pĕrĕtha* might mean "without a bridge"; and that *pĕrĕtu* would,
in the singular instrumental, form *pĕrĕthwa* or *pĕrĕtava.* I suppose, therefore, that *pĕrĕtu* may be conjoined with the preposition *à,* and then the
negative *an* have been prefixed.

But a final u may also be retained, in the form of a semi-vowel, either pure or with Guna: the latter form I recognise in ᴊᴊᴊᴊ *ydtava* (Vend. S. p. 120 ; in Olshausen, p. 7), which can only be the plural accusative of ᴊᴊᴊ *ydtu*, for it stands with ᴊᴊᴊ *agha*, "*peccata*; and in the same page in Olshausen occurs a derivative of *ydtu* in the accusative singular, viz. ᴊᴊᴊ *ydtumēntĕm*, "the magician," "gifted with magic" (according to Anquetil, *magicien*). I render, therefore, *agha ydtava* literally by "the sins of sorcery" (Anquetil, "*la magie très mauvaise*"); and in Anquetil's Vocabulary is (p. 467) ᴊᴊᴊ *ydthvanm*, the regular plural genitive of our base *ydtu*, which means, therefore, "of the sorceries"; while Anquetil faultily gives it the meaning of the derivative (*magiciens*), and, according to his custom, takes this oblique case for a nominative. An example of a neuter plural form without Guna is at V. S. p. 122, ᴊᴊᴊ *hĕndva* "the Indies"; with *hapta hĕndu*, "the seven Indies" (Anq. II. p. 270). It has the epithet *us-astar-a* ("up-starred?") in opposition to ᴊᴊᴊ ᴊᴊᴊ *daus-astarĕm hĕndum*, "to the ill-starred (?)   [G. Ed. p. 269.] Indies." An example, in which the suppressed termination in a *u* base is replaced by lengthening the final vowel, is the very frequently occurring ᴊᴊᴊ *vôhû*, "goods," from ᴊᴊᴊ *vôhu.*

233. The interrogative base *ki* (cf. *quis, quid*), which in Sanskrit forms only the singular nominative-accusative (neuter) फिम् *ki-m*, but is elsewhere replaced by *ka*; whence, in Zend, ᴊᴊᴊ *ka-t*, "what": this base, the use of which is very limited, forms in Zend the plural neuter ᴊᴊᴊ *ky-a**; and

---

* V. S. p. 341. ᴊᴊᴊᴊᴊᴊᴊᴊ *kya aĕté vacha yói hĕnti gáthdhva thris ámrúta* (erroneously *thris ámrúta*), "What are the words which are thrice said in the prayers (songs)?" The masculine forms *aĕté* and *yói* can here, according to Note at §. 231., occasion no difficulty. So also V. S. p. 85, ᴊᴊᴊ *kya* before

this form is the more important, since we still require examples which can be relied upon, in which the *i* of the base is not suppressed before the termination *a* (above, *gara* for *gairy-a*), although it may with reason be conjectured, that, in accordance with the abovementioned *hĕndv-a* and *yâtav-a*, forms also like *vairy-a* or *vairay-a*, from *vairi*, were in use. As in Gothic, neuter substantive and adjective bases in *i* are wanting, the numeral base *THRI*, "three," and the pronominal base *I*, "he," are very important for the neuter cases under discussion, in which they form *thriy-a* (*thriya hunda*, "three hundred ") and *iy-a*, according to the principle of the Sanskrit monosyllabic forms, of which the *i* sound has not passed into its simple semi-vowel, but into *iy*; thus, in Sanskrit, भिया *bhiy-â*, from भी *bhî*.

234. The Sanskrit gives, in place of the Zend-European neuter *a*, an इ *i*, perhaps as the weakening of a former *a* [G. Ed. p. 270.] (§. 6.); the final vowel of the base is lengthened, and between it and the case termination a euphonic *n* is placed (§. 133.); hence दानानि *dânâ-n-i*, वारीणि *vâri-n-i*,[*] मधूनि *madhû-n-i*.[†] The bases which terminate with a single consonant—न *n* and र *r* being excepted—prefix to it a nasal,

---

before the masculine رَتَوو *ratavô* (رَتَوو کیَ *kya ratavô*, "which are the lords"?).

[*] According to a euphonic law (Gram. Crit. r. 84[a].), an न *n* following after र *r*, and some other letters, is, under certain conditions, changed into ण *ṅ*.

[†] In the Vêdas, the *ni* in *a* bases is frequently found suppressed ; *e.g.* विश्वा *viswâ*, "*omnia*," from *viśca*. In this way the Sanskrit is connected with the Zend *viśpa*, *viśpâ-cha*: but perhaps this coincidence is only external; for as the Sanskrit nowhere uses a neuter termination *a*, विश्वा *viśwâ* cannot well be deduced from *viśpa+a*, but can only be explained as an abbreviation of the *â-ni*, which likewise occurs in the Vêdas, as also पुरु *purû*, "*multa*," "*magna*," is used for पुरूणि *purûṅi* (Rosen's Spec. pp. 9, 10).

and after *s* and *n* the preceding vowel is lengthened; hence
वचांसि *vachân-si,* नामानि *nâmân-i.*   Into relation with this *i*
might be brought the neuter inflexion of *quæ* (*quai*) and *hæ-c*
(*haic*) which stand in Latin very isolated; *quæ* is, however,
still tolerably distant from the Sanskrit कानि *kâ-n-i,* while it
is nearly identical with the neuter dual के *kê* from *ka + i*
(§. 212.). Since, however, the antiquity of this dual termination
is supported by the Zend, the plural form *kâni* stands on the
other side isolated, and its age is thereby rendered doubtful;
as, moreover, the Latin, in the verb also, has introduced a
termination originally dual into the plural*;   [G. Ed. p. 271.]
we cannot avoid recognising in the Latin plural *quæ* a
remnant as true as possible of the Sanskrit dual के *kê.*

235. We give here a general view of the formation of
the plural nominative, and of the vocative, identical with
it and the neuter accusative:

SANSKRIT.	ZEND.	GREEK.	LATIN.	LITHUAN.	GOTHIC.
m. *vrikâs,*	*vĕhrkâonhô,*†	λύκοι,	*lup'-î,*	*wilkai,*	*vulfôs.*
m. *tê,*	*tê,*	τοί,	*is-t'î,*	*tie,*‡	*thai.*
n. *dânâ-n-i,*	*dâla,*	δῶρα,	*dona,*	. . . .	*daura.*
f. *jihwâs,*	*hizvâo,*	χῶραι,	*terrae,*	*rankos,*	*gibôs.*

---

* The termination *tis* answers to तस् *thas,* Greek τον from τος, not to
त *tha* or त *ta,* Greek τε.   With respect to the otherwise remarkable
declension of *qui,* and of *hic,* which is akin to it, I would refer preliminarily to my treatise "On the Influence of Pronouns in the formation of
Words" (by F. Dümmler), p. 2.

† See §. 229.

‡ This form belongs not to the base *TA* (=त *ta*), whence, in the singular, *ta-s,* and nearly all the other cases; but to *TIA,* whence, through
the influence of the *i,* *tie* has been developed (cf. p. 174, Note* and
§. 193.); and whence, in the dative dual and plural, *tie-m, tie-ms.* The
nominative plural is, however, without a case termination. The original
form *TIA* corresponds to the Vêda त्य *tya,* mentioned in §. 194.; while
the base स्यु *syu* (श्य *shya,* see §. 55.) is fully declined in Lithuanian in the
form of *SZIE,* and in the plural nominative, likewise without inflexion,
is

	SANSKRIT.	ZEND.	GREEK.	LATIN.	LITHUAN.	GOTHIC.
f.	tás,	tấu,	ταί,	is-tae,	tes,	thás.
m.	patay-as,	paity-ô,*	πόσι-ες,	host'-ēs,†	....	gastei-s.
f.	prílay-as,	áfrity-ô,*	πόρτι-ες,	mess'-ēs,†	áicy-s,	anstei-s.
n.	vấrí-n-i,	var'-a,	ἴδρι-α,	mari-a,	....	....
n.	....	ky-a,‡	....	....	....	iy-a.
f.	bhavishyanty-as,	búshyainty-ó,*	....	....	....	....
m.	súnav-as,	pasv-ô,*	ἰχθύ-ες,	pecŭ-s,	sùnu-s,	sunyu-s.
f.	tanav-as,	tanv-ô,*	πίτυ-ες,	svcrū-s,	....	handyu-ı
n.	madhú-n-i,	madhv-a,	μέθυ-α,	pecu-a,	....	....
f.	vadhw-as,	....				
m.f.	gáv-as,	geu-s,§	βό(F)-ες,	bov-ēs,†	....	

[G. Ed. p. 272.]

is *szie*. From the pronominal declension the form *ie* (from *ia*) has found its way into the declension of the adjective also : so that the base *GERA*, "good," forms several cases from *GERIE*; viz. dat. du. *gerie-m* for *gera-m*, dat. pl. *gerie-ms* for *gera-ms*, and nom. pl. *gerì* for *gerai*. This *gerì* appears to stand in most complete agreement with the Latin nominatives of the corresponding declension (*boni, lupi*); but the difference between the two languages is this, that the *i* of *boni* (for *bono-i*) belongs to the termination, while *gerì* is void of termination, and stands for *gerie* (analogous with *tie*), but this latter for *gerie-i* (cf. *yaunikkie-i*.)

    * See p. 163, Note ‡.

    † See p. 1078.

    ‡ To this *ky-a*, from *ki-a*, corresponds surprisingly the Latin *qui-a* (*quianam, quiane*), if, as I scarce doubt, it is a plural neuter, as *quod* is a singular neuter (cf. Max. Schmidt " *De pron. Græco et Latino*," p. 34). In the meaning " that," *quia* is clearly shewn to be an accusative: the meaning " because " is less apt for this case, and would be better expressed by an instrumental or an ablative; but in the singular *quod* we must be content to see the idea "because" expressed by an accusative. On the other hand, *quo*, among other meanings, signifies " whither," a genuine accusative signification in Sanskrit grammar. Without the support of *quod* we might conjecture that an instrumental singular had been preserved in *quia*, after the analogy of ﺳﺟﻮﺟﺳﻮ *paity-a*, for *paiti*.

    § We might expect *gav-ó, gavai-cha*, " *bovesque*;" but we read ﺳﻮﺟﻮ *geus* in the Vend. S. p. 253, L. 9, in combination with the pronominal neuters ﺳﻮﻣﻮ *tá*, " *illa*," ﺳﻮﻳﻦ *yá*, " *quæ*," which, according to §. 231. Note, cannot surprise us.

SANSKRIT.	ZEND.	GREEK.	LATIN.	LITHUAN.	GOTHIC.
f. *nâv-as,*	. . . .	*vâ(F)-es,*	. . . .	. . . .	. . . .
f. *vâch-as,*	*vâch-ô,**	*ŏπ-ες,*	*vocēs,†*	. . . .	. . . .
m. *bharant-as,*	*barĕnt-ô,**	*φέροντ-ες,*	*ferent-ēs,†*	. . . .	*fiyand-s.*
m. *âtmân-as,*	*asmun-ô,*	*δαίμον-ες,*	*sermon-ēs,†*	. . . .	*ahman-s.*
n. *nâmân-i,*	*nâman-a,*	*τάλαν-α,*	*nomin-a,*	. . . .	*namôn-a.*
m. *bhrâtar-as,*	*brâtar-ô,**	*πατέρ-ες,*	*fratr-es,†*	. . . .	. . . .‡
f. *duhitar-as,*	*dughdhar-ô,**	*θυγατέρ-ες,*	*matr-es,†*	*dugter-ĕs,*	. . . .
m. *dâtâr-as,*	*dâtâr-ô,**	*δοτῆρ-ες,*	*datōr-es,†*	. . . .	.. . .
n. *vachâns-i,*	*vachanh-a,§*	*ἔπε(σ)-α,*	*oper-a,*	. . . .	. . . .

[G. Ed. p. 273.]

THE ACCUSATIVE.

236. The bases which end with a short vowel annex न्
n in Sanskrit, and lengthen the final vowel of the base;
hence, वृकान् *vrikân,* पतीन् *patîn,* सूनून् *sûnûn,* &c. We might
imagine this *n* to be related to the *m* of the singular accusative, as in the verb the termination आनि *âni* (1st pers.
sing. imperative) has clearly proceeded from आमि *âmi.* The
cognate dialects speak, however, in favour of Grimm's acute
conjecture, that the Sanskrit *n* is, in the accusative plural
masculine, an abbreviation of *ns,*‖ which has remained entire in the Gothic—*vulfa-ns, gasti-ns, sunu-ns,*—but has been
divided in the other sister languages; since the Sanskrit,
according to §. 94., has given up the latter of the two con-

---

* See p. 163. Note ‡

† See Note † in preceding page.

‡ The Gothic *r* bases annex in the plural a *u,* and can therefore be
contrasted no further with the cognate languages. *BRÔTHAR* becomes
BRÔTHRU, whence *brôthryu-s,* &c., according to the analogy of *sunyu-s.*

§ Or ᴍᴏᴏᴢᴇᴘᴍᴏ *vachenha.* Thus we read Vend. S. p 127, *nĕmĕnha,*
which, I think, must be regarded as accusative of *nimô* (नमस् *namas,*
"adoration"), and as governed by ᴍᴏᴄᴇᴏᴇᴊ *bĕrĕthra,* "from him
who brings," "from him offering."

‖ The Old Prussian, too, exhibits in the acc. pl. *ns, e.g. tâva-ns, πατέρας.*
Respecting the Veda termination *ṅr,* from *ṅs,* see §. 517. Remark.

sonants, and has lengthened, as it appears, in compensation for this, the final vowel of the base*; while the Greek
[G. Ed. p. 274.] λύκους has preserved the sibilant, but has permitted the ν to volatilize to υ.† In fact, λυκο-υς has the same relation to λυκους that τύπτουσι has to τύπτονσι, from
[G. Ed. p. 275.] τύπτοντι.‡ For πόσι-ας, ἰχθύ-ας, we could not, however, expect a πόσι-νς, ἰχθύ-νς, as the Greek makes the ι and υ bases in all parts similar to the bases which terminate with a consonant, which, in Sanskṛit, have *as* for a termination; hence पदस् *padas* = πόδας: and even in the most vigorous period of the language *ns* could not have attached itself to a consonant preceding. This *as* for *ns* may be compared with

---

* Thus *vṛikân* for *vṛikans*; as, विद्वांस् *vidwâns*, whence the accusative विद्वांसम् *vidwâns-am*, in the uninflected nominative विद्वान् *vidwân*, ("*sapiens*").

† As the ν also passes into ι (τιθείς for τιθένς, Æolic τύψαις, μέλαις for τυψαν(τ)ς, μελανς), Hartung (l. c p. 263) is correct in explaining in this sense the ι in Æolic accusative forms like νόμοις, τοὶς στρατηγοίς, &c. As regards, however, the feminine accusatives like μεγάλαις, ποικίλαις, τείμαις, quoted by him, I believe that they have followed the analogy of the masculines, from which they sufficiently distinguish their gender by the α preceding the ι; we cannot, however, thence infer, that also the first and specially feminine declension had originally accusatives in νς, as neither has the Gothic in the corresponding declension an *ns*, nor does the Sanskṛit exhibit an *n* (see §. 287., and cf. Rask in Vater's Tables of Comparison, p. 62).

‡ It cannot be said that τύπτουσι proceeded from τύπτοντσι, a truly monstrous form, which never existed in Greek, while the τύπτοντι before us answers to all the requirements of Greek Grammar, as to that of the whole base, since ο-ντι corresponds to the Sansk. *anti*, Zend ĕnti, Goth. *nt'*; and from the singular τι (Dor.), in the plural nothing else than ντι can be expected. But to arrive at ουσι from οντι it is not requisite to invent first so strange a form as οντσι; for that οντι can become ουσι is proved by the circumstance that the latter has actually arisen from it, by the very usual transition of τ into Σ, and the not rare vocalization of the Ν to Υ, as also in Sanskṛit, in all probability, उस् *us* has arisen from *nt* (cf. p. 172, Note *), of which more hereafter. But if in the dative plural, indeed, ου-σι has arisen from οντ-σι, not from ον-σι (λέουσι not δαίμουσι),

we

the Ionic αται, ατο, for νται, ντο, a form which has extended
from the places where the vocalization of the ν was necessary,
to those also where ν might be added (πεπείθαται, τετρά-
φαται; then, also, πεπαύαται, κεκλιάται, &c. for πέπαυνται,
κέκλινται). This comparison with the 3d person plural appears to me the more in point, as, in my opinion, the *n*
in the presupposed forms, like वृकंस् *vrikans*, पतिंस् *patins*,
λύκονς, has the same object that it has in the 3d person
plural; viz. allusion to plurality by extending (nasalizing)
the syllable preceding the sign of personality. The introduction of a nasal is an admixture which is least of all
foreign, and comes nearest to the mere lengthening of an
already existing vowel.

237. Feminine bases with a final vowel follow in Sanskrit the analogy of consonantal bases; but with the suppression of the *a*,* thus *s* for *as* or *ns*; they may perhaps,
too, never have had *ns*, for else hence would have arisen,
as in the masculine, a simple *n*: to the   [G. Ed. p. 276.]

---

we must remember that the abandonment of the *n* before case terminations
beginning with a consonant is a very old and therefore pro-Greek phenomenon, which is not to be accounted for in the Greek, and wherefore no
compensation is to be required for the ν, which has been dropped. But
even if it were so, we must still be satisfied, if the demand for compensation for a lost ν remains unfulfilled in several places of grammar; for
there are two kinds of euphonic alteration in all languages: the one,
which has acquired the force of a general law, makes its appearance under
a similar form on each similar occasion, while the other only irregularly
and occasionally shews itself.

* Monosyllabic bases only have preserved the *a* as the case sign in
the singular nominative (§. 137.); hence, स्त्रियस् *striy-as*, "*feminas*,"
भुवस् *bhuvas*, "*terras*," from स्त्री *stri*, भू *bhû*. There is scarce a doubt
that this form originally extended to polysyllabic bases also; for besides
the Greek, the Zend also partly evinces this (§. 238.), as also the circumstance that in the actual condition of the Sanskrit language the accusative plural shews, in general, an inclination to weaken itself, and thus
contrast itself more submissively with the imperious nominative (§. 120.).

feminine gender, too, the well-sounding Ionic *a* is more suitable than *n*. In general, the Sanskrit feminines in other parts
of grammar cast off the *n*, which is annexed by masculines
and neuters (§. 133.). Moreover, the Gothic also, in feminine
ó bases, gives no *ns*, but it appears that *thôs* = नास् *tás* (*eas*,
has) is a pure dowry from the ancestral house; and when the
feminine *i* and *u* bases in Gothic, by forms like *i-ns, u-ns*,
assimilate themselves to the masculines, this may be regarded
as a disguise of gender, or a deviation caused by the example
of the masculines. The consonant bases follow the example of the Indian, but have lost the *a*, as in the nominative (§. 227.); hence, *fiyand-s, ahman-s*, for *fiyand-as*,
ahman-as.

238. Feminines with a short final vowel lengthen it, to
compensate, as it appears, for the suppression of the *a*;
thus प्रीतीस् *príti-s* is formed from *prity-as*, and तनूस् *tanú-s*
from *tanw-as*. The Greek certainly presents, in this respect, only a casual coincidence, through forms in ῖς, ῦς.
which, however, are not restricted to the feminine, and
stand at the same time, in the nominative, for *ι-ες, υ-ες*.
The Zend, like the Greek, follows in its *i* and *u* bases the
analogy of the consonantal terminations; hence, ‍‍‍
paity-ô (paity-as-cha,) ‍ *pasv-ô (pasv-as-cha*, or, with
Guna, *paitay-ô, pasav-ô*. In feminine bases in *i, u*, occur at
times also the forms *i-s, ú-s*, corresponding to the Sanskrit;
as, ‍ *gairi-s*, "*montes*" (Vendidâd S. p. 313.), ‍
erezú-s, "*rectas*," ‍*tafnú-s*, "*urentes*," ‍ *perítú-s*,
"*pontes*."

239. Masculine bases in ‍ *a*, where they are not replaced
by the neuter (§. 231. Note), have, in the accusative, *an* (cf. §. 61.);
as, ‍*imañ*,[*] "*hos*," often occurs, ‍*mazistañ*, "*maxi-
mos*" (Vend. S. p. 65.). The sibilant is retained before the
[G. Ed. p. 277.]   particle ‍ *cha*, and these forms can be
copiously quoted; as, ‍*amëshañs-cha*, "*non-*

---

* Cf. Vêdic forms in *án*.

conniventesque"; *manthrans-cha*, "*sermonesque*"; *aẽsmans-cha*, "*lignaque*"; *vás-tryans-cha*, "*agricolasque*."[*] The form *athau-run-ans-cha*, "*presbyterosque*" (V. S. p. 65.), is remarkable, as there is no reason elsewhere to assume a theme *athauruna;* and this form would accordingly shew that consonantal bases also could assume the inflexion *ns*, with an unavoidable auxiliary vowel however; unless, indeed, we are to suppose that, in the perverted feeling of the language, it has been introduced by the preponderating analogy of the *a* bases. More important, therefore, than this *athaur-unans-cha* are the accusatives *nareus*, "*homines*," and *streus*, "*stellas*," which occur very frequently; while from *átar*, "fire," we have found, not *áthr-eus*, but *áthr-ô*, in which it is to be remarked that *átar* distinguishes itself from other words in *r* in this point also, that it forms, in the nominative singular, not *áta*, but *átars*. But how is the termination *eus* to be explained? I believe in no other way but from *ans*, by changing the *n* into a vowel, as in [G. Ed. p. 278.] λόγους; after which, according to §. 31., the *a* has become ϛ *e* : the sibilant, however, which, after *a* and *an*, is *š*, must, after *u*, appear as *s*. We actually find, too, in the V. S. p. 311, *ner-ans* in the sense of a dative:

---

[*] I formerly thought I could, through forms of this kind, quote the introduction of a euphonic *s* in Zend, according to the analogy of §. 95. But if this introduction cannot be proved by cases, in which no ground exists for the assumption of an original sibilant, preserved merely by the particle *cha* (cf. §§. 56ᵇ. 207. 228.), then the above examples are the more important, in order to supply a fresh proof that *ns* is the original designation of masculine plural accusatives of themes terminating with a vowel. The superlative *vĕrĕthraxanstĕma* (of which hereafter) may be regarded as derived from a participial nominative. Other cases, which might suggest occasion to assume, in Zend, a euphonic *s* after *n*, have been nowhere met with by me.

s

ﺩﻭﺴﻭ *ddidi* *at̤* *něrans* *mazdâ ahurd ashaond,* &c. "*da quidem hominibus, magne Ahure! puris.*"

240. As *a* in Sanskṛit occurs the most often of all letters as the termination of masculine bases, and we cannot mistake, in the history of our family of languages, the disposition in the sunken state of a language to introduce, by an unorganic addition, the more inconvenient consonantal declension into that of the vowels, I cannot therefore think that it admits of any doubt, that the New Persian plural termination *ân,* which is restricted to the designation of animate creatures, is identical with the Sanskṛit आन् *ân* in the masculine plural accusative: thus, مردان *mardân,* "homines," answers to मर्त्यान् *martyân,* "mortales," "homines."[*]

241. If, then, the termination ان *ân,* applied to animate beings, belongs to a living being in the old language, the inanimate neuter will be fitted to give us information regarding that New Persian plural termination which is appended to the appellations of inanimate objects. A suffix, in the formation of words which is peculiarly the property of the neuter, is अस *as* (§. 128.), which is still more frequently used in Zend than in Sanskṛit. In the plural, these Zend neuters form *anha* or *ěnha* (§§. 56*. 235.); and with this *ha* is evidently connected the lengthened ها *hâ* in New Persian; thus, روزها *roz-hâ,* "days," answers to the Zend *raochanha,* "lights." Many New Persian words have been compared with New German words,

[G. Ed. p. 279.] and often, too, correctly; but, except through the medium of the Sanskṛit and Zend, it could not have been conjectured that our "*Wörter*" is, in respect to its termination, related to the New Persian *hâ.* As, however, the High German has, from its earliest period, repeatedly changed *s* into *r,* and *a* into *i* (later *e*), I have no

---

[*] Thus in Spanish the whole plural has the termination of the Latin accusative.

doubt the *ir*—Middle and New High German *er*—which makes its appearance in the plural in many Old High German neuters, is identical with the Sanskṛit neuter suffix अस् *as*; *e. g. húsir,* "houses," *chalpir,* "calves" (cf. Grimm, pp. 622 and 631).*

242. Here follows a general view of the accusative formation:

	SANSKRIT.	ZEND.	GREEK.	LATIN.	LITHUAN.	GOTHIC.
m.	*vṛikå-n,*	*vĕhrka-n̂,*	λύκο-υς,	*lupō-s,*	*wilkù-s,*	*vulfa-ns.*
n.	*dånå-n-i,*	*dåta,*	δῶρα,	*dona,*	. . . .	*daura.*
f.	*jihwå-s,*	*hizvå-o,*	χώρᾱ-ς,	*terrā-s,*	*rankà-s,*	*gibó-s,*
f.	*tå-s,*	*tå-o,*	τᾱ-ς,	*is-tā-s,*	*tà-s,*	*thó-s.*
m.	*patî-n,*	*paity-ô,†*	πόσι-ας,	*host'-es,*	. . . .	*gasti-ns.*
f.	*bhiy-as,*	*åfrîty-ô,†*	πόρτι-ας,	*mess'-es,*	. . . .	. . . .
f.	*prîti-s,*	*åfrîtî-s,*	πόρτῑ-ς,	. . . .	*åwy-s,*	*ansti-ns.*
n.	*våri-n-i,*	*var'-a,*	ἴδρι-α,	*mari-a,*	. . . .	. . . .
n.	. . . .	*kya,*	. . . .	. . . .	. . . .	*iy-a.*
f.	*bhavishyantî-s, båshyaintî-s,†*		. . . .	. . . .	[G. Ed. p. 280.]	
m.	*sûnû-n,*	*paśv-ô,†*	ἰχθύ-ας,	*pecu-s,*	*sunù-s,*	*sunu-ns.*
f.	*bhuv-as,*	*tanv-ô,†*	πίτυ-ας,	. . . .	. . . .	. . . .
f.	*tanû-s,*	*tanû-s,*	πίτῡ-ς,	*socrū-s,*	. . . .	*handu-ns.*
m.	*madhû-n-i,*	*madhv-a,‡*	μέθυ-α,	*pecu-a,*	. . . .	. . . .

---

* This *ir*, however, is treated in declension as if the theme originally terminated in *a*, and would thus, in Sanskṛit, be *asa*. Hence, compared with the dative *húsiru-m* (from *húsira-m*, §. 168.), the nom. accus. *húsir* appears an abbreviation. Bu the relation of our *ir* to the Sanskṛit *as* is not thereby disturbed, because in general, most of the original consonantal terminations in High German have received unorganic vowel additions. Cf. pp. 148 and 191, G. Ed. Note. More regarding this hereafter.

† See p. 175, G. Ed. Note. ‡.

‡ This form is further confirmed by ⲛⲣⲱⲫⲱⲉⲟ *pĕiô-tanva*, from *pĕiô-tanu*, which signifies the hind part of the body (§. 199.), but is also used in the sense of "blow on the hinder part of the body"; and in this manner it occurs in the 15th Fargard of the Vend.: ⲛⲱⲣⲱⲫⲱⲉⲟ *ainhat* (*ainhåt?*) *hacha*

	SANSKRIT.	ZEND.	GREEK.	LATIN.	LITHUAN.	GOTHI
f.	vadhů-s,	....	....	....	....	...
m. f.	gd-s,*	gâu-s,	βό(F)-ας,	bov-ēs,	....	...
f.	nâv-as.	....	νᾶ(F)-ας,	....	....	...
f.	vâch-as,	vâch-ô,†	ὄπ-ας,	voc-ēs,	....	....
m.	bharat-as,‡	barĕnt-ô,†	φέροντ-ας,	ferent-ēs,	....	fiyanı
m.	âtman-as,	asman-ô,†	δαίμον-ας,	sermon-ēs,	....	ahma
n.	nâmân-i,	nâman-a,	τάλαν-α,	nomin-a,	....	namð
m.	bhrâtri-n,§	brâthr-eus?	πατέρ-ας,	fratr-es,	....	...
f.	duhitri-s,§	dughdhĕr-eus?	θυγατέρ-ας,	matr-es,	dujter-és,	....
m.	dâtri-n,§	dâthr-eus?	δοτῆρ-ας,	dutōr-ēs,	....	...
n.	vachâns-i,	vachanh-a,	ἔπε(σ)-α,	oper-a,	....	....

THE INSTRUMENTAL.

[G. Ed. p. 281.]   243. The formation of this case, and what is connected with it, has been already explained in §§. 215—224.; it is therefore sufficient to give here a comparison of the forms which correspond to one another in the cognate languages,

---

hacha skyaôthnâ-varĕza atha buvainti pĕiô-tanva, " *hac pro facti-peractione tum sunt verbera posteriori corpori inflicta* " (Anquetil, *Celui qui commet cette action sera coupable du tanafour*). In regard to the *anâpĕretha*, mentioned at §. 232., it is further to be noticed that the *ŏ th* can only be occasioned by a ϱ *w* that has been dropped (§. 47.), for the theme of the concluding substantive is ⟩ϱϱϟϱϢ *pĕrĕtu*, not *pĕrĕthu* (Vend. S. pp. 313 and 362, twice).

   * Irregularly from a theme गा *gâ* (§. 122.), for गवम् *gav-as*. The Zend ᴧᴧᴑᴧᴧᴑ *gâus* (also ᴧᴧᴑᴧᴧᴑ *gâos*), which often occurs, rests on the strengthened Sanskrit form गौ *gâu*; so that in respect of the strong and weak cases (§. 129.), the relation in this word is distorted. In the nominative, for instance, we should expect ᴧᴧᴑᴧᴧᴑ *gâus*, and in the accusative ᴧᴧᴑᴧᴑ *geus*, rather than *vice versâ*.

   † See p. 163, Note †.

   ‡ See §. 129.

   § See §. 127. Note and §. 249. Note †.

by which a summary view of the subject may be assisted.
As the German, in its singular dative,* is identical with
the Sanskrit-Zend instrumental, it is hence deducible that
its character *m* (for *b* see §. 215.), in the dative plural,
must rather be regarded as an abbreviation of भिस् *bhis*
than as belonging to the dative-ablative termination भ्यस्
bhyas; although it approaches equally near to the two old
terminations.

SANSKRIT.	ZEND.	GREEK.	LATIN.	LITHUAN.	GOTH. DAT.
m. *vriké-bhis,*	. . . .	θεό-φιν,	*vo-bis,*	. . . .	*vulfa-m.*
vriká-is,	*vēhrká-is,*	. . . .	. . . .	*wilka-is,*	. . . .
f. *jihwá-bhis,*	*hizvá-bís,*	. . . .	. . . .	*ranko-mis,*	*gibó-m.*
priti-bhis,	*áfriti-bís,*	. . . .	. . . .	*awi-mis,*	*ansti-m.*
m. *súnu-bhis,*	*pašu-bís,*	. . . .	. . . .	*sunu-mis,*	*sunu-m.*
f. *nau-bhis,*	. . . .	ναῦ-φιν,	. . . . . .	. . . .	. . . .
m. *álma'-bhis,*	*ašma'-bís,*	. . . .	. . . . . .	. . . . .	*ahma'-m.*
n. *náma'-bhis,*	*náma'-bís,*	. . . .	. . . . . .	. . . .	*namn-am.*
n. *vachó-bhis,†*	*vachó-bís,†*	ὄχεσ-φιν,†	. . . .		[G. Ed. p. 282.]

THE DATIVE, ABLATIVE.

244. Mention has already been made of the suffix of
these two cases in §. 215.   Only the *s* of the Latin *bus* has
been left in the first, second, and (according to Nonius)
occasionally, also, in the fourth declension; for the *i* of
lupi-s, terri-s, speci-s (for *speci-bus* from *specu-bus*), must be
allotted to the base.   *Lupi-s* stands for *lupo-bus,* as evinced
by *ambo-bus, duo-bus.*   From *o-bus* (by lightening the final
vowel of the base, *o, u,* from an original *a,* §. 6.), as occurs
in the beginning of compounds (*multi-plex* for *multu-plex*
or *multo-plex,* of which hereafter), the language arrived at
i-bus, (*parvi-bus, amici-bus, dii-bus,* cf. Hartung, p. 261).   In
the first declension *a-bus* has been retained with tolerable

---

* Vide §. 160. Note ‡
† See §§. 56ᵇ. and 128.

frequency, but the middle step *i-bus* is wanting; yet the language has scarcely made the spring from *a-bus* at once to *ĭ-s*, but *a-bus* has weakened the *a* of the base to *ĭ*, which, to compensate for the *bu* which has been dropped, has been lengthened; thus *terrĭ-s* from *terri-bus*, for *terra-bus*, as [G. Ed. p. 283.] *mālo* from *măvolo*. Compare,

SANSKRIT.	ZEND.	LATIN.	LITHUANIAN.
m. *vrikĕ-bhyas,*	*vĕhrkaĕi-byô,*	*lupĭ-s.*	*wilka-m(u)s.*＊
f. *jihwâ-bhyas,*	*hizvâ-byô,*	*terrĭ-s,*	*ranko-m(u)s.*
m. *pati-bhyas,*	*paiti-byô,*	*hosti-bus,*	. . . .†
f. *priti-bhyas,*	*âfriti-byô,*	*messi-bus,*	*awi-m(u)s.*
m. *bhavishyantî-bhyas,*	*bûshyainti-byô,*	. . . .	. . . .
m. *sûnu-bhyas,*	*pasu-byô,*	*pecu-bus,*‡	*sunu-m(u)s,*
f. *vâg-bhyas,*	*vâch-e-byô,*	*voc-i-bus.*	. . . .
m. *bharad-bhyas,*	*barĕn-byô.*§	*ferent-i-bus,*	. . . .
m. *âtma'-bhyas,*	*asma'-byô,*	*sermon-i-bus,*	. . . .
m. *bhrâtri-bhyas,*	*brâtar-ĕ-byô,*	*fratr-i-bus,*	. . . .

THE GENITIVE.

245. The genitive plural in Sanskrit, in substantives and adjectives, has the termination **आम्** *âm*, in the Zend *anm*, according to §. 61. The Greek ων bears the same relation to the original form of the termination that ἐδίδων does to **अददाम्** *adadâm* (§§. 4. 10.). The Latin has, as usual,

---

＊ See §. 215.

† The masculine *i* bases pass in the plural, by an unorganic increment, into a different declension. And in the dual and dative singular, also, *PATI* had to be given up (Mielcke, p. 35, Rem. 1.).

‡ I have selected the masculine base *PECU*, which occurs only in a few cases, on account of its connection with ﺎﻬ *paku*, and I have carried it through all the cases, and think, therefore, that I may here also give the original *u-bus* for the corruption *i-bus*.

§ See §. 224. Note ＊, p. 241.

preserved the labial final nasal in its original form, but
by its influence has shortened the preceding vowel; hence,
ped-um (=pad-âm), the u of which supplies the place of a
short a, as in lupum = वृकम् vṛikam, λύκο-ν.[*]   [G. Ed. p. 284.]
The German, like the Lithuanian, has dropped the final nasal.
In Gothic, however, the आ â, which has been left, shews itself
under two forms, and thereby an unorganic difference has
been introduced between the feminine genitive termination and that of the masculine-neuter; since the fuller ô
has remained only to the feminine ô and n bases.

246. Bases ending with a vowel, with the exception,
partly necessary and partly arbitrary, of monosyllables,
place, in Sanskṛit, a euphonic n between the termination and
the base, the final vowel of which, if short, is lengthened.
This interposition appears to be pristine, since the Zend
partakes of it, although in a more limited degree; for
instance, in all bases in ﺱ a and ﺱ â: hence, ﻉﺱﻝﻭﻍﻕ
věhrka-n-aṅm, ﻉﺱﻝﻭﻍﺱﻉ, jihva-n-aṅm.   To the latter correspond very remarkably the genitives (which occur in
Old High German, Old Saxon, and Anglo-Saxon, in the

---

[*] Regarding the termination i-um in consonantal bases, and, vice versâ,
respecting um in places where i-um might have been expected, we refer
the reader to §. 126.   In adjectives the feminine character î mentioned in
§. 119. may have had its effect, and may have passed over from the feminine to the other genders, according to the analogy of the Lithuanian
(p. 174. Note * §. 157.): thus the i of ferenti-um reminds us of the Sanskṛit
feminine भरन्ती bharantî.   The same is the case with the i of the neuter
form ferenti-a; it is bequeathed by the deceased feminine theme FE-
RENTI.   On the other hand, contrary to the opinion preferred in
§. 126., we must now regard the i before bus (e.g. voc-i-bus) as a conjunctive vowel, like the ç e in the Zend vâch-e-byô.   Here it is to be observed
that those consonantal bases, which admit neither i-a nor i-um, must nevertheless proceed before bus to annex an i.   In the chapter upon the adjectives we shall recur to the feminine character i; and then treat also of the
i for   in the singular ablative of the common dialect.

corresponding class of words) in *ó-n-ó*, *e-n-a*; hence, Old
High German *këpó-n-ó*, Old Saxon *gëbó-n-ó*, Anglo-Saxon
gife-n-a.

247. We find the bases in short and long *i*, in Zend, if
[G. Ed. p. 285.] polysyllabic, only with euphonic *n*: on the
other hand the monosyllabic *i* bases annex the termination
direct, either attaching Guna to the final vowel, or keeping it
pure; thus, *thry-anm* or *thray-anm*, "*trium*," from *thri*; *vay-anm*,
"*avium*," from *vi*. Bases in ꜱ *u* admit both of the annexing
the termination direct and of the insertion of the euphonic *n*;
but I find from the masculine ꙍꙍꙍꙍ *pasu* only *pasv-anm*: on
the other hand, I have found from feminine bases like ꙍꙍꙍ
tanu, "body," ꙍꙍꙍꙍ *nasu*, "corpse" (cf. *νέκυς* according to
§. 21.), hitherto only *u-n-anm*. With Guna ꙍꙍꙍꙍꙍꙍꙍ
pasav-anm would serve as a prototype for the Gothic *suniv-ê*
with Guna weakened (§. 27.).

248. Pronouns of the third person have, in Sanskrit,
साम् *sám*[*] for आम् *ám*; and this may be the original and
formerly universal form of the case-suffix, so that *ám*
would properly be only the termination of the termination,
and the *s* connected with the genitive singular would be
the chief person. If this is the case, the abbreviation of
this termination in substantives and adjectives must still
be recognised as very ancient; for the Gothic, which in the
plural nominative restricts itself so rigorously to the old
limits (§. 228.), gives to the sibilant, in the genitive also,
no wider scope; hence *thi-zê* (§. 86. s.) = *te-shám* (for *té-
sám*, according to §. 21.) "*horum*"; *thi-zo* = *tá-sám*, "*harum*." Here the *a*, like the *ó* of the base *THA, THŌ*,
appears weakened to *i* (§. 66.): on the other hand, the adjective *a* and *ó* bases, which follow the pronominal declension, have *ai-zê*, *ai-zó*; and *blindai-zê*, "*cæcorum*" (for
blinda-zê), answers exactly to the Sanskrit तेषाम् *te-shám*

---

* Cf. Old Prussian *son*, e.g. in *stei-son*, "*των*."

(from *taï-sâm*) from the base प *ta.*   The High German has
changed the old sibilant to *r*, as in many other places;
hence, in Old High German, *dë-rô* for *thi-zê* and *thi-zô*, of
which termination only the *r* has remained   [G. Ed. p. 286.]
to us.   To the Latin, in like manner, belongs *rum* for *sum*
(§. 22.); hence, *istorum, istarum.**

249. We give here a general view of the formation of
the genitive :

	SANSKRIT.	ZEND.	GREEK.	LATIN.	LITHUAN.	GOTHIC.
m.	*vrikâ-n-âm,*	*vëhrka-n-aṅm,*	λύκ'-ων,	*lupō-rum,*	*wilk'-û,*	*vulf'-ê.*
m. n.	*tê-shâm,*	*taê-shaṅm,*	τ'-ῶν,	*istō-rum,*	*t'-û,*	*thi-zê.*
f.	*jihwâ-n-âm,*	*hizva-n-aṅm,*	χωρά-ων,	*terrā-rum,*	*rank'-û,*	*këpô-n-ô.*†

---

* This *rum*, however, has, like the property of the plural nominative
(§. 228.), found its way or returned from the pronominal declension
into the entire second, first, and fifth declension, which is originally identical with the latter (§§. 121 and 137.).   The transplanting of the *rum*
termination into the declensions mentioned was the easier, as all pronouns
in the genitive plural belong to the second and first declension.   Forms,
however, remain, especially in the old languages, which evince that the
language was not always equally favourable to the bringing back the termination *rum* (*deum, socium, amphorum, drachmum, agricolum,* &c).
On the other hand, the termination *rum* appears also to have attempted
to fix itself in consonantal bases, with *e* as conjunctive vowel, if, at least, the
forms furnished by Varro and Charis.—*boverum, Joverum, lapiderum,
regerum, nucerum* (Hartung, p. 255.)—are to be regarded as correct, and
do not perhaps stand for *bovo-rum,* &c. ; as also, in Zend, the base *gô* may
extend itself to *gava.*   The Latin *rum* and Sanskrit साम् *sâm* lead us to
expect the Greek σων: this is not met with, however, even in the pronoun ; so that the Greek, in this respect, stands in the strongest opposition
to the Latin.   The forms in a-ων, ε-ων (*e.g.* αὐτά-ων, αὐτί-ων, ἀγορά-ων,
ἀγορέ·ων) point, however, to a consonant that has been dropped.   It is a
question, therefore, whether universally a Σ (cf. §. 128.), or, as the Sanskrit and Zend lead us to expect, only in pronouns a Σ, but in other words
of the first and second declension an N has been dropped, as in μεῖζω
from μείζονα.   According to this, λύκων would be to be derived from
λυκο-ν-ων, χωράων from χωρα-ν-ων , but τῶν from τοσων, τάων from τασων.

† Old High German, see §. 246.

	SANSKRIT.	ZEND.	GREEK.	LATIN.	LITHUAN.	GOTHIC.
f.	tá-sâm,	â-oṅhaṅm,*	τά-ων,	istā-rum,	t'-û,	thi-zô.
m. n.	tray-â-nâm,	thray-aṅm,	τρι-ῶν,	tri-um,	tri-û,	thriy-ê.
f.	prîti-n-âm,	âfrîti-n-aṅm,	πορτί·ων,	messi-um,	awi-û,	ansî'-e.
m.	súnû-n-âm,	paśv-aṅm,	ἰχθύ-ων,	pecu-um,	sun'-û,	suniv-ê.
f.	tanû-n-âm,	tanu-n-aṅm,	πιτύ-ων,	socru-um,	. . . .	handiv⤳
m. f.	gav-âm,	gav-aṅm,	βο(F)ῶν,	bov-um,	. . . .	. . . .
f.	nâ-vâm,	. . . .	να(F)-ῶν,	. . . .	. . . .	. . . .
f.	vâch-âm,	vâch-aṅm,	ὀπ-ῶν,	voc-um,	. . . .	. . . .
m. n.	bharat-âm,	barĕnt-aṅm,†	φερόντ-ων,	ferenti-um,	. . . .	fiyand⤳
m.	âtman-âm,	aśman-aṅm,	δαιμόν-ων,	sermon-um,	akmen-û,	ahman⤳
m.	bhrâtrī-n-âm,	brâthr-aṅm,‡	πατέρ-ων,	fratr-um,	.	. . . .

[G. Ed. p. 287.]

---

* This word often occurs, and corresponds to the Sanskrit आसाम् *â-sâm* "*harum*," "*earum*" (§. 56ᵇ.); from तद् *tâ, tâoṅhaṅm* would be expected, which I am unable to quote. The compound (polysyllabic) pronominal bases shorten the last syllable but one; hence, *aê-taṅhaṅm* not *aêtâoṅhaṅm*, as might be expected from एतासाम् *etâ-sâm*.

† Or, also, *barantaṅm*, as in the Vendidâd Sâde, p. 131, *śaochantaṅm*, "*lucentium:*" on the other hand, also, frequently *śaochentaṅm*.

‡ This and the following genitives from bases in *ar* are clearly more genuine, and are more nearly allied therefore to the cognate European languages than the corresponding ones in Sanskrit, which, in this case, has shortened *ar* to ऋ *ri*, and has then treated it according to the analogy of vowels. From *nar* frequently occurs *nar-aṅm*, with retention of the *a*, on account of the base being monosyllabic: on the other hand, *âthr·aṅm* from *âtar*, "fire," and *tisr-aṅm* "*trium*," fem. for the Sanskrit तिसृणाम् *tisri-n-âm* (Gramm. Crit. r. 255.). From *dughdhar*, we find the form *dughdhĕr-aṅm* (cf. p. 208, G. Ed. Note †): the Codex has, however, *dugdĕr-aṅm* (p. 472, L. 2.). In general, in this word the readings *dughdhar* and *dugdar* are interchanged in various passages: the former, however, is the more common.

LOCATIVE.

2 50. The character of the plural locative   [G. Ed. p. 288.]
is, in Sanskrit, **श** *su*, which is subject to be changed into **ष**
shu (§. 21.), for which, in Zend, is found ꭇꭇ *shu* (§. 52.);
while from **श** *su*, according to §. 53., has been formed ꭇꭇ *hu*.
The more usual form for *shu* and *hu* (for which, also, occur
shû and *hû*) is, however, ꭇꭇꭇ *shva*, ꭇꭇꭇ *hva*, which leads
to a Sanskrit **श्व** *swa*. This appears to me to be the original
form of the termination; for nothing is more common in
Sanskrit than that the syllables **व** *wa* and **य** *ya* should free
themselves from their vowel, and then change the semi-vowel
into a vowel, as **उक्त** *ukta* is said for *vakta* (see also §. 42.).
The supposition, therefore, of the Indian abbreviation of the
termination is far more probable than that of a Zend
extension of it by a lately-added *a*, especially as in no
other case does a similar aftergrowth admit of being established. But if **श्व** *swa* is the original form of the termination, it is then identical with the reflective-possessive
base **श्व** *swa*, of which more hereafter.[*] The same relation
which, in Latin, *si-bi* has to *su-bi* (which might be conjectured from *su-i*), or that *ti-bi* has to *tu-bi*, Sanskrit **तुभ्यम्**
tu-bhyam, the Greek dative-locative termination σι (σιν) has
to the Sanskrit **श** *su*.[†]

---

[*] Therefore, in Zend, the locative ꭇꭇꭇ *thrishva*, "*in tribus,*" is
identical with ꭇꭇꭇ *trishva*, "the third part," since the pronoun in
the latter compound denotes the idea of part.

[†] Regarding the termination *w* of the pronoun of the 1st and 2d
person see §. 222. From the Æolic form ἀμμέσιν, quoted by Hartung
(p. 260) from Apoll., I cannot infer that *w* is an abbreviation of σιν:
if it were so, the *v* also in ἡμῖν would not adhere so firmly. It appears to
me more suitable, therefore, to accord to the common declension an influence upon the transformation of the form of inflexion peculiar to the
pronouns without gender, but of the highest antiquity; an influence which
has penetrated further in σφίσι for σφίν.

[G. Ed. p. 289]   251. The bases in **व** *a* add to that vowel, as in many other cases, an *i*; but from *a + i* is formed **ए** *é* (§. 2.), to which the Greek *οι* corresponds; hence, λύκοι-σι = **वृकेषु** *vriké-shu.*   Hence the *ι* in Greek has also passed over to the bases in *α-, η-,* either preserving its full value or sub-scribed, while in Sanskrit the **व** *a* remains pure; hence, **जिह्वासु** *jihwâ-su,* with which the locatives of names of towns best agree, as Πλαταιᾶσιν, Ὀλυμπίασι, Ἀθήνῃσι (Buttmann, §. 116. R. 7. and Hartung, p. 461.).*

252. Like the Gothic, the Lithuanian has an unorganic difference between the terminations which mark the case in the masculine and feminine in the genitive plural: the first has the sound of *se,* and the latter of *sa,* with the original and more powerful *a,* which, in the masculine, has softened into *e*.   The ending *sa* is plainly from the *swa,* assumed above (p. 267, l. 7.) to be the original form, from which it is made by rejecting the semi-vowel.

253. Here follows a general view of the Sanskrit, Zend, and Lithuanian plural locatives, with the Greek datives :—

	SANSKRIT.	ZEND.	LITHUAN.	GREEK.
m.	*vriké-shu,*	*věhrkaĕ-shva,*	*wilkŭ-se,*	λύκοι-σι.
f.	*jihwâ-su,*	*hizvâ-hva,*	*ranko-sa,*	Ὀλυμπίᾱσι, χώραι-σι.
f.	*prìti-shu,*	*âfrîti-shva,†*	*áwi-sa,*	πόρτι-σι.
m.	*súnu-shu,*	*pasu-shva,*	*dangŭ-se,*	ἰχθύ-σι.
m. f.	*go-shu,*	. . . .	. . . .	βου-σί.
f.	*nau-shu,*	. . . .	. . . .	ναυ-σί.

[G. Ed. p. 290]

---

* The common termination *οις, αις* (*οι-ς, αι-ς*), formed by curtailing *οι-σι, αι-σι,* and so brought into agreement of sound with the third declen-sion, is here lost, through its apparent connection with the Sanskrit cur-tailed instrumental ending **एभिस्** *âis* (§. 219.), which had before required consideration, because the Greek dative is also used as the instrumental.

† I have no authority for the locative of the Zend bases in *i,* but it can only be analogous to that of the bases in *u,* which can be referred to in copious instances.

SANSKRIT.	ZEND.	LITHUAN.	GREEK.
f. *vák-shu,*	*vác-sva ?*	. . . .	ὀπ-σί.
m. n. *bharat-su,*	*brátar-ĕ-shva ?*	. . . .	φέρου-σι.
m. *átma'-su,*	*asma'-hva,* *	. . . .	δαίμο'-σι
m. *bhrátri-shu,*	. . . .	. . . .	πατρά-σι. †
n. *vachas-su,*	*vachó-hva,* ‡	. . . .	ἔπεσ-σι.

---

* Thus, in the Vend. Sàde, p. 499, ‏ushahva,‎ from ‏ushan,‎ and p. 500, ‏dámahva,‎ from ‏dáman.‎

† The *a* in this form is not, as is generally supposed, a conjunctive vowel, but rests on a transposition; as ἴδρακον for ἴδαρκον, and in Sanskrit द्रक्ष्यामि *drakshyámi,* "I will see," for दर्क्ष्यामि *darkshyámi* (Sansk. Gramm. §.34ᵇ.): thus πατράσι (compare τέτρασι) for παταρσι (compare τέσσαρσι), which, by preserving the original vowel, agrees with the Sanskrit base *pitar* better than πατέρα, πατέρες, &c. The same applies to the dative ἀρνάσι, since the theme of ἀρνός has, as appears from the cognate word ῥήν, ἀρήν, ἀρρήν, rejected a vowel between the ρ and ν, which again appears in the dative plural in the form of an *a,* and removed from its place. The whole *REN* appears to be a transposition of *Ner,* Sanskrit नर् *nar* (मृ *nṛi*), "a man," for ἀρήν properly means "male sheep." The *a* of ἀρνάσι is therefore etymologically identical with that of ἀνδράσι (comp. Kühner's complete Greek Grammar, §. 281. Rem. 2.). It is more difficult to give any accurate account of the *a* of υἱάσι: it is either the older and stronger form for the ε of υἱέσι, or this word must have had, besides its three themes ('YIO, 'YI, 'YIEY), a fourth, YIAT, from which came υἱάσι, as γόνασι from ΓΟΝΑΤ, the more prevailing co-theme of ΓΟΝΥ, which latter agrees with जानु *jánu.*

‡ In the Vendidàd Sàde, p. 499, we find the analogous plural locatives ‏uziróhva,‎ and ‏csapóhva.‎ Anquetil translates the former by " *au lever du soleil,*" and the latter by " *à la nuit.*" It is impossihle to pronounce these forms aught but derivatives from themes in ‏ai‎ (‏ó,‎ §. 56ᵇ.) Most of the cases of the latter word, which occurs very frequently in various forms, spring from a theme in ‏ar,‎ and the interchange of ‏csapar‎ with ‏csapó‎ is a similar case to that in Sanskrit, where अहन् *ahan,* "day," forms some cases from अहस् *ahas* (from which अहो *ahó* in अहोभिस् *ahóbhis,* &c.); and together with

[G. Ed. p. 291.]   "Remark.—From the bases in EΣ, to which
in the dative εσσι (= अस्सु as-su) properly belongs, this form
appears to have imparted itself to other bases terminating
[G. Ed. p. 292.]   differently, in which, for this case, an extension of the original theme by ες is to be adopted ; which,
in its origin, is identical with the abovementioned (§. 241.)
plural increase to the base by ir (from is and this, from as), in
Old High German forms, as hûsir, "houses," chalpir "calves,"
which are the plural themes, with which the nominative, accusative, and vocative are identical, and from which, in the
dative, by the addition of the ending for that case, arises hu-
sirum, chalpirum; as, in Greek, κύνεσ-σι, νεκύεσσι, πάντεσσι,
γυναίκεσσι, πολίεσσι, and others, from the unorganically increased themes ΚΥΝΕΣ, ΝΕΚΥΕΣ, &c., according to the analogy of 'ΕΠΕΣ.   From the doubled Σ one may then be rejected (ἀνάκτεσιν, πολίεσι, μήνεσι), or the doubling of a Σ by itself be employed ; as, for example, νέκυ-σσι, for νέκυ-σι.   This,

---

with the theme अहस् exists another, अहर् ahar. The anomaly of the
Sanskrit "day" appears, in Zend, to have passed completely over to
"night," as this latter word has also a theme in n, namely ﻣﺴﻮﻧﺪ
csapan, of which the genitive pl. ﻣﺴﻔﻨﻢ csafnanm—analogous with
अह्नाम् ahnâm, "dierum" (§. 40. relative to ف f for प p)—is found in connection with the feminine numeral ﺗﺴﺮﻧﻢ tisranm, "trium" (Vend. S.
p. 246); for we read, l. c. §. 163., asnanmcha (= अह्नांच ahnâncha),
csafananmcha (read csafnanmcha), "of days and nights."   In Sanskrit,
by the suffix अ a, the form अह्न ahna, derivative, but equal in its meaning,
has arisen out of अहन् ahan, which, however, occurs only in compounds
(as पूर्वाह्न pûrvâhna, "the early part of the day"), and in the adverbial
dative अह्न्य ahnâya, "soon," "immediately," which, therefore, it is not
necessary to deduce from the root अनु anu, with the a privative. The
Zend, however, whose night-nomenclature, in this respect also, is not out-
stripped by the Sanskrit, produces, as it appears, by a similar mutation,
ﻣﺴﻔﻨﺎ csafna from ﻣﺴﻮﻧﺪ csapan; whence we find the locative
ﻣﺴﻔﻨﻲ csafnê, which might also be taken for the dative of ﻣﺴﻮﻧﺪ
                                                                   csapan,

in most important particulars, is adopted by Thiersch, §. 128., for the developement of the forms in εσσι; only that he withdraws from the neuter bases described in §. 128., as ΒΕΛΕΣ, the Σ which belongs to them, and, by a supposition, proved to be erroneous, ΒΕΛΕ is made the theme: and he divides forms like ὄχεσφι into ὄχε-σφι instead of ὄχεσ-φι, and, by assimilation, derives ὄχε-σσι from ὄχε-σφι; while, as I believe I have proved, the forms ὄχεσ-φι and ὄχεσσι rest on entirely different case-suffixes (§. 218.), and have only the base 'ΟΧΕΣ in common with one another. An assimilation, however, may be remarked in γούνασ-σι, from γουνατ-σι, so that the first letter has assimilated itself to the second, not the reverse. In δέπασ-σι we shall leave it undecided whether the first Σ be primitive, and ΔΕΠΑΣ the theme (comp. γῆρας, §. 128.), or whether it has arisen out of τ, and so ΔΕΠΑΤ with ΤΕΡΑΤ, ΚΕΡΑΤ, belong to one class. If,

---

csapan, but that it is preceded (V. S. p. 163.) by the unequivocal adjective locative ‌ naémê (from ‌ naéma, "half"). Compare, also, l. c. §. 149., where ‌ ‌ ‌ ithra, aîné, ithra, csafné, probably means "in this day," "in this night," with the locative adverb ‌ ithra, "here," in the sense of a locative demonstrative. To the theme ‌ csafna, the plural of the same sound csafna, might also be assigned, which occurs l. c. §§. 330. 331., and in several places elsewhere: ‌ ‌ thrayó csafna, "three nights,' ‌ ‌ csvas csafna, "six nights," ‌ ‌ nava csafna, "nine nights," if here csafna be not (as in §. 231. Note ‡ it was considered to be) rather to be taken for the plural of ‌ csapan, as neuter, since, as has been before observed, the Zend uses the gender of the substantive with great laxity, especially in the plural. For the frequently-occurring ablative ‌ csapardê, however, we cannot assume another theme csapara, but we must, if the reading be correct, admit that feminine consonantal roots in the ablative adopt also the broader ending, dê for aê.

however, in all these forms, we allow only σι or σιν to be the case-suffix, and all that precedes it is referred to the true or un-organic increase of the base, it can therewith not be denied that not even to Homer himself, in forms like ἔπεσσι, not to mention unorganic forms like κύνεσσι, did the entire εσσι present [G. Ed. p. 293.] itself as pertaining to that which marked the case; for in the feeling of the speaker ἔπεσσι could present itself, during that period of the language, only as what it is, namely, as ἔπεσ-σι, while ἔπεσος, ἔπεσι, plural ἔπεσα and not ἔπεος, &c., were used in declension. But different from what has been here adopted is the assumption of Hartung (p. 260, ff.) and Kühner (l. c. §. 255. R. 8.), in the most material points following Greg. Cor. Æol. §. 35., relative to the production of the Greek plural datives. Kühner says (l. c.) " The character of the dative plural is ες (character of the plural) and ι or ιν (character of the dative singular), there-fore, εσι(ν)." I, however, think ες not the character of num-ber, but of the nominative plural, and connected with the nominative singular through its Σ: a union of the plural nominative suffix with the singular dative is, to me, not to be imagined. If it were so, how could neuter nouns, to which ες in the nominative is quite foreign, arrive, in the dative, at their identity of form with the natural sexes? It further deserves to be remarked, that, in Prâkṛit, the locative ending सु su frequently assumes an Anuswâra, and so adapts itself, by the form सुं suṅ, for su, to the Greek, σιν, for σι.

254. After laying down the laws of the formation of a single case, it may serve to facilitate the general survey if examples are adduced of the most important classes of words in their connected declension. We pass over here from the Sanskṛit, and go to the other languages in their order, according as they have, in the particular cases, most truly preserved their original form; and where one or other of them has departed entirely from the original

principle of formation, or by an unorganic increase to the base has entered the province of another declension, we there, in the place in question, exclude it from the comparison.

MASCULINE BASES IN *a*, GREEK IN *o*, LATIN IN *u*, *o*.
SINGULAR.

Nominative, Sanskrit *vrika-s*, Lithuanian *wilka-s*, Zend *vĕhrk-ô*, with *cha*, *vĕhrkaś-cha*, Greek λύκο-ς, Latin *lupu-s*, Gothic *vulf'-s*.*

Accusative, Sanskrit, *vrika-m*, Lithua-   [G. Ed. p. 294.] nian *wilka-n*, Zend *vĕhrkĕ-m*, Greek λύκο-ν, Latin *lupu-m*, Gothic *vulf'*.

Instrumental, Sanskrit *vrikĕ-n-a*, Zend *vĕhrka*, Gothic Dat. *vulfa*, Lithuanian Instr. *wilkù*.

Dative, Sanskrit *vrikâya*, Zend *vĕhrkâi*, Lithuanian *wilkui*.

Ablative, Sanskrit *vrikâ-t*, Zend *vĕhrkâ-t̤*, Latin *lup-o(d)* (see §. 181.).

Genitive, Sanskrit *vrika-sya*, Greek λύκο-(σ)ιο†, Zend *vĕhrka-hê*, Gothic *vulfi-s*, Lithuanian *wilkô*.

---

* The meaning is, in all these languages, the same, and so is the theme in its first origin. The connection of the Lithuan. *wilkas* with *vrikas* rests on the very usual interchange of the semi-vowels *r* and *l*; and this latter goes through the whole of the European sister languages. The Gothic *vulfs* shews, moreover, the equally common interchange of gutturals and labials, and follows the rule for the alteration of letters (Asp. for Tenuis, see §. 87.). In Latin the same thing takes place with regard to the supply of the guttural by the corresponding labial; but *lupus* is further altered through the loss of the initial letter *V*, as is the Greek λύκο-ς: it may, however, be assumed, that this *v* is introduced into the middle of the word in being vocalized into *u*. While therefore, in Lithuanian, in *wilkas*, *l* and *k* are united, they are, in Greek, separated by *v*.

† M. Reimnitz, whose pamphlet, "The System of Greek Declension" (Potsdam, 1831), had not been seen by me before I completed the preceding Part of this book, unfolds (l. c. p. 122 passim) the same views concerning

the

T

Locative,   Sanskrit *vriké* (from *vrika* + *i*), Zend *vĕhrkĕ*
[G. Ed. p. 295.] (*maidhyόi*, §. 196.), Lithuanian *wilkè*, Greek
                 Dat. λύκῳ (οἴκοι §. 195.) Latin Gen. *lup'-ĭ*.
Vocative,   Sanskrit *vrika*, Zend *vĕhrka*, Lithuanian *wilkè*,
                 Greek λύκε, Latin *lupe*, Gothic *vulf'*.

DUAL.

Nom.Acc.Voc. Sanskrit *vrikáu*, Vêdic *vriká*, Zend *vĕhrká*,
             Lith. Nom. *wilkù*, Voc. *wílku*, Greek λύκω.
Instr. Dat.Abl. Sanskrit *vriká-bhyám*, Zend *vĕhrkaéi-bya*, Greek
                Dat. Gen. λύκο-ιν, Lithuanian Dat. *wilka-m*
                (see §. 215.).
Gen. Loc.   Sansk. *vrikay-όs*, Zend *vĕhrkay-ό* (see Rem. 1.),
             Lithuanian *wilkú*.

PLURAL.

Nom. Voc.   Sanskrit *vrikás*, Gothic *vulfόs*.*
Accusative, Sanskrit *vriká-n*, Zend *vĕhrka-ṅ*, Goth. *vulfa-ns*,
             Greek λύκο-υς (from λύκο-νς, §. 236.), Lithu-
             anian *wilkùs*, Latin *lupō-s*.

---

the Greek οιο and its connection with the Sanskrit *a-sya* which I have, without being aware of his concurrence, brought forward in §. 189. I have,
however, in this respect, already stated my views in my pamphlet "On
the Demonstrative and the Origin of Case" (in the ·Transactions of the
Hist. Phil. Class of the Academy of Science of Berlin for the year 1826,
p. 100. Here I have only further to observe, that the Greek adj δημόσιος,
from the root ΔΗΜΟ, is, in the suffix by which it is formed, probably connected with the genitive ending in the text; and is therefore remarkable
with reference to the preservation of the *s*, which is lost in δήμοιο. With
regard to the origin of δημόσιος from the genitive, let reference be made
to the Latin *cujus, a, um*; and the identity of the Sanskrit suffix of words
like मनुष्य *manushya*, "man," as a derivative from Manu, with the genitive ending श्य *shya* for स्य *sya*, as in अमुष्य *amu-shya*, "*illius*."

* With reference to the Zend, see §. 231. Note ‡; and with regard to
the Greek, Latin, and Lithuanian forms λύκοι, *lupi, wilkai*, see §. 228.

Instrumental,	Sanskrit *vrikâ-is** (from *vrikâ-bhis*), Véda *vriké-bhis*, Zend *vêhrkâ-is*, Lithuanian *wilka-is*. Prâkrit *déve-hin* (from *déva*, "God," see §. 220.), Greek θεό-φιν,† Gothic Dat. Instr. *wulfa-m* (§. 215).
Dat. Abl.	Sanskrit *vriké-bhyas*, Zend [G. Ed. p. 296.] *vêhrkaéi-byô*, Latin *lupi-s* (*amici-bus* §. 244.), Lithuanian *wilka-m(u)s* (§. 215.).
Genitive,	Sanskrit *vrikâ-n-âm*, Zend *vêhrka-n-anm*, Greek λύκ'-ων, Lithuanian *wilk'-û*, Gothic *wulf'-ê*, Latin *lupô-rum* (§. 248.),

---

* I take the liberty, in order to separate the base and the termination, to divide the diphthongs, as above in λυκο-υς ; therefore one must here pronounce *vrikáis*, and in Lithuanian *wilkais*, not as trisyllables, but as dissyllables.

† I have remarked at §. 217., but only as a conjecture, that the ending φιν in the plural is perhaps identical with the Sanskrit भिस् *bhis*, and the thence-derived Prâkrit हिं *hin*, and the Latin *bis* in *nobis*, *vobis*; and I will not advance more than a conjecture here, also, in comparing θεό-φιν with *dévé-hin*. This only is certain, that with the syllable भि *bhi*, which in Sanskrit, lies at the bottom of the case-forms भिस् *bhis*, भ्यम् *bhyam*, and भ्याम् *bhyâm*, as their common root (see §. 215. passim), the Greek φι and φιν is also to be associated. I here willingly agree with M. Ag. Benary (Berl. Ann. July 1833, p. 51.), that φιν might be formed from the ending भ्यम् *bhyam* (§. 222.) by the contraction of य *ya* into *i* (as in ἡμῖν, ὑμῖν, τεῖν, &c. §. 222.). The third possible supposition would be the derivation from the usual dative-ablative plural termination भ्यस् *bhyas*; again with the corruption of *s* to *v*, as in the 1st person plural μεν from μες, and in the 2d and 3d person τον, τον from थस् *thas*, तस् *tas*. The fourth possible case would be the derivation from the dual termination भ्याम् *bhyâm* (§. 215.), and the changing this number of restricted plurality to that of unlimited plurality. I prefer, however, to consider φιν (φι) as from one of the multifarious terminations of the Sanskrit plural belonging to all declensions; therefore, from भिस् *bhis* or भ्यस् *bhyas*.

T 2

Locative,　　　Sanskrit *vriké-shu*, Zend *věhrkaé-shva*, Lithuanian *wilkŭse*, Greek Dat. λύκοι-σι.

NEUTER BASES IN *a*, GREEK *o*, LATIN *u, o*.

SINGULAR.

Nom. Acc.　　Sanskrit *dâna-m*, Zend *dâtĕ-m*, Latin *donu-m*, Greek δῶρο-ν, Lithuanian *géra*, Gothic *daur`*.

Vocative,　　Sanskrit *dâna*, Zend *dâta*, Gothic *daur`*.
　　　　　　The rest as the masculine.

DUAL.

Nom. Acc. Voc. Sanskrit *dâné* (from *dâna* + *i*), Zend *dâtĕ*.
　　　　　　The rest as the masculine.

[G. Ed. p. 297.]　　　　PLURAL.

Nom. Acc. Voc. Sanskrit *dânâ-n-i*, Vêdic *dânâ*, Zend *dâta*, Latin *dona*, Greek δῶρα, Gothic *daura*.
　　　　　　The rest as the masculine.

"Remark 1.—The Zend system of declension has received some valuable additions from the treatises published by Burnouf since the appearance of the First Part of this book, which I must lay before my readers.[*] First a dual case, viz. the genitive-locative, which I imagined to be lost in the Zend, as I had searched for it alone in vain, and could supply all the other dual endings in tolerable copiousness. M. Burnouf supplies this (*Yasna, Notes et éclaircissements*, p. cxxii.) by the expressions ࢸࢾࢾ ࢸࢺࢲ *ubôyô anhvô* which are to be twice found in V. S. p. 312, and on both occasions are rendered by Anquetil, whose

---

[*] First, a review of this Part in the *Journal des Savans*, which refers particularly to the Zend; then the First Part of the First Volume of a Commentary on the Yaçna; lastly, a disquisition in the Nouveau Journal Asiatique, '*Sur les mots Zends et Sanscrits Vahista et Vasichta, et sur quelques superlatifs en Zend.*"

translation is in this place particularly confused, "*dans ce
monde.*" This translation might lead us astray so much
the more easily, that ࿋ *anhvô*, according to §. 187.,
might also be the singular genitive, which frequently
occurs with a locative meaning. We await the elucidation which Neriosingh's Snnskṛit translation will give of
this passage; but, for the present, content ourselves with
the inferences deduced by Burnouf. ࿋ *ubôyô*, according to that authority, corresponds with the Sanskṛit
उभयोः *ubhayôs* (*amborum, in ambobus*), with *ô* for *a*, probably,
according to Burnouf's acute conjecture, through the
influence of the preceding *b*, and with the loss of the concluding *s*. I am the more inclined to assent to Burnouf's
opinion regarding the origin of the first *ô* of ࿋ *ubôyô*,
as I have been so fortunate as to find another example
for the hitherto missing dual cnse, in which ࿋ *ayô*, not
࿋ *ôyô*, actually occurs; because, that is to say, no letter
exercising the force of assimilation in question precedes
the *a*—I mean the form ࿋ *zaśtayô* (= Sanskṛit
hastayôs), "in the hands," from ࿋ *zaśta*, [G. Ed. p. 298.]
in a passage of the Jzeschne, which has perhaps not yet been
examined by M. Burnouf (V. S. p. 354.): ࿋
࿋ ࿋ ࿋ *kathâ ashâi drujĕm dyanm zaśtayô,*[*]
which Anquetil (p. 192) translates by "*Comment moi pur,
mettrai-je le main sur le Daroudj?*" It appears, however, that ࿋ *ashâi* can as little be a nominative as
࿋ *zaśtayô* a singular accusative; and I believe
I am not wrong in the following literal translation: "How can
I give the (Dæmon) Drudj into the hands of the pure (into
the power)?"

"Remark 2.—In the instrumental singular M. Burnouf
admits the termination *ana* in bases in *a* (Yaçna, p. 98.
passim), with *n* introduced, for the sake of euphony,

---

[*] The Codex has faultily ࿋ *aśdi* and ࿋ *drvjem.*

according to the analogy of the Sanskrit एन *ĕna* (§. 158.). He rests this, among other forms, on that of ساؤحسوسؤ *maĕsmana*, "*urina*," a word which had often attracted my attention, and from which I, in like manner, would have deduced instrumentals in *a-n-a* if I had not differed from Burnouf in the etymology of the same, as I make its theme terminate in *n*; and this word, which I remember to have seen only in the instrumental, I derive from the Sanskrit root मिह् *mih*, "*mingere*," by a suffix मन् *man*, according to the analogy of ساؤسحلس *barĕsman*, from बृह् *vrih*, "to grow," whose instrumental ساؤحسحلس *barĕsmana*, analogous with ساؤحسؤسؤ *maĕsmana*, occurs very frequently. M. Burnouf appears, on the other hand, to adopt a suffix *ma* in the word *maĕsmana*, in which we think we cannot agree with him as long as we cannot supply any cases which must indubitably belong to a theme in *a*. If, further, some words, which in their theme terminate in سس *as* (ऽ, Sanskrit अस् *as*), adopt *ana* in the instrumental form—M. Burnouf quotes, p. 100 note, ساؤحسؤ *mazana*, ساؤسسلس *srayana*, and ساؤسسجلؤ *ranhana*; still, in my opinion, bases in *a* may be assigned as the origin of these forms, and they can be divided *maza-na*, &c., only in as far as such forms have been already proved to belong to undoubted bases in *a*. But now we prefer dividing them *mazan-a*, so that the letter *s*, with which these themes originally terminate, is interchanged with a nasal, just as, [G. Ed. p. 200.] in Sanskrit, the words यकृत् *yakrit*, शकृत् *śakrit* change their *t* for *n* in the weak cases, and may substitute यकन् *yakan*, शकन् *śakan*; or as, in more remote analogy, the Greek, in the first person plural, has formed μεν from μες (मस् *mas*, "*mus*"). Besides this, M. Burnouf cites also the interrogative instrumental ساؤس *kana*, "with what?" which is the only word that brings to my mind somewhat of conviction, and had struck my attention before, in passages like ولسؤسحؤ ساؤسحؤ ساؤس *kana yazna yazdnĕ*, "with

what offering shall I sacrifice?" (V. S. p. 481.) I have not,
however, ventured to draw a grammatical deduction from
this form, because the pronominal bases are prone to
unite with one another, and because I believed I might
assume that the same pronoun which is contained in चन
ana and एन *ena* forms also the last element of ﻛﺎﻧﺎ *kana*,
if from this base the instrumental only had been evolved
or preserved, as has also occurred in the Sanskṛit
चन *ana* and एन *ena* in but a few cases. For the rest,
the Greek κεῖνος also appears connected with this ﻛﺎﻧﺎ
kana, if it is looked upon as a theme, with which the instrumental must agree in sound, for κεῖνος, if not directly
of interrogative meaning, is still plainly connected with
the old interrogative base (comp. कश्चन *kaśchana*, " whoever."). Under these circumstances I cannot yet admit
of any instrumentals in *a-n-a*, especially as also the bases
in *i* and *u* (in which the Sanskṛit in the masculine and neuter likewise introduces a euphonic *n*) in the Zend, in words
which we have noticed, have dispensed with a similar insertion
(§. 160.). In another place (*Journal des Savans*), M. Burnouf deduces the frequently-occurring instrumental ﺍﺷﻬﻴﺎ
ashayâ, " with purity," from the masculine theme ﺍﺷﺎ
asha ; and there would be accordingly ﺍﺷﺎﻳﺎ *ashaya*, an
instrumental form, at present standing alone in the Zend,
which I hesitate to acknowledge, although it would be
analogous to the Vêdic form mentioned in §. 158., स्वप्नया
swapnayâ, if one derives this, with the Indian grammarians,
from a theme स्वप्न *swapna*. But if instrumental forms of
this kind, in the Vêdas or in the Zend, are not to be produced in other undoubted instances as in the case of
adjectives in construction with masculine or neuter substantives, nothing prevents the assumption, that the form
स्वप्नया *swapnayâ* belongs to a feminine theme स्वप्ना *swapnâ*,
especially as the suffix न *na* occurs also in other abstracts
in the feminine form ना *nâ*, and therefore स्वप्नया *swapnayâ*

may be explained according to the analogy of गृष्णया *trish-*
[G. Ed. p. 300.] *ṇayd,* " with thirst." In every case I think
I may deduce the Zend ꟃꟃꟃꟃ *ashaya* from a feminine
theme ꟃ *ashâ,* as the Zend in general, in the substantive,
passes readily from one sex to the other ; and, for example,
with a masculine base ꟃ *manthra,* " a speech," occurs,
also, a feminine ꟃ *manthrâ.*

"Remark 3.—For the genitive termination ꟃ *hê* there
also exists, as Burnouf has most satisfactorily proved, a
form nearer to the Sanskrit *sya,* viz. ꟃ *hyd,* which,
although rather rare in comparison with the more
corrupt form *hê,* is still sufficiently frequent in some
chapters of the Jzeschne to satisfy one perfectly of its
signification, according to the proofs given by Burnouf.
I too had remarked words with the ending ꟃ *hyâ,*
but in passages where Anquetil's translation was little
adapted to bring to light the genitive nature of the same,
which, besides, was very much obscured through its usual
representative ꟃ *hê,* and was, moreover, concealed from
me under the appearance of an instrumental form.
However, the termination *hyâ*—for which is sometimes
found, also, ꟃ *khyâ*—approaches so very near to the
Sanskrit स्य *sya,* and agrees with it so precisely according
to rule, as far as the unorganic lengthening of the *a,* that
a single passage, with the accurate translation of Neriosingh, who, in the passages hitherto edited, follows the
original word by word, would have led us to it. Such a
passage is given, although with a different aim, by Burnouf in his Yaçna (Notes, p. cxxxix.), which we here annex,
as it is interesting in other respects, also, for grammar :—
ꟃꟃ ꟃꟃ ꟃꟃꟃ ꟃꟃꟃ ꟃꟃ ꟃꟃ ꟃꟃ
ꟃꟃ ꟃꟃ ꟃꟃ ꟃꟃ *kaìnd zanthwâ patâ
ashahyâ paourvyô kaìnd kheng strencha dât adhwânĕm.* Neriosingh translates this passage word for word, only that
he renders *kaìnd,* " which man?" (here properly not more

than "who," for the idea of man is lost in the general
signification of the whole,) not by को ना *kô nâ*, but simply,
by को *kô*, as follows : को जनने: पिता पुण्यस्य प्रथमं कः सूर्यस्य
तारकानाञ्च ददौ पदवीम् *kô jananêh pitâ punyasya prathaman**
(किल सद्व्यापारत्वङ् कस् चक्रे *kila sadvyâpâd-* [G. Ed. p. 301.]
ratvan kas chakrê, i. e. "*boni originem quis fecit?*") *kah sûr-
yasya târakânâncha daddu padavím* (किल मार्गन् तेषान् को ददौ
kila mârgan têshân kô daddu, *i. e.* "*viam ipsis quis dedit?*").
We translate from the Zend, "*Quis (qualis vir) creatione pater
est puritatis* (or *puri*) *primus? quis (qualis vir) soli stellisque
dedit viam ?*" The Zend expression ᴢᴇɴᴅ *zanthwâ*, for
which, in the lithographed codex, p. 351, is erroneously
given ᴢᴇɴᴅ *zanthâ*, is plainly the instrumental of ᴢᴇɴᴅ
zantu ; which would correspond to the theme of a Sanskrit
infinitive, जन्तुम् *jantum*, as the latter is feminine, and to which
I have, in another place, referred the ablative ᴢᴇɴᴅ
zanthwât (Gramm. Crit. p. 253.). This form is, besides, remarkable on this account, viz. that it is identical with the
Sanskrit instrumental gerund, which, from जन् *jan*, without a
conjunctive vowel and without the euphonious suppression of
the न् *n*, would sound जन्त्वा *jantwâ*. With regard, however,
to the length of the concluding *a* of the Zend form, which is
preserved contrary to the prevailing rule (see §§. 118, 158.
and 160. p. 191 G. Ed., where, however, ᴢᴇɴᴅ *janthwa* is to
be read for *zanthwa*), I do not attach any particular importance to that, because in the chapter from which this passage is taken *a*, originally short, is repeatedly to be found
lengthened. The Sanskrit जनने: *jananêh*, with which Neriosingh translates the Zend instrumental case, must be considered as an ablative, as this case often enters the department of the instrumental, and is also capable of expressing

---

* Perhaps the adverb प्रथमं *prathaman*, "*primum*," is a corruption for
प्रथम: *prathamak*, "*primus*," which answers to the original, and is to be
expected from the sense.

† Vide as to ᴢᴇɴᴅ *zanthwâ*, p. 1244 G. ed.

the preposition "through" (for example, Nal. XII. 89.).
Considered as a genitive, जननें:*jananêh* would not correspond
with *zanthwâ*, which cannot possibly be a genitive,
for the genitive of *zantu* could only be
zanteus, or, also, *zanthwô*, or *zantavô* (see
§. 187.), but in no case *zanthwâ*. Add to this, also,
that जननि *janani* is feminine, like the Zend *zantu*, and
पुण्यस्य *punyasya*, therefore, could no more pass as the epithet
of जननें: *jananêh* than, in Zend, *ashahyâ* could
pass as the epithet of *zanthwâ*. I will, however, as
concerns the Zend, lay no great stress on this circumstance,
since in it the genders of the substantive are constantly
changing. M. Burnouf, who looks upon जननें: *jananêh* as a
genitive, and refers पुण्यस्य *punyasya* to it, according to this
interpretation justly takes objection to the पुण्यस्य *punyasya*,
which does not agree with the gender of जननि *janani*, but he
confirms, however, the reading expressly by the addition of a
[G. Ed. p. 302.] *sic*. His translation runs, "*Quel est le premier père de la creation pure? qui a montré leur route au soleil
et aux astres.*" I look with anxiety for M. Burnouf's further
explanation of this passage, but expect from him rather information of value in other respects, than to find that he has
succeeded in making the forms जननें: *jananêh* and
zanthwâ pass for genitives. Anquetil's traditionary interpretation sounds, in this place, very strange, but does not
contradict my apprehension of *zanthwâ*: he makes
the genitive *ashahyâ* pass for the nominative,
and does not, therefore, throw any light on the meaning of
the termination *hyâ*; for, in the presumption that it
was right, *ashahyâ* might, perhaps, have next
been taken for an instrumental, and perhaps have been translated "father with purity." His translation is as follows:
"*Quel est le premier père pur* qui a engendré? qui a donné*

---

* In other places (V. S. p. 385) Anquetil renders (p. 137) the words

de lui même les astres qui ne sont pas a deux faces?" The
sun is here quite left out of the question; and it must be
acknowledged, that, as far as relates to etymology, it is
very much obscured in this passage; we might identify,
with reference to the form of ⟨script⟩ *kheng*, this expression
with the reflective pronoun ⟨script⟩ *kha* (as in *kha-ḍâta*, " created
of itself," which is often said of the stars, as of self-
created lights), and consider it as the epithet of ⟨script⟩
itren-cha; so that it would correspond as accusative plural
to the Sanskrit स्वान् *swân*. It is here to be remarked, that
in some chapters of the Jzeschne, ⟨script⟩ *ng* is repeatedly
found instead of a simple nasal, and, indeed, without
regard to the organ of the following initial letter. So we
read, in the V. S. p. 391, ⟨script⟩ *dushacsathreng,*[*]
⟨script⟩ *dusskyaḍlhneng,* ⟨script⟩ *dushda-
ḍneng.* Anquetil, indeed, renders these expressions as
singular nominatives, " *ce roi mechant, qui fait le mal, attaché
à la mauvaise loi*"; but they, together with [G. Ed. p. 308.]
⟨script⟩ *dushvachanhô,* ⟨script⟩ *dushmananhô,*
refer to the plural ⟨script⟩ *drĕgvatô,* and I have no
doubt of their accusative nature: the whole passage, however, like many others in the Jzeschne, can be explained
only with the help of Neriosingh's Sanskrit translation.
We can but regret that the in other respects highly valuable
elaborate exactitude of Burnouf's excellent Commentary
leaves us no hope that he will come very soon to the
elucidation of this and other passages, regarding which
I am most curious. But to return to our ⟨script⟩ *kheng,*

⟨script⟩ *patâ ashahyâ* rightly by *père de la pureté:* his
translation is, however, little calculated to throw light on the connection
of the passage referred to.

[*] The lithographed MS. has ⟨script⟩ *dusa csathreng* as
two words; the *a* is, however, clearly only a conjunctive vowel, to unite
the prefix ⟨script⟩ *dush* more conveniently with the following ⟨script⟩ *cs*.

the ‫ ‬ *kh* makes no difficulty in this expression, even in its
acceptation for the sun, for which, commonly, ‫ ‬ *hvarĕ*
is found (the Sanskrit स्वर् *svar*, "heaven,"), as ‫ ‬ *kh* is used
very frequently for ‫ ‬ *hv* (see §. 35.); but we might here
expect to find ‫ ‬ *kharĕ*, and may suppose that the
‫ ‬ *ng* has arisen out of *n*, and this letter out of *r*, as
these liquids are easily interchanged, as is shewn in Sanskrit, by the connection of अहन् *ahan*, "day," with अहर्
ahar, and, in the Zend, that of ‫ ‬ *csapan*, "night,"
with ‫ ‬ *csapar* (I write it thus, and not ‫ ‬
csaparĕ, designedly, see §. 44.). At all events I take ‫ ‬
kheng to be the accusative, if, indeed, it may not also be
conjectured that the base ‫ ‬ *hvar* may have entirely lost
its *r*, and that it may be ‫ ‬ *kheng* for ‫ ‬ *khem*, the
accusative of a base ‫ ‬ *kha*. ‫ ‬ *itren-cha*, also,
according to my opinion, is the accusative, and not, as one
might expect from the Sanskrit translation, the genitive
plural, which more frequently occurs in the form ‫ ‬
itáraṅm. Although, from this, ‫ ‬ *itren* might easily
be formed by contraction and combination with ‫ ‬ *cha*, I
nevertheless prefer acknowledging in ‫ ‬ *itrencha*, a
secondary form of ‫ ‬ *itreus*, explained in §. 239.;
so that the nasal, here vocalized to *u*, is there retained,
but the sibilant has been removed (comp. §. 239.); especially as, in other places also, ‫ ‬ *dá* is found in construction with the accusative of the person, which has been
given. In the Zend expression, ‫ ‬ *adhvánĕm*, the
Sanskrit अध्वानम् *adhwánam* cannot fail to be observed
(comp. §. 45.); but in the lithographed MS. we have instead of this, ‫ ‬ *advánĕm*, which is easily seen to be
an error. This false reading appears, nevertheless, to be an
ancient one, and widely diffused; and upon this is founded
Anquetil's, or rather his Pârsî teacher's, interpretation, which
is strangely at variance with Neriosingh's exposition; "*qui*

[G. Ed. p. 3ᴦ4.] *ne sont pas a deux faces*," so that ‫ ‬ *a* is taken for the well-known privative particle, *dva* as the number two, and the last portion finds in the Sanskrit आनन *ánana*, "countenance," its corresponding syllable.

FEMININE BASES IN *á*, GOTHIC *ó* (§. 119.).

Nominative,   Sanskrit *dhará*,[*] Greek χώρᾱ, Lithuanian *ranká*, Zend *hizva*, Gothic *giba*, Latin *terra*.

Accusative,   Sansk. *dhará-m*, Latin *terram*, Zend *hizva-ṅm*, Greek χώρᾱ-ν, Lith. *ranka-ṅ*, Goth. *giba*.

Instrumental, Sanskrit *dharay-á*, Zend *hizvay-a*, Gothic Dat. Instr. *gibai* (§. 161.), Lithuanian *ranká*.

Dative,   Sansk. *dharáy-ái*, Zend *hizvay-ái*, Lith. *ranka-i*.

Ablative,   Zend *hizvay-át*, Latin *terra(d)*.

Genitive,   Sanskrit *dharáy-ás*, Zend *hizvay-áo*, Greek χώρᾱ-ς, Latin *terrā-s*, Lithuanian *rankò-s*, Gothic *gibó-s*.

Locative,   Sanskrit *dharáy-ám* (§. 202.), Zend *hizvay-a*, Lithuanian *ranko-ye* (§. 197.).

Vocative.   Sanskrit *dharé*, Zend *hizvé* (?), Greek χώρᾱ, Latin *terra*, Lithuanian *ranka*, Gothic *giba* (?).

DUAL.

Nom. Acc. Voc. Sanskrit *dharé*, Zend *hizvé* (§. 213.), Lithuanian Nom. *ranki*, Voc. *ránki*.

Instr. Dat. Abl. Sanskrit *dhará-bhyám*, Zend *hizvá-bya*,[†] Greek Dat. Gen. χώρᾱ-ιν, Lith. Dat. *ranko-m* (§. 215.).

Gen. Loc.   Sanskrit *dharay-ós*.   [G. Ed. p. 305.]

---

[*] Means "earth," and is probably connected with the Greek χώρα, as aspirates are easily interchanged (Buttmann, §. 16. Rem. 1.). The root is य़ *dhri* (धर् *dhar*, §. 1.), "to hold," "carry;" whence, also, धारा *dhárá*, which, by reason of the long vowel of its root, approaches nearer the Greek χώρα (§. 4.), although it does not signify earth.

[†] Without being able to quote this case in Zend bases in *á*, I still have no doubt of the genuineness of the above form, since I can prove by other cognate case terminations: 1. That the *á* is not shortened; and 2. also that an *i* is not introduced into the theme by the assimilative power of the termination; hence, *e. g.* in the instr. pl. *ghnábis* (V. S. p. 308.) from *ghná* "woman" (γυνή).

FEMININE BASES IN *i*.[*]

SINGULAR.

Nominative, Sanskrit *príti-s*, Zend *áfríti-s*, Greek *πόρτι-ς*.
Latin *turri-s*, Lithuanian *awi-s*, Gothic *anst'-s*.

Accusative, Sanskrit *príti-m*, Latin *turri-m*, Zend *áfríti-m*.
Greek *πόρτι-ν*, Lithuanian *áwi-ń*, Gothic *anst'*.

Instrumental, Sanskrit *príty-á*, Zend *áfríthy-a*, Gothic Dat.
Instr. *anstai* (without case suffix, see §. 161.).

Dative, Sanskrit *prítay-ė* (or *príty-ái*, §. 164.), Zend
áfríte-ė.[†]

Ablative, Zend *áfrítói-t*, Latin *turri-(d)*.

Genitive, Sanskrit *prítė-s* (or only with the feminine
termination *príty-ás*), Gothic *anstai-s*, Zend
áfrítói-s, Greek *πόρτι-ος*, *φύσε-ως*, Lat *turri-s*.

Locative, Sanskrit *prít-áu*, (or with the feminine termination only *príty-ám*).

Vocative, Sanskrit *prítė*, Zend *áfríti*, Greek *πόρτι*.

DUAL.

Nom. Acc.Voc. Sanskrit *príti*, Zend *áfríti*(?), Lithuanian Nom.
[G. Ed. p. 306.] *awi*, Voc. *áwi*.

---

[*] It may be sufficient to give here the cases of a Sanskrit masculine in
 इ *i*, which differ from the feminine paradigms : from *agni*, " fire," comes the
instrumental singular *agni-n-á*—whilst from *pati*, " master," comes *paty-a*,
and from *sakhi*, "friend," *sakhy-á* (see §. 158.)—and in the accus. plural
अग्नीन् *agni-n*.

[†] Differing from what is stated in §. 164. p. 196. G. Ed., it is now my
opinion that the ع *e* in ـمجويـلدٮٮ *áfríteė* does not represent the ٮٮ *a* of
the original form ـمجـٮٮوٮلدٮٮ *áfrítayė*, but is the contraction of *a* and *y* ;
as, for instance, in the Prakrit चिन्तेमि *chintėmi*, from चिन्तयामि *chinta-
yámi*. ع *e* is here a weaker form of *é*=ए, and is more properly used to
represent the latter than another vowel. With regard to the Lithuanian,
see p. 218, Note †.

Instr. Dat. Abl.   Sanskrit *príti-bhyám*, Zend *áfríti-bya*, Greek
Gen. Dat. πορτί-ο-ιν, Lithuanian Dat. *áwi-m*
(§. 215.).

Gen. Loc.   Sanskrit *príty-ós*, Zend *áfríthy-ó* (?) (see p. 276.
Rem. 1.).

PLURAL.

Nom. Voc.   Sanskrit *prítay-as*, Zend *áfríthy-ó* (with *cha*
"and" *áfríthy-as-cha*), Greek πόρτι-ες, Latin
turr'-ês,* Gothic *anstei-s*, Lithuanian *áwy-s*.

Accusative,   Sanskrit *príti-s*, Zend *áfríti-s*, Greek πόρτι-ς,
Gothic *ansti-ns*, Lithuanian *áwy-s*.

Instrumental,   Sanskrit *príti-bhis*, Zend *áfríti-bís*, Lithuanian
awi-mis, Gothic Dat. Instr. *ansti-m* (§. 215.).

Dat. Abl.   Sanskrit *príti-bhyas*, Zend *áfríti-byó*, Latin *tur-
ri-bus*, Lithuanian *awi-m(u)s* (§. 215.).

Genitive,   Sanskrit *príti-n-ám*, Zend *áfríti-n-anm*, Latin
turri-um, Greek πορτί-ων, Lithuanian *awi-ú*,
Gothic *anst'-ê*.

Locative,   Sanskrit *príti-shu*, Zend *áfríti-shva* (or *áfríti-
-shu*), Lithuanian *áwi-sa*, Greek Dat. πόρτι-σι.

NEUTER BASES IN *i*.

SINGULAR.

Nom. Acc. Voc. Sanskrit *vári*, Zend *vairi*, Greek ἴδρι, Latin
mare.

The rest like the masculine.

DUAL.

Nom. Acc. Voc. Sanskrit *vári-n-í*.

The rest like the masculine.

PLURAL.

Nom. Acc. Voc. Sanskrit *vári-n-i*, Zend   [G. Ed. p. 307.]
vár'-a, Greek ἴδρι-α, Latin *mari-a*, Gothic
thriy-a (from *THRI*, "three").

The rest like the masculine.

---

* Vide p. 1078 G. ed. as to *turré-s* and similar forms.

MASCULINE BASES IN *u*.

SINGULAR.

Nominative,   Sanskṛit *sûnu-s*, Gothic *sunu-s*, Lithuanian *sunù-s*, Zend *paśu-s*, Latin *pecu-s*, Greek βότρυ-ς.

Accusative,   Sanskṛit *sûnu-m*, Latin *pecu-m*, Zend *paśû-m*, Greek βότρυ-ν, Lithuanian *sunu-ṅ*, Gothic *sunu.*

Instrumental, Sanskṛit *sûnu-n-â* (Vêda *prabdhav-â*, from *prabdhu*, §. 158.), Zend *paśv-a*, Gothic Dat. Instr. *sunau.*

Dative,   Sanskṛit *sûnav-ê*, Zend *paśv-ê*, Lithuanian *sunu-i.*

Ablative,   Zend *paśaθ-ṭ*, Latin *pecu-(d).*

Genitive,   Sanskṛit *sûnṓ-s* (from *sunau-s*), Gothic *sunau-s*, Lithuanian *sunaù-s*, Zend *paśeu-s* or *paśv-ô* (from *paśv-aś*), Latin *pecû-s*, Greek βότρυ-ος.

Locative,   Sanskṛit *sûn'-âu.*

Vocative   Sanskṛit *sûnô* (from *sunau*), Gothic *sunau*, Lithuanian *sunaù*, Zend *paśu*, Greek βότρυ.

DUAL.

Nom. Acc. Voc. Sanskṛit *sûnû*, Zend *paśû*, Lithuanian Nom. *sunù*, Voc. *sûnu.*

Instr. Dat. Abl. Sanskṛit *sûnu-bhyâm*, Zend *paśu-bya*, Greek βοτρύ-ο-ιν, Lithuanian *sunu-m* (§. 215.)

Gen. Loc.   Sanskṛit *sûnv-ôs*, Zend *paśv-ô* (see p. 276.
[G. Ed. p. 308.]   Rem. 1.)

PLURAL.

Nom. Voc.   Sanskṛit *sûnav-as*, Greek βότρυ-ες, Zend *paśv-ô* (with *cha*, *paśvaś-cha*), Latin *pecû-s*, Gothic *sunyu-s* (for *suniu-s*, from *sunau-s*, §. 230.), Lithuanian *sùnu-s.*

Instrumental, Sanskṛit *sûnu-bhis*, Zend *paśu-bîs*, Lithuanian *sunu-mis*, Gothic Dat. Instr. *sunu-m* (§. 215.).

Genitive,   Sanskrit *sûnu-n-âm* Zend *paśu-aṅm*, Latin *pecu-um*, Greek βοτρύ-ων, Gothic *suniv-ê*, Lithuanian *sun'-û.*

Locative,   Sanskrit *sûnu-shu*, Zend *paśu-shva* (or *paśu--shu*), Lithuanian *sunû-se*, Greek Dat. βότρυ-σι.

Remark.—Feminine bases in *u* in Sanskrit differ in declension from the masculine, exactly as, p. 305 G. Ed , प्रीति *prîti* f. differs from अग्नि *agni* m.

NEUTER BASES IN *u.*

SINGULAR.

Nom. Acc. Voc. Sanskrit *madhu,* Zend *madhu,* Greek μέθυ, Latin *pecu,* Gothic *faihu.*

The rest like the masculine.

DUAL.

Nom. Acc. Voc. Sanskrit *madhu-n-î.*

The rest like the masculine.

PLURAL.

Nom. Acc. Voc. Sanskrit *madhû-n-i,* Zend *madhv-a,* Greek μέθυ-α, Latin *pecu-a.*

The rest like the masculine.

FEMININE BASES IN *î.*   [G. Ed. p. 309.]

SINGULAR.

	Sanskrit.		*Zend.*
Nom.	*nârî,* "woman,"	*bhî-s,* "fear,"	*nâiri,* "woman."
Accus.	*nârî-m,*	*bhiy-am,*	*nâirî-m.*
Instr.	*nâry-â,*	*bhiy-â,*	*nâiry-a.*
Dat.	*nâry-âi*	*bhiy-ê,* or *bhiy-âi,*	*nâiry-âi.*
Abl.	*nâry-âs,*	*bhiy-as* or *bhiy-âs,*	*nâiry-âṭ.*
Gen.	*nâry-âs,*	*bhiy-as* or *bhiy-âs,*	*nâiry-âv.*
Loc.	*nâry-âm,*	*bhiy-i* or *bhiy-âm,*	*nâiry-a.*
Voc.	*nâri,*	*bhî-s,*	*nâiri.*

U

DUAL.

	Sanskrit.		*Zend.*
N.A.V.	*ndry-áu,*	*bhiy-áu,*	*ndiri*(see §. 213, p. 227.)
I. D. Ab.	*ndrí-bhyám,*	*bhí-bhyám,*	*ndiri-bya.*
Loc.	*ndry-ós,*	*bhiy-ós,*	*ndiry-ó ?*

PLURAL.

N. V.	*ndry-ás,*	*bhiy-as,*	*ndiry-áo.*
Accus.	*ndrí-s,*	*bhiy-as,*	*ndirí-s.*
Instr.	*ndrí-bhis,*	*bhí-bhis,*	*ndiri-bís.*
D. Abl.	*ndrí-bhyas,*	*bhí-bhyas,*	*ndiri-byó.*
Gen.	*ndrí-n-ám,*	*bhiy-ám,**	*ndiri-n-añm.*
Loc.	*ndrí-shu,*	*bhí-shu,*	*ndiri-shva* or *-shu.*

" Remark.—By the side of the declension of monosyllabic feminine bases in *í*, which may reject the terminations peculiar to the feminine alone, may be placed the Greek [G. Ed. p. 310.] κίς, and a remarkable similarity of inflexion will be observed, as Nom. *bhí-s,* κί-ς, Gen. *bhiy-as,* κί-ός, Loc. Dat. *bhiy-i,* κί-ί, Acc. *strí-ın,†* κί-ν, Voc. *bhí-s,* κί-ς. Plural: Nom. *bhiy-as,* κί-ες, Gen. *bhiy-ám.* κί-ῶν, Loc. Dat. *bhí-shu,* κί-σί, Acc. *bhiy-as,* κί-ας, Voc. *bhiy-as,* κί-ες. I consider, however, this coincidence as accidental, but, nevertheless, an accidental coincidence of that nature, that can only occur in languages which were originally really one: and undoubtedly the terminations, whose common sound appears so startling, are historically connected. As far, however, as concerns the theme, I believe, with Kühner (§. 287.), that the *ī* of κί was not the original concluding radical letter of the word, but that a consonant has fallen out after the *ı*. I would rather, however, leave the question as to this consonant undecided, than assume

---

* Or *bhí-n-ám.* Further, the longer case-terminations, which belong to the feminine (see §. 164.), are added at will to the monosyllabic feminines in *í,* *ú ;* for example, together with *bhiyé, bhruvé,* also *bhiyái, bhruvái.*

† Or, like the other monosyllabic words in *í,* with the termination *am, striy-am.*

that KIϜ is the true theme, and that the nominative was originally κιϜς; for if κιός, κιί, in the form in which they have been received, be analogous to Διός, Διί, from ΔιϜός, ΔιϜί, still, to establish a theme KIϜ, a proof must be brought similar to that which really attaches to ΔιϜί from its being found in inscriptions. And besides this, that which of itself is alone sufficient proof, the cognate Sanskrit word दिव् *div*, "heaven" (§. 122.) likewise attests a digamma. All ground for supposing a theme KIϜ is, however, wanting, for the long *ι* could, as in the Sanskrit भी *bhí*, and like the long *υ* in ὀφρύς, be also the real final letter of the base, only that the long *i* in the Sanskrit, except in compounds (for example गतभी *gata-bhí* m. f., " void of fear," जलपी m. f., " water-drinking," see Gramm. Crit. §§. 169. 170.), concludes only the feminine themes. We will therefore seek elucidation regarding the Greek κῖς in another way, through the Sanskrit, and we find this, as it appears to me, through a like masculine base, which approximates closely to the κί-ς, as well in form as in meaning; namely, in कीट *kíṭa*, Nom. कीटस् *kíṭa-s*, " insect " " worm," which would lead us to expect in the Greek κῖτος, Acc. κῖτον, to which κῖς, κῖν, bear the same relation as μέγας, μέγαν, to the to be presupposed μέγαλος, μέγαλον. I do not consider it requisite to assume a theme ΜΕΓΑΤ, although the Sanskrit महत् *mahat*, " great," might support it; but महत् *mahat* is a participial form, and its full and original form [G. Ed. p. 311.] (§. 129.) is महन्त् *mahant*, Nom. masc. महान्! *mahán*, which would correspond to the Greek μεγων."

FEMININE BASES IN *û*, *ū*.

SINGULAR.

	Sanskrit.		Greek.
Nom.	vadhû-s, "wife,"	bhrû-s, "eye-brow,"	ὀφρύ-ς.
Accus.	vadhû-m,	bhruv-am,	ὀφρύ-ν.
Instr.	vadhw-â,	bhruv-â,	. . . .
Dat.	vadhw-âi,	bhruv-ê (or -âi),	. . . .

υ 2

	Sanskrit.		*Greek.*
Abl.	*vadhw-ás,*	*bhruv-as* (or *-ás*),	. . . .
Gen.	*vadhw-ás,*	*bhruv-as* (or *-ás*),	ὀφρύ-ος.
Loc.	*vadhw-ám,*	*bhruv-i* (or *-ám*).	ὀφρύ-ϊ.
Voc.	*vadhu,*	*bhrû-s,*	ὀφρῦ.

DUAL.

N.Ac.V.	*vádhw-âu,*	*bhruv-âu,*	ὀφρύ-ε.
I.D.Ab.	*vadhû-bhyâm.*	*bhrû-bhyâm.*	ὀφρύ-ο-ιν.
G.L.	*vadhw-ós,*	*bhruv-ós.*	. . . .

PLURAL

N.V.	*vadhw-as,*	*bhruv-as,*	ὀφρύ-ες.
Accus.	*vadhû-s,*	*bhruv-as,*	ὀφρύ-ας.
Instr.	*vadhû-bhis,*	*bhrû-bhis,*	. . . .
D.Abl.	*vadhû-bhyas,*	*bhrû-bhyas,*	. . . .
Gen.	*vadhû-n-âm,*	*bhruv-âm* (or *bhrû-n-âm*),	ὀφρύ-ων.
Loc.	*vadhû-shu,*	*bhrû-shu,*	ὀφρύ-σι.

Remark.—The identity of स्व *bhrû* and 'ΟΦΡΥ* is
[G. Ed. p. 312.] sufficient proof that the length of the *u* is
organic (comp. §. 121.), and it is not necessary, therefore, to
suppose a theme ΟΦΡΥϜ (comp. Kühner §. 289.) so as to
consider ὀφρύς as coming from ὀφρυϜς, and the long *u* as a
compensation for the rejected Ϝ, as perhaps μέλᾱς from μέλανς.
That, however, Ϝ originally stood—for example, ὀφρύϜος—
before the terminations now commencing with a vowel, though
at a time when the language had not a Grecian form is
shewn by the Sanskrit *bhruv-as* ; by which, at the same time,
the shortening of the *u* in this case is justified, for the Sanskrit

---

* The *o* in ὀφρύς is based on the peculiar disposition of the Greek to
prefix a vowel to words which originally commenced with a consonant,
to which I have already drawn attention in another place, and by which,
among other things, the relation of ὄνυξ, ὄνομα, to नख*nakha-s,* नाम
náma, is shewn.

changes, that is to say in polysyllables, as well v as $\hat{v}$, before vowel terminations, into a simple v; but in monosyllables, in order to avoid commencing with two consonants, or to gain a polysyllabic form, the semi-vowel has its corresponding short vowel placed before it, and thus is formed उव् uv ($\breve{u}v$), as well from u as from $\hat{u}$, as, under a similar condition, इय् from i and $\acute{\imath}$: hence the two opposite forms, for example, $vadhw\text{-}as$ (not $vadhuv\text{-}as$), "women," and $bhruv\text{-}as$ (not $bhrw\text{-}as$), "the eyebrows;" as above, $bhiy\text{-}as$ (not $bhy\text{-}as$), opposed to $n\acute{a}ry\text{-}as$ ($n\acute{a}riy\text{-}as$). In the dative plural the short v of ὀφρύ-σι for ὀφρῦ-σι may be attributed to the effeminate habit of regularly shortening the v before vowel terminations."

BASES IN du (नौ),[*]

SINGULAR.

	Sanskrit.	Greek.
Nominative,	$n\acute{a}u\text{-}s,$	$ναῦ\text{-}ς.$
Accusative,	$n\acute{a}v\text{-}am,$	$ναῦ\text{-}ν.$
Genitive,	$n\acute{a}v\text{-}as,$	$ν\bar{a}(F)\text{-}ός.$
Locative,	$n\acute{a}v\text{-}i,$	$ν\bar{a}(F)\text{-}\ddot{\iota}.$
Vocative,	$n\acute{a}u\text{-}s,$	$ναῦ\text{-}ς.$

DUAL. [G. Ed. p. 313.]

Nom. Acc. Voc.	$n\acute{a}v\text{-}\acute{a}u,$	$ν\hat{a}(F)\text{-}ε.$
Instr. Dat. Abl.	$n\acute{a}u\text{-}bhy\acute{a}m,$	$ν\bar{a}(F)\text{-}o\text{-}\hat{\iota}v.$

PLURAL.

Nominative,	$n\acute{a}v\text{-}as,$	$ν\hat{a}(F)\text{-}ες.$
Accusative,	$n\acute{a}v\text{-}as,$	$ν\hat{a}(F)\text{-}ας.$
Genitive,	$n\acute{a}v\text{-}\acute{a}m,$	$ν\bar{a}(F)\hat{ω}ν.$
Locative,	$n\acute{a}u\text{-}shu,$	Dat. $ναυ\text{-}σί.$
Vocative,	$n\acute{a}v\text{-}as,$	$ν\hat{a}(F)\text{-}ες.$

"Remark.—I find no sufficient grounds, with Kühner, (l. c. §. 283.) to suppose that the base of the nominatives

---

[*] I give only the cases retained in the Greek.

in αυς, ευς, ους, originally terminated in F, so that in the
case before us it would be requisite to suppose a theme NAF:
for even if the vocalization of F to v, in order to facilitate the
junction with a consonant following, did not surprise us—
(forms like vaFς, vaFσι, could never occur);—still, on the other
hand, the transition of the sound v into its corresponding
semi-vowel, in order to avoid the hiatus, is far more
regular, and is required in the Sanskrit according to the
common rules of euphony. We will not therefore differ
from the Indian grammarians, by the assumption of a
theme नाव् *ndv* for नौ *ndu*, and गव् *gav* for गो *gô* (*bos*); although, if there were adequate reasons for it, the practice
of the Indian grammarians would not restrain us from
laying down गव् *gav* and नाव् *ndv* in the Sanskrit as the true
themes, which maintained themselves in this form only
before vowel terminations, but before consonants have
allowed the v to pass into a u, according to the analogy
of the anomalous दिव् *div*, "heaven"; whence, for example,
the instrumental plural चुभिस् *dyu-bhis* for दिव्भिस् *div-bhis*,
which would be phonetically impossible (Gramm. Crit.
§. 208.). The Latin *navis* cannot compel us to lay down a
theme *ndv* for the Sanskrit and Greek, for the Latin base
has extended itself by an unorganic *i*, as *swan*, "dog," lengthened to *cani*; and therefore it exhibits in its declension
nowhere u, but universally v.

[G. Ed. p. 314.] BASES TERMINATING WITH A CONSONANT.

SINGULAR.

	Sanskrit.	Zend.	Latin.	Greek.
Thema,	*VĀCH*,	*VĀCH*,	*VŌC*,	'ΟΠ.
Nom.	*vâk*,	*vâc-s*,	*voc-s*,	ὄπ-ς.
Accus.	*vâch-am*,	*vâch-ĕm*	*voc-em*,	ὄπ-α.
Instr.	*vâch-â*,	*vâch-a*,	. . . .	. . . .
Dative,	*vâch-ê*,	*vâch-ê*.	. . . .	. . . *

* See Locative.

	Sanskrit.	Zend.	Latin.	Greek.
		SINGULAR.		
Ablat.	....*	vâch-at,	voc-e(d),	....
Gen.	vâch-as,	vâch-ô,†	voc-is,	ὀπ-ός.
Loc.	vâch-i,	vâch-i,	D. voc-i,	D. ὀπ-ί.
Voc.	vâk,	vâc-s ?	voc-s,	ὄπ-ς.
		DUAL.		
N. Acc. V.	vâch-âu,	vâch-âo,	....	....
or	vâch-â,‡	vâch-a,	....	ὄπ-ε.
I. D. Abl.	vâg-bhyâm,	....	....	D. G. ὀπ-ο-ῖν.
G. L.	vâch-ôs,	vâch-ô ?	....	....
		PLURAL.		
N. V.	vâch-as,	vâch-ô,†	voc-es,	ὄπ-ες.
Accus.	vâch-as,	vâch-ô,†	voc-es,	ὄπ-ας.
Instr.	vâg-bhis,	....	....	....
D. Abl.	vâg-bhyas,	....	voc-i-bus,	....
Gen.	vâch-âm,	vâch-anm	voc-um,	....
Loc.	vâk-shu,	vâc-shva ?	....	D. ὀπ-σί.

"Remark 1.—I leave the terminations in [G. Ed. p. 315.] the Zend which commence with *b* unnoticed, since, contrary to my former opinion (§. 224. Note *), I look on the ۶ *e*, in forms like مودربكوبلسٱ *raochebis*, no longer as a conjunctive vowel; and therefore no longer attribute the said form to a theme بلسٱ *raoch*, but assume that مودربكوبلسٱ *raochebis*, and similar forms, have proceeded from bases in ۇ ô (from *as* §. 56ᵇ.); so that I look upon the ۶ *e* as a corruption of the ô, and to the form ۇدددربكوبلسٱ *raochehyô* I place as anterior a lost form ۇدددرپبلسٱ *raochô-byô*.§ In a similar way

---

* Like the Genitive.

† With *cha*, "and," *vâchas-cha*.

‡ See p. 230, Note *.

§ M. Burnouf, who has induced me, by his excellent pamphlet, cited at p. 276, on the Vahista (in the separate impression, p. 10, and following), to rectify my former views, leaves, p. 18 note, the question still undecided, whether forms like مودربۀربكوۇ *mazebis*, مودربۀربكوۇ *manebis*, بلاددۀربكود

[G. Ed. p. 316.] I find, in the Prâkṛit (Urvasi, by Lenz, p. 40.), अच्छरेहिं *achharêhiṅ* for अच्छरॊहिं *achharôhiṅ* (Sanskrit *apsaróbhis*); and if this form is genuine, then the ꝰ *e*, in forms like ‌‌‌‌‌ *raochebís*, appears to stand for ‌ *ê*, as generally many interchanges between ꝰ *e* and ‌ *ê* occur, although in the case before us the ꝰ *e* is very constantly written, and ‌ *ê* has not yet been pointed out in its place. If it is further considered that we often find ꝰ⊂ *ye* for ‌⊂ *yô*, "which," ꝰ‌ *ke* for ‌ *kô*, "who?" and in the pronoun of the 2d person in the plural also ꝰ‌ *ve* for ‌ *vô*; and, finally, in the pronoun of the 1st person ꝰ‌ *ne* for ‌ *nô*; then we see the change of the ‌ *ô* with ꝰ *e* is sufficiently ascertained, although it appears to be restricted to the end of words of a monosyllabic form; and in these the practice of writing the ‌ *ô* is the prevailing one, while before termi-

---

‌‌‌‌‌ *vachebís*, ‌‌‌‌‌ *raochebís*, have so arisen from the bases ‌‌‌ *mazô*, &c., that the ‌ *ô* (‌ *ai*) is suppressed, and ꝰ *e* then introduced as conjunctive vowel; or whether, before the *ô* (from *ai*) only, the *i* has been rejected, and the preceding *a* with an epenthetic *i* united with an *e*. In the former case I should not have been entirely wrong, from the analogy of *raoch-e-bis*, to deduce forms like *vách-e-bis*. I consider, however, the last view as the right one, only that I prefer letting the *ô* from the pre-supposed original form, *manô-bis, raochô-bis*, be changed in its whole force into ꝰ *e*, rather than reduce it into its elements, and mix the first of the said elements (*a*) with a conjoined *i*: for the derivation of *manebis* from *manȷibis* from *manabis*, for *manasbis*, would extend to the Sanskrit form मनॊभिस् *manóbhis*, which originally may have been *manarbhis* (*manas-bhis* was never possible). But I believe that in the Zend the form *ebis* really preceded the form *óbis*. M. Burnouf, in his review in the *Journal des Savans* (in the separate impression, pp. 30, 31), calls attention to a form ‌‌‌‌ *rághzhhyó*, for which is once found, in the Vend. Sâde, pp. 60 and 70, ‌‌‌‌ *rághĕzhĕhyó·* once ‌‌‌‌ *rághzhĕbyó*, and once ‌‌‌‌ *rághĕzhhyô*, which,

nations beginning with *b* as yet no *ó* has been pointed
out; so that *b* appears to be as repugnant to a preceding *ó*
as favourable to a following *ó*, if the conjecture of Burnouf,
mentioned at p. 297, G. Ed., is well-founded.　On this point
I was not yet clearly informed, when, at §§. 224. and 242., I
inconsiderately imagined I could deduce *vachô-bya, vachô-bís,*
from ‏فسیولب‎ *vachô* (from *vachas*).　Instead of this should be
read ‏اببعسولب‎ *vache-bya,* ‏بو_عسولب‎ *vache-bís*; and besides
this, in the locative singular, ‏بوسمسولب‎ *vachahi* for ‏لبسبوسب‎
vachanhi; since the nasal to be prefixed to the *h*, according
to §. 56ᵇ., falls away when the vowel which follows the *h*
is *i*, which has been already indicated in the paragraph
quoted, but since then fully proved by Bur-　[G. Ed. p. 817.]
nouf.　Besides, there really occurs, also, in one passage (where,
unfortunately, the lithographed MS. is faulty, and is therefore

---

which, with the conjunctive vowel ‏ع‎ *ě* (see §. 30.) introduced in different
ways, plainly represent one and the same word, and have proceeded from
‏فببعبوسولب‎ *vághzhbyô,* which itself never occurs.　Although these
forms, which had struck me likewise, clearly belong to a theme which
means "discourse," and is connected with our *vách,* I would still rather
not, with Burnouf, derive it from *vách;* so that the nominative of this,
‏بوۃسولب‎ *vács,* raised to a secondary theme, would be contained therein.
We dare not, without further authority, attribute to the Zend such a
malformation, although it derives its superlatives in ‏بوعقو‎ *těma* from
the masculine nominative, instead of from the theme.　But Anquetil, in
his Glossary, gives a form *vakhsenghě,* "parole utile," which we ought
probably to read ‏موسبوسبوۃسولب‎ *vacsanhě* (as dative), if not with long *a*
‏موسببوسبوۃسولب‎ *vácsanhě.*　This latter form would belong to a theme
‏فسبوۃسبولب‎ *vácsó (vácsas);* from which, in the dat. abl. pl., ‏فببوبوۃسسولب‎
vághzhbyô (vághčzhbyô, &c.) might proceed for ‏فببوسبوۃسسولب‎ ‏لب‎ *vácsbyó;*
as with ‏بو_عقسوۃ‎ *mazebís,* ‏بو_عقسوۃ‎ *manebís,* occur also ‏بوعقسوۃ‎
mazbís, ‏بوعقسوۃ‎ *manbís;* for the ‏بو‎ *s* of ‏فسبوۃسولب‎ *vácsó* must, as
Burnouf has shewn, in contact with *b* become ‏ۃ‎ *zh.*

impossible for me to use) the locative *vachahi*;
that is to say, in the Vend. S. p. 173, where, for
manahêchâ vachahêchâ, is to be read
manahichâ vachahichâ. In a Grammar, the lost
acquaintance with which is again to be restored, oversights
of this kind will, I trust, be excused in the first labourers;
and if, for example, Rask gives to the word *paiti* the genitive
paitôis, while, according to §. 180. p. 196, Note †, *patôis* is to
be written, still the form *paitôis* was, in its time, instructive
in the main, and first taught me that the Sanskrit genitive
termination *ê-s* corresponds to the form *ôis* in the Zend.
If, too, Rask has incorporated in his scheme of declensions
the ablative *paitôit* (for *patôit*), this was indeed a new error,
but also a new advantage for the Zend Grammar in its
then state, and brought to light a new and important fact,
which I believe I was the first to discover; namely this,
that bases in *i* form their ablative in *ôit*, for which the
proofs in the Zend-Avesta, as much as I have of it, are
neither numerous nor easily found. I make this remark
because M. Burnouf, as it appears to me, speaks too unfa-
vourably of such theoretic formations. As far as I am
concerned, I believe I may assert that my communications
regarding Zend Grammar are founded on careful reflection. I could not, however, perfectly conclude my considerations, and I am very ready to complete and adjust
them through those of M. Burnouf. For in this book
also, in regard to Zend Grammar, one must carefully
distinguish the disquisitions given in the text from the
general comparison added at the end of each rule regarding
case. In the former I give only those Zend forms which
I have seen, and I thence deduce theoretic laws: in the
latter I seek to make the deductions from the inquiries
pursued in the text evident in one select example. I am
perfectly sure of the prevailing majority of the forms
given in the tables, and can produce abundant examples

of them. I have marked some as questionable, and shewn
the limits of the probability of others, in notes; and if an
error has crept into the forms spoken of, and by me
believed to be correct, it will give me pleasure to be able
hereafter supplementarily to correct it. The form وَچَنْهِى
vachanhi was, however, only in a measure a theoretic formation; and I should not have ventured to   [G. Ed. p. 318.]
exhibit it if I had not observed, in other words of the same
declension, *i.e.* in other bases terminating with a consonant,
the locative, which has entirely escaped Rask.

"Remark 2.—One might consider the *o* of ὁποῖν instead
of a conjunctive vowel, as has been stated above (see
§. 221.), as a property of the base, *i.e.* as an unorganic
extension of it; or, in other words, regard it as a transition from the third to the second declension; a declaration which must then naturally extend itself to the dual
termination οιν of the whole third declension (ποσίο-ιν, βο-
τρύο-ιν, δαιμόνο-ιν like λύκο-ιν), and to all cases in the formation of words and arrangement of the same, where we have
represented an *o* foreign to the proper base as conjunctive
vowel. According to this, forms like μελιτόεις, μελιτοπώλης,
φυσιολογία, βοτρυόεις, βοτρυόδωρος, would be, under the presupposition of the bases ΜΕΛΙΤΟ, ΦΥΣΙΟ, ΒΟΤΡΥΟ, to be
divided into μελιτό-εις, and would lead us to expect the
nominatives μελιτο-ν, &c., which are not to be found. The
statement here given has this in its favour, that similar
cases occur also in cognate dialects, since in general that
declension which is the most in vogue and most used, is
prone, in certain cases, to receive into itself the other
declensions, which annex to their original base the final
letters of the bases of the declension more in use. The
origin of ὁποῖν from 'ΟΠΟ, of φερόντοιν from ΦΕΡΟΝΤΟ,
was as it were the first commencement of the disease,
which came to its full developement in the Pâli; since in
this language, which otherwise closely resembles the
Sanskrit, the bases which end with consonants are declined

in the old way only in the singular, but in the plural are
so corrupted, that, with the exception of the nominative
and the vocative of similar sound, and the genitive, which
at the same time supplies the place of the dative, they
have extended the old base by an unorganic a (=Greek o),
and have thus partly brought it from the Greek third
declension into the second; and in the singular, also,
most of the cases may, together with the old form, assume
more recent forms, which have originated in the manner
stated. In this manner, for example, the root चर् char, "to
go," forms its participle present partly from the original base
चरन्त् charant, or its corruption चरत् charat (see §. 129.), partly
from the augmented theme चरन्त charanta, and in part also
[G. Ed. p. 319.] arbitrarily from चरन्त charant or चरन्त
charanta, as follows (see Clough's Pâli Grammar, Colombo
1824, p. 25, and compare Burnouf's and Lassen's Essay,
p. 112 et seq.):

	SINGULAR.	
Th. *CHARANT*,	*CHARANTA*,	*CHARAT*.
Nom. *charañ,**	*charantô,*	. . . .
Acc. *charant-am,†*	. . . .	. . . .
Instr.	*charantê-n-a,*	*charat-â.*
Dat. like the Genitive,		
Abl.	{ *charanta-smâ,* or *charanta-mhâ,‡* }	*charat-â.§*

---

* The final न् n is, as in the Prâkrit (§. 10.), transmuted into the
Anuswâra, which I here express, as in the Sanskrit, by ñ.

† It might also be divided thus, *charanta-m*. and deduced from
charanta.

‡ Transposed, and with h for s (comp. §. 166.). These forms are
derived from the medial pronoun *sma* mentioned in §. 166., which, in
the Pâli also, has forced its way into the usual declension. The t, which
was to have been expected, is, as generally happens at the end of a word,
suppressed.

§ *Charatâ* is, according to appearance, identical with the instrumental,
but

SINGULAR.

Th.	*CHARANT,*	*CHARANTA,*	*CHARAT,*
Gen.	. . . .	*charanta-ssa,*	*charat-ô,*
Loc.	. . . .	{ *charantê,* or *charanta-smin,* or *charanta-mhi,* }	*charat-i,*
Voc.	{ *charan,* or *chara,* or *charâ,* }	. . . .	. . . .

PLURAL. [G. Ed. p. 320.]

Nom.	. . . .	*charantâ,*†	. . . .
Acc.	. . . .	*charantê,*	. . . .
Instr.	. . . .	{ *charantêbhi,* or *charantehi,* }	. . . .
Dat.	like the Genitive.		
Abl.	like the Instrumental.		
Gen.	. . . .	. . . .	*charat-am.*
Loc.	. . . .	*charantê-su,*	. . . .
Voc.	*charantô,*	*charantâ,*	. . . .

" If the Greek in its bases ending with a consonant had followed the declension-confusing example of the Pâli, one would have expected, for instance, from φέρων a genitive φέροντου, dative φέροντῳ; and in the plural indeed, φερόντων from

---

but is, in reality, corrupted from *charat-at,* analogous with Zend forms like *ap-at* (in ỹ. 180.): the suppressed *t* is replaced by the lengthening of the preceding vowel, as in *acharâ,* "he went," from *acharât* (Clough, p. 106.).

* If this form really belongs to a theme in *nt,* as I believe, it has sprung from the original form *charan,* by suppression of the concluding nasal (comp. Burnouf and Lassen, p. 89); and in *charâ* this deficiency is replaced by lengthening the vowel.

† According to the usual declension ending with a consonant one would expect with *charantâ* also *charantô,* from the original theme *charant;* as, for example, *gunavantô* is used with *gunavantâ,* "the virtuous"; the former from *gunavant,* the latter from *gunavanta.*

ΦΕΡΟΝΤ, but φεροντοι, φεροντους, φεροντοις, from ΦΕΡΟΝΤΟ. In this manner the form φερόντοιν in the dual, which has been lost in Pâli, would be clearly explained as derived from ΦΕΡΟΝΤΟ ; but even when standing isolated, φερόντοιν may be justly referred to a theme ΦΕΡΟΝΤΟ, as the first commencement of a corruption which was further pursued in the Pâli; and I prefer this view of the matter now to that laid down at §. 221. Both views, however, concur so far; and thus much of my opinion may be looked on as proved, that in φερόντοιν, and all other dative-genitive forms of the third declension, the o belongs neither to the original theme, which lies at the root of all the other cases, nor to the true case-suffix.

[G. Ed. p. 321.]   SINGULAR.

	Sanskrit.	Zend.	Latin.	Greek.	Gothic.
N.	bharan,	baran-s,	feren-s,	φέρων,	fiyand-s.*
Ac.	bharant-am,	barent-ĕm,	ferent-em,	φέροντ-α(ν),	fiyand.
Ins.	bharat-â,	barĕnt-a,	. . . .	. . . .	D. I.fiyand.
D.	bharat-ê,	barĕnt-ê,	see Locat,	see Loc.	see Dat.
Ab.	see Gen.	barant-at,	ferent-e(d),	. . . .	. . . .
G.	bharat-as,	barent-ô,†	ferent-is,	φέροντ-ος,	fiyand-is.†
L.	bharat-i,	barĕnt-i,	D. ferent-i,	D. φέροντ-ι,	. . . .
V.	bharan,	baran-s,	feren-s,	φέρων,	fiyand.

---

* Feind, "foe," as "hater," see §. 125. p. 138.

† See p. 210. Note §; with cha, barentai-cha ("ferentisque").

‡. I imagined, p. 210, that I must, in this case, which before was not proved to exist in ND bases, set down fiyand-s as a mutilation of fiyand-is from fiyand-as, according to the analogy of other bases terminating with a consonant (ahmin-s, brôthr-s, §. 191.); Grimm has (I. 1017.) conjectured friyôndis or friyônds from friyônds. Since this, owing to the very valuable additions made by Massmann to our Gothic authorities, the genitive nasyandis of Nasyand ("preserver, "preserving") has come to light (see his Glossary, p. 163), by analogy with which I form fiyand-is.

DUAL.

	Sanskrit.	Zend.	Greek.
N. Ac. Voc.	bharant-âu,	barant-âo, or baranta,	φέροντ-ε.
	Vêdic, bharant-â,*	. . . .	. . . .
I. D. Abl.	bharad-bhyâm,	baran-bya,†	φερόντο-ιν.‡
Gen. Loc,	bharat-ôs,	baraṭ-ô? (p. 276, R. 1.)	. . . .

PLURAL.   [G. Ed. p. 322.]

	Sanskrit.	Zend.	Latin.	Greek.	Gothic.
N. V.	bharant-as,	barĕnt-ô,§	ferent-ês,	φέροντ-ες,	fiyand-s.
Acc.	bharat-as,	barĕnt-ô,§	ferent-ês,	φέροντ-ας,	fiyand-s.‖
Instr.	bharad-bhis,	baran-bis,¶	. . . .	. . . .	. . . . **
D.Ab.	bharad-bhyas,	baran-byô,¶	ferent-i-bus,	. . . .	. . . .
Gen.	bharat-âm,	barĕnt-aṅm,††	ferenti-um,	φερόντ-ων,	fiyand-ê,‡‡
Loc.	bharat-su,	. . . .§§	. . . .	φέρου-σι.	[G. Ed.p.323.]

---

* See p. 230, Note *

† Or barĕnbya. See p. 241 Note *, and p. 210. Note §.

‡ See p. 299. Rem. 2.

§ Barentaś-cha, "ferentesque." See p. 210 Note §.

‖ This form, which, owing to an oversight, is omitted in p. 260, is found at Matth. 5. 44., and agrees with friyônds, "amicos" ("amantes"), Matth. 5. 47. as generally with the declension of a root terminating with a consonant. Comp. Grimm (I. 1017.).

¶ See p. 241 Note *, and p. 210 Note §.

** The Gothic dative, which I would have used also as the instrumental (§. 243.), does not occur in roots ending in nd.

†† Or barant-aṅm. See p. 266 Note †.

‡‡ This case certainly cannot be proved in bases in nd; but may, however, be correctly deduced from the other bases ending with a consonant, and from the elder sister dialects. See §. 245.

§§ I conjecture a transition into the a declension (comp. p. 299 Rem. 2.), by suppressing the nt; thus, perhaps, baraêshva (or -shu, or -shû, §. 250.), as Vend. S. p. 354; ꞩ drĕgvaêshû (read ꞩ shû) for drĕgvat-shû, from drĕgvat, in the strong cases (§. 129.) drĕgvant; on the supposition that the reading is correct, except the false s. See §. 52.

SINGULAR.

	Sanskrit.	Zend.	Latin.	Greek.	Gothic
N.	átmá',	aśma',	sermo',	δαίμων,	ahma'.
Acc.	átmán-am,	aśman-ĕm,	sermon-em,	δαίμον-α(ν),	ahman.
Inst.	átman-á,	aśman-a,	. . . .	. . . . D. I.	ahmin. (§. 132.)
Dat.	átman-é,	aśmain-é,	see Loc.	see Loc.	see Dative.
Abl.	see Gen.	aśman-aṭ,	sermon-é(d),	. . . .	. . . .
Gen.	átman-as,	aśman-ó,*	sermon-is,	δαίμον-ος,	ahmin-s (§. 132.)
Loc.	átman-i,	aśmain-i, D.	sermon-i,	δαίμον-ι,	. . . .
Voc.	átman,	aśman,	sermo',	δαῖμον,	ahma'.

DUAL.

	Sanskrit.	Zend.	Greek.
N. Acc. Voc.	átmán-áu,	aśman-áo, or aśman-a,	δαίμον-ε.
	Véda. átmán-a,		
Instr. D. Ab.	átma'-bhyam,	aśma'-bya,	D. G. δαιμόνο-ιν.†
Gen. Loc.	átman-ós,	aśman-ó? (p. 276, R. 1.),	. . . .

PLURAL.

	Sanskrit.	Zend.	Latin.	Greek.	Gothic.
N. V.	átmán-as,	aśman-ó,*	sermon-ēs,	δαίμον-ες,	ahman-s.
Ac.	átman-as,	aśman-ó,*	sermon-ēs,	δαίμον-ας,	ahman-s.
Instr.	átma'-bhis,	aśma'-bís,	. . . .	(δαιμόνο-φιν),D. I.	ahma'-m‡
D.Ab.	átma'-bhyas,	aśma'-byó,	sermon-i-bus,	. . . .	. . . .
Gen.	átman-ám,	aśman-ám,	sermon-um,	δαιμόν-ων,	ahman-é.
Loc.	átma'-su,	aśma'-hva,	. . . .	δαίμο'-σι,	. . . .

[G. Ed. p. 324.]   SINGULAR.

	Sanskrit.	Zend.	Latin.	Greek.	Gothic.
N.	bhrátá,	bráta,	frater,	πατήρ,	bróthar.
Ac.	bhrátar-am,	brátar-ĕm,§	fratr-ĕm,	πατέρ-α(ν),	bróthar.

---

* *Aśmanas-cha*, "cœlique."   † See p. 209, Rem. 2.   ‡ See p. 241, Note †.
§ Also ᚵᛖᚵᛁᚷ *bráthrĕm* might be expected, as Vend. Sâde, p. 357;
ᚵᛖᛈᚷ *patrem (pathrĕm?)*, contrary to the theory of the strong cases
(§. 129.), for *patarĕm*.

SINGULAR.

	Sanskrit.	Zend.	Latin.	Greek.	Gothic.
In.	bhrátr-á,	bráthr-a,	. . . .	. . . . D. Inst. bróthr (see §. 132.).	
D.	bhrátr-ê,	bráthr-ê,	see Loc.	see Loc.	. . . .
Ab.	see Gen.	bráthr-at,	fratr-e(d),	. . . .	. . . .
G.	bhrátur,	bráthr-ó,*	fratr-is,	πατρ-ός,	bróthr-s (see §. 132.).
L.	bhrátar-i,	bráthr-i,†	D. fratr-i,	πατρ-ί,	. . . .
V.	bhrátar,	brátarĕ,‡	frater,	πάτερ,	bróthar.

DUAL.

	Sanskrit.	Zend.	Greek.
N. Acc. Voc.	bhrátar-áu, Vêd. bhrátar-á,	brátar-áo or brátar-a,	πατέρ-ε.
Inst. D. Ab.	bhrátṛi-bhyám.	bratar-ĕ-bya,	πατέρο-ιν.
Gen. Loc.	bhrátr-ós,	bráthr-ó(?)	. . . .

PLURAL.§

	Sanskrit.	Zend.	Latin.	Greek.
Nom. Voc.	bhrátar-as,	brátar-ó,‖	fratr-ês,	πατέρ-ες.
Accus.	bhrátṛi-n,¶	bráthr-eus?**	fratr-ês,	πατέρ-ας.
Instr.	bhrátṛi-bhis,	brátar-ĕ-bis,	. . . .	[G. Ed. p. 325.]
Dat. Abl.	bhrátṛi-bhyas,	brátar-ĕ-byó,	fratr-i-bus,	. . . .
Genitive,	bhrátṛi-n-ám,	bráthr-aṅm,††	fratr-um,	πατέρ-ων.
Locative,	bhrátṛi-shu,	. . . .	. . . .	πατρά-σι.

---

* Vide §. 194. p. 211, l. 1. Note.

† See p. 216 Note ‖. ‡ See §. 44.

§ For the Gothic, which is here wanting, see p. 253, Note ‡.

‖ ᬝᬫᬫᬝᬘᬫᬩᬪ brátarai-cha, "fratresque."

¶ See §. 127. Note.

** Perhaps also bráthr-ó, bráthrai-cha ("fratresque"), according to the analogy of áthr-ó, "ignes," from átar. See §. 239.

†† See p. 266, Note †.

SINGULAR.

	Sanskrit.	Zend.	Greek.	Latin.
N. A. V.	manas,	manô.*	μένος,	genus.
Instr.	manas-á,	mananh-a,†	. . . .	. . . .
Dat.	manas-ê,	mananh-ê,	see Loc.	see Loc.
Abl.	see Gen.	mananh-at,	. . . .	gener-e(d
Gen.	manas-as,	mananh-ô (mananhai-cha),	μένε(σ)-ος,	gener-is.
Loc.	manas-i,	manah-i,(see p. 316, G. ed.) D.	μένε(σ)-ι,	gener-i.

---

* *Manai-cha*, "*mensque*," "*mentemque*."

† M. Burnouf remarks, in his review (in the separate impression, p. 11),
that in this class of words the instrumental ending is generally long.
I, in like manner, had remarked forms enough of this kind with a long *á*,
but in passages where also many *a's*, originally short, appear to be lengthened at the termination, and which, therefore, I was not willing to bring
into account: moreover, the cases could not be included, where, through
the particle ‸ᴕ *cha*, a preceding ‸ᴕ *á* is preserved in its original length.
After deducting these two classes from forms in *anhá*, the computation
might perhaps turn out in favour of the short *a* given above. I have,
however, as yet not applied any closer reckoning: it would, however,
surprise me if, on more exact calculation, but still in departure from the
fate of other polysyllabic words ending with a shortened *a*, the advantage
in this particular case should incline to the side of those words which
retain the long vowel, which I would then gladly restore. No one will
deny that the collation of MSS. is of great importance in deciding many
grammatical and orthographical questions, although I believe I may assert
that even a single lithographed MS. opens a rich field to inquiries and
important grammatical observations: for although it is very full of errors,
it nevertheless shews no systematic opposition to what is correct; and
many expressions, passages, and turns recur so frequently, that, taken
together, they can in a measure supply the place of a comparison of other
MSS. For the rest I had at my command the edition of Olshausen of
the three first chapters and part of the fourth of the Vendidâd, with the
various readings attached to it, so that, through these means, I was not
left entirely destitute of MSS.

DUAL.

	Sanskrit.	Zend.	Greek.
N. Ac. V.	manas-î,	....	μένε(σ)-ε.
I. D. Ab.	manô-bhyâm,	mane-bya (p. 316 G. ed.), D.G.	μενέ(σ)ο-ιν.*
G. L.	manas-ôs,	mananh-ô(?) (p. 297 G. ed.),	....

PLURAL.

	Sanskrit.	Zend.	Greek.	Latin.
N. Ac. V.	manâns-i,	mananh-a,†	μένε(σ)-α,	gener-a.
Instr.	manô-bhis,	mane-bîs,	(μένεσ-φιν,)	....
Dat. Abl.	manô-bhyas,	mane-byô,	see Loc.	gener-i-bus.
Genitive,	manas-âm,	mananh-anm,	μενέ(σ)-ων,	gener-um.
Locative,	manas-su,	manô-hva,	μένεσ-σι,	....

SINGULAR, MASCULINE AND FEMININE. [G. Ed. p. 327.]

	Sanskrit.	Zend.	Greek.
Nom.	durmanâs,	dushmanâo (§. 56ᵇ.).	δυσμενής (§. 146.)
Accus.	durmanas-am,	dushmananh-ĕm,	δυσμενέ(σ)-α(ν).
Voc.	durmanas,	....	δυσμενές.

The rest like the simple word.

DUAL

N. Ac. V.	durmanas-âu,		
Vêda,	durmanas-â,‡	} dushmananh-a (?)	δυσμενέ(σ)-ε.

The rest like the simple word.

PLURAL.

N. Voc.	durmanas-as,	dushmananh-ô (as-cha),	δυσμενέ(σ)-ες.
Accus.	durmanas-as,	dushmananh-o (as-cha),	δυσμενέ(σ)-ας.

The rest like the simple word.

---

* See p. 299, Rem. 2.

† See p. 245, Note ‡. It was, however, from an oversight that I, as was observed at p. 253, Note §. read in the Vendidâd Sâde, p. 127, ꭓꮶꮤꭾ nĕmĕnha: it should be ꭓꮶꮤꭾ nĕmanha, and may also be considered the instrumental singular; then we should have in this passage, which recurs three times, the instrumental in ꭓꮶꮢ anha in both editions three times with a short a.

‡ See p. 230, Note *.

x 2

SINGULAR, NEUTER.

	Sanskrit.	Zend.	Greek.
Nom. Ac. V.	durmanas,	dushmanô (as-cha).	δυσμενές.

The rest like the simple word.

" Remark.—It was remarked in §. 152. (comp. §. 146.), that the Σ in forms like μένος, εὐγενές, belongs to the base, and is not the nominative character; and that the Σ in forms like τετυφός has come from τ, and in like manner belongs to the theme. M. Reimnitz, who, in (p. 54, &c.) his pamphlet mentioned at p. 294, G. ed., agrees with this view, first given in my treatise "On some Demonstrative Bases," wishes to look upon the Σ in the masculine τετυφώς as belonging to the base, and arising out of τ; in which I cannot agree with him, as I, according to the view generally taken, consider the final letters of τετυφώς as marks of the nominative, before [G. Ed. p. 328.] which the final letter of the base is suppressed on account of the incompatible association of τσ (comp. §. 99.), and replaced by lengthening the preceding vowel; as, for example, in μέλας for μέλανς. The Sanskrit has a few bases in n which, differing from the ruling principle (see §. 139.), run parallel in the nominative to the Greek μέλᾱς; thus, panthâs, "the way," from panthan, accusative panthân-am. Only in this panthâs the lengthening of the a can be less regarded as a compensation for the rejected n than in the Greek, because it extends also to the other full cases (§. 129.), with the exception of the vocative; but perhaps the lengthening of the a has originally taken place only in the nominative, and has thence imparted itself, when the reason of this prolongation was no longer perceived, to those cases which otherwise stood upon an equal footing with the nominative. Thus one says महान् mahân, "great" (from the theme mahant, properly a participle present from मह् mah, " to grow "), with the vowel of the concluding syllable lengthened, according to the analogy of the Greek form, as λέγων. The Sanskrit word, however, retains the long vowel

also in the other strong cases (*mahántam* "*magnum*," *mahántas*
"*magni*," *mahántáu*, "μεγάλω"), with the exception of the vocative; while the usual participles present leave the *a* short
in all the strong cases. In most exact accordance, however,
with the Greek participle present stand the Sanskrit possessive adjectives, which are formed by the suffix *vant*
(Greek εντ for ϝεντ, in μελιτόεις and others) and *mant* (in the
weak cases *vat*, *mat*). These lengthen, that is to say the *a*
only, in the nominative singular; so, for example, *dhanaván*,
" *dives*"[*] (from *dhana*, "riches"), *dhanavant-am*, *dhanavant-áu*,
dhanavant-as, as λέγων, λέγοντα, λεγόντω, λεγόντες.

OLD SCLAVONIC DECLENSION.†   [G. Ed. p. 329.]

255. Before we enter upon the province of Sclavonic
Grammar, we must endeavour to explain its system
of sounds; and although it is not requisite to specify
all the minutiæ of the subject, we must, nevertheless,
bring into notice those parts which are indispensable to
the understanding of the Grammar. It is therefore our
principal object, in the following remarks, to exhibit the
connection of the Old Sclavonic sounds with those of the
elder languages, of which they are either the true trans-

---

* If, as has been remarked in another place, the suffix वत् *vant* has
maintained itself in the Latin in the form *lent* (as *opulents*), it would not
be surprising if the weak form वत् *vat*, without the interchange of *v* with *l*,
but with the weakening of the *a* to *i*, had its representative in the Latin
divit, which stands in the same relation to *dhanavat*, by passing over the
middle syllable, as *malo* to *mavolo*.

† It is stated by Professor Bopp, in the preface to the second published
portion of this Grammar, commencing with the formation of cases in
general, that it had not occurred to him to direct his attention at an
earlier period to the Sclavonic tongues: having subsequently considered
the subject, he found sufficient reason to include them in the same
family of languages, and accordingly devotes to its principles of declension
the supplementary section which follows.—*Editor*.

missions, or corruptions more or less vitiated. We give
therefore, for the first time, a history of the Sclavonic
sounds, in which, however, as is natural, as far as their value
is concerned, we have nothing new to bring forward; and in
this respect follow only the teaching of native grammarians.

(a.)—The Old Sanskrit व a has so far experienced, in the
Sclavonic, an exactly similar fate to that which has befallen it
in the Greek, that it is most frequently supplied by e or o
(e, o), which are always short: it very rarely remains a. In
the interior of the bases, also, ε and o are interchanged as in
Greek; and as, for example, λόγος is related to λέγω,
so, in the Old Sclavonic, is brod, "ferry," to bredû, "I wade
through;" voz, "carriage," to vezû, "I ride in a carriage."
And as, in the Greek, the vocative λόγε is related to the
theme ΛΟΓΟ, so is, in the Old Sclavonic, rabe, "O slave," to
rabo, nominative rab, "a slave." The o has more
weight than e, but a more than o; and hence a
corresponds most frequently to a Sanskrit â, so that,
for instance, in the Old Sclavonic, forms in a answer to
the feminine bases in आ â (comp. vdova, "widow," with
विधवा vidhavâ), which, in the vocative, is in like manner
abbreviated to o (vdovo!), as above o to e. As final
vowel, also, of the first member of a compound, a is
weakened to o; for instance, vodo-pad, "waterfall," vodo-
poï, "water-drinker," for voda-; just as in the Greek
Μουσο-τραφής, Μουσο-φίλης, and similar compounds, which
[G. Ed. p. 330.]   have shortened the feminine α or η to o.
Even if, therefore, a is in the Old Sclavonic a short vowel,
I nevertheless regard it, in respect to grammar, as the long
o; so that in this the Old Sclavonic stands in a reversed
relation to the Gothic, in which a has shewn itself to us as
the short of ô, and, in case of abbreviation, ô would become
a, exactly as in the Old Sclavonic a becomes o.

(b.)— इ i and ई î both appear in the Old Sclavonic as i,
and the difference of the quantity is removed, at least I

do not find that a longer or shorter *i* is anywhere spoken of. Let *schivû*, "I live," be compared with जीवामि *jîvâmi*; *sila*, "virtue," with शील *śila*; and, on the other hand, *vidyeti*, "to see," with the root विद् *vid*, "to know," to the Guna form of which, वेद्मि *védmi*, the Old Sclavonic *vyemy* (abbreviated from *vyedmy*, infin. *vyes-t* for *vyed-ti*,) "I know," assimilates itself, so that *vid* and *vyed* in the Sclavonic appear as two different roots. The short इ *i*, however, appears frequently in the Old Sclavonic also in the corruption to *e* (є), as in the Greek and the Old High German (§. 72.); that is to say, the bases in *i* shew, in several cases, *e* for *i*, and the numeral three (त्रि *tri*) appears frequently in composition in the form *tre*, e. g. *trepûtye*, "trivium." So, also, *pûte-shestvye*, ὁδοιπορία from *PŪTI* (§. 260.). The *i* is also very frequently *suppressed, e. g. in the 3d person plural *dadyat*, "they give," Sanskrit ददति *dadati*; *sût*, "they are," Sanskrit सन्ति *santi*. Where *i* forms a diphthong with a vowel preceding it, it is marked in the old writing with a short mark, which we retain, e. g. *boï*, "strife."

(*c*).—उ *u* and ऊ *û* have, in the Old Sclavonic, in the forms which are retained most correctly, both become *y*.† In this manner, for instance, *by* (infin. *by-ti*) answers to भू

---

* The suppression here noticed of final *i* refers to Dobrowsky's incorrect orthography. In point of fact, however, the final *i* in Old Sclavonic has either been retained unaltered, or has become ь *y*; e. g., that which Dobrowsky, l. c., writes *dadjat*, "they give," *sût*, "they are," should be corrected to ДАДАТЬ, *dadanty*, САТЬ *santy*. Regarding the nasalized vowels, see §. 783. Remark.

† We express, as in Polish, the *yery* or dull *i* by *y*, as, like the Greek *υ*, where it is original it supplies the place of the old short or long *u*. It is pronounced in Russian, according to Reiff (by Gretsch II. p. 666.), as in the French *oui*, spoken very short and monosyllabically; according to Heym, nearly like *ü*, in union with a very short *i* (Heym, p. 5). This does not, however, remain the same in all positions of this letter (Reiff, l. c.), and it sounds after consonants other than labials like a dull thick *i* ("*i sourd et étouffé*").

bhû, "to be;" *svekry,* "mother-in-law," to स्वश्रू *śvaśrû; mysky,* "mouse," to मूष *mûsha; syn,* "son," to सूनु *sûnu; chetyri,* τέσσαρες, with चतुर् *chatur* (in the theme), nominative masculine चत्वारस् *chatwâras.* The instances of *y* for उ *u* are, nevertheless, more rare than those where *y* corresponds to the long ऊ *û;* for the short *u,* as in the Old High German (§. 70.), has for the most part [G. Ed. p. 331.]   become *o;* and thus, for example, *snocha,* "daughter-in-law," answers to स्नुषा *snushâ; oba,* "both," to उभा *ubhâ* (Vêdic form), Zend ubâ.   Hence, also, the old *u* declension has, in many cases, become similar to the *o* declension, which, according to (*a.*), has arisen from अ *a;* and, on the other side, *o* may also, but only in substantives, participate in those forms which belong only to the genuine *u* declension: whence it is easily perceived that the genius of the language could not everywhere distinguish further the two kinds of *o,* in their history, indeed, far separated from one another, but phonetically identical.

(*d*).—Unorganic *y,* i. e. *y* as representative of original vowels other than उ *u* or ऊ *û,* is not uncommon in the grammar; that is to say, the personal termination *my* (1st person plural), like the Latin *mus,* has arisen from the more ancient *mas;* and if the bases in *a* (for आ *â*) have *y* in the nominative plural (*vdovy,* "*viduæ* "), still the *y* here is so much the less to be looked upon as a case termination, as no account could be given of *y* in this sense; and with bases in *ya* the *a* of the base is also really retained (*volya,* "*voluntates*"). But as the *y* exerts the force of an *Umlaut* on an *o* succeeding it, by which that vowel is changed to an *e,* so I think that to an *i* following the *o,* without the intervention of another letter, the force of a reactive *Umlaut* must be ascribed, even if this force is not everywhere exerted, and that some *y*'s must be declared to be the *Umlauts* of *o·* that is to say, as soon as so much has been re-

cognised in the Old Sclavonic adjectives, that their
bases all end either in *o* or *yo* (changed by the *Umlaut*
to *ye*), and are thus sister forms to the Greek, like ΑΓΑΘΟ,
'ΑΓΙΟ; and of the Sanskrit, as श्वेत *sućta*, "white," दिव्य *divya*,
"heavenly";—so soon, I say, as the abbreviation of the
base in the masculine nominative has been recognised
(*nov*, *novus*, for *novo*), then will it be no longer said with
Dobrowsky (p. 318) that the definite adjectives are derived
from the primitives (indefinite) by annexing, according
to the measure of the final letter of the primitive, either
yi̇̆ or *ii̇̆*.* If, however, I may trust that I have obtained
an accurate knowledge of the organization of the Old
Sclavonic grammar on any point, it is on this, that the affix
in the nominative singular of definite adjectives consists
not in *yi̇̆* or *ii̇̆*, but in *i* as a mutilation of *yo* from *ya*
(य *ya*), and in the feminine of *ya* from *yâ* [G. Ed. p. 332].
(या *yâ*). This also appears to me subject to no manner
of doubt, that if, for example, the compound word *svyatyi̇̆*
comes from the word *svyato*, "holy," its acknowledged
theme, the *y* is a euphonic product from *o*, through the influence of the *i* which is added to it. This *i* has, in some
cases, in which it has been dropped, still in a degree, in its
euphonic operation, left its reflection, and thereby the
proof of its former existence. Thus, for instance,
svyaty-m, "*per sanctum*," from the older *svyatyi̇̆m*,
svyaty-ch, "*sanctorum*," and "*in sanctis*," from *svyatyi-ch*,
corresponds to the indefinite forms *svyato-m*, *svyatye-ch*
(for *svyato-ch*).† At times, through the said pronominal
syllable *i*, the preceding *o* may be changed at will into *y*

---

* Dobr. also himself, p. 403, considers simple *i* or *ii* as the definitive
adjunct; but in considering, as he there does, *blagyi̇̆* as the confluence of
blag and *ii*, he appears to look upon the *y* as having arisen from the *i* of
the suffix, and not to acknowledge in it the final vowel of the simple
adjective root.

† In the oldest MSS., according to Dobr. p. 502, the more full forms
ïch, *yi̇̆m*, *yi̇̆mi* occur in the plural, for *ym*, *ych*, *ymi*

or not: thus the interrogative exhibits the forms *kyĭ*, "*quis?*" (Dobr. 500 and 343.), *kyĭm*, "*per quem?*" *kyĭch*, "*in quibus, quorum?*" *kyĭm*, "*quibus?*" *kyĭmi*, "*per quos?* with *koĭ*, *koĭm*, *koĭch*, *koĭmi*. The possessive pronouns allow no euphonic reaction at all to the demonstrative *i*, which forms the last member of them, and they always retain their radical *o*; *e. g. moĭ*, " *meus*," *moĭm*, "*per meum*," not *myĭ*, *myĭm*. As to the definite form of the adjective bases in *yo*, which Dobrowsky forms through the addition of *ŭ*, I have not the slightest doubt that here, also, a simple *i* is the defining element, for the first *i* is clearly the vocalization of the *y* of the primitive base; so that therefore, for example, *siniĭ* "the blue," is to be divided, not into *sin-ŭ*, but into *sini-ĭ*. The primitive adjective is sounded in the nominative which is deprived of all inflection and of the last vowel of the base—*siny*, the *y* of which appears as *i* in the nominative plural masculine, just as in the definite pronoun, *sini*, "*cærulei*," *sinii, oi* "*cærulei*." In order, however, here fully to explain the nature and origin of the definite declension, and not hereafter to be compelled to repeat what is already settled, it may be stated that its pronominal defining addition is identical with the Sanskrit relative base य *ya*, which is most correctly preserved in the Lithuanian, in which language **ya* signifies "he" (*ya-m*, "to him," *ya-mė*, "in him"). The nominative *yis*, "he" (for *yas*), has given the *y* an assimilating influence, as is the case with all bases in *ya* (§. 135.). The feminine, also, is pronounced in the nominative, through assimilation, *yi* for *ya*; but the genitive *yos*, and all the other cases, are easily perceived through the declension of *rankà*, "hand," and *giesme*, "song," [G. Ed. p. 333.] from *GIESMYA* (p. 169, Note). The

---

* Written *ja* in the text. This passage furnishes a good reason for writing the Germanic *j* by *y*, as has been done throughout this translation.

Old Sclavonic has, in all the masculine bases ending with a vowel, suppressed this vowel in the nominative and accusative; and since the vowel has dropped from the Sanskrit-Lithuanian base ऩ *ya, ya*—which, according to (*a.*), makes one expect *yo* in the Old Sclavonic, from which, according to (*n.*), must be formed *ye**—the *y* must be changed into a vowel; hence, *i*, "he," "him," which must, therefore, on no account be placed together with the Latin-Gothic *is*, from the base *i*. In the nominative singular masculine, however, this Sclavonic pronoun occurs in all the three genders, not isolated, but in union with the particle *sche*, which has preserved to it the old relative meaning: *i-sche* means as well "*qui*" as "*quem*"; *ya-sche*, "*quæ*"; *yû-sche*, "*quam*"; and *ye-sche* "*quod*." Now as *i* means "he," *ya*, "she," and *ye*, "it," I could not imagine how one could create the definitive adjective forms *svyaty-î*, *svyata-ya*, *svyato-e* (for *svyatoye*), accusative *svyaty-î*, *svyatâ-yû*, *svyato-e*, in their opposition to the indefinites *svyat(o)*, *svyata*, *svyato*, differently from Dobrowsky (p. 493), and perhaps other grammarians before him, have done, namely, by the addition of the pronoun here under discussion;† for this pronominal suffix supplies the place of the article of other languages; and the Lithuanian language uses the same pronoun

---

* Hence in the genitive *ye-go*, dative *ye-mû*, loc. *ye-m*, the *e* of which Dobrowsky wrongly ascribes to flexion, because he everywhere seeks the base in the nominative. However, the base *ye* has not fully maintained itself before all terminations beginning with a consonant, but become, in like manner, shortened to *i*: in *i-m*, "*per eum*," and *iis*, *i-mi* "*per eos*," *i-ch*, "*eorum*," "*in iis*," for *ye-m*, &c.

† What Grimm (by Wuk, p. xl.) remarks against this declaration has not convinced me; least of all can I, for the above, reasons, concede to him that the *i* of *svyatyi* has any thing to do with the *a* of *blinda*, "the blind" (from *blindan*, §. 140.); so that *svyatyi* would belong to the indefinite declension; and, on the other hand, *svyat*, contrary to the Sclavonic Grammarians, would be to be removed from the indefinite into the definite forms.

for the same object, *i. e.* equally in the emphatic, or,
as it is also termed, definite declension of the adjective;
and certainly so, that, through all cases, both the adjective which precedes and the pronoun which concludes are
declined, while, in the Sclavonic, in most cases the pronoun
only is provided with the inflexions of case, but in some
[G. Ed. p. 334.]   it has utterly disappeared, and in others
is still to be recognised in the *y* for *o* mentioned above.

(*e.*)—The Sanskrit diphthong ए *ê* I have found always rendered, in the Old Sclavonic, by *ye*, in similar forms; so
that after weakening the ए *ê*, to compensate for this,
the semi-vowel *y* has made its appearance, to which, in
this union, a particular legitimacy would be, according
to (*c.*), to be ascribed.   Let *pyena,* "foam," be compared
with फेन *phêna*; *svyet* "light," with श्वेत *svêta*; *vyemy,* "I
know," with वेद्मि *vêdmi.*   The most important cases in
the grammar wth *ye* corresponding to ए *ê* are the dual
case forms of the feminine and neuter, and those of the
imperative, in accordance with the Sanskrit potential of
the first conjugation.

(*f.*)—The Sanskrit diphthong ओ *ô* (from *a + u*) is represented in the Old Sclavonic by *û* (ѵ);[*]   so that the first

---

[*] Although this vowel may at times be pronounced short, still this much,
at least, is certain, that, according to its origin and its definition, it is long.
In Bohemian it appears in two forms, as *au* and *u*: the former is pronounced *ou,* but the writing points to an older and different pronunciation,
in which the *a* was accurately preserved in its place: the *u* is pronounced
short, whence, however, it cannot be deduced that this short *u* perhaps
corresponds to the Sanskrit उ and Greek ὔ, and that *au* is its intensitive
or Guna; but, on the contrary, only the *u* retained in the *au* corresponds to the Sanskrit उ *u,* and the *u* which stands alone in Bohemian
is a weakening of the *au*; so that, from this, the concluding element *u*
alone is left: etymologically, that is to say, the Bohemian *au,* as also *u,*
answers to the Sanskrit ओ *ô,* and also to the Sclavonic *û* (ѵ), only that
the former is phonetically more exact, and without the loss brought about
by time.   Hence, also, *usta* (written *vsta*) "*ora*" corresponds to the Sanskrit ओष्ठ *ôshtha,* "the lip": more complete, however, is *austne,* "by word
of

element of the Indian diphthong has assimilated itself to
the second, and, in conjunction with it, presents a similar long vowel, as, in the Greek *ʊ* (*ou*), two heterogeneous vowels, according to pronunciation, have united
themselves in a similar measure. As, according to (*u*),
the Indian short *a* has, in the Sclavonic, mostly become
short *o*, we must consider the first element in the diphthong *û* also (so we write the *ʊ*) to be *o*; and it becomes visible, too, in this form, when *û* is resolved before
vowels into *ov*, (compare βο(F)ός from Bʊ, [G. Ed. p. 335.]
§. 123.), while the Indian वो *ô* becomes *av* before a vowel
(गवि *gavi* = βοFί, from गो *gô*). Now as, in the Sanskrit, उ *u*,
ऊ *û*, rise to *ô* through Guna (§. 26.), and *stô-shyâmi*
appears as the future of *stu*, so in the Old Sclavonic,
in like manner, *y* (*ey*) is interchanged with *û*; so that *bû*
in *bû-du*, "I shall be," must pass as the Guna form of *by*
(in *byti*, "to be"): but if a class of nouns, which in the
nominative-accusative terminate in a consonant or in
yerr (see *k*.), exhibit, in many oblique cases, the syllable
ov before vowel-endings, this *ov* must neither be considered, with Dobrowsky, for an augment added to the
base, nor can it be deduced from forms like *synovi*, "from
a son" (Sanskrit सूनवे *sûnav-e*, from *sûnu*), *synov-ê*, "sons"
(सूनवस् *sûnav-as*), that *syn*, in the nominative-accusative,
is an abbreviation of *synû*; and that therefore the *yerr*,
when it is added to the form *syn*, is a representative
or weak remainder of *û*: but it is clear, from (*c*.),
that *syn*, "*filius*," "*filium*," if its final vowel, in its
most genuine form, had remained to it, would sound
syny, from which *synov* is the Guna intensitive, the
ov of which has arisen from *û* through the influence

---

f mouth"; and even for *vsta* is to be found *austa* (Dobr. Böhm. Lehrg.
.4.): *ruka* corresponds to the Lithuanian *ranka*, "hand"; and *hus* to the
anskrit हंस *hahsa*, "goose"; for which, according to p. 319. *rauka, hausa*
'as to have been expected. A distinction must here. according to §. 783.
temark q. v., be made between oy *û*, and ⅄ *uñ*.

of the vowel following it, but has remained in the
genitive plural also, after the ending has been dropped.
Let *synov,* "*filiorum,*" be compared with the Gothic
suniv-ê (§. 247.)   As, in the Sanskrit, the substantive
bases in *u* adopt the Guna form of the *u* before the
vowels of the derivative suffix, so it is very remarkable
that, in the Old Sclavonic bases in *y,* also, this vowel
appears before certain derivative suffixes in its Guna
form ; *e. g. domov-it* from *dom* (*DOMY*), "house"; *binov-at,*
"debtor," from *byn* (*BYNY*).*   Derivative substantives
and adjectives in *ov, ev* (theme *ovo, evo,* the latter for
yovo, see *n.*), correspond to the Sanskrit in चव *ava* ; as
पाण्डव *pândav-a* (nominative *as*), "descendant of Pându";
आर्तव *ârtava,* "seasonable," from ऋतु *ritu,* "season": so,
in Old Sclavonic, *Adamov,* "Adamite," from *Adam*
(*ADAMY*); *zarev* for *zaryev,* "kingly," from *zar* (theme
ZARYY).   For these formations, therefore, we must not,
with Dobrowsky (322, 323), assume a suffix *ov* or *ev.*
but we must look upon the *o* alone, which, in the nominative, is suppressed, as the derivative suffix (*ADAMOV-O,*
ZAREV-O).   Through the Vriddhi increase (§. 29.) the
Old Sclavonic *y* becomes *av,* because *a,* according to (*a.*),
usually corresponds to आ *â* : hence, from the root *by,*
"to be," comes the causal *baviti* (infinitive), as in the
[G. Ed. p. 336.]   Sanskrit भावयितुम् *bhâvayitum.*   But
though *staviti* occurs as the causal of *sta,* this form may
have arisen in the perverted feeling of the language as an
irregularly analogous word to *baviti.*   In order, then, still
more to establish, by a few other examples, the representation of the Indian ओ *ô* or चव *av* by the Sclavonic *û,* we
find *ûst,* "mouth," correspond to ओष्ठ *ôshtha,* "lip"; *shûi*
"*sinister*" (theme *SHUYO*), to सव्य *savya* ; *bûditi,* "to
awake"—a causal, whose primitive *bûdyeti* has entirely

---

* Dobrowsky supports himself in these cases by calling *ov* a prefix (p. 329).

lost the vowel of the root—to वोधयितुम् *bôdhayitum,* also
" to awake," from बुध् *budh,* " to know."   Thus *gûbiti* is
the causal of *gyb-nú* (1. P.), and *stúditi* of *styd-nú* (Dobr.
360, 361.); while *vyesiti* is the causal of *visyeti* (see *e.*), as,
in the Sanskrit, वेशयितुम् *vêśayitum,* " to cause to enter,"
from विश् *viś,* " to go in."

(*g.*)—As the nasals[*] easily resolve themselves into *u,* so
the second element of the diphthong *û* sometimes also
supplies the place of a nasal in the cognate languages;
e.g. rûka, " a hand," Lithuanian *ranka; pûty,* " a way,"
Sanskrit पन्थास् *panthâs, id.* Latin *pons; goluby,* " a dove,"
columba; gûsy, " a goose," हंस *hansa.*   The Polish has
preserved the old nasal in *golamb,* " a dove," *gansie,* " a
gosling," *gansior,* " a gander," and in many similar
cases.   Hereby the *û* in the accusative of bases in *a*
(from आ *â*), which are for the most part feminine, is
remarkably explained; compare *vdovû* from *vdova,* " a
widow," with विधवाम् *vidhavâm,* " *viduam.*"   Therefore
vdovû is to be derived from *vdovo-m* for *vdova-m* (see *a.*);
so that the *a* which is weakened to an *o* is contracted
with the nasal mark of the case to *û.*   This view is further
supported by the consideration, that in Polish, also, the
corresponding feminine declension marks the final vowel
of the base with the same sign which, in the middle of
a word, expresses a nasal, which is governed according
to the organ of the following letter, but at the end,
probably through a corruption of sound, is said to have
an equal value with a ringing *h.*   This nasalizing mark
recurs also in the Polish verb, and, indeed, exactly in
such a place where one had to expect a nasal, *i.e.* in
the 1st person singular and 3d person plural; and thus,
in Bandtke's second and third conjugation, the so
marked *ę, e.g.* in *piekę,* "I bake," supplies the place of
the *am* of the first conjugation, as *czytam,* " I read."

---

[*] Cf. §. 783. Remark.

The Old Sclavonic has, however, excepting some ano-malous remains of an older formation, *û* in all the con-jugations; and, according to what has been said, it admits of no doubt, that in the second part of this diph-thong (*o* + *ŭ*) the personal character *m*, and in the first part of the diphthong the conjunctive vowel, is retained. When therefore, in the 1st person, an *o* corresponds to the *e* (ε) of *nes-e-shi*, " thou carriest," *nes-e-t*, " he carries "—

[G. Ed. p. 337.]   for *nesû* is for *nes-o-ŭ* for *nes-o-m* from *nes-e-m*—it must be assumed that the conjunctive vowel *e*, before its confluence with the *ŭ*, which has arisen out of *m*, has passed into *o*; as in Greek *ου* arises by the contraction of *e* and *o*, through the transition of ε into *o* and *o* into *υ*. The same relation is to be found in the Old Sclavonic in the 3d person plural, where, corresponding to *nes-e-m*, " we carry," *nes-e-te*, " ye carry " (comp. λέγ-ε-τε), the form *nesent* is expected, but in place of it occurs *nesût* in sur-prising accord with the Greek λέγουσι for λέγονσι from λέγοντι. The Polish has, like the Bohemian, relinquished the character of the 3d person in the plural, as well as for the most part in the singular, but everywhere retains, in the first, the old and more powerful *a* (ᄝ), and marks this with the diacritical sign mentioned above, which, in the middle of a word, supplies the place of a nasal function; thus, *są*, " they are," corresponds to the Sanskrit सन्ति *santi*, Sclavonic *sût*. The Bohemian has also, in many conjugations, retained the old conjunctive vowel *a* in the 3d person plural, but, like the Sclavonic, permitted the *n* to dissolve into a *u*; therefore, in *wezau*, " *vehûnt* " (*wez-e-me*, " *vehimus*," *wez-e-te*, " *vehitis* "), the *u* answers to the *n* of वहन्ति *vahanti*, " *vehunt*," and the *u* which, in Bohe-mian, is united with an *a*, is essentially different from that which stands alone; for the latter answers to the Old Sclavonic diphthong *û* (ᲂ�), but the former only to the latter portion of the *û*, which, in the Old Sclavonic, never stands alone, at least never occurs as *ŭ*, but as *y* (ᲊ).

If, then, through what has been said, the vocalization of
the *m* or *n*, which is of such frequent occurrence in the Sclavonic, has been shewn with sufficient clearness, it is remarkable that conversely, also, the latter portion of the *û* (*v*) has
occasionally been hardened into a nasal; and thus *búdú*, "I
will be," is in Polish *bendę* (written *będę*).

(*h.*)—In certain cases an old *á* (आ) unorganically supplies
the place of the Sclavonic *ú*, *i.e.* in the instrumental of
pronouns without gender, and all feminines; thus,
vdovoy-ú, "through the widow," answers to विधवया *vidha-
vay-á*; and *toboy-ú*, "through thee," to त्वया *tway-á*. Denominatives also, in *áyá* (1st per. pres.), in the Old Sclavonic, correspond to the Sanskrit in नामामि *áyámi*, as शब्दायामि
śabdáyámi, "I sound," from शब्द *śabda*, "a sound,"; चिरायामि
chiráyámi, "I hesitate," from चिर *chira*, "long": thus,
in the Sclavonic, *zieláyá*, "I greet," "I kiss," from *ziel*,
(*ZIELO*), "healthy": *vdováyá* from *vdova*, "widow" (Dobr.
p. 372.). Finally, words in *án* (*ŪNO*) answer, as it appears,
to the Sanskrit participles of the middle voice, in *ána*, as
युञ्जान *yunjána*, "uniting." from युज् *yuj*; so in the Old
Sclavonic, *perún*, (*PERŪNO*), "*Deus*   [G. Ed. p. 338.]
tonans," from the root *per*, "to shake"; *byegún*, "runner"
(*BYEGŪNO*), from *BYEG* "to run" (Dobr. p. 289.).

(*i.*)—There are in the Sclavonic alphabet two marks, which
by some are called *litteræ aphonæ*, but by Gretsch semi-
vowels; I mean the so-called soft *yer*,[*] and the hard *yerr*.
The former is represented by Gretsch as half *i*, and by
his translator, Reiff (47), as answering to the tones
'mouillés' of French (compare Kopitar, p. 5); and thus
schal[b], "sympathy," and *ogon*[b], "fire," are, in respec-
to the soft *yer* compared with the pronunciation of
travail and *cicogne*. This *yer*, therefore, denotes a tone

---

[*] In the original *jer*, pronounced, however, *yer;* and hence *y* has been
substituted for *j* in all that follows.— *Editor.*

Y

which is rather to be called a *y* than an *i* [*] ; and it may be said that in *schal* [b] and *ogon* [b] one hears quite as much of a *y* as can be heard of this semi-vowel after a consonant preceding it. Hence we mark it with a *y*, and write the above words *schaly, ogony*, Old Sclavonic *ogny*. In the words, too, which end with it in the uninflected nominative and accusative singular, it occurs in several oblique cases as a distinct proper *y*, *e.g.* in *zarya*, " *regis*," *zaryu*, " *regi*," from *zary*, " *rex*," " *regem*." On the consonant which precedes it this *yer* has an influence which renders its pronunciation more mild, because its sound is somewhat broken by the *y*, which throws back its sound. Etymologically the *yer* corresponds either to a final *i* of the cognate languages, as in *yesty*, " he is " (अस्ति *asti*, ἐστί, Lithuanian *esti*), *kosty*, " bones" (अस्थि *asthi*), or in the nominative and accusative singular of masculine substantives and adjectives, to a *y* (य *y*), from which a vowel has dropped; for the theme of *siny*, " *cæruleus*," concludes neither with *i* nor with *y*, but with *yo* (euphonically *ye*, see *n*.); whose final vowel, suppressed in the nominative and accusative masculine, appears, however, in the feminine *sinya*, in its extension to *a*, while the neuter *sine* for *sinye* has rejected the *y*.

(*k*.)—The hard *yerr* is represented by Gretsch as a semi *o*, but by Reiff, more correctly in my opinion, it is compared to the French silent *e* and the Hebrew *schva*: it is therefore, to use the expression, equivalent to "nothing"; and one cannot perceive of what vowel the small, still perhaps remaining vowel part of it is the residue. Consonants preceding it have a stronger and free pronunciation ; [G. Ed. p. 339.]   and Kopitar (p. 5) tells us that they are pronounced before it sharp, and without echo, and that it is for this reason called the hard *yerr*, and not on account of its own pronunciation. We require, therefore, in the

---

[*] In the Carniolan dialect this sound has mostly disappeared; but where it has remained it is also written by a *y*; as, *kony*, "horse."

Roman character, no substitute for this mark, and Dobrowsky also omits it at the end of words. Etymologically, however, this *yerr* always represents a suppressed mute vowel, only not always an *o*, nor, as Grimm conjectures (in his valuable Preface to Wuk's Servian Gramm. p. xxxiv) a *u*. Rather, each of the three short fundamental vowels—*a* (as represented also by *o*, *e*), *i*, *u*, (for which may stand *y*, *o*),—is very frequently dropped at the end of words; and although the *i* is seldom entirely suppressed, more generally throwing back its sound as *y*, nevertheless the vowel suppressed after the *m* of *rabo-m*, "*per servum*," and in Russian replaced by *yerr*, is clearly, as we gather from the Lithuanian, an *i*.

(*l*.)—I* believe I may assert, that in the whole extent of the structure of the Sclavonic language, at least in all the conditions of its noun and verb, not a single final consonant occurs after which some termination, which, through the cognate languages can be pointed out as beginning with a vowel, has not been dropped. Thus, the base *NEBES*, "*cœlum*," forms, in the genitive plural, likewise *nebes*, but the vanished termination is, in Sanskrit, नाम् *ám* (नभसाम् *nabhasám*, "*cœlorum*"), Greek ων (νεφέ(σ)ων), Latin *um*, Gothic *è*. The real final consonants, however, which, in the truly-preserved elder dialects of the Indo-European family, stand as the foundation of the word, have utterly disappeared in Sclavonic polysyllables; *e. g.* from नस् *as*, ες is formed, in the. nominative plural, *e* (ε); and *synov-e* answers to forms like सूनवस् *súnav-as*, βότρυ-ες.

(*m*.)—As far as regards the writing of those consonants which, in the Sclavonic alphabet, properly correspond to the Roman, we express the sound of the French *j* (*zivyete*, in the Carniolan *sh*), as in Zend (§. 65.), by *sch*, that of our German *sch* (= श) by *sh* as in Sanskrit,

---

* Cf. §. 783. Remark.

and also as, in Sanskrit, the *tsch* by *ch:* for the
sound of the Greek ζ ($=ds$) we retain ζ, and use z for
the sound of our German z ($=ts$): for χ we write *ch*. In
regard to etymology, it is important to call attention
to the relation of this letter to sibilants, by means
of which *snocha*, "daughter-in-law," corresponds to
the Sanskrit स्नुषा *snushâ*. *Ch* also, in declension
and conjugation before certain vowels, passes into *s*
[G. Ed. p. 340.] (Dobr. pp. 39, 41), and in some cases
into *sh* (Dobr. 41.). Finally, in preterites like *dach*, " I
gave," *dachom*, " we gave," the *ch* returns to the *s* (स *s*, Σ)
whence it has proceeded, in the cases where a personal
ending beginning with a *t* follows it; hence, *daste*, " ye
gave," *dasta*, " ye two" and " they two gave."* As the
vowels exercise a multifarious influence in the transformation of gutturals preceding them, we will further remark that the *ch* under discussion maintains itself in the
3d person plural before *û*, but before *a* appears as *sh* ;
hence, *dasha* or *dachû*, " they gave."

(*n.*)—†For the semi-vowel y (य् *y*) the Cyrillian alphabet
gives the Greek ι, excepting in the cases for which the
inventor of the character has provided by particular
letters set together according to their value, which, at
the same time, express the y with the following vowel ;
that is to say, *ya* is never written by two letters. It
would, however, for this reason, be wrong to assume a
vowel *ya*, as this syllable, however it may be written,
still always unites in itself two sounds. For *ye*, also,

---

* Dobrowsky has, however, as t appears to me, not perceived the
irrefragable connection between the *ch* of *dach* and the *s* of *daste*, for he
considers the *ch* and *ste*, &c. as personal terminations (pp. 264. 383. 397) ;
and hence he nowhere informs us that *ch* before *t* passes into *s*. More on
this subject when we come to the verb.

† The vowels mentioned here, preceded by *y*, are, with the exception of
ѥ *ye*, and ѣ *yĕ*, nasalised vowels (see §. 783. Remark) ; and hence *pyaty*,
" five," must be pronounced *pańty* (in the original character ПАТЬ).

Cyril has provided by a simple sign, and *yú* is expressed by an *o* in conjunction with an *ι*. But *y* often appears in Sclavonic as a dialectic addition before vowels foreign to the cognate languages. Compare *yesmy*, "I am," *yam* (for *yadmy*), "I eat," *pyaty*, "five," *desyaty*, "ten," *yedin*, "one," with the corresponding Sanskrit forms, *asmi*, *admi*, *panchan*, *daśun*, *ádi* (*primus*). An *o* which follows is, in accordance with similar forms which we have observed in the Zend and Lithuanian (§. 137. and p. 174, Note*), changed into *e* through the influence of a *y* preceding it. In like manner, in accordance with the Zend and Lithuanian, the *y*, after it has assimilated a vowel following it, has often itself disappeared, and has left behind only its effect, and thereby the proof of its former existence.*

---

* Dobrowsky does not express himself with sufficient clearness regarding this form, when he says (cap. II. §. iii.) that *o* after *y* and liquid consonants is changed into *e*. According to this, one would believe that, besides *y*, certain other consonants had the power of changing an *o* following them into *e*. Dobrowsky understands—which, however, as far as I know, he nowhere expressly says—under "*consonæ liquidæ*," those which, in consequence of a following *yer* (*y*), have retained a more flowing and softer pronunciation; while he calls the consonants without *yer* "*consonæ solidæ*" (comp. l. c. p. 267); so that no consonant is by nature and of itself alone liquid, but receives this quality through a following *yer* (a *y* without a vowel). Thus, in Dobrowsky's second masculine declension, the consonants *r*, *ch*, and *ζ*, in *zary*, "king," *vrachy*, "physician," and *knyaζy*, "prince," are liquid. But as these words in the instrumental form *zarem*, *brachem*, *knyaζem*, Dobrowsky ascribes the *e* for *o* to the influence of a liquid consonant; while, according to my opinion, the consonants in these forms have no concern whatever in transforming *o* into *e*, but for *zarem*, &c. *zaryem* must originally have stood. And as in this form the *y* is the full semi-vowel, not entirely without a vowel sound, and therefore not the expression of the *yer* without a vowel which softens the consonant preceding it—as in the abbreviated nominative *zary*—so the *r* also, in *zaryem*, was not liquid, and has not, according to my opinion, become liquid after the dropping of the semi-vowel; at least, I find it nowhere
stated

[G. Ed. p. 341.]   256. We must now, in order to be able
to compare the true case-suffixes of the Old Sclavonic with
those of the cognate languages, first of all endeavour to ascer-
tain the final letter of the kinds of base which occur, as they
have for the most part been rubbed off in the singular
nominative, whence it has appeared as if these letters,
where they again present themselves in the oblique cases,
either belonged to the case termination, or were an addition
equally foreign to the base and to the termination, which has
been termed "augment" by Dobrowsky.   After becoming
[G. Ed. p. 342.]   acquainted with the true base, the case terminations assume, in many points, an entirely different shape
from what Dobrowsky has represented (p. 460), with whom
we cannot concede to the neuter a nominative termination
o or *e*, but perhaps the advantage of having preserved, in preference to the masculine, the final vowel of the theme in this
case.   For the practical use of the language, and to keep
simply within the limits of the Sclavonic language, all might,
notwithstanding, be assumed as inflexion which is usually
represented as such.   It is not, however, here our object
to consider those syllables as supplying the place of grammatical relations which present themselves to the feeling
of the speaker as such, but only those which may be so
traced through the history of the language, and which, for
thousands of years, have subsisted as Grammatical forms.

257. To the masculine and neuter bases in ⴅ *a* correspond, in the Old Sclavonic as well as in Greek, bases in
o,* which vowel has disappeared in the nominative and

---

stated that the *r* and other consonants, in forms like *zarem, knyaʒem,
golúbem, lebedem,* are differently pronounced from what they are in *pirom,
voʒom, lobom, adom,* of Dobrowsky's first masc. declension. The difference
in the two classes of words is only this, that the former have a *y* for the last
letter but one of their theme, which, by the power of assimilation, has
changed the following *o* into *e*, which *e*, after the *y* has been dropped, does
not again become *o*.

* Dialectically the older *a* has, in certain cases, maintained itself, as in

accusative singular: so the corresponding *a* has disappeared in Gothic, except in the neuter (as Gothic *blinda-ta*, "*cœcum*," in contrast with *blind'-s*, "*cœcus*"): it has also maintained itself frequently in the beginning of compounds in the Gothic and Old Greek, where, according to the oldest principle, the naked theme is required; as, *nov*, "*novus*," appears in many compounds as *novo* (*novo-grad*, "new-town"), but is then not to be considered as the neuter *novo*, "*novum*," but as the common theme [G. Ed. p. 343.] of the masculine and neuter, in which as yet no difference of sex is pointed out. The clearest proof that the class of nouns under discussion corresponds to the Indian, Lithuanian, and Gothic nouns in *a*, is afforded by their feminine bases in *a* (for वा *á*); so that to the form *rab* (for *rabo*), "servant," corresponds a feminine *raba*, "a maid": that is to say, all Old Sclavonic primitive adjectives, *i.e.* those with an indefinite declension, correspond to the Sanskṛit in *a-s*, *á*, *a-m*, Greek *o-ς*, *η(a)*, *o-ν*, Latin *u-s*, *a*, *u-m;* much as one might be led astray by outward appearance to seek in the adjectives, which in the nominative masculine end in *y* (*yer*), and in the neuter in *e*, as *siny*, "*cœruleus*," *syne*, "*cœruleum*," an analogy to Latin adjectives like *mili-s*, *mile*.

258. But I recognise in adjectives like that just mentioned, and in similarly-constituted substantives, as *knyaζy*, "prince," *more*, "the sea," bases of such a nature as, without the euphonic form mentioned at §. 255. (*n.*), must have terminated in *yo*, whence *ye*; and hence, in the nominative masculine—according to the suppression of the final vowel of the base, *y* in this case—and in the neuter *e* retaining the vowel and dropping the *y*. These bases, therefore, correspond to the Indian in व *ya*, the Greek and Latin in

---

the Carniolan, before all inflections beginning with *m* in the three numbers, as *posla-m*, "through the domestic," *posla-ma* "the two domestics." This word appears to be identical with पुत्र *putra*, "son," Persian *pisar* "son," "boy," "young man," and to owe its meaning to familiar address.

io, iu (ἄγιο-ς, ἄγιο-ν, *sociu-s, prœliu-m*); that is to say, *serdze* (nominative and accusative neuter), "heart," corresponds to the Sanskrit हृदयम् *hridaya-m*, which is likewise neuter. The feminines, again, afford a practical proof of the justice of this theory, for the Sclavonic bases in *ya* correspond to the Sanskrit या *yá* Greek *ια*, Latin *ia*); and this form, in the uninflected nominative, stands opposed to the masculine termination *y* and neuter *e*, as *sinya*, "*cœrulea*," to *siny*, "*cœruleus*," and *sine*, "*cœruleum*."

[G. Ed. p. 344.]   When an *i* or other vowel precedes the last *y* but one of the base, the *y* in the nominative, and accusative masculine is changed into the vowel *ĭ*; as, *nyetĭĭ*, "*nepos ex sorore*" (Dobrowsky, p. 282). The corresponding feminine form is *iya*, and the neuter *ye*, the *y* of which has arisen from *i* of the form *iye*, which is to be supposed the original, after dropping the last *y* but one. To the Sanskrit सव्यस् *savya-s*, सव्या *savyá*, सव्यम् *savyu-m* (*sinister, a, um*), correspond thus *shǎi, shǎya, shǎe* (compare Dobrowsky, p. 285).

259. The Old Sclavonic masculine and neuter bases in *yo*,[*] with their feminines in *ya*, are, according to their origin, of four kinds :—1. Those in which, as in *SHŪYO=*सव्य *savya*, both the semi-vowel and the vowel following, from the earliest period of the language, belong to the base of the word; and this case is perhaps the most rare. 2. Such as originally end in *i*, to which an unorganic *o* has been added; as, in the Lithuanian, the bases in *i*, in many cases, change into the declension in *ia* (*ie*) (§. 193. and p. 174, Note *). To this class belongs *MORYO*, nom. *more*, "the sea," the *e* of which therefore differs widely from

---

* Where I fix the theme, I leave the euphonic law contained in §. 255. (*n.*) unregarded, and I give *SERDZYO* as the theme of *serdze* ("heart," nom. acc.), although the latter is no other than the theme modified according to that euphonic law, *i.e.* without inflection, as in the Sanskrit *vách* is laid down as the theme, although *ch* cannot stand at the end of a word, but passes into *k*, as in the nominative *vák*, which is properly identical with the theme.

the *mare* in Latin, corrupted from *mari*; so that the
Sclavonic *y*, which again makes its appearance in the genitive *morya*, dative *moryû*, corresponds to the Latin *e* spoken
of. The Latin word must, however, in order to be
classed with the Sclavonic, be pronounced in the nominative
mariu-m. Neuter bases in *i*, without an unorganic augment,
are entirely wanting in the Sclavonic. [G. Ed. p. 345.]
Among the masculines of this class of words *chervy*, "a worm"
(theme *CHERVYO*), answers to the Sanskrit कृमि *krimi*
and the Latin *VERMI*, Old High German, *WURMI*; and
ζyaty (*ζYATYO*), "*gener*," to the Sanskrit जाति *jâti*,
feminine, "*familia*," "*genus*," from जन् *jan*, "to be born."[*]
The third kind of bases in *yo* is that where the unorganic *y*
precedes a final *o*, according to the euphonic disposition
mentioned in §. 255. (*n.*). So *gûsy* (*GŪSYO*) corresponds to
the Indian हंस *hansa*, "goose" (§. 255. *g.*). In the fourth
place there exist among bases in *yo* the words in which the *y*
as well as the following vowel is an unorganic addition.
Thus †nouns of agency in *TARYO* correspond to the
Sanskrit in तर् *tar* (तृ *tri*, in the strong cases तार् *târ*,) to the
Latin in *tôr*, and to the Greek in τηρ, τωρ; hence the nominatives *my-tary*, *schi-tary*, and *ζlatary* (Dobrowsky, p. 295), and,
with *y* for *a*, *pas-tyry*, "shepherd." Of this kind, also, are
the nouns of agency in *TELYO*, the *l* of which is clearly
an interchange with *r* (§. 20.), so that this suffix also con-
forms itself to the Sanskrit तर् *tar*; hence the nominatives
blayo-dyetely, "*beneficus*," *pye-tely*. "a cock," from the root
pye. "to sing," *schately*, "*messor*," *spas-i-tely*, "*salvator*."[‡]

---

[*] ζ frequently answers to the Sanskrit ज *j*, and for example ज्ञा *jnâ*,
"to know," is in the Sclavonic ζna (infinitive ζnati).

[†] But see p. 879. Note §. 647.

[‡] As these words stand in analogy with the infinitive in *ti*, in so far
that their suffix begins with a like consonant, Dobrowsky (pp. 292, 293)
derives them from the infinitive, and allows them simply *ely* as suffix (as
also simple *ary* for *tary*), as it has been the custom to derive also, in
the Latin, *tor* and *turus* from the supine. However, it is certain
                                                 the

260. To the Sanskrit feminine bases in **आ** *â* correspond
as has been already remarked, Old Sclavonic in *a*. To
[G. Ed. p. 346.]   this class of words, however, belong also
some masculines, particularly proper names, which are then
declined entirely as feminines, as in Latin *nauta, cœlicola* ,&c.
(§. 116.), on which we will not here dwell further. Among
the bases in *i* there are, in Old Sclavonic, no neuters, and only
a very small number of masculines — as in Lithuanian —
which Dobrowsky, p. 469, represents as anomalous, as
though they were only irregulars of his second declension
masculine: they are, however, in reality, foreign to it, for
this very reason, that they end their theme with *i*, but
the former with *yo*, and in part with *yy*, (§. 263.). It is only
in the nominative and accusative singular that these three
classes of words, from various reasons, agree; and, *gosty*,
"guest," from *GOSTI** (Gothic *GASTI*, Latin *HOSTI*)
agrees with *knyaζy*, "prince," from *KNYAζYO*, and *vrachy*,
"*medicus*," from *VRACHYY*. The masculine bases originally ending with *n*—there are but a few of them—form
most of their cases from a base augmented by *i*; *KAMEN*,
"stone" (Sanskrit **अश्मन्** *aśman*), is extended to *KAMENI*,
and then follows *GOSTI*.

261. To the Sanskrit feminine bases in **इ** *i* correspond
numerous Old Sclavonic bases of a similar termination
(Dobrowsky, decl. fem. iv.);. that is to say, the Sclavonic
agrees with the Sanskrit in the formation of feminine ab-

---

the suffixes *TOR, TURU* and the Sclavonic *TARYO, TELYO*, used to
borrow their *t* not at first from another syllable of formation so commencing. They form primitive words from the roots themselves, and not
derivatives from other words.

* Thus, also, *PŪTI*, "a way" (Sanskrit **पथिन्** *pathin*), and *LYŪDI*, pl.
num, nom. *lyúdy-e*, "people," Gothic *LAUDI*, nom. *lauths*, "a person," the
au of which, according to §.255. (*f.*), is represented by *ú* (*y*), and, according
to §.255. (*m.*), has gained a prefixed *y*. *GOSPODI*, "a master" (comp. **पति**
pati, Lithuan. *PATI* and Gothic *FADI*) is in fact irregular, as it passes
into several kinds of theme in its declension.

stracts in *TI*, as *PA-MYA-TI*, "memory," nom. *pamyaty*, from the root *MAN*, as in Sanskrit मति *mati* (for *manti*), "spirit," "meaning," from मन् *man*, "to think "* (compare *memini*). These words weaken, indeed, in   [G. Ed. p. 347.] the nominative and accusative, their *i* to *yer*, but in no case overstep their original base by an unorganic addition; and hence they must not, on any account, be looked upon as of the same base with the majority of masculines terminating similarly in the nominative and accusative singular. But Dobrowsky's third feminine declension is of a mixed nature (*zerkovy*, "a church"): in this we recognise some words which have, by Guna, changed a Sanskrit final अ *û* to *ov*; and from this form several cases, as from a base ending with a consonant—*e. g.* *zerkv-e*, genitive singular and nominative plural—but so that the *o* is suppressed before vowel terminations. In some cases the theme extends itself by an unorganic *i*, in others by *a*; and also before these extensions of the base the *o* of the syllable *ov* is suppressed†; *e. g.* *zerkviy-û*, "*per ecclesiam*," *zerkvi*, "*ecclesia*," *zerkvii*, "*ecclesiarum*," *zerkva-m*, "*ecclesiis*," *zerkva-ch*, "*in ecclesiis*," *zerkva-mi*, "*per ecclesias*." The dative locative *zerkvi* is doubtful, as this case could have no other sound than *zerkvi*, whether it come from *ZERKOV* or from *ZERKVI*.

---

* Dobrowsky (p. 355) imputes, in my opinion wrongly, the *n* of *pomyanû*, "I remember," and some similar bases, to derivation, instead of supposing that the radical *n* is suppressed before *t*, in analogy with the Sanskrit, and as, in Greek, τάσις from TAN, Sanskrit तनिस् *tati-s*, "a line" (as extended), for तन्तिस् *tanti-s*.

† The example given by Dobrowsky, *zerkovy*, "a church," nevertheless does not apply to monosyllables, as *krovy*, "blood" (Sanskrit क्रव्य *kravya*, neuter, "flesh"), nor to those polysyllables in which two consonants precede the syllable *ov*; for *yatrvach* and *krvach* would be equally impracticable (comp. Gretsch by Reiff, p. 163). *Brovy*, "eyebrow," also appears to form all its cases from a theme *BROVI*, an extension of the Sanskrit भ्रू *bhrû*, feminine, by the addition of *i*, with a Guna of the अ *û*. The nominative plural is hence *brovi* (Dobrowsky, p. 115), not *brov-e*.

Some words of this class have, in the nominative, *y,* and
[G. Ed. p. 348.]   thus *svekry* agrees with स्वस्रू *śwaśrû-s,*
" *socrus* " (§. 255. *c.*); others have, at will, *ovy* or *vi,* with
o suppressed ; hence *zerkovy* or *zerkvi.*

262. Among bases in *u* (Greek *v*) of the cognate languages, only masculines have maintained themselves in the
Old Sclavonic.   They, like the bases in *o,* suppress their
.final vowel in the nominative and accusative, but in the
remaining cases this letter shews itself either with Guna
changed to *ov* or *û* (§. 255. *f.*), or without Guna, as *o*
(§. 255. *c.*); and in the latter form it appears also in the
beginning of compound words as a naked theme.   Hence
it is more probable, that anciently for *syn,* "*filius,*" "*filium,*"
stood *syno* rather than *syny* (§. 255. *c.*).*   With this similar conformation of theme of the old bases in *a* and *u,* it
is not surprising that two kinds of bases, which in their
origin are widely different, run very much into one another
in the Sclavonic declension ; and that, in the more modern
dialects, these two declensions, which were originally so
strictly separate, have fallen almost entirely into one.

263. As in the *o* bases which have arisen from व *a,* a *y*
preceding introduces a difference of declension, which we,
in §. 258., have represented as purely euphonic, the same phenomenon makes its appearance also in the *y* bases, by means
of which their Guna form is articulated *ev* (for *yev*) instead

---

* We term this class of words, nevertheless, bases in *y* ; for although
their final letter never occurs as *y,* still, according to §. 225. (*c.*), *y* is the
most legitimate, even if it be the most rare, representative of the Sanskrit
उ *u.* But should it be wished to call them bases in *o,* they would not be
distinguished from the order of words, which, according to §. 257., bear
this name with more right.   The term *u* bases would be appropriate only
so far as here, under the *u,* might be understood, not the Old Sclavonic *ъ*
(etymologically = ओ *ô*), but the Sanskrit उ *u* or the Latin *u* of the
fourth declension, which, in the Old Sclavonic, has no real existence.

of *ov*.* If, however, with Dobrowsky, we di- [G. Ed. p. 349.]
vide the Old Sclavonic masculines—with the exception of the
bases in *i*, §. 260.—into two declensions, and in doing this desire, as is natural, to ground the division on the final letters of
the bases, we must place *knyaζy*, "prince" (nominative) of
Dobrowsky's second declension in the first, and by the side
of *rab*, "a servant": on the other hand, the words *syn*,
"son," and *dom*, "a house," of Dobrowsky's first masculine
declension must be transferred to the second declension
as mutilated *y* forms. Of the paradigma here given by
Dobrowsky, *vrachy*, "*medicus*," adheres most strictly to the
true *y* declension, and, according to §. 255. (*n.*), opposes
ev to the *ov* of *SYNY*. On the other hand, words inflected
like *zary*, "a king" (nominative), clearly form the nominative and genitive plural from bases in *i*; hence *zary-e*,
"kings," *zarii*, "of kings," from *ZARI*; as *gosty-e*, "ho-
spites," and *gostii*, "hospitum," from *GOSTI*. In the dative
plural and instrumental singular the form *zare-m* is doubtful: in this and other words, also, of obscure origin, it remains uncertain whether the more contracted theme in *i*,
or the more extended in *yy*, is the older; but it is certain
that several old *i* bases have migrated into this declension
by an unorganic addition; for instance, *ogny*, "fire" (nom.),
dative *ognev-i*, from *OGNYY*, agrees with the Sanskrit अग्नि
agni, Latin *IGNI*, Lithuanian *UGNI*.† It [G. Ed. p. 350.]

---

* Without Guna, the final of the base is pronounced *e* for *ye* from *yo*
(§. 255. *n.*); and hence, in the cases without Guna the *yy* bases are just
as little to be distinguished in their inflection from the *yo* bases, as, in
the instrumental singular, *syno-m* (from the theme *SYNY*) from *rabo-m*
(theme *RABO*). In the beginning of compound words, also, the *yy* bases
end like those in *yo*, with *e* for *ye*.

† As regards words inflected like *mravŭ*, the only proof which could
bring them under the head of the *y* bases is the vocative sing. *mruviyŭ:*
that they, however, although they have borrowed this case from the *y*
declension, originally belong to the *o* declension, is proved by their
feminine in *iya* and neuters in *iye* or *ye* (Dobrowsky, p. 282).

deserves here to be further remarked, that in the more modern
dialects of the Sclavonic stock, the two masculine declensions
here spoken of have been transfused almost entirely into one,
which has taken several cases regularly from the old *u*
declension, in which, however, from the point of view of
the more recent dialects, *e.g.* in the genitive plural of
the Polish and Carniolan, *ov*, *ow*, form an exception as a
case termination.   In the Old Sclavonic, also, *rab* (theme
RABO), "a servant," may optionally form several cases from
a theme *RABY* (for *rabŭ*); and for *rab*, "*servorum*," we
may also have *rabov :* and in the nominative plural of
this class of words we find also *ov-e*, according to the
analogy of *synov-e*.   On the other hand, the adjective
masculine *o* bases (the indefinites) of the *y* declension have
admitted no irregular trespassings any more than the
pronouns.

264. Bases ending in a consonant are, under the limitation of §. 260., entirely foreign to the masculine: on the
other hand, there are neuter bases in *en*, *es*, and *at* (*yat*),
which are important for the system of declension, because
the case suffix, commencing with a vowel, divides itself so
much the more distinctly from the base ending with a
consonant.   The bases in *en* correspond to the Sanskrit
in अन् *an*, and have preserved, too, in the uninflected
nominative, accusative, and vocative, the old and more powerful *a*, but with the euphonic prefix of a *y* (see §. 255. *n*.),
and with the suppression of *n* of the base (see §. 139.).
All of them have an *m* before the termination *en*; so that
men is to be considered as the full formative suffix of the
word, which answers to the Sanskrit मन् *man*—*e. g.* in कर्मन्
karman neut., "deed"—and to the Latin *men;* that is to say,
SYEMEN (nominative *syemya*, "seed," from the base *sye*)
answers to the Latin *se-men;* and *imen*, "a name," is a
mutilation of नामन् *nâman*, "*nomen*." The bases in *es*
answer to the Sanskrit neuter bases in *as*, as *nebes*,

."heaven," Sanskrit नभस् *nabhas*.   In the [G. Ed. p. 351.] nominative, accusative, and vocative, they relinquish the concluding *s* (according to §. 255. *l.*), and afterwards strengthen the *e* to *o* (§. 255. *a.*).   We cannot, therefore, any longer compare the *o* of *nebo* with the Sanskrit-Zendian *o*, which has arisen out of *a* + *u*.   As in this abbreviation of *es* to *o* the neuter *es* bases in the cases mentioned become similar to the *o* bases, it is then—on account of the influence of these cases, and because the nominative principally gives the tone in the declension, and shews in the oblique cases as inflection that which is in itself deficient,—it is then, we say, not surprising, if the original *o* bases at times admit an *es* in the oblique cases, particularly when we consider the original great extension of these neuter bases terminating in *s* (compare §. 241.), which induces the conjecture, that many words, now declined as *o* bases, were originally domiciled in the bases in *es*.   On the other hand, Dobrowsky proves that there is no admixture of *es* in the thoroughly legitimate adjective *o* bases.   It is also clear, from §. 255. (*l.*), that the bases in *yat* * in the uninflected cases must lay aside the *t*, and follow σῶμα, not महत् *mahat* ("*magnum*") and *caput*.

265. Of the class of words in *r* mentioned in §. 144. two feminine words have remained in the Old Sclavonic which derive most of their cases from the genuine *r* bases, but in others increase the original base by an unorganic *i*, or also by *ya* (compare the Lithuanian in §. 144.): in the nominative singular, however, in accordance with the Sanskrit and Lithuanian, they suppress the *r*.   These are, *mati*, "mother," and *dshchi*, "daughter"; in the latter only occurs the increase of the base by *ya* (in the nominative accusative and dative plural); the declension of the former springs   [G. Ed. p. 352.]

---

* They are all derivatives from names of animals, and denote the young of the animal mentioned.

partly from *MATER*, *e. g.* *mater-e*, "*matris*," and *matres* (μᾱτέρ-ες), partly from *MATERI*, *e. g.* *matery*, "*matrem.*"

266. *In order now to pass over to the formation of cases, the nominative and accusative have lost the case-signs *s* and *m*, with the exception of the bases in *a*, which present in the diphthong *û* (*ъ*), a contraction of the vocalized nasal with the final vowel of the base shortened to *o*, (see §. 255. *g.*); hence *vodû*, "*aquam*," from *vodo-ŭ*. The instrumental has, in the feminine, and the pronouns which have no gender preserved the genuine Sanskṛit inflection; but it is to be remarked of the feminine bases in *i* that they change this vowel before the termination *û*, (for *û*, see §. 255. *h.*), not into simple *y*, but into *iy*; so that in this respect the Old Sclavonic agrees more closely with the Pâli, which, in the corresponding class of words, changes the final *i* before all the vowel endings into *iy*, than with the Sanskṛit. Hence, let *kostiy-û*, from *KOSTI*, "bones," be compared with the Pâli पीतिया *pítiy-â* (from *píti*, "joy"), for the Sanskṛit प्रीत्या *príty-â*. Masculines and neuters have *m*† for their instrumental ending; and this is, I have no doubt, an abbreviation of the Lithuanian *mi*, and comes therefore from *bi* (§. 215.).

267. The dative has, in the singular, a common ending with the locative, and, in fact, the Old Sanskṛit *i* (§. 195.); hence, *imen-i*, "*in nomine*," and "*nomini*"; *synov-i*, "*filio*," *brachev-i*, "*medico*," from *SYNY* and *BRACHYY* (§. 263.), with Guna.‡ If the case-sign is suppressed, the preceding *ov*

[G. Ed. p. 363.]   becomes *û*, and *ev* (from *yov*) becomes *yû*; hence, also, *synû*, "*filio*," with *synov-i*, and *zaryû*, "*regi*," with

---

* Cf. §. 783¹.

† For *m*, according to Dobrowsky, we should read мь *my*.

‡ Hence I am now disposed, contrary to §. 177., to assume for the Lithuanian a common origin for the two cases, although in their received condition they are externally separated from one another, as is the case in Old Sclavonic, also, in several classes of words.

the *y* bases, but prefer, however, the abbreviated form *û*; hence *rabû*, from *RABO*, more rarely *rabov-i*. The *o* bases of the adjectives, and of these there are, in the masculine and neuter, only *o* bases, and those of neuter substantives have alone the uninflected form iu *û*; hence, *e. g. blayû,* "*bono,*" masc. neut.; *sinyû,* "*cœruleo,*" masc. neut.: *slovû,* "*verbo,*" *moryû,* "*mari*": not *blagov-i, sinev-i, slovov-i, morev-i.* In masculine names of inanimate things this uninflected form in *û* extends itself also to the genitive and locative; hence *domû,* "of the house," "to" and "in the house": but in the dative is also found *domov-i,* and in the locative *domye.** The pronouns of the 3d person masculine and neuter—with exception of the reflexive—have in the dative, in like manner, the uninflected *û*; for the form *mû* in *to-mû,* "to this," is clearly from the Sanskrit appended pronoun स्म *sma* (§. 165. &c.), which has extended itself in the cognate European languages so much, and under such different forms, and this, in the Old Sclavonic, would necessarily give the base *SMO,* from which, after dropping the *s,* would come the dative *mû,* as *rabû* from *RABO.*

268. While the *o* bases, as has been shewn above, have borrowed their dative from the *y* declension, the *y* bases appear, in the locative, to have intruded on the *o* class; for *synye* answers to *rabye,* from *RABO* from *RABA* (§. 255. *a.*); but the *ye* of *rabye* is. according to §. 255. (*e*), clearly from the Sanskrit ए *é* of वृके *vriké* from वृक *vrika,* and answers to the Lithuanian *wilké* from   [G. Ed. p. 354.] *WILKA* (§. 197.). As, however, in Lithuanian, from *SUNU* comes *sunu-ye,* so may also the Old Sclavonic *synye* require

---

* Masculine names of inanimate things all follow the declension of *dom* (theme *DOMY*), although very few among them, according to their origin, fall into the class of the old उ *u, i.e.* of the Latin fourth declension. but for the most part correspond to Sanskrit bases in अ *a.*

z

to be divided into *syn'-ye* : and this is rendered the more probable, as the feminine *a* bases, also, have in the locative *ye*
for *a-ye*; hence *vod'-ye*, "*in aqua*," from *VODA*, answers to
the Lithuanian *ranko-ye* (for *ranka-ye*) from *ranka.*[*]   In bases
in *i*, masculine and feminine, it might appear doubtful
whether *i*, with which they end in the dative and locative—*e. g.*
páti, "in the way," *kosti*, "in the bone"—is to be ascribed
to the theme or to the inflection: as, however, in the
genitive, (to which belongs an *i*, though not through any
inflection), they have just the same sound, and otherwise
never entirely give up the *i* of the base, except in the instrumental plural, it is more natural to consider the forms
páti, *kosti*, uninflected, just like *domú*, "in the house." We
may also look upon the *i* in the dative and locative of those
bases, which have *y* as the last letter but one, as nothing
else than the vocalization of this *y*; the *i*, therefore, of
knyaζi, *mori*, *brachi*, *voli*, represents nothing else than the *y*
of the masculine bases *KNYAζYO*, *VRACHYY*, and of
the neuter *MORYO*, and feminine *VOLYO*.

269. In the genitive the terminations *as, os, is,* which
in the cognate languages, are joined to bases ending with a
consonant, must, according to §. 255. (*l.*), drop the *s*, but the
[G. Ed. p. 355.]   vowel appears as *e* in all the bases ending
with a consonant (§§. 260. 264.): hence *imen-e*, "of the name,"

---

[*] It must be allowed that here occurs the very weighty objection, that
the feminine form *rankoye* in the Lithuanian, and *vodye* in the Sclavonic,
might stand in connection with the Sanskrit आयाम् *áyám* in जिह्वायाम्
jihwáy-ám (§. 202.) ; so that, after dropping the *m*, as in the Zend (§. 202.),
the preceding vowel, which in the Zend is already short, would, through
the euphonic influence of the *y*, become *e*. As the bases in *i* in the
Lithuanian, down to a few exceptions, are feminine, so might also *awiye*
from *awi-s*, "a sheep," be divided into *awiy-e*, and compared with मत्याम्
maty-ám, from *mati* or भिय्याम् *bhiy-ám* from *bhi* (comp. in §. 266. *kostiy-ú*,
for *kosty-ú*, from *KOSTI*).

answers to नामनस् *námn-as, nomin-is ; ncbes-e,* " of the heaven," to नभस् *nabhas-as,* νέφε(σ)-ος ; *mater-e* to *matr-is,* μητρός. The pronominal forms also follow this analogy : *men-e,* "*mei,*" *teb-e,* "*tui,*" *seb-e,* "*sui,*" because, in the oblique singular cases, *MEN, TEB, SEB* are their themes. We recognise the fuller Sanskrit genitive ending स्य *sya* in the pronominal genitive termination *go,* as *to-go =* तस्य *ta-sya* (§. 188.). This comparison might alone be sufficient in place of all proof; but, over and above, is to be remarked the easily adopted hardening of the semi-vowel *y* to *g* (comp. p. 121 G. ed.), and in the Prâkrit to ज *j* (§. 19.); finally, let the high degree of improbability be considered, that the Sclavonic should have formed an entirely new genitive termination, foreign to all the cognate languages. Now, if the *g* of the termination *go* is taken for a hardening from *y* (य *y*), then the Old Sclavonic has preserved exactly as much as the Greek of the termination *sya ;* and *go* answers to the Greek *ιο,* and *to-go,* "*hujus,*" to the Greek το-ῖο. As, however, in Sclavonic, the sibilants are easily interchanged with gutturals (see §. 255. *m.*), one might also conjecture the *g* of *go* to be a corruption of the Sanskrit *s* and the semi-vowel of स्य *sya,* which had been lost. This conjecture cannot entirely be put aside; but in any case, even in this supposition, the termination *go* remains connected with स्य *sya* and *ιο.* As, however, in the Old Sclavonic, *g* is elsewhere exchanged only with ζ and *sch* (Dobr. p. 41), but not with *s,* in my opinion the derivation of *g* from *y* (य *y*) is to be preferred to that from *s.*

270. The substantive and adjective (indefinite) *o* bases, in disadvantageous comparison with the pronouns which hold fast the old form, have lost the genitive termination *go;* but for it, in compensation for the lost termi-   [G. Ed. p. 356.] nation, they have retained the old *a* of the base, instead of, according to §. 255. (*a.*), weakening it to *o;* hence *raba,* "*servi,*" *nova* (=Sanskrit *nava-sya*) "*novi.*" Now, although the *y* bases

z 2

in the genitive end in *a*, the comparison of the form *syna*, "*filii*," with the Lithuanian and Gothic *sunaú-s*, *sunau-s*, and the Sanskrit *súnô-s* (from *súnau-s*), teaches that the *a* here is only a Guna element, but foreign to the proper base, as well as to the case-suffix, which, according to §. 255. (*b.*), must disappear.

271. The feminine bases in *a*, with the exception of those which have a penultimate *y*, change that *a* in the genitive into *y;* hence *vody*, "*aquæ*," from *VODA*, but *volya*, "*voluntatis*," with unaltered base, from *VOLYA*. I ascribe that *y*, as well as that in the nominative plural, to the euphonic influence of the *s*, which originally ends the form (see §. 255. *d.*): this, however, does not obtain if a *y* precedes the *a*; hence *volya*, "*voluntatis*," is identical with the theme. On the other hand, the feminine pronominal bases in *a* have preserved a remarkable agreement with the Sanskrit pronominal declension; for if *ta*, "this" (at the same time the theme), forms *to-ya* in the genitive, I do not doubt of the identity of the ending *ya* with the Sanskrit *syâs* (§. 172.), as in the word तस्याः *tasyâs*, of the same import, for the final *s* must, according to §. 255. (*l.*), give way; but the *a* of the Sclavonic *ya* directs us, according to §. 255. (*a.*), to an Indian आ *â*, just as the preceding *o* points to a short व *a*. The irregularity, therefore, in the shortening of the Sclavonic termination lies only in the dropping of the sibilant before *y*, as, in the Greek, τοῖο, from तस्य *ta-sya*, and in the *to-go*, for *to-(s)yo*, mentioned in §. 269.

272. In the vocative, which in the cognate languages is without any case-suffix (§. 204.), *o* is weakened to *e* (ε) and *a* to *o* (§. 255. *a.*); hence *nove* (from *NOVO*, "new"), for

[G. Ed. p. 357.] Sanskrit नव *nava*, is identical with the Latin *nŏvĕ*, and answers to the Greek νέ(F)ε: from *VODA*, "water," comes *vodo;* but from *VOLYA*, according to §. 255. (*n.*), *vole* for *volyo*: and so from *KNYAZYO*, "prince," *knyashe** for

---

* ζ before *e* becomes *sh*.

knyaζye. Bases in *yy* change their *y* by Guna to *û* (§. 255.*f*.),
in analogy with §. 205.; hence *vrachyû*—more commonly,
with *y* suppressed, *vrachû*—"*medice!*" from *VRACHYY*. On
the other hand, *y* bases without *y* for their penultimate letter
commonly omit the Guna, and weaken their final vowel,
like the *o* bases, to *e*; hence *syne*, •oh son!" more rarely
synû (Dobr. p. 470), =Gothic *sunau*, Lithuanian *sunaù*, Sanskrit *sûnô* from *sunau*.

DUAL.

273. By preserving a dual, the Old Sclavonic surpasses
the Gothic, in which this number is lost in the noun:
it exceeds, in the same, the Lithuanian in the more true
retention of the terminations, and it is richer than the
Greek by one case. The agreement with the Sanskrit
and Zend is not to be mistaken: let the comparison be
made.

	SANSKRIT.	ZEND.	OLD SCLAVONIC.
N. Acc. V. m.	*ubhâ (ambo* Vêdic),	*ubâ,*	*ʋba.*
f. n.	*ubhê,*	*ubê,*	*obye* (§. 255. *n.*).
I. D. Ab. m. f. n.	*ubhâ-bhyâm.*	*ubôi-bya,* I. D.	*obye-ma* (§. 215.).•
G. L. m. f. n.	*ubhay-ôs,*	*ubôy-ô,*	*oboy-û.†*

• The *ye*, which precedes the termination *ma*, may be compared with
the Sanskrit *ê* in plural forms, as वृकेभ्यस् *vrikêbhyas: ye-ma,* however,
occurs in the Old Sclavonic only in *drye-ma,* "duobus," "per duos," and
some pronouns. The usual form of substantive *o*-bases before this ending
is that with an unchanged *o*, as *sto-ma,* from *sto,* "a hundred"; and the
final *a* of feminine substantives also remains unchanged, as *dyeva-ma,* from
DYEVA, "a girl."

† The form *û*, for the Sanskrit ending *ôs*, is, according to §. 255. (*f.*)
and (*l.*), necessary: the Zend certainly approaches the Old Sclavonic in
casting away the *s* voluntarily. The *oy*, which precedes the termination *û*, clearly corresponds to the Sanskrit अय् *ay* (see §. 225.) and the
Zend

[G. Ed. p. 358.]   The Sanskṛit *ubhê*, as neuter, comes, according to §. 212., from the theme *ubha*, in union with the case-suffix *í*; and the feminine *ubhê* is an abbreviation of *ubhay-áu*, and is therefore without a case termination (§. 212.). The Old Sclavonic, which runs parallel to the Sanskṛit in both genders, and, according to §. 255. (*l.*), opposes *ye* to the Indian द *é*, no longer recognises the origin of this *ye*, and regards it entirely as a case-suffix before which the final vowel of the theme appears to be suppressed.   Therefore, also, neuter bases ending in a consonant make *ye* their termination, if the *imenye*, "two names," given by Dobrowsky, p. 513, actually occurs, and is not a theoretic formation.   In feminines, however, the termination *ye* extends, exactly as in Sanskṛit, only to bases in *a* (for Sanskṛit *á*. §. 255. *a.*); but in such a manner, that those with *y* as the last letter but one in the theme reject the termination *ye*, and vocalize the *y* of the theme; hence *dyerye*, "two girls," from *dycva*, but *steζi*, "two steps," from *STEζYA*.   The feminine bases in *i*, in the dual case under discussion, answer to the Sanskṛit and Lithuanian forms mentioned at §§. 210. 211., as *patí*, "two sirs," from पति *pati ;*

[G. Ed. p. 359.]   *awí*, "two sheep," from *AWI;* only that, according to §. 255. *b.*), the *i* in the Sclavonic is not lengthened; as *dlani* from *DLANI* (nominative singular

---

Zend *ôy* or *ay* (see p. 277); but that occurs only in *dvoy-û*=Sanskṛit *dway-ôs,* "of two," "in two" m. f. n., and in *toy-û*=Sanskṛit *tay-ôs,* "of these two," m. f. n.   The genitives and locatives of the two first persons also rest on this principle, only retaining the older *a — noyú*, *váyú*. For the rest, however, the final vowel of the theme is rejected before the termination *û*, as *st'-û* (Sanskṛit *shatay-ôs*) from *STO*, "a hundred," *dyev-û* from *DYEVA*, "a girl"; and thus occurs, also, together with *dvoyú*, the syncopated form *dvû*.   Although the Lithuanian generally does not drop the final *s*, still the *û* mentioned in §. 225. may be identical with the Sclavonic *û*; as in the Zend, also, in this termination the *s* is often dropped.

dlany), "*vola manus*." On the other hand, the masculine *y*
bases do not follow this principle, but suppress the final
vowel before the case-suffix *a*; hence *syn'-a*, "two sons,"
from *SYNY*.

274. In the plural, the masculine nominative termination *e* (ε) for the most part answers to the Greek ες, and,
according to a universal rule of sounds, omits the *s*
(§. 255. *l.*); hence *synov-e*, "the sons," सूनवस् *sûnav-as* :
compare βότρυ-ες, *kamen-e*, "the stones," for अश्मानस
asmân-as (§. 21.); compare δαίμον-ες, *gosty-e*, "guests" (theme
GOSTI), for the Gothic *gastei-s*, and Greek forms like πόσι-ες.
The bases in *o* take, as in Lithuanian do the corresponding
bases in *a, i* as their termination (see §. 229.), but before
this reject the *o* of the base; hence *rab'-i*, "servants," for
rabo-i (comp. λύκο-ι), as in Latin *lup-i* for *lupo-i*. Neuters
have *a* for their ending, like the cognate dialects, with the
exception of the Sanskrit with *i* for *a*; nevertheless, *slova*,
"*verba*," from *SLOVO*—as δῶρα from ΔΩΡΟ—answers to
Vêdic forms like *vand*, "woods," from *vana;* and the same
thing obtains which, §. 231. p. 267 G. ed., has been said of
Gothic, Greek, and Latin, regarding the relation of the *a* of
the termination to the *o* of the theme. As regards the bases
ending in a consonant, let *imen-a*, "names," be compared
with the Latin *nomin-a* and Gothic *namôn-a; nebes-a*, "the
heavens," with νεφε(σ)-α; and *telyat-a*, "calves," with Greek
forms like σώματ-α. Feminines, with the exception of the
class of words in *ov* mentioned at §. 261., have lost the nominative ending; hence *volya*, "*voluntates*," is the same as
the theme and the nominative singular; and   [G. Ed. p. 360.]
from *KOSTI*, "bones" (Sanskrit *asthi*, neuter) comes the
nominative singular *kosty*, and the plural like the theme.

275. The accusative plural is, in feminine and neuter
nouns, the same as the nominative, and therefore in the former

mostly without inflection, exactly as in the few masculine
bases in *i*; hence *gosti* for the Gothic *gasti-ns*. Bases in *o*,
without *y* preceding, like *RABO*, change this *o* into *y*, as
raby, "*servos*"; at least I cannot believe that this *y* is to
be looked upon as the case-suffix; and I pronounce it to be
the euphonic alteration of the *o* of the base, through the
influence of the consonant of the inflection which has
been dropped (comp. §. 271.): as in Lithuanian, also, the
corresponding class of words often changes the final vowel
(*a*) of the base into *u*; hence *wilkù-s*, "*lupos*," answering
to the Gothic *vulfa-ns* and Sanskṛit *vrikả-n*. But if the
Old Sclavonic bases in *y*, of animate creatures, form
owy in the accusative plural, and thus *synovy*, "*filios*,"
answers to the Lithuanian *sunù-s* (from *SUNU*), this
very Lithuanian form, as well as the Gothic and Sanskṛit
sunu-ns, सूनून् *sûnù-n*, prove that the Sclavonic form is
unorganic, and formed from an augmented theme *SYNOVO*,
according to the analogy of *raby*. Bases in *yy* in this case
follow bases in *yo* (from *ya*, §. 255. *a.*), which, preserving the
old *a* sound, give *ya*, as in the genitive singular (see §. 270.);
hence *vrachya*, "*medicos*," like *knyaζya*, "*principes*": but
forms, also, like *doschdevy*, analogous with *synovy*, occur, following the euphonic rule, §. 255. (*n.*).

276. The view here given is the more incontrovertible,
as in the dative, also, *synovo-m*, "*filiis*" (compare *rabo-m*),
is clearly formed from a theme *SYNOVO*, increased by *o*,
corresponding to the Lithuanian *sunu-ms*. This dative
suffix *m*, for the Lithuanian *ms* (from *mus*, §. 215.), according
[G. Ed. p. 361.]　　to §. 255. (*l.*), extends itself over all classes
of words, and appears to be attached by a conjunctive vowel
e to bases terminating with a consonant; but, in fact, it is
to be considered that these, in the cases mentioned as also in
the locative (see §. 279.), pass over into the *i* declension, as
a final *i*, before the signs of case *m* and *ch*, becomes *e*: and a
similar metaplasm occurs in the Lithuanian, and indeed, to a

much greater extent (§. 125. *sub finem*, comp. §. 126.); hence *imenc-m, imene-ch*, from *IMENI* from *IMEN*, "names," as *koste-m, koste-ch*, from *KOSTI*, "bones."

277. Less general is the instrumental ending *mi*, answering, subject to the loss required by §. 255. (*l.*), to the Lithuanian *mis*, Sanskṛit *bhis*, and Zend *bis*. This termination *mi* is, however, in masculine and neuter nouns for the most part lost (comp. Dobr. pp. 473 and 477); and is preserved principally, and indeed without exception, in feminines, as well as in a few masculine *i* bases: a final *i* of the base is, however, suppressed before the termination *mi*. Let *kost'-mi* be compared with अस्थिभिस् *asthi-bhis*, from अस्थि *asthi*, "bone"; *vdova-mi* with विधवाभिस् *vidhavá-bhis*, from विधवा *vidhavá*, "a widow." The instrumentals *raby, synovy*, are, like the accusatives of similar sound, uninflected (§. 275.); the *i* of *knyaζi, vrachi*, is the vocalization of the *y* of the bases *KYNAζYO, VRACHYY*, after the loss of the final vowel; and the *y* of neuters terminating in a consonant, like *imeny "per nomina,"* is to be explained by a transition into the *o* declension, and is therefore analogous to *raby, slavy*, similarly to the *o* of the Greek dual forms like δαιμόνοιν (p. 318 G. ed. Rem. 2.).

278. Dobrowsky (p. 461) represents *ov, y, ĭ, ev, en, yat,* and *es*, as plural genitive terminations; but in reality the suffix of this case has entirely disappeared, and in bases in *o, a*, and *y*, has also carried away those final vowels with it, while bases in *i* double that vowel; hence *rab*, [G. Ed. p. 362.] "*servorum*," from *RABO*; *vod*, "*aquarum*," from *VODA*; *syn*, "*filiorum*," from *SYNY*; *kostĭ*, "*ossium*," from *KOSTI*; *imen*, "*nominum*," from *IMEN*; *nebes*, "*cœlorum*," from *NEBES*. The *n* and *s* of *imen, nebes*, would, without the former protection of a following termination have been dropped, as in Sclavonic we have only a second generation of final consonants; while the former, with the exception of a few monosyllabic forms, has, according to §. 255. (*l.*), disappeared.

279. The termination of the locative plural is *ch* throughout all classes of words, and has been already, at §. 255. (*m.*) recognised as identical with the Indian सु *su*, and therefore, also, with the Greek σι: compare, also, the Zend ﺧﻮ *kha*, for the Sanskrit *swa*, in §. 35. Before this *kh*, *o* passes into *ye*, exactly as the corresponding Sanskrit व *a* into ए *é* (see §. 255. *e.*); hence *rabye-ch*, "*in servis*," answers to वृकेषु *vriké-shu*, "*in lupis*." Bases in *yo*— and those in *yy* follow their analogy—suppress, however, before this *ye*, their preceding *y*, as in similar cases; hence *knyaζye-ch*, "*in principibus*," not *knyaζyy-ch* from *KNYAζYO*. A final *a* remains unchanged; hence *vdova-ch*, "*in viduis*," answers to the Sanskrit *vidhavi-su*. For bases in *i*, and consonants, see §. 276.

280. For an easier survey of the results obtained for the Old Sclavonic case-formation, we give here, in order to bring under one point of view all the kinds of theme existing in Old Sclavonic, and to render their comparison with one another easy, the complete declension of the bases: *RABO*, m. "a servant," *KNYAζYO*, m. "a prince," *SLOVO*, n. "a word," *MORYO*, n. "a sea" (Dobr. p. 476, §. 11.), *VODA*, f. "water," *VOLYA*, f. "will," *GOSTI*, m. "a guest," *KOSTI*, f. "a bone," *SYNY*, m. "a son," *DOMY*, m. "a house," *VRACHYY*, m. "a physician," *KAMEN*, m.

[G. Ed. p. 363.] "a stone," *IMEN*, n. "a name," *MATER*, f. "a mother," *NEBES*, n. "heaven," *TELYAT*, n. "a calf."* In

---

* The above examples are arranged according to their final letters, with the observation, however, that *o* represents an original short *a*, and hence precedes the *a* for Sanskrit *á* (§. 225. *a.*). All bases in *t* have a *y* before the preceding *a*; this semi-vowel is, however, readily suppressed after sibilants; hence *ovcha* for *ovchya*, Dobr. p. 475; and hence, also, from *lizyo* come (nom. *lize*) the genitive, dative, and nominative accusative plural *liza*, *lizá*, for *lizya*, *lizyá*. If in bases in *yo*, m. n., and in feminines in *ya*, an *i* precedes the semi-vowel, this involves some apparent variations

those forms of the following table in which a part of the word is not separated from the rest, thereby shewing itself to be the inflection, we recognise no inflection at all, *i.e.* no case-suffix; but we see therein only the bare base of the word, either complete or abbreviated; or also a modification of the base, through the alteration of the final letter, occasioned by the termination which has been dropped (compare §. 271.). In some cases which we present in the notes, base and termination have, however, been contracted into one letter, by which a division is rendered impossible. With respect to the dual, which cannot be proved to belong to all the words here given as specimens, we refer to §. 273.

---

variations in the declension, which require no particular explanation here (see, in Dobr. *mravii*, m. p. 468; *ladiya*, f. p. 478; and *úchenye*, n. p. 474. With regard to *zary*, "a king," see §. 263).

SINGULAR.

THEME.	NOM.	ACCUS.	INSTR.	DATIVE.	GEN.	LOC.	VOC.
RABO, m.[1]	*rab'*,	*rab'*,	*rabo-my*,	*rabŭ*,[18]	*raba*,[21]	*ralye*,[25]	*rabe*.
KNYAƵYO. m.[2]	*knyaƶy'*,	*knyaƶy'*,	*knyaƶe-my*,	*knyaƶyŭ*,	*knyaƶya*,[21]	*knyaƶi*,	*knyaƶchu*
SLOVO. n.[3]	*slovo*,	*slovo*,	*slovo-my*,	*slovŭ*,	*slova*,[21]	*slovye*,[25]	. . . .
MORYO, n.[2]	*more*,	*more*,	*more-my*,	*moryŭ*,	*morya*,[21]	*mori*,	. . . .
VODA, f.[4]	*voda*,	*vodŭ*,[15]	*vodoy-ŭ*,[16]	*vod'-ge*,[19]	*vody*,[22]	*vod'-ye*,[25]	*vodo*.
VOLYA, f.[4]	*volya*,	*volyŭ*,[15]	*voley-ŭ*,[16]	*voli*,	*volya*,	*voli*,	*vole*.
GOSTI, m.[5]	*gosty*,	*gosty*,	*goste-my*,[17]	*gosti*,[20]	*gosti*,	*gosti*,[20]	*gosti ?*
KOSTI, f.[5]	*kosty*,	*kosty*,	*kostiy-ŭ*,[16]	*kosti*,[20]	*kosti*,	*kosti*,[20]	*kosti*.
SYNY, m.[6]	*syn'*,	*syn'*,	*syno-my*,[17]	*synov-i*,	*syna*,[21]	*synye*,[25]	*synŭ*.[26]
DOMY, m.[7]	*dom'*,	*dom'*,	*domo-my*,	*domov-i*,	*domŭ*,	*domŭ*,	*dome*.
VRACHYY,m.[8]	*vrachy'*,	*vrachy'*,	*vrache-my*,	*vrachev-i*,	*vrachya*,[23]	*vrachi*,	*vrachyi*
KAMEN, m.[9]	*kamy'*,[14]	. . . .	*kamene-my*,	*kamen-i*,	*kamen-e*,[24]	*kamen-i*,	. . . .
IMEN, n.[10]	*imya*,	*imya*,	*imene-my*,	*imen-i*,	*imen-e*,[24]	*imen-i*,	. . . .
MATER, f.[11]	*mati*,	. . . .	. . . .	*mater-i*,	*mater-e*,[24]	*mater-i*,	. . . .
NEBES, n.[12]	*nebo*,	*nebo*,	*nebese-my*,	*nebes-i*,	*nebes-e*,[24]	*nebes-i*,	. . . .
TELYAT, n.[13]	*telya*,	*telya*.	*telyate-my*,	*telyat-i*,	*telyat-e*,[24]	*telyat-i*,	. . . .

---

[1] Comp. p. 273, &c.   [2] See §§. 258. 259   [3] Comp. pp. 275, 276.   [4] Comp. p. 28?

[5] Comp. p. 286.   [6] Comp. p. 288.   [7] See p. 337, Note.   [8] See §. 263.

[9] Comp. p. 304.   The cases wanting come from *KAMENI* (see §. 260.); whence also, *kamene-m*, *kamene-ch* (§. 266.); and whence, also, might be derived the dativ and locative *kamen-i*, which I prefer, however, deriving from the original theme, jus as in *MATER*.

[10] Comp. §. 139.   [11] See §. 265. and comp. p. 305.   [12] Comp. p. 306. and §. 147.

[13] See §. 264.   [14] Dobr. p. 287.   [15] See §. 266.

[15] Comp. Sanskrit *jihway-á*, &c. See §. 266.   [17] Comp. Lith. *pati-mi*, *sunu-m*

[16] Or *rabori*, §. 267.   [19] See §. 268.

[20] The *i* may also be ascribed to the mark of case, and the dropping of the final letter of the base may be assumed ; but in the genitive of the same sound, the *i* clearly belong to the theme.

[21] See §. 270.   [22] See §. 271.

[23] More commonly *vracha*, and in the vocative, *vrachŭ*. See p. 347, Note.

[24] See §. 269.   [25] See §. 268.   [26] Or *syne*.

PLURAL. [G. Ed. p. 365.]

NOM. VOC.[1]	ACCUS.[3]	INSTR.[5]	DATIVE.[6]	GEN.[7]	LOCATIVE.[8]
rab'-i,	raby,	raby,	rabo-m,	rab',	rabye-ch.
knyaǵi,	knyaǵya,	knyaǵi,	knyaǵe-m,	knyaǵy',	knyaǵe-ch
slova,	slova,	slovy,	slovo-m,	slov',	slovye-ch,
morya,	morya,	mori,	more-m,	mory',	morye-ch.
vody,[2]	vody,	voda-mi,	voda-m,	vod',	voda-ch
volya,	volya,	volya-mi,	volya-m,	voly',	volya-ch.
gosty-e,	gosti,	gost'-mi,	goste-m,	gostii,	goste-ch.
kosti,	kosti,	kost'-mi,	koste-m,	kostii,	koste-ch.
synov-e,	synovy,[4]	synovy,[4]	synovo-m,[4]	synov,	synovye-ch.[4]
domov-e,	domy,	domy,	domo-m,	domov,	dome-ch.
vrachev e,	vrachya,	vrachi,	vrache-m,	vrachev,	vrache-ch.
. . . .	. . . .	. . . .	kamene-m,	. . . .	kamene-ch.
imen-a,	imen-a,	imeny,	imene-m,	imen,	imene-ch.
mater-e,	. . . .	mater-mi,	matere-m,	. . . .	. . . .
nebes-a,	nebes-a,	nebesy,	nebese-m,	nebes,	nebesye-ch.[9]
telyat-a,	telyat-a,	telyaty,	telyate-m,	telyat,	telyate-ch.

---

[1] See §. 274. [2] See §. 271. [3] See §. 275.

[4] From *SYNOVO*, see §.275. In the locative occur also *synovo-ch* and *synove-ch*.

[5] See §. 277. [6] See §. 276. [7] See §. 278. [8] See .279.

[9] One would expect *nebese-ch*; but in this case *ech* and *yech* are frequently interchanged with one another, and the form *yech* appears to agree better with the preceding *s* (comp. Dobrowsky, p. 477).

ADJECTIVES.

[G. Ed. p. 366.]   281. The declension of the adjective is not distinct from that of the substantive; and if some inflected forms, which in the Sanskrit and Zend belong only to the pronouns, have, in the cognate languages, emerged from the circle of the pronouns, and extended themselves further, they have not remained with the adjectives alone, but have extended themselves to the substantives also. As regards the Greek, Latin, and Sclavonic, we have already explained at §§. 228. 248. and 274. what has been introduced from pronominal declension in those languages into general declension: we will here only further remark that the appended syllable *sma*, in §. 165. &c., which, in Sanskrit, characterises only the pronominal declension, may in the Pâli be combined also, in several cases, with masculine and neuter substantive and adjective bases, and indeed with all bases in *a*, *i*, and *u*, including those which, originally terminating in a consonant, pass by augment or apocope into the vowel declension; thus the ablative and locative singular of *kêsa*, "hair," is either simply *kêsâ* (from *kêsât*, see p. 300), *kêsê*, or combined with *sma* or its variation *mha*, *kêsa-smâ*, *kêsa-mhâ*, *kêsa-smiñ*, *kêsa-mhi*. In the Lithuanian, this syllable, after dropping the *s*, has, in the dative and locative singular, passed over to the adjective declension, without imparting itself to that of the substantive, and without giving to the adjective the licence of renouncing this appended syllable; as, *gêram*, "*bono*," *geramé*, "*in bono*." According to this principle it would be possible, and such indeed was lately my intention,

to explain the agreement of the Gothic full adjective dative,
as *blindamma* (from *blindasma*, §. 170.), with   [G. Ed. p. 367.]
pronominal datives like *tha-mma*, "to this," *i-mma*, "to him";
but the examination of the Old Sclavonic declension, in which
the indefinite adjectives remove themselves from all admixture of the pronominal declension, and run entirely parallel
to the German strong substantive, not to the weak, has
led me to the, to me, very important discovery, that
Grimm's strong and Fulda's abstract-declension-form of
adjectives diverges in not less than nine points from the
strong substantives (*i. e.* those which terminate in the
theme in a vowel), and approaches to the pronominal declension for no other reason than because, like the definite
adjectives in the Sclavonic and Lithuanian, they are compounded with a pronoun, which naturally follows its own
declension.   As, then, the definite (so I now name the
strong) adjectives are defined or personified by a pronoun
incorporated with them, it is natural that this form of declension should be avoided, where the function of the inherent pronoun is discharged by a word which simply precedes it; thus we say *guter*, or *der gute*, not *der guter*, which
would be opposed to the genius of our language; for it
still lies in our perception that in *guter* a pronoun is contained, as we perceive pronouns in *im*, *am*, *beim*, although the pronoun is here no longer present in its original
form, but has only left behind its case-termination.   In
comprehending, however, the definite adjective declension,
the science of Grammar, which in many other points had
raised itself far above the empirical perception of the language, was here still left far behind it; and we felt, in
forms like *guter*, *gutem*, *gute*, more than we recognised, namely,
a pronoun which still operated in spirit, although it was no
longer bodily present.   How acute, in this respect, our perception is, is proved by the fact that we place the definite form of
the adjective beside the *ein* when deprived   [G. Ed. p. 368.]

of its definitive pronominal element; but, in the oblique
cases, beside the definite *eines, einem, einen*, the indefinite:
ein grosses, eines grossen (not *grosses*), *einem grossen* (not
grossem). In the accusative, *grossen* is at the same time
definite and indefinite; but in the former case it is a bare
theme, and therefore identical with the indefinite genitive
and dative, which is likewise devoid of inflection; but in
the latter case the *n* evidently belongs to the inflection.

282. The pronominal base, which in Lithuanian and
Old Sclavonic forms the definite declension, is, in its original form, *ya* (= Sanskrit य *ya*, "which"); and has, in the
Lithuanian, maintained itself in this form in several cases
(see below). In the Old Sclavonic, according to §. 255. (*a.*),
yo must be formed from *ya*; and from *yo* again, according to §. 255. (*n.*), *ye* or *e*: but the monosyllabic nature of the form has preserved it from the suppression of
the *y*, which usually takes place in polysyllabic words. In
some cases, however, the *y* has vocalized itself to *i* after
the vowel has been dropped. It signifies in both languages "he"; but in Old Sclavonic has preserved, in union
with *sche*, the old relative meaning (*i-sche*, "which"). The
complete declension of this pronoun is as follows :—

SINGULAR.

	LITHUANIAN.		OLD SCLAVONIC.		
Nominative,	m. *yis* f. *yi*,	m. *i*,[*]	f. *ya*,[*]	n. *ye*.[*]
Accusative,	m. *yin*, f. *yen*,	m. *i*,	f. *yû*,	n. *ye*.
Instrumental,	m. *yû*, f. *yè*,	m. n. *im*.	f. *yeyû*,	
Dative,	m. *yám*, f. *yei*,	m. n. *yemû*,	f. *yeï*,	
Genitive,	m. *yo*, f. *yôs*,	m. n. *yego*,	f. *yeya*,	
Locative,	m. *yamè*, f. *yoyè*,	m. n. *yem*,	f. *yeï*,	

---

[*] Occurs only as the relative in union with *sche*.

PLURAL.

		LITHUANIAN.		OLD SCLAVONIC.
Nominative,	m.	*yie (yi),* f. *yos,*	m. *i,** f. n. *ya.**
Accusative,	m.	*yûs,* f. *yes,*	m. f. n. *ya.*
Instrumental,	m.	*yeis,* f. *yomis,*	m. f. n. *imi.*
Dative,	m.	*yiems,* f. *yoms,*	m. f. n. *im.*
Genitive,	m. f.	*yû,*	m. f. n. *ich.*
Locative,	m.	*yûsè,* f. *yosà,*	m. f. n. *ich.*

DUAL. [G. Ed. p. 369.]

		LITHUANIAN.	OLD SCLAVONIC.
Nominative,	m.	*yu (yû),* f. *yì,*	. . . .
Accusative,	m.	*yuǹ,* f. *yin,*	. . . .
Dative,	m.	*yièm,* f. *yom,*	Instr. Dat. m. f. n. *yima.*
Genitive,	m. f.	*yû,*	Gen. Loc. m. f. n. *yeyû.*

283. The Lithuanian unites, in its definite declension, the pronoun cited—which, according to Ruhig (Mielcke, p. 52.), signifies the same as the Greek article—with the adjective to be rendered definite; so that both the latter, and the pronoun, preserve their full terminations through all the cases; only the pronoun in some cases loses its *y,* and the terminations of the adjective are in some cases somewhat shortened. *Géras,* "good," will serve as an example.

MASCULINE.

	SINGULAR.	DUAL.	PLURAL.
Nominative,	*gérasis,†*	*gerûyu,*	*gerieyi.*
Accusative,	*gerańyań,*	*geruyuń,*	*gerûsus,*
Instrumental,	*gerûyu,*	. . . .	*geraiseis.*
Dative,	*geramyam,*	*giriemsiom,‡*	*geriemsiems.*
Genitive,	*geroyo,*	. . . .	*gerûyû.*
Locative,	*geramyame,*	. . . .	*gerûsûse.*
Vocative,	*gerasis,*	*gerûyu*	*gerieyi.*

---

* See Note on preceding page.

† Or *gerassis,* by assimilation from *gerasyis,* as, in the Pràkṛit *y* frequently assimilates itself to a preceding *s,* as *tassa,* " hujus," for तस्य *tasya.*

‡ The *s* of the adjective is here not in its place, and appears to be borrowed from the plural.

FEMININE.

	SINGULAR.	DUAL.	PLURAL.
Nominative,	*geroyi,*	*gerieyi,*	*gerosos,*
Accusative,	*geranyčn,*	*geriyin,*	*gerases.*
Instrumental,	*geraye,*	. . . .	*geromsomis.*
Dative,	*geraiyei,*	*gerómsom,*[*]	*geromsoms.*
Genitive,	*gerosiés,*	*gerúyú,*	*gerúyú.*
Locative,	*geroyoye,*	. . . .	*gerososa.*
Vocative,	*geroyi,*	*geriyi,*	*gerosos.*

[G. Ed. p. 370.]   284. The Old Sclavonic, differing from
the Lithuanian, declines only in some cases the adjective
together with the appended pronoun, but in most cases the
latter alone. While, however, in the Lithuanian the appended
pronoun has lost its *y* only in some cases, in the Old Sclavonic
that pronoun has lost, in many more, not only the *y* but also
its vowel, and therefore the whole base. Thus the termination alone is left. For more convenient comparison we
insert here, over against one another, the indefinite and
definite declension: *svyat* (theme *SVYATO*), "holy," may
serve for example:

SINGULAR.

	MASCULINE.		FEMININE.	
	Indef.	*Def.*	*Indef.*	*Def.*
Nominative,	*svyat,*	*svyaty-ĭ,*[1]	*svyata.*	*svyata-ya.*
Accusative,	*svyat,*	*svyaty-ĭ,*[1]	*svyatú,*	*svyatú-yú.*
Instrumental,	*svyatom,*	*svyaty-m,*[1]	*svyatoyú,*	*svyato-yú.*[3]
Dative,	*svyatú,*	*svyato-mú,*	*svyatye,*	*svyato-i.*[4]
Genitive,	*svyata,*	*svyata-go,*	*svyaty,*	*svyaty-ya.*
Locative,	*svyatye,*	*svyato-m,*[2]	*svyatye,*	*svyato-i.*[4]

---

[*] See Note 1 on preceding page.

[1] See §. 255. *d.*   [2] Or *svatye-m,* in which, as in the Lithuanian, the
adjective is inflected at the same time.

[3] The indefinite and definite forms are here the same, for this reason,
that *svyato-yeyú,* as the latter must originally have been written, has dropped
the syllable *ye.* The adjective base *svyata* has weakened its *o* to *a*
before the pronominal addition (§. 255. *a.*), just as in the dative and locative *svyato-i,* where an external identity with the indefinite form is not
perceptible.   [4] Or *svyatye-i.* Comp. Note 2.

PLURAL.

| | MASCULINE. | | FEMININE. | |
	Indef.	Def.	Indef.	Def.
Nominative,	svyati,	svyati-i,	svyaty,	svyaty-ya.
Accusative,	svyaty,	svyaty-ya,	svyaty,	svyaty-ya,
Instrumental,	svyaty,	svyaty-imi,[5]	svyata-mi,	svyaty-imi.[7]
Dative,	svyatom,	svyaty-imi,[5]	svyata-m,	svyaty-im.[7]
Genitive,	svyat,	svyaty-ich,	svyat,	svyaty-ich.
Locative,	svyatyech,	svyaty-ich,[5]	svyata-ch,	svyaty-ich.[7]

| | SINGULAR. | | PLURAL. | |
| | NEUTER. | | | |
	Indef.	Def.	Indef.	Def.
Nom. Accus.	svyato,	svyato-e,	svyata,	svyata-ya.

The rest like the masculine.

---

[5] I give those forms which, according to Dobrowsky (p. 302.), occur in the oldest MSS., in place of the more ordinary forms, which have lost the *i* of the pronominal base: *svyaty-mi, svyaty-m, svyaty-ch.*

[6] Although in the pronominal declension the genitive plural is externally identical with the locative, we must nevertheless, in my opinion, separate the two cases, in respect to their origin. I find, however, the reason of their agreement in this, that the Sanskrit, which in this case is most exactly followed by the German and Sclavonic, in pronouns of the third person begins the plural genitive termination with a sibilant, Sanskrit *sâm*, Gothic *zê* (for *sê*, §. 248.). This *s*, then, has, in Old Sclavonic, become *ch*, just like that of the locative characteristic स *su* (§. 279.). The nasal of साम् *sâm* must, according to rule, be lost (§. 255. *l.*): the vowel, however, has, contrary to rule, followed it, as also in the ordinary declension the termination *âm* has entirely disappeared (§. 278.); and the same relation which *imen*, "*nominum*," has to the Gothic *naman-ê*, *tye-ch*, "*horum*," has to *thi-ze.* This *tye-ch*, however, answers as genitive to the Sanskrit तेषाम् *tê-shâm*, and as locative to तेषु *tê-shu*; *ye* being used in both cases for ए *ê*, according to §. 255. (*e.*)

[7] See Notes 5 and 6. The identity with the masculine and neuter forms arises from this, that the grave *a* of the feminine adjective base is changed into the lighter *o*; and this again, as in the masculine neuter, is converted, according to §. 225. (*d.*), into *y*.

[G. Ed. p. 371.] 285. As in the Sanskrit the preponderating majority of adjective bases end in the masculine and neuter in *a*, and in the feminine in *d*; and as this class is, in the Old Sclavonic, only represented by bases in *o, yo* in the masculine and neuter (see §. 257.), and *a, ya* in the feminine it is not surprising that in German also, with the exception of a few in *u* (of the comparative and participle present), all other adjective bases, in their original condition, end in *a*, feminine *o* for *d* (§. 69.). It is, however remarkable, and peculiar to the German, that its adjectives in their indefinite condition, have all lengthened their theme

[G. Ed. p. 372.] by an unorganic *n*, and that in substantives the class of words in *n* appears to be the most generally made use of, inasmuch as a large number of words, whose bases in Gothic terminate in a vowel, have, in the more modern dialects, permitted this to be increased by *n*. The reason however, why the indefinite adjectives—not simply in part and for the first time in the more modern dialects, but universally, and so early as in Gothic—have passed into the *n* declension, is to be sought for in the obtuseness o the inflection of this class of words, which, according to §§. 139. 140., in common with the Sanskrit, Latin, and Greek, omits the nominative sign, and then, in variance from the older languages, dispenses also with the dative character, upon the loss of which, in Old High German has followed, also, that of the genitive character. This absence of the animating and personifying mark of case might belong to the indefinite adjective, because it feel itself more exactly defined through the article which precedes it, or through another pronoun, than the definite adjective, the pronoun of which, incorporated with it, has for the most part left behind only its case terminations In the Lithuanian and Sclavonic, in which the article is wanting, and thereby an inducement further to weaken the declension of the indefinite adjectives, the latter stand on a equal footing with Grimm's strong declension of substantives, *i.e.* they maintain themselves, without an unorganic consonantal augment, in the genuine, original limits of their base.

286. As the feminine, where it is not identical, as in adjective bases in *i* in the Sanskrit, Greek, and Latin, with the theme of the masculine and neuter, is always, in the Indo-European family of languages, made to diverge through an extension or an addition to the end, it is important for German Grammar to remark—and I have already called attention to this point in another place— that the feminine of the German indefinite adjective, in variance from the principle which has been   [G. Ed. p. 378.] just given, has not arisen from its masculine, but from an older form of the feminine; *e.g.* the primitive feminine *BLINDA* m. n. "blind," has extended itself in the indefinite to *BLINDAN*, and the primitive feminine *BLINDŌ* to *BLINDŌN*: one must not, therefore, derive the latter, although it is the feminine of *BLINDAN* m., from this, as it is entirely foreign to the Indo-European family of languages to derive a feminine base through the lengthening of the last letter but one of the masculine and neuter. As far as regards the declension of *BLINDAN* m., it follows precisely that of *AHMAN* (p. 322 G. ed.), and *BLINDAN* n., that of *NAMAN* (p. 176 G. ed. &c.); the fem. *BLINDŌN* differs from the masculine only by a more regular inflection, since its *ō* remains everywhere unchanged, while *a*, in the genitive and dative singular, is, according to §. 132., weakened to *i*; therefore—

MASCULINE.		NEUTER.		FEMININE.	
Theme, *BLINDAN.*		*BLINDAN.*		*BLINDŌN.*	
SINGULAR.	PLURAL.	SINGULAR.	PLURAL.	SINGULAR.	PLURAL.
N. V. *blinda',*[1]	*blindan-s,*	*blindŏ',*[2]	*blindŏn-a,*[2]	*blindŏ',*	*blindŏn-s.*
Acc. *blindan,*	*blindan-s,*	*blindŏ',*[2]	*blindŏn-a,*[2]	*blindŏn,*	*blindŏn-s.*
Dat. *blindin,*[1]	*blinda'-m,*	*blindin,*[1]	*blinda'-m,*	*blindŏn,*	*blindŏ'-m,*
Gen. *blindin-s,*[1]	*blindan-ĕ,*	*blindin-s,*[1]	*blindŏn-ĕ,*[2]	*blindŏn-s,*	*blindŏn-ŏ.*

---

[1] See §. 140.   [2] See §. 141.   [3] See §. 245.

287. In order, then, to examine the definite declension of
adjectives in Gothic, we will, in the first place, for the purpose of bringing into view their agreement and discrepancy
with substantives and simple pronouns, place by the side
of each other the declension of the definite *BLINDA* m. n.
and *BLINDŌ* f., and that of *VULFA* m., " wolf," *DAURA*
n., "a gate," *GIBŌ* f., a gift," and the interrogative
[G. Ed. p. 374.]   *HVA* m. n., " who? " what ?" *HVŌ* f.; further,
that of *MIDYA* m. n. (*medius*), *MIDYŌ* f., by that of *HARYA*
m., "an army," *BADYA* n., "a bed," *KUNTHYŌ* f., "news,"
and *HVARYA* m. n., " who ?" " what ?" *HVARYŌ* f.

MASCULINE.

	SINGULAR.			PLURAL.		
N.	*vulf's,*	*blind's,*	*hva-s,*[1]	*vulfōs,*[2]	*blindai,*	*hvai,*[3]
A.	*vulf',*	*blindana,*	*hva-na,*	*vulfa-ns,*	*blindans,*	*hva-ns.*
D.	*vulfa,*[4]	*blindamma,*	*hva-mma,*[5]	*vulfa-m,*	*blindaim,*	*hvai-m.*
G.	*vulfi-s,*	*blindis,*	*hvi-s,*	*vulf'-ē,*	*blindaizē,*	*hvi-zē.*
V.	*vulf',*	*blind's,*	. . . .	*vulfōs,*	*blindai,*	. . . .
N.	*haryi-s,*[6]	*midyis,*[7]	*hvaryi-s,*	*haryōs,*[2]	*midyai,*	*hvaryai.*[3]
A.	*hari,*[8]	*midyana,*	*hvarya-na,*	*harya-ns,*	*midyans,*	*hvarya-ns.*
D.	*harya.*	*midyamma,*	*hvarya-mma,*	*harya-m,*	*midyaim,*	*hvaryai-m.*
G.	*haryi-s,*	*midyis,*	*hvary-is,*	*hary-ē,*	*midyaizē,*	*hvaryaizē.*
V.	*hari,*	*midyis,*	. . . .	*haryōs,*	*midyai,*	. . . .

---

[1] See §. 135.   [3] See §. 228.   [5] See §. 171.

[2] See §. 227.   [4] See §. 160.

[6] From *harya-s,* see §. 135.

[7] The nominative in adjective bases in *ya* does not occur, unless perhaps
in the fragments which have last appeared ; and I have here formed it by
analogy with *haryis* and *hvaryis.* Grimm gives *midis* (I. 170.). If, l. c., the
form *yis* is considered as unorganic, and, in regard to *midis,* if its analogy
with *hardus* is remembered, then Grimm is wrong in taking *MIDI* for the
theme, as in reality *HARDU* is the theme of *hardus.* The true theme
MIDYA occurs, however, in the comp. *midya-sveipains,* "deluge," and

answers

NEUTER.

SINGULAR.   PLURAL.

N. A. V. *daur'*,   *blindata,*[9] *hva.*[9]   *daura,*   *blinda,*   *hvô.*
     The rest like the masculine.

N. A. V. *badi,*   *midyata,*[9] *hvarya-ta,*   *badya,*   *midya,*   *hvarya.*
     The rest like the masculine.

FEMININE.   [G. Ed. p. 375]

SINGULAR.   PLURAL.

N. *giba,*	*blinda,*	*hvô.*	*gibôs,*[2]	*blindôs,*[2]	*hvôs.*[2]
A. *giba,*	*blinda,*	*hvô.*[11]	*gibô-s,*	*blindôs,*	*hvô-s.*
D. *gibai,*[12]	*blindai,*[12]	*hvizai.*[13]	*gibô-m,*	*blindaim,*	*hvai-m.*
G. *gibô-s,*	*blindaizôs,*[13]	*hvizô-s.*[13]	*gib'-ô,*	*blindaizo,*	*hvi-zô.*
V. *giba,*	*blinda?*	. . . .	*gibôs,*	*blindôs,*	. . . .
N. *kunthi,*[14]	*midya.*	*hvarya.*	*kunthyôs,*[2]	*midyôs,*[2]	*hvaryos.*[2]
A. *kunthya,*	*midya,*	*hvarya.*	*kunthyô-s,*	*midyôs,*	*hvaryô-s.*
D. *kunthyai,*[12]	*midyai,*[12]	*hvaryai.*[12]	*kunthyô-m,*	*midyôm,*	*hvaryô-m.*
G. *kunthyô-s,*	*midyaizôs,*	*hvaryaizôs.*[13]	*kunthy-ô,*	*midy'ô,*	*hvary'ô.*
V. *kunthi,*	*midya.*	. . . .	*kunthyôs,*	*midyôs,*	*hvaryôs.*

---

answers to the Sanskrit मध्य *madhya.* Formed from *midya* as theme, *midyis* would be clearly more organic than *midis.* Adjective *i* bases, which could be referred to *hardu-s* as *u* base, do not exist, but only substantive, as *GASTI,* nom. *gasts.*

[8] Compare Zend forms like ꞔ𝑗᠑𝑗𝑔𝑝 *tûirîm,* "quartum," from ᠊ᢍᢈᢈ᠑᠑᠑𝑔𝑝 *tûirya* (§. 42.).

[9] *Hva,* with suppressed termination, for *hvata,* Old High German *huaz,* see §§. 155. 156.; for *blindata* also *blind;* and so for *midyata* also *midi.*

[10] The form *hvô,* which, like some others of this pronoun, cannot be shewn to occur, is, by Grimm, rightly formed by analogy from *thô,* "*hæc.*" Grimm here finds, as also in the accusative singular, the *ô* in opposition to the *a* of *blinda* surprising: the reason of the deviation, however, is fixed by §§. 69. 137. 231.

[11] See p. 173, Note †.   [12] See §. 161.   [13] §. 172.

[14] For *kunthya,* from *kunthyô,* by suppression of the final vowel of the base, which again appears in the accusative, but shortened *to a* (see §. 69.); but here, also, the final vowel can be dropped; hence *kunthi* as accusative. Luc. 1. 77.

If, then, it is asked which pronoun is contained in the German definite adjective, I answer, the same which, in Sclavonic [G. Ed. p. 376.] and Lithuanian, renders the adjective definite, namely, the Indian relative *ya* (य *ya*). This pronoun in German, indeed, in disadvantageous comparison with the Lithuanian and Sclavonic, does not occur isolated in its inflected state; but it is not uncommon in the history of languages, that a word has been lost in regard to its isolated use, and has been preserved only in composition with other words. It should be observed, too, that a demonstrative *i* base must be acknowledged to belong to the Sanskrit, which, in Latin, is completely declined; in Gothic almost completely; but in Sanskrit, except the neuter nominative accusative *idam*, "this," has maintained itself only in derivative forms, as इति *i-ti*, इत्थम् *it-tham*, "so," इयत् *iy-at*, "so much," ईदृश *í-drisa*, "such." The case is the same in Gothic, with the pronominal base *ya*: from this comes, in my opinion, the affirmative particle *ya*, as in other languages, also, affirmation is expressed by pronominal forms (*i-ta*, तथा *ta-thá*, "so," οὔτως), and further *yabai*, "if," analogous with *ibai*, "whether," *ibaini*, "lest"; as also, in Sanskrit, यदि *yadi*, "if," comes from the same base, and to this, as I now believe, the Greek εἰ—the semi-vowel being laid aside—has the same relation as in Prâkrit, in the 3d person singular present, *ai*, e.g. भमइ *bhamai*, "he wanders" (Urvasi by Lenz, p. 63), has to the more usual अदि *adi*, for the Sanskrit अति *ati*. In Prâkrit, too, जइ *jai* (l. c. p. 63 on *j* for *y*, see §. 19.), really occurs for *yadi*; so that in this conjunction, as in the 3d person of the present λέγει from λέγετι), the Greek runs parallel to the corruption of the Prâkrit. If, however, in εἰ the Sanskrit य *y* has disappeared, as in the Æolic ὔμμες=Sanskrit *yushmé*, it appears as *h* in ὅς, which has nothing to do with the article ὁ, ἡ, where *h* falls only to the nominative masculine and feminine, while in ὅς it runs through all the cases, as

in Sanskrit the य् *y* of यस् *ya-s.* To this [G. Ed. p. 377.]
यस् *yas,* ὅς, in regard to the rough breathing, bears the same
relation as ὑμεῖς to युष्मे *yushmê,* ἅζω, ἅγιος to यज् *yaj,* "to
worship," "to sacrifice," यज्य *yajya,* "to be worshiped;" ὑσμίν
to युध् *yudh,* "to strive," युध्म *yudhma,* "strife" (comp. Pott,
pp. 236. 252.). But to return to the Gothic *YA,* let us further
observe *yah,*[*] "and," "also," with *h* enclitic, of which hereafter,
and *yu,* "now," *i. e.* "at this time," "already" (comp. Latin *jam*).
It also clearly forms the last portion of *hvar-yis* (for *yas*), as,
in the Sclavonic, this pronoun often unites itself with almost
all others, and, for example, is contained in *ky-i,* "who?"
although the interrogative base also occurs without this
combination.

288. In Gothic definite adjectives the pronominal base
YA shews itself most plainly in bases in *u.* Of these,
indeed, there are but a few, which we annex below,† but
a *ya* shews itself in all the cases, and these in *blinds* differ
from the substantive declension, to such an extent that
before the *y* the *u* of the adjective is suppressed, as in
Sanskrit before the comparative and superlative suffixes
iyas, ishtha; e.g. *laghîyas,* "more light," *laghishtha,* "most
light," for *laghv-îyas, laghv-ishtha* from *laghu;* and as,
even in Gothic, *hard'-izô,* "more hard" (according to

---

[*] The *h* may assimilate itself to the initial consonant of the following
word, and thus may arise *yag, yan,* and *yas,* and in conjunction with *thê:*
yatthê, "or" (see Massmann's Gloss.).

† *Aggvus,* "narrow," *aglus,* "heavy," *glaggvus,* "industrious," *hardus,*
"hard," *manvus,* "ready," *thaursus,* "dry," *thlaqvus,* "tender," *seithus,*
"late," *filus,* "much," and, probably, *hnasqvus,* "tender." Some occur
only as adverbs, as *glaggvu-ba,* "industriously." In addition to the adverb
filu, "much," since Grimm treated this subject the genitive *filaus* has been
found (*filaus mais,* "for much more," see Massmann's Gloss.), which is
the more gratifying, as the adjective *u* bases had not yet been adduced in
this case.

[G. Ed. p. 378.]   Massmann, p. 48), for *hardv-izô,* from *HARDU.* Hitherto, however, only the accusative singular masculine *thauri-yana,* "*siccum*," *manv'-yana,* "*paratum*"; the accusative singular neuter *manv'-yata;* the dative plural *hnasqv'-yaim* are adduceable, if Grimm, as I doubt not, is right in ascribing to this word, which is not to be met with in any other case, a nominative *hnasqvus.** Finally, also, the accusative plural masculine *unmanv'-yans,* ἀπαρα-σκευάστους (2 C. 9. 4.), although, in this case, *blindans* is not different from *vulfans.* These examples, then, although few, furnish powerful proof; because, in the cases to be met with, they represent an entire class of words—viz. the definite adjective in *u*—in such a manner, that not a single variety of form occurs.   It may be proper to annex here the complete definite declension of *MANVU,* as it is either to be met with, or, according to the difference of cases, is, with more or less confidence, to be expected:—

	MASCULINE.		FEMININE.	
	SINGULAR.	PLURAL.	SINGULAR.	PLURAL.
N.	*manvu-s,*	(*manv'-yai*),	*manvu-s,*	(*manv'-yôs*).
Ac.	*manv'-ya-na,*	*manv'-ya-ns,*	(*manv'-ya,*)	(*manv'-yôs*),
D.	(*manv'-ya-mma*),	*manv'-yai-m,*	(*manv'-yai*),	(*manv'-yaim*).
G.	*manvau-s,*	(*manv-yaizê*),	(*manv'-yaizôs*),	(*manv'-yaizô.*

[G. Ed. p. 379.]   NEUTER.

| | SINGULAR | PLURAL. |
| Nom. Accus. | *manv'-ya-ta,†* | (*manv'-ya*). |

---

* I am the more inclined to agree with him, as a few other adjective bases in *vu* occur.   Perhaps a euphonic influence of the *v* on the vowel which follows it is also at work; as at times one finds in the Prâkṛit a final *a* changed through the influence of a preceding अ *n,* र *r,* or ळ *l,* to उ *u.* So Urvasi, p. 72, *âlu, tâlu, âvaraṇu,* for *kâla, tâla, âvaraṇa;* p. 71, *manôharu* for *manôhara.*

† Without inflection and pronom. *manvu,* as स्वादु *svâdu,* ἡδύ, Lithu-anian *darkù.*

" Remark 1.—Grimm finds (I. 721.) the identity of the feminine with the masculine remarkable, since he, as it appears,
looks upon *s* as an originally mere masculine termination
(comp. l. c. 824, 825. [2, 3]). That, however, the feminine has
equal claim to *s* as the nominative character, and that it is
entirely without inflection where this is wanting, I think
I have shewn in §§. 134. 137. Adjective bases in *i*, which
in the Gothic, as in the Lithuanian and Sclavonic, are
wanting, end, in the Sanskrit, Greek, and Latin, in the
nominative of both genders, in *is*; and only the neuter is
devoid of inflection : compare सुचिस् *suchi-s* m. f., "clean,"
suchi n., with ἴδρι-ς, ἴδρι, *facili-s, facile*. Adjectives in *u*, in
Sanskrit, frequently leave, in like manner, the feminine base
undistinguished from the masculine and neuter, and then
end, according to §. 234., in the nominative in *u-s*; so *pándu-s*
m. f., agrees with *manvu-s* above, and the neuter *pándu*
with *manvu*. If two consonants do not precede the final
उ *u*, as in *pándu*, the feminine base may, except in compound words, be lengthened by an *í*, which is particularly
characteristic of this gender; and thus स्वाद्वी *swádwí*, " the
sweet" (theme and nominative), answers to the Greek
word ἡδεῖα, which is lengthened by an unorganic *a* (§. 119.),
for ἡδϜια; and *swádu-s* answers both as feminine and masculine nominative to the Gothic *manvus*. In the Sanskrit,
also, a short *u* in the feminine base may be lengthened, and
thus the feminine of तनु *tanu*, "thin," is either *tanu* or
tanú, whence the nominative *tanú-s; and *tanuí*, as substantive, means the " slender woman." The Lithuanian has
adjective bases in *u*, as *szwiesu-s*, m. " light," " clear,"
(compare श्वेत *swéta*, " white,") which nevertheless, in several cases, replace the *u* by *a*; as *szwiesám dangui*, "to the
bright heaven": in some, too, they prefix an *i* to the *a*,
the assimilating power of which changes the *a* into *e*
(comp. p. 169 Note); as, *szwiesiems dangums*, "to the bright
heavens." The feminine is, in the nominative, *szwiesi*, the

[G. Ed. p. 380.] final *i* of which is evidently identical with the Sanskrit इ *í* in *swádwí*. In the oblique cases, however, an unorganic *a* also is added to the Lithuanian *i*, as it has been in ἡδεῖα: this *ia*, however, becomes either by euphony, *e* (comp. p. 174, Note *), *e. g.* accus. *szwieseń*, accus. plural *szwieses*; or it happens, and that, indeed, in the majority of cases that the *i* is entirely suppressed, so that *SZWIESA* passes as the theme; as *szwiesòs rankòs*, "of the bright hand" (gen. *szwiesai rankai* (dat.). The *i* of *ia*, however, appears, as with the participles, to have communicated itself from the feminine to the masculine,

"Remark 2.—With the accusative *manvyana* which has been cited, the conjectured dative *manvyamma* is least doubtful. That Grimm should suggest forms like *hardv-amma, hardv-ana*, arises from his regarding *amma, ana*, as the dative and accusative terminations of the pronoun and adjective; while, in fact, the terminations are simply *mma* and *na*. When, therefore, *HARDU*, in the dative and accusative, without annexing a pronoun, follows nevertheless the pronominal declension, the cases mentioned must be written *hardu-mma, hardu-na*, analogous with *tha-mma, tha-na, i-mma, i-na*. If, however, contrary to all expectation, forms like *hardvamma, hardvana*, shew themselves, they must be deduced from *hardu-ya-mma, hardu-ya-na*; so that after suppressing the *y*, the preceding *u*, in the place in which it would be left, has passed into *v*. With regard to *blindamma, blindana, blindata*, it is doubtful whether they ought to be divided *blind'-(y)amma, blind'-(y)ana, blind'-(y)ata*, as analogous with *manv(u)-yamma, manv(u)--yana, manv(u)-yata*, or *blinda-(ya)mma*, &c.: I have therefore left them, as also the corresponding forms from *MIDYA*, undivided. If the division *blinda-mma*, &c. is made, nothing is left of the pronoun, as in the Old Sclavonic dative *svyato-mú*, and as in our expressions like *beim, am, im*, except the case-termination, and the adjective base has preserved its *a*. If, however, the division *blind'-amma*, &c. is made, to which I now give the preference, and which is also adopted by Grimm, though from a different point of view, then the pronoun has only lost its *y*, as in some cases of the Lithuanian definite, *e.g.* in *gerûs-us* for *gerûs-yus* (see p. 353); and with respect to the *y* which has been dropped and the vowel which is left, *blind'-amma* would have the same relation to *blind'-yamma* as *midums*, " the middle man" (theme *MIDUMA*), to its Sanskrit cognate form of the same import, मध्यम *madhyama*, whose relation to *MIDUMA* I thus trace—the latter has softened the first *a* to *i*, and has changed the middle *a*, through the influence of the liquid, into *u*; and both, however, have, according to §. 66., suppressed the semi-vowel.

" Remark 3.—Although, in the accusative plural masculine, *blindans* is not different from *vulfans*, and the simple word *BLINDA* could not form aught but [G. Ed. p. 381.] *blinda-ns*; nevertheless the word *manv-yans*, mentioned above, which is of the highest importance for the Grammar, as well as the circumstance that where any inflections peculiar to the pronoun admonish us of the existence of an inherent pronoun in the definite adjective, this inheritance really exists ;—these two reasons, I say, speak in favour of dividing thus, *blind'-ans*, and of deducing it from *blind-yans*. Just in the same manner the dative *blindaim*, both through the *aim*, which occurs elsewhere only in pronouns, as through the word *hnasqv'-yaim*, mentioned above, declares itself to be an abbreviation of *blind'-yaim*; but *blindai* proves itself only by its pronominal inflection (compare *thai*, *hvai*, Sanskrit ते *tê*, के *kê*) to be an abbreviation of *blind'-ya*.

" Remark 4.—In the Sanskrit, in some cases an *i* blends itself with the final *a*, which, with the *a* of the base, becomes *ê*: hence the instrumental plural of the Vêda dialect and of the Prâkrit, अश्वेभिस् *aśvê-bhis* from *aśva*, कुसुमेहिं *kusumê-hiñ* from *kusuma*. To this *ê* answers the *ai* in

Gothic pronominal datives like *hvai-m,* "*quibus,*" *tha-im,*
"*his*"; as the German dative, in accordance with its origin,
is identical with the old instrumental. We were, however,
compelled, before we had a reason for seeking the pronoun
YA in the Gothic definite adjective, to give to the extension of the base in German a wider expansion by an *i*
which means nothing, than it has in the Sanskṛit; while we
have now every reason, where, in Gothic definites, an *i*
unsubstantiated by the oldest grammar shews itself, to recognise in the *i* a remnant of the pronominal base *YA,*
either as a vocalization of the *y,* which so often occurs in
the Sclavonic (see p. 354), or the *i* may be considered as
an alteration of the *a* of *YA,* as in the Lithuanian *geras-is*
for *geras-yis,* (p. 353). The latter view pleases me the better because it accords more closely with *blind'-amma,*
blind'-ana, &c., from *blind'-yamma, blind'-yana.* The vowel,
then, which in *blind'-amma,* &c., maintains itself in its
original form, appears, in this view, as *i* in the feminine
singular genitive *blindaizôs*—which is to be divided *blinda-*
izôs—from *blinda-yizôs* ; and this *yizôs* is analogous with
hvizôs, thizôs, from *hvazôs, thazôs,* = Sanskṛit *kasyâs, tasyâs*
(§. 172.). We must not require *blindô-izôs* — because
BLINDŌ is the feminine adjective base—for there is
a reason for the thinning of the *ô,* in the difficulty of
placing the syllables together, and *a* is the short of *ô*
(§. 69.). For the rest, let it be considered, that in
the Sclavonic the graver feminine *a* before its union
with the pronoun is weakened to the lighter masculine *o*
(p. 354, Note 3.); and that a diphthong *oi* in the Gothic
[G. Ed. p. 382.] is never admissible; on which account
salbô, " I anoint," in the subjunctive suppresses the *i,* which
belongs to this mood (*salbôs, salbô,* for *salbôis, salbôi*). In the
feminine dative one should expect *blindaizai* for *blindai,*
which is simple, and answers to *gibai,* while the remaining
German dialects are, in this case, compounded in the very

same manner: in Old High German the genitive is *plintera*,
and the dative *plinteru*.* In the genitive plural masculine and neuter the *ai* in *blindaize* might be substantiated
through the Sanskrit ए *ê* of the pronominal genitive, as
तेषाम् *têshâm*, "*horum*"; and therefore the division *blindai-ze*
or *blind'-(y)aize* should be made: as, however, the monosyllabic pronominal bases, in which one would rather expect a firm adherence to the old diphthong (comp. §. 137.), do
not retain it, and *thi-zê*, "*horum*," *hvi-zê*, "*quorum*," as weakened forms of *tha-zê*, *hva-zê*, are used; and in the feminine
thi-zô, *hvi-zô*, for *thô-zô*, *hvô-zô*,=Sanskrit *tâ-sâm*, *kâ-sâm*;
I therefore prefer to substantiate in a different way the *ai*
in *blindaizê* m. n., and *blindaizô* f., than by the Sanskrit *ê*
of *tê-shâm* m. n. (f. *tâ-sâm*), which, moreover, would not be
applicable to the feminine form *blindaizô*; and I do it, in
fact, by the pronominal base *ᛣA*, so that *blinda-izê blindaizô*, is the division to be made according to the analogy of
blinda-izôs.

"Remark 5.—The nominative masculine and feminine has
kept itself free, in Gothic, from union with the old relative
base, and has remained resting upon the original, as
received from the Sanskrit, Greek, and Latin. The masculine *blinds*, also, through the very characteristic and
animated *s* (see §. 134.). has cause to feel itself personified
and defined determinately enough. Even if *blinds* could be
looked upon as an abbreviation of *blindeis* (comp. *altheis*,
"old," from the base *ALTHᛣA*, according to Massmann),
or of *blindais*, to which the Old High German *plinter*
would give authority, I should still believe that neither the
one nor the other has existed in Gothic, as even the *u* bases,

---

* The Gothic *ai* would lead us to expect *ê*, and this, too, is given by
Grimm. As, however, with Kero, the doubling of the vowel, and, with
Notker, the circumflex is wanting, I adopt in preference a shortening of
the *e*, or leave the quantity undecided.

like *manvu-s* above, which, in the oblique cases, shew so
clearly the pronominal base Ұ*A*, have not received it in
the nominative singular of the personal genders. In Old
High German, however, the pronoun spoken of has had
time, in the space of almost four centuries which intervene
between its oldest memorials and Ulfilas, to raise itself up
from the oblique cases to the nominative; which was the
more desirable, as the Old High German substantive declen-
[G. Ed. p. 383.] sion in the nominative masculine, in disadvantageous comparison with the Gothic, omits the mark of
case. *Plintêr* (the length of the *ê* is here rendered certain)
is contracted from *plinta-ir* (for *plinta-yir*); for the Old High
German *ê* corresponds, according to §. 78., to the Gothic *ai*.
In the feminine, therefore, the form *plintyu*, which occurs
in the chief number of strict Old High German authorities, and those which, as Grimm remarks, are the oldest
of all, has good substantiation, and corresponds very fitly
to the masculine *plintêr;* and in the nominative and accusative plural and neuter the form *plint-yu*, with regard to the
retaining the *y* of the pronoun, is more genuine than the
Gothic *blind-a* for *blind-ya*. The form *plintyu*, moreover,
answers to feminine pronominal forms like *dyu*, "the" (f.),
syu, "she," *dësyu* (*dë-syu*), "this"* (f.), and to the instrumental masculine and neuter *dyu* (in the interrogative *huiu*),
where all authorities concur in retaining the *i* or *y*; while
in the adjective, Otfrid, and, as Grimm remarks, here and
there Isidore and Tatian, have *u* for *yu*, For explanation,

---

* As in the Old High German *i* and *j* (*y*) are not distinguished in
writing, it remains uncertain in many, if not in all cases, in what places of
the memorials which have come down to us the sound *j*, and in what that
of *i* is intended; as even where the Gothic has a *j*, it may become *i* in
the Old High German. If, however, in the analogous adjective forms
like *plintju* one reads *j*, which is supported by the Gothic (p 362), we
must, in my opinion, leave it in the above forms also. Grimm writes *diu*,
siu, but *dësju ;* and expresses, p. 791, his opinion regarding the *i*.

however, of the pronominal forms which have been mentioned, it is important to consider, that in the Sanskṛit the pronominal base *ta*, or the *sa* which supplies
its place in the nominative masculine and feminine, unites
itself with the relative base स *ya*, by which the first pronoun loses its vowel. Compare, then—

SANSKRIT.	OLD HIGH GERM.	OLD SCLAVONIC.
स्या *syâ* (= *syâ,*) "*hæc,*"	*syu, dyu,*	*ta-ya.*
त्याम् *tyâm,* "*hanc,*"	*dya,*	*tû-yû.*
ते *tyê,* " *hi,*"	*dyê,*	*ti-i.*
त्याम् *tyâs,* "*hæ,*" "*has,*"	*dyô,*	*ty-ya.*
त्यानि *tyâni,* "*hæc,*"	*dyu,*	*ta-ya.*

Here, then, in a manner as remarkable as convincing, the
relation is proved in which the Old High German forms
mentioned stand to the Gothic *sô, thô, thai,* [G. Ed. p. 384.]
thôs, thô : one must first transpose these into *syô, thyô,* &c.,
before they can pass as original forms for the Old High German. Our mother tongue, however, in the case before us,
obtains more explanation through the Sclavonic, where the
demonstrative base *TO* may indeed be simply inflected
through all the cases: in several, however, which we have
partly given above, it occurs also in union with *YO.* It is
most probable, that in the Old High German the combination of the base of the article with the old relative pronoun
has extended itself over all the cases of the three genders;
for that it does not belong to the feminine alone is seen
from the masculine and neuter instrumental form *dyu*
(*d'-yu*), and from the dative plural, where together with
dêm occurs also *dyêm* (*diêm*), and, in Notker, always
dien. According to this, I deduce the forms *dër, dës, dëmu,*
&c., from *dyer, dyes* (for *dyis*), *dyemu* (from *dyamu*); so
that, after suppression of the vowel following the *y,* that
letter has vocalized itself first to *i* and thence to *ë.* According to this, therefore, *dës,* and the Gothic genitive

B B

thi-s, would be, in their origin, just as different as in the accusative feminine *dya* and *thô*. In the neuter, on the other hand, *daz*—for *dyaz*, as Gothic *blind'-ata* for *blind-yata*—the vowel of the base *DYA* is left, and the semivowel, which above had become *ë* (from *i*) has disappeared. Further support of my views regarding the difference of bases in the Gothic *tha-na* and the Old High German *dë-n* (I give the accusative intentionally) is furnished by the demonstrative *dësêr*, which I explain as compounded, and as, in fact, a combination of the Sanskrit त *tya*, mentioned at p. 383 G. ed., for *taya*, and स्य *sya* for *sa-ya*, the latter of which has a full declension in the Old Sclavonic, also, as a simple word. *Dësêr* stands, therefore, for *dya-sâir* (*ë=ai*); and our Modern German *dieser* rests, in fact, upon a more perfect dialectic form than that which is preserved to us in the above *dësêr*, namely, upon *dya-sêr* or *dia-sêr*; referred to which the Isidorean *dhëa-sa*, mentioned by Grimm (I. 795.), at least in respect of the first syllable, no longer appears strange, for *dhëa* from *dhia* for *dhya*,* answers admirably to the Sanskrit त *tya*, and the final syllable *sa* answers to the Sanskrit-Gothic nominative form *sa* (Greek ὁ), which has not the sign of case.

"Remark 6.—The adjective bases which from their first origin end in *ya*, as *MIDYA*=Sanskrit *madhya*, are less favourable to the retention of the *y* of the definite pronoun; for to the feminine or plural neuter *plint'-yu* for *plintu-yu* a *midy'-yu* would be analogous, which, on account of the diffi-
[G. Ed. p. 385.] culty of pronouncing it, does not occur, but may have originally existed in the form *midya-yu*, or *midya-ya*; for the masculine nominative *midyêr* is from *midya-ir* for *midya-yar*, as, in Gothic, the feminine genitive-form *midyaizôs* from *midya-yizôs*. If, however, according to this, even *hvar-yaizôs* (from *hvar-ynyizôs*) be used, and analogous

---

* *D, th,* and *dh* are interchanged according to different authorities.

forms in several other cases, so that the base YA is therein doubled, we must recollect, that in the Lithuanian also the base YA, besides its composition with adjectives, combines itself, also, with itself, for stronger personification; and, indeed, in such a manner, that it is then doubly declined, as *yis-sai* (for *yis-yai**), 'he'; *yo-yo*, 'of him,' &c."

289. The participle present has, in Gothic, preserved only the nominative singular masculine of the definite declension, *e.g.* *gibands*, "giving," which may be deduced as well from a theme *GIBAND*, according to the analogy of *fiyand-s* (see p. 164), as from *GIBANDA*, according to the analogy of *vulf'-s* (§. 135.). The Pâli (see p. 300) and Old High German support the assumption of a theme *GIBANDA*, as an extension of the original *GIBAND*; whence, then, by a new addition, the indefinite theme *GIBANDAN* has arisen, as, above, *BLINDAN* from *BLINDA*; and it is very probable that all unorganic *n* bases have been preceded by an older with a vowel termination: for as all bases which terminate in a consonant (*nd, r,* and *n,* §. 125.) are in their declension, with the exception of the nominative *nd-s,* alike obtuse; [G. Ed. p. 386.] so it would not be necessary for *GIBAND,* in order to belong, in the indefinite adjective, to a weak theme, or one with a blunted declension, to extend itself to *gibandan* (compare p. 302), unless for the sake of the nominative *gibanda* (see §. 140.).

290. In the Pâli, no feminine theme *charantí* has been formed from the unorganic theme *charanta*, mentioned at p. 319 G. ed.

---

* Ruhig (by Mielke, p. 68) wrongly gives *ai* as the emphatic adjunct, as the doubling of the *s* in *tassai, szissai, yissai* is clearly to be explained through the assimilative power of the *y* (see p. 353, Note †). The termination *ai* answers to the neuter *tai*, mentioned at §. 157., for *tat*, which latter is contained in the compound *tat-tai* (comp. *kok-tai, tok-tai*). After two consonants, however, the *y* is entirely dropped; hence *e.g. kurs-ai*, not *kurs-sai*.

for the masculine and neuter form *charanta* has arisen from
the necessity of passing from a class of declensions terminating in a consonant into one more convenient, terminating
with a vowel in the theme.   The Sanskrit, however, forms
from bases terminating in a consonant the feminine theme
by the addition of a vowel (*î*, see §. 119.) ; *e. g.* from *charant* m.,
comes *charantî*, and there was therefore no reason in the
Pâli to give also to the more recent form *charanta* a
feminine theme *charantâ*.   Here, again, the Gothic stands
in remarkable accordance with the Pâli, for it has produced no feminine base *GIBANDŌ* from the presupposed
GIBANDA; and therefore, also, the indefinite *GIBANDAN*
has no feminine, *GIBANDŌN*, nom. *gibandô*, answering to
it (as *BLINDŌN* to *BLINDAN*); but the feminine form
gibandei (*ei*=*î*, §. 70.), which has arisen from the old
theme *GIBAND*, in analogy with the Sanskrit *charantî*,
has become *GIBANDEIN*, by the later addition of an *n*.
Hence, according to §. 142., in the nominative *gibandei*
must have arisen.   It is not, however, right to regard this
nominative as a production of the more recent theme, but
as a transmission from the ancient period of the language,
for it answers to the feminine Sanskrit nominative *charantî* (§. 137.), and to Lithuanian forms like *sukanti*, "the
turning," for which a theme *sukantin* is nowise admissible.   In Latin, bases in *i* or *î*, originally feminine, must
have arisen from adjective bases terminating with a
consonant ; thus *FERENTI* from *FERENT* (compare
§. 119. *genitrí-c-s*) : and this feminine *i*, as is the case in
Lithuanian, as well with the participles (see p. 174, Note) as
[G. Ed. p. 387.]   with the adjective bases in *u* (p. 363), has
in some cases no longer remembered its original destination,
and been imparted to the other genders : hence the ablatives
in *i* (for *i-d*), genitive plural in *i-um*, neuter plural in *ia*
(*ferenti(d)*, *ferenti-um*, *ferenti-a*) ; and hence is explained,
what must otherwise appear very surprising, that the

participles, when standing as substantives, freely take this
i, which is introduced into them from the feminine adjective (*infante, sapiente*).

"Remark.—In the *yu* of *këpantyu*, the Old High German
feminine of *këpantêr*, I recognise the regular defining element, as above in *plintyu*, answering to the masculine *plintêr*.
On account of the participial feminines in *yu*, therefore,
it is not requisite to presuppose masculines in *yêr*, according to the analogy of *midyêr, midyu, midyaz*, partly as
këpentêr and *këpantaz*, incline, in none of their cases, to the
declension of *midyêr, midyaz*, and also as the derivative
indefinite base in *an* has sprung from *KĔPANTA*, and not
from *KĔPANTYA*: therefore m. *këpanto* (=Gothic *gibanda*),
f. n. *këpanta* (=Gothic *gibandô*). This only is peculiar
to the Old High German participle present, in relation to
other adjectives, that in its uninflected adverbial state it
retains the defining pronominal base *YA* in its contraction to *i*; therefore *këpanti*, "giving," not *kepant*, like *plint*.
It is, however, to be observed, that there is far more
frequent occasion to use this form divested of case terminations in the participle present, than in all other adjectives, as the definite form in *nds* in Gothic, in the
nominative singular masculine, corresponds to it; and as
it may be assumed, that here the *i* supplies the place of
the case termination, which has been laid aside; so that it
is very often arbitrary whether the definite form of the
participle, or the uninflected form in *i*, be given. So in
Grimm's hymns (II. 2.), *sustollens* is rendered by the uninflected *ufpurrenti*, and *baptizans* by *taufantêr*, although the
reverse might just as well occur, or both participles might
stand in the same form, whether that of the nominative
or adverbial. As regards the Old Saxon forms mentioned by Grimm, namely, *slâpandyes* or *slâpandeas*,
"*dormientis*," *gnornondyê*, "*maerentes*," *buandyum*, "*habitan-
tibus*," they should, in my opinion, be rather adduced in

proof of the proposition, that the participle present has, in the dialect mentioned, preserved the defining element more truly than other adjectives; and that those forms have maintained themselves in the degree of the Gothic [G. Ed. p. 388.] forms like *manvyana*, mentioned at p. 362, than that a theme in *ya* belonged to the Old High German participle present before its conjunction with the pronominal syllable."

DEGREES OF COMPARISON.

291. The comparative is expressed in Sanskrit by the suffix *tara*, feminine *tarâ*, and the superlative by *tama*, feminine *tamâ*, which are added to the common masculine and neuter theme of the positive; *e.g.* *punya-tara*, *punya-tama*, from *punya*, "pure"; *śuchi-tara*, *śuchi-tama*, from *śuchi*, "clean"; *balavat-tara*, *balavat-tama*, from *balavat*, "strong." In the Zend, through a perversion of the language ᳚ᳲᳱ᳴ *tara* and ᳚ᳲᳱ᳴ *tĕma* unite themselves with (in place of the theme) the nominative singular masculine; *e.g.* ᳚ᳲᳱ᳴ *huskôtara* (Vend. S. p. 383) from *huska*, nominative masculine ᳚ᳲᳱ᳴ *huskô*, "dry"; ᳚ᳲᳱ᳴ *śpĕntôtĕma* from *śpĕnta*, "holy"; ᳚ᳲᳱ᳴ *vĕrĕthrazaṅstĕma* (Vend. S. p. 43) from *vĕrĕthrazant*, nom. *vĕrĕthrazaṅs*, "victorious" (literally, "Vritra-slaying ").* According to my opinion ᳚ᳲ *tara* owes

---

* The participle present *sant*, the nominative of which I recognise in ᳚ᳲ *vĕrĕthra-zaṅs*, rests on the analogy of the frequently-occurring ᳚ᳲ *upa-zôit*, "let him strike"; since, in fact, the root *zan* (Sanskrit ᳚ᳲ *han*) suppresses its final vowel, and has treated the *a* which remains according to the analogy of the conjugation vowel of the first and sixth class (see p. 104). The Sanskrit radical ᳚ᳲ *han*, "slaying," which appears in ᳚ᳲ *Vritra-han*, "Vritra slaying," and similar compounds, has, in Zend, taken the form *jan*, the nominative of which is ᳚ᳲ *jâo* (Vend. S. p. 43),

its origin to the root र् *tri* (*tar*, §. 1.), "to   [G. Ed. p. 389.]
step beyond" "to place beyond" (*e. g.* "over a river"); hence,
also, the substantive *tara*, "a float." In the Latin, as Lisch
has acutely remarked, with this root are connected the preposition *trans*, and also *terminus*, as that which is overstepped,
and probably also *tra*, in *in-tra-re, penetra-re*. The superlative suffix I derive, with Grimm (III. 583.), from that of the
comparative, although I assume no theoretic necessity that the
superlative must have been developed through the degree of
the comparative. But *tama*, as a primitive, presents no satisfactory etymology. I formerly thought of the base तन् *tan*,
"to extend," whence, also, ταρος could be explained; but then
तम *tama* would be no regular formation, and I now prefer
recognising in it an abbreviation of *tarama*, partly because the superlative suffix इष्ठ *ishtha* may be satisfactorily considered as derived from its comparative *íyas*,
through the suffix *tha*, which, in the Greek, is contained in
the form of το, as well in ισ-τος as in ταιος, for ταρτος or
ταροτος. In this manner, therefore, is formed ταιο-ς and
तमस् *tama-s* : they both contain the same primitive, abbreviated in a similar manner, but have taken a different derivative suffix, as in πέμπ-τος contrasted with पञ्चम *panchama*,
"the fifth": the vowel, however, is more truly retained
in the derivative ταιος than in its base τερος. In Latin,
तमस् *tama-s* has become *timu-s* (*optimus, intimus, extimus,*
ultimus); and, by the exchange of the *t* with *s*, which
is more usual in Greek than in Latin, *simus*; hence,

---

p 43), and is analogous to the Sanskrit *panthás*, from *panthan*, mentioned
at p. 308. More usually, however, *do* in Zend nominatives stands in the
place of the Sanskrit *án* of the suffix *vant* and *váns*; so that, in Zend, the
sign of the nominative has taken the place of the Indian *n*, the said sign
being *o* for *s*, according to §. 56°. In ᎒᎒᎒ *vdo*, from वान् *váns*, the Zend
o may also be looked upon as belonging to the base (comp. Burnouf's
Yaçna, Notes, p. cxxviii. &c.).

maximus (*mac-simus*) for *mag-simus*.   However, the *simus* is generally preceded by the syllable *is*, which we will hereafter explain.

292. As in comparatives a relation between two, and in [G. Ed. p. 390.] superlatives a relation between many, lies at the bottom, it is natural that their suffixes should also be transferred to other words, whose chief notion is individualized through that of duality or plurality: thus they appear in pronouns, and कतरस् *katara-s* is "which of two persons?" and कतमस् *katama-s*, "which of more than two persons?" एकतरस् *ékataras* is "one of two persons," and *ékatama-s*, "one of more than two." It is hardly necessary to call attention to similar forms in Greek, as πότερος (for κότερος), ἑκάτερος. In ἕκαστος the superlative suffix (στος for ιστος) presents a different modification from that in *ékatama-s*, and expresses "the one of two persons," instead of "the one of many persons." In Latin and German, indeed, the suffix *tara* is not in use in genuine comparatives, but has maintained itself in pronouns in Latin in the form of *TERU* (*ter, teru-m*), and in Gothic in that of *THARA*; hence *uter,· neuter, alter*; Gothic, *hva-thar*,[*] "which of two persons?" Old High German, [G. Ed. p. 391.] *huëdar*, which has remained to us in the adverb *weder*, as an abbreviation of the Middle High Ger-

---

[*] The Gothic resembles the Latin in withdrawing the sign of the nominative from its masculine bases in *ra*, as the latter does from its corresponding bases in *ru*. Hence, above, *hvathar* for *hvathar(a)s*, as *alter* for *alterus*; so also *vair*, "man," = Latin *vir* for *viru-s*. This suppression has, however, not extended itself universally in both languages. In the Gothic, as it appears, the *s* is protected by the two preceding consonants; hence *akrs*, "a field" (comp. Grimm, p. 599); still the adjective nominatives *gaurs*, "mournful" (theme *Gaura*, comp. Sanskrit घोर *ghôra*, "terrible"), and *svêrs*, "honoured," occur, where this cause is wanting, where, however, the preceding long vowel and the diphthong *au* may have operated. In *vair*, indeed, a diphthong precedes; but the *a* is here first introduced through the euphonic law 82. If, in Latin, in adjective bases in *ri*, only the masculine has predominantly given up the *s*, with the preceding

man, combined with a particle of negation *newëder*. *Anthar*, also, our *anderer*, belongs here, and answers to the Sanskṛit षमारस antara-s, whose initial syllable is the same which in षन्य anya, "*alius*," has united itself with the relative base य ya. From this षन्य anya comes anyatara, "*alter*." If, however, षनार antara means, in general, "the other," the comparative suffix is here intended to denote the person following after, passing over this thing; so is, also, the Latin *ceterus* to be considered, from *ce* as demonstrative base (compare *ci-s*, *ci-tra*); and so, also, in Sanskṛit, *itara*, "the other," comes from the demonstrative base *i*, as, in Latin, the adverb *iterum* from the same base."[*] In our German, also, *wieder* is the comparative suffix, and the whole rests, perhaps, on a pre-existing Old High German word *huia-dar* or *huyadar*, with a change of the interrogative meaning into the demonstrative, as in *weder*, *ent--weder*. The *wie* in *wieder*, therefore, should be regarded as, p. 370, *die* in *dieser;* and herein we may refer to the Isidoric *dhëa-sa*.

293. In prepositions, also, it cannot be surprising if one finds them invested with a comparative or superlative suffix, or if some of them occur merely with a comparative termination. For at the bottom of all genuine prepositions,

---

preceding *i*, while *e.g.* the feminine *acris* might have permitted its *is* to have been removed, just as well as the masculine, I can find the reason of this firm adherence of the feminine to the termination *is* only in the circumstance that the vowel *i* particularly agrees with that gender, as it is in Sanskṛit (although long), according to §. 119., the true vowel of formation for the feminine base. In Gothic, the suppression of the nominative sign *s* is universal in bases in *sa* and *si*, in order that, as the final vowel of the base is suppressed, two *s* should not meet at the end of the word; hence *e.g.* the nominative *drus*, "a fall," from *DRUSA ;* *garuns*, "a market," from *GARUNSI*, f.

[*] I have traced back the comparative nature of this adverb, which Voss derives from *iter*, "the journey," for the first time in my Review of Forster's Sanskṛit Grammar in the Heidelb. Jahrb. 1818. i. p. 479.

at least in their original sense, there exists a relation between
[G. Ed. p. 392.]   two opposite directions — thus, " over,"
"from," "before," "to," have the relations " under," "in," "towards," " from," as their counter-poles and points of comparison, as the right is opposed to the left; and is always
expressed in Latin, also, with the comparative suffix, *dexter*
(दक्षिण *dakshina*), *sinister.*   As, however, the comparative nature of these formations is no longer recognised in the present
condition of the Latin, the suffix *ter* admits of the further
addition of the customary *ior* (*dexterior, sinisterior,* like
exterior, interior); while the superlative *timus* has affixed
itself to the core of the word (*dextimus* or *-tumus, sinistimus*).
The prepositions which, in Latin, contain a comparative
suffix, are *inter, præter, propter,* the adverbially-used *subter,*
and probably, also, *obiter* (compare *audacter, pariter*).*   To
inter answers the Sanskrit अन्तर् *antar,* "among," "between ";
for which, however, a primitive *an* is wanting, as in Sanskrit
the relation "in" is always expressed by the locative. Notwithstanding this, *antar,* in regard to its suffix, is an analogous
word to प्रातर् *prâtar,* " in the morning," from the preposition
[G. Ed. p. 393.]   *pra,* "before,"† with a lengthened *a,* as in the

---

* I was of opinion, when I first treated this subject (Heidelb. Jahrb.
1818, p. 480), that *ob-i-ter* must be so divided, and *i* looked upon as the
vowel of conjunction. As, however, the preposition *ob* is connected with
the Sanskrit अभि *abhi,* " to," " towards," the division *obi-ter* might also be
made, and the original form of the preposition recognised in *obi* : observe
the Sanskrit derivative अभितस् *abhi-tas,* "near," from *abhi* with the suffix
tas. The common idea, however, that *obiter* is compounded of *ob* and
iter cannot entirely be disproved, partly as then *obiter* would be a similar
compound to *obviam.*

† Comp. *ni, pari, prati,* for *ni,* &c. in certain compounds. Formations
which do not quite follow the usual track, and are rendered intelligible by
numerous analogies, are nevertheless frequently misunderstood by the
Indian Grammarians. Thus Wilson, according to native authorities,
derives अन्तर् *antar* from *anta,* "end," with *râ,* " to arrive at," and the
analogous

Greek πρωΐ from προ. For the relation "under," the Sanskṛit has the preposition अधस् adhas, which I have elsewhere explained as coming from the demonstrative base
अ a; from which, also, come अधर a-dhara and अधम, a-dhama,
"the under one," or "the most under," to which inferus and
infimus are akin, as fumus to धूमस् dhûma-s, "smoke," and,
with a nasal prefixed, as in ἀμφί in relation to अभि abhi,
and in ἄμφω, "ambo," answering to उभौ ubhâu, Old Sclavonic oba. The suffixes धर dhara and धम dhama are, in my
opinion, only slightly-corrupted forms of the tara and tama
mentioned in §. 291.; as also in प्रथम prathama, "the
first," m. from pra, "before," the T sound of the suffix is
somewhat differently transposed. The suffix dhas of adhas,
"beneath," however, has exactly the same relation to tas,
in अतस् atas, "from here," as dhara, dhama, have to tara,
tama; and therefore adhas, as a modification of atas, is, in
respect to its suffix, a cognate form of subtus, intus. The
usual intention of the suffix तस् tas, like that of the Latin
tus, is to express distance from a place. In this, also, the
Greek θεν (from θες, comp. §. 217.) corresponds with it,
which, in regard to its T sound, rests on the form धस् dhas
in अधस् adhas (§. 16.), as the latter also serves as the pat-
tern of the Old Sclavonic suffix dû, which only occurs in
pronouns, and expresses the same relation as तस् tas, θεν,
tus: e.g. ovo-ûdû, "hence,"[•] ono-ûdû, "thence." The form
dû, however, corresponds to the euphonic alteration, which
a final as in the Sanskṛit must suffer before [G. Ed. p. 394.]
sonant letters (§. 25.), viz. that into ð (see §. 255. f.), which in
Zend has become fixed (§. 56ᵇ.).

---

analogous word prâtar from pra, with at, "to go." A relation, nevertheless, between anta, "end," and antar, "among," cannot perhaps be
denied, as they agree in the idea of room. They are, however, if they
are related, sister forms, and the latter is not an offshoot of the former.

[•] The demonstrative base OVO answers remarkably to the Zend
ανανα ava, with o for a, according to §. 255. (a.).

"Remark.—Dobrowsky p. 451 gives *ûdû* 'as the full form of the suffix, just as he also lays down a suffix *ûdye*, which forms adverbs of place, as *kûdye*, "where?" *onûdye*, "there." As, however, the definitive pronoun, which has been treated of at p. 353, &c., exists in these two adverbs, *ûdû*, *ûdye*, and forms, with *sche*, *ûdûsche*, *ûdyesche*, for *yûdû*, &c.; and as this pronoun is, in general, so frequently compounded with other adverbs, there is every reason to assume that it is also contained in *ovo-ûdû*, *ono-ûdû*, *on'-ûdye*, *ĉ-ûdye*, and others. But how is the *û* itself in *u-dû*, *yû-dye*, to be explained? I cannot speak with confidence on this point; but as, according to §. 255. (*g.*), in the last element of the diphthong *û* a vocalised nasal is sometimes recognised, *yudû*, *yûdye*, might be regarded as corruptions of *yondû*, *yondye*, and, in respect to their nasal, be compared with the Latin *inde*, *unde*, from *I, U.* *Yûdye*, *yûdyû*, might also have proceeded from the feminine accusative *yû*, which would again conduct us to a nasal (§. 266.): this accusative would then stand as theme to the derivative adverb, as our preposition *hinter*, Old High German *hintar*, has arisen from *hin*, a petrified accusative, on which the Gothic *hina-dag*, "this day," "to day," throws light. Before the suffix *dye*, however, elder form *de*, occur also the pronouns in a simple form, as *gdye*, "where?" (more anciently *kde*, with the final vowel of the base *KO* suppressed); *zdye* (older *sde*), "here"; *idyesche*, "where" (relative). As *e* (ε), according to §. 255. (*b.*), frequently stands as the corruption of an older *i*, I recognise in the suffix *de* the Sanskrit धि *dhi*, from अधि *adhi*, "over," "upon" "towards," (from the demonstrative base *a*), which, in Greek, is far more widely diffused in the form of θι (πόθι, ἄλλοθι)"

294. In German, even more than in Latin, the prepositions shew themselves inclined to combine with the comparative suffix. To the Sanskrit अन्तर् *antar*, Latin *inter*, mentioned above (at p. 392, G. ed.), corresponds our *unter*, Gothic

undar, with *u* for the old *a*, according to §. 66.* If, however, the, in my opinion, incontrovertible original identity
of the latter with the two former is recognised, [G. Ed. p. 305.]
one must not, with Grimm (III. 260.), derive *undar* from the
preposition *und*, " as far as," &c., by a suffix *ar*, and so again
divide the *dar;* for *undar*,† as transmitted from an ancient
period of the language, was already formed, before the
existence of a German dialect, and the abovementioned
preposition has only to dispose itself according to the
relations of sound mentioned in §§. 66. 91. The matter
is different with the Old High German *af-tar*, " after,"
for the primitive language, or languages, transmit to
us only अप *apa, ἀπό*, " from "; to which, in the spirit of
अन्तर *antar, inter, subter*, &c., the old comparative suffix
has first united itself upon German ground. In Gothic,
aftra means " again." which I look upon as an abbreviation of *aftara*, as in Latin *extra, intra, contra*, and others,
as feminine adjectives, from *extera*, &c. In regard
to the termination however, *aftra*, and similar forms
in *tra, thra*, appear to me as datives, *i. e.* original instrumentals (§. 160.), as also, in the Sanskrit, this case occurs
as an adverb, *e. g.* in अन्तरेण *antarêna*, " between." Perhaps, also, the Sanskrit pronominal adverbs in *tra*, although
they have a locative meaning, like यत्र *yatra*, " where,"
are to be regarded as instrumental forms, according to
the principle of the Zend language (§. 158.), and of the
gerund in य *ya*, (Gramm. Crit. §. 638. Rem.), so that their
tra would be to be derived from तरा *tard* : compare forms
like मनुष्यत्रा *manushya-trá*, " *inter homines* " (Gramm. Crit.

---

* Regarding *dar* and *tar* for *thar*, see §. 91.

† Grimm however, also, at II. 121. &c., divides *bróth-ar, vat-ar*
(" brother," " father "), although the many analogous words denoting relationship in the German and the cognate languages clearly prove the *T* sound
to belong to the derivative suffix (see Gramm. Crit. §. 178. Rem.).

§. 252. suff. *trá*).   As *aftra* is related to *aftar,* so is the Gothic
vithra, "against," to the Old High German *widar*, our *wider*,
the primitive of which is supplied by the Sanskrit through its
[G. Ed. p. 396.]   inseparable preposition फि *vi*, which expresses separation, distraction, *e.g.* in *visrip*, "to go from one
another," "to disperse."   Exactly similar is the Sanskrit
फि *ni*, to which I was the first to prove the meaning "below"
to belong,* and whence comes the adjective नीच *nícha*, "low"
(Gramm. Crit. §. 111.), the base of our *nieder*, Old High Ger-
[G. Ed. p. 397.]   man *ni-dar*.†   From *hin-dar*, Old High
German *hin-tar*, comes our *hin-ter* which has already been
discussed (p. 394, G. ed. compare Grimm. III. 177. c.).
In the Old High German *sun-dar*, Gothic *sun-dró*,
"*seorsim*," afterwards a preposition, our *sondern*, *dar* is,
in like manner, clearly the comparative suffix, and the
base appears to me, in spite of the difference of signi-

___

* It is usual to attribute to it the meaning "in," "into," which cannot
in any way be supported.

† Grimm assents to my opinion, which has been already expressed in
another place, regarding the relationship of फि *ni* and *nidar* (III. 258,
259): he wishes, however, to divide thus *nid-ar*, and to suppose a Gothic
verb *nithan*, *nath*, *nêthun*, to which the Old High German *ginâda* (our
Gnade) may belong.   Does, however, *gi-nâda* really signify *humilitas*?
It appears that only the meaning *gratia* can be proved to belong to it;
and this is also given by Grimm, I. 617. and II. 235. *gratia, humanitas*,
where he divides *ki-nâ-da*, which appears to me correct, and according to
which *nâ* would be the root, and *da* the derivative suffix; as in the etymologically clear *ki-wâ-da*, "*afflatus*," to which the Sanskrit gives वा *wa*,
"to blow," as root, the Gothic gives *vô* (§. 69.) (*vaia, vaivó*).   To *gi-nâ-
-da*, indeed, the Sanskrit supplies no root *nâ*, but perhaps *nam*, "to bend
oneself," the *m* of which, according to the laws of euphony, is suppressed
before *t*, which does not produce Guna; as *nata*, "bent," *nati*, "bending,"
with the preposition *sam, san-nati*, which Wilson explains by "reverence,"
"obeisance," "reverential salutation."   As the Gothic inseparable preposition *ga*, Old High German *gi* or *ki*, is, as Grimm first acutely remarked,
identical with the Sanskrit *sam*, *gi-nâ-da* has much the same formation
with *san-na-ti*: it would, however, still better agree with the feminine
                                                                 passive

fication, related to the Sanskrit सम् *sam*, "with" (compare
Gothic *samath*, "together with," Old High German *samant*),
and the *u*, therefore, is from *a*, according to §. 66. The
Latin *con-tra*, however, is nearly just as much opposed in
meaning to its primitive *cum*; and as *cum* (compare σύν)
belongs, in like manner, to सम् *sam*, so *sundar*, *sundrô*, and
contra, would be, in a double respect, sister forms. Observe,
also, the Gothic *samath*, Old High German *samant*, "together with": the latter answers surprisingly to the
Sanskrit समन्त *samanta* (from *sam + anta*, "an end"), the
ablative of which, *samantât*, as also the adverb, *samantatas*,
mean "everywhere." Perhaps, too, in all other Old High
German adverbs in *nt* (Grimm. III. 214.), the said अन्त *anta*
is contained, for the meaning "end," cannot be unexpected
in adverbs of place and time, and, like *Mitte*, "mid,"

---

passive participle *san-na-tâ*. Be that as it may, so much is certain, that
there is no necessity for a hypothetic Gothic base *nith* or *nath*, either for
the substantive *gi-nada* or for the preposition *nidar*, as they can be fully
set at rest by the existence of a Sanskrit primitive नि *ni*, "below," and
the comparative suffix *dar*, which frequently occurs in prepositions. And
as the circumstance that genuine original prepositions never come from
verbs, but are connected with pronouns, I must, with regard to its etymology, keep back every verb from our *nidar*. Grimm wishes also to divide
the Gothic preposition *vi-thrâ*, Old High German *wi-dar*, into *vith-ra*,
wid-ar, and to find their base in the Anglo-Saxon preposition *widh*,
English *with*, Old Sclavonic *wid*, Old Norman *vidh*, Swedish *vid*, Danish
ved, which mean "with," and, according to appearance, are wanting in
the Gothic and High German. If, however, one considers the easy and
frequent interchange of *v*, *b*, and *m* (वारि *vâri*, "water,"=mare, βρότός==
मृतस् *mritas*, "mortuus"), one would rather recognise, in the above prepositions, dialectic variations of sound from the Gothic *mith*, which is of
the same import with them (=the Zend ꝏꝏ *mat*), and which, in most
of the dialects mentioned, maintains itself equally with the other forms;
as it often occurs, in the history of languages, that the true form of a word
is equally preserved with a corruption of it.

(compare *inmitten*, "in the midst") and *Anfang*, "beginning," it attaches itself first to the prepositional ideas:
therefore *hinont*, "this side," *enont*, "that side," would be
the same as "at this end," "at that end." With regard
to the comparative forms there is, further, the Old High
German *for-dar, fur-dir* ("*porro*," "*amplius*"), our *für-der*
to be mentioned, whence *der vordere, vorderste*.

[G. Ed. p. 398.] "Remark 1.—As we have endeavoured
above to explain the Gothic *af-tra* and *vithra* as datives, I believe I can with still more confidence present the forms in
thrô or *tarô* as remarkable remains of ablatives. Their meaning corresponds most exactly to that of the Sanskrit ablative,
which expresses the withdrawing from a place, and to that of
the Greek adverbs in θεν; thus *hva-thrô*, "whence?" *tha-thrô*,
"thence," *yain-thrô*, "hence," *alya-thrô*, "from another
quarter," *inna-thrô*, "from within," *uta-thrô*, "from without," *af-tarô*, "from behind," *dala-thrô*, "from under," and
some others, but only from pronouns, and, what is nearly the
same, prepositions. I might, therefore, derive *dalathrô*,
not from *dal*, "a valley," but suppose a connection with
the Sanskrit अधर *adhara*, "the under person," with aphæresis of the *a* and the very common exchange of the *r*
with *l* (§. 20.). Perhaps, however, on the contrary, *thal* is
so named from the notion of the part below. As to the
ablative forms in *tarô, thrô*, the *ð* corresponds to the Sanskrit *ât* (§. 179.), with *ð*, according to rule, for आ *â* (§. 69.),
and apocope of the *t*; so that *ð* has the same relation to
the to-be-presupposed *ât* that in Greek οὕτω has to οὕτως,
from οὕτωτ (§. 183. Note * p. 201). Many other Gothic adverbs in *ð*, as *sinteinô*, "always," *sniumundô*, "hastily," *sprantô*,
"suddenly," *thridyô*, "thirdly," &c., might then, although
an ablative meaning does not appear more plainly in them
than in the Latin *perpetuo, cito, subito, tertio*, and others, be
rather considered as ablatives than as neuter accusatives of
indefinite (Grimm's weak) forms; so that *thridyô* would

answer to the Sanskrit ablative *tritíyât*, while the common
Gothic declension extends the ordinal bases in *a* by an
unorganic *n*; thus *THRIDYAN*, nom. *thridya*. It must
be further observed, that all unorganic adjective bases in
an are, in general, only used where the adjective is rendered definite through a pronoun preceding it; that therefore the forms in *ô*, which pass for adverbial, are, for the
very reason that no pronoun precedes them, better assigned to the definite (strong) declension than to the indefinite; especially as most of them are only remains of
an old adjective, which is no longer preserved in other
cases, and, according to their formation, belong to a period
where the indefinite adjective declension had not yet received the unorganic addition of an *n*. As to the translation of τοὐναντίον, 2 Cor. ii. 7., by *thata andaneithô*, here of
course *andaneithô* is the neuter accusative; but the inducement for using the indefinite form is supplied by the
article, and τοὐναντίον could not be otherwise literally rendered. The case may be similar with 2 Cor. iv. 17., where
Castiglione takes *thata andavairthô* for the [G. Ed. p. 399.]
nominative, but Grimm for the adverbial accusative : as it
would else be an unsuitable imitation of the Greek text,
where τὸ does not belong to αὐτίκα, but to ἐλαφρόν. In my
opinion, however, it can in no case be inferred from these
passages that the adverbs in *ô*, without an article preceding
them, belong to the same category. Moreover, also, *andaneithô* and *andavairthô* do not occur by themselves alone ad-
verbially. As, then, *thrô* has shewn itself to us to be an
abbreviation of *thrôt*, it is a question whether the suppression of the *t* by a universal law of sound was requisite, as
in Greek, and in the Prâkṛit, all *T* sounds are rejected
from the end of words, or changed into Σ. It is certain
that the *T* sounds (*t*, *th*, *d*), which, in the actual condition of the Gothic, are finals, as far as we can follow their
etymology, had originally a vowel after them, so that

c c

they are final sounds of a second generation, comparabl
in that respect to the Sclavonic final consonants (§. 255. *l*.
This holds good, for example, with regard to *th, d*, in th
3d person singular and plural, and the 2d person plura
= Sanskrit ति *ti*, अन्ति *anti*, थ *tha* or त *ta* ; and I explain th
th or *d*, which, in pronominal bases, expresses direction t
a place, as coming from the Sanskrit suffix ध *dha* (ह *ha*)
which, in like manner, in pronouns expresses the locativ
relation.   The passing over from the locative relation t
the accusative, expressing the direction whither, cannot b
surprising, as, even in Sanskrit, the common locative ad
verbs in *tra*, and the ablatives in *tas*, occur also with accu
sative meaning, *i. e.* expressing the direction to a plac
(see *tatra* in my Glossary).   The Sanskrit suffix ध *dh*
appears, in common language, abbreviated to *ha*, and i
found, indeed, only in *i-ha*, "here," from the pronomina
base *i* and सह *sa-ha*—in the Vedic dialect and Zend *sa-dha*—
which I derive from the pronominal base *sa*.   It ought
according to its origin, and consistently with the usua
destination of the suffix *dha*, to mean "here *or* there": i
has, however, become a preposition, which expresses "with.'
The adverb इह *iha*, "here," is, in Zend, ‌ *idha*,* and fre

[G. Ed. p. 400.]   quently occurs in combination with ‌ *na*
"not"; so that ‌ *naēdha*† means "nor," answering t
‌ *nōit*, "neither" (literally "not it," from *na + it*, §. 33.)
From ‌ *ava* and ‌ *aēta*, "this" (mas.), comes ‌

---

* Vend. Sâde, p. 868. several times: ‌ ‌ ‌ ‌ ‌.
iman idha vachô framrava, "*hæc hic verba enuntia*," which Anqueti
translates by "*en prononçant bien ces paroles*."   In the same page als
occurs repeatedly ‌ *adha*, with the same meaning, from the demon
strative base *a*, as in the Vêda's अध *adha* (Rosen's Sp. p. 10), withou
perceptible meaning.

† *a + i* makes *ē*, according to §. 2. ; and from *nēdha* is formed, by §. 28.
naēdha.

avadha and ᨈᨌᨕᨁᨈ *atta-dha* (Vend. S: p. 164). To the Zend-Vêdic suffix *dha* corresponds most exactly the Greek *θα*, in *ἔνθα* and *ἐνταῦ-θα*, "here." Perhaps *ἔνθα* and ᨌᨁ *i-dha*, इह *iha*, are, with regard to their base, identical ; *ἔνθα*, therefore, is for *ἴνθα* from *ἴθα* (comp. *in*, *inde*), as nasals are easily prefixed to another consonant, and thus *ἀμφί* answers to अभि *abhi*, *ἄμφω* to उभौ *ubháu*, Old Sclavonic *oba* ; but *αὐθα*, in the triple compound *ἐν-τ'-αῦθα*, is completely the Zend ᨌᨁᨕᨕᨌ *avadha*, whose theme *ava* has been contracted in the Greek to *αὐ* (compare *αῦ-θι* and *αὐ-τός*, the latter being combined with the article), but in the Old Sclavonic it is more correctly preserved in the form of *OVO*.[*] To the word इहत्य *ihatya*, "of this place," which is derived from इह *iha* through the suffix त्य *tya*, corresponds the Greek *ἐνθάσιος*, with *σ* from *τ* ; compare, with regard to the suffix, the Latin *propitius* from *prope*, and, in the Gothic, *frama-thya*, "a foreigner," through which the preposition *fram* shews itself to be an abbreviation of *frama*. As in the Sanskrit the suffix त्य *tya* belongs only to local adverbs and prepositions, so might also the Gothic *ni-thyis*, "cousin" (for *ni-thyas*, §. 135.), as *propinquus*, or one who stands somewhat lower in relationship than a brother, &c.,[†] be derived from the   [G. Ed. p. 401.]

---

[*] Before my acquaintance with the Zend, and deeper examination of the Sclavonic, I believed I could make out the Greek base *αὐ* to agree with the Sanskrit *amu*, "*ille*," by casting out the *m* (as *κοῦρος* with *kumára*): now, however, अव *ava* and *OVO* have clearly nearer claims to take the Greek forms between them.

[†] Terms of relationship often express the relation, of which they are the representatives, very remotely, but ingeniously. Thus नप्तृ *naptri*, "a grandson," is, I have no doubt, compounded of *na*, "not," and *pitri*, "father"; and "not-father" is regarded as a possessive compound, "not having as father," in relation to the grandfather, who is not the father of the grandson. In Latin it would be difficult to find the etymology of *nepos* (*nepot-*)—and the same may be said of our word *neffe*—without the aid of the word *Vater*, which is fully preserved from the Sanskrit. In the

meaning

ancient preposition *ni*, mentioned at p. 382, from which,
in Sanskrit, *nitya* actually comes, but differently related,
and with a signification answering less to the meaning
of the preposition, namely, *sempiternus.* In consideration
of the aspirates in Greek being easily interchanged, and,
e.g. in the Doric, ῎ΟΡΝΙΞ is said for ῎ΟΡΝΙΘ, one may also
recognise in the syllable χο, in forms like παντα-χό-θεν,
παντα-χό-σε, πολλαχόσε, and others, a cognate form of the
suffix θα, *dha,* or of the corrupted ह *ha* (comp. §. 23.).   At
the bottom of these forms lies, in my opinion, as the theme,
the plural neuter, which need not be wondered at, as πάντα
and πολλά are also used as first members of compounds
(πολλά-σημος, παντά-μορφος).   Πανταχο might, in the identity of its suffix with θα, *dha,* or *ha,* mean "everywhere";
whence may then be said πανταχό-σε, "from everywhere,"
&c., as we combine our locative adverbs *wo* and *da* with
her and *hin* (*woher, wohin*); and in Greek, also, ἐκεῖθι, ἐκεῖσε,
ἐκεῖθεν, which might literally mean *in illic, versus illic, ab
illic,* as ἐκεῖ is a local adverb.   Forms in χο, however, are in
a measure raised to themes capable of declension, though
only for adverbs, and develope, also, case-forms, as πανταχοῦ,
πανταχοῖ (old locative and dative), πανταχῇ.   The addition
of new suffixes or terminations to those already existing,
but which are obsolete, appears to me assuredly more natural
than, as Buttmann supposes, the introduction of an un-
meaning αχ or even αχο, in which case we should have
to divide παντ-αχό-θεν, &c.   But as the χο under discussion has arisen from θα, *dha,* I think I recognise in the
χι of ᾗχι a corruption of the suffix θι, from f़ि *dhi*;   in
which respect might be compared ἄγχι, as a sister form to

---

meaning of *Neffe* the negation of the relationship of father points to the
uncle.   The Indian Grammarians, according to Wilson, see in *naptri* the
negation, but not the father, but the root *pat,* "to fall," and a Unâdi
suffix *tri.*

अधि *adhi*, "to," "towards," with a nasal introduced. As a
third form in which the Vêdic-Zend suffix *dha* appears in
Greek, I notice σε, with σ for θ, ध *dh*, as μεσος from मध्य
madhya, "midst," the *y* of which has assimilated itself,
in the form μέσσος, to the σ. The suffix σε, however, in
that it is altered from its original intention to denote
rest in a place, to the expression of motion to a place,
answers to the Gothic *th* or *d*, whence we set out in this
examination, in forms like *hva-th*, πό-σε, "whither?" also
hvad—John xiii. 3. *hvad gaggis*, ποῦ ὑπάγεις—*yain-d*, ἐκεῖ-σε,
alya-th, ἄλλο-σε. To the Zend *idha*, Greek ἔνθα, corresponds
i-th; which, however, contrary to the original intention of
the form, does not mean "thither," but is used as a conjunction—"but," "if," "then" (1 Cor. vii. 7.). To this class,
also, belongs *ath*, which only occurs in combination with *than*
—*ath-than*, "but," like *ith-than*; and it has   [G. Ed. p. 402.]
the Vêdic-Zend *a-dha* as prototype (§. 399.). *Thad*, in combination with the relative particle *ei*, which is probably connected with य *ya*, has preserved the original locative
meaning together with the accusative, and *thad-ei* may be
cited as "where" and "whither." The *d* in these forms,
answering to the Greek θ, agrees with the rule for the transmutation of sounds (§. 87.); and it is to be observed that medials
at the end of a word freely pass into aspirates—compare *bauth*,
bu-dum (§. 91.);—so that the Gothic *T* sound of the suffix
under discussion, after it has, in one direction, diverged from
the Greek, has, in another, again approached it.

"Remark 2.—As we have above recognised ablatives in
the formations in *thrô*, *tarô*, so we find in this comparative
suffix, also, a remnant of the Sanskrit locative; in which,
however, as in the adverbs in *th*, *d*, the expression of
repose in a place is changed into that of motion to a
place—in *hidrê*,* "hither," Mark xi. 3. Luke xiv. 21.; *hva-drê*,
"whither?" John vii. 35. On the other hand, *yaindrê* ac-

---

* Vide §. 991.

tually occurs with a locative meaning; *tharei leik, yaindrê galisand sik arans,* '*ὅπου τὸ σῶμα, ἐκεῖ συναχθήσονται οἱ ἀετοί.*' Compare these forms with the Sanskrit, as, *adharê,* " in the lower," and the Lithuanian *wilkė* (§. 197.). That, however, the Gothic *ê,* which in the genitive plural masculine and neuter answers to the Sanskrit आ *â* (§. 69.), moreover corresponds to ए *ê,* is proved by preterites like *nêmum,* 'we took,' answering to the singular *nam*; as, in Sanskrit, नेमिम *nêmima,* 'we bent ourselves,' answers to ननम *nanama* or नमाम *nanâma,* 'I bent myself.' "

295. The superlative suffix तम *tama* occurs in the Gothic also in the form of *TUMAN,* nominative *tuma,* or, with *d* for *t* in prepositional derivations, either simply or in combination with the common superlative suffix *ISTA*; thus, *af-tuma,* "*posterus,*" *af-tumists,* "*postremus,*" *hin-dumists,* " *extremus.*" If one considers the Indian suffix तम *tama,* to have suffered apocope of the *a* — as in Latin, also, *timus* appears abbreviated to *tim* in adverbs like *viri-tim, caterva-tim,* which I have already, in another place (Heidelb. Jahrb. 1818. p. 480), explained, together with forms like *legi-timus,* as superlatives—one may look for that *tam* in the Gothic cor-

[G. Ed. p. 403.]   rupted to *tana,* after the analogy of the accusative masculine of pronouns, like *tha-na =* तम् *tam,* τόν, *hva--na =* कम् *ka-m,* " whom?"; and accordingly regard the prepositional derivations in *tana, dana,* as superlative forms; thus, Gothic *af-tana,* " behind"; *hinduna,* πέραν, Old High German *ni-dana,* "under" (compare our *hie-nieden,* "here below." As, however, in Old High German there exist, also, formations in *ana* without a preceding *t* sound (Grimm III. 203, &c.), it is a question whether *innana* " within," *ûzana* "abroad," *forana* shortened to *furna* "from the beginning," *fèrrana* "πόρρωθεν," *rûmana* "from a distance," *hôhana* " ὑψόθεν," *heimina* "οἴκοθεν," have lost a *t* or a *d* preceding the *a*; or if they are formed after those in *tana, dana,* in the notion that the whole of the suffix consists merely of *ana*; or, finally, whether they rest on some other principle.

The preposition *obar*, "over," Gothic *ufar*, which answers to the Sanskrit उपरि *upari*, Greek ὐπέρ, has, in the same manner, an adverb *obana*, "above," corresponding to it.

296. In the Sanskrit the appellations of the quarters of the heavens come from prepositions in combination with the root अन्च् *anch*, "to go"; thus the east is denoted as "that which is before," by प्राच् *prânch*, from प्र *pra*, "before"; the west as "that which is over against it," by प्रत्यच् *pratyanch*, from प्रति *prati*, "opposite"; the south as "that below," by अवाच् *avânch*, from अव *ava*, "below"; and its opposite pole, the north, as "that above," is called उदच् *udanch*, from उत् *ut*, "up." Now it is remarkable that in German the names of the quarters of the world shew themselves through their terminations, Old High German *tar* and *tana*, or as they so frequently occur in prepositions, *dar*, *dana*, to be derivations from prepositions, though the nature of their origin has become obscure. The custom of the language disposes of the forms in *r* and *na* in such a manner, that the former expresses the direction whither (Grimm. III. 205.), the latter the direction whence, which, however, was not, perhaps, the original intention of the terminations, both which seem adapted to express the same direction; the former comparatively, with a glance at   [G. Ed. p. 404.] that which is opposite, the latter superlatively, in relation to all the quarters of the globe, as, p. 376, एकतर *ékatara*, "one of two persons," but एकतम *ékatama*, "one of many persons." The west may perhaps be most satisfactorily explained, and in fact, as being etymologically pointed out to be that which lies over against the east, as in Sanskrit. For this object we betake ourselves to the prepositional base *wi*, mentioned at p. 382, whence the comparative *wi-dar*. We do not, however, require to deduce *wës-tar*,*

---

* By writing *wĕ*, Grimm marks the corruption of the *e* from *i*, in which I readily agree with him.

" towards the west," *wës-tana*," from the west," from
the derivative *widar*; but we may keep to its base *wi*,
with the assumption of a euphonic *s*; as in the Sanskrit,
also, some prepositions terminating in vowels in certain
combinations, and before consonants which are disposed
to have an *s* before them, assume this letter; *e. g. pra-
tishkaśa* for *pratikaśu*; and as in Latin *abs*, *os* (for *obs*),
from *ab*, *ob* (§. 96.). But if it were preferred to deduce
wëstar, *wëstana*, from the derivative *widar*, it would
then be necessary to force the *d* of derivation into
the base, and, according to §. 102., change it into *s*.
The east is more difficult of explanation than the west
—Old High German *ôs-tar*, "towards the east," *ôs-tana*,
" from the east,"—for several prepositions start up together that would gladly sustain this quarter of the heavens.
It is not necessary that the preposition after which the
east is named should elsewhere, also, be received as a
German preposition; for in this appellation a preposition might have incorporated itself, which, except in this
case, is foreign to the practice of the German language.
[G. Ed. p. 405.] It may therefore be allowable for us,
first of all, to turn to a preposition which, in the Indian
language, is prefixed to the south, and, in the German,
may have changed its position to the east; the more so,
as, with prepositions, the principal point is always where
one stands, and the direction to which one is turned;
and one may, with perfect justice, turn that which is at the
bottom to the uppermost, or to the front. In Zend, *ava*,
which in Sanskrit signifies " below," exists as a pronoun,
and means " this"; and as this pronoun is also proper to
the Sclavonic (*OVO*, nom. *ov*), and occurs in Greek as αὐ,
(αὐ-θι, αὐτός, see p. 387), it need not surprise us to find an
obsolete remnant of this base in German, and that the
east is taken as the side opposed to the west. Here it
may be necessary to observe, that in Sanskrit the preposition *ava*, in like manner, annexes a euphonic -*s*; from

avas, therefore, by suppressing the last *a* but one, would
arise (as in Greek *αὐ*) *aus* (different from our *aus*, Old
High German *úz*, Gothic *út*, in Sanskrit उत् *ut*, " up "),
and hence, according to §. 80., *ôs:* the old northern form
is *austr, austan*. The Latin *aus-ter* might then—to which
Grimm has already alluded (Wiener Jahrb. B. 28. p. 32)—
be placed with more confidence beside the Old High
German as a sister form, and led back by the hand of our
comparative suffix to the preposition, which in Sanskrit
has given its name to the south, bold as it at the first
glance might appear, if we declared *aus-ter* and अवाच् *avânch*
(*ava + anch*), "southern," to be related. The derivations
from *haurio*, or *αὔω*, certainly deserve less notice. As,
however, the juxta-position of *austar* with the Latin *auster*
and the Indian preposition *ava, avas*, is most suitable,
we refrain from giving other prepositional modes in
which one might arrive at the appellation of the east in
German. As the most natural point of departure, we
cannot place it in so subordinate a position to the west as to
mark it out as "not west" (*a-ustar* from *a-*   [G. Ed. p. 406.]
-wëstar). We turn now to the south, in Old High German *sun-dar*, " towards the south," *sundana*, "from the
south," the connection of which with the *sundrô, sundar*,
mentioned at p. 383, is not to be mistaken. The south,
therefore, appeared to our ancestors as the remote distance, and the reason for the appellation of this quarter
of the heavens being clearly in allusion to space, is a new
guarantee for the prepositional derivation of the names for
east and west, as also for the fact that the designation of the
north, too, has subjected itself to a preposition, although it is
still more veiled in obscurity than that of the three sister
appellations. We cannot, however, omit calling attention to the Sanskrit preposition निस् *nis*, which signifies
" out, without," and before sonant letters, to which *d* belongs
(§. 25.) according to a universal law of euphony, appears

in the form of *nir*, which it is also usual to represent as the original form.

297. In the Old Sclavonic the Indo-Greek comparative suffix occurs in *vtoryi*, "the second" (m.), in which the definitive pronoun is contained (p. 352): *vtory-i*, then, is formed from *vtoro-i* (§. 255. *d*.), in which the cardinal number *dwa* is melted down to *v*, corresponding in this respect to the Zend *b* in *b-yarĕ*, "two years," but singular, with *b* as a hardened form from *v*.   To the Sanskrit कतर *katara*, "which of two? m." (Gothic *hva-thar*) and यतर *ya-tara*, "which of both," corresponds etymologically, the Old Sclavonic *ko-tory-i* (as definitive), older *ko-tery-i* and *ye-ter*, feminine *ye-tera* (γε-τερα), neuter *ye-tero*.   The origin of these two pronouns is, however, forgotten, together with their comparative meaning ; for *kutoryi* means "who?" and *yeter*, "some one" (compare p. 352).   Dobrowsky (p. 343), however, in which he is [G. Ed. p. 407.] clearly wrong, divides the suffix into *ot-or;* for although the interrogative base *KO* may lay aside its *o*, and combine with the demonstrative base *to* (*kto*, "*quis?*" Dobr. p. 342), still it is more in accordance with the history of language to divide *ko-toryi* than *kut-oryi* or *koto-ryi*, as the formation *or* would there stand quite isolated ; and besides this the pronoun *i*, "he," from *yo*, does not occur in combination with the demonstrative base *to*, and yet *ye-ter* is said.

298. A small number of comparatives are formed in Sanskrit by ईयस् *íyas*, and the corresponding superlative by इष्ठ *ishtha*, in which *ishtha*, as has been already remarked (p. 389.), we recognise a derivation from *íyas* in its contraction to *ish* (compare *ish-ta*, "offered," from *yaj*), so that the suffix of the highest degree is properly थ *tha*, through which, also, the ordinal numbers चतुर्थस् *chatur-thas* (τέταρ-το-ς), and षष्ठस् *shash-thas* (ἕκ-τος), are formed, for the notion of the superlative lies very close to the ordinal

numbers above two, as that of order does to the superlatives, and hence the suffix तम *tama* occurs in ordinal
numbers; *e.g.* विंशतितमस् *vinśati-tama-s*, " the twentieth,"
wherefore *ma*, in forms like पञ्चमस् *pancha-ma-s*, " the fifth,"
may be held to be an abbreviation of *tama*. To the form
ish, contracted from *íyas*—euphonic for *is*—in Greek and
Zend *is*, corresponds the Latin *is*, in the superlatives in
is-simus, which I deduce through assimilation from *is-timus*
(comp. §. 101.); the simple *is*, however, which, viewed
from Latin, is a contraction of *iōs* (§. 22.), appears in the
simple form in the adverb *mag-is*, which may be compared
with μεγις in μέγισ-τος. In the strong cases (§. 129.) the
Indian comparative shews a broader form than the *íyas*
above, namely, a long *á* and a nasal preceding the *s*, thus
इयांस् *íyáns* (see §. 9.), This form, how- [G. Ed. p. 408.]
ever, may originally have been current in all the cases,
as the strong form in general (§. 129.), as is probable
through the pervading long *ō* in Latin, *iōris, iōri,* &c., if
one would not rather regard the length of the Latin *o* as
compensation for the rejected nasal: compare the old
accusative *mel-iōsem*, mentioned in §. 22., with Sanskrit
forms like गरीयांसम् *gar-íyáns-am* (*graviorem*). The breadth
of the suffix, which is still remarkable in the more
contracted from *íyas*, may be the cause why the form
of the positive is exposed to great reductions before
it; so that not only final vowels are rejected, as generally before Taddhita suffixes* beginning with a vowel, but
whole suffixes, together with the vowel preceding them,
are suppressed (Gramm. Crit. §. 252.); *e. g.* from मतिमत्
mati-mat, " intelligent," from *mati*, " understanding," comes
mat-íyás; from *balvat*, " strong " (" gifted with strength,"

---

* The Taddhita suffixes are those which form derivative words not
primitives direct from the root itself.

from *bala + vat*), *bal-íyas;* from *kṣhipra*, "quick" (from
the base *kṣhip*, "to throw"), comes *kṣhêp-íyas;* from
kṣhudra, "insignificant," *kṣhêd-íyas;* from *tripra*, "satisfied," *trap-íyas;* since with vowels capable of Guna the
dropping of the suffix is compensated by strengthening
the radical syllable by Guṅa, as in the Zend *vaêdista;*
which Burnouf (Vahista, p. 22) deduces, as it appears to me,
with equal correctness and acuteness from *vîdvas* (*vîdvô*,
§. 56ᵇ., Sanskṛit *vidwas*), "knowing." With respect to
trapíyas, from *tripra*, let it be observed that *ar*, as Guna of
ri, is easily transposed to *ra* (Gramm. Crit. §. 34ᵇ.): compare
the Greek ἔδρακον for ἔδαρκον; πατράσι for παταρσι (see
p. 290, G. ed.). In a similar manner M. Ag. Benary explains
the connection of *varíyas* with *uru* "great," with which he
rightly compares the Greek εὐρύς (Berl. Jahrb. 1834. I.
[G. Ed. p. 409.]　pp. 230, 231). But *varíyas* might also
come from *vara*, "excellent," and *uru* might be an abbreviation of *varu*, which easily runs into one. To the superlative वरिष्ठ *varishṭha*, which does not only mean *latissi-
mus* but also *optimus*, the Greek ἄριστος (therefore Ϝάριστος)
is without doubt akin, the connection of which with εὐρύς one
could scarcely have conjectured without the Sanskṛit. Remarkable, too, is the concurrence of the Greek with the
Sanskṛit in this point, that the former, like the latter, before the gradation suffix under discussion, disburthens itself
of other more weighty suffixes (compare Burnouf's Vahista,
p. 28); thus, ἔχθιστος, αἴσχιστος, οἴκτιστος, κύδιστος, μήκιστος,
ἄλγιστος, from ἔχθρος, &c., exactly as above *kṣhêpishṭhas* and
others from *kṣhipra;* and I believe I can hence explain, according to the same principle, the lengthening of the vowel in
μήκιστος, μᾶσσον, from μακρός, on which principle also rests
the Guna in analogous Sanskṛit forms—namely, as a compensation for the suppression of the suffix. The case is
the same with the lengthened vowel in forms like θᾶσσον,
ἄσσον, where Buttmann (§. 67. Rem. 3. N. **) assumes that

the comparative *ı* has fallen back and united itself with
the α (ą); while, in my opinion, a different account is to be
given of what has become of the *ı* in forms like θάσσων,
βράσσων (§. 300.). The formation of μέγιστος from μέγας,
from μέγαλο-ς, is similar to the origin, in Sanskrit, of
बंहिष्ठ *bańhishtha*, from *bahula*, " much "; from *bahu*, " much "
comes *bhûyishtha*; and μέγ-ιστος, in relation to ΜΕΓΑΛΟ, has
lost as much as *bańh-ishtha*, compared with *bahula*, only that
the Sanskrit positive base is compensated for the loss of *ula* by
the addition of a nasal; which therefore, as Ag. Benary
(l. c.) has very correctly remarked, rests on the same
principle with the Guna in *kshépishtha*, &c.*

" Remark.—It will then, also, be necessary   [G. Ed. p. 410.]
—as Burnouf (Yaçna, p. 131) first pointed out, but afterwards
(Vahista, p. 25), in my opinion, wrongly retracted—to explain
the ए *é* of *sréyas*, " better," *sréshtha*, " the best," as coming
from the *i* of *srî*, " fortune," by Guna, instead of the common
view, in which I formerly concurred, of substituting a useless
sra as positive, and hence, by contraction with *íyas*, *ishtha*,
forming *sréyas*, *sréshtha*. From *srî* comes the derivative *srî-
mat*, " fortunate," from which I deduce *sré-yas*, *sré-shtha*, by
the prescribed removal of the suffix,† although one might

---

* The Guna, however, in the gradation forms under discussion, might
also be accounted for in a different way, namely, by bringing it into connection with the Vriddhi, which occurs before many other Taddhita
suffixes, especially in patronymics, as वैवस्वत *vaivaswata*, from विवस्वत्
vivaswat. On account of the great weight of the gradation suffixes *íyas*,
ishtha, which has given rise to the suppression of the suffix of the positive
base, the initial vowel also of the same would accordingly be raised by
the weaker Guna, instead of by the Vriddhi, as usual (§. 26.). Be that
how it may, one must in any case have ground to assume an historic connection between the Grecian vowel-lengthening in μήκιστος, θᾶσσον, and
others, and that of Sanskrit forms like *kshépíyas*, *kshépishtha*.

† If there existed, as in Zend, a *srîra*, one might hence also derive the
above gradations.

expect in the superlative *śray-ishṭha*, euphonic for *śrê-ishṭha ;*
and on this ground it is that Burnouf takes his objection.
But as in Greek ἔκα-στος, ὁπό-στος (see p. 376), in spite of
the want of the *ι* of *ιστος,* are nevertheless nothing else than
superlative forms, I do not see why, in certain cases, in
Sanskrit, also, the suppression of an *i* may not hold good.
This happens, moreover, in *sthê-shṭha* from *sthi-ra,* " fast,"
sphê-shṭha from *sphi-ra,* " swollen," and *prê-shṭha* from *priy-a,*
" dear." In the latter case, after removing the suffix *a,*
the preceding *y,* also, must retire, since *priy* is only a
euphonic alteration of *pri* (Gramm. Crit. §. 51.) As to the
derivation, however, of the meanings *melior, optimus,* from
a positive with the meaning " fortunate," it may be further
remarked, that, in Sanskrit, " fortune " and " splendour "
are generally the fundamental notions for that which is
good and excellent ; hence, *bhagavat,* " the honourable," " the
[G. Ed. p. 411.] excellent," properly, " the man gifted with
fortune "; for our *besserer, bester,* also Gothic *bat-iza, bat-ists,*
are associated with a Sanskrit root denoting fortune (*bhad,*
whence *bhadra,* " fortunate," " excellent "), which Pott was
acute enough first to remark (Etymol. Inquiries, p. 245), who
collates also *bôlyan,* " to use." The old *d* gives, according
to §. 87., in the Gothic *t,* and the Sanskrit *bh* becomes *b.*
It might appear too daring if we made an attempt to refer
melior also to this root ; but cognate words often assume the
most estranged form through doubled transitions of sound,
which, although doubled, are usual. It is very common for
d to become *l* (§. 17.), and also between labial medials and the
nasal of this organ there prevails no unfrequent exchange
(comp. §. 63.). If, also, the Greek βελτίων, βέλτιστος, should
belong to this class, and the τ be an unorganic addition, which
is wanting in βέλ-τερος, βέλ-τατος, βελ would then give the
middle step between भद् *bhad* and *mel.* The ideal positive
of βελτίων, namely ἀγαθός, might be connected with अगाध
agâdha, " deep," with which, also, the Gothic *gôths* (theme

gôda) is to be compared, with *ô*, according to rule, for **श** *d*
(§. 69.), and medials for Greek aspirates, according to §. 87.

299. From the strong theme **ईयांस** *íyâns*, mentioned at
§. 298., comes the nominative *íyân*, with the suppression
of the final letter rendered necessary through §. 94. The
vocative has a short *a*, and sounds *íyan*. To *íyan* answers
the Greek *ἴων*, and to the vocative *íyan* answers *ἴον*; to
the neuter *íyas* (N. A. V.), identical with the weak theme,
corresponds the Latin *ius* (§. 22.). The Greek, however,
cannot become repossessed of the *s*, which is abandoned
in Sanskrit in the nominative and vocative masculine for
legitimate reasons, since it declines its comparative as
though its theme terminated from the first with *v*; hence
accusative *ἴον-α* for the Sanskrit **ईयांसम्** *íyâns-am*, Latin
iôr-em (*iôs-em*, §. 22.), genitive *ἴον-ος* for *íyas-as*, *iôr-is*.
However, one might, as Pott has already, I believe, noticed
somewhere, reduce the contracted forms like *βελτίω*,
βελτίους, to an original *ἰοσα, ἰοσες, ἰοσας*, corresponding to
íyânsam, *íyânsi* (neuter plural), *íyâns-as*, *íyas-as*, the *σ* of
which, as is so common between two vowels, would be
rejected.* On the other hand, *v*, except in   [G. Ed. p. 412.]
comparatives, on the presupposition that the contracted forms
have rejected an *v* and not *σ*, is suppressed only in a few
isolated words (*Ἀπόλλω, Ποσειδῶ, εἰκώ, ἀηδοῦς*, and a few
others), which, however, the theoretic derivation of the comparative *Σ* renders very embarrasing. We would therefore
prefer giving up this, and assuming, that while the Sanskrit
in the weak, *i.e.* in the majority of cases, has abandoned
the former consonant of *ns*, the Greek, which was still
less favourable to the *vσ-*, has given up the latter, as
perhaps one may suppose in the oldest, as it were, pre-
Grecian period, forms like *βελτιονσα*. It is, however,
remarkable, that while all other European sister lan-

---

* Comp. p. 325 G. ed.

guages have only preserved the last element of t
comparative *ns*—the Latin in the form of *r*—and wh
the Sanskrit also shews more indulgence for the *s* th
for the *n*, the Greek alone has preserved the nas
so that in the comparative it differs in this resp
from all the other languages. Without the interventi
of the Sanskrit and Zend it would be hardly possible
adduce from the European sister languages a cogn
termination to the Greek ἴων, ἴον; or if *iōr* and ἴων shot
be compared, one would think rather of a permutation
liquids,* than that after the Greek ν the prototype of t
Latin *r*, namely σ, has originally existed.

300. In Zend, the superlatives in ⲁⲉⲟⲩⲩ *ista* are mc
numerous than the corresponding ones in Sanskrit, and i
quire no authentication. With regard to their theo
Burnouf has rendered important service, by his excelle
[G. Ed. p. 413.] treatise on the Vahista; and his remarks a
also useful to us in Sanskrit Grammar. In form ⲁⲉⲟ
ista stands nearer to the Greek ιστο-ς than the Indian *ishti*
and is completely identical with the Gothic *ista*, nom, *isi*
(§. 135.), as the Zend frequently exhibits *t* for the Sansk
aspirates. The comparative form which belongs to *ista*
much more rare, but perhaps only on account of the want
occasion for its appearance in the authorities which have be
handed down to us, in which, also, the form in *tara* c
only scantily be cited. An example of the comparati
under discussion is the feminine ⲁⲩⲣⲟⲩⲩⲩⲁⲅ *masyĕhi*, whi
occurs repeatedly, and to which I have already elsewhe
drawn attention.† It springs from the positive ba

---

* Comp. §. 20.

† Berl. Jahrb. 1831. I. p. 372. I then conceived this form to be t
arrived at, that the *y* of the Sanskrit *iyasi* had disappeared, as in the ge
tive termination *hĕ*, from ख्य *sya*; after which the *s* must have passed int
Still the above view of the case, which is also the one chosen by Burn

ᴊᴊᴊᴊᴊ masas, "great" (masŭ, masah, masanh, §§. 56ᵃ. 56ᵇ.),
and confirms, like other Zend forms, the theory which holds
good for the Sanskrit, that other suffixes fall away before
the exponents of the comparative and superlative relation
under discussion. If yêhî is compared with the Sanskrit
feminine base íyasí, the loss of the í shews itself, and then
the a has, through the power of assimilation of the y (§. 42.),
become ê, and s has, according to §. 53., become h. In
the loss of the í the Zend coincides with the Sanskrit forms
like srê-yas, mentioned at p. 397, with which, also, bhû-yas,
"more," and jyâ-yas, "older," agree. Greek comparatives
with a doubled σ before ων, as κρείσσων, βράσσων, ἐλάσσων,
are based on this; which, according to a law of euphony
very universally followed in Prâkrit, have assimilated the y to
the preceding consonant, as elsewhere ἄλλος [G. Ed. p. 414.]
from ἄλγος, Gothic alya-, Latin aliu-s, Sanskrit anya, are
explained (Demonstrative Bases, p. 20). In Prâkrit, in the
assimilations which are extremely common in this dialect,
the weaker consonant assimilates itself to the stronger,
whether this precedes or follows it; thus anna, "the
other," from anya, corresponds to the Greek ἄλλος; the Sanskrit tasya, "hujus," becomes tassa; bhavishyati, "he will
be," becomes bhavissadi,* divya, "heavenly," divva; from

---

is simpler, and closer at hand, although the other cannot be shewn to be
impossible; for it is certain that if the y of íyas had disappeared in Zend,
it would fall to the turn of the preceding í to become y.

* Comp. ἴσσομαι, from ἴσγομαι, with स्यामि syâmi, in composition with
attributive verbs. It may be allowed here preliminarily to mention
another interesting Prâkrit form of the future, which consists in this, that
the Sanskrit s passes into h, but the syllable य ya is contracted to i,
herein agreeing with the Latin i in eris, erit, amabis, amabit, &c.; as,
karihisi, "thou willst make," from karishyasi; sahihimi, "I will endure,"
from sahishyâmi, instead of the medial form sahishyê (Urvasi, by Lenz.
p. 59).

D D

which it is clear that *v* is stronger than *y*, as it also is more powerful than *r*; hence *sarva* from *sarva*, "everyone." It is remarkable that the *i* also of *iti* "thus" assimilates itself to the following *t*; hence, *tti*, which, in pronunciation, naturally leans upon the word preceding. Therefore one might thus also, without presupposition of a form *ywv*, establish the assimilation from *ῖων*. As to the transition of the consonant of the positive base into σ (κρέισ-σων, βράσ-σων, βάσ-σων, μάσ-σων, ἐλάσ-σων, &c.), to which the *y* has assimilated, the transition of τ, δ, θ, into σ need least of all surprise us (see §. 99.); but with regard to the gutturals, the Old Sclavonic may be noticed, in which, besides what has been remarked in §. 255. (*m*.), *y*, *i*, and *e*— which latter comes very near the vowel combined with a *y*, and is frequently the remainder of the syllable *ye*— exert an influence on a guttural preceding them, similar [G. Ed. p. 415.] to that which the comparative *y* or *ı* produces in Greek. Before the *i*, namely, of the nominative plural, and before *ye* in the dative and locative singular, as before *i* and *ye* of the imperative, *ch* becomes *s*; *e.g. gryes-i* from *gryech*, as θάσ-σων from θάσ-γων, from ταχ-; *g* becomes ζ, *e. g. prŭzi* from *prŭg*, as μείζων, ὀλίζων, from μειζγων, ὀλιζγων, from μεγ-, ὀλιγ-; *k* becomes *ch*, while in Greek κ is modified in the same way as χ   On account of the contracted nature of the ζ (= δσ) no assimilation takes place after it, but the *y* entirely disappears, or, in μείζων, is pressed into the interior of the word (comp. §. 119.), as in ἀμείνων, χείρων, which latter may be akin to the Sanskrit अधर *adhara*, "the under (m)," consequently with aphæresis of the *a* (comp. §. 401.). With the superlative μέγιστος compare the Zend ꞏꞏꞏꞏꞏꞏ *mazista*, where ς *z*, according to §. 57., answers to the Sanskrit *h* of महत् *mahat*, "great"; while in the above ꞏꞏꞏꞏꞏꞏ *masyêhi*, as in the positive *masas* (euphonically *masâ*), *s* stands irregularly for *z*, as if the Zend, by its permutation of consonants in this word, would vie with the Greek; but

we find, Vend. S. p. 214, ⟨ᵫᵫⳋ⟩ *mazyô*, with *z*, which I hold
to be a neuter comparative; thus, ⟨ᵫᵫⳋ⟩ ⟨ᵫᵫⳋ⟩ *mazyô
vîdvâo*, "the more (literally greater) wise."

301. As in the Latin comparative a suffix has raised
itself to universal currency, which in Sanskṛit and Greek
is only sparingly applied, but was, perhaps, originally,
similarly with the form in *tara*, τερο-ς, in universal use; so
the German, the Sclavonic, and Lithuanian, in their degrees
of comparison everywhere attach themselves to the more
rare forms in Sanskṛit and Greek; and indeed in the Gothic
the suffix of the comparative shews itself in the same shortened form in which it appears in the Sanskṛit, Zend, Greek,
and Latin, in its combination with the superlative suffix
(see §. 298. p. 395 &c.), namely, as *is*; and this most plainly
in adverbs like *mais*, "more," whose con- [G. Ed. p. 416.]
nection with comparatives in the Sanskṛit, &c., I first pointed
out in the Berl. Jahrb. (May 1827, p. 742). We must divide,
therefore, thus, *ma-is*; and this word, as well in the base as
in the termination, is identical with the Latin *mag-is* (comp.
μέγισ-τος, p. 402); whence it is clear that the Gothic form
has lost a guttural (compare *ma-jor* and *mag-ior*), which, in
mikils, "great"—which has weakened the old *a* to *i*—appears,
according to the rule for the removal of letters (§. 87.), as *k*.
Mais, therefore, far as it seems to be separated from
it, is, in base and formation, related to the Zend *maz-yô*
(from *maz-yas*), which we have become acquainted with
above (p. 415 G. ed.) in the sense of "more."

"Remark.—There are some other comparative adverbs
in *is*, of which, the first time I treated of this subject, I
was not in possession, and which Grimm has since
(III. 589, &c.) represented as analogous to *mais*. He has
however, afterwards, l. c. p. 88, agreed, with Fulda, in viewing
hauhis, ἀνώτερον, as the genitive of the positive *hauhs*, "high."
Yet *hauhis* stands in exactly the same relation to *hau-
hiza*, "the higher," that *mais* does to *maiza*, "major."

Compared with the Zend *maz-yô* and Greek $\mu\epsilon i\zeta\text{-}\omega\nu$, one
might believe the *z* in *maiza* belonged to the positive base,
particularly as the Old High German adds a second comparative suffix to its adverb *mêr*, answering to the Gothic *mais*
(*mêriro*, '*major*') because in *mêr* no formal expression of the
comparative relation was any longer felt. *Raihtis*, which
Grimm wishes to leave under the forms which, III. p. 88,
are considered as genitive, seems to me properly to signify
potius, or our *rechter*; and I consider it, therefore, as a comparative, although the Old High German *rëhtes*, examined
from the point of view of the Old High German, can only
be a genitive, and the comparative adverb is *rëhtôr*. The
comparative *ga-raihtôza*, '*justior*,' which may be cited in
Gothic, does not prevent the assumption that there may
have been also in use a *raihtiza*, as in all adjectives
iza may just as well be expected as *ôza*; for, together
with the comparative adverb *frumôzô*, 'at first' (R. xi. 35),
occurs the superlative *frumists*.   Perhaps, however, the
genius of the Old High German language has allowed itself
to be deceived through the identity of the comparative
suffix *is* with the genitive termination *i-s*; and taking some
obsolete comparatives, which have been transmitted to it
[G. Ed. p. 417.] for genitives, left them the *s*, which, in
evident comparatives, must pass into *r*; but is also still retained as *s* in *wirs*, '*pejus*.' I prefer to consider, also, *allis*,
'*omnino*,' as a comparative, in order entirely to exclude the
Gothic apparent genitive adverbs from the class of adjectives.
In the Old High German, together with *alles*, '*omnino*,' exists
alles, '*aliter*,' which, according to its origin, is an essentially
different word—through assimilation from *alyes*, as above
(p. 414 G. ed.) $\H{\alpha}\lambda\lambda o\varsigma$—in which the comparative termination,
in the Latin *ali-ter* and similar adverbs, is to be observed. The
probability that these forms, which, to use the expression,
are clothed as genitives, are, by their origin, comparatives,
is still further increased thereby, that together with *eines*,

'*semel*,' and *anderes*, '*aliter*,' there occur, also, forms in the
guise of superlatives, namely, *einest*, 'once' (see Graff,
p. 329), and *anderest*, 'again.' Some comparative adverbs
of this sort omit, in Gothic, the *i* of *is*; thus *min-s*,
'less' (compare *minor*, *minus*, for *minior*, *minius*), perhaps
vair-s, 'worse,' which is raised anew into *vairsiza*, '*pejor*,'
and may be connected with the Sanskrit *avara*, '*posterus*,'
as above χείρων was compared with म्र *adhara* ; *seith-s*,
'*amplius*' (from *seithu*, 'late'); and probably, also, *suns*,
'*statim*,' and *anaks*, '*subito*.'"

302. The comparative-suffix *is* required in Gothic, where
the consonant *s* is no longer capable of declension,* an unorganic addition, or otherwise the sibilant would have been
necessarily suppressed. The language, however, preserved
this letter, as its meaning was still too powerfully perceived, by the favourite addition *an*, which we have seen
above, though without the same urgent necessity, joined to
participial bases in *nd* in their adjective state (§. 289.). As,
then, *s* comes to be inserted between two [G. Ed. p. 418.]
vowels, it must, by §.86. (5.), be changed into *z*: hence the
modern theme *MAIZAN*, from the original *MAIS*, which
has remained unaltered in the adverb. The nominative masculine and neuter are, according to §§. 140. 141., *maiza*, *maizô*.
On the other hand the feminine base does not develope itself
from the masculine and neuter base *MAIZAN*—as in general
from the unorganic bases in *an* of the indefinite adjectives

---

* A base in *s*, as the abovementioned *mais*, would not be distinguished
from the theme in all the cases of the singular, as also in the nominative and
accusative plural, as, of final double *s*, the latter must be rejected (comp.
drus, "fall," for *drus-s* from *drusa-s*, §. 292. 1st Note). In the nominative
and genitive singular, therefore, the form *mais-s* must have become *mais*;
just as, in the nominative and accusative plural, where *ahman-s* comes
from the theme *ahman*. The dative singular is, in bases ending in a consonant, without exception devoid of inflection ;, and so is the accusative,
in substantives of every kind.

no feminines arise—but to the original feminine base in *î*,
which exists in the Sanskrit and Zend, an *n* is added, as in
the participle present; thus *MAIZEIN* (*ei = î*, §. 70.), from
mais + ein, answers to the Zend feminine base of the same
import, ⲙⲁⲥⲩⲉⲏⲓ *masyêhî*, and Sanskrit forms like गरीयसी
garîyas-î, from *garîyas*. The nominative *maizei* may then,
according to §. 142., be deduced from *MAIZEIN*, or may
be viewed as a continuation of the form in Zend and Sanskrit which, in the nominative, is identical with the theme
(§. 137.); in which respect again the participle present
(§. 290.) is to be compared. These two kinds of feminines,
namely, of the said participle and the comparative, stand
in Gothic very isolated; but the ground of their peculiarity,
which Jacob Grimm, III. 566, calls still undiscovered (compare I. 756), appears to me, through what has been said, to be
completely disclosed; and I have already declared my opinion
[G. Ed. p. 419.] in this sense before.* The Old High German

---

* Berl. Jahrb. May 1827, p. 743, &c.   Perhaps Grimm had not yet,
in the passage quoted above, become acquainted with my review of the
two first parts of his Grammar; since he afterwards (II. 050.) agrees with
my view of the matter. I find, however, the comparison of the transition
of the Gothic *s* into *z* with that of the Indian स *s* into ष *sh* inadmissible, as the two transitions rest upon euphonic laws which are entirely
distinct; of which the one, which obtains in the Gothic (§. 86. 5.), is just
as foreign to the Sanskrit, as the Sanskrit (§. 21. and Gramm. Crit. 101*.)
is to the Gothic. It is further to be observed, that, on account of the
difference of these laws, the Sanskrit ष *sh* remains also in the superlative,
where the Gothic has always *st*, not *zt*. In respect to Greek, it may
here be further remarked, that Grimm, l. c. p. 651, in that language, also,
admits an original *s* in the comparative; which he, however, does not
look for after the *ν* of *ιων*, as appears from §. 299., but before it; so that
he wishes to divide thus μεί-ζων, as an abbreviation of μεγίζων; and regards
the ζ not as a corruption of the γ, as Buttmann also assumes, but as
a comparative character, as in the kindred Gothic *ma-iza*. The Greek
ων, ον, would, according to this, appear identical with the unorganic Gothic
an in *MAIZAN*; while we have assigned it, in §. 299., a legitimate
foundation, by tracing it back to the Sanskrit *dns*.

has brought its feminine comparatives into the more usual path, and gives, as corresponding to the Gothic *minnizei,* "the lesser" (fem.), not *minniri,* but *minnira.* The Gothic sibilant, however, was, in the High German comparatives, in the earliest period transmuted into *r,* whence, in this respect, *minniro, minnira,* has more resemblance to the Latin *minor* than to the Gothic *minniza, minnizei.*

303. The comparative suffix in the Gothic, besides *is, iz-an,* exhibits also the form *ôs, ôz-an:* it is, however, more rare; but in the Old High German has become so current, that there are more comparatives in it in *ôrô* (nominative masculine), *ôru* (nominative feminine and neuter), than in *iro, ira,* or *ëro, ëru.* The few forms in *ŌZAN* which can be adduced in Gothic are, *svinthôza,* "*fortior*" (nominative masculine), *frôdôza,* "*prudentior,*" *frumôza,* "*prior,*" *hlasôza,* "*hilarior,*" *garaihtôza,* "*justior,*" *framaldrôza,* "*provectior ælate,*" *usdaudoza,* "*sollicitior,*" *unsvikunthôza,* "*inclarior*" (Massmann, p. 47), and the adverbs *sniumundôs,* "*σπουδαιοτέρως,*" and *alyaleikôs,* "*ἑτέρως.*" How, then, is the *ô* in these forms to be explained, contrasted with the *i* of *IS, IZAN?* I believe only as coming from the long *a* of the Sanskrit strong themes *iyâns* or *yans* (§§. 299. 300.), with *ô,* according to rule, for ग *â* (§. 69.). If one starts from the latter [G. Ed. p. 420.] form, which, in the Zend, is the only one that can be adduced, then, beside the nasal, which is lost also in the Latin and in the weak cases in the Sanskrit, *yâns* has lost in the Gothic either the *â* or the *y* (=*j*), which, when the *â* is suppressed, must be changed into a vowel. The Gothic *ôs, ôz,* and still more the Old High German *ôr,* correspond, therefore, exactly to the Latin *ôr* in *minor, minôr-is,* for *minior.* There is reason to assume that, in the Gothic, originally *y* and *ô* existed in juxta-position to one another; and that for *minniza,* "the lesser," was used *minnyôza,* and for *frôdôza,* "the more intelligent," *frôdyôza.*

The forms which have lost the *y* are represented in Latin
by *minor, minus,* and *plus,* and those with *ô* suppressed by
mag-is. One cannot, however, in Gothic, properly require
any superlatives in *ÔSTA,* nom. *ôst'-s,* corresponding to the
comparatives in *ôs, ôz;* because this degree in the Sanskrit, Zend, Greek, and Latin always springs from the
form of the comparative, contracted to *is, ish.* It is, however, quite regular, that, to the *frumôza,* "*prior,*" corresponds
a *frumists,* "*primus,*" not *frumôsts.* To the remaining
comparatives in *ôza* the superlative is not yet adduced;
but in the more recent dialects the comparatives have
formed superlatives with *ô,* after their fashion; and thus,
in the Old High German, *ôst* usually stands in the superlative, where the comparative has *ôr:* the Gothic furnishes
two examples of this confusion of the use of language, in
lasivôsts, "*infirmissimus*" (1 Cor. xii. 22.), and *armôsts,* "*miser-
rimus*" (1 Cor. xv. 19.).

304. In the rejection of the final vowel of the positive base
before the suffixes of intensity the German agrees with the
cognate languages; hence *sut'-iza,* from *SUTU*[*], "sweet";
[G. Ed. p. 421.]   *hard'-iza,* from *HARDU,* "hard"; *seith-s*
(*thana-seiths,* "*amplius*"), from *SEITHU,* "late"; as in the
Greek ἡδίων from ῾ΗΔΥ, and in the Sanskrit *laghîyas* from
laghu, "light." *Ya* is also rejected; hence *spêd'-iza,* from
SPEDYA, "late" (see p. 358, Note 7.); *reik'-iza,* from
REIKYA, "rich." One could not therefore regard the *ô,* in
forms like *frôdôza,* as merely a lengthening of the *a* in *FRÔDA*
(§. 69.), as it would be completely contrary to the principle
of these formations, not only not to suppress the final vowel
of the positive base, but even to lengthen it. The explanation of the comparative *ô* given at §. 303. remains therefore
the only one that can be relied upon.

---

[*] The positive does not occur, but the Sanskrit *swâdu-s* and Greek ἡδύ-s
lead us to expect a final *u.*

305. In the Old Sclavonic, according to Dobrowsky, p. 332, &c., the comparative is formed in three ways, namely,

(1) By masculine *iĭ*, feminine *shi*, neuter *yee*; as, *ŭniĭ*, " the better (m.) "; *ŭnshi*, " the better (f.) "; *ŭnyee*, " the best (n.)," from a positive which has been lost, as *bntizn*, *melior*, and ἀμείνων; and it is perhaps connected in its base with the latter, so that α may have become o (§. 255. a.), but μ, *ŭ*, as frequently occurs with *n*; and this *ŭ*, with the preceding o, has become *ŭ* (*ᴠ*).* *Mniĭ*, " the lesser, (m.)," fem. *menshi*, neuter *mnyee*, spring, in like manner, from a positive which has been lost. *Bolii*, " the greater," fem. *bolshi*, neuter *bolyee*, may be compared with the Sanskrit *balĭyân*, " the stronger " (p. 396), fem. *b:lĭyasĭ*, neuter *balĭyas*.† For [G. Ed. p. 422.] *boliĭ* is also used *bolyeĭ*; and all the remaining comparatives which belong to this class have *yeĭ* for *iĭ*, and thus answer better to the neuter form *yee*. If, as appears to be the case, the form *yeĭ* is the genuine one, then *ye* answers to the Sanskrit *yas* of *jyâ-yas*, *bhû-yas*, *srê-yas*, &c. (§. 300.), and the loss of the *s* is explained by §. 255. (*l.*): the final *i* of *ye-ĭ*, however, is the definitive pronoun (§. 284.), for comparatives always follow, in the masculine and neuter, the definite declension. In the feminine in *shi* it is easy to recognise the Sanskrit *si* of *iyas-i*, or *yas-i*, and herewith also the Gothic *zei* (oblique theme *ZEIN*,

---

* The *a* in ἀμείνων appears to me to be privative ; so that μείνων would seem to be a sister form to the Latin *minor*, Gothic *minniza*, Sclavonic *mnii* ; and ἀμείνων would properly signify " the not lesser," " the not more trifling." Perhaps this word is also inherent in *omnis ;* so that *o* for *a* would be the negation, which, in Latin, appears as *in* ; where it may be observed, that, in Sanskrit, *a-sakrit*, literally " not once," has taken the representation of the meaning " several times."

† The positive *veliĭ*, with *v* for *b* and *e* for *o*, occurs only in this definite form (Dobr. p. 320) ; the primitive and indefinite form must be *vel*. With respect to the stronger *o* corresponding to the weaker letter *e* (§. 255. a.), *boliĭ*, in the positive, answers to the manner in which vowels are strengthened in Sanskrit, as mentioned at §. 208.

p. 418 G. ed.); that is to say, *bol-shi*, "the greater (fem.), " corresponds to the Sanskrit बलीयसी *baliyasi*, "the stronger (f.)," and *menshi*, " the lesser," to the Gothic *minn-izei*. While, therefore, the Sclavonic masculine and neuter have lost the *s* of the Sanskrit *yas*, the feminine has lost the *ya* of *yas-i*.* This feminine *shi*, also, in departure from (2) and (3), keeps free from the definite pronoun. There are some comparative adverbs in *e*, as the abbreviation of *ye* (§. 255. *n.*), which in like manner dispense with the definite pronoun; thus, *úné*, "better"; *bole*, "greater"—in Servian MSS. *únye*, *boiye*;

[G. Ed. p. 423.]   *pache*, " more," probably related to παχύς, πάσσων; so that (which is very obscure) the final vowel of *pache* for *pach-ye*, for reasons which have been given before, is, in fact, identical with the Greek σο of πᾶσ-σον, for πασ-γον. The *ch* of *pache* may, according to p. 415 G. ed., be regarded as a modification of *k*, as the first σ of πᾶσσον has developed itself from χ. Thus the ζ of *dolζ-yre*, "longer" (neuter and adverbial), as euphonic representative of the *y* of *doly, dolga, dolyo* (*longus, a, um*), answers remarkably to the Greek ζ in μείζων, ὀλίζων, for μείγων, ὀλίγων. That, however, the positive *dolg* is connected with the Greek δολιχός needs scarce to be mentioned. Somewhat more distant is the Sanskrit दीर्घस् *dirgha-s*, of the same meaning, in which the frequently-occurring interchange between *r* and *l* is

---

* It may be proper here to call remembrance to the past gerund, properly a participle, which in the strong cases *váns*, nom. masc. *ván* for *vans*, fem. *ushi*, neuter *vat* (for *vas*), corresponds to the Sanskrit of the reduplicated preterite in *vas*. The Old Sclavonic has here, in the nominative masculine, where the *s* should stand at the end, lost this letter, according to §.255. (*l.*), as *by-v*, "*qui fuit*," but *by-vshi*, "*quæ fuit*"; and in the masculine also, in preference to the comparative, the *s* again appears in the oblique cases, because there, in the Sanskrit, after the *s* follow terminations beginning with a vowel; so in *rek-sh*, "*eum qui dixit*," the *sh* corresponds to the Sanskrit *váis-am*, as *rurud-váns-am*, "*eum qui ploravit*."

to be noticed (§. 20.). The ι of δολιχὸς, however, shews itself, by the evidence of the Sclavonic and Sanskrit, to be an organic addition. Let *garyee*, "*pejus*," be compared with the Sanskrit *garîyas*, "*gravius*," from *guru*, "heavy"— according to Burnouf's correct remark from *garu*, as this adjective is pronounced in Pâli—through the assimilating influence of the final *u*, to which the kindred Greek βαρὺς has permitted no euphonic reaction.

(2) The second, by far the most prevalent form of the Old Sclavonic comparative, is nominative masculine *shiï*, feminine *shaya*, neuter *shee*. The *i* of *shiï* is the definitive pronoun, which, in the feminine, is *ya*, and in the neuter *e* for *ye* (§§. 282. 284.). After the loss, then, of this pronoun, there remains *shi, sha, she;* and these are abbreviations of *shyo, shya, shye*, as we have seen, p. 332, G. ed., the adjective base *SINYO* (nominative *siny*), before its union with the defining *i*, contracted to *sini* (*sini-ï*, neuter *sine-e* for *sinye-ye*. The definite feminine of *SINYO* is *sinya-ya;* and as to the feminine comparatives not being *shya-ya* but *sha-ya*, this rests on the special ground that sibilants gladly free themselves from a following *y*, especially   [G. Ed. p. 424.] before *a* (Dobrowsky, p. 12); so in the feminine nominatives *dûsha, sûsha, chasha*, for *sûsya*, &c. (Dobr. p. 279). The relation of the comparative form under discussion to the Sanskrit यस् *yas* and Zend ﺳﺲ *yas* (p. 401) is therefore to be taken thus, that the *ya* which precedes the sibilant is suppressed, as in the above feminines in *shi;* but for it, at the end, is added an unorganic *YO*, which corresponds to the Gothic-Lithuanian *YA* in the themes *NIUYA, NAUYA*, " new," answering to नव *nava*, *NOIU*, NEO, Sclavonic *NOVO*. This adjunct *YO* has preserved the comparative sibilant in the masculine and neuter, which, in the first formation, must yield to the euphonic law, §. 255. (*l.*) Examples of this second formation are, *ûn-shiï*, " the better (*m.*)," feminine

ûn-shaya, neuter *ûn-shee; pûst-shiĭ* from *pûst,* theme *PŪSTO,*
" desert." Hence it is clear that the final vowel of the
positive base is rejected, as in all the cognate languages,
however difficult the combination of the *t* with *sh.* Even
whole suffixes are rejected, in accordance with §. 298.; as,
glûb-shŭ from *glûbok,* " deep" (definite, *glûboky-ĭ*), *sladshiĭ*
from *sladok,* " sweet."*

(3) Masculine *yeĭshiĭ,* feminine *yeĭshaya,* neuter *yeĭshee ;*
but after *sch, sh,* and *ch, aĭ* stands for *yeĭ :* and this *aĭ* evidently
stands only euphonically for *yaĭ,* since the said sibilants, as
[G. Ed. p. 425.]　　has been already remarked, gladly divest
themselves of a following *y :* hence *blasch-aĭshiĭ,* " the
better" (masculine), from *blag* (theme *BLAGO*), " good,"†
since *g,* through the influence of the *y* following, gives
way to a sibilant, which has subsequently absorbed
the *y ;* compare ὀλίζ-ων, for ὀλίγ-ίων, ὀλιγ-γων (p. 402):
so *tish-aĭshiĭ,* from *tich* (theme *TICHO*), " still,"‡ as in
the Greek θάσ-σων from ταχύς. As example of the form

---

* I hold *ko,* whence in the nom. masc. *k,* for the suffix of the positive
base, but the preceding *o* for the final vowel of the lost primitive ; and
this *o* corresponds either to a Sanskrit *a,* according to §. 255. (*a.*), or to an
उ *u,* according to §. 255. (*c.*); for example, *tano-k,* " thin," theme
TANOKO, corresponds to the Sanskrit *tanu-s,* " thin," Greek τανυ ; and
slado-k to the Sanskrit *swâdu-s,* " sweet," with exchange of the *v* for *l,*
according to §.20. Thus the above *slad-shiĭ* shews itself to be originally
identical, as well in the suffix of the positive as of the other degrees with
the Greek ἡδ-ίων and Gothic *sut-iza* (§. 304.), far as the external difference may separate them ; and to the Sclavonic is due, as to the truer
preservation of the fundamental word, the preference above the Greek
and Gothic, although, on account of the unexpected transition of the
v into *l,* the origin of the Sclavonic word is more difficult to recognise.

† Dobrowsky says (p. 334) from *blagyi* (this is the definite, see §. 284.) :
it is, however, evident that the comparative has not arisen from the adjective compounded with a pronoun, but from the simple indefinite one.

‡ Compare the Sanskrit adverb *tûshnîm,* " still, silent," and refer to
§. 255. (*m.*).

with *yeĭ*, *yŭn-yeĭshiĭ*, "junior," from *yŭn*, may serve. Whence comes, then, the *yeĭ* or *aĭ* (for *yaĭ*), which distinguishes this formation from the second? It might be supposed that to the first formation in *yeĭ*, where, for example, also *yŭn-yeĭ*, "the younger (m.)," occurs, that of the second has also been added, as in Old High German *mêrero*, "the greater" (masculine), and in Gothic, probably, *vairsiza*, "the worse" (p. 405), are raised twice to the comparative degree; and as, in Persian, the superlatives in *terín*, in my opinion, contain, as their last element, the comparative इयास् *íyáns*, which forms, in the nominative masculine, *íyán*, and from this could be easily contracted to *ín*. In Persian the comparative is formed through *ter*; as, *behter*, "the better," whence *behterín*, "the best." Now it deserves remark, that in Old Sclavonic the formation before us frequently occurs with a superlative meaning, while in the more modern dialects the superlative relation is expressed through the comparative with *nai*, "more," prefixed (probably from *maĭ* = Gothic *mais*, according to §. 225. *l.*). The only objection to this mode of explanation   [G. Ed. p. 426.] is this, that the element of the first formation *ye-ĭ* has not once laid aside the definitive pronoun *i*, which is foreign to the comparative; so that therefore in *yŭn-yeĭ-shiĭ* the said pronoun would be contained twice. There is, however, another way of explaining this *yeĭshiĭ* or *(y)aĭshiĭ*, namely, as an exact transmission of the Sanskrit *íyas* or *yas*, from which the second formation has only preserved the sibilant; but the third, together with this letter, may have retained also that which preceded. Still, even in this method, the *i* of *yeĭ*, *(y)aĭ*, is embarrassing, if it be not assumed that it owes its origin to a transposition of the *í* of *íya*.

306. As to the remark made at p. 400, that among the European languages the Greek only has preserved the nasal, which the Sanskrit shews in the strong cases of the comparative suffix *íyáns*, I must here admit a limitation in

favour of the Lithuanian, which, exceeding in this point the Greek, continues not only the nasal,* but also the comparative sibilant through all the cases.　For an example, *gerésnis*, "the better" (m.), may serve, with which we would compare the Sanskrit *garíyдñsam*, "*graviorem*" (nominative *garíyдn*).　It may be, but it is not of much consequence to us, that *gerésnis* and *garíyдñs* (strong theme) are also connected in the positive base; so that, as according to p. 398, in Greek and Gothic goodness is measured by depth, in Lithuanian it is measured by weight.　The Sanskrit comparative under discussion means, also, not only "heavier," or "very heavy," but also, according to Wilson, "highly venerable."　In order, however, to analyze the Lithuanian *gerésnis*, we must observe that *gerésnis* stands for *gerésnias*, and the theme is clearly *GERÉSNIA*; hence genitive *gerésnio*, dative *gerésniam*; as *géro*, *gerám*, from *géra-s*.

[G. Ed. p. 427.]　The termination *ia*, therefore—for which *ya* might be expected, the *y* of which, as it appears for the avoiding of a great accumulation of consonants, has been resolved into *i*—corresponds to the unorganic addition which we, p. 411, have observed in Sclavonic comparatives.　We have now *geresn* remaining, which I regard as a metathesis from *gerens*,† through which we come very near the Sanskrit *garíyдñs*.　But we come still nearer to it through the observation, that, in Lithuanian, *e* is often produced by the euphonic influence of a preceding *y* or *i* (§. 193).　We believe, therefore, that here also we may explain *gerésn* as from *geryasn* (*geryans*), and further recall attention to the Zend ꞁꞁꞁ *maśyéhí* (§. 300.).

---

* In the Lith. comparative adverbs like *daugiaus*, "more," *mažaus*, "less," I regard the *u* as the vocalization of the *n*; thus *daugiaus* from *daugians*, where *ians*=Skr. *íyдns* of the strong cases.

† This has been already alluded to by Grimm (III. 635, Note *), who has, however, given the preference to another explanation, by which *esnis* is similarly arrived at with the Latin *issimus*.

The emphasis upon the *e* of *géresnis* may be attributable to the original length in the Sanskrit strong theme *gariyáns*. Hence the astonishing accuracy may justly be celebrated with which the Lithuanian, even to the present day, continues to use the Sanskrit comparative suffix *íyáns*, or rather its more rare form preferred in Zend *yáns*.

307. The Lithuanian superlative suffix is only another modification of the comparative. The nasal, that is to say, which in the latter is transposed, is, in the superlative, left in its original place: it is, however, as often happens, resolved into *u*,* and to the *s* which ends the theme in the Sanskrit, which, in Lithuanian, is not declinable (§. 128.), is added *ia* : hence *GERAUSIA*, the nominative of which, however, in departure from *gerésnis*, has dropped, not the *a*, but the *i* ; thus *gerausa-s*, gen. *gerausio*, and, in the feminine, *gerausa, gerausiôs* ; in which forms, [G. Ed. p. 428.] contrary to the principle which is very generally followed in the comparative and elsewhere, the *i* has exercised no euphonic influence.

"Remark.—With respect to the Sanskrit gradation-suffixes *tara, tama*, I have further to add, that they also occur in combination with the inseparable preposition उद् *ut* ; hence *ut-tara*, 'the higher,' *ut-tama*, 'the highest,' as above (§. 295.) *af-tuma*, and in Latin *ex-timus, in-timus*. I think, however, I recognise the base of *ut-tara, ut-tama*, in the Greek ὑς of ὕσ-τερος, ὕσ-τατος, with the unorganic spir. asp., as in ἑκάτερος, corresponding to the Sanskrit *ékatara-s*, and with σ from τ (compare §. 99.), in which it is to be remarked that also in the Zend for *ut-tara, ut-tama*, according to §. 102., *us-tara, us-téma*, might be expected.

* Comp. §. 255. (*g.*) ; in addition to which it may be here further remarked, that in all probability the *u* also in Gothic conjunctives like *haitau, haihaityau*, is of nasal origin.

NUMERALS.

CARDINAL NUMBERS.

308. I. In the designation of the number *one* great difference prevails among the Indo-European languages, which springs from this, that this number is expressed by pronouns of the 3d person, whose original abundance affords satisfactory explanation regarding the multiplicity of expressions for *one*. The Sanskrit *éka*, whose comparative we have recognised in the Greek ἑκάτερος, is, in my opinion, the combination of the demonstrative base *é,* of which hereafter, with the interrogative base *ka*, which also, in combination with *api*, "also" (nom. masc. *kâ'pi*), signifies "whoever"; and even without this *api*, if an interrogative expression precedes, as Bhagavad-Gîtâ, II. 21, कथं स पुरुष: पार्थ कं घातयति हन्ति कम् *kathañ sa purushañ Pârtha kan ghâtayati hanti kam*, "How can this person, O Pârtha, cause one to be slain, (or) slay one?" The Zend ᚐᚍᚊᚅᚐᚍ

[G. Ed. p. 429.] *aéva*, is connected with the Sanskrit pronominal adverbs *éva*, "also," "only," &c., and *évam*, "so," of which the latter is an accusative, and the former, perhaps, an instrumental, according to the principle of the Zend language (§. 158.). The Gothic *ain'-s*, theme *AINA*, our *einer*, is based on the Sanskrit defective pronoun *éna* (§. 72.) whence, among others, comes the accusative masculine *éna-m*, "this." To this pronominal base belongs, perhaps, also the Old Latin *oinos*, which occurs in the Scipionian epitaphs, from which the more modern *ûnus* may be deduced, through the usual transition of the old *ŏ* into *u*, which latter is lengthened to make up for the *i* suppressed. Still *ûnus* shews, also, a surprising resemblance to the Sanskrit *ûna-s*, which properly means "less," and is prefixed to the higher numerals in order to express diminution by one; as, *ûnaviñshati*, "*undeviginti*," *ûnatriñshat*, "*undetriginta*." This *ûnas* could

not have appeared in Latin, more accurately retained than
under the form of *ûnu-s*, or, more anciently, *ûno-s*. The
Greek 'EN is founded, it is highly probable, in like manner,
on the demonstrative base एन *êna*, and has lost its final
vowel, as the Gothic *AINA*, in the masculine nominative
uins: with respect to the *é* for *ê* compare ἑκάτερος. On the
other hand, οἶος, "*unicus*," if it has arisen from οἶνος compare
οἶνος), as μείζω from μείζονα, has retained the Indian diphthong more truly, and has also preserved the final vowel
of एन *êna*. If ὄνος, the number one in dice, really has
its name from the idea of unity, one might refer
this word to the demonstrative base अन *ana*, Sclavonic
ONO (nominative *on*, "that"), which also plays a part
in the formation of words, where ονη corresponds to
the Sanskrit suffix *anâ* (feminine of the masculine and
neuter *ana*), if it is not to be referred to the medial
participle in *âna*, as μονη to *mâna*. The Old Sclavonic, *yedin*,
"one," is clearly connected with the Sanskrit आदि *âdi*, "the
first," with *y* which has been prefixed according to §. 255. (*n.*):
on the other hand, in the Lithuanian *wiena-s*, [G. Ed. p. 430.]
if it is connected with the Gothic *AINA* and Sanskrit एन
êna, an unorganic *w* has been prefixed. In regard to
to the *ie* for ए *ê* compare, also, *wies-te*, "knowledge," with
वेद्मि *vêdmi*, "I know."

"Remark.—The German has some remarkable expressions, in which the number *one* lies very much concealed
as to its form, and partly, too, as to its idea: they are, in
Gothic, *haihs*, "one-eyed," *hanfs*, "one-handed," *halts*,
"lame," and *halbs*, "half." In all these words the number one is expressed by *ha*; and in this syllable I recognise a corruption of the abovementioned Sanskrit क *ka* for
एक *êka*, "one," which is founded on the universal rule
for the mutation of consonants (§. 87.). It would be
erroneous to refer here to the Zend ﻬﻭ *ha* of ﻬﻭﻙﻩﻭﻬﻭ
ha-kěrět, "once" (Sanskrit सकृत् *sakrit*), as the Zend ﻭ *h*

E E

stands, without exception, for the Sanskrit स् *s,* to which
the *h* in Gothic never corresponds.* J. Grimm compares
haihs with *cæcus* (II. 316), not with the purpose of following
out the origin of these cognate words, but in order to
prove the transition of the tenuis into the aspirate ; for the
simple aspiration stands in Gothic instead of *kh,* which
is wanting. These words are, however, so far connected,
that, in both, the word *eye* is contained. It is only the
question whether the one-eyed in Latin has also lost the
other eye, and if the blind (*cæcus*), in regard to etymology,
has not preserved one eye left. This appears to me
more probable than that the blind in Gothic should reco-
ver his sight, though but with one eye. The theme of
haihs is *HAIHA :* one may, then, divide *HAIHA* into
HA-IHA or into *H-AIHA* ; thus the latter portion of this
compound word is assuredly connected with the word अक्ष
akṣha, "eye," in Sanskrit, which only occurs at the end of
compounds ; so that of the compounded क्ष *kṣh* only the first
portion is left, while the Zend ᭜᭜ *ashi,* "eye"—which, in
like manner, I have found only at the end of compound words,
as ᭜᭜᭜᭜᭜ *csvas-ashím,* "the six-eyed"—has preserved the last element : the Latin *ocus,* however (the primitive base of *oculus*), preserves only the first like the Gothic. If
in *HAIHA* the diphthong *ai* is left entirely to the share of the
eye, we must assume that the *a* is introduced through the
euphonic influence of the *h* (§. 82.), and that *AIHA* stands for
[G. Ed. p. 431.]   *IHA,* and this for *AHA* ; as *fimf* from
पञ्च *pancha; fidvôr* from चत्वार् *chatwâr.* But if the *a* of *HAIHA*
is allotted to the numeral, which appears to me more correct,
then the *h* in this word has not introduced any euphonic *a,*
because, with the aid of the first member of the compound, the

---

* Connected, however, with this designation of " one," which is taken
from the pronominal base *sa* (Greek ὁ), may be the Greek ἁ in ἁ-πλοῦς.

disposition of the *h* to *ai* was already satisfied. We must further recall attention to the Latin *cocles*, in which, however, the notion of unity is evidently represented only by the *c*, for the *o* must be left to the *ocles* as a derivative from *oculus*: *cœcus*, however, if *œ* is the correct way of writing, and if the number one is contained therein, would spring from *ca-icus*; and the Indian *a*, therefore, is weakened, as in Gothic, to *i*, which, in Latin compounds, is the usual representative of an *a* of the base (§. 6.). Let us now examine the one-handed. Its theme is, in Gothic, *HAUFA*, nominative abbreviated *haufs*; so that here, as in a skein, two bases and a pronominal remnant, as mark of case, lie together. The numeral is here the most palpable element: it is more difficult to search out the hand. In the isolated state no theme *nfa* could be expected; but in compounds, and also in prefixed syllables of reduplication, a radical vowel is often rejected; as, in the Sanskrit जग्मिम *jagmima*, "we went," of the root गम् *gam*, only *gm* is left; and in the Greek, πίπτω for πιπέτω, ΠΕΤ, which corresponds to the Sanskrit पत् *pat*, "to fall," is abbreviated to ππ. We shall, therefore, be compelled to assume that a vowel has fallen out between the *n* and *f* of *HA-NFA*. If it was an *i* which was displaced, then *NIFA* might pass as a transposition of the Sanskrit पाणि *páni*, "hand," with *f* for *p*, according to §. 87. In *HA-LTA*, "lame"—nominative *halts*—must *ha* again pass for a numeral, and *ha-lta* may originally signify "one-footed," for it is (Mark ix. 45.) opposed to the Gothic *tvans fóluns habandin*, "having two feet," where it is said 'it is better for thee to enter into life with one foot, than having two feet to be cast into hell.' It is at least certain, that a language which had a word for one-footed would very fitly have applied it in this passage. If the last element, however, in *HA-LTA* means the foot, we must remember that, in Sanskrit, several appellations of this member are derived from roots which mean "to go." Now, there is, in

Gothic, a root *LITH,* "to go," with an aspirated *t,* indeed; but in compounds the consonants do not always remain on the same grade which they adopt in the simple word; [G. Ed. p. 432.] *e.g.* the *t* of *quatuor* appears as *d* in many derivatives and compounds, without this *d* thereby dissembling its original identity with the *t* of *quatuor* and चतुर् *chatur.* So, then, *HA-LTA* may stand for *HA-LITHA;* and it may be remarked, that from the root *LIT* comes, also, *lithus,* "the limb," as that which is moveable. Before I pass on to the explanation of *halb,* I must mention that J. Grimm divides the pronoun *selber,* as it appears to me very properly, into two parts; so that the syllable *si* of the Gothic *silba* devolves on the reciprocal (*sci-na, si-s, si-k*). With respect to the last portion, he betakes himself to a verb *leiban,* "to remain," and believes that *silba* may, perhaps, have the meaning of "that which remains in itself, enduring." Be this as it may, it is clear that *halbs* —the theme is *HALBA*—might be, with equal right, divided into two parts; and it appears to me, that, according to its origin, this word can have no better meaning than, perhaps, "containing a part"; so that the ideas *one* and *a part, remnant,* or something similar, may be therein expressed, and, according to the principle of the Sanskrit possessive compounds, the notion of the possessor must be supplied, as in the already explained *haihs,* "having one eye." In the Gothic, also, *laiba* means "remnant." It scarcely needs remark, that *halb* is no original and simple idea, for which a peculiar simple word might be expected, framed to express it. The half is one part of the whole, and, in fact, equal to the absent part. The Latin *dimidius* is named after the middle through which the division went. The Zend has the expression ᬔᬓᬭᬵᬚᬚ *naéma,* for *halb,* according to a euphonic law for *néma,* which in Sanskrit, among other meanings, signifies "part": this is probably the secondary meaning, and the half, as part of the whole, the original. If it is so, नेम *néma* appears to me a very ingenious designation for a half, for it is a regular contraction of न *na*, "not," and इम *ima*, "this or that"; and the démonstrative therefore points at the "this or that" portion of the whole excluded by the negative *na*. In Sanskrit, *halb* is termed, among other appellations, सामि *sámi*, in which one recognises both the Latin *semi* and the Greek ἥμι; and the three languages agree in this also, that they use this word only without inflection at the beginning of compounds. As to its origin, सामि *sámi* may be viewed as a regular derivative from सम *sama*, "equal," "similar," by a suffix *i*, by which the suppression of the final vowel, and widening of the initial vowel of the primitive, become necessary. If this explanation is well founded, [G. Ed. p. 433.] then in this designation of *halb* only one part of the whole, and, indeed, one equal to the deficient part, would be expressed, and the सामि *sámi* would be placed as ἕτερον over against the deficient ἕτερον; and the Sanskrit and German supply each other's deficiencies, so that the former expresses the equality, the latter the unity, of the part; *i.e.* each of the two languages only semi-expresses the half. As to the relation, however, of the Greek ἥμισυς to ἥμι, it follows from what has been already said—that the latter is not an abbreviation of the former, but the former is a derivation from the latter; and indeed I recognise in συ the Sanskrit possessive *swa*, "*suus*," which, remarkably enough, in Zend enters into combinations with numerals with the meaning " part "; *e.g.* ⲗⲟⲡⳛⳡⳚ *thri-shva*, "a third part," ⲗⲟⲡⳡⳚⲟⲥ *chathru-shva*, "a fourth part." In the accusative these words, according to §. 42., are written ⳡⲟⲡⳛⳡ *thri-shú-m*, ⳡⲟⲡⳡⲟⲥ *chathru-shúm*, of which the last member comes very near to the Greek συν of ἥμισυν. Ἥμι-συς means therefore, "having one equal part," and the simple ἥμι means only the equal. The Sanskrit designation of "the whole" deserves further to be mentioned, सकलस *sa-kala-s*,

which, as signifying that which joins the parts and unites them,
is opposed to the German *halb* as applying to one part, and
in a measure furnishes a commentary and guarantee for the
correctness of my view of the latter. The word सकल *sakala*
consists, though this is scarcely perceptible, of स *sa*, " with,"
and कला *kalá*, " part," so that, if the latter is regarded
in the dual relation—and the last member of a compound
may express each of the three numbers—सकल *sakala* expresses that in which the two parts are together. Thus the
word समग्र *sam-agra*, " full," is used especially in regard to
the moon, as a body with points, *i. e.* that in which the two
points touch one another. Transposed into Greek relations of
sound *sakala-s* would give, perhaps, ὁκαλος, or ὁκελος, or
ὁκολος; but from this the present ὅλος has rejected the middle
syllallable, as is the case in κόρος, κοῦρος, compared with
कुमारस् *kumára-s*, "a boy."

309. II. The theme of the declension is, in Sanskrit, *dwa*,
which is naturally inflected with dual terminations: the
Gothic gives for it *tva*, according to §. 87., and inflects it, in
the want of a dual, as plural, but after the manner of pronouns:

[G. Ed. p. 434.]   nominative *tvai, tvós, tva ;* dative *tvaim ;* accusative *tvans, thvós, tva.*[*]   The Sanskrit displays in the dual

---

[*] One would expect *tvô*, on account of the form being monosyllabic
(§. 231.). In the genitive masculine and neuter I should look for *tvi-zé*,
after the analogy of *thi-zé*, " *horum*," from *THA*, or *tvaizé*, according to the
analogy of the definite adjectives (§. 287. p. 374 G. ed.), and according to the
common declension *tv'-é* (p. 276). However, the form *tvaddyé* occurs three
times in the sense of *duorum ;* whence it is clear that the genitive of the
base *TVA* was no longer in use in the time of Ulfila.   The form *tvaddy'-é*
belongs to a theme *TVADDYA* (as *hary'-é* from *HARYA*), and appears,
from the ordinal number, which in Sanskrit is *dwi-tíya* for *dwa-tíya*, to
have introduced itself into the cardinal number.   From *tvaddyé*, by
rejecting both the *d*—of which one is, besides, superfluous—and by
changing the *y* into a vowel, we arrive at the Old High German *zueió*,
according to Isid. *zueiyó*, as *fior* from *fulvor ;* also definite, *zueiéró*, which,
in Gothic, would be *tvaddyaizé*.   Grimm appears, on the other hand, to
                                                                                    have

no difference between the pronominal declension and the ordinary one, and *dwâu* is declined like *vrikâu* (p. 274), *dwê* feminine like *dhârê* (p. 285), and *dwe* neuter like *dânê* (p. 276). As, however, the notions of number are much akin to those of the pronouns; and as वस्य *alpa*, "a little," forms, in the nominative plural masculine, वसे *alpê* (§. 228.); so from the masculine theme *dwa*, if it had a plural, might be expected *dwê*, to which, according to §. 78., the Gothic *tvai* would correspond, which it is not requisite to regard like adjectives terminating similarly, as if com- pounded with a definite pronoun, espe- [G. Ed. p. 435.] cially as a genitive *tvaizê*, which would make the latter view necessary, does not occur. To *tvai* corresponds, also, *bai*, "both," from the theme *BA*, neuter *ba*, dative *baim*, accu- sative masculine *bans*, which is to be deduced through aphæresis from the Sanskrit base *ubha*, Old Sclavonic *oba* (nominative and accusative dual), from the base *OBO*. In Zend the masculine of the number two is ꦱ *dva* (for *dvâ*, §. 208.), with which the Old Sclavonic *dva* is identical, while the feminine neuter *dvye* answers to the Sanskrit *dwê* (§. 255. *e.*). The Zend neuter is *duyê*, with euphonic *y* (§. 43.), and the *v* resolved into *u*. In the Greek and Latin δύω, δύο, *duo*, the

---

have taken occasion, from the Old High German forms, to suppose a Gothic *tvaiyê* and *tvaiaizê*, in which I cannot agree with him. The Old Northern, by exchanging the dental medials with gutturals, gives *tvaggya* for the Gothic *tvaddyê*. In the accusative plural feminine is found, in Gothic, together with *tvôs* also *tvcihnôs*, which presupposes a masculine and neuter base *TVEIHNA*. fem. *TVEIHÑO;* and in which the an- nexed *HNA* reminds us of the appended pronoun स्म *sma*, discussed at §. 165. &c., which, by metathesis, and with the alteration of the *s* into *h*, has in Prâkrit and Pâli taken the form *mha* (comp. §. 169.). On this Gothic *TVEIHNA* is based the Old High German nominative and accusative masculine *zuênê* with loss of the *h*. The feminine, however, appears in Old High German free from this addition, and is in the nomi- native and accusative *zuô*, also abbreviated *zua* (comp. §. 69.).

old *v* is, in the same way, resolved into the *u*, but the final
vowel of the base is not abandoned: δύω answers to the
Vêdic masculine *dwâ* (§. 208.); but in distinguishing the
genders the Greek is surpassed by the Latin and the
other European sister languages. The Lithuanian has *du*
in the nominative masculine, and *dwi* in the nominative
feminine; with the closer explanation of which, and
their dual declension, we will not here occupy ourselves
further. It is, however, to be remarked of the Sanskṛit numeral, that the *a* of *dwa* is, in the beginning of compounds,
weakened to *i* (compare §. 6.): hence *dwi*, which is represented by the native grammarians as the proper theme
(comp. p. 102). The Greek, in which δϝι is inadmissible,
gives in its stead δι; hence, διμήτωρ = द्विमातृ *dwimâtri* (theme),
"having two mothers." The Zend and Latin agree in
the corruption of this *dwi* very remarkably, in this point,
that they have both dropped the *d* and have both hardened
the *v* to *b*; hence ⲁⲓⲡⲉⲩⲣⲡⲟⲥⲟⲩⲉⲗⲕⲕ *bipaitistana*, "with two
nipples," like *biceps, bidens,* and others. From this abbreviated *bi*, comes, in both languages, also the adverb *bis*,
"twice," in contrast to the Sanskṛit *dwis* and Greek
δίς: the Greek δι, however, in compounds, cannot be regarded as an abbreviation of δίς, as is wont to be done.
The German dialects, with exception of the Old High Ger-
[G. Ed. p. 436.]   man, require, according to §. 87., *tvi* for *dvi*,
as the initial member of compounds; this is furnished by the
Anglo-Saxon in compound words like *tvi-féte,* "*bipes*," *tvi-finger,*
"*duos digitos longus*," *tvi-hive,* "*bicolor*." The Old High
German gives *zui* (=*zwi*) or *qui*; *e. g. zui-beine,* "*bipes*,"
qui-falt, "*duplex*" (Grimm III. 956.). The adverb *zuiro,*
more fully *zuiror,* also *quiro,* "twice," belongs, according to
its formation, but not without the intervention of another
word, to the above *dwis,* δίς, *bis;* but it is clear, from the
Old Northern *tvis-var,* that *ro* has arisen from *sva* by
apocope of the *a* and vocalization of the *v,* perhaps more

anciently to *u*, and thence to *o* (§. 77.) as in *dëo* (also *diu*),
"a servant," genitive *diwe-s*, from the base *DIWA*.
Whence comes, however, the Old Northern *svar*, which
occurs also in *thrisvar*, "thrice," and with which the English *ce* in *twice, thrice*, is connected. I believe that
the *s*, which precedes the *var*, is certainly identical with
the *s* of द्विस् *dwis*, δίς, and त्रिस् *tris*, τρίς, but the annexed *var* corresponds to the Sanskrit substantive *vâra*,
which signifies period and time; hence *ékavâra*, "once"
(see Haughton), and *vâramvâram*, "repeatedly." Hence
comes the Persian *bâr*, e.g. *bâr-i*, "once"; and as the
original meaning of this word is "time," and we have
already seen, in Persian, the transition of the *v* into *b*, we
may hence very satisfactorily explain the Latin *ber* in
the names of months; and *Septem-ber*, therefore, is literally
the seven-time, *i.e.* the seventh time-segment of the year.
But to return to the Old Northern *svar*, in *trisvar, thrisvar*,
which we must now divide into *tris-var, thris-var*, according to the explanation which has been given, the idea of
time, is expressed therein twice, which is not surprising,
as in the Old High German *mériro*, also mentioned above,
the comparative suffix is twice contained, because it is no
longer felt the first time, by the genius of the language,
with sufficient clearness. As then, in Old High German,
first the *r*, and more lately also the *o* (from *v*), of *s-var* has
been dropped, we see, in the Middle High   [G. Ed. p. 437.]
German *drir*, from *dris*, the form again returned into the
original limits of the Sanskrit-Greek *tris*.

310. III. The theme is, in the Sanskrit, Greek, Latin,
Lithuanian, and Old Sclavonic, *TRI*, whence in the
Gothic, according to §. 87., *THRI*, and exactly the same in
Zend, according to another law of sound (§. 47.). The
declension of this base is, in most of the languages
mentioned, perfectly regular: it is only to be remarked
of the Gothic, in which, however, all the cases cannot be

adduced, that on account of the word being monosyllabic, the *i* is not suppressed before vowel terminations, but becomes *iy* (compare the Pâli, §. 226.): hence the genitive *thriy-ê*, and nominative neuter *thriy-a* (§. 233.). Besides these, the dative *thri-m* and the accusative *thri-ns* may be cited. The Sanskrit forms the genitive from an extended theme *traya*, hence *trayâ-n-âm ;* while the Zend *thry-anm* or *thray-anm* comes from the original base. Both languages, however, agree in this, that फि *tri,* ड्री *thri,* is only a theme of the masculine and neuter; and although, according to its termination, it might quite as well be assigned to the feminine, nevertheless the feminine number has an appellation peculiar to it, which is rather different from *tri, thri,* of which the theme is *tisar* (तिस्रि *tisri,* §. 1.), the *a* of which, in the Sanskrit nominative, accusative, and vocative, is irregularly suppressed ; hence तिस्रस् *tisras*† for *tisaras,* Zend ﻟﺲ *tisarô.*

[G. Ed. p. 438.] 311. IV. The Sanskrit feminine theme चतस्र् *chatasar (chatasri)* follows the analogy of the *tisar* just mentioned ; and the similarity between the two forms is so great that it appears, which is perhaps the fact, that the number three is contained in the fourth numeral; so that *tisr-as* would be a weakened form of *tasr-as,* and the *cha* prefixed to the number four would be identical with the particle, which means "and," and which, in other places, is attached to the end of the word. If one wished to press still farther into the deep mystery of the appellations of numbers, one might moot the question whether

---

* With this extended theme one may compare the Old High German nominative masculine *driê* in Isidor, which belongs to a theme *DRIA*, with pronominal declension. The feminine *driô,* from the base *DRIÔ*, of the same sound, presupposes in like manner a masculine and neuter theme *DRIA.*

† In the accusative, *tisras* is more organic than तिस्रिस् *tisris,* as it must stand according to the common rule (comp. §. 242.).

the syllables *tasa* in the theme *cha-ta-sar*, might not be considered as identical with the demonstrative bases of the same sound. I do not think, at least, that any language whatever has produced special original words for the particular designation of such compound and peculiar ideas as three, four, five, &c.; and as the appellations of numbers resist all comparison with the verbal roots,[*] the pronominal roots remain the only means by which to explain them. Without attempting to resolve the difficulties in the individual numbers, we will express the conjecture, that the operation of speech with regard to the numbers might originally be expounded nearly in this manner—that one might perhaps say, " it, this, that, and it, and this," &c.: thus the pronouns might actually suffice better than they appear to do in the forms of numerals which lie before us. But an obscuration of the original clearness of this method, which would occur in the course of time, would be owing also   [G. Ed. p. 439.] to this, that a simple or compound word might undertake immediately to designate this or that number, and no other one, though equally adapted to denote it.

312. The masculine and neuter of the number four have, in Sanskrit, चत्वार *chatwâr* as the strong theme, and चतुर् *chatur* as the weak[†]; hence, nom. masc. *chatwâr-as*, accus. *chatur-as*, nom. accus. voc. neut. *chatwâr-i*: the gen. masc. and neut. is irregularly *chatur-n-âm* for *chatur-âm*, since, according to the analogy of bases terminating with a vowel, a nasal

---

[*] Only in three might one perhaps think of the Sanskrit root त्रि *tri*, " *trans-gredi*," and consider three, therefore, as the more (than two). This verbal notion of passing over, adding, is, however, also the only possible one which could be blended with the names of numbers.

[†] To §. 129. is further to be added, that from the strong theme springs also the form of the nom., acc., and voc. plural of the neuter; while this kind forms the whole singular and dual from the weak theme.

is introduced (§. 246.). In the Zend the strong theme is
chathwâr, according to §. 47.; hence, nom. masc.
chathwârô; and the weak theme is, by transposition, *chathru*; as, *chathru-mâhîm*, "four months"
(accus. sing.), Vend. S. p. 248. For the Sanskrit genitive
चतुर्णाम् *chaturnâm*, we find *chathrusnanm* (l. c.
pp. 204 and 206, with *a* inserted, *chathrusa-
nanm*); but in the beginning of compound words it is
more frequently found *chathwarĕ*; so that the
weakening consists merely in the shortening of the *â*, and,
according to §. 44., an *ĕ* is added to the *r*; as *chatwarĕ-
paitistanyâo*, "of her with four teats" (gen. fem., Vend. S.
p. 83). As to the European sister languages, one must
expect, according to §. 14., for *ch*, gutturals and labials,
hence, in Gothic *fidvôr*, and aspirates for smooth letters,
according to §. 87. This *fidvôr* is based on the strong theme
चत्वार् *chatwâr*, but in the state of declension extends the
theme by an unorganic *i*, hence dative *fidvôri-m*, the only
adduceable case. In Old Northern the nom. masc. is *fiôri-r*.

[G. Ed. p. 440.] The original theme *fidvôr* appears in the
compound *fidvôr-tiguns*, "forty" (accus.): on the other hand,
fidur in *fidur-dôgs*, "four days," is referable to the Indian
weak theme *chatur*; whence, however, it should not be
said that the weak theme of the German, Lithuanian, and
Sclavonic has been brought from an Asiatic original site;
for it was as easy for the Gothic, by suppressing the last
vowel but one, to contract its *fidvôr* to *fidur*—like *thiu-s*,
"servant," from *thiva-s*, gen. *thivi-s*—as for the Sanskrit to
abbreviate *chatwâr* to *chatur*. The Lithuanian theme follows the example of abbreviation in its interior, but
extends the theme at the end; the masc. nom. is *keturi*,
and the feminine *keturios*: *KETURIĀ* serves the latter as
theme: the masculine *keturi* is analogous with *geri*, "the
good" (see p. 251, Note ‡), and therefore has *KETURIE*,
euphonic for *KETURIA*, as its base. The genitive and

accusative masculine *keturi-û, keturi-s*, proceed from the base *KETURI*. The Old Sclavonic gives *CHETYRI* as the masculine and feminine theme, and inflects the masculine like *GOSTI*, and the feminine like *KOSTI* (p. 349); hence nom. *chetyry-e, chetyri*, just as in the third numeral *triy-e*, "*tri*"; and the feminine form may, in both, represent also the masculine, and always supplies the neuter. But the collective *chetvero*, and the ordinal number *chetverty-ĭ*, stand in closer agreement with the Indian strong theme चत्वार् *chatwâr*: the Latin *quatuor*, also, which, in disadvantageous comparison with the cognate languages, has lost the capability of declension, and the Greek τέσσαρ-ες, τέτταρ-ες, rest on the strong चत्वारस् *chat.râras*; so that τέτταρες, just like the Pâli form चत्तारो *chattârô*, has gained its last *t* by assimilatson of the semi-vowel. The Prâkrit form, also, which I am not able to quote, will scarcely be other than *chattârô* (comp. §. 300 p. 414 G. ed.). With regard to the initial τ let reference be made to §. 14., by which this τ is accommo-   [G. Ed. p. 441.] dated with the Æolic πίσυρες, which refers itself to the weak theme चतुर् *chatur*. With the Zend transposition of the weak theme to *chathru* (p. 439 G. ed.), at the beginning of compounds, agrees surprisingly the Latin *quadru*, in *quadrupes* and other words. The adverbial *s*, by which द्विस् *dwis*, "twice," and त्रिस् *tris*, Zend *thris*, "thrice," are formed, is, in the Sanskrit *chatur*, suppressed by the rule of sound mentioned in §. 94.; hence *chatur*, "four times," for *chaturs*. That the latter has originally existed one learns from the Zend transposed form ᴡᴏᴌ*chathrus*. The Latin has already, in the number three, without being forced by a compulsory law, dropped the *s*, and hence *ter* and *quater* appear only as internal modifications of the cardinal numbers.

313. V. Sanskrit पञ्चन् *panchan*, Zend ᴘᴀɴᴄʜᴀɴ *panchan*, Lithuanian *penki*,* Greek πέντε, Æolic πέμπε, Gothic

---

* This is the nominative masculine; the feminine is *penkios*, and holds the

fimf,[*] Latin *quinque*, Old Sclavonic *pyaty*.[†] The Sanskrit-
Zend *panchan* is the theme, and the genders are not dis-
[G. Ed. p. 442.]   tinguished in this and the following numbers; hence the nominative, accusative, and vocative have
always singular neuter forms (therefore *pancha*, according to
§. 139.): the other cases shew plural terminations; as, genitive पञ्चानाम् *panchánám*, Zend ꭓ᭄ᬮᬸᬳ *panchananm*
(Vend. S. p. 52). By this irregularity in the declension the
Sanskrit and Zend prepare us in a measure for complete want
of inflection in Greek and Latin. Moreover, it is remarkable that not one of the European languages will at all recognise the final nasal, while, nevertheless, that of *saptan*,
navan, and *daśan* is found also in Gothic and Lithuanian;
and in Lithuanian, also, that of अष्टन् *ashṭan*, "eight"
(*asztûni*). The Greek has frequently preserved an old *α*

---

the same relation to it that *keturios* does to *keturi* (p. 428). The same
obtains with the appellations of the numbers 6, 7, 8, 9, of which we give
only the masculine.

[*] Occurs only uninflected: in the declined theme, the unorganic addition of an *i* must be expected, as in *FIDVORI*; and as is also actually
the case in Old High German in this number, and the appellations for the
six to ten inclusive. In Gothic, however, occur also *saihs*, "six," *sibun*,
"seven," *ahtau*, "eight," and *taihun*, "ten," only uninflected, and therefore without the unorganic *i*; but from *niun*, "nine," comes the genitive
niun-ê, which indeed might also have proceeded from a theme *NIUN* or
NIUNA, but which I doubt not comes from *NIUNI*.

[†] The theme is *PYATI*, and is inflected like *KOSTI* (p. 348), and
with singular terminations; so that one has to look upon this numeral as a feminine collective, beside which the object numbered stands
in apposition in like cases. The same obtains with the appellations for
the numbers 6 to 10 inclusive. As to the formal relation of *PYATI*
to *panchan*, we must observe, that of the latter, in Sclavonic, only the
syllable *pa* is represented by *pya* (§. 225. n.); but *TI* is a derivational
suffix, as in *SHESHTI*, "six," *DEVYATI*, "nine," and *DESYATI*,
"ten," and corresponds to the Sanskrit suffix *ti* in the multiplied numbers
vinśati, "twenty," *shashṭi*, "sixty," &c.

before a nasal originally there, while it has preferred weakening the same to *e* before other consonants; hence ἔτυψα(μ, ν), ἔτυψαν, but ἔτυψε(τ); τέτυφα(μι) but τέτυφε(τι); and so ἕπτα, ἐννέα, δέκα: not πέντα, however, but πέντε. It might therefore well be assumed, that the nasal in Indo-Zend numerals is a later addition, but that *cha* is the particle signifying "and," which, in the number four, we have taken for the prefix (§. 311.). In Latin, also, *quinque* is, in regard to its termination, similar to words connected with the particle *que*, as in πέντε the enclitic τε, which is akin to *que* and *cha* (see §. 14.) appears to be contained. This being the case, I would prefer regarding *pan* in पञ्च *pancha* as euphonic for *pam*, and the *m* as a neuter case-sign; but the *pa* which remains over as a pronoun, and indeed as identical with the *ka* which occurs in the number one (§. 308), in regard to which one might advert to the   [G. Ed. p. 443.] old Latin *pidpid* for *quidquid*, ποῖος for κοῖος, &c. Five would, therefore, literally mean "and one," and in fact that one which is to be added to four.*

314. VI. Sanskrit षष् *shash*, Zend ᴍᴍᴍᴍᴍᴍ *csvas*, Lithuanian *szeszi*, Old Sclavonic *shesty* (theme *SHESHTI*, p. 430, Note †), Gothic *saihs* (see §. 82.), Latin *sex*, Greek ἕξ. One may justly suppose that the guttural which begins the Zend word has also existed in Sanskrit, for instance, षष्

---

* Ag. Benary, who likewise recognises in *pancha* the particle "and," seeks to compare the preceding syllable with *páni*, "hand" (Berl. Jahrb. 1833. 11. p. 49). If, however, a connection exists between the appellations of the hand and five, the former word might be named from the number of the fingers; as one might also venture an attempt to explain *digitus* and δάκτυλος with the number "ten," and our "finger," Gothic *figgrs* (= *fingrs*), theme *FIGGRA*, with *fünf* (*fimf*); so that in this word no transition of the guttural organ into the labial has taken place. I do not think it probable that *finger* is named from *fangen*, "to seize"; also, as far as regards the Greek and Latin, the appellation of each single finger is more likely to be derived from the total number than from pointing (δείκνυμι).

kshash, for *sh* is otherwise not an initial syllable in Sanskrit, and also no original sound, but that sibilant which is only admissible with a preceding *k* (§. 21.). In Latin, Greek, and German the guttural appears to be transposed, for *sex* is the transposition of *xes*.

315. VII. Sanskrit सप्तन् *saptan*, Zend ᚻᚫᚹᛞᚫᚹ *haptan*, nominative and accusative सप्त *sapta*, ᚻᚫᚹᛞᚫᚹ *hapta* (see §. 313.), Greek ἑπτά, Latin *septem*, Lithuanian *septyni*, Old Sclavonic *sedmy* (theme *SEDMI*). The *m* of *septem* and *sedmy* seems to me to have been introduced from the ordinal number, which is, in Sanskrit, *saptama*, nom. masc. *saptama-s*, and in Sclavonic *sedmyi*. The same holds good of the termination of *osmy*, "eight," and the Latin *novem*, *decem*, Sanskrit *navama-s*,

[G. Ed. p 444.] "the ninth," *dasama-s*, "the tenth"; for it is not probable that the *n* of the Sanskrit cardinal number has become *m* in the abovementioned languages, as *m* is very frequently corrupted to *n*, especially at the end of words, where, in Greek, this transition is necessary; while the reverse method of the *n* to *m* scarcely occurs anywhere.

316. VIII. Sanskrit अष्टन् *ashtan* or अष्टौ *ashtâu*; from the former the nominative and accusative *ashta*, from the latter again *ashtâu*; Zend ᚻᚫᚹᛞᚫᚹ *astan*, nominative ᚻᚫᚹᛞᚫᚹ *asta*, Lithuanian *asztûni*, Gothic *ahtau*, Greek ὀκτώ, Latin *octo*, Old Sclavonic *osmy* (theme *OSMI*). The Sanskrit *ashtâu* and the analogous ὀκτώ appear, as it were, in a dual dress (see §. 206.); nevertheless, *ashtâu* is, in my opinion, just as much as *ashtan*, a bare theme, and has perhaps proceeded from the latter form, which occurs only in Zend, by the resolution of the *n* to *u*, which is so common (comp. p. 415, Note), and the lengthening of the *a*; if it is not preferred to develope it from *ashtas*, according to the analogy of §. 206. From अष्टौ *ashtâu* comes, by suppression of the last element of the diphthong, *ashtâ-bhis*, *ashtâ-bhyas*, *ashtâ-su*, as *râ-bhis*, &c., from *râi*, "thing," "riches," while *ashtân*, in the cases mentioned, forms regularly *ashtabhis*, *ashta-*

bhyas, ashtásu (comp. p. 304). The genitive has only one
form, namely, अष्टानाम् *ashtánám.*   The strength of the *du*
of *ashtáu* is preserved, also, in the cognate languages, and
indeed in the Latin *octav-us,* Greek ὄγδοος for ὄγδοϝ-ος, and
in German forms as *ahtowe-n,* dative, according to Notker
the cardinal number from *ahtowi-m,* from the theme
AHTOWI.   But if *ashtáu* were connected in its base with
चतुर् *chatur,* "four," there would be strong reason for considering the former form as the dual, expressing four twice,
and for assuming that an unorganic corruption of a dual
termination, which made its appearance in the earliest
antiquity, has grown up with the theme.

317. IX. Sanskrit नवन् *navan,* Zend [G. Ed. p. 445.]
navan (nominative and accusative *nava*), Gothic *niun*
—by contracting the *va* to *u* and weakening the *a* to *i*, as is
so common, §. 66.—Latin *novem* (see §. 315.), Greek ἐννέα,
Lithuanian *dewyni,* Old Sclavonic *devyaty* (theme *DEVYATI*).
The last two appellations appear foreign to the system of
the other sister languages: they are based, however, as I
have already remarked in another place,[*] on the facile
interchange of a nasal with the organically corresponding
medial on which, among others, rests the relation between
βροτός and मृतम् *mritas,* "*mortuus.*"   As regards the origin
of this numeral term, there exists a close connection in respect of form with the expression for "new" (Sanskrit *nava*).
That, however, a relation of ideas actually exists between
the two designations, as Ag. Benary first acutely conjectured (Berl. Jahrb. 1832. ii. p. 50), appears to me likewise
probable; for without recognising a dual in *ashtáu,* and
without excluding the thumbs in reckoning by the fingers,
the number nine can still only be thought of with reference to the earlier numbers, and as next to eight; and

---

[*] Historical and Philological Transactions of the Academy of Letters for
the year 1833, p. 168.

nine, in contrast with eight or all the preceding numbers,
is just as much a new number, as that which is new itself
is always a something later and successive, a *this* corresponding to the old *that.*   As a case in point, observe
the Latin *secundus* from *sequor.*   One must also admit that
it would not be surprising if any former number whatever, excluding one, were named after the idea of that
which is new, and that this origin is most intimately connected with the pronominal origin of other numerals.

[G. Ed. p. 446.]   318.   X.   Sanskrit दशन् *daśan,* Zend
ﺪﺳﻥ *dasan* (nominative and accusative *daśa*), Greek δέκα,
Latin *decem,* Lithuanian *deszimt, deszimt'-s* and *deszimtis* (the
two first indeclinable), Old Sclavonic *desyaty* (theme *DESYATI,*
see §. 313. Note †), Gothic *taihun.*   Concerning the *ai* and *u* of
taihun, see §§. 66. and 82.: the consonants have obeyed the law
of removal (§. 87.).   The Greek, rather than the Sanskrit,
therefore serves as prototype to the Gothic in regard
to the second consonant; and we have laid down in
§. 21. the Sanskrit श *ś* as a proportionably modern sound.
If, then, in this corruption, the Lithuanian and Sclavonic
agree with the Sanskrit, this may be so explained, that
these languages, guided independently by the Sanskrit and
Zend, but with the same euphonic feeling, have transformed
an old guttural to a sibilant;* in which change of sound, however, the Sclavonic, in other cases, goes farther than the
Sanskrit (comp. p. 415 G. ed.).   If, however, we desire to base
on historical tradition the peculiar coincidence with the Sanskrit and Zend in the case before us, and some others, we
must arrive at this through the assumption that the Lithuanian and Sclavonic races at some period wandered
from their original settlement in Asia, when corruptions

---

* But not universally, where, in Sanskrit, श *ś* is found; for *aśman,*
"a stone," nom. *aśmá,* is, in Lithuanian, *AKMEN,* nom. *akmù* (§. 139.),
and in Old Sclavonic *KAMEN',* nom. *kamy* (§. 264).

had already entered into the language, which did not exist at the time when the Greeks and Romans transplanted the Asiatic original language to Europe.

319. XI—XX. The smaller numbers are combined with the expression for ten : Sanskrit रूकादशन् *ékádasan*, द्वादशन् *duádasan*, त्रयोदशन् *trayódasan*, चतुर्दशन् *chaturdasan*, &c. ; Zend ﺟﻤﻬﻮﺭﻳﻬ *aévandasan* (?), ﺟﻤﻬﻮﺭﻳﻬ *dvadasan ;** Greek ἔνδεκα, δώδεκα, τρισκαίδεκα, τεσσαρεσ- [G. Ed. p. 447.] καίδεκα; Latin *undecim, duodecim, tredecim, quatuordecim;* Lithuanian *wienolika, dwylika, trylika, keturólika;* Gothic *ainlif* (1 C. xv. 5.), *tvalif,† fimftaihun,* "fifteen"; Old Sclavonic *chetyrinadesyaty,* "fourteen," *pyatynadesyaty,* "fifteen," &c.

"Remark.—Before the simple *dasan* (from *dakan*) had been changed in the Gothic into *taihun,* according to the

---

* These may be deduced from the ordinals *aévandaia, dvadaia* (Vend. S. p. 120). So also *chathrudaian,* "fourteenth," *panchadaian,* "fifteenth," from *chathrudaia,* "the fourteenth," *panchadaia,* "the fifteenth." The nasal in *aévandaia* appears to have proceeded from *m,* and to be an accusative sign, for the whole stands l. c. in the accusative (*aévandaiëm*). By this, doubt is thrown on the *aévandasan* given above, and perhaps *aévódaian,* or, according to the original principle of the compound, *aévadaian* might be expected. In one other passage, indeed, occurs the nominative of the ordinal *aévandaió* (l. c. p. 230): it is, however, clearly a false reading, and the sense requires the accusative, as governed by ﺟﻤﻬﻮﺭﻳﻬ *frásnaóiti,* which Anquetil renders by *a atteint;* thus, ﺟﻤﻬﻮﺭﻳﻬ ﺟﻤﻬﻮﺭﻳﻬ *aévandaiëm frásnaóiti,* "*decimum attingit*"; and in the following analogous constructions the ordinal number also stands always in the accusative. The form *aévandaiëm,* from *aévamdaiëm,* is remarkable, also, in a phonetic respect, because elsewhere in Zend a final *m* is not governed by the organ of the following letter.

† I do not take the *tva* here, with Grimm (11. 947.), for the neuter, but, according to the principle of genuine compounds, for the theme (compare §. 112.), whence the nom. masc. *tvai. Tva* may also—and this appears to me more correct—be regarded, without the Gothic being conscious of the formation, precisely as the abbreviation of the Sanskrit *dwá,* which is a lengthening of the theme *dua,* as *éká* from *éka.*

comparatively recent law for the alteration of sounds
(compare § 92.). it may have happened that, through the
very widely-diffused disposition for exchanging the *d* with
l, and through the not less common permutation between
gutturals and labials —through which, among others, the
relation of *fidvôr* to the Lithuanian *keturi* and Latin *quatuor*
becomes explicable—the *daśan* contained in *ekâ-daśan*
"eleven," and *dwâ-daśan*, "twelve" (from *dakan*), may have
passed, in Gothic, into *LIBI*. Through the dative *tva-libi-m*,
genitive *tva-lib'-ê*, *LIBI* is preserved, in fact, as the true
theme; so that each *a* of *daśan* is weakened to *i*. The *f* of
[G. Ed. p. 448.]   the uninflected *tvalif* is, therefore, not to be
explained according to §. 37., but according to §. 93ª.; and if
the theme *libi* has not obeyed the law for the mutation of
sounds, the objection, which has been raised by Graff
(Old High German Thesaurus, p. 317) against my explanation, is removed by what has been remarked in
§. 89., for we refer to *fidvôr*, not *fithvôr*. The Latin
quadraginta, also, for *quatraginta*, and the Greek ὄγδοος for
ὄκτοος, ἕβδομος for ἕπτομος, and several others, may be
noticed, in support of the proposition that the numeral formations in the choice of the degree of the organ of
the consonants have not always remained in the customary path; and in cumbrous compounds the medials are
more admissible than the smooth letters and aspirates.* To remove the objection which may be taken
on the ground that *LIBI* is so very different from
the form of *taihun*, we may remark, that, in French

---

* The Anglo-Saxon *endleofan*, *endlufan*, compared with *twelf*, and
the Old Friesian *andlova* with *twilif*, should not make us doubt, since
the Anglo-Saxon *eo* corresponds to the Sanskrit *a* of *daśan* and Gothic *i*
of *lif*, as in the relation of *seofon* (Old Friesian *siugon*) to the Sanskrit
saptan, Gothic *sibun*. Let, then, the Old Friesian *o* of *lova* be regarded
like that of *siugon*. To the Sanskrit *chatwâr*, Gothic *fidvôr*, correspond
the Anglo-Saxon *feover*, Old Friesian *fiuwer*.

also, the number ten, in compounds like *on-ze*, *dou-ze*, *trei-ze*, is so remote from the expression of the simple ten, that one would hardly venture to pronounce the syllable *ze* to be akin, or originally identical with *dix*, if it were not historically certain that *onze*, *douze*, &c., have arisen from *undecim*, *duodecim*, and that therefore *ze* is a corruption of *decim*, as *dix* is a less vitiated form of *decem*. If, then, *onze*, *douze*, &c., have assumed the appearance of uncompounded words through the great alteration of the expression for the number ten contained in them, the same holds good with regard to our *eilf* and *zwölf*, in which, perhaps, as in *onze* and *douze*, a connection with *ein* and *zwei* may be recognised, but none with *zehn*; and in the English eleven, also, the relation to one is entirely obliterated. But with regard to our using for thirteen, fourteen, &c., not *dreilf*, *vierlf*, or similar forms in *lf*, but *dreizehn*, *vierzehn*, &c., in which *zehn* is just as unaltered as the *drei* and *vier*, this arises from the Germans having forgotten the old Indo-European compounds for these numbers, and then having compacted the necessary expressions anew from the elements as they exist uncompounded. Nay, even   [G. Ed. p. 449.] the Greek has reconstructed afresh, as well as it could, its numerals from thirteen upwards, after that the old more genuine compounds had fallen into disuse; but this has been done, I must say, in a clumsy, awkward fashion, by which the addition of a particle signifying *and* was found requisite in an attempt at extreme perspicuity, while ἕνδεκα, δώδεκα, move more freely, and are suited to the spirit of the ancient compounds. The literal meaning, too, of τρισκαίδεκα (for τρίδεκα) is "thrice and ten," and the numeral adverb τρίς, instead of the bare theme τρι, is here just as much a mistake as the masculine plural nominative serves as a reproach to the τεσσαρεσκαίδεκα, and is inferior in purity to the Sanskrit *chatur-daśan*, not *chatvdras-daśan* (*chatvârô-daśan*). On the other hand, the Sanskrit, in the designation of the number thirteen, commits a similar error, and awkwardly gives instead of *tri-dasan, trayô-dasan*—euphonic for *trayas-dasan*—where the masculine plural nominative instead of the theme, which is adapted for all genders, is not well selected. The Latin *tre-decim* is therefore a more pure formation, as it dispenses with a case-sign in the first member of the compound : just so the Lithuanian *try-lika*, not *trys-lika*. This *lika*, which concludes the form, in all Lithuanian adding numerals (eleven to nineteen), exchanges the old *d* for *l*, as in German, and is therefore as far estranged from the simple *deszimt's* as the Gothic *libi* from *taihun ;* partly, as the second consonant in *lika* has maintained itself in its oldest form received from the Greek, and has not become a sibilant; so that *lika* and δέκα resemble each other very closely. The Lithuanian *lika*, therefore, is derived, like the Gothic *libi* and the French *ze* in *onze, douze,* &c., from the old compound which has been handed down, and cannot, therefore, be censured for its want of agreement with the simple number ten: it is no longer conscious of its meaning, and, like an inanimate corpse, is carried by the living inferior number. As, however, the smaller number in these compounds is still living, so that in the feeling of the speaker the numbers *wieno-lika, dwy-lika,* &c., do not appear as independent simple designations of numbers—as, perhaps, *septyni* is felt to be independent of each of the earlier numbers—so, naturally, in these compounds the first member has kept tolerably equal pace with the form which it shews in its isolated state; on which account *wieno-lika*, if it is regarded as an ancient compound from the time of the unity of language, or perhaps as derived from रवादशन् *êkâ-dasan,*

[G. Ed. p. 450.]   has nevertheless undergone, in its initial member, a renovation; as also in Gothic *ainlif*, in Greek ἕνδεκα, in Latin *undecim*, have regulated their first member according to the form which is in force for the isolated number one. On the other hand, δώδεκα is almost entirely the Sanskrit *dwâ-dasa* (ω for *ñ*, according to §. 4.), and is as similar to it as possible, as υ (F) in Greek cannot be pronounced after consonants, and in the first syllable, also, could not assimilate itself to the preceding consonant (compare τέτταρες from τέτϝαρες), for δδώδεκα could not be uttered.   In Latin, *duodecim* has formed its first member exactly after the simple form : on the other hand, the French has paid no regard to the form in which the preceding number appears in its isolated state, but has left the composition entirely in the old form, only with the abbreviations which time has by degrees introduced.   With reference to the isolated state of the smaller number, it would have been, perhaps, necessary in French to have said *unze, deuze, troize,* &c.   After what has been stated, I think no one can any longer doubt, that in our *eilf* (*elf*) and *zwölf,* strange as it at the first glance may appear, a word is contained expressing the number ten, and identical in its origin with *daśan,* δέκα, and *zehn.*   If, however, the older *LIBI, lif,* and Lithuanian *lika,* be regarded without the suspicion arising, that in them corrupt though very common permutations of sounds may have preceded, then one would propose in Lithuanian a root *lik,* and in Gothic *lif* or *lib* (Gothic *af-lifnan,* "*relinqui, superesse,*" *laibôs,* "*reliquiæ*"), which both signify "to remain," and are also connected with each other and with the Greek λείπω (ΛΙΠ).   Grimm, who has recognised (II. 946) the original identity of our *lif* and the Lithuanian *lika,* has perhaps allowed himself to be led astray by Ruhig in the meaning of these expressions, and deduces the latter from *likti,* "*linqui, remanere,*" the former from *leiban,* "*manere.*"   Ruhig, according to Mielcke, p. 58, holds *lika* for the 3d person plural, since he says, "Composition in the cardinal numbers from ten to twenty takes place by adding the 3d person plural number present indicative *lika* (from *likù* s. *liekmi*) ; scil., the tenth remains undisturbed with the simple number, *e.g.* one, two, &c.; which addition, however, in composition degenerates into a declinable noun of the feminine gender, according to which, also, the preceding

[G. Ed. p. 451.]   simple number must be regulated."[*]   The
languages, however, do not proceed so pedantically; and if
they hold any thing understood, as very commonly happens,
they do not expressly state that any thing remains over to
be expressed.   It is certain, however, that the Sclavonic languages, in their expressions for eleven to twenty, do not keep
back any thing to be understood, but form those expressions,
after the loss of the old, no longer intelligible compounds,
anew, with the annexed preposition *na*, "over"; *e.g.* in Old
Sclavonic, where the numbers eleven, twelve, thirteen, no
longer occur, *chetyri-na-desyaty*, "four over ten."   The ordinal numbers for eleven and twelve are *yedinyĭ-na-desyaty*,
" the first over ten," *vtoryĭ-na-desyaty*, " the second over ten."
In the same manner proceeds the twin sister of the Lithuanian
—accompanying it, but corrupted—the Lettish, in which
weenpazmit signifies "eleven," as it appears to me, with contraction of the *d(e)s* of *desmit*, "ten," to *z*, and overleaping the *e*.
This procedure in Lettish has no doubt originated from the
older *lika* being no longer intelligible.   If it was to be so
understood, as Ruhig has taken it, its form would be palpable,
and the Lettians might have been satisfied with it.   With reference to the composition of the numerals under discussion,
there remains to be noticed a most remarkable coincidence
of the Lithuanián and German with a Prâkṛit dialect,
which coincidence, when I formerly touched upon this

---

* Grimm's view is certainly much more natural, "ten and one over,
two over."   Only it would be to be expected, if the language wished to
designate the numbers eleven and twelve as that which they contain more
than ten, that they would have selected for combination with one and
two a word which signifies "and over, or more," and not an exponent of
the idea "to leave," "to remain."   It would, moreover, be more adapted
to the genius and custom of the later periods of the language, not to
forget the number ten in the newly-formed compounds, like the Lettish
and Sclavonic.   J. Grimm, in his "History of the German Language,"
p. 246, agrees with my explanation of *eilf*, *zwölf*, and analogous forms in
Lith. and Sclavonic.

subject,* was not yet known to me, and which has been since then observed by Lenz in his edition of Urvasi (p. 219). In this dialect, then, the number ten is pronounced simply दह *daha*—approaching closely to the Gothic *taihun*—but at the end of the compounds under notice *raha*: *r* and *l*, however, are, according to §. 17., most intimately connected. Hitherto only, बारह *vdraha*, "twelve," from द्वादश *dwâdasa*, and अठारह *althâraha*, "eighteen," from अष्टादश *ashtâdasa*, can be cited, but still from them it is probable that the other numerals too, which fall under this cate- [G. Ed. p. 452.] gory, have an *r* for *d*, apparently to lighten the word loaded by the prefixing of lesser numbers, by exchanging the *d* for a weak semi-vowel. Now it is a remarkable coincidence that if we were desirous of not seeing a mutation of letters in this *ruha* we should be led to the root *rah*, "to leave," which is probably identical with the verb, to which recourse has been had for the explanation of the corresponding Lithuanian and German numeral forms.† I thought I had exhausted this subject, when I was led by other reasons to the Hindûstânî grammar, where I was agreeably surprised by perceiving that here, also, the number ten, in the designation of eleven, twelve, &c., has taken another lighter form than in its simple state, in which it is pronounced *das*.‡ But in the compounds under discussion this becomes *rah*,‡ and, for example, *bârah*,

---

* Influence of the Pronoun on the formation of Words, p. 27; and Histor. Philol. Trans. of the Academy for the year 1833, p. 178, &c.

† The *a* of *rah* has been weakened in the cognate languages to *i*: hence *linquo*, Lithuanian *likù*, Greek λείπω (ἔλιπον), Gothic *of-lif-na*. In respect to the consonants, we refer the reader to §§ 20. 23.: remark, also, the connection of the Lithuanian *lakù*, "I lick," with the Sanskrit root *lih*, "to lick." Since writing this note, I have come to the conclusion that it is better to concur with Benfey, in assigning the Latin *linquo*, Greek λείπω, Gothic *af-lif-na*, to the Skr. root *rich*, from *rik*, "to leave."

‡ The text has *des* and *reh*, but as these sounds are incorrect, I have altered them, as well as some other inaccuracies in the Hindûstânî numerals which follow.—*Translator.*

"twelve," answers to the abovementioned Prâkrit बारह
bâraha, and, like this, has proceeded directly from the
Sanskrit original form द्वादश duâdasa, without heeding
the form of the simple do, "two," and das, "ten." It
may be proper here to quote all the Hindûstânî compounds
which belong to this subject, together with the corresponding Sanskrit words of which they are the corruptions. We annex, also, the number twenty, and nineteen which is related to it as being twenty less one, as
also the simple lower numbers in Hindûstânî.

[G. Ed. p. 453.]

HINDÛSTÂNÎ.				SANSKRIT, NOMINATIVE.	
êk	1,	igâ-rah,	11,	êkâdasa	11.
do	2,	bâ-rah	12,	duâdasa	12.
tín	3,	têrah,	13,	trayôdasa	13.
châr	4,	chau-dah	14,*	chaturdasa	14.
pânch	5,	pand-rah	15,	panchâdasa	15.
chhah	6,	sô-lah	16,†	shôdasa	16.
sât	7,	sat-rah	17,	saptadasa	17.
âth	8,	athâ-rah	18,	ashtâdasa	18.
nau	9,	unnís	19,	ûnavinsati ("undeviginti") 19.	
das	10,	bís	20,	vinsati	20.

320. XX—C. The idea of ten is expressed in Sanskrit
by शति sati, शत् sat or ति ti; in Zend by ساوات saiti, ساوات
sata, or ساو ti; and the words therewith compounded are
substantives with singular terminations, with which, in
Sanskrit, the thing numbered agrees in case, as in apposition, or is put, as in the Zend, in the genitive, as

---

* The retention of the d is here clearly to be ascribed to the circumstance that the lesser number ends with r, although in the Hindûstânî
corruption this is no longer present. The Bengâli has assimilated the r
to the following d, hence châuddo; but, as a general rule, the Bengâli in
these compounds changes the d into r, and in all cases suppresses the
Hindûstânî h; as êgâro, "eleven," bâro, "twelve," têro, "thirteen."

† This form merits particular notice, as, through its l for the r found
elsewhere, it comes so near to the Lithuanian and German lika, lif. The
Bengâli is shôlo.

dependent upon it. Occasionally, too, one finds these numerals in Sanskrit used adjectively, with plural endings. Compare, [G. Ed. p. 454.]

	SANSKRIT.	ZEND.	GREEK.	LATIN.
20,	विंशति viṅśati,	᭬ viśaiti,	εἴκατι,	viginti,
30,	त्रिंशत् triṅśat,	thriśata,	τριάκοντα,	triginta.
40,	chatwâriṅśat,	chathwarēśata,	τεσσαράκοντα,	quadraginta.
50,	panchâśat,	panchâśata,	πεντήκοντα,	quinquaginta.
60,	shaṣhṭi,	csvasti,	ἑξήκοντα,	sexaginta.
70,	saptati,	haptaiti,	ἑβδομήκοντα,†	septuaginta.
80,	aśíti,	. . . .	ὀγδοήκοντα,	octoginta.
90,	navati,	navaiti,	ἐνενήκοντα,	nonaginta.
100,	śata-m,	śatĕ-m,	ἑ-κατό-ν,	centu-m.

"Remark.—I hold śati, śat, śata, ti, to be abbreviations of daśati, daśat, daśata, and therefore derivations from daśan, "ten," by a suffix ti, ta, or t: the former is,

---

* The numerals in śata, answering to the Sanskrit forms in śat, are neuters, and occur, like the forms in ti, very frequently in the 6th and 12th Fargard of the Vendidâd, but only in the accusative singular, in which śatĕm might also belong to a theme śat. That, however, śata is the theme and the neuter form is clear from Vend. S. p. 230. (in the 7th Fargard), where pancha śatĕm (panchâśatĕm), "fifty," stands as nominative. From csvasti, "sixty," haptâiti, "seventy," and navaiti, "ninety," we find the accusative csvastim, haptâitim, navaitim: on the other hand, in the 12th Fargard, occurs several times viśaiti (also written viśati and viśati) as accusative of viśaiti, which perhaps is a dual neuter form (two decades), and according to this would stand for viśaiti (§. 210.). But if the final vowel is retained in its original form it is a singular neuter. It is, however, remarkable, that only this final i, and no other, is again found in the cognate Latin and Greek forms.

† This and the following number are renovated forms, in which the first member proceeds unorganically from the ordinal number. We might have expected ἑπτήκοντα, ὀκτώκοντα, for the latter Ion. ὀγδώκοντα. In ἐνενήκοντα the two ν are separated from each other: the epic form ἐννήκοντα is more genuine.

in Lithuanian and Sclavonic, already contained in the
simple *deszimťs, deszimtis,* Old Sclavonic *desyaty.* With
regard, however, to the ten being expressed without
abbreviation in the languages mentioned, in compounds,
also—as in Lithuanian *dwideszimti* (or *tis*), "twenty,"
trysdészimti (or *tis*), "thirty," and in Old Sclavonic *che-
tyridesyaty,* "forty."* *pyntydesyaty,* "fifty"—I do not consider
[G. Ed. p. 455.]   this as a more true retention of the original
form, but as a new formation. The Lithuanian, too, from
forty upwards, separates the two numbers, and puts the
former in the feminine plural, *e. g. keturios deszimtis,* "forty,"
penkios deszimtis, "fifty"; in which it is surprising that
deszimtis, also, does not stand in the plural. The Gothic
method in this numeral category is of comparatively
recent date: it has lost, as in thirteen, &c., the ancient
compound, and gives, in the numbers under seventy
(sixty does not occur), *tigus,* masculine, as the expression
for ten, and declines this, and in twenty, thirty, the lesser
number also, with regular plural terminations: hence the
accusatives *tvanstiguns, thrinstiguns, fidvŏrtiguns, fimftiguns,*
genitive *thriyétigvé.* The substantive *tigus,* however, is
the etymological quaver to *taihun,* and *LIBI*: it is related
to the former essentially, the aspirate having become a
medial (see §. 89.), thus rendering the *a,* which, in *taihun,*
is brought in by the rule of sound mentioned in §. 82.,
superfluous. Advert, also, to the Latin medials in *ginti,*
ginta, contrasted with the Greek κατι, κοντα, which answer
better to δέκα. *Tigu-s* may be identical with the Sanskrit ordinal *dasa,* nominative masculine *dasa-s,* which
occurs only in compounds, as *duádaśn-s,* "the twelfth."
To this *daśa-s,* therefore, is related *tigu-s* in regard to
its *u,* as *fŏtu-s* to *páda-s,* "a foot." In the numbers
seventy, eighty, and ninety, ten is denoted by the neuter

* Twenty and thirty do not occur.

substantive *tĕhund* (theme *TEHUNDA*, genitive *tĕhundi-s*); hence *sibun-tĕhund*, "seventy," *ahtau-tĕhund*, "eighty," *niun-tĕhund*, "ninety." The *ĕ* of this *TEHUNDA* stands as the representative of the *ai* of *taihun*, and I hold *DA* to be the ordinal suffix, which has introduced into the common ordinals another unorganic *N*, or, according to Grimm, follows the weak declension; hence *TAIHUNDAN*, nominative *taihunda*, "*decimus*." Hereby, then, it becomes still more probable that the abovementioned *tigus* also is originally an ordinal number. In our New German this word has transformed itself to *zig* or *ssig* (*dreissig*), and is found also in *siebenzig, achtzig, neunzig*, Old High German *sibunzog, ahtozog, niunzog*, or *-zoc*, and *zëhanzog* (*zoc*), Gothic *taihuntĕhund*, "a hundred." The Sanskrit-Zend *sata*, "a hundred," which is a neuter substantive—nominative शतम् *satam*, ₵₴ℂⱮⱮⱮ *satĕm*—in my opinion owes its designation to the number ten (*dasan*), whence it is formed by the suffix *ta*—the suppression of the final nasal is regular;—so that it is to be regarded as an abbreviation of *dasata*, as above, शति *sati*, शत् *sat*, and the Zend ⱮⱮⱮⱮⱮ *sata* for *dasati*, &c. This abbreviation, however, which has given to the word the stamp of a primi- [G. Ed. p. 456.] tive expression specially created for the idea "a hundred," is proved to be of the highest antiquity by the consentaneous testimony of all the cognate languages, Greek κατόν (ἑκατόν is, verbatim, "one hundred"), Latin *centum*, Lithuanian *szimta-s* (masculine), Old Sclavonic *sto* (at once theme and nominative and accusative neuter).* The Gothic *hund* and Old High German *hunt* (theme *HUNDA, HUNTA*) occur only in compounds, as *tva-hŭnda, thria-hunda, zuei-hunt, driu-hunt*, where the lesser number is likewise inflected. That also शति *sati*, शत् *sat*, and the corresponding words

---

* In Zend *ita* occurs frequently for *sata*, and just so in the numbers compounded therewith.

in the cognate languages, have in the earliest periods lost the
initial syllable of the number ten, and with it the lingual ·
remembrance of the same; and that in विंशति *vinśti*, ٮۯڛڛ *viśaiti*, εἴκατι, εἴκοσι, *viginti*, the single elements have lain
together undisturbed for thousands of years, affords a fresh
proof of the agreement of the languages which have most
faithfully preserved their ancient construction.   I would
not, however, wish to maintain that the loss of the *d* of
the number two in the above forms falls under the period
of the unity of languages ; and that it may not have happened that each of the four individual languages, having
become weary of the initial double consonant in a word
already encumbered by composition, may have disbur-
thened itself of the initial sound, as we have above seen
the Latin and Zend, independently of each other, produce
bis from *dwis*, and *bi* from *dwi*, and as, in agreement with
the abbreviation of विंशति *vinśuti*, the Prâkṛit dialect mentioned at p. 451 G. ed. has laid aside the *d* in the number
twelve also (*vâraha* for *dwâraha*).   It is remarkable that the
four oldest and most perfect languages of the Indo-European
family in the category of numerals before us, have lost
exactly as much of the number ten as the French in the
forms for eleven, twelve, &c.; and the *ze* of *douze* is
therefore identical with the Sanskṛit *śa* of विंशति *vinśati*.
The Sanskṛit and Zend, however, in a later corruption
which is unsupported by the Greek and Latin, have
caused the word *daśati* to be melted down to the derivation suffix *ti*, and this *ti* corresponds to the French *te*
of *trente*, *quarante*, &c.   The numbers which have been
thus far abbreviated begin, in Sanskṛit and Zend, with
sixty, षष्टि *shashti* (*ti* euphonic for *ti*), ڛۏڛڛۿۺۏڟ *csvasti*.   To
the *śati* of विंशति *vinśati* ٮۏڛڛ *viśati*, regularly corresponds
the Doric κατι of εἴκατι, while in the Latin *ginti* the smooth

[G. Ed. p. 457.]   letter has sunk to a medial, as in *ginta* = κοντα
of the higher numbers.   In Sanskṛit the *n* of *vinśati*,

triṅśat, chatwâriṅśat, is surprising, and one might imagine a transposition of the nasal, so that in the Latin *ginti, ginta, centum,* and in the Gothic *HUNDA,* "one hundred," it would stand in its proper place. For the rest, *chatwâriṅśat* shews its relation to the neuter *chatwâri* (see §. 312.); as also τρια, τεσσαρα in τριάκοντα, τεσσαράκοντα, are, in my opinion, plural neuter forms, with the termination length-ened in τριᾱ, and originally, also, in τεσσαρα, as the Ionic τεσσαρήκοντα, Doric τετρώκοντα,* Latin *quadraginta,* prove. These forms excite the conjecture, that, in Sanskṛit, the introduction of the nasal may, contrary to the explanation attempted above, have the same object that, in Greek, the lengthening of the termination has, namely, an emphatic repetition of the prefixed number, which is also percep-tible in the long *i* of the Zend *vîsaiti,* as in the long *a* of वचाशत् *panchâśat,* ६ᠷᠷᠣᠠᠣᠣᠣᠷᠣᠣᠣᠣ *panchâśatĕm* from *panchan* (§. 318.), and to which again the length of πεντήκοντα, *quinquaginta,* runs parallel. The Zend *chathwarĕ,* in ᠣᠣᠣᠷᠣᠣᠣᠣᠣᠣᠣ *chathwarĕśata,* "forty" (Vend. S. p. 380), is likewise stronger than *cha-thru-śata,* which might have been expected from §. 312. As ᠣᠣᠣᠣ *śata* is a neuter, to which, in Greek, κατον or κοντον would correspond, κοντα therefore, and the Latin *ginta,* are best explained as neuters in the plural, by which the neuter nature of τριᾱ and τεσσαρα is still more authenticated. An auxiliary vowel, which merely facilitated the combination, and which might be assumed in ἑξήκοντα, would at least be very superfluous in the theme ΤΡΙ; and it is much more probable that ἑξη, too, is a lengthened plural neuter. Compare ἑξά-κις, ἑξαπλοῦς, and the remarks on πάντα and πολλά, p. 401, G. ed.

---

* The ω for ᾱ is explained by §. 4. As to the suppression of the vowel before the ρ, τετρω answers to τετρα in τετράκις, τετραπλοῦς, which in like manner are based on plural neuter forms instead of the theme.

ORDINAL NUMBERS.

321. While, in designating the number one, the greatest variety obtains amongst the Indo-European languages, they are [G. Ed. p. 458.] almost unanimous in their designation of *the first*, which idea none of the languages here treated of derives from the corresponding cardinal number : Sanskrit प्रथमस् *prathama-s* (nom), Zend ⟨glyph⟩ *frathēmō* (§. 56ᵇ.), Latin *primu-s*, Lithuanian *prima-s*, Gothic *frum'-s* (for *fruma-s*, §. 135.), or indefinite *fruma* (theme *FRUMAN*, §. 140.), or, with newly-added superlative suffix, *frumist'-s*, Old High German *éristêr*, usually indefinite *éristo* (from the adverb *ér*, " before "), Greek πρῶτος, Old Sclavonic *pervyi*. प्रथम *prathama*, from the preposition *pra*, has been already discussed (p. 393 G. ed.); so the Greek πρῶτος is derived from the corresponding preposition πρό, the lengthening of which to πρω accords with the Sanskrit *prá* in *prátar*, " in the morning" (see p. 392 G. ed.). The suffix TO is an abbreviation of the Sanskrit *tama* or *thama*, which occurs even in Sanskrit in चतुर्थस् *chatur-tha-s*, " the fourth," and षष्ठस् *shash-tha-s*, " the sixth," as also in Latin in the form of *TU* in *quartus*, *quintus*, *sextus*, while in Greek this abbreviation extends to all the ordinal numbers, exclusive of δεύτερος, ἕβδομος, and ὄγδοος. In Lithuanian the corresponding *TA* of four runs through all, but in such wise, that together with *septintas*, *asztuntas*, occur also *sékmas*, *úszmas*, which correspond to the Sanskrit सप्तमस् *saptama-s*, अष्टमस् *ashtama-s*, in which the last portion of the superlative suffix *tama* or *thama* has remained ; of which kind of division, also, पञ्चमस् *panchama-s*, नवमस् *navama-s*, and दशमस् *dasama-s*, partake, which therefore complete, by their suffix, the *tha* of *chaturtha*, so that both united present the perfect word. The Zend agrees herein with the Sanskrit, only that its ⟨glyph⟩ *haptathô* agrees more with *septintas* than with सप्तमस् *saptama-s* and *septimu-s*; and

that also ‏ڢڡہو‎ pug-dhŏ, " the fifth," belongs more to
the European cognate languages, in which it comes nearest
to the Lithuanian *penk-ta-s.* The Lithuanian, however, is
more true to the original form, as its sister, the Zend, has
softened two original smooth letters, as   [G. Ed. p. 459.]
in Greek, ὄγδοος for ὄκτοος ; and, besides this, has aspirated
the last, rejected the nasal (comp. p. 94, *busta* from *bandh*),
and irregularly. changed the *a* to *u*, as in ῎ΟΝΥΧ, corresponding to the Sanskrit नख *nakha,* "a nail." In the
numbers from eleven to twenty the superlative suffix, in
Sanskrit and Zend, is abbreviated still more than in the
simple दशम *daśama,* ‏ڗڡڗڛڡو‎ *daśĕma,* and of all the derivational suffix only the *a* is left, before which the *a* of the
primitive word must fall away, according to a universal
principle for the derivation of words; as, द्वादश *dwd-
daśa,* ‏ڗڛڛڡڛ»ڡ‎ *dvadaśa,* "the twelfth"; चतुर्दश *chaturdaśa,*
‏ڗڛڛڡڡ؍ڱڛٯ‎ *chathrudaśa,* "the fourteenth." The Latin
appears to prove that this abbreviation is comparatively of
recent date, and it goes beyond both the Asiatic sisters by
its *undecimus, duodecimus,* not *undecus, duodecus;* but has, as it
were, exhausted itself in the effort which the continuance of
these heavier forms has cost it; and has given up the analogous formations in the very place in which the German
cardinal numbers have lost the old compound in *lif*: hence,
tertius decimus for the lost *tredecimus,* &c. An imitation, however, of the abbreviation which we have just remarked in the
Sanskrit-Zend *daśa* is supplied by the Greek and Latin in the
forms *octav-us,* ὄγδο(F)-ος, where, of the ordinal suffix, in like
manner, only the final vowel is left: we might have expected
ὄγδομος, *octomus.* In the very remarkable coincidence which
here exists between the said languages, it must seem strange
that, in the remaining designations of the ordinal numbers,
the Latin is a much truer colleague to its Asiatic sisters
than to the Greek; and it preserves this character, also, in
annexing, from twenty upwards, the full superlative suffix
simu-s (from *timu-s*=तमस् *tama-s*); thus *vicesimus* or *vige-*

[G. Ed. p. 460.] *simus, trigesimus,* as in Sanskṛit *viṅśatitama-s, triṅśattama-s.** In Latin, however, the termination *nti* or *nta* of the primitives is rejected, and in compensation the preceding vowel is lengthened in the form of *ē.* Compare, in this respect, the comparative formations discussed in §. 298. The Greek shews its more rare superlative suffix, corresponding to the Sanskṛit इष्ठ *ishṭha,* in the ordinal numbers like εἰκοστός, τριακοστός, with the loss of the ι of ιστος, as in ἕκαστος, πόστος. Here also, therefore, as in Latin, the τι, σι, and ντα of the cardinal number are rejected. The German languages employ in like manner the superlative suffix in numbers from twenty upwards: hence, Old High German *drî-zugôsto,* "the thirtieth," *fior-zugôsto,* "the fortieth": but in the numbers from four to nineteen the *TAN* or *DAN,* in Gothic, corresponds, according to the measure of the preceding letter (§. 91.), to the suffix of the cognate languages, as in चतुर्थस् *chaturtha-s,* τέταρτο-ς, *quartu-s, ketwir-ta-s.* The *N,* however, is an unorganic addition, after the principle of the indefinite adjective declension (§. 285.), which is followed by the ordinal numbers, with the exception of 1 and 2 in the older dialects; while the New German has also introduced the definite—*vierter,* "fourth," *fünfter,* "fifth," &c.; hence, Gothic *FIMFTAN,* nom. masc. *fimfta.*†

[G. Ed. p. 461.] 322. From the weakened base द्वि *dwi* "two" (p. 424), and from the त्रि *tri,* "three," contracted to त्रि *tṛi,* the Sanskṛit forms the ordinal numbers by a suffix *tîya;* hence *dwi-tîya-s, tritîya-s.* This suffix is easily recognised in the Latin *ter-*

---

* However, this and the higher numbers may follow the analogy of *êkâdaśa-s,* "the eleventh"; hence, also, *viṅśa, triṅś-a,* &c. In Zend I am unable to quote the ordinal numbers from twenty upwards.

† In compounds like *fimftataihunda,* "the fifteenth," the lesser number has either preserved the original theme while still free from the *n,* which was added more lately,—for the lesser number in these compounds does not partake of declension,—or *fimfta* is here the regular abbreviation of the theme *FIMFTAN,* since, as I have already elsewhere remarked (Berl. Ann. May 1827. p. 759), bases in *n,* in strict accordance with the Sanskṛit, drop the *n* in the beginning of compounds.

tius, as also in the Old Sclavonic *tretiï*, fem. *tretiya*, which, like all the ordinal numbers, has only a definite declension, in which, however, the particular case occurs, that the defining element is brought with it direct from the East, while the *tyï* of *chetwertyï* and others, in which, in like manner, a connection with तीय *tíya* might be easily conjectured, is, in fact, connected with the थ *tha*, TO, *TU* of चतुर्थ *chaturtha*, τέταρτος, *quartus*, and has arisen from the indefinite theme in *TO* (comp. the collective *chetvero*, §. 312.), according to §. 255. (*d.*), although the simple word in most of the formations falling under this category no longer exists. The same relation, then, that *chetvertyï*, *shestyï*, have to *chaturtha-s*, *shashtha-s*, *sedmyï*, *osmyï*, have to सप्तम *saptama*, अष्टम *ashtama ;* and *pervyï*, " the first," to पूर्व *púrva*, " the former ;" which expressions, in Sclavonic, remain only in combination with the pronominal base *YO* (§. 282.). The Zend has rejected the *i* of the suffix *tiya*, and abbreviated *dwi* to *bi;* hence ꭕ*bitya*, ꭕ*thritya*, in which it is to be remarked that the *y*, which is thus by syncope united with the *t* at a comparatively later period, has gained no aspirating influence (§. 47.). To this Zend *tya* corresponds, by similar suppression of the middle *i*, the Gothic *DYAN* (from *dya*, §. 285.) in *THRIDYAN*, nom. masc. *thridya*, the *y* of which in the Old High German *dritto*, has assimilated itself to the preceding *t*, in analogy with the Prâkrit forms and Greek comparatives, like θάσσων, κρείσσων, κρείττων, mentioned at p. 402. Still closer, however, lies the comparison with διττός, τριττός (δισσός, τρισσός), which are evidently, in [G. Fd. p. 462.] their origin, one with the corresponding Sanskrit-Zend ordinal numbers; and, in respect of their reduplicated consonant, have the same relation thereto that the Old High German *dritto* has to the Gothic *thriyda*. Regarding *tvaddyê*, " *duorum*," see p. 422, Note *: the place of the ordinal number is supplied by the pronoun *anthar* (see p. 377), Old High German *andar*, Middle High German *ander*. Our *zweiter*, however, is a new unorganic formation. The Old Sclavonic *vtoryï* (see §. 297.)

answers, in respect to its derivation, to the Greek δεύτερος, and, in abbreviation of the base, to the Zend *bitya*, only that it has lost also the *i* of the Sanskrit *dwi-tiya*, in regard to which we have, in §. 297., adverted to the Zend ع‌ها‌یرٍ‌ب *b·yárĭ**, " two years."

323. We give here a general view of the ordinal numbers in the feminine nominative singular, since in this case the agreement of all the languages strikes the eye more than in the nominative masculine. The Gothic forms which do not occur we give in parentheses, formed theoretically, and according to the Old High German.

[G. Ed. p. 463.]　　　　NOMINATIVE FEMININE.

SANSKRIT.	ZEND.	GR. DOR.	LATIN.	GOTHIC.	LITHUANIAN.	OLD SCLAVONIC.
prathamá,	frathĕma,[1]	πρώτᾱ.	prima,	fruma,	pirmà,	pervn-ya.
dwitiyá,	bitya,	δευτέρᾱ,	altera,	anthara,	antrà,	vtora-ya.
tṛitiyá,	thritya,	τρίτᾱ,	tertia,	thridyó',	trĕchià,	treti-ya.
chaturthá,[2]	túirya,	τετάρτᾱ,	quarta,	(fidvórdó'),	ketwirtà,	chetverta-ya.
panchamá,	pugdha,	πέμπτᾱ,	quinta,	fimftó',	penktà,	pyata-ya.[3]
ṣhaṣhṭhá,	cstvá,[4]	ἕκτᾱ,	sexta,	saihstó',	szĕszta,	shesta-ya.
saptamá,	haptatha,	ἑβδόμᾱ,	septima,	(sibundó'),	sĕkma,	sedma-ya.
aṣhṭamá,	astĕma,	ὐγδόᾱ,	octava,	ahtudó',	ászma,	osma-ya.
navamá,	náuma,	ἐννάτᾱ,	nona,	niundó',	dewintà,[5]	devyata-ya.[5]
daśamá,	daśĕma,	δεκάτᾱ,	decima,	taihundó',	deszimtà,	desyata-ya.
ékádaśá,	aévandaśa,[6]	ἐνδεκάτᾱ,	undecima,	(ainliftó'),	wienólikta,	yedina-ya-na-desyat,
vinśati-tamá,	visaititĕma ?	εἰκοστᾱ,	vicesima,	....	dwideszimtà,	vtoraya-na-desyaty.

------

* We should read thus §. 297. for *byarĕ*, as accusative singular (see Olshausen, Vend. S. 43).

[1] More usually *paoirya*, masc. *paoiryó*, by which the Sclavonic *perryi*, *pervaya*, is, as it were, prepared.

[2] Also *turiyá*, masc. *turiya-s*, on which is based the Zend *túirya*, masc. *túiryó*. The suppression of the syllable *cha* might announce th looser connection of the same with the remaining portion of the wor and thereby support the conjecture expressed at §. 311.

[3] The *t* of *pyataya*, masc. *pyatyi*, has nothing in common with the *t* of the cardinal number *pyaty*; the proper primitive is *pya* (see p. 430 Note †), whence *PYATI* by the suffix *TI*, and *PYATO*, fem. *PYATA*, by the suffix *TO*, fem. *TA* (see §. 322.). The same holds good with regard to *shestaya* in relation to *shesty*, &c.

[4] By transposition and syncope from *csvasta*, as must be expected from the cardinal number ا‌هاو‌س‌یرٍ‌ع *csvas*.

[5] Regarding the *d* for *n*, see §. 317.　　　[6] See §. 319, Note *, p. 435.

"Remark.—As the old *a* of the preposition व *pra* has been weakened to *i*—as in *quinque*, answering to *panchan* —the Latin *prima* appears distinct from the preposition *pro*, and is decidedly not derived from a Roman soil, but is, as it were, the continuance of the Indian *prathamâ*, the middle syllable being cast out. A similar weakening of the vowel is exhibited in the Greek adverb πρίν, which is hereby, in like manner, brought into connection with the preposition πρό. In the comparative *prior* only the *pr* of the preposition, which forms the base, is left, as the *i* belongs to the comparative suffix. In Lithuanian the *m* of the superlative formation has introduced itself also into the preposition *pirm*, 'before'; but the unaltered *pra* stands as prefix. To the same base, however, belongs also *pri*, 'by, before,' as well isolated as prefixed. The Gothic *fruma* shews the same relation to *prathamâ* that the Latin [G. Ed. p. 464.] and Lithuanian do: the *u* of *fru* has arisen from *a* through the influence of the liquid (§. 66.). In the cognate preposition *fram*, 'before, by,' &c., the original vowel has remained, and in this form, as in the Lithuanian *pirm*, the superlative *m* is contained. On व *pra* is based, also, *faur*, 'before,' with transposition of the *u* of *fru-ma*, and with *a* prefixed, according to §. 82.

NUMERAL ADVERBS.

324. The adverbs which express the ideas "twice," "thrice," "four times," have been already discussed (p. 435. G. ed.). Let the following serve for a general view of them :—

SANSKRIT.	ZEND.	GREEK.	LATIN.	OLD NORTHERN.
dwis,	*bis*,	δίς,	*bis*,	*tvis-var* (p. 436 G. ed.).
tris,	*thris*,	τρίς,	*ter*,	*thris-var*.
chatur,*	*chathrus*,	. . . .	*quater*,	. . . .

---

* According to §. 94. for *chaturs*.

BIBLIOBAZAAR

The essential book market!

Did you know that you can get any of our titles in our trademark **EasyRead**™ print format? **EasyRead**™ provides readers with a larger than average typeface, for a reading experience that's easier on the eyes.

Did you know that we have an ever-growing collection of books in many languages?

Order online:
www.bibliobazaar.com

Or to exclusively browse our **EasyRead**™ collection:
www.bibliogrande.com

At BiblioBazaar, we aim to make knowledge more accessible by making thousands of titles available to you – quickly and affordably.

Contact us:
BiblioBazaar
PO Box 21206
Charleston, SC 29413

Lightning Source UK Ltd.
Milton Keynes UK
12 December 2009

147426UK00001B/51/A